A History of
Scandinavian Literature
1870-1980

The University of Minnesota Press
gratefully acknowledges publication assistance from
The Clara Lachmann Foundation for the Promotion
of Scandinavian Solidarity, Gothenburg
and
The Society for the Advancement of Knowledge of
Danish Literature Abroad, Copenhagen

A History of Scandinavian Literature 1870-1980

Sven H. Rossel

Translated by Anne C. Ulmer
in association with the
University of Minnesota Press

University of Minnesota Press ● Minneapolis

Copyright © 1982
by the University of Minnesota.
All rights reserved.
Published by the University of Minnesota Press,
2037 University Avenue Southeast, Minneapolis MN 55414
Printed in the United States of America.

Library of Congress Cataloging in Publication Data

Rossel, Sven Hakon.
   A history of Scandinavian literature,
1870-1980.

   (The Nordic series; v. 5)
   Updated translation of: Skandinavische
Literatur, 1870-1970.
   Bibliography: p.
   Includes index.
   1. Scandinavian literature — 20th century —
History and criticism. 2. Scandinavian
literature — 19th century — History and criticism.
I. Title. II. Series.
PT7078.R6713   1981   839'.5   81-14654
ISBN 0-8166-0906-3   AACR2
ISBN 0-8166-0909-8 (pbk.)

The University of Minnesota
is an equal-opportunity
educator and employer.

To Eva Maria
my beloved daughter

THE NORDIC SERIES
Volume 5

Preface

This work is directed not only to scholars and students of Nordic and comparative literature, but also to those who would like to learn about the literary and cultural life of the five Nordic countries. Rather than writing a complete, hence a more superficial, survey, I have restricted myself to a small number of outstanding authors who are considered to be characteristic of an epoch, a stylistic trend, or a social group. This, however, does not imply that only well-established authors and works are included. Indeed, many talented writers who—undeservedly—have remained unrecognized, even in their home-country, have been given special attention here.

I would like to express my deepest gratitude to my wife, Marianne, for her continuous help and support. Thanks are also due to my translator, Dr. Anne C. Ulmer, to Mr. John Ervin, Jr., Director, University of Minnesota Press, for his enthusiastic support of this project, and to Ms. Beverly Kaemmer, University of Minnesota Press, for her valuable editorial assistance. I am also very much indebted to my former teacher at the University of Copenhagen, Professor F. J. Billeskov Jansen, for his advice and support throughout the years; he secured the two grants that have contributed to the publication of this volume: The Clara Lachmann Foundation for the Promotion of Scandinavian Solidarity, in Gothenburg, and the Society for the Advancement of Knowledge of Danish Literature Abroad, in Copenhagen. Finally I would like to thank colleagues, students, and staff in the Scandinavian Department, and A. Gerald Anderson, Luzzallo Library, for help, advice, and support.

Sven H. Rossel

Introduction

When one decides to write a history of Danish, Norwegian, Swedish, Finnish, and Icelandic literature for English-speaking readers, the first question to arise is on what basis should one select the literature to be discussed. Should one select the same works one would include in a literary history written for readers in the Nordic countries? Or should only those works be discussed that will be of interest to English-speaking readers? Or should one include only works that have already been translated into English?

Because most English-speaking readers are not very familiar with Nordic literature, the first possibility would result in a selection too broad and diverse for this audience. The second and third solutions would yield a very limited and superficial presentation. I have attempted in this book to find a middle way, to discuss not only standard works and well-known authors but also those who, undeservedly, have remained unknown.

Why a *Nordic* literary history? Literature and culture do not develop independently and in isolation, but in a process of continual interrelationship. Denmark, Norway, Sweden, Iceland, and, to some extent, Finland share not only a historical, ethnic, and linguistic heritage but also a homogeneous culture which had its Golden Age in the ninth century — even before the introduction of Christianity — and which continues to influence the literary tradition in these countries. Although this is a Nordic literary history, the literature is placed in an international context, since the reciprocal literary influences between the five Nordic countries and the rest of the world are critical in the development of this literature.

Because it would be impossible to present an exhaustive literary history of the Nordic countries in a single volume, I selected works from the period 1870 to the present. (My choices were dictated in part by subjective evaluation. The closer one is to the period in which the works were written, the more difficult it is to evaluate literary high points and trends.) I chose 1870 because it marks the decisive breakthrough of modern thought—first in Denmark with the famous university lectures of Georg Brandes which stimulated a rich literature. Before this, the Nordic countries had been primarily "receivers" of culture from other countries. Now they became one of the European centers of realism and naturalism, and were transformed into a uniquely creative cultural area.

Contents

Part I The Late Nineteenth Century

Chapter *1*

The Modern Breakthrough in Denmark

Denmark's victorious naval battle against the English fleet off Copenhagen in 1801 produced a wave of national self-confidence. However, that self-confidence was soon shaken by defeats in the same war, which forced Denmark into an alliance with Napoleon. With the French collapse in 1814, Denmark was forced to cede Norway to Sweden. The war had so exhausted the country economically that it declared itself bankrupt. Despite the difficult economic situation, the country experienced a cultural "Golden Age." The feeling of defeat gave way to an enthusiastic Scandinavianism, its zenith coming in 1829 when the great romantic Adam Oehlenschläger was crowned with laurel by Swedish poet Esaias Tegnér.

The Danes began to isolate themselves from everything that came from outside and to rock themselves contentedly in memories of their glorious past. This was particularly true after the successful suppression, involving volunteers from Norway and Sweden, of the insurrection in Schleswig-Holstein, incited by Prussia (1848–50). The Scandinavians organized against the growing Prussian imperialism, but this front broke down only a few years later (1864) in the Prussian/Austrian war of aggression, in which Denmark lost the Danish province of North Schleswig. This collapse of national dreams kindled a heated debate about the relationship of the ideal and the real, of faith and knowledge—an omen threatening upheaval in the Danes' spiritual life. At the same time, they became intensely politically aware.

ROMANTICISM AND NATURALISM

The reaction against romantic literature, much influenced by German literature, cast its scattered shadows ahead. Harsh criticism had been leveled by Søren Kierkegaard in his thesis *Om Begrebet Ironi* (On the Concept of Irony, 1841). Poet Poul M. Møller depicted ironically, yet sympathetically, the romantic good-for-nothing in *En dansk Students Eventyr* (The Adventures of a Danish Student, 1843), and J. L. Heiberg, in *En Sjæl efter Døden* (A Soul after Death, 1841) ridiculed the romantically brought-up petty bourgeois. The severest attacks, however, came with Fr. Paludan-Müller's *Adam Homo* (1842–49) and Hans E. Schack's *Phantasterne* (The Phantasts, 1857). The latter novel, a shattering psychological portrayal of the struggle of three young men against their world of self-absorbing daydreams, was far ahead of its time.

Except for these reactions against romanticism, literature was stagnant. In the theater, comfortable student comedies and weak late-romantic dramas were staged. Poets attempted to reconcile the threatened idealism with reality, and critics advocated an ethical literature. It was a time of imitations. Epoch-making, however, was the creation in the 1830s by minister and poet N. F. S. Grundtvig (1783–1872) of the "school for life"; it was realized in the establishment of numerous folk high schools, which sought to bring about a popular and Christian revival among the Danish peasantry. This pedagogical and social experiment proved viable outside Denmark as well.

New currents became manifest in public debate. From the 1830s on, women's liberation was discussed in the Scandinavian press, and there were occasional demands for suffrage. This was brought into sharper focus by Georg Brandes's translation of John Stuart Mill's *On The Subjection of Women* in 1869. In the 1840s radical German biblical criticism, primarily the work of David Friedrich Strauss and Ludwig Feuerbach, caused widespread discussion. Socialistic and atheistic agitation informed two pamphlets written by Frederik Dreier in 1848 —the year of the *Communist Manifesto*. In the sciences, Auguste Comte's positivistic philosophy and Charles Darwin's evolutionary theory opened new vistas.

In France these currents were transformed into a rational view of life in a literary movement that rejected all things supernatural: naturalism. Scientific objectivity broke through with Gustave Flaubert's *Madame Bovary* (1857) and was carried further by Émile Zola. The critic Sainte-Beuve developed the naturalistic aesthetic. He conceived of a literary work as a manifestation of human action, whose interpretation was to be found in the poet's individuality. Hippolyte Taine, on the other hand, employed a strictly methodical approach to history and philosophy, and made literature the object of painstakingly detailed analysis.

Georg Brandes

The sudden breakthrough of these new ideas in Denmark at the beginning of the 1870s is primarily attributable to Georg Brandes (1842–1927). With his lectures at the University of Copenhagen on Main Currents in Nineteenth Century Literature (begun on November 3, 1871 and published in six volumes between 1872 and 1890; Eng. tr. 1901–5), he became the pivotal figure in the "Modern Breakthrough." Brandes, the son of a Jewish businessman, grew up in an entirely nonreligious atmosphere. When he encountered Christianity, it was to him a strange teaching, which, because of Kierkegaard's uncompromising proclamations, made a great impression on him. A religious crisis lasting many years gave way in about 1863 to a wholly atheistic view of life.

Through his eloquent style and his gift for empathy, Brandes attracted attention as an aesthetician and essayist. In 1866 he began to publish his literary criticism and theater reviews, which were later collected and published in *Æsthetiske Studier* (Aesthetic Studies, 1868) and *Kritiker og Portraiter* (Critiques and Portraits, 1870). Brandes's academic training was the dominant one of the time, rooted in Hegel's dialectic. After 1865 his study of the critics Taine and Sainte-Beuve caused him to move gradually from an abstract to a concrete method of looking at history. The literary and biographical essay became Brandes's favorite genre; he brought it to its epitome in his essay collection *Danske Digtere* (Danish Poets, 1877). In 1870 he wrote his inaugural dissertation on Taine: *Den franske Æsthetik i vore Dage* (French Aesthetics in Our Day), a book in which he both admired and critically dismissed the French critic. Brandes distanced himself most sharply from Taine's conception of the genius as a manifestation of *Zeitgeist* and national character. Underlying Brandes's opposition to this idea was his growing conviction that criticism is an art rather than a science.

In 1870–71 Brandes traveled to England, Italy, and France, where, influenced by the Mediterranean climate, Renaissance art, and antiquity, he opened himself to the new thoughts of the time. On this trip occurred the change from complacent nationalism to merciless criticism of the old-fashioned educational ideals and the narrow horizons of his homeland. This change was reinforced by his encounter with Norwegian dramatist Henrik Ibsen, in whom he found a "comrade in arms" for the fight that loomed.

After Brandes drafted the first outlines of his lectures on Main Currents, he returned to Copenhagen determined to "open the doors from the inside to the outside." The lectures that followed were a declaration of war on the status quo. This portrayal of romanticism's victory over the ideas of the French revolution, and the resulting liberal upheaval led by Shelley and Byron in England, Hugo and his followers in France, Heine, Börne, and "the young Germany," contained clear allusions to conditions in Denmark, where, in Brandes's opinion, people were forty years behind the rest of Europe. It was his goal to awaken the country from its self-satisfied romantic dreaming and to proclaim "the belief in the right of free research and the final victory of freedom of thought."

The lecture series between 1871 and 1887 was more agitation and polemics than science. It excited enthusiasm but also the embittered opposition of the church, the university, and the press. Even his more positive "program" did not find unmixed approval. From this program comes the famous paragraph:

> That a literature exists in our time is shown by the fact that it sets up problems for debate. Thus, for instance, George Sand debates the question of marriage, Voltaire, Byron and Feuerbach debate religion, Proud'hon private property, the younger Alexandre Dumas the relationship between the sexes, and Émile Augier the societal relationships. For a literature not to raise any question for debate is the same as for it to set out to lose all significance.

All these themes, which idealistic literature had previously avoided as unpoetic, were now to be taken up by the young writers. Brandes demanded a literature that would be an organ "of the great thoughts of liberty and the progress of humanity," a committed literature written in grandiose forms, with highly gifted, passionate characters.

For a time, Brandes seemed to have lost the battle: the magazine he had founded with his brother, Edvard, *Det nittende Aarhundrede* (The Nineteenth Century), had to cease publication in 1877 after only three years, and his hope for a professorship of aesthetics miscarried. He left Denmark and lived for five years in Berlin, where he laid the groundwork for his later European renown. When he returned to Denmark in 1882, he had, in reality, been victorious. Intellectual life around 1880 was dominated almost exclusively by the ideas of the Main Currents lectures. Politically, "Brandesianism," through its association with the great Farmer's Party, had become a political force, which in 1884 founded its own radical daily newspaper, *Politiken*. This decade also became a time of battle for Brandes, who had himself outgrown the ideas of the 1870s. Now he declared openly that he was not interested in the opinions of the people. In 1888 he was the first to draw attention to Friedrich Nietzsche, whose disregard for the average person was largely responsible for leading Brandes away from the social agitation and naturalistic program of his university lectures. The reformer became an aristocratic individualist.

In his Main Currents lectures, Brandes had demonstrated more interest in individuals than in ideas and literary movements. During his stay in Berlin, he published a series of outstanding monographs: *Søren Kierkegaard* (1877), *Esaias Tegnér* (1878), *Benjamin Disraëli* (1878; Eng. tr. *Lord Beaconsfield*, 1924), *Ferdinand Lassalle* (1881; Eng. tr. 1911), followed in 1884 by *Ludwig Holberg*.

Brandes understood and found useful the positivist Nietzsche who wrote *Zur Genealogie der Moral* (On the Genealogy of Morals, 1887), Nietzsche the Voltairian and anti-Christian. But he was far removed from the religiosity of *Zarathustra*. In 1889, in the treastise *Aristokratisk Radikalisme* (Aristocratic Radicalism), Brandes presented his new program. He set the earth-bound quality of naturalism in opposition to the great personality, the source and goal of culture. True art should no longer content itself with the ideas and ideals of the average and moderate; it should lift itself above the ordinary and seek its independence and self-will in defiance. Brandes became preoccupied with great figures. His monograph on *William Shakespeare* (1895–96; Eng. tr. 1898) is in the spirit of Nietzsche. Debatable as a scholarly study owing to its method—a parallelization of Shakespeare's dramas and his life—it was brilliant literary psychology and aesthetic analysis.

World War I marked the beginning of a new fruitful period in Brandes's literary activity. Apart from two books about the war and the concluding peace, studded with bitter expressions of an increasing scorn for humanity, he wrote, at a very advanced age, four extensive and popular monographs in which Nietzschean ideas are evident: *Wolfgang Goethe* (1914/15; Eng. tr. 1942), *François Voltaire* (1916/17; Eng. tr. 1930), *Cajus Julius Cæsar* (1918; Eng. tr. 1924), and *Michelangelo Buonarotti* (1921).

Brandes became an unmatched source of controversy in Nordic intellectual life. While he—in the wake of the change of political power in 1901—became officially recognized, the same period marked the beginning of his ideological quarrels with his younger critics. Even his last, insignificant, antitheological studies—for instance, *Sagnet om Jesus* (The Legend of Jesus, 1925)—provoked the most strenuous protests.

Brandes's greatest significance does not lie exclusively in his scholarly qualities. As a philosopher, he was a pronounced eclectic; as a literary scholar, he lacked methodological rigor and patience in the critical investigation of source material; as a writer, his strength was in psychological portrayal. In fact, his major accomplishments were his literary portraits and essays—unsurpassed in any of the Nordic countries.

Intuitive and alertly intelligent, he was the discoverer of an entire generation of Danish writers: J. P. Jacobsen, Holger Drachmann, K. Gjellerup, and others, whom he introduced in his book *Det moderne Gjennembruds Mænd* (The Men of the Modern Breakthrough, 1883). He also influenced a number of high-ranking Scandinavian authors, such as Bjørnson, Hamsun, Ibsen, and Strindberg, and made them known in Europe, not least through his extensive correspondence and his personal contact with such well-known writers as Paul Bourget, Anatole France, André Gide, Paul Heyse, and Romain Rolland. Brandes also discovered several great figures of European cultural life: He was the first to call attention to Paul Claudel, Henrik Ibsen, and Friedrich Nietzsche.

THE NEW PROSE AND LYRIC POETRY

Georg Brandes's true followers in the 1870s distinguished themselves more by their faithful adherence to his ideas than by their talent. Edvard Brandes (1847–1931) wrote a series of dramas of social criticism, Sophus Schandorph (1836–1901), a number of rigid and tendentious works, and Erik Skram (1847–1923), several erotic problem novels. Vilhelm Topsøe (1840–81) opposed the radical political ideas of Brandesianism, but accepted its demands for the true depiction of life; he wrote sensitive realistic novels and short stories in the 1860s and '70s. As an observer with deep psychological insight, he equals the better-known J. P. Jacobsen. For Jacobsen, as well as for Holger Drachmann, whose future literary development took other directions, Brandes's example resulted in a significant intellectual and spiritual liberation.

Jens Peter Jacobsen

Jacobsen (1847–85), born in the North Jutland provincial town of Thisted, was originally a botanist. Darwin influenced him decisively. He wrote about Darwin's theories in the new radical journal *Nyt dansk Maanedsskrift* (New Danish Monthly, 1870–74), and translated his two primary works in 1871–73 and 1874. Darwin's theory of evolution provided him a new view of life, determined by nature alone. His study of the biblical criticism of the Germans Strauss and Feuerbach led him to atheism.

The literary criticism of the young Brandes was particularly important for Jacobsen's aesthetic education. His study of Brandes's work clarified for him the goal and the means of literature. It led him to French literature and to the artistic ideal he espoused after being preoccupied with the works of Sainte-Beuve, Flaubert, and Stendhal. Stimulated by Brandes, he gained the courage to step forward with his own innovative work, the novella *Mogens* (1872), the story of a young, naive dreamer.

Jacobsen was by nature a dreamer, and the essential motif of his work, revealed in his early poetry, is the constant struggle between dream and reality. His poetic fantasy was inspired by intense reading, which included the collected works of Goethe and Shakespeare. From Hans Christian Andersen he learned to master everyday speech. Kierkegaard sharpened his stylistic sense and awakened his interest in psychological experimentation.

Jacobsen's total lyrical output is small, but significant because of its uniqueness and poetic power. During his lifetime, he published only six poems; not until 1886, when Edvard Brandes published his *Digte og Udkast* (Poems and Sketches) could one get an overview of Jacobsen's lyrical output. It is a poetry in which the young natural scientist personally expresses his inner self, after a long struggle with form and content. Nordic ancient and medieval motifs are treated in an epic or romance-like mode, usually in regular strophes. In the poem cycle *Gurresange* (Gurre Songs, completed in 1869 and set to music in 1913 by Arnold Schönberg) his lyric poetry lost its imitative features. The medieval Danish legend of King Valdemar and his beloved Tove, often a subject for the romantics, is presented here in a modern psychological manner: The painful loss of his beloved causes the king to rebel against God. In lyrical monologues, Valdemar's defiance of God and Tove's passionate love find linguistic expression that completely bursts the bounds of the romantic tradition.

Jacobsen's best poems are filled with pithy thoughts, illuminated by sense impressions and colors. He reaches his zenith in the speculative poem "Det bødes der for" ("One Atones for That"), in the atheistic death poem "Saa standsed'—" ("Thus Ended—"), and in two grandiose arabesques, poems with strangely complex language and theme, "Arabesk til en Haandtegning af Michel Angelo" ("Arabesque on a Sketch by Michelangelo") and "Har du faret vild i dunkle Skove?" ("Have You Gone Astray in Shadowy Forests?"):

Have you gone astray in shadowy forests?
Do you know Pan?
I have felt him,
Not in the shadowy forests,
While all things silent spoke,
No! that Pan I have never known,
But I have felt the Pan of love,
When all things speaking fell silent.

In warm sunny regions
There grows a mysterious plant,
Only in deepest silence,
Beneath the blaze of a thousand sunbeams,
Will its blossom open out
A fleeting second,
Looking like the eye of a crazed man,
Like the ruddy cheeks of a corpse.
This I have seen,
This, in my love.

She was like the sweet-smelling snow of the jasmine,
It was poppy blood that beat in her veins,
Her cold, her marble-white hands
Would rest there in her lap
Like water-lilies in the deepest lake.
Her words fell softly
Like apple-blossom petals
On wet dewy grass;
But there were hours
Where cold and clear they would twine
Like jets of water climbing.
There were sighs in her laughter,
Jubilation in her weeping;
Unto her all things must yield,
But two there were that dared defy her,
Her own two eyes.

From the dazzling chalice
Of the poisonous lily
She drank to me;
To him who is dead,
And him who now kneels at her foot.
With all of us she drank
—and then were looks obedient to her—

THE MODERN BREAKTHROUGH IN DENMARK

A cup of vows of unfailing fidelity
From the dazzling chalice
Of the poisonous lily.

It is all over!
On the snow-covered plain
In the brown forest
There grows a lonely hawthorn,
The winds inherit its leaves.
One by one,
One by one,
It drips its blood-red berries
Into the white snow;
Its glowing berries
In the cold snow.—

Do you know Pan?

Tr. David Colbert

Jacobsen's maturity as a naturalist and an artist was established with *Mogens*, the first naturalistic novella in Danish literature. It had the effect of a revelation on the youth of the time. Here they found the program of the new realism carried out with astonishing talent: a precise depiction of impressions from nature, a portrayal of humankind that perceived humans not only as spiritual, but also as physiological creatures. The sustaining motif is the maturation of the dreamer Mogens through unhappiness and doubt. This story of a male character's development, during which he is introduced to many secondary female characters, appears in Jacobsen's subsequent work.

A year after the publication of *Mogens*, Jacobsen suffered a hemorrhage in Florence. The poet, hopelessly ill with tuberculosis, spent his remaining twelve years in Thisted, in Copenhagen, and in Switzerland and Italy, using his time energetically in exceedingly self-critical creative work. During these years he wrote his two great novels, a few poems, and a collection of novellas and sketches.

Jacobsen needed time to give his impressions a completely congruent linguistic form. Slowly and hesitatingly, his new book, the historical novel *Fru Marie Grubbe* (1876; Eng. tr. *Marie Grubbe*, 1917 and later), subtitled Interior Scenes of the Seventeenth Century, took shape. Probably influenced by Flaubert's *Madame Bovary*, Jacobsen had wanted to give a complete portrayal of a human fate and had selected for his purpose the Jutland noblewoman Marie Grubbe, who as a young girl became the wife of a prince, but after a hectic life with him ended up the contended wife of a poor, primitive ferryman. Marie's circumstances—

her inherited tendencies, her upbringing, and her environment—are portrayed with Flaubertian sensitivity. Unquestionably naturalistic also is the psychological idealization of Marie "downward," toward the "human animal." As a social being, she has sunk through the social strata into the depths, from castle to hut; in human terms, however, she has not been destroyed, for she has found the strong man who can dominate her and satisfy her needs. *Marie Grubbe* signifies a renewal of the historical novel: Realism was the goal, and the means to that goal was an exhaustive study of sources in archives and libraries, the result a magnificently executed period piece.

Niels Lyhne (1880; Eng. tr. 1919 and later), on the other hand, is a contemporary novel. Niels, a budding poet, embodies the generation of dreamers that suffered defeat as a result of the war of 1864. The novel ends in the year in which Niels dies of his war wounds. The arguments of the 1870s between old and new left their imprint on the book, which to a much greater extent than the objective *Marie Grubbe* is based on Jacobsen's personal experiences. It is not only a novel of development about a man who is ill-suited for life and who flees into dreams because he expects too much from reality, but also a problem novel about a freethinking heart that cannot keep pace with a freethinker's brain and that longs in decisive moments for "a god to accuse and to worship." *Niels Lyhne* is also a book about the ending of life. Niels achieves little in life. For a time he overcomes his dreaming and grasps reality, but we do not learn much about this. His love is either hopelessly demanding or a dream game, because he is too weak, or it lasts too short a time; death destroys his happiness.

After completing *Niels Lyhne*, Jacobsen thought of writing something "bright and light and glorious." Nothing came of it; he wrote only a few pages more, among them the splendid novella "Fru Fønss" ("Mrs. Fønss")—his own melancholy balancing of accounts with life. It appeared in *Mogens og andre Noveller* (1882; Eng. tr. *Mogens and Other Stories*, 1921 and later) with "Pesten i Bergamo" ("The Plague in Bergamo"), a colorful Italian renaissance piece and Jacobsen's greatest stylistic achievement, "Et Skud i Taagen" ("A Shot in the Fog"), a Poe-inspired analysis of a pathological case, and "To Verdener" ("Two Worlds"), a story of the predetermined fates of happiness and unhappiness.

Jacobsen had learned much about psychological portrayal from French literature. His depiction of women and his psychology of love are influenced by Stendhal's *De l'Amour* (On Love), his many-faceted analysis of personality by Flaubert. But Jacobsen was no French naturalist. His acute understanding of human beings and melancholy tone are more similar to the Russian novelist Turgenev, whose books were very popular at that time in all Nordic countries.

Jacobsen's exquisite style corresponds to his refined psychology. Using Kierkegaard and Hans Christian Andersen as his closest Danish models, he created an exceedingly individualistic prose, whose strengths were objective precision, a keen sense of beauty, and intense imagery. This style, often admired and imitated, sometimes seems artificial and florid, but the portrayal of human beings, the absorption with the secret depths of the soul, is impressively forceful.

Jens Peter Jacobsen is undoubtedly a major figure of the modern movements of the 1870s and '80s. Characteristic of his time are his Darwinistic view of life, the themes of his works, and his naturalistic techniques. But unlike Brandes, for example, Jacobsen builds up rather than tears down: He does not ridicule his opponents and never seeks to awaken tendentious sympathies or antipathies in his readers.

Whereas Jacobsen joined ranks with Brandes on the strength of Brandes's naturalistic view of life, it was the social-critical aspect of his program that inspired the second great writer of the decade, Holger Drachmann. Stormy and melodramatic, with a distinct sense of theatrical effect, he was the antithesis of the ironic, introverted Jacobsen.

Holger Drachmann

Drachmann (1846–1908), a son of a Copenhagen physician, began to write poems at a very early age. As a young adult, he moved in radical circles and at first was a painter. A long sea trip to Scotland and southern Europe influenced both brush and pen, but not until a six-month stay in London in 1871 did he develop a distinctive style. In the company of dockworkers and political refugees from France, he experienced the after-effects of the Paris Commune and was deeply impressed by the social distress and the dawn of socialism. When he returned to his homeland, he again joined the rebellious radical movement, and he attended Brandes's lectures. He wrote a few polemical articles about academic Danish painting, which caused Brandes to seek him out as a comrade-in-arms and to promote him as a poet.

The best known of Drachmann's early poems is the melodramatic and theatrical "Engelske Socialister" ("English Socialists"). It appeared in *Digte* (Poems, 1872), a collection of poetry that immediately made Drachmann famous. If it was the revolution in Brandes's message that had inspired Drachmann, then in this and in his next volume of poetry, *Dæmpede Melodier* (Muted Melodies, 1875), the inspiration was social contrasts and the struggle between the reactionary old and the victorious new. Besides politically radical lyric poems, one finds bohemian songs in which Drachmann appears as a sailor, peasant, or vagabond without bourgeois inhibitions. One also encounters enchanting, intimate verses in which bright nights and the sea are images of freedom and of the poetic spirit, pointing beyond naturalism.

In the years following, Drachmann's poetic personality fully unfolded, given wings by a new love—his first marriage had been dissolved after only two years. Encounters with women were always an essential element in his writing. In the novel *En Overkomplet* (A Supernumerary, 1876), in which Drachmann employed Turgenev's favorite motif of a strong woman versus a weak man, a more intense spirituality is perceptible. His feelings of guilt toward his first wife gave his later poetry a deeper tone that also found expression in the poem "Sakuntala." The poem, inserted in the novel, is named for the title character in Indian playwright Kalidasa's drama *Abhijnana-shakuntala*; it is one of the more beautiful and well-known poems in Danish literature:

I could not sleep for yearning,	O Thou! whose calm eyes lower
A wind of flowers	like hazy stars
awoke my dreams,	to gaze on me,
pouring warm through my window	as if at this hour the magic
in rich Himalayan streams.	ring were bestowed on thee;—
I heard the tall palm's music,	it is not one hour, one day
and a word	that divides
they wept to sing;	our souls' blown spheres
I heard it blown on the winds of spring:	but thousands of years, withered years,
Sakuntala, Sakuntala.	Sakuntala, Sakuntala.
(. . .)	(. . .)

(Tr. by Robert Silliman Hillyer)

While experiencing this spiritual intensification, Drachmann sought to rise above national party struggles and political controversies. In his travel book *Derovre fra Grænsen* (Over There from the Border, 1877), in which he glorified the national struggle of Danish North Schleswig and scorned Danish internal politics, he set himself apart from the modern breakthrough. Drachmann, with his craving for beauty, his admiration for the extraordinary and heroic, now looked upon ideological literature as confining. In the antinaturalistic poem *Prinsessen og det halve Kongerige* (The Princess and Half the Kingdom, 1878), he decisively rejected gray tendentious literature in favor of the poesy of the fairy tale. This new orientation was most clearly manifest in three collections of poems, *Sange ved Havet* (Songs by the

Sea, 1877), *Ranker og Roser* (Vines and Roses, 1879), and *Ungdom i Digt og Sang* (Youth in Poem and Song, 1879)—the high points of his youthful poetry.

This poetry has many precursors. Among Nordic poets, one could mention Oehlenschläger, Ibsen, and Bjørnson; among foreign poets, Goethe and Heine contributed to Drachmann's songlike tone; the broad metric forms are reminiscent of Swinburne; the self-worship and preference for the heroic attitude remind one of Byron. However, Drachmann created his poems entirely from his own experience, formed them with his poetic personality. Never before in Danish literature had there been such a candid revelation of an artist's entire personality, such exuberant fantasy, such artistic and wide-ranging linguistic virtuosity. Drachmann experimented with changing, undulating rhythms, with new and complicated verse forms. The allusive and dreamy quality of his poems shatters the clarity and firmness of earlier Danish lyric poetry. A basic motif in his writing, the animated dream vision of beauty which is hunted in vain, is now carried further and reshaped to perfection in a number of Venetian fantasies in *Songs by the Sea*.

The section "Sange til en Søster" ("Songs to a Sister") in the collection *Youth in Poem and Song* marked another turning point in Drachmann's life. In 1879 he married for the second time. From then on, he praised domesticity instead of free love and returned to a national, bourgeois poetry. Drachmann threw down the gauntlet before the "critical-Jewish-French" spirit and officially broke with Georg and Edvard Brandes. Both the fairy-tale poem *Østen for Sol og Vesten for Maane* (East of the Sun and West of the Moon, 1880), and the fairy-tale comedy *Der var engang* (Once upon a Time, 1885), which became a major stage success owing to its national flavor and pomp, belong to this period. The only outstanding poems from the period are in the collection significantly titled *Gamle Guder og nye* (Old Gods and New, 1881), which was based on such ideals as the sanctity of home, mother, and child. Striking are the two philosophical poems "Det tabte Paradis" ("The Lost Paradise") and the cycle "Vor Moders Saga" ("The Saga of Our Mother"), a homage to motherhood culminating with "Ved Arnen" ("At the Hearth")—characterized by Brandes as "as great in its style as a choral passage of a Greek tragedian."

By the late 1880s, Drachmann's poetic power had diminished. He longed for the artist's life of his youth, fell in love with a cabaret singer whom he called Edith, proclaimed himself a revolutionary, and deserted his wife and children. Edith became the inspiration for his last significant works, the poetry volume *Sangenes Bog* (Book of Songs, 1889) and the novel *Forskrevet* (Signed Away, 1890).

Book of Songs portrays the new love experience, the renewed youth of the poet, but the joyful tone is mixed with pain. Behind the hectic happiness lurks anxiety about approaching old age. *Signed Away* is Drachmann's argument with himself and his time. He has divided his own persona, which he condemns in penetrating self-criticism, into the two main characters: The painter Henrik Gerhard is the correct working man, the poet Ulf Brynjulfsen is the bohemian artist. Ulf destroys himself and Gerhard *signs* himself *away* to the soulless, hypocritical time, until Edith, the embodiment of all purity and beauty, frees him from the middle-class existence to which he had pledged himself through his marriage. The portrayal of characters is so mature and intense that it far surpasses the realistic works of the period. The protagonists are presented as unpredictable beings, placed in an existence determined by a dark fate. *Signed Away*, as self-confession and self-defense, is a psychological document of the greatest value; its poetry is so lively and rich that it will survive inspite of the fact that it has elements of the period novel and *roman à clef*, and that its structure is weak. Stylistically, the book is a high point of impressionistic prose, interwoven with dreamlike moods and lyrical scenes.

For some years, Drachmann's writing was heavily influenced by Edith, but the relationship was slowly dissolving. Drachmann's despair following their breakup is most clearly expressed in his so-called melodramas, lyrical plays with powerful characters and scenes. The most significant of these is *Vølund Smed* (Wayland the Smith, 1894), in which Drachmann, influenced by Shakespeare and Wagner, transformed the famous smith of the edda into a new and towering symbol of his poetic persona.

When the Edith period ended, Drachmann was an old man. In the last ten years of his life, he wrote a series of works that are pale reflections of his earlier writing, with the exception of the melancholy novella *Kirke og Orgel* (Church and Organ, 1904). The main theme is the poet's grief over his lost youth, which for a short while can be recaptured through an experience of true love. Drachmann's position in the literary world was assured. At the beginning of the 1890s he was reconciled with Georg Brandes, and around the turn of the century he was hailed as the Danish poet laureat.

He considered freedom and beauty the main ideas of his creative work. As a spendthrift Renaissance type and an incorrigible dreamer, he lived outside his time, which was sober and objective. Holger Drachmann's significance for later Danish poetry is extraordinary, owing to the greatness of his exceptional artistic personality and the infinite wealth of rhythms and moods in his poetry.

Chapter *2*

The Modern Breakthrough in Norway

Until the mid-nineteenth century, Norwegian intellectual life was predominantly politically oriented and was determined by the decisive national events of 1814 as well as by contemporary social problems. In literature, the short stories of Mauritz Hansen and the plays of H. A. Bjerregaard from the 1820s and 1830s, characterized by imitation of the romantics, were widely popular in their time. Not until the work of Henrik Wergeland (1808–45) did the newer Norwegian literature become original. In his major work, the dramatic poem *Skabelsen, Mennesket og Messias* (Creation, Man, and Messiah, 1830), he combined eighteenth-century rationalism and romantic philosophy with modern ideas of liberty. Wergeland's best poetry is sustained by an eruptive, ecstatic force and bold imagination. He is regarded as the greatest Norwegian lyric poet, and his influence was deeply felt, not only in Norwegian *literature*, but also on the national political scene. Unlike Wergeland, his opponent and critic J. S. Welhaven (1807–73) stressed solidarity with Danish culture; a fierce debate raged between the two men throughout the 1830s. Welhaven's main contribution was the polemical collection of sonnets *Norges Dæmring* (The Twilight of Norway, 1834), but his most valuable and tightly structured poetry takes its motifs from a personal love experience and from Norway's nature and folk life.

Romanticism did not actually break through in Norway until the 1840s when the young nation had to create a new historical and cultural foundation. The Norwegians wanted to reach back to the time of the old Norway, before its union with Denmark. This longing marked the onset of the era of romanticism.

In the years 1841–44, two volumes, *Norske Folkeeventyr* (Norwegian Folktales) appeared, collected by P. Chr. Asbjørnsen and J. Moe. These fairy tales were recounted in a form of the Norwegian language that retained the freshness and originality of the oral tradition. At the same time, interest awakened in the old dialect and folk songs. Wergeland had already prophesied that there would be a new written language, based on the village and mountain dialects. The self-taught philologist Ivar Aasen (1813–96) pursued this. With his *Prøver af Landsmaalet i Norge* (Examples of the Norwegian Landsmaal, 1853), he created, from various dialects, a purely Norwegian written language, the *landsmål* (after 1929 *nynorsk*), which was to replace the official state language, the *riksmål* (after 1929 *bokmål*). In the journal *Dølen* (The Valley Inhabitant, 1858–70), published by A. O. Vinje (1818–70), the *landsmål* was developed further and used for literary purposes in the travelogue *Ferdaminni* (Recollections from a Journey, 1861); its capricious structure is clearly related to German poet Heinrich Heine's *Reisebilder* (Travel Pictures).

The atmosphere of the 1850s and '60s was the worst conceivable for poetry. It was a time of practical interests, of economic and industrial development. The old romanticists sought in idyllic fantasy an alternative to the impending machine age, or they actively rebelled against the spirit of the new time; the younger ones were uncertain. From the predominant philosophy, a rigid Hegelianism, no help was to be expected. Politics were equally somber. To be sure, the first socialist workers' organizations had created a little unrest, but this died out in the bureaucratic society.

The active optimism of the young nation had some time earlier yielded to a growing pietism, the so-called Haugeanism (named after its founder, H. N. Hauge); the movement met with strong approval in the lower strata of society and in the country. In the cities, an aesthetic view of life was spreading, influenced by Danish late romanticism. Often strong idealistic aspiration lay behind the pietism and aestheticism, an aspiration that had been strongly promoted by the works of Kierkegaard. The most popular poet of the time was Heine. In his works, readers no longer sought ideals of freedom and democracy but concentrated on his ironic and introspective approach.

The center of gravity in literature was the lyric. The novel was an almost neglected genre. The first modern novel, *Amtmandens Døttre* (The Governor's Daughters, 1854–55), was written by Camilla Collett (1813–95), Wergeland's sister. With this artistically rather insignificant book, she not only paved the way for realistic problem fiction, but also introduced the subject of the social position of women, which was carried further by Ibsen and Lie, and ended in the tendentious works of Kielland. On the other hand, Andreas Munch (1811–84) followed in the footsteps of Adam Oehlenschläger's romanticism with a number of national Christian dramas. He was the most productive and popular author of the 1850s, but in the same decade had to defer to the greater talents of Ibsen and Bjørnson.

When Georg Brandes encountered Ibsen at the train station in Dresden, the latter said to him challengingly, "You go home and annoy the Danes; then I will annoy the Norwegians." With his university lectures, Brandes began to carry out this charge, but the decisive, victorious advance, and the realization of the new ideas, took place not in Denmark but in Norway.

Henrik Ibsen

Ibsen (1828–1906) was born in Skien in southern Norway, the son of a well-to-do merchant. Soon, however, the family faced bankruptcy, hence social humiliation, which overshadowed Ibsen's entire youth. The oppressive atmosphere in his later family dramas is not fiction, but personal experience. Influenced by the February revolution of 1848 in France, he wrote banal, provocative freedom poems and his first drama, *Catilina* (Eng. tr. *Catiline*, 1921 and later), which was published in 1850 after he had completed his university entrance examinations in the same year in Christiania.

If one compares it with Ibsen's later creative efforts, *Cataline*, which was not staged, is barely worth mentioning. Ibsen matured slowly; for a long time he vacillated between the influences of Oehlenschläger and Norwegian romantics Wergeland and Welhaven, and sought his motifs in folk ballads, Icelandic sagas, and in the present. Ibsen achieved a minor dramatic success in 1850 with the totally unoriginal romantic one-act play *Kjæmpehøjen* (Eng. tr. *The Burial Mound*, also published as *The Warrior's Barrow*, 1921 and later); this was the sole recommendation he brought to his post as playwright and director of the National Stage in Bergen. The theater had been founded in 1850 as a counterpoise to the Christiania Theater, which was under Danish management.

From 1851 to 1857 the young dramaturgist was active at the theater. The stay in Bergen was not successful for Ibsen, but these years of apprenticeship provided knowledge that would be useful later. In Bergen he also began to write his national dramas. The first drama that demonstrates mastery, *Fru Inger til Østråt* (1855; Eng. tr. *Lady Inger at Östraat*, 1890 and later), a shattering tragedy of mother love, was written here. In this play, one of Ibsen's major themes surfaced, the significance of vocation. The demand for "all or nothing" is set out clearly for the first time. Ibsen showed himself to be sophisticated in dramatic technique. Modeled on the plays of French dramatist Eugéne Scribe, the intrigues are worked out to the tiniest detail, the sequence of scenes is boldly calculated, and the plot precisely constructed.

The most artistically successful of Ibsen's youthful works is the saga play *Hærmændene paa Helgeland* (1858; Eng. tr. *The Warriors of Helgeland*, also as *The Vikings of Helgeland*, 1890 and later). By contrast to the intrigues and complications of *Lady Inger at Östraat*, *The Warriors of Helgeland* has the brevity and clarity of the saga form and its sharpness of characterization. Here we find a major figure in Ibsen's writing: a woman who shows to a man the high goals, the ideals of life. The drama was printed only after Ibsen had left Bergen and become the artistic director of the new Norwegian theater in Christiania in 1857.

The Christiania period of 1857–64 was the most difficult in Ibsen's life. The theater went bankrupt in 1862, and his financial situation was desperate. He was filled with uncertainty and indifference, and was judged to be a talent who had not fulfilled his promise. For about ten years he was entirely overshadowed by the younger Bjørnson.

In the satiric contemporary drama *Kjærlighedens Komedie* (1862; Eng. tr. *Comedy of Love*, 1900 and later), which drew destructive criticism, Ibsen attempted to write himself free of his preoccupation with the antitheses of ideal and real, dream and actuality. In this tragicomedy the "ideal demand" of love is set up and confronted with reality. Generally accepted attitudes toward profession, engagement, marriage, and love are mercilessly mocked in the name of beauty and poetry.

A drama of the Middle Ages, *Kongs-emnerne* (1863; Eng. tr. *The Pretenders*, 1890 and later), is replete with more profound personal experiences. There are several levels: an explicit portrayal of the battles of succession to the Norwegian throne around 1250, strongly influenced by Shakespeare's history plays and Snorri's sagas of the kings; a concealed representation of Ibsen's relationship to his successful rival Bjørnson; and a merciless balancing of the poet's accounts with himself. The figure of the doubter, Skule, who lacks faith in his call to the throne, and who, therefore, despite all his abilities, must remain a "stepchild of God on earth," mirrors the doubts that the

poet has now overcome. Ibsen's breakthrough to self-confidence inspired the conception of King Haakon, who has faith in his vocation.
Although *The Pretenders* demonstrates Ibsen's conclusive victory
over the doubts he had so long entertained about his vocation as a
poet, the Christiania period, so filled with misfortune, was not yet
overcome. Added to that was Ibsen's greatest disappointment, the
collapse of Scandinavianism, when in 1864 Norway and Sweden de-
clined to enter the Schleswig War on Denmark's behalf. In that same
year, Ibsen turned his back on Norway, not to return and remain
there permanently until twenty-seven years later. For the first four
years, he lived in Rome, where *Brand* and *Peer Gynt* were written.
After that he traveled to Dresden, where his next play, *The League of
Youth*, was published. In these cities and Munich he spent the greatest
part of his "voluntary exile."

The dramatic works *Brand* (1866; Eng. tr. 1891 and later) and *Peer
Gynt* (1867; Eng. tr. 1892 and later) are the foundation of Ibsen's
writing. They were conceived as a unity: *Brand* portrays an idea and
Peer Gynt the relationship to that idea. Ibsen said that he wanted, in
these works, to hold up a mirror to his countrymen. *Brand* was the
mirror and *Peer Gynt* that which was reflected in it. Brand chose a
life of uncompromising obedience to the vocation he received from
God. In Brand's battle against the state church and against the "spirit
of compromise," Ibsen was above all popularizing Kierkegaard's ideas.
Brand is the pastor in a destitute valley. He risks everything to live according to his absolute faith. He risks his life to bring salvation to a
sinner, but refuses to go to his mother's deathbed because she had not
been willing to give up worldly riches. Brand is forced to sacrifice his
own happiness. Although neither his wife, Agnes, nor their child can
live in the unhealthy climate of the valley, he refuses to give up his
post. When the child dies, he forbids Agnes to mourn and demands
that everything which reminds him of the dead boy be destroyed.
Agnes, however, does not possess his strength, and she also dies. With
his mother's inheritance, Brand now builds a large church, but when
he discovers that the congregation has not grasped the significance of
his house of God, he locks the doors of his church and moves up into
the mountains, into the "ice church." For the first time he is tempted,
and he pleads with God for help. At this moment an avalanche thunders
down and buries him, and from heaven he hears the answer to his
despairing question: "God is love." Brand has lived for a great idea;
his death is the tragedy of merciless idealism. In his strict adherence
to elevated ideals, he has forgotten the most important thing: humility
and love for his fellow human beings.

If *Brand* is the tragedy of the isolated personality, then *Peer Gynt* is the farce of self-satisfaction and mediocrity. Peer Gynt is the anti-thesis of Brand; he worships the "spirit of compromise," dreams and fantasizes himself out of reality. Brand's uncompromising conception of life is replaced with Peer's life principle: "Go round about." Ibsen bestowed the full power of poetic genius on this phrase-filled dreamer. In no other drama is his humor as free and uninhibited, his irony as merciless, his language as powerful.

Peer's mother raised him with fairy tales and accustomed him to a world in which one finds happiness without struggle and personal effort. When he is older, his tall tales give him a bad reputation. He meets the gentle Solvejg who sacrifices everything for him, but he does not wish to accept this devotion and goes "round about." He bungles life through compromise and cowardice. When, after many years, Peer returns to his homeland, old and worn out, he discovers that all of his acquaintances are leading happy lives. In a series of symbolic encounters, he is brought face to face with his forsaken ideals, and he is called to account. "The Buttonmoulder," considering him "useless goods," would like to put him into his pot and melt him down. Then he encounters again Solvejg, who has faithfully waited for him. Through her waiting her life has received meaning, and when he asks her where, in all these years, "he himself" has been, she responds, "In my faith, in my hope, in my love." Now the transformation occurs: Through awareness of his sins and repentance Peer is purified, and through Solvejg's love he is saved from destruction, as Dante was through Beatrice, Faust through Gretchen, and Adam Homo (see p. 4) through Alma.

With the major works *The Pretenders*, *Brand*, and *Peer Gynt*, Ibsen's romantic period reached its zenith. If he had ended his creative work with these plays, and with the forceful and epigrammatic collection *Digte* (Poems, 1871), he would have been a great Nordic writer. He had exhausted his rich poetry, exposed his restless soul, and demonstrated his comprehensive dramatic ability. But at the age of fifty, Ibsen decided to conquer the world. He now wrote plays which, in less than twenty years, were to make him the sole sovereign of the European stage.

Ibsen was aware that his last romantic drama, *Kejser og Galilæer* (1873; Eng. tr. *Emperor and Galilean*, 1876 and later) was not successful. In the play, using German chancellor Bismarck's cultural battle as factual background, he portrayed the persecution of the Christians by the Roman Emperor Julian and his defeat, inevitable because suppression always gives new strength to the believers. Influenced by

Brandes, he now began to write modern problem plays. As early as 1862, with *Comedy of Love*, he had written a contemporary piece. With the satiric comedy *De unges Forbund* (1869; Eng. tr. *The League of Youth*, 1890 and later), he created the first Norwegian conversation play of social criticism, in itself insignificant, but interesting because it is Ibsen's first attack on political liberalism.

The conclusive turning point came in 1877 with *Samfundets Støtter* (Eng. tr. *Pillars of Society*, 1888 and later), which established Ibsen's world reputation. In the portrayal of the circle around Consul Bernick, conventional hypocrisy is exposed and attacked. The *true* pillars of society are freedom and truth. The piece is a typical tendentious drama, even though the plot is still too reminiscent of popular comedy, the characterization too conventional, and the treatment of the problems too superficial. In at least one respect, the play is of interest to us: For the first time, Ibsen consistently used retrospective methods in constructing the plot. When the curtain goes up, everything is predetermined. While the plot unfolds, the earlier history is gradually unveiled and actively participates in the events on the stage. When, at the end of the play, the past is fully revealed, the fate of the characters has been decided. This so-called analytical technique, familiar from Greek tragedy, is developed by Ibsen with increasing virtuosity, until in *Little Eyolf* the entire plot is unraveled in the first act.

More significant is *Et Dukkehjem* (1879; Eng. tr. *A Doll's House*, 1880 and later). Here Ibsen meets Brandes's challenge and debates the issue of marriage; he assigns priority to the right of women to develop as human beings, over attention to their duties as wives and mothers. *A Doll's House* inspired vigorous debate and was used by both sides on the questions of women's liberation, although Ibsen was using this problem as a motif to champion his basic idea: the right of the individual to live his or her own life. As in the previous play, an unveiling occurs. The "pillar of society" is the solid husband, Helmer, and the bearer of the "ideal demand" is his wife, Nora. To save her sick husband, she has forged a promissory note. When Helmer learns of this, he fears a public scandal, and Nora understands that bourgeois convention is more important to Helmer than love. From "a little lark" she develops into a free personality and deserts her home and children.

A Doll's House aroused debate, but the tragedy *Gengangere* (1881; Eng. tr. *Ghosts*, 1885 and later), which was first performed in Chicago, horrified and shocked the public; in Norway, Bjørnson alone defended it. In this play, the attack was much sharper, the theme far more sinister. Darwinism is the presupposition for the unnerving proclamation that the sins of the fathers are visited upon the children. The dissolute life of Captain Alving has had many consequences: His wife's life has been destroyed, his son suffers from an incurable venereal disease which will eventually lead to imbecility, and unknowingly he is about to enter into an incestuous relationship with his sister, Regine. The play is an attack on the conventions that have forced Mrs. Alving to remain with her husband, as well as on the morals of a society that virtually demands such hypocrisy and forces Mrs. Alving into martyrdom.

The reception of *Ghosts* enraged Ibsen and forced from him a second reckoning with the liberals in *En Folkefiende* (1882; Eng. tr. *An Enemy of the People*, 1890 and later). In the figure of Dr. Stockmann, who wants to be of use to his hometown and who is accused of being an enemy of the people, Ibsen turns energetically against democracy, "the damned, compact, liberal majority," and proclaims that "the strongest man in the world is he who stands most alone." Ibsen takes up a more far-ranging conflict in the pessimistic tragedy *Vildanden* (1884; Eng. tr. *The Wild Duck*, 1891 and later). Through the skeptic, Dr. Relling, Ibsen expresses his own nihilistic world view and demonstrates his belief in the impossibility of improving humankind in his rejection of the "ideal demand" for truth. This demand is made by Gregers Werle, a naive idealist, of the untruthful and contemptible phrasemonger Hjalmar Ekdal. Werle's reward is calamity; he is the cause of the tragic death of Hjalmar's little daughter Hedvig.

The varied assortment of characters, as well as the tension-laden atmosphere, make *The Wild Duck*, without question, Ibsen's most mature and outstanding play. Hjalmar Ekdal is among Ibsen's most inspired portrayals. Technically, too, the drama is a landmark. In his earlier works, a number of symbols are used sporadically; this entire piece is dominated by a single symbol: the wounded wild duck in the loft, whose well-being is an image of the delusive life of most of the major characters.

The Wild Duck is the last of Ibsen's polemical social dramas. Influenced by Brandes, who had been distancing himself during these years from democratic ideas and approaching Nietzsche's philosophy, Ibsen turned to the problems and crises of individualism, and deserted the realistic in favor of the symbolic. In *Rosmersholm* (1886; Eng. tr. 1889 and later), Johannes Rosmer is Ibsen's superhuman ideal. He is by nature a Christian, but he has abandoned the teachings of Christ. He seeks, through his spiritual view of life, to ennoble the demonic, heathen Rebekka. She struggles to win him, but an insuperable obstacle stands between them: the awareness that the two of them are not without guilt in the death of Rosmer's wife. They seek a death of atonement in the millstream.

Ibsen's next two dramas are also concerned with two people living together, and the theme of ennoblement reappears. In *Fruen fra Havet* (1888; Eng. tr. *The Lady from the Sea*, 1890 and later), the primitive natural force of Ellida and the power of a strange sailor over her spirit are tamed and overcome. This half-acknowledged attraction is finally acknowledged, and Ellida is free to choose between her husband and the mysterious stranger. In *Lille Eyolf* (1894; Eng. tr. *Little Eyolf*, 1894 and later) the erotically passionate and egotistical Rita Allmers is transformed through the death of her young son Eyolf, who had been crippled as the result of his parents' inattention. Through her guilt, she experiences the "law of transformation" and finds a degree of happiness in idealistic self-sacrifice.

In these works, a weakness of Ibsen's dramas becomes clear: His earlier great characters embodied ideas behind which lay particular theories; many of the characters in these plays proved to be dead creations, the distinctive, individualizing reply often giving way to pompous, hollow diction. Symbolism which earlier had been so skillfully woven into the plot is employed too restrictively. Even Ibsen's stage technique, earlier very confident, is no longer sure.

In Hedda Gabler, Ibsen once more created a living character. *Hedda Gabler* (1890; Eng. tr. 1891 and later) is an extremely pessimistic drama not in the symbolic style. Neither is it a problem play; it is a psychological study of a middle-class woman who yearns for beauty but whose emotional life has become sterile, owing to the conditions of present-day society and her own drive for power. Forcefully, Ibsen portrays Hedda Gabler and condemns her life-destroying aestheticism.

Ibsen's three "dramas of genius" form a distinct group. In them he advocates a fruitful, loving human life in opposition to the cold genius who pays for his successes with the happiness of others, as well as with his own.

Bygmester Solness (1892; Eng. tr. *The Master Builder*, 1893 and later) is a masterpiece, the tragedy of an artist, the builder, who wants the impossible and so is struck down by punishing fate. He has sacrificed everything to build "homes for people"; with his strong will, he has removed or suppressed everything that stood in his way. To achieve this victory he has sacrified his own and his wife's happiness. For a time he is liberated from his guilt about failures in his private life by the encounter with the girl Hilde, who demands that he "climb as high as he builds." However, he does not succeed in erecting "castles in the air on a firm foundation," for his conscience is too burdened. While standing at the top of his last creation, he loses his balance and plummets to the ground.

In spite of several weak spots, *John Gabriel Borkman* (1896; Eng. tr. 1897 and later) is also deeply effective, owing to the characters whose spiritual indifference has virtually turned them to stone. Former bank director Borkman is a great dreamer, a self-righteous one, like Skule and Solness, whose greatest sin is not his betrayal of his bank but his destruction of a woman's loving life.

The sculptor Rubek does the same thing in Ibsen's last work about the limits of genius, the dark and fascinating play *Når vi døde vågner* (1899; Eng. tr. *When We Dead Awaken*, 1900 and later). Ibsen characterized it as the epilogue of his writing. It treats of the relationships between life and art, realism and idealism, symbolized by the old sculptor who has abandoned the idealistic strivings of his youth in order to create portrait busts, "men and women with dimly suggested animal faces." He encounters the woman Irene, who once stood nude before him as the model for his masterpiece, while he chiseled her soul into the art work without ever getting close to her. His relationship with this woman is a failure: He sacrificed the human being in himself and the happiness of another on the altar of art. After a violent argument, both seek death under an avalanche and "return to their graves." The drama is a poem of redeeming death.

This despairing play—which questions whether all artistic striving, all renunciation for art, is worth the sacrifice—is a shattering confession by Ibsen, his last judgment of his own act of creation. Ibsen's development is reminiscent of Solness's: The architect first wanted to build churches, then "homes for people," and finally "castles in the air on a firm foundation"; Ibsen's works developed from the romantic through the realistic to the symbolic. Common to the three phases is the emphatic longing for wholeness and strength of personality.

Without doubt, Henrik Ibsen's dramas belong to world literature. He became famous first in Germany and then in all of Europe. To a significant degree, he formed the history of drama at the turn of the century. Gerhart Hauptmann, George Bernard Shaw, and Arthur Miller are among his students. His importance lies in his total mastery of stage technique, in his renewal of analytical drama, and in his treatment of varied subject matter. He is one of the great questioners who seldom provide answers—if they do, they only hint darkly. Ibsen dazzles his audiences and readers through suggestive and aphoristic slogans that counterfeit a wider perspective than is actually present. He is a decided relativist, skeptical of all absolute political and social programs. Even if one senses an affected escapism in his lack of engagement, his creativity is still a passionate delving into personality, his entire work a mercilessly honest self-judgment.

Bjørnstjerne Bjørnson

Bjørnson (1832–1910) as human being and writer is the perfect antithesis of Ibsen: Ibsen is the skeptical critic, Bjørnson the born folk orator. Ibsen represents aristocratic individualism, Bjørnson praises democratic brotherhood. Bjørnson, who was four years younger than Ibsen, influenced the cultural life of his country long before Ibsen did. He was not only a lyricist, dramatist, and writer of novellas, but also a cultural politician and humanist who drew the attention of the entire world to himself through his writings and lecture tours in Europe and the United States (1880–81).

Bjørnson grew up in Romsdalen, where his father was a country parson. The countryside, which was at once wildly romantic, fruitful, and benevolent, became the source and setting of his later stories of rural life. Although he had earlier written poems, novellas, and dramas, the real summons to the poetic art came on a student excursion in 1856 to Uppsala. After his return, he wrote the one-act play *Mellem Slagene* (Between the Battles, 1857), the first Nordic saga drama in prose, a new form that Ibsen took over a year later in *The Warriors of Helgeland*. That same autumn, Bjørnson traveled to Copenhagen. Here, in a foreign environment, he recalled his childhood experiences and wrote a series of peasant tales, which ensured his popularity in his own country and his fame abroad as a modern successor of Jeremias Gotthelf, Berthold Auerbach, and Danish romantic Steen Steensen Blicher. The most important of the tales are *Synnøve Solbakken* (1857; Eng. tr. under various titles, 1858 and later), *Arne* (1859; Eng. tr. 1866 and later), *En glad Gut* (1860; Eng. tr. *A Happy Boy* and various other titles, 1869 and later) and *Fiskerjenten* (1868; Eng. tr. *The Fisher Girl* and various other titles, 1869 and later).

The predominant theme of these stories is a major motif in all of Bjørnson's works: the overcoming of force and the ennobling of defiant strength by love. This moral goal exerts little influence on the dispassionate characters who typically indulge in terse, suggestive exchanges of words. The impressionistic vitality of his language he owes to Hans Christian Andersen, to the fairy-tale language in Asbjørnsen and Moe's collection (see p. 18), and not least to the sagas. Naturalistic critics spoke scornfully of Bjørnson's muted treatment of eroticism and of his idealized portrayals of peasant life. When measured against the criteria of national romanticism, however, Bjørnson's narratives contain many very realistic passages.

As Ibsen's successor, Bjørnson worked energetically from 1857 to 1859 to bring the theater in Bergen, which was in the process of dissolving, back to its artistic and financial heights. For some time in the 1860s he took over the management of the theater in Christiania and the editorship of various newspapers; in 1874 he acquired the farm Aulestad, in order to help realize Danish romantic N. F. S. Grundtvig's ideas of a folk high school and adult education (see p. 4). During these years Bjørnson revived Norway's past in a series of historical dramas, epic romances, and short lyric prose.

The most interesting of his stage works is the trilogy *Sigurd Slembe* (1862; Eng. tr. 1888), in which he used material from Snorri's sagas of the kings. Young Sigurd has all the qualifications to become king, but cannot win the crown because he cannot conquer himself. In his despair, he attempts to seize the rights to the throne. He murders the king, but thereby forfeits his right of succession to the throne. *Sigurd Slembe* parallels Ibsen's *Pretenders*: Like Skule, Sigurd lacks the actual right to power. The play was developed primarily in Rome, where Bjørnson, with his longing for the harmonious, was converted to classicism. *Sigurd Slembe* was written under the influence of Schiller's trilogy *Wallenstein*, and his *Maria Stuart* gave Bjørnson the idea for his next work, *Maria Stuart i Skotland* (1864; Eng. tr. *Mary, Queen of Scots*, 1912), a Renaissance drama whose setting and style are noticeably influenced by Shakespeare. Although it is poorly constructed, the play contains effective crowd scenes and interesting character studies: the implacable John Knox and the weak Darnley, with his Othello-like jealousy. The sole Bjørnson figure is Bothwell, a Viking spirit reminiscent of characters in Bjørnson's Nordic writings.

The smaller forms are the most successful. In the monologue romance "Bergliot" (in *Poems and Songs*, 1862) Bjørnson's portrayal of Bergliot's mourning for her murdered husband and son penetrates deeply the psyche of a saga character. Equally imposing is the epic poem *Arnljot Gelline* (1870; Eng. tr. 1917). As in *Sigurd Slembe*, Bjørnson chooses an insignificant historical figure, a born ruler who finally atones for his crimes by serving King Olav and dying at his side in the Battle of Stiklestad in 1030.

From the numerous poems scattered through the short stories and dramas, one might conclude that Bjørnson was a productive lyricist. However, he published only one collection, *Digte og Sange* (1870; Eng. tr. *Poems and Songs*, 1915), which was expanded in later editions. His lyricism took the form of poems only under great pressure. They were born of particular situations; this is true not only of his poems to famous contemporaries, and those to Denmark in 1864, but also of his more personal poems. Bjørnson's style is grandiose—influenced by Grundtvig—particularly in poems in the saga mold or when linked to historical situations, as in the Norwegian anthem "Ja, vi elsker dette landet" ("Yes, We Love This Land"). One cannot generalize about his versatile poetry. In his situational and mood lyrics, and in the erotic poems, an intimate subjectivity dominates; in the more public poems, there is a strong metaphorical power; common to both is a direct and simple style.

Around 1870 Bjørnson, like Ibsen, left his romantic youthful writing behind him. The succeeding years brought the most violent battles of his life. He too had called for Scandinavian aid for Denmark (see p. 3), but after France's defeat in 1871, Bjørnson began to orient himself toward Germany. In 1872 he demanded in a speech that the Scandinavian countries "change their signals" toward their southern neighbor. And when Bjørnson declared himself in favor of Pan-Germanism, he ignited a momentous argument in Denmark and Norway, the "Signal Feud."

To find a peaceful surroundings in which he could work, Bjørnson traveled in 1873 to Rome, where he wrote the two plays that introduced the modern problem drama in Norway, *Redaktøren* (1875; Eng. tr. *The Editor*, 1914) and *En Fallit* (1875; Eng. tr. *The Bankrupt*, 1914). The first attacked partisan fanaticism and malicious journalism, the other dishonesty in business. Both have significant artistic weaknesses, but the latter play, owing to its modern theme, became a great success in Europe and was a precursor of Ibsen's *Pillars of Society*. Typical of Bjørnson is the conversion of dishonest businessman Consul Tjælde, signifying a victory of public morals over the selfishness of the individual; by contrast, in Ibsen's drama the conversion of Bernick is a victory over hypocritical society.

Bjørnson's next dramas are typical discussion and problem plays. *Det ny System* (1879; Eng. tr. *The New System*, 1913) demonstrates how difficult it is to express oneself truthfully in a restrictive society; it contains severe attacks on the institution of the church, on its clergy, and on bureaucracy. *Leonarda* (1879; Eng. tr. 1911 and later) defends the right of a divorced woman to make her own decisions.

Through the "Signal Feud" Bjørnson had won new, liberal friends, and through Brandes he had become familiar with current intellectual trends on the continent. In the years 1876–79 he experienced a religious crisis that led to his break with Christianity. At first Bjørnson was influenced by radical biblical criticism (see p. 4); later he became interested in the natural sciences and was an eager follower of Darwin's evolutionary theories. He attempted in the 1880s, to a greater degree than other Nordic authors of the time, to enrich his writing with these theories.

In the tragedy *Over Ævne, Første Stykke* (1883; Eng. tr. *Beyond*

Human Power I, also as *Pastor Sang*, 1893 and later) Bjørnson attacks Christianity because it demands the impossible from people. However, Pastor Sang is such an objective and sympathetic character that it becomes a gripping drama of a religious genius. Sang has boundless faith. By nature he loves his neighbor; he is strict with himself and understanding of others. Only when he takes the challenges of Christianity unto himself does he cross the borders of human possibility and go beyond his own power: He succeeds through prayer in bringing his crippled wife to the point where she can walk. She comes toward him, but dies in his arms. In the same instant he is seized by doubts and falls dead beside her. Humans should not try to transcend their natural limitations: This is Bjørnson's answer to Ibsen's *Brand* and Kierkegaard's religious idealism.

Beyond Our Power I is now considered a major work of Bjørnson's. In his own time, it did not arouse as much interest as *En Handske* (1883; Eng. tr. *A Gauntlet*, 1886 and later). In *Leonarda* he had opposed the tendency of public opinion to very quickly judge the morality of husbands and wives. In *A Gauntlet* the morality of both sexes is analyzed. The main character, Svava, demands chastity from men as well as from women; when she learns that her fiance does not live according to this demand, she throws her gauntlet in his face.

This play aroused displeasure in radical circles, as did the novel *Det flager i byen og på havnen* (1884; Flags are Flying in City and Harbor; Eng. tr. *The Heritage of the Kurts*, 1892), which follows closely Ibsen's *Ghosts*. It portrays a mother convincing her son to adopt her own healthy view of life. Bjørnson now prepared a sharp attack against the sexual anarchism of the literary left and kindled the "Gauntlet" or "Morality Feud," in which Brandes and Strindberg were among his opponents.

After 1890 Bjørnson deserted his exclusively polemical approach to literature and concentrated on psychologically subtle characterization. In 1895 another high point: *Over Ævne, Andet Stykke* (Eng. tr. *Beyond Human Power II*, and various titles, 1914 and later), a social drama in which the major characters are Pastor Sang's children, Elias and Rakel, and the major theme the tension between wealth and poverty. Bjørnson places anarchist Elias between socialist workers and representatives of a Nietzschean superman morality. Elias blows both classes of his opponents and himself into the air out of idealistic motives. The message is that neither anarchistic assassinations nor the implacability of the upper class can create a future. Both extremes have stretched their power too far. At the end, through Rakel, love and reconciliation are prophesied.

Beyond Human Power II does not match the first part in dramatic expression and structure. Bjørnson's next work, however, his most significant play from his later period, is a perfect whole. *Paul Lange og Tora Parsberg* (1898; Eng. tr., 1899) mirrors his bitter experience in politics and continues his fight against Nietzsche's philosophy. Much earlier in *The Editor*, Bjørnson had drawn a picture of political persecution; in this play too—with less tendentiousness and greater psychological empathy—he analyzes intolerance. He sets forth the hatred of the professional politician for the righteous but weak Paul Lange, who is doomed to defeat in this unequal battle. In vain his beloved, the strong and self-sacrificing Tora Parsberg, attempts to save him through her love; in the last act he takes his own life.

After this, Bjørnson's work began to decline. In the following years he wrote several more dramas, but they are not impressive. Not until he was 77 years old did he write his last success, the cheerful and youthfully fresh family play *Når den ny vin blomstrer* (1909; Eng. tr. *When the New Wine Blooms*, 1911).

Bjørnson was above all a prophet. His poetry represents a struggle to uphold ethical ideals. He was never an aesthete; he wanted to teach that human goodness is deep within us, that evil is created by external circumstances. Bjørnson was an evolutionist and a democrat, with a firm faith in the fellowship of humankind. Because of the idealism in his work, he was the first Scandinavian to receive the Nobel Prize for literature in 1903. As an artist he does not indulge in deep analyses of the human soul, but he is capable of capturing and communicating the essence of his characters. Although his aesthetic taste may be somewhat less certain than Ibsen's, his human portrayals are warmer and more alive than those of his great adversary.

Jonas Lie

During the 1870s the work of Ibsen as well as that of Bjørnson was clearly influenced by Brandes. But Jonas Lie (1833–1908), who had scarcely any contact with Brandes, was inhibited by the radical intellectual movement. He was deeply mystical, a dreamer whose visionary fantasies were fully expressed in his essentially realistic writing.

Lie, who was born in Hokksund, west of Christiania, grew up in Tromsø, the capital of Nordland. The eight years he spent north of the Arctic Circle left enduring impressions. A lawyer, Lie later oc-

cupied himself with the wood trade and became involved in speculations which led to his bankruptcy in 1868. From then on he wanted
to live exclusively by his pen and pay off his debts. As a writer he
spent most of his time abroad, particularly in Dresden and Paris, and
did not return to Norway until 1906.

In 1870 his first novel appeared. Titled *Den Fremsynte* (Eng. tr.
The Visionary, 1894), it embodied the mysticism of Nordland. This
wonderful world, in which the borders between the real and the un-
real are blurred under the influence of powerful nature and the secret
anxiety about evil powers—forms the background for a melancholy
love story of two young people, a story interwoven with legends. The
novel became an instant success, and Lie was praised by critics as the
poet of Nordland. He received a scholarship for a trip to Tromsø, for
which he expressed his gratitude with a new Nordland novel: *Tremas-
teren "Fremtiden"* (1872; Eng. tr. *The Barque "Future,"* 1879), a romantic depiction of life at sea and the first Norwegian merchant novel.
More significant is Lie's next book, *Lodsen og hans Hustru* (1874;
Eng. tr. *The Pilot and His Wife*, 1876), in which realistic experiences
of sailors are portrayed, and behind which is concealed the story of
growing alienation of two married people.

The following years brought many disappointments for Lie. Without success he tried his hand at a few novels dealing with the psychology of artists and a drama, *Grabows Kat* (Grabow's Cat, 1880),
in which he defended a vague conservative viewpoint against the new
Brandesian ideas which, through Ibsen and Bjørnson, had influenced
Norwegian intellectual life. The critics preferred his Nordland stories
and sailors' novels. Therefore, he wrote two more successful works in
this genre: *Rutland* (1880) and *Gaa paa!* (Go Ahead!, 1882). In the
latter, one of Lie's best books, one finds the new ideas—criticized by
the author. An old family, threatened by destruction, victoriously
wages its battle for renewal. An isolated village society, in which
everything is stagnating and degenerating, becomes a symbol of the
stagnant intellectual life of Norway.

Earlier Lie had portrayed mostly people of an older generation.
Now he turned to the present and represented the ideas of youth. His
subsequent novel, *Livsslaven* (The Life Convict, 1883; Eng. tr. *One
of Life's Slaves*, 1895), treats the problem of poverty and social dis-
parities. The empathic story of an illegitimate child, Nikolai, who becomes a criminal and is condemned to life imprisonment because he
committed a crime of passion is an attack on societal injustice. The
novel shows that Lie had developed into a writer of modern problem
novels, yet his partisanship never interfered with the artistic quality

of his work. Characterization is essential: Lie portrayed not *problems* but, as his Danish student Herman Bang put it, *human fates*.

In the same year that *The Life Convict* appeared, *Familjen paa Gilje* (1883; Eng. tr. *The Family at Gilje*, 1894 and later) was published—a major Norwegian literary work and Lie's "classical" novel. The plot is set in a mountain village in about 1840. Protesting a marriage of convenience, Inger-Johanna breaks her engagement, thus sacrificing an advantageous match, but does not get the man she really loves. She is resigned, and when she later discovers that he has drunk himself to death, her sole response is: "He gave me something to live for"—quiet words concealing profound human drama. In this novel, Lie found the form that enabled him to practice his art while conveying new ideas. Although he rejected doctrinaire naturalism, he detailed every trait, every small peculiarity of his characters. His description of the Biedermeier milieu is masterfully sharp and honest.

In *Kommandørens Døttre* (1886; Eng. tr. *The Commodore's Daughters*, 1892), the title of which refers to Camilla Collet's novel (see page 18), the question of the emancipation of women, already touched on in *The Family at Gilje*, is treated in a completely undogmatic way. Two of the daughters, each in her own fashion, fall prey to social conventions and morality. Cecilie loves young Fasting, but etiquette forbids her to show her feelings. He perceives her reserve as rejection, and marries the second, less complicated, sister. The youngest, Marthe, loves her cousin, a sailor. She becomes pregnant, his ship sinks, and he is lost. The life and happiness of both sisters are crushed by hypocrisy and fear of scandal: The proud Cecilie ends her days in pain and bitterness, and the warm-hearted Marthe is forced to bear her child in secret and to deny it.

In the 1890s, Lie abandoned problem literature and began to write subjectively. Two small volumes of tales, *Trold* (Trolls, 1891–92) lie entirely outside the realm of realism, with their intensive portrayal of mystical nature and the unconscious life of the soul. They contain simple fairy tales and pensive parables but also witty satires on modern society, including women's liberation.

The conception of a demonic lower stratum in the soul dominated Lie's next works, giving a symbolic character to many of them. It is clear that he had shifted his sympathies, which in most of his previous work were with youth, hence new ideas. In *Niobe* (1893; Eng. tr. 1897) it is the guilt of the young generation—with its grand phrases and its dislike of honest work and responsibility—which causes the destruction of an entire family. The catastrophe occurs after the suicide of the despairing father; the mother blows up herself and her three older ill-bred children.

The only outstanding work in Lie's late novels is *Naar Jernteppet falder* (When the Iron Curtain Falls, 1901). The characters are passengers on a steamship from all social classes, the ship becoming symbolically a microcosm. Among these carefree people the rumor suddenly spreads that a bomb is hidden in the cargo. In the face of impending death, all masks fall, and concealed thoughts and character traits are revealed. But the writer allows the danger to pass—the world remains whole.

Lie wrote poems and plays, but only his novels are significant. Many of them are tendentious, and Lie, like his Norwegian colleagues, is a writer of problem pieces. But he prefers the *indirect* method. He deserts the role of omniscient, realistic narrator, and stands invisible behind his characters. Human fate is always of primary interest to him. He deals with the great problems in the fortunes and misfortunes of little people. Émile Zola's broad and pathetic style became a dangerous model for many not highly talented Nordic naturalists. Lie's work more closely resembles that of another French author, Alphonse Daudet. Lie is humorous and empathic, his style terse and lively.

One finds in Lie's novels scarcely any lengthy descriptions and portrayals of characters. He created a delicate impressionistic style from fleeting allusions and striking details which appeal to the sympathy of the reader. The characters reveal themselves through their individualistic responses. "You never tell us anything, you show us everything," wrote Herman Bang to his teacher Lie.

Chapter *3*

Nordic Literature in the 1880s

The decade of the 1880s in Norway and Denmark was quite different from the previous one. The fighting spirit of the years of the "modern breakthrough" was gone; pessimism and skepticism became increasingly widespread. Problem literature was no longer as dominant as before, and the evangelistic mission to instill new ideals was succeeded by a more aesthetic approach to literary creativity. Instead of attempting to alter opinions and arouse debates, many of the younger writers were satisfied simply to shock the bourgeoisie. In Sweden, Finland, and Iceland, the modern breakthrough did not take place until the 1880s, in Sweden partly because of a strong idealistic tradition, in the other two countries because of the dominance of national romanticism. This romanticism lingered in Finland because of an interest in the national past and in the creation of a Finnish literary language. In Iceland it remained because of their struggle for independence from Danish rule throughout the nineteenth century. However, toward the end of the decade, these countries also reacted against the naturalistic ideology; in Finland Leo Tolstoy's religious and social ideas were a strong influence. Characteristics of the years 1880-90 is the dominance of the novel in all five countries: Drama is pushed aside—only in Sweden is there original work—and poetry finds no outstanding champion.

THE CRISIS OF DANISH NATURALISM
When George Brandes surveyed Danish naturalism in 1883 in *The Men of the Modern Breakthrough*, this group of writers was already

in the process of dissolving. Jacobsen, whose novel about the unhappy freethinker *Niels Lyhne* had disappointed Brandes and his other radical friends, died in 1885. In the same year that Brandes's book appeared, Drachmann published the travelogue *Skyggebilleder* (Shadow Pictures, 1883), an ethical argument against naturalism. He then returned for a time to Brandes's camp. However, the defection of another radical author, Karl Gjellerup (1857-1919), was permanent. Influenced by Turgenev and Dostoevski, he wrote the novels *Minna* (1889; Eng. tr. 1913) and *Møllen* (The Mill, 1896); his later writings were influenced first by Nietzsche and Wagner, then by Schopenhauer and Buddhism. In 1917 Gjellerup shared the Nobel Prize for literature with Henrik Pontoppidan; today he is undeservedly forgotten.

Outside of the Brandes camp stood the two greatest figures of the 1880s, Herman Bang and Henrik Pontoppidan. One finds the most penetrating criticism of the morality of naturalism in Pontoppidan's exposure of the unfounded belief in the magnificence of liberated human nature. The other critical realist, Bang, emphasized that realism is an art form, not partisan writing. This doubt about the value of the ideas of the breakthrough was in no way related to the desire for progress in Danish society. The collaboration of the "Literary Left," led by Edvard Brandes, and the Farmer's Party (see p. 6) collapsed in 1883 owing to religious and national differences, but the Farmer's Party remained Denmark's largest. It demanded that it be allowed to take over the government and that parliamentary rule be introduced, which finally occurred in 1901. The governing right-wing party under its minister Estrup, who had been reigning dictatorially since 1885 by imposing provisional Finance Acts, fought these ideas. The struggle over parliamentarism splintered the nation. Even the simultaneous economic and social advances (the cooperative movement began in 1882, and labor unions were established during the 1870s and '80s) did not prevent political acrimony and apathy among the populace. This mood characterized the leading writers of the period, who utilized primarily personal themes, permeated with deep pessimism.

Herman Bang

This tendency is clear in the work of Bang (1857-1912). His first novel, confiscated because it was deemed immoral, bears the revealing title *Haabløse Slægter* (Generations without Hope, 1880). Faith in the triumph of progress has been replaced by renunciation of life and mixed sympathy and contempt for humankind. After Bang's youthful dreams of being an actor were destroyed when the Royal Theater in

Copenhagen rejected him in 1877, he created for himself an influential position as a journalist and critic for the conservative press—which brought him into cultural and political opposition to Brandes and his adherents. Around 1900 Bang exerted a significant influence on the Danish theater as a stage director; in Paris he even staged Bjørnson and Ibsen.

In *Generations without Hope*, the protagonist is a writer, Bernhard Hoff. It is not Bang's self-portrait, but Hoff is characteristic of the decadent type that Bang introduced into literature. Hoff's blase, affected demeanor became a mask for Bang, behind which he concealed his despair and suffering. He was brutally derided by his contemporaries because he was homosexual, which is probably the explanation for his profound feelings of isolation and homelessness.

Generations without Hope is significant beyond its value as a document of the times. It is plotted as a naturalistic novel of inheritance, in which the main character and his family decline and fall, a theme basic of Bang's creative work and derived from the French naturalists Balzac and Zola. Another major theme, the transformation of tenderness into sexual desire—this urge being the cause of all misfortune—is found in his next novel, *Fædra* (1883).

Of greater value are the subsequent collections of short stories, which Bang wrote on a European trip. *Excentriske Noveller* (Eccentric Short Stories, 1885) treat of people who, like Bang, live outside of society; *Stille Existenser* (Quiet Existences, 1886) is a series of tragic idylls. This volume contains Bang's most mature work, "Ved Vejen" ("By the Wayside"), a story about life in a small provincial city. Katinka Bay—lonely in her marriage to a primitive stationmaster—longs for tenderness. When her feelings are returned by the farm foreman Huus and the two become aware of their love, they separate. Katinka languishes in a lonely, quiet existence, until she dies. In this portrayal of everyday people experiencing tragedy, Bang pays superlative attention to their surroundings. With admirable clarity he works many tiny and precise observations into a mosaic of reality. Nothing is *told* about the people. Bang, using a purely filmic technique, presents them alive before the reader. No work in Danish literature deals more understandingly with the unnoticed, the neglected, with their disappointed hopes and stunted feelings.

This line is continued in the collection *Under Aaget* (Under the Yoke, 1890), bitter novellas dedicated to Bang's stylistic teacher, Jonas Lie. In "En dejlig Dag" ("A Lovely Day"), he portrays with good-natured irony the tragi-comic contrast of the impoverished existence of a teacher's family and a great, festival experience which turns everything upside down: A famous female pianist performs in the tiny provincial city, and after the concert, along with the local notables, is a guest in the teacher's modest home. More tragic is the story of the faded spinster, "Frøken Caja" ("Miss Caja"), whose expectations of life have come to nothing and who now lives on as an observer of the happiness of others. Purely tragic—infinitely sad and gripping—is "Irene Holm," a wholly destitute dance teacher, whose illusions of becoming a great ballerina are brutally destroyed during her solo dance in a village by the derisive laughter of the onlookers.

Bang's work from 1886 to 1890 is the high point of his creativity. During this time he wrote two novels. Stylistically influenced by Lie and thematically by Zola, Bang portrays in *Stuk* (Stucco, 1887) the spiritual hollowness and economic fraud behind the abortive attempt of Copenhagen to transform itself from a provincial city into an international metropolis. This ambition is symbolized in the erection of a great theater which subsequently proves unprofitable for the small Copenhagen and goes bankrupt. In an accelerating tempo, Bang shows us scenes and characters from all social levels. For the first time, a writer attempts to condense all of modern, demoralized Copenhagen life into one impression; the result is the creation of the first Danish big-city and collective novel.

Another characteristic picture of the time is presented in *Tine* (1889). The plot is set in the South-Danish island of Als, Bang's birthplace, at the time of the Schleswig war of 1864. The masterful chapter "Dannevirkenatten" ("The Night at Dannevirke") portrays the collapse of Denmark's political illusions in a night of military retreat. Against this background plays the tragic love story of Tine, a servant girl who perishes in the passion of the war. When the wife of the forest ranger leaves because of the unsettled times, Tine's solicitude for him develops into a serious passion. When he later rejects her in disgust, the despairing Tine drowns herself: a new variation on the theme of sexual desire. This plot is only secondary for Bang, however, and recedes behind an abundance of episodes from the theater of the war: the anxiety of the soldiers, the cries of the dying, the general apathy after the retreat—all portrayed with Bang's overpowering impressionistic art.

Tenderness, desire, and destruction are again stages of development in the novel *Ludvigsbakke* (1896). Here Bang, like Strindberg, portrays the relationship of husband and wife as a torture leading to the destruction of life. The kind-hearted nurse Ida Brandt falls into the hands of an unprincipled young nobleman whom she has known since her childhood on the estate "Ludvigsbakke," where her father was the foreman. He egotistically exploits and seduces Ida, only to reject her in favor of a match with a wealthy woman. Although this plot may seem thin and banal, and Ida Brandt is somewhat sentimentally portrayed, Bang's ability to hint at experiences between human beings with incomparable discretion conjures up pictures that are unforgettable.

The end of the century marked a new subjective period in Bang's writing. In addition to the two poetic, somewhat sentimental books of reminiscences, *Det hvide Hus* (The White House, 1898) and *Det graa Hus* (The Gray House, 1901), he wrote two lengthy "artists novels," which are highly autobiographical. The main character of the first, *Mikaël* (1904), is the French painter Claude Zoret, an embodiment of Bang's own artistic dreams. Zoret loves his young pupil Mikaël, but a woman comes between them and lures Mikaël away. Because the morality of his time prevented Bang from dealing openly with the tragedy of his own life in his description of the relationship between the two artists, the spiritual tension of the novel is expressed in a complicated, often forced, style, which seems old-fashioned compared with his earlier works.

His last novel, *De uden Fædreland* (1906; Eng. tr. *Denied a Country*, 1927), is marred by a mannered style and hysterical tone. Bang describes the unfortunate fate of the homeless violin virtuoso Count Joán. One day he happens upon a national idyll in a small Danish frontier town in which he is to appear. He is immediately taken with the simplicity and geniality of the provincial milieu, and he dreams of a harmonious marriage to Gerda, the young daughter of a merchant. But during a party, this dream is destroyed. All the defects and weaknesses of the nation—manifest in the guests at the party—are revealed: conceit, half-heartedness, and jealousy. Gerda is tied to her milieu and cannot marry Joán, and he is forced to realize that this land cannot become his home.

Denied a Country shows to the fullest extent Bang's stylistic technique. The main plot is played out in one afternoon, the essential background information having been given in the prologue. As in Bang's other great impressionistic works, everything happens before the eye of the reader. The novel is drama. Nothing is reported, described, or analyzed; everything is situation, action, and direct speech, often in scenes involving many characters—as in the ball and dinner scenes.

This "scenic" technique is central to Bang's impressionistic style, a technique that bears the influence not only of Jonas Lie but clearly also of Hans Christian Andersen's novels. Bang has a fine eye for the actions of his characters. Like no other Danish writer, he mastered the individualized, lifelike response, introducing the finest nuances. These overlooked, "quiet existences" Bang portrayed, as had his patron and teacher Vilhelm Topsøe, without any social or ideological polemic. Remaining from naturalism is the pessimism that informs the work: hopelessness, degeneration, and decadence as the prevailing way of life. More important than naturalism, however, is Bang's compassion for people who, like himself, have been brutally dealt with by their fellow creatures and, indeed, by life itself.

During a recitation tour through the United States, Bang was found gravely ill in the train going from Chicago to California; he died in Ogden, Utah.

Henrik Pontoppidan

The pessimism of the late decades of the nineteenth century, which determined Bang's view of life, found even more powerful expression in the works of Pontoppidan (1857–1943). He was a confirmed realist, an opponent of complacency, but he also sharply criticized naturalism. Scorn and biting irony lifted his writing to an irrational sphere of passion and fantasy. He was born in the Jutland city of Fredericia, the son of a minister. Rebelling against the gloomy atmosphere of the parsonage, Pontoppidan went to study at the Polytechnical Institute in Copenhagen. He quit school shortly before final examinations, left Copenhagen, and until 1910 lived in North Sealand, where the peasant environment offered him new inspiration. Then he settled in Copenhagen. In 1917 he shared the Nobel Prize with Karl Gjellerup.

The best-known piece in his first collection of short stories, *Stækkede Vinger* (Clipped Wings, 1881), is "Kirkeskuden" ("The Ship Model"). It deals with the orphaned gypsy youth Ove, who is raised, like a bird with clipped wings, by a minister and his wife. Ove perceives a comrade in suffering in the votive ship that hangs in the church, and he sets it into the water, where it immediately sinks. This allegory of the immutable force of environment is varied by Pontoppidan in later works; in the two novel cycles *Det forjættede Land* (The Promised Land) and *Lykke-Per* (Lucky-Per), and in the fable "Ørneflugt" ("Eagle's Flight"), a counterpiece to Hans Christian Andersen's fairy tale "Den grimme Ælling" ("The Ugly Duckling") with its faith in genius. Other major themes are present in "The Ship Model": rebellion against the parsonage, as well as a crassly realistic and satiric presentation of the materialistic, wealthy farmers.

While the farmers were organizing in Grundtvigian folk high schools and in the Parliament, the lower, impoverished classes found a champion in Pontoppidan. He published two volumes of short stories, *Landsbybilleder* (Village Pictures, 1883) and *Fra Hytterne* (From the Cottages, 1887). There is no idealization; they are realistic accounts of the misery of the country proletariat told sternly and unsentimentally. A comparison of stories in the two collections reveals a stylistic development from doctrinaire naturalism to pellucid objectivity, a development that continues in the books he wrote later. In the novel *Isbjørnen* (The Polar Bear, 1887), which portrays a maverick priest struggling against his "civilized" colleagues, gray realism is succeeded by delight in poetic narration. This cheerful satire modulates into cruel derision in the short-story collection *Skyer* (Clouds, 1890), stories about city and country in the years of the Estrup government (see p. 36). In "Den første Gendarm" ("The First Gendarme"), the village inhabitants prepare for a military reception of the first "Estrup" gendarme, but when he appears, high on horseback, they all simply stand there and gape. In this volume, Pontoppidan's "double viewpoint" becomes clear: He is attacking and deriding not only the misuse of power by the conservative government, but also the cowardice of the Left and of the people who tolerate these offenses.

Pontoppidan's trilogy *Det forjættede Land* (1881–95; Eng. tr. *The Promised Land Emanuel; or, Children of the Soil*, 1896) is also a satiric portrait of the times. It is at the same time a penetrating study of the soul of a religious dreamer and the tragedy of an idealist, and as such is a counterpart of Bjørnson's *Beyond Our Power I*. Young Pastor Emanuel Hansted is isolated not only from the Copenhagen bourgeoisie from which he came, but also from the rural population. As a country minister, he eagerly participates in the political and spiritual life of his community; he walks behind a plow and he marries a farmer's daughter, Hansine. But his attempt to find "the promised land" proves unsuccessful. When he is totally isolated by a Grundtvigian adversary, he loses faith in the people and in his profession, he turns away from his infatuation with nature and deserts his office, wife, and children. He flees to Copenhagen but does not find peace there either. In his personal and religious quest, he brings the enmity of his surroundings upon himself. The encounter with the cosmopolitan woman Ragnhild plunges him into an erotic-religious crisis which robs him of his last contact with reality. He buries himself deeper and deeper in mystical religiosity; at first he believes that he is a prophet sent by God, then that he is Christ himself; finally he dies in a mental institution. Seen from the perspective of intellectual history. Emanuel is a weak echo of Rousseau's and Tolstoy's anti-cultural messages. As a national type, he enters the great gallery of dreamers in Danish literature. Pontoppidan does not condemn him; here, too, his double viewpoint is evident. Although Emanuel's idealism shatters when it encounters external reality, his striving is serious; even in his madness he has an acute self-awareness which the author presents reverently.

As in *The Promised Land*, the next novel cycle, *Lykke-Per* (Lucky-Per, 1898–1904) contains autobiographical material. Like Emanuel, Per Sidenius is searching for happiness, but in an entirely different way. Whereas Emanuel pursues great, unselfish goals, and perishes as a result, Per is interested only in his own happiness and finds it by finally losing everything except himself. He is the son of a pietist priest in a Jutland provincial city. His upbringing is characterized by strong authority, against which he rebels by deciding to study engineering rather than theology in Copenhagen. Here he begins to work out a major project designed to transform Denmark into a great industrial country. Although he rebels against his family, he is incapable of cutting himself off from them. He is unable to accomplish his great technical projects because his inheritance, his Sidenius nature, cripples his ability to act at decisive moments. Per settles in Jutland and finds consolation in idyllic traditional Christianity. He believes he has found a harmonious existence. Only later, influenced by medieval mysticism and pietism, does he discover his innermost self, and thereby also his happiness, in a lonely area in northern Jutland.

As a *roman à clef*, *Lucky-Per* provides a lively and richly populated picture of the last years of the nineteenth century. The sharp satire of land and people is informed with Pontoppidan's usual double viewpoint. Like Emanuel, Per is a national type: The Danes are a people of "Sideniuses"—passionate, lyrically gifted, but weak when action is necessary. All this is perceived sympathetically. Per sees the spiritual strength of his ailing mother as a symbol of the nation after 1864, which is rescuing itself through inner strength from catastrophe. He himself founders on the shoals of life, but achieves a sense of inner reality.

Pontoppidan wrote a series of shorter novels and stories at the beginning of the twentieth century that can be considered a prelude to *The Realm of the Dead*, the major work of the last period of Pontoppidan's authorship in which destruction and nihilism predominate. *Borgmester Hoeck og Hustru* (Mayor Hoeck and Wife, 1905) is permeated with anxiety about the secrets of the soul, which can erect insuperable walls between people. In the story *Det store Spøgelse* (The Great Ghost, 1907) fear of fellow humans is combined with mystical anxiety in the face of nature. Universal fear pervades the long novel *De Dødes Rige* (The Realm of the Dead, 1912–16).

By 1901 the transition to parliamentary government had been made. But as a picture of contemporary Denmark at the turn of the century, *The Realm of the Dead* again reveals the author's disappointment with political developments. Pontoppidan condemns his epoch by showing how the characters, in their conflicts with moral and political conditions, demean themselves or are even destroyed. The basic theme of the novel is the emptiness of human existence owing to the absence of love, the relationships of the major characters to their fellow human beings being measured by their ability to love. Pontoppidan applies this criterion most strictly to the politician Enslev. He cannot achieve his democratic goals because he pursues his career selfishly and wants to change people according to his own willful ideas. Enslev is not only the major character, he is also the major cause of the transformation of the realm of the living into the realm of the dead. He personifies Pontoppidan's gloomy view of life and his attitudes toward humankind. After all, is the longing for freedom anything but a powerless rattling of the chains of the imprisoned? Is love anything more than a deceptive dream? This opinion is shared by the landowner Torben Dihmer. A miracle medicine slows the pace of his fatal illness, but when young Jytte Abildgaard deserts him and he realizes he cannot find happiness, Torben withdraws to his estate to die alone. Jytte, because she is egotistical, is incapable of yielding to love. After the break with Torben, she ponders about herself, but understanding less than ever, she plunges into the sparkling artistic life of Copenhagen. When she hears of Torben's death, she praises her dead friend happily: "He had been released from the terrible world where everything was deception—except for disappointment." After a year, she herself dies: "Now I am dying, and yet I have never lived." This grandiose work is sustained by a shattering feeling of ennui. The religious experience of the nothingness of life, combined with the moral experience of its valuelessness, makes it unique in Nordic literature.

Pontoppidan's last novel, *Mands Himmerig* (Man's Heaven, 1927), portrays the tragedy of a ruthless authoritarian figure. The author's concern here is with the threatening moral decline of the Danish nation during World War I. In contrast to the unconcerned populace, Thorsen, a journalist, thinks Denmark has an obligation to participate in the war; through his impotent criticism, he destroys his happiness and his wife's. Although Thorsen, with his absolute demand, *politically* echoes Emanuel Hansted's religious vision, Pontoppidan does not treat him in his usual ironic fashion. He is firmly on Thorsen's side.

The basic theme in Pontoppidan's work is a demand for the liberation of the individual, which cannot be accomplished within the confines of a deterministic world view. As late as 1894, in the "artist's" novel *Nattevagt* (Night Watch), he accepted radical naturalism on equal terms with the poetic, religious renaissance of the 1890s. However, after 1900 one senses in his books an ever-increasing metaphysical emphasis. Henrik Pontoppidan characterized himself as a "popular storyteller." This modest self-characterization by an inspired epic writer corresponds to his clear style, which "de-lyricizes" language. No other modern Danish author has been able to paint so precisely a complete picture of his time—its intellectual movements and its people.

SWEDEN BETWEEN IDEALISM AND NATURALISM

In Sweden the new intellectual and literary movements were not established until around 1880. August Strindberg's novel *The Red Room* is a landmark. Whereas in Denmark and Norway realism and naturalism already prevailed, Sweden was still dominated by an idealistic poetic, whose outstanding representatives were Carl Snoilsky (1841-1903) and Victor Rydberg (1828-95). In his early poetry Snoilsky writes enthusiastically of Poland and Italy's fight for freedom, but the democratic and social sentiments of his later, stylistically impeccable poetry are less convincing. A poet who wavers between idealism and cultural pessimism, Victor Rydberg is a major figure in Swedish literature. Rydberg's humanistic idealism is evident in his cultural, historical novel *Den siste athenaren* (1859; Eng. tr. *The Last Athenian*, 1869), in which a synthesis between ancient humanism and liberal Christianity is advocated; idealism is even more succinctly expressed in his lyric poetry. Rydberg clearly rejects materialism and atheism, which were being proclaimed by the emerging radical naturalists.

The rudiments of realistic prose written around 1850 exerted only a minor influence on the literary developments of the 1880s. However, in the writings of romanticist C. J. L. Almqvist (1793-1866) one sees signs of realistic description. The heroine of his novel *Det går an* (1839, It Can Be Done; Eng. tr. *Sara Videbeck*, 1919) argues against marriage as an institution, an alarming topic which led to heated public debate. Whereas both Almqvist and Camilla Collett in Norway wanted to change the structure of traditional marriage, the first Swedish female emancipator, Fredrika Bremer (1801-65)—approximately fifty of her works have been translated into English—wanted to change society itself. The general title of her prose fiction, begun in 1828, is *Teckningar utur Hvardagslifvet* (Sketches from Daily Life), a series of novels that introduced realism into Swedish literature. Another pioneer of realism was August Blanche (1811-68), who in his first novel,

Jernbäraren (The Carrier of Iron, 1845), wrote of the working class as a positive contrast to the upper social classes. His descriptions of Swedish society in the 1840s have earned Blanche the reputation of being the most prominent portrayer of Stockholm between Gustavian poet Bellman and Strindberg.

However, it was the radical European ideas transmitted through Brandes, together with the tendencies toward social commentary and moral challenges for truth in the works of Ibsen and Bjørnson, that provided the impetus for revolt against the dominant views. As in Denmark and Norway, the theoretical basis of the modern breakthrough in Sweden was to be found primarily in French and English intellectual life; later the direct influence of German philosophy was evident. The younger generation rejected Rydberg's Christian-Platonic idealism as unrealistic speculation and turned to positivism and the theory of evolution (p. 4). Running parallel to the optimistic faith in the positive development of humankind was, in the mid-1880s, a nihilistic, pessimistic movement originating with Arthur Schopenhauer and his pupil Eduard von Hartmann. Hartmann's *Philosophie des Unbewussten* (Philosophy of the Unconscious, 1869) in particular, with its combination of scientific methods and metaphysical goals, found a wide audience and prepared the way for the great interest of the time in occult experiments.

The social and political transformations in the country provided fruitful soil for these new movements. Until the nineteenth century, Sweden had definitely been an agrarian country. Around 1850 the development toward industrialization began, bringing with it the gradual dissolution of the feudal agrarian structures, the creation of a city and country proletariat, and mass emigration to the United States. To be sure, the parliamentary reform of 1865 meant that a certain democratization did occur, but the right to vote was restricted at first and the workers were not represented in the Parliament. Although most of the younger writers came from the bourgeoisie, they sympathized with the upward-striving working classes; however, most of them lacked deep insight into social problems. Both writers and workers demanded a change in society. The most valuable artistic formulation of this demand was articulated in the critical novels of August Strindberg.

August Strindberg

To a far greater degree than Georg Brandes, Strindberg (1849–1912) was a symbol of contradiction. He was alternately a Darwinist, Rousseauist, Socialist, Nietzschean, and Christian mystic. But at the center stands the gigantic personality: a sensitive, always searching spirit—embittered, irreconcilable, occasionally self-torturing and melancholy. Strindberg was born in Stockholm. His father was a merchant and later commissioner of shipping. His mystically inclined, devout mother had served as a servant to his father and so was on a different social level. In his autobiography, *Tjänstekvinnans son* (1886–1909; Eng. tr. *The Son of a Servant*, 1913–14 and later), Strindberg gave a moving, but one-sided portrayal of his childhood and youth. He was abnormally sensitive and shy, and at times his latent feelings of anxiety shifted suddenly into a deep depression for which he later sought to compensate through aggressive behavior.

After passing university entrance examinations in 1867, Strindberg attended the University of Uppsala. While there, he made a living as a tutor and schoolteacher, attempted in vain to become an actor, and at the same time wrote his early, immature dramas. In 1872 he left the university without a degree and worked as a journalist and an assistant at the Royal Library in Stockholm. In addition, he translated a number of American humorists, such as Mark Twain, Bret Harte, and Artemus Ward. In 1877 he married the actress Siri von Essen, who brought some balance into his unharmonious life.

During his early years in Stockholm, Strindberg was influenced by many new ideas. Kierkegaard attacked official Christianity and demanded that the integrity of the individual be recognized. In Ibsen's dramas Strindberg encountered not only a firm belief in the importance of vocation (*Brand*), but also the program of realism (*The League of Youth*). Through Brandes's provocative writings and the relativistic viewpoint of English historian Thomas Buckle concerning the mutability of "official truths," his tendency toward social commentary was bent in a radical direction.

All of this can be found in *Mäster Olof* (1872; Eng. tr. *Master Olof*, 1915 and later), a drama of the greatness and tragedy of the vocational summons. The title character, a historical personage, believes himself called to win Sweden for the Lutheran faith. On the one side, Strindberg places Olof, vacillating between idealism and skepticism; opposite him is the fanatic Gert the bookprinter, more a political than a religious revolutionary, who misuses Olof as a tool in his fight against King Gustav Vasa. Olof knows of the conspiracy against the king, and when the plot is revealed, he is imprisoned and condemned to death, along with Gert. Olof begs forgiveness so that he may complete his work of religious reformation, while Gert, the real hero of the drama, hurls at him the damning word "apostate."

Success did not come to Strindberg until he published the novel

Röda rummet (1879; Eng. tr. *The Red Room*, 1913), which offers a cross-section of bourgeois society. The lower classes are represented less by the working classes than by a bohemian proletariat of poets, painters, and actors. The major character, Arvid Falk, moves into this artistic milieu, after having given up his career as an official, and attempts to live as a writer. As a journalist with the liberal press and later at a workers' paper, whose editor combines a lust for power with servility before the mighty, Falk loses all his illusions, not only about society but also about himself. He regrets that he did not remain an official. Like Strindberg's first great drama, this novel ends with a defection. Falk looks for a position at a school, becomes engaged to a teacher, and finds his niche in a marriage based on freedom and equality.

What makes *The Red Room* a breakthrough is the often biting criticism of economic and political conditions in Sweden. The novel was written in the aftermath of the economic crisis of the late 1870s, which interrupted the boom and its often unsound stock-market speculations. The novel gives a comprehensive portrait of the early rise of capitalism. In spite of the satire and indignation, the mood of the book is not embittered. Strindberg's style sparkles with subtle observations and impressionistic technique—an example is the famous panorama of Stockholm in the early pages of the novel.

After he had suddenly become famous and *Master Olof* had finally been staged, Strindberg turned to new subjects. On the basis of exhaustive source studies, he wrote a cultural history entitled *Svenska folket i helg och söcken* (The Swedish People on Holidays and Weekdays, 1880–82), with the intention of reforming the official writing of national history. However, much of the material was not sufficiently thought through, and the strange mixture of poetic fantasy and fact provoked the irate criticism of expert historians.

Angered by these attacks, Strindberg published a pamphlet with the ironic title *Det nya riket* (The New Kingdom, 1882), a malicious satire of official Sweden. His experiences in school and at the university gave him material for ridiculing cultural politics, and he also sharply attacked officials and the military. *The New Kingdom* provoked much indignation and sparked the first great feud in Strindberg's life. It was generally thought that he wrote the book to gain personal revenge. In Denmark he was accused of antisemitism, and Strindberg's private life was strongly attacked. As a result, he and his family moved precipitately to Paris in 1883.

During his stay in Paris, Strindberg regularly saw the Norwegian writers Bjørnson and Lie. In Switzerland, where he lived—with short interruptions—from 1884 to 1887, he became a cultural critic, using

Rousseau as his model. Even though Strindberg demanded radical reforms of most aspects of the social order, his attitude toward the women's movement of the 1880s was astonishingly negative. In the short stories *Giftas I* (1884; Eng. tr. *Married*, 1913 and later), the women's-rights advocates and *modern* marriage are derided. Strindberg interpreted them as feminist attacks on men. He still believed, however, that women should enjoy the same upbringing and the same schooling as men. Only the woman who wants to lead an independent life *outside* the family is censured by Strindberg, as in "Ett dockhem" ("A Doll's House"), a parody of Ibsen's *A Doll's House*. In the introductory story "Dygdens lön" ("The Reward of Virtue"), Strindberg advocates the free unfolding of the life of the senses and protests Bjørnson's demand for chastity before marriage. This novella contains a blasphemous description of the Last Supper, which resulted in his indictment on this charge. In late October Strindberg appeared in court in Stockholm. He was acquitted, but his sensitive nerves were shattered. He saw himself the victim of persecutions by an international league of women, accused his wife of infidelity, and believed that she wanted to have him locked away in a mental institution. This pathological mistrust led to irreconcilable frictions, and the marriage was finally dissolved in 1891.

The key to understanding the difficult crises of these years is given in *Le plaidoyer d'un fou* (1887–88, publ. 1895; Eng. tr. *The Confession of a Fool*, also as *A Madman's Defense Manifesto*, 1912 and later). Strindberg himself characterized this autobiography as "a terrible book." It gives the psychological background for his expressed hatred of women, as it is developed fully in *Giftas II* (1886; Eng. tr. *Married*, 1913 and later). In contrast to the first collection, many of these novellas were written when the author was suffering from hysteria. The woman is seen as a ruthless tyrant and an exploiter of the man. Strindberg's earlier democratic optimism has given way to a dark nihilism wherein every moral ideal is denied. Life is dominated by egoism and selfishness. Rousseau's deism is succeeded by cynical atheism. Within a few years Strindberg wrote a series of dramas permeated with hatred and disillusionment.

The wife succeeds in her male-destructive ambitions in the tragedy *Fadren* (1887; Eng. tr. *The Father*, 1899 and later). This play, portraying the struggle of power-seeking Laura for her daughter, has the shattering effect of an antique tragedy of fate. Laura finally gains power over her husband, the cavalry captain, by awakening a distrust in him that destroys his will: She causes him to doubt that he is the father of her child and that he is sane. His jealous thoughts deepen into despair, which reaches its highest pitch when he hurls a lamp at Laura. Now no one doubts that he is mentally ill. When he dies, tormented to death in a straitjacket, she has won her victory and her child.

Fröken Julie (1888; Eng. tr. *Miss Julie*, also as *Countess Julia, Julie,* and *Lady Julie,* 1911 and later) was written during Strindberg's stay in Denmark between 1887 and 1889. It contains a remarkable theoretical introduction, in which Strindberg explains his new naturalistic form of the drama: The unalterable, consistent development of character should be abolished, for modern humans are complicated and vacillating, and should be presented as such on stage. The dialogue should also be shaped more naturally and should be interrupted, as in reality, by sudden thoughts and associations. The plays should be short, without intrigues, the primary focus being on the psychological aspects.

In *Miss Julie* the plot is even more concentrated than in *The Father.* On a midsummer eve, the young noblewoman Julie is drawn into a love affair with her servant Jean, falls under his power, and can atone for her shame only through suicide. Julie goes to her destruction even more quickly than the cavalry captain: He is a victim of fate, but she provokes her own tragic fate.

In his next play, *Fordringsägare* (1889; Eng. tr. *Creditors,* also as *The Creditor,* 1910 and later), Strindberg uses his naturalistic dramatic theories even more consistently. The action of the plot, limited to the conflict situation, accounts for the entire playing time; the stage setting does not change, and only three characters are on stage. Tekla, a vampire figure, has been made into a successful writer by her second husband, Adolf. When she has drained his strength, she fears for her career and flirts with young admirers to awaken Adolf's jealousy. He continues to love her until her first husband appears and discloses her true nature. When he succeeds in proving that Tekla would be ready to enter into a relationship with him, he strikes Adolf a destructive blow, thereby revenging himself on both him and Tekla. The man is now as cruel to the woman as she was to the man in *The Father;* but his cruelty is a *just* revenge.

The second half of the 1880s was a time of great creativity for Strindberg. In addition to the dramas, he wrote articles on psychology, literature, and theater, travel descriptions from Italy and France, and his best-loved book, the novel about people and nature in the Swedish archipelago, *Hemsöborna* (1887; Eng. tr. *The People of Hemsö,* also as *The Natives of Hemsö,* 1959 and later), which was written in Bavaria and influenced by Jeremias Gotthelf's peasant novels. A foreman from the mainland, Carlsson, comes to the island to bring order to a farm that was neglected after the owner died. He attempts to win the hand of the widow Flod to gain financial security, but throws away his chances because of his desire for a younger woman. The entire novel is characterized by a joy in story-telling; it contains marvelous descriptions of nature and episodes that range from the idyllic to the exceedingly comic. Although the book ends tragically with Carlsson's death at sea, the basic mood is cheerful and fresh.

In the "women's" dramas that Strindberg wrote in the 1880s, the man is always superior, the woman inferior; but often she, owing to her meanness, is stronger. *Miss Julie* showed, above all, the struggle between upper and lower classes. Carlsson in *The People of Hemsö*, although he belongs to the lower class, represents a superior type of human being. Strindberg was, therefore, ready when Brandes called his attention, in 1888, to the writings of Nietzsche. Strindberg even exchanged several letters with Nietzsche—a contact that was broken off by Nietzsche's mental illness, clearly evident at the end of the year. Strindberg was strongly influenced by Nietzsche's hatred of Christianity and his homage to strong personalities; the superman theory found its way into the novella *Tschandala* (1889), in which an educated man, a Swedish scientist, struggles with a gypsy, a representative of the lowest level of society, and is victorious owing to his intellectual superiority. Here culture triumphs over nature in direct contrast to Strindberg's earlier infatuation with Rousseau.

In his second archipelago novel, *I havsbandet* (1890; Eng. tr. *On the Seaboard*, also as *By the Open Sea*, 1913 and later), which Strindberg wrote in 1889 after his return to Sweden, he goes a step further: The novel has an explicitly antidemocratic prejudice. The superman is Borg, the inspector of fisheries and Strindberg's alter ego, an almost hysterical disdainer of women and Christianity. Strindberg portrays him sympathetically as an absolute individualist and a being with superior intelligence, who does constant battle against a world of mediocrities. But he also shows the inadequacy of the purely materialistic approach to life. Behind Borg's apparent strength lurks insecurity. The fishermen, old-fashioned and simple, regard him with enmity. He falls in love with a young girl who abandons him in favor of a less worthy man. Fear overcomes him, his weak nerves fail, and on Christmas Eve he goes out to sea in his boat, never to return.

During this stay in Sweden, which lasted until 1892, Strindberg tried in vain to found his own theater. He was entangled in a divorce case with his wife, there were public scandals, but in spite of the difficult situation, he was astonishingly productive. His works include the comedy *Leka med elden* (1897; Eng. tr. *Playing with Fire*, 1930 and later), which deals with adultery that has no real consequence, since the man is ready to give up the other woman. Strindberg also wrote *Bandet* (1897; Eng. tr. *The Bond*, also as *The Link*, 1912 and later). This important drama signifies his departure from marriage, from atheism, and from naturalistic drama. He brings his own divorce case onto the stage in the embittered argument of a married couple over their child, whom the court eventually denies to both of them.

In 1892 Strindberg went to Berlin. In the next few years he traveled all over Europe while his disposition became increasingly gloomy. In 1894 he settled in Paris and occupied himself with alchemistic experiments and occult phenomena—related to the theosophical and mystical movements current at the turn of the century. His periods of melancholia returned periodically from then to his death. After 1894 he experienced a number of religious crises which lasted until 1896 and led him to espouse nonsectarian Christianity. This was the "inferno crisis," the course of which Strindberg sketched in diary entries in the confessional books *Inferno* (1897; Eng. tr. also as *The Inferno*, 1912 and later) and *Legender* (1898; Eng. tr. *Legends*, 1912 and later).

The confession begins in the autumn of 1894, when he leaves his second wife, the Austrian Frieda Uhl, about which he speaks with strong self-accusation. His fear that he would be assassinated by his enemies caused hallucinations which several times drove him to attempt suicide. Strindberg also felt persecuted by supernatural forces. His reading of Emanuel Swedenborg and other mystics strengthened his conviction that these powers were punishing spirits, destined to drive the repudiator of God to repentance and submission. After a period of intense anxiety, the sinner was converted. But the power of sin remained, and Strindberg was convinced that he had been chosen by God to suffer more than others in order to lead humanity on the path to atonement.

In *Till Damaskus* (1898–1904; Eng. tr. *To Damascus*, also as *The Road to Damascus*, 1913 and later), a three-part dramatic paraphrase of his inferno crisis, Strindberg himself appears as "The Stranger" who after painful wandering is driven to submit to "The Invisible One." The Stranger has left his wife and children, and waits for forty years for happiness. Gradually he experiences the guidance of the heavenly powers and senses that he must humiliate himself before God; he resists this, however. He admits that his pessimism and his hatred for humankind impede his salvation. Sick and chastized, The Stranger seeks admission to a monastery, where his Confessor speaks the judgment against him: "Because thou servedst not the Lord, Thy God, when thou livedst in security, thou shalt serve him in hunger and thirst, in nakedness and in want; and He shall put a yoke of iron upon thy neck, until He has destroyed thee!" The trials continue, now increased by "The Tempter," who characterizes the remorse and atonement of The Stranger as weakness. He attempts to awaken the jealousy of The Stranger against his wife, and here Strindberg again has the opportunity to give free rein to his misogyny, which stands in marked contrast to the prophecy of humanity and resignation with which the drama—somewhat abstrusely—ends. All the characters and events in *To Damascus* are seen through the veil of a dream; natural and supernatural are inexplicably interwoven. The problems and struggles of the soul are not presented primarily through the responses of the main character, or with allegorical figures, but through a crystallization of thoughts and wishes in characters or scenes.

After the nightmare of the inferno crisis, Strindberg's plan matured to write historical dramas modeled on Schiller and Shakespeare. There followed a series of stage works that dramatize segments from Swedish history from the Middle Ages to the Rococo period. Strindberg had always worked with historical sources rather casually. Now, too, he treated the facts very freely. By way of compensation for that, the dramas are more full of pulsing life than are most historical plays. Scenes change often and arbitrarily, and events from different epochs are placed next to each other, sometimes in a single scene for dramatic effect and tension—a Shakespearean technique.

In none of these stage works do the dramatic tension and the power of the dialogue emerge as strongly as in *Gustav Vasa* (1899; Eng. tr. also as *Gustavus Vasa*, 1916 and later). Strindberg links the play to his youthful work *Master Olof*, whose title character now plays a significant role as Schoolmaster Olaus. Olaus has matured with the years, is loyal and humble, but is also critical of his king. It is humility that Olaus teaches to Gustav Vasa, whose brutal domestic measures have aroused great dissatisfaction among the people. Olaus compels him to write to a rebellious leader of the peasants; as a result, the population of Dalecarlia, which has been so hard and thanklessly treated, comes to the king's aid in his darkest hour of need.

Strindberg's second drama of kings, *Erik XIV* (1899; Eng. tr. 1931 and later), is one of his most personal stage works. It contains an interesting portrait of a man, half-genius, half-psychopath, who is the personification of Strindberg's own psychic conflicts. Erik has extreme mood swings, and is, like Strindberg, insane at times, or assumed to be so by others. His figure is not drawn with the same openness as the queen in *Kristina* (1903; Eng. tr. *Queen Christina*, 1955), a drama which, with *Gustav III* (1903; Eng. tr. 1955), shows Strindberg's ability to write elegant and spirited conversation pieces. In contrast to the other royal dramas, *Gustav Adolf* (1900; Eng. tr. 1957), is based on an exhaustive study of Swedish history. Strindberg wanted to portray how the devastating religious war of 1618–48 was permeated with intrigue and power politics. Gustav Adolf, who wavers between the commandment to be just and the necessity of being ruthless, gradually becomes convinced that he must fight for a goal entirely different from the one that caused him to enter the war: He devastates Germany, which, as a good Protestant, he wanted to save, and is even forced to ally himself with a Catholic power, France. After prolonged doubts about the justification of his conduct in the war, the king establishes his ideal of religious freedom. The Protestants are to be freed from the tyranny of the Catholics, and *they* are not to suppress anyone. Strindberg linked this humanistic proclamation to Lessing's drama of tolerance, *Nathan der Weise* (Nathan the Wise).

In addition to the historical dramas that Strindberg worked on until 1908, he wrote the following: *Easter* and *A Dream Play*, in which the religious mystery play lives on; the sinister marital drama *The Dance of Death*; and the short chamber plays written in the spirit of the 1880s.

The central theme in *Påsk* (1901; Eng. tr. *Easter*, 1912 and later) is that suffering improves humankind. The milieu is described realistically: the everyday life of an unhappy family whose paterfamilias is in prison for misusing property belonging to his wards. His wife and his son Elis feel threatened in their difficult struggle for existence by the return to the city of the family's heaviest and, they fear, most implacable creditor. Another great sorrow: Elis's sister Eleonora is retarded, but through the girl's suffering, happiness and love again find their way into the family. The creditor renounces his financial claim when he thinks back on a good deed the father of the family had done him many years earlier. This plot, which is set on the last three days of Holy Week, has a shimmering overlay of dream and mysticism. The passion play achieves its tense yet exalted mood through the transformation of the gloomy hopelessness of Maundy Thursday and the anxiety-laden suffering of Good Friday, into the peace and joy of the radiant evening before Easter.

In the same year—1901—*Dödsdansen* (Eng. tr. *The Dance of Death*, 1912 and later) appeared. It contains Strindberg's most desperate portrayal of human beings, which, in contrast to the marital dramas of the 1880s, is now presented in an entirely impartial manner. Captain Edgar and his wife, Alice, have been living for twenty-five years in a marriage that has long been true hell. Filled with mutual hatred, they remain chained to each other—and lonely. Isolated through their malice, they live in a fortress tower on an island. Alice's cousin Kurt comes to visit them, and the couple harass him with their complaints. He attempts to help them out of their misery, but is pulled into the vicious circle when Edgar attempts to draw him into his camp, in order to find out what Kurt's thoughts and opinions of him are. Although in the first part of the drama, Edgar is portrayed with some sympathy, in the second, the portrayal is wholly negative. The characters are masks through which an almost demonic hatred is expressed. Punishment strikes the captain: He dies of a stroke. Interest then is concentrated on his daughter Judit and her love for Kurt's son. The relationship is drawn in somewhat brighter colors, but in Judit's character, too, there is the germ of a new dance of death.

In his productive years around the turn of the century, Strindberg also wrote a series of works in which his romanticizing tendency peaked. A very significant experience was his brief marriage to the young actress Harriet Bosse between 1901 and 1904. This late love inspired Strindberg to write his best lyric poetry, published in the small volume *Ordalek och småkonst* (Wordplays and Miniatures, 1905). This love also set the mood of the romantic fairy-tale plays *Kronbruden* (1902; Eng. tr. *The Crown Bride*, also as *The Bridal Crown*, 1914 and later) and *Svanevit* (1902; Eng. tr. *Swanwhite*, 1909 and later), as well as of the lyrical and fantastic *Ett drömspel* (1902; Eng. tr. *A Dream Play*, 1912 and later).

The basic theme of *The Crown Bride*—which, in Strindberg's words, was "an attempt . . . to penetrate Maeterlinck's world of beauty"—is atonement after despair and suffering. *Swanwhite* treats of self-sacrificial love, whereas *A Dream Play* is a fantasy of resignation and redemption. The daughter of the God Indra descends from heaven as a mediator between God and humankind, and shares the fate of humankind in order to investigate their complaints about the absurdity of existence. The play consists of the dream fantasies of the various characters and develops into the author's own dream. The latter is personified through one character—actually three—for the "characters are split, double, and multiply; they evaporate, crystallize, scatter, and converge. But one consciousness stands above all: that of the dreamer." (Preamble.) First he is an officer who waits faithfully, but in vain, for his beloved; then he changes into a lawyer, whose profession compels him to see the meanness and malice of human beings; then he becomes a poet. Indra's daughter falls in love with the lawyer and marries him, but the marriage becomes a new hell. However, not just the main character, but all humans suffer, and the poet in the play finally concludes that death is the only release. He hands the daughter of the God a written petition with the complaints of humankind. To prove that life is miserable, she sacrifices herself in the flames of the burning palace and returns to heaven. *A Dream Play* is constructed in the same way as *To Damascus*. In order to create the dream atmosphere, time and space are suspended; the suggestive scenes change and symbolically illuminate the hopelessness and monotony of existence.

After *A Dream Play* Strindberg returned to prose. In the novel *Götiska rummen* (The Gothic Rooms, 1904), a continuation of *The Red Room*, he sharply criticizes Swedish society and writes of his thoughts and opinions that have altered since his youth, particularly regarding religion. He criticizes the Lutheran state church, accusing it of making its pastors worldly, and he finds words of appreciation for Catholicism. Strindberg is also congenial to the great men of naturalism such as Zola and Darwin. The more he approaches social questions, the stronger his old views become, as he strikes out unrestrainedly right and left.

In the novel *Svarta fanor* (Black Banners, 1907), a *roman à clef,* the major themes from *The Gothic Rooms* are repeated. Here the uninhibited attacks are directed particularly against the literary present. It is a biting satire far removed from reality. Strindberg's fantasy made it grotesque, and his paranoia and misogyny are again evident. The lofty values and morals of the spiritual and religious life are sharply contrasted with the surroundings that Strindberg renders with such hatred. The protagonist, Falkenström, characteristically withdraws into a monastery to be with kindred spirits.

The religious and natural philosophical speculations and conversations that take place in this monastery were continued in *En blå bok* (A Blue Book, 1907; Eng. tr. *Zones of the Spirit,* 1913); in 1908 and 1912 further sequels followed. The book is a mixture of observations and dreams, meditations and polemics. It also contains psychological sketches, socio-political observations, sharp attacks on the materialism of the time, anecdotes, and a good complement of pseudoscientific essays—all of them shot through with Strindberg's fascinating temperament.

While Strindberg set down his struggles with himself and his time in *A Blue Book,* he attempted once more to realize his theatrical plans. This time, thanks to the strong support of the theatrical director and actor August Falck, he was successful. The name of the new theater, "Intima teatern," which opened its doors in 1907, describes its purpose, which Strindberg formulated as follows: "In the drama we look for the strong, significant theme, but with limitations. In shaping it we want to avoid all artificial superficiality, all calculated effects, pauses for applause, star roles."

For this theater he wrote four plays in 1907, which he called "kammarspel" after Max Reinhardt's "Kammerspiel-Haus" in Berlin. Common to all these "chamber plays" are the symbolic treatment of everyday life and a unique mixture of dream atmosphere and naturalism. The contents are predominantly unharmonious and pessimistic. That is particularly true for the first piece, *Oväder* (Eng. tr. *The Storm*, also *The Thunderstorm* and *Stormy Weather*, 1913 and later). The main character, an older gentleman, looks back with resignation on his broken marriage. His wife reappears and disturbs his peace for a time, but is punished for this by her second husband's betrayal. Only when she has made amends for her crime against the husband she deserted—like the wife in *The Father* she has disputed his paternity of their children—is she rescued from the betrayer. The dialogue is clear and subtly shaded, the atmosphere of peace and loneliness troubled only temporarily by hatred and bitterness.

In *Brända tomten* (Eng. tr. *After the Fire*, also *The House That Burned* and *The Burned House*, 1913 and later) this calm is conclusively destroyed. The traveler returns to his ancestral home after a long stay in America, but finds the house burned down. In his memory he begins to reconstruct it. The recent inhabitants, his family, and the neighbors come back to life, and are mercilessly exposed by the traveler. Everything is different, and worse than he had thought. Many possible crimes come to light, and at last all of humankind stands naked before his condemning eyes. The house has become an image of the entire world.

This fantastic symbolism intensifies to a surrealistic nightmare in *Spöksonaten* (Eng. tr. *The Ghost Sonata*, also *The Spook Sonata*, 1916 and later). The apparently solid middle-class home of a colonel is revealed, with macabre expressiveness, to be a chamber of horrors. Originally Strindberg planned to name the piece *Ghost Supper* for the eerie meal in the second act, which is eaten in a dreamlike, grotesque atmosphere. The participants, who are bound to one another like ghosts by crimes, secrets, and guilts, unmask one another and wait for death. An old cripple reveals that the fortune of the colonel rightfully belongs to him, that the noble colonel is a former servant, and that he, the cripple, is the father of the colonel's daughter. But the cripple too wears a mask. The wife of the colonel unmasks him as a usurer and murderer. He collapses and on her command hangs himself.

In the third act, a pair of young lovers meet: a student and the young daughter. During their time together, he is confronted, through the vampire character of the cook, with the deceptiveness of material existence. When he learns in his conversation with the young girl of the hatefulness and hardship of everyday life, he loses all illusions about his life and their future together. In despair, he calls to Christ for help and liberation; the girl falls dying to the ground. The drama closes with words of longing for salvation.

Pelikanen (Eng. tr. *The Pelican*, 1916 and later) technically is reminiscent of the naturalistic plays of the 1880s, which distinguishes it from the other chamber plays. The number of characters is limited, and the plot proceeds in a compressed and effective manner. The basic theme is the same as in the *Ghost Sonata*, but it is presented even more implacably: Life is filled with hatred and gloom, and most people are burdened with heavy guilt. The father has died because of his wife's malignity. Now, unavoidably as in Greek tragedies of fate, revenge catches up with her. Her children perceive that she tormented their father to death and permitted them, as small children, to go cold and hungry. She is, therefore, not a pelican, which sacrifices its blood for its young. The father was the pelican, the mother a vampire. The son sees no other way out of their misery than to set the house on fire; the mother plunges from the balcony, and while the two siblings ecstatically re-experience their childhood—in a vision of paradise—they die in the flames.

In 1909 Strindberg published his last drama, *Stora landsvägen* (Eng. tr. *The Great Highway*, 1954 and later). He, himself, without much camouflage, appears in the figure of the hunter who climbs down from the mountains to begin his last trip, to death. The drama is actually a great lyrical, philosophical monologue without a plot, often interrupted by satiric and polemic invective. All the other characters in the play give cues or make supplementary remarks; the central event is a great, lonely, and homeless genius bidding farewell to his art and to the world.

In the context of world literature, Strindberg's fame and major significance are attributable to his dramas. The models for his first masterpiece, *Master Olof*, were Ibsen and Kierkegaard; his stylistic teachers were Schiller, the young Goethe, and, above all, Shakespeare. In the 1880s he picked up ideas from Zola's essay *Le Naturalisme au théâtre* (Naturalism in the Theater), and created the three works, *The Father*, *Miss Julie*, and *Creditors*, that brought naturalistic theater to its highest point. After the inferno crisis, Strindberg wrote his great cycle of history dramas, which, in spite of their national themes, found a response and pointed out new directions in other countries as well. It is unthinkable that Bernard Shaw's *Saint Joan* and Eugene O'Neill's *Mourning Becomes Electra*, with their modern psychological approach and dialogue, could have been written without the examples of Strindberg's history plays. With *To Damascus* and the chamber plays, Strindberg created the modern irrational/visionary and expressionistic theater. Even after World War II, Strindberg was significant as stimulus and pioneer. Thus, for instance, *To Damascus* and *A Dream Play* had a great influence, through their atmosphere, style, and structure, on the works of the French Absurdist Arthur Adamov, Tennessee Williams, Sean O'Casey, Sartre, Ionesco, Pinter, Peter Weiss, and Edward Albee have also found inspiration in Strindberg's plays, and he has had a continuing and strong influence on Swedish filmmaker Ingmar Bergman.

If the themes in Strindberg's works are too often bound to himself and his environment, the best of his dramas are never too private. They provide naturalistic clarity and conciseness, and a dreamlike and metaphysical world of fantasy. August Strindberg was the boldest and most poetic experimenter in modern drama. "For me," said O'Neill (he and Luigi Pirandello were Strindberg's most significant students), "he remains . . . in his sphere the master, today even more modern than any of us . . . the greatest genius of all modern dramatists."

"YOUNG SWEDEN"

In the 1880s Sweden was faced with entirely new problems in its economic and political life. The economic crisis was particulary serious because the greatest part of the population was still involved in agriculture. Certainly this important branch of the national economy was advancing—improved farming methods had been introduced—but the importation of cheap foreign grain caused the prices to plunge, so that the farmers and the flourishing industry demanded tariff-protection for domestic products. After the establishment of customs boundaries in 1888, industry was able to develop further. Factories and railroads were built and the wood-export industry found a wealthy market in the European industrial countries. However, neither the industrial workers nor the economically weaker groups in the population benefited from this economic improvement, nor did they have a place in the political life of the country. For the time being they did find compensation in the incipient worker's movements and in the Free Church organizations which originated health and unemployment insurance, and training programs for the lower classes.

The unrest and hopes of this period found expression in a group that called itself "Young Sweden." Their influence on the spiritual life of the country was notable, although they left behind only a few works of artistic merit. The writers belonging to this group wanted to mirror reality in all its everyday banality and tragedy; they demanded personal truth in their views and in their art, and in the spirit of Brandes, took passionate positions on current problems. They thereby developed the beginnings of social realism in the 1840s into a much sharper and more relentless naturalism, uncircumscribed by any aesthetic prejudices.

Next to Strindberg, the spiritual leader of this group, Victoria Benedictsson (pseudonym Ernst Ahlgren [1850-88]), was the most interesting figure of the 1880s, in spite of the fact that her short stories and novels of marriage *Pengar* (Money, 1885) and *Fru Marianne* (Mrs. Marianne, 1887) did not have any great artistic value. The driving force behind the Young Sweden group, the very productive Gustaf af Geijerstam (1858-1909), was a more typical representative of the pessimistic outlook of the period. The title of his first volume of novellas, *Gråkallt* (Gray Cold, 1882) is characteristic of his dark naturalism. Later, in accordance with the movements of the 1890s, Geijerstam developed into an inward-directed, psychological author; his novels, for instance *Vilse i livet* (Astray in Life, 1897), became very popular and achieved an undeserved reputation for profundity.

Ola Hansson

One finds a tendency toward the provincial in the work of the greatest lyrical talent of the 1880s, Ola Hansson (1860-1925). In his youth he wrote insignificant social propaganda poems, but in his second collection, *Notturno* (1885), he created a nature poetry influenced by J. P. Jacobsen, based on exact observation, and permeated by a soft and musical tone. His short stories *Sensitiva amorosa* (1887) are also characterized by a lyrical tone and combine a mood of refined eroticism and psychological analysis. The philosophical pessimism present in the poems now intensifies—influenced by Hartmann and Schopenhauer—into a dread of life and leads beyond the moralizing naturalism of the 1880s.

From 1889 on, Hansson spent virtually all his time in Germany. Edgar Allan Poe and Nietzsche became his models. The stories of crime *Parias* (Pariahs, 1890) are marked by somber fatalism and strongly stress the irrational. Hansson was led by Nietzsche's superman philosophy, which he expresses in the prose poems *Ung Ofegs visor* (The

Songs of Young Ofeg, 1892), to the then popular book by Julius Langbehn, *Rembrandt als Erzieher* (Rembrandt as Educator, 1890); the book won him over to Pan-Germanism and kindled his peasant nationalism. Mysticism and subjectivism are further steps in the development of his metaphysical and transcendent life view. The final result of this development was Catholicism, to which Hansson became a convert in 1898, and which is anticipated in his valuable autobiographical novel *Resan hem* (The Journey Home, 1895).

Ola Hansson's work was of no great direct significance for Swedish literature, but through his pronounced sensitivity and his feeling for the mystical, it mirrors the intellectual movements of Europe. Thereby he, and Gjellerup in Denmark, Aho in Finland, Garborg in Norway, and Strindberg, hastened the dissolution of naturalism, and the transition to the symbolic and neo-romantic poetry of the next epoch.

REALISTIC PROPAGANDA LITERATURE IN NORWAY

In Norway in the 1880s, naturalism took on a much more bellicose character than it did in Denmark. Doctrinaire writing became a force in society, writers responding to Brandes's urgings that they write about critical, sharply discussed, social, political, and religious problems. A great stir was caused by a radical group of artists and writers, the so-called Kristiania-Bohême, who vehemently argued about morality with Bjørnson (see page 30). Their model and prophet was the young Strindberg, and their leaders were the painter Christian Krohg (1852–1925) and the anarchist Hans Jæger (1854–1910). Jæger's novel *Fra Kristiania-Bohêmen* (From the Christiania Bohemia, 1885) represented "free love" and prostitution as being socially caused; therefore it was banned.

In Norway, as in Denmark, the novel was the favored genre. Kristian Elster (1841–81), whose art was strongly influenced by Turgenev, his view of life by Kierkegaard, wrote the significant novel *Farlige Folk* (Dangerous People, 1881), contrasting the modern ideas of progress and their reception in a small Norwegian provincial city. For Amalie Skram (1846–1905), Brandes's program was personally significant, giving her the courage to break up an unhappy marriage in 1877 and to choose a career as a writer. She became the most consistent representative of naturalism in Scandinavia. The lives of many of her heroines were based on private experience; in the cycle of novels *Hellemyrsfolket* (The People from Hellemyr, 1887–98), she penetratingly portrays a woman's unsatisfied desire for love in a deterministic, desolate world.

Alexander Kielland

While Elster and Skram openly expressed their hopeless view of life in their work, Kielland (1849–1906) concealed it behind the elegance of his style. During a stay in Denmark in 1881, he made friends of the leading naturalists and followed Brandes's program in his subsequent writing. Kielland came from a respected merchant family in Stavanger and lived until 1879 in the city of his birth as a lawyer and owner of a brickyard. In that year he published his first book, a collection of witty and elegant *Novelletter* (Novelettes; Eng. tr. *Tales of Two Countries*, 1891), scarcely influenced by the radical demands of the modern breakthrough.

Kielland's first novel, *Garman & Worse* (1880; Eng. tr. 1885) was received with even more enthusiasm than his *Novelettes*. He worked with his own recollections and gave an excellent picture of the merchant aristocracy in Stavanger. In the center stand the two Garman brothers, Richard, a lonely lover of nature who has become a lighthouse-keeper instead of a diplomat, and Christian Frederik, "the young consul," the capable head of the trading firm. His oldest son, Morten, also called "the wholesaler," is totally overshadowed by his charming wife, Fanny, who captivates everyone. Between these characters a plot full of intrigue and drama is played out in which social satire is dominant. A very effective contrast to this world is the cottage of the old dockworker Anders, representing the world of the poor workers. The young among them are rebellious and speak of the "bloodsuckers," while Anders remains true to the Garman family. When his daughter is buried on the same day as the consul, there is absolutely no doubt in his mind: He must attend the funeral of the head of the firm.

In *Skipper Worse* (1882; Eng. tr. 1885) the early history of the trading firm of Garman & Worse is portrayed. Kielland tells how former sailor Jacob Worse used his fortune to save the firm of Christian Frederik Garman, which had gone into bankruptcy, and became a partner. The author places even greater weight on the portrayal of the social and religious surroundings, on the circle of Haugeans (see page 18), in whose center stand the preacher Hans Nielsen Fennefos and the pious and slyly calculating widow Torvestad. With a mixture of irony and understanding, Kielland shows how she lures the elderly Jacob Worse into a marriage with her daughter Sara, although Sara is in love with Hans Nielsen. Disappointed, Nielsen leaves Norway as a missionary. The Worses' marriage becomes unhappy. The old sailor, previously so cheerful and coarse, is intimidated by his dark and confining environment, and is destroyed by it. Although Kielland, with scarcely concealed glee, unmasks the hypocritical mix of Christianity and business in some of the Haugeans, he does understand this popular lay movement, which he can play against the official state church.

The novels *Gift* (Poison, 1883) and *Fortuna* (1884; both tr. as *Professor Lovdahl*, 1904) are above all attacks on the upbringing of children and education in the schools, and on the dishonesty of society in general. The main character, Abraham Løvdahl, was originally a healthy and uninhibited character. He is brought up by his father to unthinkingly obey authority, while his mother attempts to show him the importance of personal honesty. His father's influence triumphs, and Abraham renounces sincerity in favor of a successful career.

Kielland's last novel, *Jacob* (1891), is a sharp satire of the vulgar careerist in a democracy. The portrayal of the peasant oaf Tørres Snørtevold, who with insatiable greed and brutal ruthlessness fights his way up to the position of the most powerful businessman and politician of the city, is a convincing vote of no confidence in the new democratic society by a previously very progressive author.

Alexander Kielland was the sharpest satirist and ironist of his generation. His moral and social indignation, as well as the demands of Kierkegaard for the integrity of the individual, were decisively significant for his work. He passionately fought any kind of mendacity within the public sphere and the state church, but he never attacked Christianity itself. In spite of this emphasis on day-to-day problems, in spite of the topicality of his themes, his best novels are masterpieces, owing to their vivid psychology and their linguistic virtuosity; they completely burst the confines of the naturalistic novel.

Arne Garborg

An even more typical transitional figure is Garborg (1851–1924), whose life was shattered by serious existential crises. He was always spiritually seeking and asking, and his entire work is informed by a dread of life and by religious longing. To a large extent, Garborg's importance is linguistic. He wrote almost all of his works in *landsmål* (see page 18), which, after his works were published, became the second literary language of Norway.

Garborg was a farmer's son from Jæren, to the south of Stavanger. His father, a melancholy brooder and strict pietist, committed suicide in a fit of religious depression. In spite of his poverty, Garborg succeeded in becoming a teacher at an elementary school. Later, as a Christian journalist writing for a conservative newspaper, he at first opposed Brandes and Bjørnson; but after intensive study of Brandes,

Kierkegaard, Taine, and Darwin, he changed his mind. In 1878 he published the novel *Ein Fritenkjar* (A Freethinker), which clearly shows this shift in opinion; the novel made Garborg one of the leaders of Norwegian naturalism in the succeeding decade.

A Freethinker tells of the disappointment of a radical theologian in orthodox Christianity, which is for him a caricature of the true faith. The novel suffers from an excess of theory and tendentiousness. Not until the crassly realistic novel *Bondestudentar* (Peasant Students, 1883), an outstanding portrait of student life in Christiania in the 1870s, based on the cultural tension between country and city, is Garborg's significance as a writer manifest.

His subsequent books, with their doctrinaire intentions, are typical naturalistic novels. *Mannfolk* (Menfolk, 1886) is a declaration of solidarity with the Kristiania-Bohême and portrays an eerie, dark picture of the miserable and disillusioned existence of the academic and artistic proletariat. More muted in its presentation, but equally depressing, is *Hjaa ho Mor* (Living with Mother, 1890), the broad and overlong story of the development of a young girl. In this novel one already senses Garborg's rising doubt that naturalism could solve all social and individual problems.

In 1891 came the clear renunciation; in *Trætte Mænd* (Weary Men), Garborg repudiated the materialism and dogmatic atheism of the time. In diary form, he portrayed the spiritual despair and self-criticism, and finally the conversion to Christianity, of the main character, Gabriel Gram—a conversion against which he had long struggled. Influenced by Nietzsche, Garborg confirmed the absurdity of democracy and the bankruptcy of science. Gram felt himself attracted by a mystical longing for eternity, which flowered into a religiosity with Catholic overtones. With this conclusion, *Weary Men* marked a turning point in Norwegian literature which clearly paralleled the conversion novels of J.-K. Huysmans in France.

In his next works, probably the most significant that Garborg wrote, the religious theme is expressed even more clearly. He turned from city life to his rural home; his deep feeling for nature gives abiding beauty to these books. In the tragic novel *Fred* (1892; Eng. tr. *Peace*, 1929), Garborg analyzes the melancholy pietism of his parental home, one of the most important influences on his creative work. His father is the model for the main character, the farmer Enok Hove, one of the greatest spiritual portrayals in Norwegian literature. Enok sinks deeper and deeper into religious speculation and tormenting self-condemnation. Eventually his awareness of the disparity between the strict demands of Christianity, which he inexorably attempts to obey, and the frail potential of weak human nature to fulfill them, drives him to death, where he finally finds peace.

In the drama *Læraren* (The Teacher, 1896), Paulus Hove breaks with the pietism of his father. As a follower of Christ, he sacrifices everything he loves to help the poor and to console the despairing. Paulus attracts adherents, hence power, and becomes a danger to society; the play ends with his arrest. In this figure, who passionately attempts to live the Christian ethic, Garborg presents his undogmatic religion. Influenced by Tolstoy, he shows us the practice of Christianity as the active love of one's fellow humans.

The sequel, the lyrical novel *Den burtkomne Faderen* (1899; Eng. tr. *The Lost Father*, 1920), has no plot, but is Garborg's most accomplished work stylistically. Paulus's brother, Gunnar, has gone out into the world to win power and wealth. He had married for money and destroyed his wife's love by his egoism. After she has left him, he in his emptiness longs for his homeland and for God, his lost father. In an encounter with Paulus and his preaching, Gunnar's skepticism is conquered; he finds his faith and thereby his peace.

These books about Enok Hove and his sons are inspired by the religious movements around 1900; the poem cycles *Haugtussa* and *In Hell* express a more *literary* symbolism. *Haugtussa* (1895) portrays, in musically expressive strophes, the visionary peasant girl Veslemøy and her struggle against the dark powers. The simple plot, interwoven with her fantastic visions and with poetic representations of nature and the peasant life in *Jæren*, makes *Haugtussa* one of the lyrical masterpieces of Norwegian *landsmål* literature.

The supernatural element is also a theme and starting-point for the sequel *I Helheim* (In Hell, 1901); Veslemøy is led in a dream vision through the realm of the dead, where everyone receives his or her deserved fate. The poem, whose models are Dante's *Inferno* and the late medieval Norwegian poem *Draumkvedet* (The Drama Ballad), is not transcendental, but symbolically presents earthly life and Garborg's arguments with the negative forces of the time: the lust for money and power.

Arne Garborg was not only an outstanding portrayer and defender of Norwegian peasantry and culture; he was also an emphatically European writer, always receptive to contemporary impulses and problems. He possessed a sharp intelligence and showed himself to be a philosophical skeptic and a brooder who advocated a religious view of life without theology and dogmatism. Writing such as Garborg's would have been unthinkable in the 1880s. His creativity blazed the way for the new intellectual movement of symbolism.

NATIONAL AND RADICAL REALISM IN FINNISH AND FENNO-SWEDISH LITERATURE

Swedish supremacy over Finland, established in the Middle Ages, was threatened by a number of Russian victories in the eighteenth century and ended with the loss of the entire country in 1808-9 and the installation of a Russian governor-general. The Russian promise to let Finland retain the exceptional position it occupied under Swedish rule was kept, on the whole; however, in 1850 the printing of books in Finnish was banned, with the exception of economic and religious literature.

In 1863 Finnish, which is not a Scandinavian language but a member of the Fenno-Ugric family of languages, was made equal with Swedish. This caused a schism between the Swedish party, representing the nobility and most of the bourgeoisie, and the numerous "fennomans," supported by the clergy and the peasantry. Around 1900 there was general opposition to increasing "Russification." Following the Russian revolution in 1917, preceded by a civil war in which the anti-Communist forces were victorious, Finland declared its independence.

The Finnish written language was created by the first Lutheran bishop of Turku (Åbo), Mikael Agricola (c. 1510-57), but an original, national literature did not arise until the nineteenth century. The cultural language was primarily Swedish, the scholarly language Latin.

The folk literature was very rich. The epic *Kalevala* (Eng. tr. 1888) was published in 1835 (enlarged ed. 1849), largely owing to the influence of nationalistic romanticism. The content, numerous songs dealing with heroic mythological persons and themes, was collected by Elias Lönnrot (1802-84), particularly in the distant and isolated Karelia, where these legends from the early Middle Ages had been preserved. Lönnrot also published the extensive collection of lyrical folk poetry *Kanteletar* (1840); this and the *Kalevala* constitute the major national works in Finnish literature. Many generations of poets, painters, and composers, such as Jean Sibelius, have found inspiration and motifs here; it was the inspiration for Longfellow's epic ballad, *The Song of Hiawatha*.

Lönnrot's publications laid the foundation for an independent Finnish literature and a national revival, culminating in J. L. Runeberg's heroic cycle of poems, *Fänrik Ståls sägner* (1848-60; Eng. tr. *The Songs/Tales of Ensign Stål*, 1925 and later), an idealization of Finnish feats during the war of 1808-9. Both here and in a number of other epic poems and idylls, Runeberg introduced into literature common people, Finnish folk life, and nature. Zacharias Topelius (1818-98) also attempted to promote Finnish nationalism through literature. He found the material for his long series of novels, *Feltskärns berättelser* (1853–67; Eng. tr. *The Surgeon's Stories*, 1883–87 and later), in historical events in Sweden and Finland during the seventeenth and eighteenth centuries. Influenced by the historical novels of Walter Scott and of Sir Edward Bulwer-Lytton, he added excitement and adventure to his skillful narratives.

Both Runeberg and Topelius wrote in Swedish. A Finnish literary language was not created until Aleksis Kivi wrote the first Finnish drama and novel. Hereafter the Finnish and Fenno-Swedish literature developed in different directions. This happened in part because of linguistic politics and in part for social reasons, since the Fenno-Swedish literature was created and supported by the upper class on the west coast. Today the Fenno-Swedes make up less than 8% of the population, and for every nine Finnish books, only one Swedish book is published—and the editions are small.

Aleksis Kivi

Kivi (1834–72) won the prize of the Society for Finnish Literature in 1860 with his first drama, *Kullervo* (1864). It is a rather immature five-act tragedy, loosely structured and based on the *Kalevala*. A masterpiece is the comedy *Nummisuutarit* (The Cobblers on the Heath, 1864). Here Kivi was in his proper domain: He describes his southern Finnish birthplace and its common people with a humorous realism reminiscent of Cervantes and Danish eighteenth-century playwright Ludvig Holberg.

Shortly before his death, Kivi published his major work, the novel *Seitsemän veljestä* (1870; Eng. tr. *Seven Brothers*, 1929 and later). He tells how seven adventurous brothers leave their ancestral farm, become settlers in the wilderness, and through hardship mature into social-minded citizens, whereupon they return to civilization. In addition to being a novel that fluctuates between romanticism and realism, baroque humor and seriousness, it is a myth of the development of the Finnish people into a cultural nation. It became an important model for later Finnish literature, with its theme, the conflict between the individual and his or her surroundings; its view of humankind, the worship of the anti-social hero; and its style, a mixture of colloquial language and pathos.

Literary activity was at a standstill for almost a decade after Kivi's death, but this trend was reversed around 1880. At that time, Finnish literature was strongly influenced first by French and Scandinavian naturalism, later by Tolstoy's preaching of altruism, self-denial, and social responsibility. Common people, everyday life, and the socially oppressed were increasingly made the objects of literary treatment by young writers, who in 1885 formed a group called *Nuori Suomi* (Young Finland); the leaders were Minna Canth, Juhani Aho, and Arvid Järnefelt.

Minna Canth

The Finnish Theater, founded in 1872, had given a performance of Ibsen's *A Doll's House* in 1880 that caused a sensation. It was primarily the issue of women's emancipation which caused Canth (1844–97) to become active as a writer, dealing with controversial issues. *Työmiehen vaimo* (The Worker's Wife, 1885) is a passionate protest against stuffy Finnish society, which was especially hard on women. The short story *Köyhää kansaa* (Poor People, 1886) depicts poverty and illness in a large working-class family and blames the wealthy for this misery. The same motif is found in her drama *Kovan onnen lapsia* (Children of Hard Destinies, 1888); artistically weak, its social indignation is powerful—an armed labor disturbance is regarded as the only solution to injustice.

Influenced by Tolstoy, Minna Canth's bitterness softened and was followed around 1890 by a more balanced and objective view of humankind and society. She wrote her most important dramas during this period. In *Papin perhe* (The Family of a Clergyman, 1891) she attempted to bridge the gap between an older, conservative generation and rebellious youth. In *Sylvi* (1893), influenced by Flaubert's *Madame Bovary*, she dealt with a married woman's tragic love for a younger man, which drives her to murder her husband.

A complex of ethical problems was evident in Minna Canth's last and well-rounded drama, *Anna Liisa* (1895), about a child-murderess, who, tortured by the memory, admits her crime on her wedding day and is left to society's punishment, but is pardoned by the minister in accordance with the religious concept of the educative influence of suffering and trouble.

Juhani Aho

Aho (1861–1921), who grew up in a pietist rectory in northern Savo, a province in Middle Finland, was also affected by the antinaturalistic tendencies of the 1890s. As a student in Helsinki (Helsingfors) he had been influenced by Norwegian and French naturalism. He wrote a number of stories dealing with the conflict between the old and the new. Among them are *Siihen aikaan kun isä lampun osti*

(1883; Eng. tr. *When Father Brought Home the Lamp*, 1893) and *Rautatie* (The Railroad, 1884); the latter deals with two settlers in the wilderness, their ideas of the railroad, which they have never seen, and their trip to see this modern invention. Psychological analysis is stressed in *Papin tytär* (The Daughter of a Clergyman, 1885), Aho's first attempt at a tendentious depiction of the middle class. The main character, Elli, is one of those passive human beings, destined to suffer in tragic resignation because of their unsympathetic surroundings—a typical motif in Nordic literature of the 1880s—found, for instance, in the novels of Jonas Lie and Herman Bang. The tone becomes sharper when Aho describes student life in *Helsinkiin* (To Helsinki, 1889), as Arne Garborg had done in *Peasant Students* in 1883.

Around 1900 Aho moved from Zola-influenced realism toward a new, introverted, emotional art related to the French fin-de-siècle authors Bourget and Huysmans. This is most apparent in the eight volumes *Lastuja* (Shavings, 1891–1921). They contain stories, reminiscences, travel sketches, reflections, and allegories; the earlier works especially show the strong influence of the warm sensibility so characteristic of Alphonse Daudet's short stories. The collections demonstrate that Aho's realism had been replaced by an impressionistic, lyric technique. This is clearly reflected in the masterpiece *Papin rouva* (The Wife of a Clergyman, 1893), a sequel to the novel of 1885. Here description and epic elements are secondary; instead, the emphasis is on the psychological analysis of the minister's wife and of her brief passion, doomed from the outset, for a blasé, cosmopolitan house-guest.

The novel, *Panu* (1897) is a product of national romantic sentiment during the 1890s, the so-called Karelianism, and of Aho's love for the *Kalevala* tradition. Set in the seventeenth century, the novel is dominated by his interest in numerous cultural, historical details. Not until *Juha* (1911), a major epic work in Finnish literature, did Aho succeed in combining the romantic and realistic elements into a lively, but tightly structured plot undoubtedly inspired by Selma Lagerlöf's *Gösta Berling's Saga*. The novel describes the cripple Juha who is driven to destruction by his passionate infatuation with the woman who has left him for her lover and seducer.

Arvid Järnefelt

The religious sentiments of the period are most convincingly expressed by Tolstoy disciple Järnefelt (1861–1932). In his early psychological novels, the autobiographical *Heräämiseni* (My Awakening, 1894) and *Veljekset* (The Brothers, 1900), Järnefelt dealt with a number of moral and religious questions, whereas in his later works, such as *Maaemon lapsia* (Children of Mother Earth, 1905), he attempted to reform social ills from a Christian standpoint. After World War I, Järnefelt abandoned his social theories and concentrated on describing human destines, as in the novel *Greeta ja hänen Herransa* (Greeta and Her Lord, 1925). However, he remained a rationalistic Christian and Utopian in Tolstoy's spirit, rejecting the dogmatic side of Christianity but accepting its practical moral: the teaching of charity.

Karl A. Tavastjerna

A more complicated personality was Tavastjerna (1860–98), whose poetry and prose made him the leading exponent of realism in the Fenno-Swedish literature of the 1880s and the 1890s; his novel *Barndomsvänner* (Childhood Friends, 1886) is actually one of the first critical portrayals of Finnish petty-bourgeois society of the times. The social pathos is increased in Tavastjerna's most skillfully structured novel, *Hårda tider* (Hard Times, 1891), in which the miserable lot of the poor during the famine years of 1867–68 is depicted.

In *Childhood Friends* the main character, Ben Thomén, represents social revolt, in addition to being a Turgenev-inspired Rudin figure, a fin-de-siècle character, dominating the work of a number of Scandinavian authors, such as Bang, Jacobsen, and Söderberg. Decadent mysticism becomes a major ingredient in the novel *I förbund med döden* (The Alliance with Death, 1893), testifying to the fact that the interest in spiritualism and hypnosis was quite widespread. Influenced by Tolstoy, Tavastjerna had allowed a humanistic, altruistic view of life to dominate the individualistic upper-class attitude in *Hard Times*, but in his novel *En patriot utan fosterland* (A Patriot without a Country, 1896), Tavastjerna speaks out against the narrow Finnish nationalism through his hero, von Steven, a cosmopolitan individualist whose tragic fate is isolation and homelessness.

Tavastjerna's poetry shows a similar development. Whereas naturalism forms the basis for the early, uneven collections from the 1880s, the tone becomes darker and more passionate in the following decade, *Dikter* (Poems, 1896) marking Tavastjerna's final maturing as a lyric poet. The sudden swing of mood between defiance and resignation, manifest in the novel written in the same year, is present here. However, a passive melancholy dominates, and the language is melodious and evocative rather than realistic.

A passionate love affair toward the end of Tavastjerna's life resulted in another climax in his lyrical creativity and was expressed in

Laureatus (The Laureate, 1897). His search for classic simplicity and his worship of antiquity—like that of his Swedish contemporaries Heidenstam, Fröding, Levertin, and Hallström—is combined with the strong influence of Nietzsche's superman philosophy as interpreted by his friend Ola Hansson. This is personified in the figure of the lonesome genius, who, in his struggle for freedom, leaves the narrow world of humans and encounters his beloved out in nature. But the happiness he experiences with her turns out to be only his dream, and the poet's individualism ends in disillusion and isolation.

Through his rejection of both national and personal human fellowship, through his worship of human freedom with all its consequences, Tavastjerna does not mark the final step in a literary tradition, but clearly points toward the Fenno-Swedish modernism prevalent during World War I.

NATIONALISM AND SOCIAL REALISM IN ICELAND

The Lutheran Reformation in the sixteenth century marked the beginning of a new Icelandic literature. The period between 800 and 1300 had been a literary Golden Age in Iceland, with its edda, skaldic, and saga literature. The period after 1300 was characterized politically by an increasing dependence on Norway until both Norway and Iceland came under Danish rule in 1387. Literary production at that time consisted essentially of copying and translating not only medieval European romances but also numerous scientific, philosophical, and didactic works.

After the Reformation, Denmark's monopoly on all trade proved fatal to Iceland's economy and certainly contributed to the cultural isolation of the country. Contact with European cultural life was not very extensive until the eighteenth century, and it is not possible to speak of a romantic movement until about 1830. The leading spokesmen were the patriotic poets Bjarni Thorarensen (1786–1841) and Jónas Hallgrímsson (1807–45); the latter's lucidly written poems about the nature and history of Iceland made him the national poet. The major historical events during this period were the re-establishment of the parliament, the *Atling*, in 1845 and the abolition of the Danish trade monopoly in 1854. From 1849, the year of the first Danish constitution, Iceland's disagreements with Denmark increased under the leadership of Iceland's national hero, the politician and philologist Jón Sigurðsson; the country finally achieved political and financial autonomy in 1874 and received its own constitution.

Since Iceland did not have its own university until 1911, young

Icelanders had to study in Copenhagen. It was here that Bjarni Thorarensen was exposed to romanticism, and that two other prominent writers, Matthías Jochumsson (1835-1920) and Grímur Thomsen (1820-96), encountered Byron's works. Thomsen's thesis, completed in 1845, was the first Scandinavian study of the English poet. It was also in Copenhagen, around 1880, that Icelandic realism and naturalism developed, under the influence of Georg Brandes. However, these currents were not as influential and did not give rise to as much innovation as they did in the other Nordic countries, primarily owing to the absence of urban areas and an industrial proletariat. Economically, the 1870s and '80s were very hard years; during these decades one-fourth of the nation emigrated to North America and population growth stopped temporarily.

The new views, attacking established institutions and traditional ideas, were proclaimed in the periodical *Verðandi* (1882), published in Copenhagen. The foremost representatives were the two poets Þorsteinn Erlingsson and Hannes Hafstein, and the two prose writers Gestur Pálsson and Einar H. Kvaran.

Þorsteinn Erlingsson

Erlingsson (1858-1914), who lived in Copenhagen from 1883 to 1896, became a particularly controversial figure through his anticlerical and socialist poetry, printed in various journals during the 1880s. His first collection *Þyrnar* (Thorns), was not published until 1897 (enlarged eds. in 1905, 1918, 1943). Besides bitter political and social satires, it contains a number of rather traditional, patriotic poems about Iceland, and sensitive, melancholy love poetry, exquisite in form and language. Lyric beauty and social satire are combined in Erlingsson's major work, a cycle of narrative poems, *Eiðurinn* (The Oath, 1913), composed on a tragic love theme. In *The Oath*, Erlingsson used folk tales that he himself had collected. He shared the romantics' admiration for the Iceland of the past, unlike the cosmopolitan Hannes Hafstein.

Hannes Hafstein

Although Hafstein (1861-1922) ridiculed excessive romantic nationalism, he became his country's first prime minister in 1904. All his poems, published in *Verðandi* while he was a student in Copenhagen, supported the new ideas, which sought to awaken the apathetic Icelandic nation and spur it to greater progress. When he returned home in 1886, Hafstein continued his attacks on Icelandic literature, specifically its antiquated themes and narrow nationalism in a time of growing individualism and technical growth.

Hafstein's poems did not appear in book form until 1893 in a volume entitled Ýmisleg ljóðmæli (Various Poems; later eds. in 1916, 1925). As in the poetry of Holger Drachmann and Heinrich Heine, Hafstein's artistic models, nature and love motifs dominate his later poetry, with no trace of naturalistic determinism. His writing is marked by straightforwardness and virility—not depth of feeling—corresponding to his pragmatic, optimistic view of life.

Gestur Pálsson

Pálsson (1852-91) was the most consistent representative of Icelandic naturalism. After interrupting his theological studies in Copenhagen, he founded the journal Suðri (In the South, 1883-86) in Reykjavík, which became the main voice of Brandes's views in Iceland. Apart from Brandes, Turgenev and Kielland appealed most to Pálsson. Their choice of topics and their style, especially Kielland's irony and sarcasm, are echoed in his short stories, the most complete edition of which, Ritsafn (Works), was published in 1927.

Pálsson made his debut with some indifferent poems (1874), but he was the most brilliant prose writer in Verðandi, to which he contributed his first short story "Kærleiksheimilið" (Home of Charity), a bitter satire on the tyranny of the rich and their mistreatment of the poor. From then on, injustice and the hypocrisy that justifies social abuses are the main motifs in his short stories. Plot is never allowed to overshadow the penetrating psychological descriptions of characters. The collection Þrjár sögur (Three Stories, 1888) contains Pálsson's two masterpieces, "Vordraumur" (Spring Dream) and "Tilhugalíf" (Engagement), a harsh satire on the provincial and petty bourgeois life in small Reykjavík.

Pálsson's pessimistic view of humankind and society contributed to his feeling of isolation and homelessness, which, in 1890, made him leave for Canada to become the editor of an Icelandic weekly in Winnipeg.

Einar H. Kvaran

The most productive writer in the Verðandi group was Kvaran (1859-1938). After studying in Copenhagen, he became an editor, first in Winnipeg (1885-95) where he was the co-founder of two Icelandic newspapers, then in Iceland. He made his debut in 1890 with a successful short story, Vonir (Hopes) about the disappointments immigrants encounter in America. This was followed by a collection of poetry, *Ljóðmæli* (Poems, 1893), characterized by a melancholy fin-de-siècle mood never before encountered in Icelandic literature. After his success with *Hopes*, Kvaran wrote a number of short stories published in three volumes (1901–13), some of which—when the sentimentality that often characterizes Kvaran's work is absent—are among the best Icelandic literature.

Most of the stories reflect life in the countryside, focusing on the exploitation of children, servants, and poor farmhands. However, his early attacks on conservatism gave way to psychological portrayal, not of the oppressors, but of the oppressed, devoid of any propagandistic tendency. This development, influenced by William James's theories of the subconscious, is also manifest in Kvaran's novels. The two-volume novel *Ofurefli* (Overwhelming Odds, 1908) and *Gull* (Gold, 1911) provides the first realistic depictions of the bourgeoisie of Reykjavík, the main theme being the victorious fight of liberal theology against dogmatic orthodoxy. However, in *Sálin vaknar* (The Soul Awakens, 1916), a murder story in which a young editor is transformed by clairvoyant visions from an ambitious social climber to a passionate humanitarian, a belief in immortality and in spiritualism becomes the main motif. The same is true in the novels that follow. The male villain or doubter is always redeemed through a self-sacrificing woman. In the historical play *Lénharður fógeti* (1913; Eng. tr. *Governor Lenhard*, 1936), the villian is turned into a chivalrous knight by the heroine, a beautiful, farmer's daughter; in the contemporary drama *Syndir annara* (Sins of Others, 1915) a wife's ability to forgive her husband's sins is put to the test. Kvaran's remaining works are dominated by this optimistic outlook on life, as indicated by the title of his last novel, *Gæfumaður* (The Fortunate Man, 1933); God forgives us and we should forgive each other.

Kvaran's style, following the demands of realism, was simple and clear. Both as artist and as thinker, he exerted an enormous influence in his country, arousing debates and controversies.

Chapter *4*

Nordic Literature in the 1890s

Symptomatic of a new intellectual epoch in the Nordic countries was the great interest that George Brandes had awakened in Nietzsche (see p. 7). Not only Nietzsche the philosopher but also Nietzsche the cultural critic and master of style influenced Nordic writers greatly. In Sweden Rydberg had fought Nietzsche's anti-humanistic teachings; but Strindberg, Ola Hansson, and later Heidenstam, Fröding, and Vilhelm Ekelund were influenced for a time by Nietzsche's superman theory. The Norwegians Kielland, Garborg, Heiberg, and later Hamsun, as well as writers of Finnish literature in the 1890s, were also influenced by Nietzsche's theories and ecstatic lust for life. However, Nietzsche's ideas exerted only a slight influence on Fenno-Swedish and Icelandic literature of the period. In the early 1890s in Denmark, a Nietzschean contempt for the masses appeared in a few plays by Gjellerup; the young poets of the symbolist movement were inspired by Nietzsche's expressive linguistic art but took issue with his philosophy.

The new movements of the 1890s were closely connected to the general cultural situation on the continent. As had been true during the Enlightenment in the eighteenth century, there were strong romantic undertones in the naturalistic epoch, especially in French literature. Pierre Loti turned to exotic themes, Maurice Barrès to nationalism, and J.-K. Huysmans to Christianity; generally the 1890s marked a return to church and religion. Huysmans converted to Catholicism, as did Johannes Jørgensen in Denmark and Ola Hansson in Sweden. In England, Oscar Wilde described his conversion in *De*

Profundis. Not until this decade did Dostoevsky's works become known in Western Europe. In them readers discovered a new awareness of metaphysical problems, an emphasis on the irrational elements of inner life. Freud had basically worked out his theories of the subconscious by 1900. Psychology and psychiatry employed objective, scientific methods; the hypnosis experiments at the Salt petrière Hospital outside Paris inspired writers throughout Europe, such as Rilke and Strindberg.

Almost all the literary transitional figures were prose writers; however, the most significant protest against naturalism came from the symbolist poets. Baudelaire had already proclaimed his poetry collection of 1857, *Les Fleurs du Mal* (Flowers of Evil), as the last blossom of an effete culture. He was the forerunner of symbolism, whose great poets, Verlaine, Mallarmé, and Rimbaud, wrote only of the incomprehensible and ethereal. They created their own language, full of musical sounds and vivid beauty, and suppressed scientific observation in favor of mystical suggestion. Symbolism was interested neither in reforming the social order nor in imitating external reality; the poet was no longer seen as the prophet of social reforms or of radical ideologies, but as a seer. The influence of French symbolism was felt least in Iceland; in Denmark and Norway it was a dominant influence. Also, the decadent fin-de-siècle mood, which, to a certain degree, was an influence in the 1890s in Denmark and Norway, was only slightly evident in the literature of the other Nordic countries.

Generally, the 1890s in the Nordic countries were characterized by a contrast to the preceding years—in Sweden, Finland, and Iceland perhaps less than in Norway and Denmark. But in these countries also neo-romanticism and symbolism are set in opposition to naturalism and realism. The ethical demand for truth was succeeded by the aesthetic demand for beauty. Heroic and noble deeds were admired, at the cost of the practical; and against anti-religious nationalism there arose a new metaphysics and a mystically colored religiosity. Nature and history now became the favored sources, and lyric poetry, which had been totally neglected, blossomed anew in all five countries.

NEO-ROMANTICISM IN SWEDEN

The naturalistic epoch in Sweden, which began in 1879 with Strindberg's novel *The Red Room* lasted only a short time. It was brought to an end in the early 1890s when a number of young, talented writers emerged. The greatest difference between the decades of the 1880s and '90s is aesthetic rather than ideological. A thoroughgoing break with the earlier world view did not occur. In contrast to the romantics at the beginning of the century, poets evinced only a faint interest in philosophical speculation; even social and political questions were of little interest to them. In fact, they tended to react negatively to the earlier democratic leveling and study of primitive instincts, passionately affirming the joy of life. Even though Ola Hansson was influenced by Paul Bourget, there was really no Swedish representative of the French fin-de-siècle movement until Hjalmar Söderberg.

Verner von Heidenstam

The new program was formulated by the leader of the movement, Heidenstam (1859-1940), in the short polemical work *Renässans* (Renaissance, 1889) and in the literary satire *Pepitas bröllop* (Pepita's Wedding, 1890, written with Oscar Levertin). Here he battles the gray "shoemaker's realism" of the 1880s and praises creative fantasy as the most important challenge to a writer. Heidenstam turns against foreign models and demands personal and national independence for writers. Whereas the 1890s brought to Denmark, above all, a rediscovery of the soul, and to Norway a new conception of nature, which became manifest in symbolistic poetry, in Sweden emphasis on the country's past and its great figures gave rise to neo-romantic poetry.

The aesthetic program was expressed in Heidenstam's first collection, *Vallfart och vandringsår* (Pilgrimage and Wander-Years, 1888), a glorification of the carefree life of the East. The partly allegorical novel *Hans Alienus* (1892), combining a historical with an imaginative treatment of antiquity, is also a typical work of the period. A strong bond to the homeland characterizes his major work, the lyrical *Dikter* (Poems, 1895). Enjoyment of life gives way to feelings of isolation, and Heidenstam forms an ideal conception of the value of death and of heroism, which raises his historical novellas *Karolinerna* (1897-98; Eng. tr. *The Charles Men*, also as *A King and His Campaigners*, 1902 and later) to the level of tragic national epic. These tales of a warlike king deal not only with victory, but also with defeat. The king is the central figure, to be sure, but the actual hero is the common and suffering people, on the battlefield as well as at home in impoverished Sweden.

Folkungaträdet (1905-7; Eng. tr. *The Tree of the Folkungs*, 1925), a novel in two volumes, is Heidenstam's greatest accomplishment as a historical writer. In contrast to *The Charles Men*, this work is composed as a unit and is far more objective. Heidenstam thoroughly studied medieval culture and society to provide an accurate historical picture of the period and a rendering of the language. A humanistic world view underlies descriptions of national events, a view that blossoms in Heidenstam's last work, *Nya dikter* (New Poems, 1915). In short, well-formed strophes, he confesses to a transfigured, fervent belief in life and a melancholy resignation toward death. The romantic has become a classicist, like his models Runeberg and Goethe. In 1916 he was honored with the Nobel Prize in literature.

Oscar Levertin

Heidenstam's friend and fellow combatant Levertin (1862-1906) began his career in the 1880s as a writer of short stories, in the naturalistic coterie around Geijerstam. However, when he published *Legender och visor* (Legends and Songs) in 1891, he became a true representative of the spirit of the 1890s. In *Nya dikter* (New Poems, 1894), the longing for eternity, as expressed in the Ulysses poem "Ithaka," is contrasted to a Nietzschean lust for life, as in the poem about the wise and foolish virgins of the Gospel, "De visa och de fåvitska jungfrurna." But the Nietzschean influence was short-lived. In *Dikter* (Poems, 1901) Levertin wrote as a national humanist attempting to replace his ingenious, often oriental and ornate imagery with a simpler style. The basic tone is now weariness, resignation, and longing for rest.

Levertin was an outstanding literary critic and essayist. His last work, the cycle of romances *Kung Salomo och Morolf* (King Solomon and Morolf, 1905), contains both a farewell to life and poetry, and a confession in which the author attempts to create a synthesis between his Jewish heritage and Western culture.

Per Hallström

Hallström (1866-1960) is the master of the novella among the writers of the 1890s. His first collection, *Vilsna fåglar* (Strayed Birds, 1894)—still dominated by naturalistic themes—is composed of empathic stories about the neglected elements of society, sensitive characters who are out of touch with reality and fall prey to brutal life. The novellas in *Purpur* (Purple, 1895) also portray the painful clash of dream with reality; but here romanticism breaks through. The themes are from distant times and countries, and the language is exquisitely beautiful, lyrical and rich in images.

The basic mood of Hallström's novellas is pessimism, influenced by Schopenhauer, which is at once bitter and resigned. He wrote of death as the final liberator in his masterful collection *Thanatos* (1900). In a series of scenes, now from the Middle Ages, now from the present, he portrays people encountering overpowering death, in whose presence everything is changed and revalued. Hallström's creativity is characterized by versatility, evident in his choice of the most varied themes, and by his brilliant refined style.

Selma Lagerlöf

Prose writer Lagerlöf (1858-1940), like Heidenstam and Hallström, turned from naturalism. She was born on the small estate Mårbacka in the province of Värmland, where people still related old tales and family traditions. This wealth of material was a decisive influence in her artistic development. In 1882-85 when she was attending teacher's college in Stockholm, she had thought of collecting this treasure of romantic stories. However, it was not until the late 1880s, after she had developed her own style—a lyrical, impressionistic style influenced by English author Thomas Carlyle—that she wrote a longer and her best work, the two-volume novel *Gösta Berling's Saga*.

Gösta Berlings saga (1891; Eng. tr. *Gösta Berling's Saga*, also as *The Story of Gösta Berling*, 1898 and later) is a modern lyrical and dramatic epic. In place of the logical, firmly constructed plot of the naturalistic novel is a series of loosely joined episodes held together solely by unity of place: Värmland and the old estate Ekeby. Ekeby is owned by Major Samselius and his wife, considered the absolute mistress of the estate. On one of her inspection trips, she encounters the alcoholic Pastor Gösta Berling, who has been removed from his position, and she puts him up in the "Cavalier wing" of Ekeby. Here reside several strange individuals, adventurers, drunks, and artists, who form the always cheerful but irresponsible bodyguard of the major's wife. Sintram, "the Dark One," a symbol of evil, incites the cavaliers against her. They reveal that the source of the couple's great wealth is the deceased lover of the major's wife. She is forced to flee. Now the cavaliers, half in jest, enter into a bet with the devil: They will give him their souls if they undertake anything useful within the next year. Thus begins the uninhibited and frivolous reign of the cavaliers, which ends with the plundering and eventual devastation of Ekeby. But before the year is over, the major's wife returns to her estate, after the angry peasants have stormed Ekeby and captured the cavaliers, to force them to make good the damage they have done. Pastor Berling, who is at the center of most of the adventures, is morally condemned by the author, even though she is fascinated by his odious dealings. Thus Berling becomes an ambiguous hero, related to Byron's Childe Harold and Don Juan. This epic is essentially different from these romantic accounts because it has a reconciling conclusion. Lagerlöf solves the moral problem, which is linked to the guilt-atonement theme: After the pact with the devil and the rebellion, the cavaliers change their lives, submitting to duty and work.

Gösta Berling's Saga was coolly received by the Swedish critics and readers. Not until two years after it was published, when Brandes awakened greater interest in the work with an appreciative review, did it become a success. Lagerlöf then published several collections of short stories, but the decisive renewal of her creative efforts did not occur until the novel *Antikrists mirakler* (1897; Eng. tr. *The Miracles of Antichrist*, 1899 and later). In 1895 she had traveled to Italy, where she found the material for her new book in a small Sicilian city. Captivated by the colorful peasant life and Catholic piety, she was at the same time confronted with the greatest social conflict of the time, the contrast between poor and rich. *The Miracles of Antichrist* tells of an old painting of Christ that hangs in a church in the city of Diamante; it is replaced by a counterfeit painting which bears the inscription "My realm is only of this world." With this picture the Antichrist has come to humankind: He can perform miracles, but is able to fulfill only requests of a material nature. This fills the people with courage, but cannot free them from their suffering. For Lagerlöf the Antichrist represents socialism; she is in sympathy with the humanitarian aspects of socialism, but is unequivocally at odds with its materialism. As a novel of ideas, the book is not entirely successful, but Lagerlöf's naive attempt to present social problems in a legendlike style, and to unite the two differing world views in a social Christianity does create a striking artistic effort.

During a trip to Jerusalem in 1899-1900, Lagerlöf visited a colony of Swedish farmers who had experienced a religious awakening in the province of Dalecarlia in 1896. They had left their farms and their families, and had emigrated to Jerusalem to practice works of mercy and to await the second coming of Christ. The material she collected about the group, both there and in Sweden, she used in the novel *Jerusalem* (1901-2; Eng. tr. 1903 and later). The first volume is the most significant, with its marvelous portrayal of an old farming family, the Ingmar sons, and the world of their thoughts. Into this family, characterized by a strong attachment to the soil and a sagalike cohesiveness, there suddenly intrudes a religious awakening sparked by a preacher. The result is confusion and sectarianism. It seems almost incomprehensible that these strong, self-aware farmers should be so seized by this experience. Basic to the work is the conflict of two opposing forces: a sense of duty toward their inherited land and a commitment to religious demands that they be free of earthly goods.

Lagerlöf's psychological realism triumphs in the first part of her novel. However, in the second part, which is set in the Holy Land, there are too many sentimental scenes and poorly articulated observations; a loose episodic narrative, similar to that of *Gösta Berling's Saga*, supplants the tight organization of the first part of the novel.

Some of Lagerlöf's early short stories contained materials from old legends, and many episodes in *The Miracles of Antichrist* also have a legendary character. In 1904 she published two collections of legends in novella form, *Kristuslegender* (Eng. tr. *Christ Legends*, 1908 and later) and *Legender* (Legends). Some legends were preserved in the oral tradition, some in the Apocrypha. The first nine legends of the *Christ Legends* treat of the birth, life, and death of Jesus. Almost all of them portray the moral transformation of the main characters through humility and mercy. This is true of the rough Roman mercenary who is unable to kill the Christ child ("I Nazaret" ["In Nazareth"]) and of the brutal knight of the crusades who wants to bring a flame from the Holy Grave to Florence without letting it go out, and through the perils of the trip is transformed into a noble human being ("Ljuslågan" ["The Flame of Life"]). The point of departure is always a small detail upon which the entire story is constructed; from the simplest themes arise very thoughtful small works of art, possessing great beauty.

Lagerlöf was in total agreement with the national movements of her time when, in 1906-7, she published her next masterpiece, *Nils Holgerssons underbara resa genom Sverige* (Eng. tr. *The Wonderful Adventures of Nils*, 1907 and later), which was written as a geography reader for the elementary schools. Nils, an ill-mannered farm lad, is changed into a Tom Thumb and carried off by a wild goose. The idea of a child living among animals who are familiar with human speech is from Kipling's *The Jungle Book*. Lagerlöf is not content merely to play out the main plot of the trip; she links it to many fairy tales, legends, and short stories, all designed to spur little Nils's moral development toward honesty and a sense of duty. The book naturally leans toward the novel of education; but what makes it so fresh and alive even today is neither this didactic intention nor the faith in national progress, which is expressed in the enthusiastic description of the development of industry and agriculture. Rather, it is the masterly portrayal of people in the city and country, as well as of animate and inanimate nature seen from a bird's point of view.

When Selma Lagerlöf received the Nobel Prize in 1909, she repurchased her family estate, where she lived for the rest of her life. At Mårbacka she again came into contact with the folk tradition of Värmland, but it did not renew her writing. Not until 1925 did she again publish a major work, the first volume of the Löwensköld trilogy, *Löwensköldska ringen* (The Löwensköld Ring), followed by *Charlotte Löwensköld* (1925) and *Anna Svärd* (1928) (complete Eng. tr. *The Ring of the Löwenskölds*, 1931).

The cycle has two parts: the fable of the Löwensköld family with the ring motif and the story of the degenerate Pastor Ekenstedt. The first part builds on a legendary motif and is carried by a suspenseful plot set in motion after the theft of the family ring. In the second part, Lagerlöf comes closer to the present and uses a more realistic style without giving up the complicated intrigues. She attempts here to answer the question of how the pious and respectable Ekenstedt has been so totally ruined, and she strongly rejects the fanatical pietism that, in company with Ekenstedt's self-satisfaction, has destroyed his personality. Opposite him stands his fiancée, the optimistic and cheerful Charlotte, an incarnation of Lagerlöf's own ideal of humanity. Her actions give to the volume a humorous mood, although the last part has a significantly dark tone. Apart from the conclusion, which is intended to take up again all the threads of the preceding volumes, this novel is doubtless the high point of the trilogy and forms the worthy termination to a great career.

Selma Lagerlöf was often unable to differentiate between original and banal effects. However, she possessed a great epic talent and the ability to construct a colorful and dramatic plot with numerous surprising elements and to create living characters with her intuition and rich fantasy. Frequently she was inspired by legends and other folk literature, and she fused stylistic elements and motifs of the oral tradition into works that represent a popular renewal of the Swedish art of narration.

Gustaf Fröding

Like the other great romantics Esaias Tegnér and Selma Lagerlöf, Fröding (1860-1911) was born in the province of Värmland, growing up on his father's estate in the vicinity of Karlstad. In 1880 he went to the University of Uppsala as a student; he did not complete his examinations, but was active in literary circles. Influenced by Brandes, Ibsen, and Kielland, he absorbed the radical ideas of the 1880s. In 1885 he returned to Värmland. Already an inherited predisposition to mental illness was becoming apparent. In 1889 Fröding went for a cure in the hospital of Görlitz (Silesia). Here he avidly read Goethe and Heine, Burns and Byron, and wrote his first collection of poetry, *Guitarr och dragharmonika* (Guitar and Concertina, 1891).

His humorous, witty pictures of peasant life in Värmland were entirely new to Swedish poetry. These poems were received enthusi-astically by readers, but Fröding's melancholy, wistful poems were overlooked. With virtuoso realism he portrayed types from the city and the country, such as the two quarrelsome farmers, "Jan Ersa och Per Persa" ("Jan Ersa and Per Persa"), the cheerful "Stina Stursk," and the old servant of the pastor and his horse, "Jonte och Brunte" ("Jonte and Brunte"). In several of these poems one senses that the author feels kinship with the disreputable and unhappy characters; Fröding's feelings of ineffectuality and failure pervade all of his poetry. His artistic treatment of these peasant motifs was novel: the language was terse and clear, with no extraneous words, no uncertainty of structure, indeed there is musical virtuosity in the rhyme and rhythm.

Scenes from Värmland, many of them written in the local dialect, form the first part of the next, even more significant collection, *Nya dikter* (New Poems, 1894). Here, too, Fröding portrays folk figures from the countryside, such as a sanctimonious gathering in "I bön-huset" ("In the House of Prayer"), or from the city, as in "Skalden Wennerbom" ("The Bard Wennerbom") when he sympathetically portrays the unhappy fate of this degenerate poet. In the long "heroic poem" "Balen" ("The Ball"), in which the young journalist dreams himself and the celebrated queen of the ball into heaven, Fröding combines satire of the small-town milieu with exuberant fantasy, far removed from the literary tendencies of the 1880s.

Fröding's pictures of peasant life, in spite of their apparent objectiv-ity, also have a personal flavor, which comes clearly to the fore in his nature poetry. As a nature poet Fröding primarily conveys subjective moods: "I skogen" ("In the Woods") expresses his own *Weltschmerz* through a gloomy picture of nature; the popular folk-songlike "Säf, säf, susa" ("Sigh, sigh, sedges") contains a motif that recurs often in Fröding's work, that of the seduced girl who encounters the hard judgment of society:

Sigh, sigh, sedges,
Flow, waves, flow!
Now tell me of young Ingalil,
Which way may she go?

Like the wing'shattered gull's was her cry as she sank in the mere —
'Twas when Spring was in green last year.

They were wroth with her, the good folk of Östanålid,
And it made her young heart bleed.
(. . .)

Tr. C. D. Locock

This dark and melancholy tone is also to be found in the brooding poems "Bibliska fantasier" ("Biblical Phantasies"), in which Samson, King Saul, and the preacher in Ecclesiastes become spokesmen for the pain in Fröding's own soul. There are poems in the last part of *New Poems*, not based on the Värmland theme, that deal with such varied figures as Don Quixote, Friederike Brion, and Ahasver, and also a series of outstanding stylistic imitations, such as the rococo parody "Corydon till Chloe" ("Corydon to Chloe").

In 1894 Fröding became ill again, more seriously than before. He was plunged into a severe emotional crisis characterized by crippling anxieties and hallucinations, which form the transition to the dream moods and visions of his artistically most significant book, *Stänk och flikar* (Splashes and Rags, 1896). One still encounters the old cheerfulness in several of the children's poems; but the new elements in this collection are the boldly beautiful erotic poems, such as "En morgondröm" ("A Morning Dream") and "Gudarna dansa" ("The Gods Dance"), which led to Fröding being accused in court of immorality, and the shattering self-accusations and gripping personal confessions ("Narkissos"). "A Morning Dream" shows how greatly Nietzsche's teaching of the reassessment of all values had influenced Fröding. In the philosophical poem "En fattig munk från Skara" ("A Poor Monk from Skara"), which ends the first collection, Fröding's subject was the problem of Good and Evil: Influenced by Goethe's monism, Fröding sought to obliterate the border between these opposites. Now the problem reappears with renewed violence and occupies the poet for the rest of his life. He casts doubt on the contradictory concepts of Good and Evil through his Nietzschean concept of humankind as combining virtue and desire in a Tolstoy-inspired harmonic synthesis.

In the poem "Sagan om Gral" ("The Story of the Grail") Fröding attempts to present this reconciliation mystically in the symbol of the Grail. This motif, which Fröding drew from Wagner's operas *Lohengrin* and *Parsifal*, appears more clearly and frequently in various poems in the collections *Nytt och gammalt* (New and Old, 1897) and *Gralstänk* (Grail Splashes, 1898). The Grail is located at the core of substance and essence. The ordinary human cannot see it, hence cannot perceive the unity of the universe. The discovery of the Grail, ensuring the introduction of a new world order, is the task of the Seeker of the Grail, who is none other than that superhuman being presented in the poem "Aningar" ("Presentiments") from *Splashes and Rags* —the poet, singer, and warrior in a single person.

From approximately 1895 on, Fröding's poetry became more

personal, speculative, confessional, and intellectual. During these years he also returned to realistic poems about the life and people in Värmland, which may be found, among others, in *New and Old* and in two books of dialect poems, *Räggler och paschaser* (Anecdotes and Fairy-Tales, approximate title, 1895 and 1897). Fröding spent six years, from 1898 to 1905, in a mental Institution in Uppsala, where he attempted suicide several times. He spent his last years in continual convalescence at Djurgården near Stockholm, where he published two more collections of poetry and prose, *Efterskörd* (Aftermath, 1910) and *Reconvalescentia* (1913).

Gustav Fröding's writing is characterized by an astonishing variety of expression: humorous portraits of Värmland folk types; stylistic imitations demonstrating his unique ability to familiarize himself with the expressions and habits of mind of times long past; and, not least, subjective, impassioned nature poetry. Fröding's poems were much read and admired, and they were set to music by composers such as Jean Sibelius. He meant more to the Nordic readers of his time than any other poet of the 1890s.

Erik Axel Karlfeldt

For Karlfeldt (1864-1931), as for Selma Lagerlöf and Gustaf Fröding, his home province was the source of poetic inspiration, his writing expressing a longing for and recollection of a vanished idyll. He was born in Dalecarlia into an old farming family. Economic reasons forced the family to leave their ancestral farm, and Karlfeldt's early years of philology study at the University of Uppsala, which he concluded in 1898, were filled with uncertainty and privation.

Dalecarlia has one of the loveliest landscapes in Sweden; even more significant, its population, which played an important role in the nation's history, maintained intact its distinctive culture and art until the country was industrialized. Most of Karlfeldt's better poems are portrayals, rather glorifications, of nature and the folk life of Dalecarlia.

His first collection, *Vildmarks- och kärleksvisor* (Songs of the Wilderness and of Love, 1895), contains a series of motifs that evince Karlfeldt's poetic uniqueness. He achieved his first real success with *Fridolins visor* (Fridolins Song's, 1898), followed three years later by *Fridolins lustgård* (Fridolin's Garden of Delights, 1901). In the figure of the bachelor Fridolin, the poet portrays himself. Fridolin is a "well-read chap of a farm family," who has returned to the work of his fathers. He is scholarly and positive by nature, enjoys drinking, and is a successful lover. In these two volumes one encounters not only dancing and happiness, but also disharmony and melancholy, which gives depth to Karlfeldt's Fridolin poetry. He transforms old rural notions of natural events into animated natural mysticism, and uses legends, folk piety, and superstition to create a rich, original world of symbols. As a counterpoise to the harmonious Fridolin, he creates the figure of the unknown stranger, "Löskerkarlen" ("The Vagrant"), an anarchistic individualist whose poems embody Karlfeldt's romantic restlessness and longing.

Fridolin's Garden of Delights also contains poetic fantasies inspired by wall paintings in old farmhouses. Karlfeldt portrays scenes from the Bible in a primitive style, like the style of the old peasant artists who painted biblical figures in local costumes and in local settings. The result is a unique mixture of burlesque comedy ("Jone havsfärd" ["The Voyage of Jonah"]), tender visionary poetry ("Jungfru Maria" ["The Virgin Mary"]), and religious confession ("Yttersta domen" ["The Day of Judgment"]).

Karlfeldt's next collection of poems, *Flora och Pomona* (Flora and Pomona), did not appear until 1906. It contains many of the themes of the previous volumes, but the tone is more serious and reflective. In solemn poems like "Höstskog" ("Autumn Forest") the poet bids a melancholy farewell to his youth and to the world so much praised by Fridolin, which now belongs irrevocably to the past; only in death can he rejoin his forefathers. Karlfeldt's portrayal of love also changes: from an idyllic and unproblematic, albeit sensuous, portrayal of the erotic, through a more subjective and complex conception, to a discovery of the fateful and demonic traits of the loving woman in the poetic series "Häxorna" ("The Witches").

Karlfeldt's fame as a poet grew with the years. In 1904, as the first neo-romantic, he was elected to the Swedish Academy, and in 1931 he was posthumously awarded the Nobel Prize for literature. During World War I he wrote the collection *Flora och Bellona* (Flora and Bellona, 1918). In addition to popular songs like "Svarta Rudolf" ("Black Rudolf") and the confessional "Sjukdom" ("Illness"), portraying the spiritual crisis Karlfeldt experienced in 1913 after a serious illness, this volume contains a series of poems that witness to his reactions to the social and political movements of the new century; among these is the rhetorical "En pesthymn" ("A Plague Hymn"), in which he rebels directly against the powers of the time, Communism in the East and the cult of Mammon in America.

In his last work, *Hösthorn* (The Horn of Autumn, 1927), Karlfeldt returned to Fridolin's world. The mood is still one of resignation, but it is mixed with humility and gratitude for life, as in the hymn "Vinterorgel" ("Winter Organ"), the self-portrait "Sub luna," and "Höstpsalm" ("Autumn Hymn"), a clear avowal of Christianity. Karlfeldt's writing was inspired by the confrontation of modern urban culture with the dying world of the Swedish farmers, and was related to the romantic idealization of the peasantry which had become a literary fashion in the 1890s, influenced by Julius Langbehn's theories (see p. 60). Karlfeldt's language originally bore the influence of Heidenstam, Fröding, and the folk song, but later it became more decorative and archaized, with elements from the local dialect, the Bible, and particularly from the Swedish baroque. Especially significant are Karlfeldt's artistic mastery of form and rhyme, and his melodious language. In his poetry, the Swedish neo-romantic movement found its perfect conclusion.

THE LYRICAL AND RELIGIOUS BREAKTHROUGH IN DENMARK

The new generation of poets was characterized not as it was in Sweden, by the rediscovery of the national past, but by the rediscovery of the soul, a lyrical reaction to the predominant naturalistic prose and materialistic philosophy. The four primary figures—Johannes Jørgensen, Viggo Stuckenberg, Sophus Claussen, and Helge Rode—were friends, who had begun their careers in the 1880s as faithful adherents of Brandes and who introduced a new epoch in Danish literature influenced by Jacobsen, Drachmann, Nietzsche, and modern French literature.

Jørgensen became the leading exponent and theoretician of Danish symbolism. As early as 1891 he used the term "the New Denmark," and in following years, in articles on Baudelaire, Huysmans, Mallarmé, Verlaine, and Poe, he attacked the everyday, matter-of-fact realism of his time and the unproductive debates about contemporary problems. The periodical he founded, *Taarnet* (The Tower, 1893-94), to which Rode, Claussen, and Stuckenberg contributed, was much read and discussed, and received more approbation with each issue. From Germany, Stefan George sent him his journal *Blätter für die Kunst* (Pages for Art), but it fell sharply into disfavor when it became clear that the key concepts in the articles—symbolism, metaphysics, and mysticism—were tending toward a dogmatic faith. When *The Tower* ceased publication, the friends went their separate ways: Rode had turned in 1890 to nonsectarian religiosity, Jørgensen was approaching Catholicism, Stuckenberg divorced himself from Christianity, and

Claussen espoused the Hellenistic ideal of beauty and a universal Epicureanism.

Johannes Jørgensen

Jørgensen (1866-1956) wrote a frankly confessional work, *Mit Livs Legende* (The Legend of My Life, 1916-28; Eng. tr. *Jørgensen, An Autobiography*, 1928-29), which as a psychological document stands with the *Confessions* of Augustine and Rousseau. This half-fictional autobiography shows Jørgensen as the most persistent self-analyst in Danish literature. The leit motif that pervades all his works is his inner struggle with the reality of eternity and his eventual victorious acceptance of it through an act of God's providence.

Jørgensen, who was born in Svendborg on the island of Funen, began his study of zoology along Darwinist lines in Copenhagen, a declared freethinker. Later he gave up zoology in favor of creative writing and journalism. Gradually the metaphysician in him won the upper hand against the doctrines of naturalism. A fleeting enthusiasm for Goethe's *Faust* and for Shelley eventually gave way to the influence of Catholic philosophy and French symbolism, which paved the way for the turning point in Jørgensen's life: his conversion to Catholicism, which occurred in 1896 on a trip to Italy. After the outbreak of World War I, he lived for years in Assisi, until his return to Denmark in 1953.

Jørgensen's first collection of poetry, *Vers* (Verses, 1887)—strongly influenced by Jacobsen, Gjellerup, and Swinburne and by an excessive use of adjectives—is the expression of an estranged soul. This feeling of melancholy and longing becomes stronger in the five short novels written from 1888 to 1894, stories of uprooted students from the provinces who yield to the temptations of big-city life. This monotonous theme smolders in an oppressive atmosphere of despair and weariness with life. But another danger contributes to the basic mood of anxiety: the threat of a naturalistically limited existence.

The spiritual struggle leads in *Bekendelse* (Confession, 1894) to a religious breakthrough; the title poem closes with the cry: "Eternity! I am in your hands." The early poems still bear traces of pantheism, but in the concluding "Confiteor," Christianity is victorious. In *Confession*, Jørgensen—influenced by Baudelaire—abandons his earlier, highly descriptive language and seeks a much more concentrated form of expression, in which outer and inner worlds unite.

In the next collections, *Digte* (Poems, 1898), *Blomster og Frugter* (Flowers and Fruits, 1907), and *Af det Dybe* (Out of the Depth, 1909), this striving for a simple, image-free style becomes clearer, and in *Der er en Brønd, som rinder* (The Well That Flows, 1920) Jørgensen's poetic art reaches its zenith. Like Verlaine's, it is a poetry of simple meters and rhythmic forms in which the poet's ideas are conveyed solely by means of the intensity of the expressed feelings, the most insignificant word imbued with new potency and meaning.

After his conversion Jørgensen achieved a place as an international Catholic author, with his travel books from Germany and Italy, and his extensive, knowledgeable biographies of the saints, *Den hellige Frans af Assisi* (1907; Eng. tr. *Saint Francis of Assisi*, 1912), *Den hellige Katerina af Siena* (1915; Eng. tr. *Saint Catherine of Siena*, 1938), and later *Den hellige Birgitta af Vadstena* (Saint Birgitta of Vadstena, 1941-43), which combine scholarship with penetrating psychological insight. In these works Jørgensen achieved an admirable mastery of the Danish language, his prose characterized by striking purity and beauty.

The hallmark of Jørgensen's writing is lyricism. Perceptible also is his wide-ranging knowledge of European literature. The early strong influence of Goethe, Eichendorff, and Heine was later opposed by the growing influence of Baudelaire and Verlaine. Goethe and Verlaine in particular were critically important in Jørgensen's development of his unique poetry: lucid poems with a simple songlike style, very evocative of intimate moods.

Viggo Stuckenberg

Closely linked to the 1880s was Stuckenberg (1863-1905). His first publication, a collection titled *Digte* (Poems) appeared in 1886; this was followed by two naturalistic stories portraying young, radical students, *I Gennembrud* (Breaking Through, 1888) and *Messias* (Messiah, 1889), detailed period pieces influenced by Strindberg's *The Red Room*.

Stuckenberg had married in 1887, and experiences from the later unhappy years of his marriage provided a recurring theme. In a number of stories from the 1890s he describes both felicity and failure in relationships of men and women. More significant are Stuckenberg's poetry collections *Flyvende Sommer* (Gossamer, 1898) and *Sne* (Snow, 1901). Little remains of the young rebellious naturalist. Loneliness and the search for happiness are the two poles around which his poetry is now concentrated, based on melancholy moods of stoic resignation.

Sophus Claussen

In contrast to the other young poets of the 1890s, Claussen (1865-1931) was almost exclusively a lyricist. Since his death, he has been recognized as one of the greatest Danish poets of the twentieth century. He perceptibly influenced many Danish poets, particularly those of the 1940s and '60s.

Claussen was born on the South Danish island of Langeland. Before he dedicated himself exclusively to imaginative literature, he was active as a provincial journalist. He traveled to France and Italy, where he was able to remain for several years, since he was financially independent. Claussen wrote two realistic travel books during this time, *Antonius i Paris* (Antonius in Paris, 1896) and *Valfart* (Pilgrimage, 1896). With the exception of these volumes and a few later volumes of essays — valuable because they contribute to an understanding of him as an artist and of his aesthetic theories — Claussen's prose is a series of rather insignificant lyrical idyllic stories with fleeting erotic moods.

Claussen's collections of poems entitled *Pilefløjter* (Willow Pipes, 1899) and *Djævlerier* (Diableries, 1904) established his greatness. They are broadly expressive, from the darkly macaber to the exuberant and enchanting. He studied the French symbolists and was the first Danish poet to consistently follow the symbolist aesthetic. Other models were Byron, Shelley, Heine, and Drachmann, as well as the Danish romantic poets. He produced sparkling translations of Heine, Shelley, and Baudelaire.

Willow Pipes was primarily influenced by Heine and Danish romantic Emil Aarestrup. The setting of these poems — except for a few with Copenhagen themes — is the province. The new element in this collection is the objective characterization of diverse, individualized female figures, as in "Balaften" ("Evening of the Ball"). In addition, there are several subjective love poems, the most exquisite, perhaps, "I en Frugthave" ("In an Orchard"), in which nature and love melt impressionistically into a whole.

> Did storm fall on suncalm surface?
> My soul fluttered up like a cloth,
> and a lightning-torn cascade of thunder
> poured rain over green leaves.
> When it grew quiet, you were mine.
>
> (. . .)
>
> The earth is wet to your foot, pure one,

and spiced like the air of the orchard.
Let us kiss in silence and alone!
We ourselves are like two appleboughs:
we shall blossom and bear fruit.

                    Tr. Poul Borum

The collection closes with the symbolic travel sketch "Røg" ("Smoke"), the major poem of this period. Claussen lets his thoughts and moods drift along with changing clouds of smoke, which become symbols of his encounter with reality (coal smoke) and his reunion with his wife (white steam).

Diableries have Italian and French motifs. With Baudelaire as model, Claussen is inspired to an artistic "Satanism," whose erotic central theme is woman as vampire. "Trappen til Helvede" ("The Staircase to Hell") provides insight into the demonic regions of the human heart, which "feels the joy of the mortal sin owing to his offense." "Il letto" portrays the Queen of Sheba, who, having been rejected by King Solomon, finds revenge by taking a black slave as lover. And, finally, "Sorte Blomst" ("Black Flower") is a cynical poem about a prostitute whose soul is as black as soot, but whose desires are "carnation red." But *Diableries* should not be considered merely erotic poetry. It treats all the problems that life poses for the poet, as, for instance, in "Afrodites Dampe" ("Aphrodite's Steam"): The poem is, to be sure, a glorification of passion, but at the same time it is a thoughtful poem about the plight and prospects of the creative person.

In *Danske Vers* (Danish Verses, 1912), Claussen returned to his home province. Side by side with pantheistic symbolistic hymns in praise of nature, there is again a predominance of erotic poems, more profound and bold than before, such as "Livets Kermesse" ("The Fair of Life"), about the dangerous snakecharmer Miss Wanda, who embodies joy of life and passion, in contrast to a lifeless mechanical doll. There are also melancholy commemorative verses to Herman Bang, which bear witness to Claussen's deep understanding of the human psyche. The cosmic poem "Imperia" is austere and triumphant, a melodramatic counterpart to the humorous satire on the power of routine, "Visen om Himperigimpe" ("The Song of Himperigimpe"), a metaphor for the severity of barren nature.

Claussen called his next book *Fabler* (Fables, 1917), meaning poems and symbols that transcend wisdom and progress: "We don't always believe in 'the power' and cables. We believe the world is deep with fables." Juxtaposed with allegorical period pieces, such as "Digteren og Daarskaben" ("The Poet and Foolishness"), stand dark and magical verses about the relationship of the creative spirit to art and to the modern materialistic world, and lines celebrating the power and immortality of the word, as in "Mennesket og Digteren" ("The Human and the Poet"): "The world is a sarcophagus—but I possess the word eternally, even though I live but a single day."

In Claussen's last significant collection, *Heroica* (1925), his world view becomes exalted. With poetic force he tames the language of grandiose hexameter hymns into expressions that reconcile contradictory aspects of himself: exuberance and passion/mildness and friendliness. The "Hexameter-Hymne til Pan og Giovanni" ("Hexameter-Hymn to Pan and Giovanni") presents humorously the remorse of his friend Johannes Jørgensen, a convert to Catholicism, over their shared youth, and combines Christ, Pan, and the Virgin Mary into a symbol of humanity. Claussen's religious humanism emerges powerfully—in the context of an awareness of the dangers of a technological culture—in the prophetic final poem "Atomernes Oprør" ("The Revolt of the Atoms"), where he issues a call for reconciliation and peace "in order to save our planet."

Sophus Claussen's writing is a protest for fantasy and beauty against the closed horizons of naturalism and materialism. Like the other symbolists, Claussen wanted to express the inexpressible, and, in accordance with symbolist aesthetics, he wanted to form all words and emotions in his poetry into images of a truth that we can only intuit, a dark prophecy of the ultimate union that underlies external reality.

Helge Rode

Although in the opinion of their contemporaries Jørgensen, Stuckenberg, and Claussen stood at the forefront of the symbolist breakthrough, Rode (1870-1937) appears to posterity to be the central figure in the dispute with naturalism. During a stay in Norway in 1891, Rode had a profound religious experience that caused him to abandon the pessimistic world view that had characterized his youth. He tried to capture and preserve that mystical moment in the ecstatic poems of his first collection, *Hvide Blomster* (White Flowers, 1892). His basic mood was one of expectation and wonder toward life, which in his lyrical and dramatic works he formed into images of unique beauty. *White Flowers* is a major work in the literature of the 1890s; more than any other book of the time, it proclaims the existence of the self as the center of life and of eternity.

Around 1894 Rode joined the circle of the journal *The Tower* (see

p. 87) and during a long stay in Norway was influenced by Sigbjørn Obstfelder. Inspired by symbolism, he created the major works of his youth, the drama *Kongesønner* (Sons of the King, 1896), influenced by Maeterlinck, and the collection *Digte* (Poems 1896), in which his tragic knowledge of human loneliness and isolation is conveyed in masterfully concentrated form. In the two sons, Rode personifies the two primal forces of life: life and death, which also represent two powers within the poet: speculative spirit and practical nature. The same dualism forms the basis of the later Tolstoy-inspired drama, the tragedy of an idealist and a materialist, *Grev Bonde og hans Hus* (Count Bonde and His House, 1912).

In the first decade of the twentieth century, Rode concentrated primarily on dramatic writing. The dark tragedy of fate, *Kampene i Stefan Borgs Hjem* (The Battles in Stefan Borg's Home, 1901), portrays the conflict of passion and respectability. The core of the drama, reminiscent in its presentation of diabolical evil of Strindberg's *Dance of Death*, is linked to Rode's mystical experience: Death alone gives life coherence.

The last period of Rode's writing is dominated by his major lyrical work, *Ariel* (1914), the title covering only those portions of the collection in which the poet, influenced by Shelley, pays homage to an ethereal spirituality. In "Vaaren i Frederiksberg Have" ("Spring in Frederiksberg Garden"), a paraphrase of Shelley's "The Sensitive Plant," the mystical conviction is proclaimed, in a supple and inspired manner, that love and beauty—here manifest in nature— suffer no alteration, no death. A conflicting view in "Atlantis" sees nature as the ruthless enemy of humankind. We stand outside nature, and our closeness to it is mere illusion.

In the volume of historical and philosophical essays *Krig og Aand* (War and Spirit, 1917), Rode attacks Georg Brandes and his books on World War I, in which Brandes condemned the war as a manifestation of the infinite stupidity of humankind. Rode asserted that Brandes himself belonged to the ruthlessly destructive intellectual movement that culminated in Darwinism and finally in Nietzsche's cult of the superman. Rode's argument with rationalism and materialism extended through several critical works that appeared during the 1920s. He reached back to the mystical experience of his youth in his major religious work, *Pladsen med de grønne Trær* (The Square with the Green Trees, 1924). His earlier uncertainty had now become an approximation of a firm belief based on the Bible. Rode gained more readers through his religious writing than through his poetry. For forty years he was a major figure in Danish intellectual life.

NATURE WORSHIP AND
NATIONAL LITERATURE IN NORWAY

The upheaval and reorientation in the Norwegian literature of the 1890s is perceptible in the works of many older authors—for instance, Lie's *Trolls*, Garborg's *Weary Men*, and *The Master Builder* by Ibsen, who had already proclaimed this revolution in *The Wild Duck* and *Rosmersholm*. Widespread opposition to naturalism was clearly evident. The fruitless debates and analyses had grown wearisome, and disappointment over the inconclusiveness of radical ideas led to a skeptical attitude toward democracy, as, for instance, on the part of Hans E. Kinck and Knut Hamsun.

The literature of the 1880s had a predominantly international character, but there awakened now—because of problematic union politics (see p. ix) and the advance of modern industry—an enthusiasm for national cultural values. Writers turned from the city to the village and to untouched nature; general social problems yielded to individual psychology, and scientifically objective description to suggestible impressionism.

Gunnar Heiberg

Heiberg (1857-1929), the greatest Norwegian dramatist at the beginning of the twentieth century, was a transitional figure, the neo-romantic and spiritual breakthrough coming later with lyricist Sigbjørn Obstfelder. Heiberg sharply attacked the moralizing tendentious literature of the 1880s. His early work consists of sarcastic and light-hearted social satires and political comedies. In his first work, *Tante Ulrikke* (Aunt Ulrikke, 1883), he drew a series of realistic portraits of people of the period, glorifying *the* great personality— here a woman—at the expense of the representatives of party politics.

Far more significant are Heiberg's erotic dramas. *Balkonen* (1894; Eng. tr. *The Balcony*, 1922) praises love as an uncontrollable, natural power which can overcome any cultural or moral convention. The main character, Julie, refuses to be tamed either by her first, materialistic, husband or by her second, idealistic, husband. The first lost his right to her love through his calculating attitude toward her; the second has to give way because he wants to transform ecstatic love into tenderness. Not until Julie meets the erotic superman, the man of instinct, does she succumb to passion.

The kind of relationship that Julie and her second husband have forms the theme of *Kjærlighetens tragedie* (1904; Eng. tr. *The*

Tragedy of Love, 1921). The love of the major character, Karen, has a spiritual aspect which recalls the metaphysical views of the neo-romantic movement. For Karen, love is the highest and most real form of life. For her husband, Erling, love within marriage is transformed into a social institution, a solid foundation for a successful career. These two views cannot be reconciled, and when Karen feels that Erling is slowly slipping from her, she commits suicide.

The muted tone and the beauty of the dialogue are well suited to the tragic theme. Heiberg was an exceptional stylist; his language, both powerful and lyrical, is consonant with that of the symbolists of the younger generation. In his clear renunciation of the utilitarian mission of literature and in his glorification of antidemocratic individualism, which forms a Norwegian parallel to Brandes's Nietzsche studies, Heiberg marks a transition to the new literary movements.

Vilhelm Krag and Nils Collett Vogt

Krag (1871-1933) and Vogt (1864-1937) are also transitional figures. Krag was a fashionable author of the 1890s; his poetry in *Digte* (Poems, 1891) was charming and elegant, but hardly original, revealing an obvious indebtedness to Danish poets J. P. Jacobsen and Drachmann. Vogt's debut collection, *Digte* (Poems, 1887), was closely related to the radical social trends of the 1880s; his first great success, *Fra Vaar til Høst* (From Spring to Autumn, 1894), in the spirit of Schiller and Swinburne, praises antiquity and also manifests the intoxication with life expressed by Nietzsche and especially by Heidenstam. Gradually Vogt's poetry changed. *Musik og Vaar* (Music and Spring, 1896) contains religious poems about transitoriness and eternity, and in *Det dyre Brød* (The Precious Bread, 1900) Vogt's relationship with Norway and its nature becomes the focal point. He also wrote novels and short stories.

Tryggve Andersen

A far more important prose writer was Andersen (1866-1920). Like the German romantic E. T. A. Hoffman, whom he admired greatly, Andersen had a dual existence: He was a prosaic clerk and an imaginative dreamer with a preference for the strange and morbid, evidently influenced by Edgar Allan Poe. Andersen's reputation as one of Norway's greatest writers of short stories rests on *I Cancelliraadens dage* (1897; Eng. tr. *In the Days of the Councillor,* 1969), a collection of stories whose source of inspiration is the author's strong feeling for tradition. This work is an exceptional portrayal of the culture of a village around 1800, in Andersen's own East Norwegian home province.

Spiritual disintegration became a major motif in the pessimistic contemporary novel *Mot kvæld* (Toward Evening, 1900), a final offshoot of the fin-de-siècle literature, confusing in its structure but a deeply personal confession characteristic of the period. Both works were succeeded by a number of masterful short stories, brought together in *Samlede fortællinger* (Collected Stories, 1916).

Sigbjørn Obstfelder

The poet who best expressed the "spiritual breakthrough" in Norway and who came to typify the fin-de-siècle mood in Norwegian poetry was the pietistically raised Obstfelder (1866-1900). He began his university career studying Old Norse, became an engineer, and spent the period from 1890 to 1891 in the United States; but he never felt at home there. His writing has its point of departure in his notion that he "seems to have come to the wrong planet" and is an expression of his longing for the eternal truth underlying the world of material appearances. The religious mystical idea in Obstfelder's works is the pantheistic wish to merge with the infinite, the divine, in this life.

His speculative poetry, *Digte* (1893; Eng. tr. *Poems*, 1920), unrhymed prose poems often of extraordinary beauty, is with its free suggestive form and mystical attitude a characteristic example of the symbolism of the 1890s, signifying a decided break with naturalism. Obstfelder attempts to penetrate to the innermost spiritual processes through eliminating everything superfluous and thereby creating a distinctive feeling of estrangement:

> Christmas Eve!
> (...)
> I wandered alone in the streets
> and listened to the children's songs.
> I sat down on the steps
> and thought of my dead mother.
> And I walked out into the fields
> out—beneath the stars.
> My shadow slid over shadows
> of the dead branches of the trees
>
> Tr. Marianne Forssblad

Related to the longing for eternity is Obstfelder's cult of love, in which eternity is present. The woman is seen not only as an instinctual person but also as a divine mystery. This is the basic idea of the first novella, "Liv" ("Life"), in the collection *To novelletter* (Two Novelettes, 1895), as well as in the novel *Korset* (The Cross, 1896). In all of Obstfelder's work, the spiritual dominates the material, as in the drama *De røde dråber* (The Red Drops, 1897), which deals with a current problem—spiritual needs in a technological age.

Among those who influenced Obstfelder are Kierkegaard, Jacobsen, Strindberg, Maeterlinck, Whitman, Schopenhauer, and Dostoevsky; he was also in contact with the Danish symbolists who wrote in the journal *The Tower* (see p. 87). As a poet, however, he was an independent personality, the major representative of Norwegian lyrical symbolism, a melancholy dreamer who suffered from existential anxiety, which he sought to escape through his longing for eternal life. This feeling was most convincingly expressed in the posthumously published *En præsts dagbog* (The Diary of a Minister, 1920), in which, as in all of Obstfelder's prose, the language is lyrically beautiful.

Hans E. Kinck

The most outstanding representative of the neo-romantic movement as a national art form is Kinck (1865-1926). He is half poet, half cultural philosopher, with a wide-ranging knowledge of history and psychology. His central themes concern periods of transition and decay in which two cultures battle each other, or a human being comes into conflict with society. Kinck began as a dogmatic naturalist, with two skillful but impersonal novels (1892-93). After a stay in Paris, where he was much influenced by Jonas Lie, he shifted to a style rich in fantasy and symbols, apparent in the short-story collection *Flaggermus-vinger* (Bat's Wings, 1895).

With the exception of the forceful peasant tales in *Fra hav til hei* (From Sea to Mountain, 1897), which shows the humorous and ironic side of his art, Kinck continued his new style in a number of erotic stories, such as *Naar kjærlighed dør* (When Love Dies, 1903) and *Livsaanderne* (The Spirits of Life, 1906). Seldom does eroticism bring happiness; rather, a feeling of loneliness in love predominates. Kinck masterfully portrays puberty, first love and youthful eroticism. More characteristic is his preoccupation with the instinctive life of the spirit and his portrayal of suppressed feelings that are never released and that degenerate into hatred or pathological fantasies.

In his novels, Kinck combines his erotic short stories and his peasant tales. They contain very successful single scenes and impressively drawn characters, but the plots are often arbitrary and are weakened by lengthy, reflective passages. In *Herman Ek* (1896-98, reworked in 1923) Kinck portrays the clash between the old peasant culture and the modern, European urban culture. The title figure is a "romantic" spirit who vacillates even as a youth between his mother and her bond with nature, and the more refined character of his father. Later Ek lives entirely in a world of his own moods, unable to relate easily to life. As a student he becomes involved in the confused debate about the meaning of life that characterized the 1890s. Tired of student life, Ek returns to his home province to become a farmer. He is disappointed, however, for he remains a stranger among the inhabitants. He wants a life with the people, but he also wants to retain his independence, which proves to be his undoing.

The novel trilogy *Sneskavlen brast* (The Avalanche Broke, 1918-19) collects within its framework all the essential themes in Kinck's work: inhibited eroticism and tenderness that is rejected, a child's suffering because of adults' arguments, and the binding force of marriage. But above all we again find his central motif: the relationship of the farmer to the civil servants and estateholders. The poverty of the farmers gives rise to their claim to wealth and their desire for revenge against the "important people," who, for their part, are living in spiritual poverty and degradation, which Kinck demonstrates in his portrayal of their erotic behavior. The young girl Sofie rises above this wretchedness, but she is not strong enough to bear the misery of others; first she must learn to overcome the problems in her own disappointing marriage. In the last part, the major figure is the wily and power-hungry Geirmund, a representative of the victorious peasant class. But the peasants arrogantly take over the life-style against which they fought; the class struggle thus has been futile and meaningless.

The most personal expression of Kinck's art is the dramatic poem *Driftekaren* (The Drover, 1908), an overpowering work, difficult to understand largely because Kinck's highly peculiar form of writing defies all the rules of traditional metrics. Vraal is a peripatetic cattle driver, but his figure has superhuman dimensions. He is at the same time a poetic genius and a tragic symbol of the Norwegian peasant character, torn between homesickness and longing for travel, doubts and recollections. Like Herman Ek, Vraal returns to his home province and his kindred, but he finds the village divided by arguments. He attempts through great visions and inflammatory words to drive the peasants to great deeds, but they are unable to follow him and they send him away. Like Ibsen's Peer Gynt, he is redeemed from his loneliness only by the persistent love of a woman, and with her he leaves civilization and seeks the way back to nature.

Kinck works with similar motifs in his dramas. They are technically weak, but imbued with lyrical beauty and philosophical depth, containing exceptional descriptions of setting and character. The tragedy *Den sidste gjæst* (The Last Guest, 1910) portrays the last, vain struggle of Renaissance satirist Pietro Aretino, the struggle between *joie de vivre* and death. *Mot karneval* (Toward Carnival, 1915) dramatizes the tragedy of Machiavelli, who loses his battle with the masses.

Kinck's figures are always shown in their relationship to the milieu from which they come. He always portrays the mind of a people or of an individual interacting with nature, and constantly emphasizes the subconscious. He is barely interested in external events, which represent for him only unfocused and counterfeit pictures of the inner world of the psyche. To achieve this reality, he intentionally represents the environment in distorted form. For this reason, Kinck is one of the least accessible and least read of the newer Norwegian authors, though he is one of the greatest.

Knut Hamsun

Hamsun (1859-1952) was also in search of the primitive and the natural. His enthusiasm for nature is expressed in lyrical prose. Hamsun spent his childhood in the Lofote islands; that environment, with its clear nights, woods, and mountains, provoked intense feelings for nature. As a young man he tried his hand as a teacher, sculptor, and road worker; later, in 1882, he traveled to the United States, where he remained until 1888, with the exception of a brief interruption in 1885, and made his living as a streetcar conductor, speaker, and farm laborer.

By the time he was eighteen, Hamsun had already written several peasant novellas in the style of Bjørnson. However, he did not achieve public notice until 1890, with his novel *Sult* (Eng. Tr. *Hunger*, 1899 and later). The book, which is partly autobiographical, portrays the hopeless struggle for existence of an unsuccessful, poverty-stricken writer in Christiania. Tormenting hunger is described in all its stages with consistent, brutal realism, as it slowly destroys his nervous system and his self-control, and causes feverish fantasies. Thus the novel has a typically naturalistic theme. However, a comparison with Garborg's *Peasant Students*, which also portrays bleak, incessant hunger, reveals that Hamsun deliberately avoids all social and political perspectives. Learning much from Dostoevsky, he concentrates on subjectively describing the spiritual experiences and the psychological behavior of a young genius in a style full of nuances and lyricism. He thereby introduces a new epoch in Norwegian literature.

Hamsun's next book *Mysterier* (1892; Eng. tr. *Mysteries*, 1927 and later), is formless, polemical, and strains for effects. The main character, enigmatic Johan Nagel, suddenly appears by chance one day in a small Norwegian city. Like the poet in *Hunger*, Nagel is "a stranger in life," whose appearance is as challenging as it is accidental. But since he is not starving, his situation is not extraordinary. Indeed Hamsun makes no attempt to explain his behavior, wanting to demonstrate the mysterious depths of the human soul. In Nagel he has collected all the irrational and instinctive elements of existence, and has placed them in opposition to the bourgeois world with its everyday morality. The portrayal of Nagel as a rebellious intellectual aristocrat living his life asocially and governed by romantic ecstasy was definitely influenced by Hartmann's *Philosophie des Unbewussten* (Philosophy of the Unconscious, 1869) and Nietzsche's philosophy of the superman. Hamsun also takes issue with the other great prophets of the time, Ibsen and Tolstoy, in Nagel's long monologues.

The Nagel type appears again, but in a different magnitude and with the powerful landscape of the Nordland region as a backdrop, in the lyrical narrative *Pan* (1894; Eng. tr. 1920 and later), written in the first person singular. Lieutenant Glahn is also a lonely wanderer, a hunter and a man of nature, weary of modern civilization; through his encounter with Edvarda, he experiences love as an intoxicating ecstasy, and he succumbs to it. In an epilogue another first-person narrator reports his encounter with Glahn in India, where the latter tells him, broken-heartedly, of the most wonderful moments of his life during that Nordland summer. On a hunting trip Glahn is shot accidentally and killed—civilization has achieved victory over nature, the lieutenant. Glahn's recollections, his life in the woods, are permeated by a pantheistic natural mysticism and a lyrical mood that raise events into an inspired fantasy world of powerful dimensions.

The lyrical element had been an essential characteristic of Hamsun's work from the beginning, and his portrayal of the moods of nature matures in the poetry volume *Det vilde Kor* (The Wild Chor-

us, 1904) into a perfected art. The poems are an anti-humanistic indictment of the hollowness of civilization and a hymn of praise to
the eternal power of poetry.

Closely related to *Pan* are the short, somewhat sentimental, erotic
fantasy *Victoria* (1898; Eng. tr. 1923 and later), one of the most
popular love stories in world literature, and a number of impressive novels glorifying natural humanity. Among these are *Under
Høststjærnen* (Under the Autumn Star, 1906), *En Vandrer spiller
med Sordin* (A Wanderer Plays with Muted Strings, 1909; both
vols. tr. as *Wanderers*, also as *The Wanderer*, 1922 and later), *Den
siste Glæde* (The Last Joy, 1912; Eng. tr. *Look Back on Happiness*, 1940), collected in the trilogy *Vandreren* (The Wanderer),
and *Sværmere* (1904; Eng. tr. *Dreamers*, also as *Mothwise*, 1921).
In his novel Hamsun's wanderer is a strange telegraph operator,
Ove Rolandsen, who manages in spite of his temperament to win
ambitious Elise, the proud daughter of a rich merchant; in the trilogy he appears as an aging vagabond, Knut Pedersen, Hamsun's
real name. Common to these volumes is the contrast between the
free individual and the city person, between nature and culture.
Knut Pedersen travels about through Norway's woods, far from the
city, from farm to farm, working as circumstances dictate and trying to find his way back to a simple primitive way of life in order
to heal his uprooted spirit. But he does not succeed in tearing himself loose from the city—no matter how far he wanders, he will
return again one day.

As early as *Dreamers* a change had been evident in Hamsun's
writing. He moved from the subjective first-person narrative to a
stronger, more objective mode, which unfolds fully in the epic
Segelfoss novels. In *Børn av Tiden* (1913; Eng. tr. *Children of
the Age*, 1924) Hamsun, who before took an interest only in his
major characters, succeeded in creating a wide-ranging realistic portrayal of the milieu of the Nordland region, with all of its social
types. In the form of social criticism, he portrayed the clash between
the old, patriarchal feudal system and material progress. The loser
in this battle is the landowner Holmsen, the tragic figure of the
book. In the sequel, *Segelfoss By* (1915; Eng. tr. *Segelfoss Town*,
1925), Hamsun reports in the same humorous and yet sharply ironic
manner how life develops in the small city after the upstart Holmengraa returns from America as a millionaire and reforms the entire
region in the spirit of modern capitalism. Above this new lifeless
society of parvenues and rogues stands Hamsun's spokesman, the
telegraph operator Baardsen, who has come down in the world; he

is an embodiment of the soul and of poetry, related to the wanderer type, and he becomes a symbolic figure when, at the end of the novel, he is discovered dead in Holmengraa's basement.

Hamsun's message seems more positive in the nature epic *Markens Grøde* (1917; Eng. tr. *Growth of the Soil*, 1921 and later), the novel that won him world fame and the Nobel Prize in 1920. Hamsun tells the story of the settler Isak, who stubbornly and with great effort clears the woods in the Nordland region, making the wilderness arable and establishing his own farm. This lonely man is joined by the proud and capable Inger, who has a harelip. Their everyday life is destroyed when she kills one of her children—who also has a harelip —and is condemned to eight years in prison. But Inger accepts her punishment, rises above it, and, when free, again takes over the responsibility for house and family. Isak's estate grows, other settlers move out into the wilderness, and a new self-supporting community is formed. The work thereby becomes a pantheistic prose hymn to the fruitful earth and the people who live on it—a fresh interpretation of Rousseau's gospel of nature.

This optimism yields to social bitterness and criticism in Hamsun's following two books. *Konerne ved Vandposten* (1920); Eng. tr. *The Women at the Pump*, 1928) portrays with great disdain human fate in a poor village, and caricatures civilization in the figure of a grotesque parasite, the castrato Oliver. Isak, in *Growth of the Soil*, constantly develops his nature through work, even becomes a part of nature; but Oliver lives *against* nature. The sick people in *Siste Kapitel* (1923; Eng. tr. *Chapter the Last*, 1929) have removed themselves from nature. They stay in a sanatorium—as in Thomas Mann's *Der Zauberberg* (The Magic Mountain, 1924), a symbolic world of indifference and degeneration—which is destroyed one day by a fire. The miserable death of these city people is sarcastically contrasted with death in nature, which is a natural part of the whole—for nature itself can never be destroyed.

Hamsun again takes up the wanderer motif in the next novels, *Landstrykere* (1927; Eng. tr. *Vagabonds*, 1930), *August* (1930; Eng. tr. 1931), and *Men Livet lever* (1933; Life Goes On; Eng. tr. *The Road Leads On*, 1934 and later); the three volumes form an ironic and humorous trilogy of the adventuresome experiences of the charming and boastful daydreamer August and his comrade Edevart. Now, however, Hamsun views his vagabond as a Peer Gynt type, lacking substance. Vagabondism leads to rootlessness and, in turn, to sterility. Therefore he condemns his hero, although he remains deeply fascinated by him. In Hamsun's last novel, *Ringen sluttet*

(1936; Eng. tr. *The Ring Is Closed*, 1937), the wanderer appears again in the figure of an asocial maverick named Abel Brodersen, who, however, in contrast to August, turns his back in aristocratic disdain on bourgeois society.

Hamsun's mystical attachment to the soil, his glorification of the superman, inspired by Nietzsche, his anti-Americanism, and his success in Germany, where his romantic portrayal of the peasants in *Growth of the Soil* was particularly enthusiastically received and imitated by representatives of the *Heimat* literature, such as Karl Heinrich Waggerl and Ernst Wiechert—all of these elements drove him into the arms of national socialism. After the liberation of Norway in 1945, he was indicted for treason, but because of his "weakened mental condition" was given only a fine. The ninety-year-old author convincingly refuted the notion of any debility in his defense, *Paa gjengrodde Stier* (1949; Eng. tr. *On Overgrown Paths*, 1967), an autobiography permeated with lyricism and wise self-irony.

Knut Hamsun's impressive writing includes both pathetic melodrama and refined poetry, both biting scorn and very tender infatuation; and his narrative technique masterfully mixes direct and indirect speech, objective attitudes and authorial omniscience. His works form an organic whole, held together by the primitive, yet modern personality of their creator.

NEO-ROMANTICISM AND LYRICAL REVIVAL IN FINLAND

FINNISH LITERATURE

"The time of exposure is over, the time of confession is coming," Minna Canth had prophesied in 1894 on the occasion of Järnefelt's autobiographical *My Awakening*. Simultaneously Juhani Aho had become interested in the spiritual problems of Pietism and the *Kalevala* tradition, abandoning analysis of contemporary society in favor of historical description. Writers and their readers had grown tired of discussing women's rights and other social problems; neither did they accept the optimistic belief in progress characteristic of the 1880s. Typically enough, the young neo-romantics remained passive in the tense political situation caused by the systematic Russian oppression after 1899, which culminated in the assassination of the hated governor-general Bobrikov in 1904.

They found their motifs not only in Finnish history and folklore, but also in distant countries, antiquity, mythology, and the Bible.

They were in close contact with the corresponding currents abroad. Nietzsche's cultural pessimism, his superman theories and rejection of the Christian "slave morality," Selma Lagerlöf's imaginative narrative art, the Swedish poets of the 1890s—especially Fröding— Hamsun's cult of nature, and Maeterlinck's and Verlaine's symbolism all evoked a clear response; however, the decadent and morbid aspects of the fin-de-siècle movement had scarcely any influence.

Eino Leino

The most talented writer and the most productive—his work comprises more than 70 volumes—of the new generation was Leino (1878-1926). His favorite authors and models were—besides Finnish and other Nordic writers—Goethe, Heine, Nietzsche, Shakespeare, and Anatole France. Generally, Leino's works before 1900 were impersonal finger exercises in poetic technique, playing with fantasy and words. Characteristic was a feeling of the pantheistic solidarity of nature and humanity; although Heine's influence is clear, pessimism and denial of life are absent. With the collection *Kangastuksia* (1902; Mirages), a more personal commitment and sensitivity is perceptible: the demand for a total dedication of one's life to art and the conviction that loneliness is the basis for the development of the individual.

A hike through eastern Karelia in 1897 left a strong imprint on Leino's poetry. In 1903 Part One of *Helkavirsiä* (Helka Songs; Eng. tr. *Whitsongs*, 1978) was published, followed in 1916 by Part Two, a bold attempt to give the old *Kalevala* motifs a modern historical and symbolic interpretation in concentrated, stylized language. Both a national and a purely cosmic view of life is expressed here, influenced by the theosophic ideas of reincarnation.

The climax in Leino's lyric period was reached with the two collections *Talviyö* (1905; The Winter Night) and *Halla* (1908; The Frost). The first contained a suite of erotic and sensuous poems with oriental settings, while the later was dominated by depressive and melancholy moods, reflecting the end of Leino's first marriage. Nietzsche's influence now became evident, as in the short poem titled "Minä" ("I").

> At the beginning was I
> I
> grew close to the Almighty
> and that I was all
> Your Self is the most wonderful power

which you received at your birth:
Never give it away!
Tr. Jaakko Ahokas

Leino also wrote several lively but superficial novels describing contemporary life in Helsinki. Of higher quality are a number of short plays, published in six volumes, entitled *Naamioita* (1905-11; Masks). Influenced by Hauptmann's, Maeterlinck's, and d'Annunzio's symbolist works, he attempted to create a form of neo-romantic drama that through stylization and simplification would work its effect through poetic beauty. The best of these plays deal with historical topics. They project a certain dreamlike mood, and the action passes in front of the audience as a series of lyrical images.

Leino had overcome his depression by about 1916 and continued to write poetry, first motivated by the Finnish civil war to compose a number of patriotic poems, later inspired by a universal belief in humanist values. He turned to myth and history, working with motifs from antiquity, as in the collection *Bellerophon* (1919).

Leino's works brought about a radical renewal of Finnish poetry. His pantheistic religion and universal humanism originated in Scandinavian and German literature, but Finland's mythology and folklore supplied him with the most valuable impulses. In *Kalevala* and *Kanteletar* Leino found the natural spontaneity, the exuberant imagination, and the clarity and precision that characterize his own writing.

Otto Manninen

The second great neo-romantic poet, Manninen (1872-1950), was a striking contrast to Leino—he was very sophisticated and not easily accessible. In his lifetime he was not much read, but his poetry has become increasingly appreciated. Manninen created his own style by extracting from language the most expressive and precise expressions possible. His writing is never sentimental or tedious; he succeeds in keeping a subtle balance of intellect and feeling. In the four collections published during his life, *Säkeitä, I-II* (1905-10; Verses), *Virrantyven* (1925; Dead Water), and *Matkamies* (1938; The Wayfarer)—and in two posthumous collections—there are several poems representing traditional poetic genres: patriotic and historical poems, satires, and humoresques. Manninen's best works are his subjective lyrics, which, without illusion but with occasional irony, revolve around the dominating forces of life—love and death—praising love's omnipotence over humans even when that love is hopeless. Death does not imply devastating emptiness; it is the gateway to "the summer of eternal sleep." External narrative and description are reduced as much as possible; sometimes they are almost nonexistent, being replaced by an inner feeling, the inexplicable mood of which is expressed symbolically.

Veikko Koskenniemi

As a poet Manninen was completely overshadowed during his lifetime by Veikko Koskenniemi (1885-1962), whose writing was marked by a development from neo-romanticism to classicism. In 1921 he took a position as professor of the history of literature at the Finnish University in Turku (Åbo), and in 1948 he became a member of the Finnish Academy. Experiences as a student in Helsinki and on the plains of his home province supplied him with the material for his first collection, *Runoja* (1906; Poems), which clearly foreshadows Koskenniemi's position as a poet of loneliness and the night, dreams and death. In his third collection, *Hiilivalkea* (1913; Charcoal Fire), Koskenniemi's pessimism, influenced by Schopenhauer's philosophy, is more intensely expressed. The collections *Elegioja* (1917; Elegies) and *Sydän ja kuolema* (1919; The Heart and the Death) evince an increasing enthusiasm for Greek and Roman antiquity, a development that can also be observed in Koskenniemi's Swedish models Heidenstam and Ekelund. Employing antique motifs and, occasionally, rhetorical technique, he proclaims humankind's absolute loneliness, lamenting the destruction of beauty, the barrenness and lowliness of our lives. However, a number of love poems present a brighter view of life, confirmed by collections such as *Kirkiaura* (1930; The Wedge of the Cranes) and *Tuli ja tuhka* (1936; Fire and Ashes). The increasingly patriotic tone of his work culminates in *Latuja lumessa* (1940; Tracks in the Snow), inspired by the war against Russia in 1939-40.

Besides poetry, Koskenniemi published a novel, a number of excellent travel books, and collections of essays. Time has dealt harshly with his writing: The importance of his artistic contribution has waned. But Koskenniemi's intimate love poetry, his clear and tightly structured reflective poetry, and simple nature verses retain their vitality and general validity.

Johannes Linnankoski

The most typical prose writer of the neo-romantic period was Linnankoski (1869-1913). In 1900 he left his job as chief editor of a newspaper in Porvo (Borgå) and lived in various places in southwest Finland, where he systematically prepared for his career as a writer by studying the masters of world literature from Aeschylus to Tolstoy. Influenced by Byron's *Cain* and Milton's *Paradise Lost*, he wrote a pathetic and incoherent tragedy, *Ikuinen taistelu* (1903; The Eternal Struggle), describing within the framework of Cain's and Abel's destinies the fight between God and Lucifer, a conflict characteristic of Linnankoski's later writings.

His next work, the novel *Laulu tulipunaisesta kukasta* (1905; Eng. tr. *The Song of the Blood-Red Flower*, 1920), was just as uneven, but became a tremendous success and has been published in more than twenty-five editions. Linnankoski utilized a motif from world literature, the Don Juan story, set in contemporary Finland among lumberjacks and timber floaters. A total failure was *Taistelu Heikkilän talosta* (1907; The Struggle over Heikkilä Farm), a crime story in a rural setting in which the crime is discovered in part through the supernatural apparition of the victim. But in the novel *Pakolaiset* (1908; The Refugees) Linnankoski created a masterpiece. The descriptions of nature and the environment are now limited in favor of dramatic suspense and psychological analysis based on the motif of a young wife's faithlessness to her older husband and his inner development, after a fierce mental struggle, when he discovers her deception.

Linnankoski wrote three more plays, one of which, *Kirot* (The Curse, 1907), is highly readable. The play is an allegorical description of political life and the fight against the Russification of Finland in a partly mythological setting. As in all of Linnankoski's works, good prevails: A burning belief in the eternal value of ethical ideas dominates all his books.

A lyrical revival also took place within Fenno-Swedish literature about 1900. The poets gathered around the periodical *Euterpe* (1902-5), whose strong cosmopolitan, aesthetic, and exclusive tendencies corresponded to the privileged social background of its contributors. The two greatest poetic talents of this group, though essentially different, were Bertel Gripenberg and Arvid Mörne.

Bertel Gripenberg

With his debut collection, *Dikter* (1903; Poems), Gripenberg (1878-1947) showed himself to be an amorist, a worshiper of youth, action, and courage. But as early as *Gallergrinden* (The Iron Gate, 1905) the hedonist man of the moment began to sing the praises of duty, loyalty, and sacrifice. From *Svarta sonetter* (Black Sonnets, 1908) on, Gripenberg's vitality became increasingly imbued with a tragic tinge caused by personal disappointments and the realization that he belonged to an upper class which would never have any influence in the new Finnish democracy. Such feelings of defeat are most exquisitely expressed in *Aftnar i Tavastland* (Evenings in Tavastland, 1911). Death is regarded as a welcome rest, a merciful end to a wasted life. The contrast between the shadow of death and the splendor of the heroic deed characterizes Gripenberg's three collections of poems about the civil war of 1917-18, in which he clearly took the side of the anti-Communist party.

After 1920 Gripenberg became an increasingly visible leader of the conservatives and was criticized especially by the advancing modernists. But the collection *Skymmande land* (The Land That Sinks into Darkness, 1925) introduced a rich period in his work, culminating in the last and most important collection, *Sista ronden* (The Last Round, 1941). The fervor of youth reappears in images from the poet's own life, depicted as a duel, a courier's ride, or a game of chess, in which death is the superior adversary.

Arvid Mörne

Mörne (1876-1946) clearly broke with the *Euterpe* ideas in his third collection, *Ny tid* (A New Time, 1903). Here the poet is manifest as a political writer with socialist sympathies who fights to improve the conditions of the Swedish working class. Mörne's disappointment with the outcome of his social and political commitments is reflected in the title of the collection, *Döda år* (Dead Years, 1910). He finds solace in nature, the west-coast archipelago becoming a particularly important source of inspiration. This landscape seems to the poet to combine freedom and sanity with loneliness and fierceness. The language in Mörne's nature poetry is sensitive and varied, stringent and exact, thereby pointing toward the lapidary reflective poetry which is his greatest achievement. The eleven collections from this subjective period, beginning in 1924 with *Vandringen och vägen* (The Journey and the Road) and concluding in 1944 with *Sfinxen och Pyramiden* (The Sphinx and the Pyramid), are completely dominated by the poet's preoccupation with the meaninglessness and brutality of life.

Mörne wrote a number of political poems in the 1930s that were aimed at the dictatorships in Germany and Italy. But these poems had an even wider purview. Mörne stepped forth as a spokesman of humankind, employing a blend of sympathy and contempt. He was a humanist equal to Norway's Arnulf Øverland and Sweden's Pär Lagerkvist. His writing became increasingly bitter in tone, marked by loneliness and isolation, and a feeling of being unappreciated and not understood. Yet Mörne stands as the greatest Fenno-Swedish poet of the old school between the two World Wars, undeservedly over-shadowed by modernistic trends.

Mikael Lybeck

Lybeck (1864-1925) also made his debut as a lyrical poet in the 1890s. With his realistic descriptions of everyday life, he remained within the world view of naturalism. He is primarily remembered as an author of novels, of which *Tomas Indal* (1911) is considered one of his best. It analyzes the breakdown of a man who has betray-ed his ideals, but who defends himself by arguing that he is only a product of his heredity and environment. At the end, the book embraces the view that life is totally worthless. The same hopelessness is characteristic of Lybeck's stylistic masterpiece, the epistolary novel *Breven till Cecilia* (Letters to Cecilia, 1920), which concludes with the death of the main character, who kills himself because his beloved is unfaithful.

The victory of brutality and blind instinct over idealism and good-ness is also the theme of Lybeck's dramas, which show the strong influence of European symbolism. In *Bror och syster* (Brother and Sister, 1915), the conflict is erotic, whereas in *Dynastin Peterberg* (The Peterberg Dynasty, 1913) and *Den röde André* (Red André, 1917) it is political, with motifs from the Russian oppression of Fin-land and from the Revolution. Lybeck's work demonstrates a devel-opment from naturalism to neo-romanticism and symbolism. His last drama, however, *Domprosten Bomander* (Canon Bomander, 1923), points toward modern existentialism; the title character has come to the awareness that responsibility for good and evil rests entirely on humankind alone. Similarly, the burlesque novel *Samtal med Lackau* (Conversations with Lackau, 1925), a parody of J. P. Eckermann's day-to-day record of his talks with Goethe between 1836 and 1848, points with its warm-hearted and relaxed comedy, beyond the highly emotional literature of ideas characteristic of the period.

NATIONAL REVIVAL AND POETRY IN ICELAND

Iceland's struggle for independence, which in 1874 had produced a new constitution, was in 1904 crowned with the establishment of home rule. In 1918 the country became a sovereign state in a union with Denmark, which was denounced by Iceland in 1944. An optimistic belief in material and spiritual progress had become dominant after 1900. The extensive emigration to America that began in the last decades of the nineteenth century soon stopped, the fishing fleet was modernized, the cities grew, and regular connections with the surrounding world were established through the telephone and telegraph—decisive signs that the medieval peasant society was in the process of being transformed.

Naturalistic literature was not clearly on the decline. In 1897 the first neo-romantic writer, Einar Benediktsson, made his debut; Hannes Hafstein had become a strong nationalist, and Einar H. Kvaran had adopted a humanitarian and spiritistic outlook. National assertiveness brought a renewed interest in the old artistic traditions; the languishing medieval *rímur* poetry, metrical romances originally sung during dancing, enjoyed a revival, and a generation of conservative peasant writers came forward, contributing substantially to the prose written after 1900.

In his poems and short stories, the self-taught Guðmundur Friðjónsson (1869-1944) warns of the demoralizing effects of civilization, contrasting it with the frugality and toughness of the peasant. In his two novels *Leysing* (Spring Floods, 1907) and *Borgir* (Castles, 1909) Jón Trausti (pseud. for Guðmundur Magnússon [1873-1918]) deals with contemporary social problems and displays deep sympathy for the old peasant traditions. But his best novels are based on his childhood experiences in the northernmost part of the island. *Halla* (1906) and its sequel *Heiðarbýlið* (The Farm on the Moor, 1908-11) depict the hard life of the isolated mountain crofters in northeast Iceland. From their narrow horizon the perspective is widened to span the entire landscape, its people and their lives. The psychological makeup of the characters is revealed in the magnificent portrayal of the fight for daily bread. In his aristocratic view of the materialistic time, Trausti resembles Hamsun; in his very strong ties with kin and tradition, he shows an affinity with the Dane Jakob Knudsen, whom he knew and admired.

The period's foremost poets, Stephan G. Stephanson and Einar Benediktsson, are two of Iceland's greatest writers.

Stephan G. Stephansson

Stephansson (1853-1927) grew up in Skagafjörður in the North; at the age of nineteen he emigrated to the United States with his family and later became a hard-working farmer in Alberta, Canada. Much of his most valuable poetry, written in Icelandic, was published in six collections, entitled *Andvökur* (Wakeful Nights, 1909-38). Here he praises not only his adopted country, as in the cycle "Á fer og flugi" ("With the Greatest Speed," 1900), in which he draws a series of magnificent pictures of the prairie and pioneer life, but also of Iceland, to whose cultural traditions he was inextricably linked. As Stephansson grew older, he increasingly included incidents from the Eddas, sagas, and legends in his most powerful and original poems, and he interpreted these incidents in such a way that they took on symbolic and universal significance. He always had his own age in mind, and he criticized violence and oppression very sharply. He was a glowing pacifist, vehemently denouncing modern warfare and condemning the political leaders on both sides. Stephansson was equally radical in his rejection of capitalistic exploitation and of dogmatic religions, which made him numerous enemies among his Icelandic compatriots in America. However, his most personal poems dealt with his relationship to poetry, work, and all of existence, and they are characterized by deep human interest, idealism, and above all, a progressive spirit. The goal is happiness for everyone in this life; we are all responsible for our actions, and humans live on what they have achieved—the moral of the Old Norse *Hávamál* poem.

Stephansson's poems combine intellectuality with warmth and poetic spirit. But the form may seem rough and the style heavy because he did not take the time to polish his work. Still, the variety of his verse forms is very great and matches the range of his themes, and the vocabulary is enormous, with many striking innovations.

Einar Benediktsson

Politically Benediktsson (1864-1940) belonged to the opposite wing from Stephansson. His debut collection, *Sögur og kvæði* (Stories and Poems, 1897), opened with a group of patriotic poems; he himself became a radical spokesman for changing Iceland into an industrial, and later an imperialistic, superpower, with Greenland as a colony. He published and edited the first Icelandic daily, *Dagskrá* (1896-98), in which he introduced the new European symbolism—demanding of the young writers a reverence not only for beauty, infinity, and eternity, but also for national greatness and history such as he found in the writings of the Swedish neo-romanticist Heidenstam. As a poet, Benediktsson gradually created his own universe and style—exclusive, hence not readily accessible—a reflection of this ideal of humankind, which is close to Nietzsche's philosophy of the superman.

Benediktsson published four more volumes of poetry, *Hafblik* (Calm Waters, 1906), *Hrannir* (Waves, 1913), *Vogar* (Billows, 1921), and *Hvammar* (Grass Hollows, 1930). Next to Halldór Laxness, he is Iceland's most universal writer. He is able to capture in one short poem the essential elements in the atmosphere of great cities, from Paris to New York, to describe with great suggestive power factories and gigantic machines, as well as art and music, churches and other monumental buildings. Cosmopolitan as he was, Benediktsson was, nonetheless, fundamentally nationalistic, delighted to be writing on Icelandic subjects. This expression of love for his home country was combined with a deep-rooted faith in the future and the mission of his people. Benediktsson excelled in natural description, picturing the striking scenic contrasts of Iceland with great affection. But usually outer reality led to inner life:

> But behind my eyelids suns go down,
> there the regions of sleep arise and the day draws to an end
> beneath the power circling round earth and sea.
> There a world like the external is arching.
> Mirrored in the brain heavens glow,
> there rivers meet, flames are lit,
> and oceans of dreams sink, rise
> beneath the wings of the magnetic storm.
>   Tr. Marianne Forssblad

Benediktsson wrestled, especially in his numerous purely philosophical poems, with the deepest problems of human existence: the ultimate meaning and goal of human life. He was obsessed with a boundless pantheistic longing to perceive and understand the mysteries of the universe, to unite the incompatibility of good and evil, life and death.

The influence of Einar Benediktsson is readily traceable in the works of his contemporaries and of younger Icelandic poets. Because of the violent tensions in his poetry, expressed within a firmly structured frame, he has been referred to as an Icelandic Robert Browning. Benediktsson was a master of the use of contrast, and all his poems bear the unmistakeable stamp of his individuality and his stylistic and thematic originality.

Part II The Early Twentieth Century

Chapter 5

Early Twentieth-Century Nordic Literature

It would be incorrect to consider the year 1900 as a sharp demarcation in the literary history of Scandinavia. To speak of a single dominant artistic direction is also impossible, for movements and tendencies that earlier had succeeded one another were now running parallel or were inextricably interwoven. The period from 1900 to the beginning of World War I leaves a much more confused impression than did the 1890s. Still, one can speak of a general reaction in European literature by young poets against the predominance of the symbolism and neo-romanticism of the preceding decade. However, the symbolist aesthetic did create a tradition that can be traced down to our time, which includes such poets as T. S. Eliot, Gottfried Benn, and Saint-John Perse.

The new poetry was reacting primarily against the focus on the self; it opened new thematic areas, such as the realities of industry and the metropolis, and experimented with language. Psychological realism is also perceptible in the drama and the novel, often focusing on problems, frequently of a socialist cast. In addition, realistic regional literature blossomed. The literature of farmers and workers was no longer written by academicians, who often idealized their subjects, but by the farmers and workers themselves; occasionally it had a marked revolutionary tone.

SWEDISH LITERATURE

THE FIN-DE-SIÈCLE AND AN AFFIRMATION OF LIFE

The new century brought a period of economic expansion, better working conditions, and greater social justice. Yet some important social problems remained in 1891 health insurance was made compulsory, and in 1901 industrial accident insurance was introduced. In all forms of Swedish literature these changes had an influence. An early result of the new educational opportunities was the rapid expansion of a culturally aware public and a hitherto unheard of increase in the production of books. Literature became much more representative of the country's social classes that it had been previously; however, throughout the first decade, the writers of the 1890s maintained their leading position, and many of the younger authors began as neo-romantics. The most significant among them lost their naturalistic faith in evolution, but maintained their belief in its scientifically conditioned determinism. The influence of the 1890s can be recognized in the mood of disillusionment and refined skepticism—expressed earlier in European literature in the works of Oscar Wilde, Anatole France, and Herman Bang, among others, and now finding an outstanding representative in Hjalmar Söderberg (1869–1941).

Hjalmar Søderberg

The protagonist in Söderberg's novel *Martin Bircks ungdom* (1901; Eng. tr. *Martin Birck's Youth*, 1930), unstable and melancholy, is a typical child of the period. Among the best passages of the work are the semi-autobiographical childhood recollections, dreamlike in mood. The plot of the novel is generally subordinated to feelings and thoughts; distinctive are the shattering of Martin's illusions about his life task and love, and his distanced role as an ironic observer of existence.

A similar lonely and reflective human being is the character of the doctor in the psychological novel *Doktor Glas* (1905; Eng. tr. *Doctor Glas*, 1963 and later). Filled with revolutionary ethical and social ideas, he kills the unsympathetically presented Pastor Gregorius, to free the pastor's young wife for her new love. His deed is futile, however; Mrs. Gregorius is deserted by her lover—life remains meaningless. Söderberg was a rationalist critic of Christianity, and his constant polemic against theology weakens the artistic quality of the book, whose value lies less in its complex of problems than in the impressive mood pictures of Stockholm and the lyrical melancholy language.

Söderberg's four collections of short stories are of higher quality. The first, *Historietter* (Historiettes, 1898) was influenced by Herman Bang and J. P. Jacobsen, but the actual models for these little masterpieces of witty and pointed art are, above all, Guy de Maupassant and Anatole France. They are tautly constructed and precisely written, most of them containing a single situation or a particular observation.

The others are symbolic expressions of the poet's view of life, of his skepticism, the ironic tone concealing weariness and emptiness.

Bo Bergman

Related to Söderberg's work is that of Bergman (1869–1967). However, his pessimism is *melancholy*. He expresses his version of the *fin-de-siècle* mood in the lines, "We are born old, and our race / grows gray hair in the cradle." His collections of short stories also reflect a fascination with age and death: They are dominated by a deterministic belief in blind faith, the feeling of the brevity and hopelessness of life, and the constant shipwreck of dreams.

Bergman's first collection of poems bears the characteristic title *Marionetterna* (The Marionettes, 1903) and contains satiric poetry on contemporary themes, influenced by Ibsen and Heine, and melancholy scenes of Stockholm, in addition to tender love poems and melodious songs. Stanzas on the themes of death and transitoriness predominate, according with Bergman's conception of life as a stern fatalistic game. In the collections that follow, this bleak view yields to a more positive one, which finally leads to a freeing and kindling of the spirit of life. *Trots allt* (In Spite of All, 1931) and *Gamla gudar* (Old Gods, 1939) contain, in addition to love poetry, primarily melodramatic and satiric contemporary poems, sharp attacks on political violence and deception by an idealistic humanist.

We find these same themes in Bergman's late volumes of poems, *Blott ett är ditt* (One Thing Only Is Yours, 1960) and *Makter* (Powers, 1962). His expressive power and lucid style are scarcely impaired. These characteristics place Bergman in the classical humanistic tradition of Swedish literature, from Tegnér to Runeberg and Rydberg.

Vilhelm Ekelund

Nietzschean views and the cult of beauty in the 1890s found an outstanding representative in young Ekelund (1880–1949). He made his debut in 1900 with the collection *I skilda färger* (In Various Colors), inspired by Ola Hansson and soon followed by other volumes. His early poetry captures moods of anxious loneliness and impressionistic pictures of nature. However, influenced by French symbolists Baudelaire and Verlaine, as well as by the Germans Dehmel and George, Ekelund developed his artistic individuality in *Syner* (Visions, 1901) and *Melodier i skymning* (Melodies in Twilight, 1902). His nature poetry lost its descriptive character and became the expression of emotional states; in lyrical ecstasy the poet seeks to unite nature and eternity, which gives peace to his restless soul.

Influenced by German classicism, Ekelund sought a way out of his romantic melancholy and his symbolic dream world in Greek antiquity. This attempt led to a new intellectual and ethically oriented poetry in the volumes *Elegier* (Elegies, 1903) and *In Candidum* (1905). The poems circle analytically around Ekelund's own ego, and the basic tone, resulting from his tragic longing, is melancholy and weary. Only by experiencing beauty or resignation does the poet manage to liberate himself briefly from these emotions. In 1906 Ekelund's most remarkable collection, *Dithyramber i aftonglans* (Dithyrambs in Evening's Splendor), was published. It was inspired by a boundless love for a woman and by a powerful feeling for nature.

More clearly than in his rather inaccessible lyric poetry, Ekelund sought to portray his heroic ideal in a series of prose works. He closed himself off from reality and glorified geniuses. In *Antikt ideal* (The Classical Ideal, 1909) he portrays his literary models—among others Nietzsche, whose paradoxical prose style had strongly influenced Ekelund, as had Plato, Hölderlin, and Leopardi, who had become symbols of his constant search for the "right" attitude toward life. Later, Nietzsche's heroism gave way to a humanness influenced by Goethe and Emerson. In the volume of aphorisms entitled *Metron* (1918), Ekelund presented his ethical ideal as "moderation," that is, peace and equilibrium. This concept is broadened to include not only the tradition of antiquity, but also that of Christian mysticism.

Ekelund's inclination toward verbal conciseness and personal coloration of words developed over the years, for instance in *Concordia animi* (1942), into a cryptic style which can be interpreted only with difficulty. Nevertheless, he exerted a great influence on the modernistic movements in Swedish and Fenno-Swedish literature.

Anders Österling

Like Ekelund, Österling (1884–) was originally a disciple of Ola Hansson and was influenced by French and German symbolism, particularly by Stefan George. His first independent collection, the sonnets *Årets visor* (The Songs of the Year, 1907), consists of sober descriptions of the countryside and people in southern Sweden. The intimate everyday language—learned from Sophus Claussen—is also present in *Blommande träd* (Flowering Trees, 1910); these well-formed nature poems point back to the "Lake School" of poetry of William Wordsworth in their combination of realism and romanticism.

The major part of Österling's writings expresses the same basic mood. Behind the harmony of his classical imagery and quiet rhythms lies the search for a positive world view. He sets his faith in life against an anxiety-filled pessimism, and strives to return to the soil and to the everyday things in life. In his poetry from the two World Wars *Sånger i krig* (Songs during War, 1917) and *Livets värde* (The Value of Life, 1940), Österling goes beyond his usual motifs in rather insignificant philosophical poems. Here he, like Bo Bergman, defends a world of humanness against the brutality of the times.

Hjalmar Bergman

Among the writers of the first decade, Bergman (1883–1931) had the most expansive imagination. He, too, around 1900, progressed from neo-romanticism to realism; the transition was stylistic and thematic, but did not affect his imaginativeness or his works, which were symbolic tales. Bergman was born the son of a bank director in Örebro, the economic center of the central Swedish ore district, Bergslagen. He studied philosophy and history in Uppsala, but left Sweden in 1901, and lived, with brief interruptions, until 1917 in Italy, where he wrote his early works. The philosophical basis of his youthful writing was a fatalism inspired by Schopenhauer; this is expressed in *Maria, Jesu moder* (Mary, Mother of Jesus, 1905), a lyric drama closely bound to the text of the Gospels, which elucidates through the life of Jesus Bergman's conception of the powerlessness of love.

The short-story collection *Amourer* (Amorous Stories, 1910), greatly influenced by Maupassant, and the novel *Hans nåds testamente* (Testament of His Grace, 1910), with its fantastic burlesque portrayal of life in a small Swedish town, mark a turning point in Bergman's writing. Now he makes contact with his home province and his childhood reminiscences by making Bergslagen the locale of virtually all his contemporary novels. The main theme is the relationship between sixteen-year-old Blenda, daughter of the baron, and Jacob, the son of the housekeeper, who is in love with her. In these two characters, and underlying the comic developments and imaginatively portrayed intrigues surrounding the drawing up of a will, are Bergman's major motifs: Jacob's passionate jealousy when Blenda appears to be turning to another man and their disappointment in the nature of the adult world.

In the gloomy trilogy of stories *Komedier i Bergslagen* (Comedies in Bergslagen, 1914–16), Bergman creates a colorful and realistic world as the background to his own half fairy-tale world. Through the portrayal of suffering humans and their diseased spiritual life, reminiscent of Dostoevsky, this world becomes an inspired expression of Bergman's pessimism. The work is composed of episodes and dramatic scenes, all of which unmask the demonic forces in life: the violent, brutal quarrels between father and son; the tormenting jealousy and unhappy love of disappointed people.

A tighter structure and more uniform style characterizes the masterpiece *Mor i Sutre* (Mother at Sutre, 1917). In the description of the authoritarian, but sympathetic mother, Boel, and in the portrayal of her love for her son Daniel, Bergman demonstrates his keen observation of human nature. The Sutre Inn is the setting of the turbulent plot. The degenerate Count Arnfelt seeks refuge there with his young mistress; the authorities are searching for him, and he is hunted and forced into the woods by his starving foresters. His arrival sets off a series of events that culminates in the unintended murder of his favorite son.

In the family chronicle *En döds memoarer* (Memoirs of a Dead Man, 1918), through the portrayal of the battle between the Arnfelt and Arnberg families, two types are set opposite each other, types that constantly appear in Bergman's works: the active realistic man and the dreamer who is unsuited for life. The novel is characterized by the dark fatalism and funereal mood of the Bergslag trilogy.

In his succeeding novels—*Markurells i Wadköping* (1919; Eng. tr. *God's Orchid*, 1924) and *Farmor och Vår Herre* (1921, Grandmother and Our Lord; Eng. tr. *Thy Rod and Thy Staff*, 1937), characterized by baroque exuberance and a tragic narrative—Bergman finally found recognition from readers and critics. In humorous, colloquial language, these novels show how people are robbed of their illusions. The braggardly upstart Markurell discovers that Johan, whom he loves above all else, is not his son, but the son of the provincial governor, whose financial fate lies in his hands. The plot, in part exuberant farce, is thereby transformed into a psychological drama, in which the disappointed Markurell, is elevated to a tragic figure whose desire for revenge is conquered by his fatherly love.

Like Markurell, the strong-willed grandmother in *Thy Rod and Thy Staff*, Agnes Borck, is also forced to renounce her love. She fantasizes herself back into her youth and discusses with God how she, a poor girl, married the rich merchant Borck and slowly gained power over him and her entire family. She is disappointed when her children reproach her with the fact that her despotism has repressed their feelings; the lifelong illusions of the old woman are conclusively destroyed when she discovers that not even her beloved grandson Nathan needs her motherly tenderness any longer.

In contrast to the Wadköping novels, the epic plot retreats behind a thoroughgoing psychological analysis of the subconscious spiritual life of a businesswoman—a psychological approach influenced more by Dostoevsky than by Freud—in Bergman's last great prose work, *Chefen fru Ingeborg* (1924, The Boss, Mrs. Ingeborg; Eng. tr. *The Head of the Firm*, 1936). She is incapable of overcoming her erotic feelings toward her son-in-law and is able to solve this moral conflict only by suicide.

Bergman's strong ethical sense and his rich psychological gifts are manifest in his prolific writing for the stage. He is considered the most significant Swedish dramatist after Strindberg, whose chamber plays inspired him. The plays of his youth are technically immature and clearly show the influence of Ibsen's social, critical works and Maeterlinck's symbolic dramas. On the other hand, the three *Marionettspel* (Marionette Plays, 1917) are particularly original; the collective title indicates the main theme: the control of grim fate over helpless humankind.

In *Herr Sleeman kommer* (Eng. tr. *Mr. Sleeman Is Coming*, 1944 and later) the dramatic atmosphere is established through the anxious waiting of young Ann-Marie, who loves another but is waiting for the arrival of the sickly Mr. Sleeman, whom she is supposed to marry. The same motif underlies *En skugga* (A Shadow): the conflict between a jealous old man and two young people. It portrays, in a half-unreal world, the abduction by young Erik of the girl Vera from her wedding to a hunch-backed bridegroom. The old man attempts to convince Vera that her erotic dreams are unrealistic; only when she discovers Erik dead does she realize that her love was not merely fantasy. Whereas *A Shadow* is an elegantly stylized play, reminiscent of the work of Alfred de Musset, in *Dödens arlekin* (The Harlequin of Death) setting and plot are more explicitly drawn, although they also have a symbolic function. The central theme is embodied in the powerful Consul Broman's being forced on his deathbed to loosen his grip on his fellow human beings: Death takes over the role of ruler. Like Strindberg in *The Pelican*, Bergman is seeking to analyze the reaction of those who are left behind, their rebellion against oppressive parental authority.

Less original than these dramas is the comedy *Swedenhielms* (1925; Eng. tr. *The Swedenhielms*, 1951 and later), Bergman's most famous stage work and one of the more successful Scandinavian comedies. Although the intrigue and the center of dramatic action are conventional—the old engineer Swedenhielm suspects his frivolous sons of having signed IOUs in his name—the dialogue sparkles with life and spirit, and each scene is brilliantly constructed.

Even though Bergman suffered throughout his life from illness and depression, his creative work was voluminous. In addition to novels and plays, he published fairy tales, a series of short stories, and wrote more than thirty screen plays—from 1923 to 1924 Bergman lived in Hollywood. In 1927 he also began to write for the radio; his last novel, *Clownen Jac* (Jac the Clown, 1930), a gripping self-confession and coming to terms with his art, first appeared as a radio piece.

Bergman always combined psychological acuity with a sympathetic attitude toward his characters, whose moral struggles he portrayed as they fought with their own evil and the gruesome game of fate. All of his work is an inspired attempt to compensate for his tragic view of life through humor and satire—learned from Dickens and Balzac—and to free himself through art from anxiety and disharmony.

BOURGEOIS REALISM

A number of realistic authors of Bergman's generation contributed, as did he, to an artistic mapping of Sweden's cities and provinces. Part of the heritage these prose writers received from the 1890s was the philosophy of the great individualists Nietzsche and Schopenhauer. However, these writers took their motifs exclusively from contemporary reality, displaying deep interest in social questions. The dissolution of Sweden's union with Norway in 1905 and the general strike of 1909, which occurred despite a progressive reform movement, brought about a fierce political and economic debate concerning the future of the country. The fictional heroes were no longer misunderstood exceptions, but active extroverts in a bourgeois milieu.

Ludvig Nordström

If central Sweden was Bergman's domain, northern Sweden became Nordström's (1882-1942). His early works, such as *Landsortsbohème* (A Village Bohemian, 1911), are broad, provincial novels in the style of Alexander Kielland, characterized by exuberant imagination and disrespectful humor, indicating that French Renaissance author Rabelais was one of his models. During the interwar period Nordström developed a social and religious view of life, a mystical progressive optimism which parallels H. G. Wells's utopian fantasies. Nordström's attempts in the novel cycle *Petter Svensks historie* (The Story of Petter Svensk, 1923-27) to realize his "totalism" in literary form failed; the characters became abstractions and theory predominated.

Gustaf Hellström

Less programmatic—but also less imaginative—was Hellström (1882-1953). He made his debut in 1904, as a disciple of Söderberg and Bang, with the short-story collection *Ungkarlar* (Bachelors)—refined, ironic stories on the morality of the bourgeoisie. The southern Sweden of Hellström's childhood became the setting of his autobiographical novel cycle *En man utan humor* (A Man without Humor, 1921–25). He also used this setting for his two major works, *Snörmakare Lekholm får en idé* (1927; Eng. tr. *Lacemaker Lekholm Has an Idea*, 1930), which follows three generations up and down the ladders of society, and *Carl Heribert Malmros* (1931), in which analyses of the period dominate the plot.

Elin Wägner

Wägner (1882–1949) was a writer of the same type. Her early novels give an accurate picture of the women's liberation movement in Sweden. In 1918 she chose a new topic for *Åsa-Hanna*, her major novel: the events of a peasant parish in the province of Småland. Whereas the title character of the book is a finely drawn objective psychological portrait, Wägner, in her numerous succeeding novels, turned from this unbiased realism to an increasingly stronger moralism.

Sven Lidman

Lidman (1882–1960) wrote a cycle of novels about the Silferstååhl family (1910–13), which succeeded his earlier symbolist poetry, influenced by Levertin, and his lyrical dramas with exotic themes. His portrayal of characters reached its height in the brilliant novel *Huset med de gamla fröknarna* (The House with the Old Ladies, 1918), in which Lidman tells of the struggle of four old ladies to retain their human dignity in a materialistic and unsympathetic world. After his conversion to the Pentacostal movement, related in the novel *Såsom genom eld* (As through a Fire, 1920), Lidman's work consisted of sermons and religious commentaries. His autobiographical works from 1952–57, beginning with *Gossen i grottan* (The Boy in the Cave), are outstanding contributions to regional literature, a genre so characteristic of Sweden.

Sigfrid Siwertz

The only portrayer of Stockholm among these authors is Siwertz (1882–1970), who, like Hellström, made his debut in the self-centered, decadent style of the 1890s. Although influenced by Henri Bergson's philosophy, Siwertz came to terms with the paralyzing concept of determinism. *Eldens återsken* (The Reflection of the Fire, 1916) proclaims the right of will and action as opposed to negativism and passivity. It is a period novel that deals with the atmosphere in neutral Sweden during World War I and contains strong attacks on the war profiteers. This theme forms the basis of Siwertz's most important artistic achievement, the novel *Selambs* (1920; Eng. tr. *Downstreams*, 1922). This work is the story of five siblings, whose minds have, through heritage and childhood experiences been poisoned and petrified into an egotism which destroys them—Siwertz was well-acquainted with Freudian psychology. In his later novels, short-story collections, and dramas, Siwertz clearly steps forth as an untendentious realist, as an author who wants to portray human fate rather than to preach.

NORWEGIAN LITERATURE

ROMANTICISM AND SOCIAL REALITY

In Norway, too, one can follow the development from symbolic idealism to new realism—in which many of the older writers participated. After 1900 Heiberg turned to political themes, Kinck to social problems, and even Hamsun developed into a satirical social critic. The younger generation attempted to unite a sense of reality and the social criticism of the older naturalism with the impressionistic techniques and the national feeling of the 1890s. Art for art's sake was sharply renounced in favor of a sense of engagement with basic existential and social problems.

The central political event of the period was the dissolution of the union with Sweden in 1905. National independence led to strong economic development: Fisheries and shipping experienced an upswing, and modern industry was established. The introduction of hydroelectric power made it possible for industrialization to proceed at tempo unknown in the other Nordic countries. The working class grew at the same pace, and the rapid population shift from the country to the city and the factories led inevitably to political radicalization. The factory workers of Christiania found their first spokesman in Oskar Braaten (1881-1939). But the radicalization is mirrored most clearly in the work of Johan Falkberget and Kristofer Uppdal.

Johan Falkberget

Falkberget (1879-1967) is the romantic among the new authors. Underlying his portrayals of the difficult struggle for existence of the workers and mountain peasants in the north of Norway is his vision of life as a fabulous tale, a vision that casts a glow of reconciliation over misery and distress. In Falkberget's books, the miner appears for the first time in Norwegian literature: In the trilogy *Christianus Sextus* (1927-35) a mine is actually the main character. The events are set in the 1720s, but Falkberget has masterfully blended the historical material with impressions from his turbulent present; the result is one of the great epic works of the period between the wars, full of fantastic figures, baroque themes, and suspenseful situations.

In *Nattens brød* (Bread of Night, 1940-59) Falkberget created a second major work. Here he draws unforgettable pictures of the fateful upheaval in the life of the Norwegian peasants when they gave up their soil in the latter half of the seventeenth century to work in the foundaries. Falkberget creates a both realistic and romantic world in which his religiously colored optimism is victorious in the figure of the ox-driver An-Magritt, whose ennobling love raises her to a symbol of humanity and the strength of the people.

Kristofer Uppdal

It became the task of Uppdal (1878-1961) to describe the workers as a *class* and to be the founder of the modern Norwegian social novel. His uneven novel cycle in ten volumes, *Dansen gjenom skuggeheimen* (The Dance through the Shadow Land, 1911-24), is based on the clash between workers and the traditional view of a peasant society, between the feudal structures of the villages and modern industry, which forces its way into the world of the farmers, tempting them from their farms and thereby changing and proletariatizing them.

Peter Egge

More traditional are the realistic novels of Egge (1869-1959), which focus on psychological questions. The naked realism of his early works is transformed in his later novels into more compassionate portraits of exploited, but strong and independent women. Among these novels are *Inde i fjordene* (In the Fjords, 1920) and *Hansine Solstad* (1925; Eng. tr. *Hansine Solstad: The History of an Honest Woman*, 1929).

Johan Bojer

This point of moral criticism, which can be traced back to Ibsen and Bjørnson, became more distinct with Bojer (1872-1959), who combined it with pessimistic social criticism. After experiencing the impact of World War I, Bojer turned against technological progress in the novel *Den store hunger* (1916; Eng. tr. *The Great Hunger*, 1918 and later), preaching an optimistic religiosity. Not until the third period of his writing, when he abandoned didacticism, was he able to freely express his epic talent. Bojer used material with which he was familiar from his childhood: the life of the farmers and fishermen of northern Norway. The three volumes *Den siste viking* (1921; Eng. tr. *Last of the Vikings*, 1923 and later), *Vor egen stamme* (1924, Our Kindsmen; Eng. tr. *The Emigrants*, 1925 and later), and particularly *Folk ved sjøen* (1929; Eng. tr. *Folk by the Sea*, also as *The Everlasting Struggle*, 1931) were the culmination of his writing. Here humans and nature have merged into a fascinating description of the bitter disappointments of Norwegian immigrants in the United States and of the dreary poverty in Norway.

Ole E. Rølvaag

The major works of Norwegian-American novelist Rølvaag (1876–1931), the trilogy *I de dage* (1924, In Those Days; Eng. tr. *Giants in the Earth*, 1927), *Peder Seier* (1928; Eng. tr. *Peder Victorious*, 1929), and *Den signede dag* (1931, The Blessed Day; Eng. tr. *Their Father's God*, 1931) also deal with psychological conflicts inherent in immigrant life.

Rølvaag was born on Dønna, an island just below the Arctic Circle, and emigrated to South Dakota in 1896. This experience forms the basis for *Amerikabreve* (1912, America-Letters; Eng. tr. *The Third Life of Per Smevik*, 1971), which recounts events in the life of a young emigrant Norwegian farmhand. Rølvaag's account of the pioneer's struggle to find an American identity is not solely a naturalistic narrative. He skillfully uses sensitive, poetic language to convey his vision of his characters' destinies as a universal, almost mythical experience.

Two Norwegian authors stand above most of the Nordic writers of the epic in the twentieth century. The first is Sigrid Undset, world-renowned Nobel prize winner, the other the more inaccessible and less well-known Olav Duun.

Olav Duun

Duun (1876–1939) was born on the island of Jøa to the north of Trondheim; this is the setting of his works, most of which are written in the dialect of Duun's native village. His work is limited to a correspondingly narrow scope: the land and the people of a certain location. But precisely because he was intimately familiar with his characters, able to penetratingly understand their mentality and their everyday problems, Duun was able to write his masterpiece, the six-volume family saga *Juvikfolke* (1918–23; Eng. tr. *The People of Juvik*, 1930–35).

With epic breadth and objectivity he relates the story of a peasant family over a one-hundred-year period, up to the end of World War I. The story, however, reaches back about 400 years, through a total of twelve generations. We follow the fate of the many-branched Juvik family: the story of the pagan patriarch Per Anders, who establishes the family farm, of his grandson, the wise and aristocratic Anders, of his daughter Åsel, who is the strongest personality of the family in a time of decline, down to her grandson Odin, who has all the positive family characteristics. In this work Duun focuses on one of his preferred motifs, the relationship of the individual to his or her environment; the novel becomes a collective portrait of the spiritual life of the Norwegian people and their development from feudalism to a society with social and ethical consciousness.

The first volume is set in a world of superstition and mysticism. Per Anders is dominated by primitive drive for power, and lives instinctively and without reflection, in contrast to the next generation, in which conscience and some doubts awaken concerning its own strength. Anders, the central figure of the second volume, arrests the decline of the family. He makes peace with God and the Church, but Viking blood still flows in his veins. He is the last one for whom the old family feeling and the power principle are alive. And yet he orients himself outward: builds a large farm, lays down new streets, and builds a church. The next volume reports the great revolts among the peasantry in the 1870s and their effect on the people of Juvik. These are times of decay, out of which Odin, the main character in the last three volumes, leads his family. The fourth volume contains a description of Odin's childhood, full of fantasy and unique in its degree of sensitivity to the world of a child. The next volume describes Odin's youth, his encounter with two women and his relationship with the bank manager Lauris, the enemy and rival of his youth. The cycle closes with the portrayal of Odin's lonely battle against the inhabitants of the village. He decides to murder Lauris and compels him to go out with him onto the stormy ocean. The boat capsizes; Odin is the stronger of the two and has Lauris in his power—but now he achieves a definitive victory through his recognition that he cannot save his own life at the expense of another human being. He sacrifices his life to save that of his mortal enemy.

Following the very accessible and humorous story Olsøygutane (The Boys from Olsøy, 1927) and the novel Carolus Magnus (1928), the mocking unmasking of a hypocrite and swindler, Duun returned to a major theme from The People of Juvik, the struggle between good and evil forces in human beings. In the trilogy Medmennneske (Fellow Man, 1929), Ragnhild (1931), and Siste leveåre (Last Year, 1933), Duun relates the dramatic life story of a peasant woman, Ragnhild, who, like

Odin, is a good person, but who, unlike Odin, feels herself compelled to destroy evil with force. This evil is embodied in her psychopathic father-in-law, Didrik. Ragnhild recognizes that he is capable of destroying the world around him. To rescue her husband, Håkon, she follows an instinctive sense of justice and murders Didrik; she then confesses voluntarily to the authorities and pays the penalty of imprisonment. The last two volumes of this masterpiece, so perspicuous in portraying human beings, concern themselves with Ragnhild's relationship to the inhabitants of the village and to her weak husband, showing his growing understanding of her action.

Duun's last book, *Menneske og maktene* (1938; Mankind and the Powers; Eng. tr. *Floodtide of Fate*, 1960), in which all the essential ideas and motifs of his work are present, is a vision of the impending world catastrophe. According to an ancient prophecy, the inhabitants of a small island will be swallowed up by the sea; meanwhile, they live in anxious expectation of their ruin. After the first warning of the misfortune, the life stories of the people are told. Each scene is viewed from more than one character's perspective, Duun demonstrating his mastery of this modern point-of-view technique. In the grandiose final chapter, the forces of nature rage. To the degree that as the water rises and floods the island, not only fear but also the will to live rises correspondingly, a new fellow feeling emerges, which finally triumphs over nature.

Olav Duun died several months after this work appeared. A few weeks before his death the catastrophe struck that he had feared and felt impending—World War II.

Sigrid Undset

Undset (1882–1949), the daughter of a Norwegian archaeologist, was born in the Danish city of Kalundborg, but grew up in Oslo. After the early death of her father, she had to give up her career as a painter. However, on the basis of her first publications, she received a travel grant to Rome in 1909, after which she dedicated herself entirely to her writing. From these years stem the materials for most of her early realistic contemporary works. She introduced the modern professional woman into Norwegian literature—without any social polemic. The high point of her first creative period, and a resounding success, is the tragic novel *Jenny* (1911; Eng. tr. 1921 and later), in which a young emancipated female, a painter, has a dramatic relationship with an older man. Jenny is shattered when she discovers that her ideal of love has not been realized. She is so bound to this ideal that real love can never be a part of her life.

The short-story collection *De kloke jomfruer* (The Wise Virgins, 1918), portraying women who are married but not really loved because they are sexually unattractive, is Sigrid Undset's last piece of contemporary writing. She then turned to the Norwegian Middle Ages, producing two historical novels that are substantial contributions to world literature: the trilogy *Kristin Lavransdatter* (1920–22); Eng. tr. 1923 and later), and *Olav Audunssøn* (1925–27); Eng. tr. *The Master of Hestviken*, 1928 and later).

Kristin Lavransdatter, set in the first half of the fourteenth century, begins with the struggle of the proud and passionate title figure for the man she loves, the courtly but frivolous Erlend, and their defiant marriage. The second part tells of her troubled marriage to a husband who has become unfaithful to her and of his ruinous political adventures. The last part is filled with the destructive crises in their life together, the struggle between love and contempt, and Kristin's anxiety that her children might take after their unreliable father. After Erlend's sudden death, Kristin's life becomes a humble pilgrimage; she finally finds peace in a life of renunciation and service to God and her fellow humans. She enters a convent in Trondheim, where she, like several of her sons, is struck down by the plague. She dies poor and alone, but with a rich heart.

In this work we encounter a multitude of people and fates, unforgettable situations and dramatic events—a piece of the Middle Ages enlivened by a powerful poetic fantasy. Through her exhaustive descriptions of setting, rich in historical detail, Sigrid Undset provides an all-encompassing picture of holiday and everyday life and introduces realism into the historical novel. This external accuracy corresponds to an inner historical truth: Kristin and all the major figures are fictional people who live at a time when Old Norse morality encounters the world view, the spirit and the order, of the Catholic church; the characters' actions and judgments are repeatedly, whether consciously or unconsciously, guided by religious motives. Yet the novel of the Middle Ages is a gripping story of everyday life: the tragedy of a wife and mother, who experiences many disappointments and few joys.

Sigrid Undset's earlier writing had hinted at metaphysical motivation underlying her moral message. Doubtless the shift of focus to the Middle Ages, influenced by English writer G. K. Chesterton, had deepened her religious conviction, and in 1925 Sigrid Undset converted to Catholicism. Whereas the Catholicism in *Kristin Lavransdatter* appears gradually, in accordance with the increasingly Christian coloration of Kristin's spirit and life, *The Master of Hestviken* is from the beginning a glorification of the power of religion. Both parts are set in the thirteenth century and portray a story of tragic love and marriage. As in *Kristin Lavransdatter*, the major motif is the struggle of a human being between willfulness and obedience to God's law. Olav, who had fled to Denmark because he committed a murder, finds when he returns that his beloved, Ingunn, is pregnant; he forgives her, but secretly kills her seducer. The marriage is burdened by the guilt of both transgressors; Olav, a believer, is tormented all his life by religious brooding about the murder, until his defiant soul finds true repentance shortly before his death. Olav's unhappy life is portrayed with broad realism, and there are many un-reworked and monotonous passages in the novel paralleled by the somewhat superficial structure.

After writing the medieval works, for which she received the Nobel Prize in 1928, Undset returned to the present. The two-volume novel *Gymnadenia* (1929; Eng. tr. *The Wild Orchid*, 1931) and *Den brændende busk* (1930; Eng. tr. *The Burning Bush*, 1932) portrays the conflict-ridden development of a young man from humanist to Catholic. Like Olav, Paul Selmer must choose between God and his own selfish nature. By choosing faith, he discovers reality and his responsibility toward his fellow human beings.

In the 1930s Undset wrote two more novels of marriage, *Ida Elisabeth* (1932; Eng. tr. 1933) and *Den trofaste hustru* (1936; Eng. tr. *The Faithful Wife*, 1937), to be read as strong counterweights to the materialistic optimism of the twentieth century. Shortly before World War II came the humorous novel *Madame Dorthea* (1939; Eng. tr. 1940), a festive period piece of the beginning of the nineteenth century, which, unfortunately, remained only a fragment of an intended larger work. Perhaps Undset's most interesting creative works of these years are her collections of essays: *Etapper* (1929, 1933; Eng. tr. *Stages on the Road*, 1934 and later), excellent literary essays, and *Saga of Saints* (1934; publ. in Norwegian in 1937 as *Norske helgener*), a spiritual history of Norway. At the same time she fought with her pen against national socialism, and escaped to the United States when the Germans occupied Norway. During the war she published in English the travelogue *Return to the Future* (1942) and the memoirs *Happy Times in Norway* (1942). In 1945 she returned to her native country.

THE LYRICAL BREAKTHROUGH

While drama moved into the background, poetry and prose dominated the early decades of the century. With the work of four somewhat younger poets—Olav Aukrust, Herman Wildenwey, Olaf Bull, and Arnulf Øverland—a link to the poetry of the 1890s was reestablished;

however, whereas that period had been melancholy and inner-directed, a positive attitude now predominated (Wildenwey), with a will to experience things (Bull) and a turning to the external world (Øverland). Neo-realism is evident: The province (Aukrust) and the metropolis (Bull) find a place in poetry.

Olav Aukrust and Tore Ørjasæter

The difference between *riksmål* poetry and *landsmål* poetry is not only that between city and country, but also between different traditions. For the *landsmål* poet, religious, ethical, and national themes have a far greater significance, as for instance in the poetic work *Himmelvarden* (Cairn of Heaven, 1916), which brought Aukrust (1883–1929) into the forefront of Norwegian lyricists. There is no epic substance in the single poems; rather, they bear witness to the struggle of good and evil powers in the anxious soul of the poet. Through powerful pictures and symbols, modeled on medieval visionary poetry, Aukrust depicts this argument between Christ and Satan, a struggle that ends with divine victory and the salvation of the soul, which has been purified through suffering.

In his religious prophecy, Aukrust was influenced by Swedenborg, Grundtvig, Kierkegaard, and Bergson, and by the anthroposophy of Rudolf Steiner; however, he created his works independently of literary movements. To be sure, his works are related, through their passionate tone, fantasy, and occasionally chaotic display of imagery, to the romantic poetry of Henrik Wergeland; however, he stood far removed from the other Norwegian authors of his time.

The only exception is the *landsmål* poet Tore Ørjasæter (1886–1968). His major work, the epic lyric trilogy *Gudbrand Langleite* (1913–27; revised 1941) analyzes the encounter of ancient peasant culture with modern industrial society, and the contrast between life in the secluded Norwegian village and the cosmopolitan world. However, Ørjasæter focuses primarily on his inner turmoil; he is torn between a longing to break with his milieu and an oppressive feeling of duty, between a religious need and materialistic impulses. Finally, Gudbrand, the peasant and poet—and Ørjasæter's alter ego—reaches a state of harmony through realizing that Christ is the only guide and the will is the decisive creative force.

Herman Wildenwey

Wildenwey (1886–1959) received an enthusiastic response to his first collection, *Nyinger* (Bonfires, 1907), which reveals him as a poet without tendentiousness. In his impressionistic poems—the best from his youth are collected in *Digte i utvalg* (Selected Poems, 1917)— Wildenway praises summer, wine, and women. He seeks not the abstruse, but the cheerful and light, which are expressed in the charming rhythms and exquisite musicality of his language.

In his later poetry, such as the volumes *Dagenes sang* (Song of the Days, 1930) and *Stjernernes speil* (Mirror of the Stars, 1935), his tone is more serious and inner-directed, and autumn is the predominant season; even religious moods are present. Wildenwey's erotic poetry was newly inspired in the 1930s by his preoccupation with the tension between the transitory and the permanent. At the same time, his motifs took on a cosmic dimension, the universe being drawn into his poetry.

Wildenwey also wrote dramas, short stories, and memoirs of varying quality. But it is as a lyricist that he transformed the influences of such varied writers as Hamsun, Kipling, and Sophus Claussen into original poetry; he learned the charming *parlando* of his verse from Fröding and Karlfeldt, and his mixture of realism, fantasy, sensitivity, and irony from Heine.

Olaf Bull

Two years after Wildenwey's triumphant debut came an even more attention-arousing collection, with the modest title *Digte* (Poems, 1909); to be sure, it lacked Wildenwey's elegance and carefree quality, but it offered far greater visual and symbol-creating power. The author, journalist Olaf Bull (1883-1933), was unanimously recognized by the critics for what he was: a genius. He called himself a nomad "shrouded in my coat, my home," and his life became, to a large extent, the restless existence of a bohemian in Oslo, Copenhagen, and, above all, Paris; it was there that he discovered his decisive source of inspiration, Henri Bergson's philosophy and the literature of symbolism. He squandered his powers and died at the early age of 49. At the time of his death, Bull had published ten volumes of poetry, all of which are among the most outstanding accomplishments in Norwegian literature.

Bull has been compared with the poets Wergeland, Bjørnson, and Collett Vogt. Certainly his visual fantasy recalls the romantic Wergeland, but his writing possesses nothing of the optimism of Wergeland's poetry, and nothing of the idyllic quality of Bjørnson's work; nor does he share the social and political interest of both. For Bull, as for Collett Vogt, the experience of reality is the point of departure. Homelessness and spiritual unrest are the decisive tragic experiences of his life; in vain he longs to exchange oppressive loneliness for a sense of community. Through portrayals of nature Bull attempts to free his thoughts and feelings, but he finds no consolation, since his sense of nature is strong, but not spontaneous. He is the man from the city who seeks out nature for the sake of contrast. His images of nature reflect sharp observation of detail, blended with his inner world. In the flower poem "Miniatur-ballade" ("Miniature Ballad") one can trace, stanza by stanza, how his fantasy increasingly pushes aside reality, as the poem is transformed into a fairy tale. This process is characteristic of Bull and finds its most beautiful expression in the poem "Gobelin" from *Nye digte* (New Poems, 1913); here the poet fantasizes about a game he plays with his little daughter involving the embroidery of a cushion, which turns into a thoughtful and melancholy picture of the struggle between dream and inexorable reality.

This painful contrast also sets the serious underlying tone of Bull's erotic poems, such as the exquisite title poem in the collection *Oinos og Eros* (Oinos and Eros, 1930), an unforgettable portrayal of female beauty, of sensuous power and spirit. But we are always confronted by Bull's brooding spirit: either in elegies about the brevity of life, as in "Emerence Christence" and "Clare Eugenie," or in despairing accusations against God in "Molok" ("Moloch") and "Julenat" ("Christmas Night"). Life and pain are fulfilled only in death, and gain meaning as the self is immersed in all-encompassing nature.

The collections *Stjernerne* (The Stars, 1924) and *Metope* (1927) mark a shift in Bull's poetry in relation to external reality. His themes are the same as before. The title poem *Metope* gathers many of his central themes into an overpowering unity: the intense experience of love and pain, the awareness of transitoriness; however, memory and reflection are now even more strongly evident. Poetic reality, created by observing objects, dissolves into a longing for eternity and ecstatic fantasy, external life dying within his soul.

The university cantata "Ignis ardens" (written in 1929, printed in 1932 in the collection of the same name) is a cosmic fantasy on the creation and evolution of the universe. In this cantata, which has its climax in a hymn to the spirit of humanity, Bull presents his world view. He succeeds here in giving grandiose poetic expression not only to his vision of reality, influenced by Bergson, as being accessible only through recollection, but also to his conception of Einstein's new world view.

Olaf Bull's poetry is strongly philosophical. He always attempted to unite lyricism and logic, strove for strict artistic precision, and was a tireless aesthetic self-critic. He thereby created a poetic universe full of beauty and temperament, of pain and ecstasy.

DANISH LITERATURE:
THE MATERIALISTIC BREAKTHROUGH

The lyrical, introverted poetry of the 1890s was followed in Denmark around the turn of the century by a new realistic and rationalistic wave, differentiated from the naturalism of the 1870s and '80s by a decidely materialistic approach and occasionally by socialistic ideas. The poetry of Johannes Jørgensen expresses the longing and yearning for eternity of a spiritual man. However, the central writer was Johannes V. Jensen, who, influenced by the imperalistic writing of Kipling, portrayed extroverted, pragmatic characters. Jensen glorified the technical age and the Industrial Revolution, which had begun in 1870 and had ended with the establishment of the labor unions and employer's association before 1900.

Two directions can be distinguished in the literature of this period: regional literature and social agitatory writing. Regional literature, written primarily by Jutland authors, was dominated by two vastly different writers—Johannes V. Jensen and Jakob Knudsen. Other regional writers were Johan Skjoldborg (1861–1936), Jeppe Aakjær (1866–1930), and Gustav Wied (1858–1914). Skjoldborg is notable primarily for his novel *En Stridsmand* (A Fighter, 1896). Aakjær's most important novel, *Vredens Børn* (The Children of Wrath, 1904), indignantly attacks the abuse of the farm workers by the well-to-do farmers; his dramatic works, and the novel *Arbejdets Glæde* (Joy of Work, 1914), defend the peasant society against industrialization. Aakjær's prose writings are problematic: Revolutionary agitation dominates and character portrayal is rather sketchy. However, he was an important writer of popular and melodious verses, especially in the collection *Rugens Sange* (Songs of the Rye, 1906). He was also an excellent translator of Robert Burns. The very popular Gustav Wied followed directly the path of doctrinaire naturalism. Motifs reminiscent of Herman Bang—family degeneration and love seen as purely instinctual—are employed with crass cynicism in a number of novels and closet dramas, the "satyr plays." The high point among these is *Dansemus* (Dancing Mice, 1905), in which Wied's tragic nihilistic view of life is revealed through caustic satire and rollicking comedy. Social agitatory writing was present in the regional literature of Skjoldborg and Aakjær, but the main writer in this vein was proletarian writer Martin Andersen Nexø.

But the ideas of the 1890s also continued, as in the lyrical and critical writings of Helge Rode (see p. 92), in the simple and intimate nature poetry of Ludvig Holstein (1864–1943), and in the not very accessible prose of Harald Kidde (1878–1918), whose major work was the exceptional novel *Helten* (The Hero, 1912). This novel, inspired by Kierkegaard, teaches the Christian, pietistic doctrine of happiness achieved only through humility and unselfishness; in many ways the work is a forerunner of Martin A. Hansen's modern masterpiece *The Liar* (see p. 218).

Jakob Knudsen

Like most of the writers around 1900, Knudsen (1858–1917) was born in Jutland. He was active at first as a folk high-school teacher, then as a clergyman until he finally withdrew to live as a writer and lecturer. In his portrayals of peasants, his work belongs to the genre of regional literature, but his horizon, like that of the great Norwegian epic writers of his time, is far wider. The point of departure of his work is the novella *Et Gjensyn* (A Reunion, 1898), a tale about his childhood and his capturing of it many years later. The contrast between childhood and adult experience is a frequent theme in Knudsen's works.

Knudsen's first major work, the novel *Den gamle Præst* (The Old Pastor), appeared in 1899. Count Trolle, in a fit of anger, kills young Magnus when he tries to rape his daughter. The count finds himself in a moral conflict typical of Knudsen's work: He has committed a murder and must give himself up to the punishment of the law. But since his sick wife would not be able to bear this shame, the old conservative Pastor Castbierg advises him to keep the deed a secret. When Magnus's father attempts to exploit his son's death to blackmail the count, the count, with the pastor's blessing, takes his own life. As in *A Reunion*, the relationship with God is understood without consideration for any external dogmatic and legal precepts. Human beings have total responsibility in their relationship to God. Thus they are at the same time free and bound—the paradox in Knudsen's work. This destructive conflict between society's official morality and obedience to one's conscience excited a great deal of attention.

There followed, one after another, Knudsen's great novels. The partially autobiographical two-volume novel *Gjæring-Afklaring* (Fermentation-Clarification, 1902) portrays with sharp satire, but also with great empathy, the spiritual situation of Knudsen's own generation. The work contains valuable insights into the circles of the peasants and the folk high-school students in the 1870s and '80s, thus forming a counterpiece to Pontoppidan's novel *Lucky Per*. With the story of the development of young Karl Wintrup, Knudsen intends to show how a childhood shaped by faith and illusions breaks down when it is confronted with reality, in order to be won back in a more intense manner.

Until this point, peasants had been merely secondary figures in Knudsen's works. In his artistically most significant novel, *Sind* (Temper, 1903), nature and the rural population become the leading elements. Anders, a young Jutland peasant, comes forward like a Kleistian Michael Kohlhaas, with an instinctive sense of justice, to oppose the encroachment of others on his land. When he becomes involved in an argument with a fraudulent neighbor, the man's accomplice, a corrupt country official, has Anders's farm set afire one night. Deliberately Anders kills the official, but is himself shot to death. Justice is thus victorious, official morality has its sacrifice, and world order is reestablished.

In *Fremskridt* (Progress, 1907) Knudsen treats the relationship of the external world to the necessity of the inner world of freedom. He confronts the old peasant culture with modern reform politics by investigating the spiritual reality that underlies the social, political, and spiritual development of a Jutland community. According to Knudsen, the basic mistake of modern times lies in the destruction of the spirit through leveling and mechanization. Ideally, societal and individual development would rest on firm social rules, but complete freedom would prevail in all spiritual matters.

Knudsen's novels confront existential problems in the social and religious spheres. They also set up "problems for debate," as Brandes had demanded, but here it is the deepest problems of human existence. Knudsen's work is simultaneously repellent, owing to the primitive brutality with which he crushes his opponents, and attractive, not only by virtue of his delicate style and the poetry that is woven through all the scenes, but also by the intensity and subjectivity of the presentation. He often intentionally leaves himself open to criticism because his psychological portrayal of characters is not realistic. His emphasis on personal commitment and an existential attitude toward the surrounding world is something Knudsen learned from Kierkegaard. This accentuated his tendency toward the paradoxical, the inexorability of his demands and his ability to analyze incongruities.

Johannes V. Jensen

One of the literary pathfinders in twentieth-century Denmark, and the writer who had the greatest influence on the later development of

Danish literature, was Jensen (1873–1950). He was born in the North Jutland region of Himmerland, the son of a veterinarian; his ancestors were peasants and village craftsmen. He portrays his encounter with Copenhagen as a young medical student in his early novels *Danskere* (Danes, 1896) and *Einar Elkær* (1898), influenced by Johannes Jørgensen and the young Hamsun. Both novels are written in the decadent mood of the 1890s and have as their protagonists perplexed narcissistic students from the provinces. Between the two novels lies Jensen's first trip to America, after he had disrupted his studies; this trip, during which he experienced the modern life-style, technology, and accelerated tempo of America, was a significant event of his youth.

A new freshness is perceptible in Jensen's first masterpiece, written at this time, *Himmerlandsfolk* (Himmerland People, 1898; later collections: *Himmerlandshistorier* [Himmerland Stories], 1904, 1910); he reaches back to his childhood and immortalizes his home region. Its legends, tales, and traditions are realistically rendered, and the population and its eccentricities are vividly portrayed. By preference, the author depicts, with a mixture of sympathy and criticism, heroic fates, as in "Cecil," tough and honest characters, as in "Mortens Juleaften" ("Morten's Christmas Eve"), and monumental figures, "Tordenkalven" ("The Thunder Calf").

Jensen spent the summer of 1898 in Spain, and here he began his activity as a correspondent, which led him through most of Europe, and later around the world. Like Hans Christian Andersen, he was enthusiastic about the progress of the times, and his interest in technology made him the ideal reporter for the World Exhibition in Paris in 1900. He collected his excellent articles in the philosophical travel book *Den gotiske Renaissance* (The Gothic Renaissance, 1901), which reaches its pinnacle in a glorification of the energetic yet well-balanced spirit of the "gothic," that is to say, the Anglo-Saxon race, as the leading force in human history.

In the regional setting of the plot, the novel *Kongens Fald* (1900–1; Eng. tr. *The Fall of the King*, 1933) is linked to *Himmerland Stories*. It is set at the beginning of the sixteenth century and focuses on the figure of the great Renaissance king Christian II, the last ruler to govern the three Scandinavian countries. The king himself is merely a secondary character, but his skepticism, which leads to the dissolution of all plans and energy into reflection and dream, becomes a symbol for the inability to act which Jensen perceived in the Danish nation. In the foreground of events, Jensen places the Jutland peasant student and later mercenary Mikkel Thøgersen; he, like the king and the major characters of the two youthful novels, is a divided and fantasizing type. In real life, he is unable to find any use for the feelings of power and the longing of his youth, and he can act only when his impotent jealousy leads him to violence and murder. Like his master, King Christian, whose imprisonment he voluntarily shares, Mikkel achieves symbolic significance as a personification of the history of Denmark.

Scenes of often ruthless naturalism alternating with passages of exquisite lyric beauty have given the novel the reputation of being a highly inspired work of art. *The Fall of the King* is, as far as the content is concerned, a historical novel—the most significant in Danish literature—but Jensen broke decisively with the historical naturalism of Flaubert and Jacobsen. The work is much more than the attempt to draw brilliant scenes, to re-form the historic material into a portrait of the present, or to analyze psychologically the basic traits of the national character that Jensen perceived as the cause of the country's defeatism after 1864 (see p. 3). The apparently accidental juxtaposition of tableaus and situations creates a mythical fantasy about the universal human—about loneliness and happiness, transitoriness and death.

A second journey to the United States in 1902–3 resulted in the two novels *Madame D'Ora* (1904) and *Hjulet* (The Wheel, 1905), both of which witness to Jensen's confrontation with the modern American metropolis. They contain brilliant descriptions of New York and Chicago, but also stereotyped suspense effects. At the same time, they turn against all belief in immortality and speculative philosophy, as this is represented by the Faustian inventor Hall, in *Madame D'Ora*.

Jensen's finest narrative art—aside from *The Fall of the King*—is in the smaller prose pieces *Myter* (Myths), which appeared in eleven volumes between 1907 and 1944. The myth is a genre offering existential perspectives on life and determined more by these visionary universal views than by concrete plot. The treatment is intensely poetic, yet lucid and concise, the action not restricted by considerations of time and space. In *Myter* Jensen symbolically presents his basic ideas in the form of essays and prose sketches describing nature, animals, and journeys. He embraces reality—to which all longing returns because it originates there, as in "Fusijama" ("Fujiyama")—ever-revitalizing nature, as in "Nordisk Foraar" ("Nordic Spring")—and the deepest recollections in the history of the human race.

Several of these myths are studies for the great series of novels *Den lange Rejse* (1908–22; Eng. tr. *The Long Journey*, 1922–24). This history of humankind, which begins with primitive existence in the tropical Jutland forest before the Ice Age and encompasses the epochs of the tribal wanderings and Viking raids to the discovery of America, tells of the progenitors of the "Gothic race," of their longing for distance places, and finally of their departure from their northern homeland toward the lost land before the Ice Age. In this epic, influenced by Darwin's evolutionary view of humankind, Jensen attempts to explain not only Nordic, but universally human symbols and conceptions, purely on the basis of practical and materialistic experience. The same themes recur again and again: the great individual as a creator, and the battle against the cold as the driving force of cultural progress. Jensen sees the yearning for distant places as a basic trait in the character of the people of the North. He explains the religiosity of the "Gothic race" as the longing for warmth and sunshine, which sets off the Viking migrations, and finally the voyage of the "Goth, Columbus," toward the fabled land of India, which, however, ends in the discovery of America—and of reality.

Jensen's prose is in a strongly lyrical vein, many of his works containing poems. Some are nearly perfect in form, others are rough; some glow with ecstasy, others are soberly cold. They are collected in five volumes, of which the first, *Digte* (Poems, 1906), containing all of the youthful poems, is a milestone in the development of modern Danish lyric poetry. The most characteristic texts, and those of epoch-making significance, are the prose poems—linked in their imagery to the modern life of technology and metropolis—in which Jensen expresses his firm belief in the joy of the present moment and his untrammeled longing; in the confession "Interferens" Jensen portrays the "perception of a world brimfull with wonder" which "intersects my conviction of the finality of all things," whereby the "transcendental vibrations of pain that are the form of my innermost self" are released.

Three poetic forms are present in Jensen's lyrical work: the oldest rhythmic prose, modeled on Goethe's and particularly on Heine's free verse; the second, alliterative poems in the Old Norse style; and finally the traditional closed verse form, which predominates in Jensen's work after 1920. In classic calm and harmony, he expresses his experiences, as, for instance, in the poem "Graven i Sne" ("The Grave in the Snow") about the romantic Adam Oehlenschläger, with whose vivid art he felt a strong kinship. Jensen praises woman as wife and mother, the child, and Danish nature, sometimes grandiosely, as in "Den jydske Blæst" ("The Jutland Wind"), sometimes very intimately, as in "Envoi":

The elder spreading
her dew-cool hands
toward the summer moon

A year later:

The self-same beeches
and twilit nights,
the same elation!

A year later:

The blackbird twitters,
spring breezes swell
once again, my love!

Nine years later:

The self-same beeches
and twilit nights,
the same elation!

Tr. David Colbert

Jensen formulated the basic idea underlying his writing after the turn of the century in the book *The Gothic Renaissance*: the rebirth of a practical form of life and spirit, the reinstatement of things and facts, after the degeneration of speculative naturalism, that led to a "breakthrough of the soul." Still he belonged to the generation of the 1890s. He heaped scorn on the tradition, but wrote with reverence about his ancestors, rejoiced in reality, and was himself a dreamer. Johannes V. Jensen is a major figure in Danish intellectual life. He was honored with the Nobel prize in 1944.

Martin Andersen Nexø

Nexø (1869–1954) was the first significant literary representative of the Danish workers' movement, a pioneer who introduced new material into literature. He was the first great writer to make the proletarian a central figure in his work. Nexø was born in the slums of Christianshavn in Copenhagen, the son of a stone-mason. He spent his youth as a shepherd, shoemaker's apprentice, and mason's assistant on the island of Bornholm. In 1896 he attended a teacher's college in Copenhagen, and he worked between 1898 and 1901 as a substitute teacher; after that he made his living as a free-lance writer and journalist. A Communist, Nexø spent several years during World War II as a refugee in Sweden, thereafter in the Soviet Union; from 1961 until his death he lived in East Germany. His youth, spent in poverty and hard labor, and described in detail in his memoirs, *Erindringer* (Recollections, 1932–39), forms the background for his two major novels. Nexø's short stories *Skygger* (Shadows, 1898) deal with the milieu that was to become his special domain: the world of the destitute. The novel *Dryss* (Life Drips Away, 1902), indicates the extent of his link with the decadent pessimism of the 1890s. A change occurred in the travel book *Soldage* (1903; Eng. tr. *Days in the Sun*, 1929), characterized by a sense of solidarity with the international working class, whose spokesman Nexø became with the novel *Pelle Erobreren* (1906–10; Eng. tr. *Pelle the Conqueror*, 1913–16). Here the author traces the successful development of the Danish workers' movement in the last decades of the nineteenth century; he elevates his portrayal "of the worker's heavy stride across the earth on his endless, semi-conscious wandering toward the light" (preface) to a general representation of the human being striving to move ahead. The achievement of this light is symbolized in the idealized title figure.

The beginning of *Pelle the Conqueror* is clearly autobiographical. Nexø masterfully portrays the life of little Pelle and his poor Swedish father, Lasse, as servants on an estate on Bornholm. But it is precisely the striving, a basic attribute of Pelle's, which leads him beyond his childhood milieu. The second part, essentially a social portrait of the times, describes his stay in a small town as a shoemaker's apprentice and his encounter with emerging socialism in the figure of the roaming artisan Garibaldi. However, individual artisanship succumbs to the new factory industries, and Pelle leaves his workshop and travels to Copenhagen. In the third volume, Nexø portrays two worlds: the social-democratic worker's movement, which is organizing itself, and the old, apathetic proletariat in the dilapidated tenement house "The Ark," the squalor of which transforms Pelle into an inflammatory agitator of the workers. After he has led the big labor fight to victory, he is arrested under the pretext of having committed forgery. After his stay in prison, Pelle returns, to once again conquer life through his optimism, and here—in the fourth part of the novel—a decisive change occurs in the work: In prison Pelle has turned more strongly within himself and finds his way back to his wife, Ellen, who has not wanted to sacrifice either her home or her individuality for his struggle. For the first time the individual is placed above the masses. Pelle feels himself briefly pulled toward the syndicalist and anarchist movements, until he begins to bring his new ideas to realization: to conquer society through cooperative workers' activities. *Pelle the Conqueror* closes with this life task.

The novel contains many agitatory conflicts, and many of the political features of the last two parts are Utopian and naive, and do not have the artistic merit of the earlier volumes. Nevertheless, *Pelle the Conqueror* is a masterpiece that is carried along by the epic power of the narrative and by Nexø's social passion. This work became a classic, and its author, in the opinion of many critics, stands second only to Maxim Gorki.

Nexø's second major work, *Ditte Menneskebarn* (1917–21, Ditte, Child of Man; Eng. tr. *Ditte: Girl Alive, Ditte: Daughter of Man, Ditte:*

Toward the Stars, 1920-23) is no political companion piece to *Pelle the Conqueror*, although it is based on the same human and social concerns. Like Pelle, Ditte begins at the very bottom. She too is characterized by ambition and a hunger for life, but her fate is different. Whereas Pelle becomes involved in political work to build a new social order, Ditte must fight alone against poverty; she succumbs as a result. She is brought up by her grandmother, who is for Ditte what Lasse was for Pelle, a refuge when reality becomes too merciless. After her confirmation, Ditte takes a position on a large farm. Out of sympathy, she allows herself to be drawn into a relationship with the shy son of the woman who owns the farm; she has a child, but is thrown out. Alone she must bear the consequences of her compassionate heart, the same heart which later, in Copenhagen, is exploited by employers and members of her own class. Nothing, however, can destroy Ditte: The more she sinks into misery and distress, the more her heart brims over with love and willingness to help others. Finally, at the age of twenty-five, she dies, worked to death.

The entire narrative is concentrated on Ditte, whom Nexø makes into a symbolic and actual representative of the true social attitude of the proletariat. Politics are left out; the organized labor movement is only sketched and has no influence on the protagonist's fate. As in *Pelle the Conqueror*, the descriptions of childhood and youth are clearly the high points of the work. The aesthetic and psychological value of the two last parts of the book is variable—the structure is weak and Nexø often lacks the necessary self-discipline.

The novel *Midt i en Jærntid* (1929, In an Age of Iron; Eng. tr. *In God's Land*, 1933) is a satirical attack on the abuses by the Danish farmers during the trade boom of World War I. *Morten hin Røde* (Morten the Red, 1945-57), again picks up characters from Nexø's earlier work, albeit in a manner which is satiric of the times, showing Nexø's sharply tendentious conflict with the Danish social-democratic party. Pelle has become a bourgeois social-democratic minister; the spirit of rebellion, which had formed his youth, is now to be found in the poet Morten, Nexø's alter ego.

Martin Andersen Nexø is the only Danish writer of his generation whose literary creativity rests on a Marxist world view. But there is an easily discernible difference between him and the socialist authors of the 1930s: Nexø still believes in human goodness, believes that it asserts itself in spite of everything—cutting across all social and economic relationships.

FINNISH LITERATURE:
THE FENNO-SWEDISH AESTHETICIANS

The early decades of the twentieth century were very dramatic. In January 1918 civil war broke out. It was regarded by the non-socialist "Whites" as a struggle for liberty, by the "Reds" as a fight for a new social and political system. The savage clash became a national tragedy, but the separation from Russia resulted in an upsurge of energy and initiative in everyday life. In literature a skeptical and apocalyptic mood prevailed, particularly among the Fenno-Swedish writers who had to give up their social privileges gradually. A melancholy attitude and a hedonistic cult of the moment had become popular; the *flaneur* became a literary type. The model for this short-lived fin-de-siècle trend was, above all, Hjalmar Söderberg: Observation became impressionistic, with life in Helsingfors the preferred theme.

Runar Schildt

The greatest writer representing the *flaneur* attitude was Schildt (1888–1925), whose life and suicide became symbolic of the period: the barren emotional life of the intellectual, the refined man's spleen, indeed the total life situation of the Fenno-Swedish upper class. His first short stories, collected in *Den segrande Eros* (The Victorious Eros, 1912), are written in Söderberg's witty and elegant style. However, the novel *Regnbågen* (The Rainbow, 1916) is characterized by a more matter-of-fact attitude and a new setting—the author's native home in southern Finland. The collection *Perdita* (1918) contains one of Schildt's finest short stories, "Den svagare" ("The Weaker"), in which careerist Johnnie Claësson lures a young woman from her husband, the petit bourgeois Blomqvist, who represents blind dependency, doomed, because of his goodness, to be defeated in life's struggle.

The collection *Hemkomsten* (Coming Home, 1919) consists of four stories, three of which deal with the civil war; Schildt attempts, despite war, to maintain a humanistic attitude, which is contrasted with a feeling of loneliness and impotence, characteristic of Schildt himself. This attitude resulted in a certain distance from events, which had been present in the *flaneur* attitude of the early books, and in the collection *Häxskogen* (Witchwood, 1920) becomes clearly tragic in the character of the poet Casimir in the title story. In the manner of Thomas Mann, life and art are juxtaposed. Uncommitted to life, Casimir indifferently attempts to artistically describe, and even to utilize, the tragedies of his own life.

Casimir is the alter ego of the author, who was, himself, no longer able to make his emptiness creative. Schildt's decision to commit suicide was made in 1922; he delayed only because he was determined to complete a number of dramatic works. The one-act play *Galgmannen* (1922; Eng. tr. *The Man of the Gallows*, 1944) poses questions about guilt and redemption, whereas Schildt's two last plays, *Den stora rollen* (The Big Part, 1923) and *Lyckoriddaren* (The Adventurer, 1923), revolve around the death motif, the end of life and the end of a career.

Schildt's works constitute the climax of the *flaneur* generation's prose. His writing survives primarily because of his language: a clear, concise style combined with sharp observation. He was unable to find his place in life, and he consistently defended the suffering human being.

Jarl Hemmer

The civil war also exerted a definite influence on the other major prose writer, Hemmer (1893–1944). The numerous collections of poetry between *Rösterna* (The Voices, 1914) and *Över dunklet* (Over the Darkness, 1919), which delineate the poet's development from pagan intoxication with life to romantic idealism, are rather traditional. Hemmer's early prose is lyrical. In the novel *Onni Kokko* (1920), however, the civil war forms a realistic and threatening background to an ethical complex of problems: the never-answered question of the role of suffering in a just world order. Connected with this is the question about guilt feelings and conscience, a motif that is dealt with in the short story "Skottet" ("The Shot") from the collection *De skymda ljusen* (The Shaded Lights, 1921). Ethical problems are given a Christian coloration in the poems of *Skärseld* (Purgatory, 1925), the novel *Fattiggubbens brud* (The Bride of the Poor Man, 1926), and especially in his major work, the Dostoevsky-like novel *En man och hans samvete* (1931; Eng. tr. *A Fool of Faith*, 1936), an expression of the depression the author experienced after the war. With existential commitment Hemmer analyzes human restlessness and guilt, suffering and death, the search for consolation and explanation in religion, and, finally, the belief in sacrificial death and suffering for others as a possible means of salvation for oneself.

After this novel Hemmer's creative power was spent. His prose and poetry became stereotypical and uneven. Much of it was inane, but his best poetry is remarkable by virtue of its burning intensity and concise symbolic language, which raise a number of poems to the level of brilliance. It is the same intense lyricism that creates the high points of Hemmer's prose. The feeling of inner emptiness gradually became so dominant that it led to the author's suicide.

ICELANDIC LITERATURE: NEO-ROMANTIC POETRY AND DRAMA

The national unity that had prevailed during the struggle for independence disappeared during World War I and was replaced by social and political conflicts involving strong class differences. The same restlessness characterized literature. In prose writing the revolt against old forms and attitudes did not begin until about 1925, but even before the war Icelandic drama had its first and most important bloom. In addition, national boundaries were transcended by a number of writers who made their debuts around 1900 and wrote some of their books in Icelandic, some in Danish.

Hulda

Purely neo-romantic was the poet Hulda, pseudonymn for Unnur Benediktsdóttir Bjarklind (1881-1946). Her melodious light poetry deals with a great variety of subjects, ranging from nature and eulogies of rural life to topics from antiquity. Her first volume *Kvæði* (Poems) was published in 1909, her seventh and last, posthumously in 1951. Her most original contribution was her imitations of Icelandic folk poetry, notably the þulur: rhapsodies and nursery rhymes, which inspired many younger poets to write in the same style.

Örn Arnarson

The older epic, the *rímur*, was revived in the twentieth century in the epigrammatic and satiric collection *Rímur af Oddi sterka* (Rhymes by Oddr the Strong, 1938) by Arnarson, the pen name of Magnús Stefánsson (1884-1942). Strong social satire characterizes his collection *Illgresi* (Weeds, 1924), championing the cause of the working class, whereas the neo-romantic tendency dominates Arnarson's numerous and very popular poems about the sea and seamanship, embodying the ancient, heroic Icelandic spirit.

Jóhann Sigurjónsson

The greatest dramatic talent of the period was Sigurjónsson (1880-1919), who after the turn of the century spent most of his time in Copenhagen; he published his plays in Danish, although he wrote them

in both Danish and Icelandic. His two best-known dramas freely utilize Icelandic legends and are based on events from the eighteenth
century. *Bjærg-Ejvind og hans Hustru*, (1911; Eng. tr. *Eyvind of the
Hills*, 1916 and *Eivindur of the Mountains*, 1961) was Sigurjónsson's
greatest success, staged not only in Scandinavia but also in England
and the United States. It is a drama about the futile struggle of heroic,
self-sacrificing love against hunger and isolation. The widow Halla
gives up her rich farm to become an outlaw, even sacrifices her children in order to live with the man she loves, who is a thief. Finally,
when she feels that her love is fading, she goes out into the snowstorm
to die. *Ønsket* (1915; Eng. tr. *Loftur*, 1939 and *Loft's Wish*, 1940) is
inspired by a Faust-like legend about a student, Loftur, who wishes
to win full control over evil forces. Contrasted with him are a number
of figures who represent goodness, the drama thus becoming a symbolic play about the fight between good and evil ending with the destruction of the main character because of his longing for the infinite
and unattainable. Less successful was Sigurjónsson's last play. *Løgneren*
(The Liar, 1917), which is a recreation of *Njáls saga*; it lacks the dramatic intensity and sustained romantic symbolism of his earlier works.

Guðmundur Kamban

Sigurjónsson's success was a great challenge to other Icelandic writers. Older authors such as Einar H. Kvaran began to write dramas, and
among the young, Kamban (1888–1945), who wrote in both Danish
and Icelandic, became Iceland's most important playwright next to
Sigurjónsson. In Copenhagen Kamban studied philosophy, literature,
and drama. He began as a neo-romantic with two plays in Sigurjónsson's style. *Hadda Padda* (1914; Eng. tr. 1917) and *Kongeglimen*
(Wrestling before the King, 1915). However, he became very interested in social and ethical problems, and his style grew more realistic.
A stay in New York from 1915 to 1917 turned him into a social critic
with a special interest in the nature and psychology of crime and the
effects of punishment. Thus the hero of *Marmor* (Marble, 1918), a
judge and criminologist, concludes that not only criminal law but
punishment itself is immoral and should be abolished.

With *Vi Mordere* (1920; Eng. tr. *We Murderers*, 1970) Kamban's
and perhaps Iceland's, best-written drama, he began a series of works
on modern marriage. The play deals with marital problems, with guilt
and innocence, and it depicts with sympathetic understanding a husband who in exasperation kills the real offender, his indolent and
flighty wife. The novel *Ragnar Finnsson* (1922), which like the two

preceding dramas takes place in the United States, also deals with help-less characters who have turned into criminals because of their environ-ment and the social system. Kamban's remaining novels deal with Ice-landic topics from the Middle Ages to the present. A monumental work is *Skálholt* (1930–34; Parts 1 and 2 Eng. tr. *The Virgin of Skálholt*, 1935), a psychological study of love and a broad depiction of every-day life in the seventeenth century, based on extensive historical study.

In *30. Generation* (30th Generation, 1933) Kamban returns to con-temporary Iceland in an enthusiastic portrayal of Reykjavík, and his last novel, *Jeg ser et stort, skønt Land* (1936; Eng. tr. *I See a Wondrous Land*, 1938), is a retelling of the stories about the discovery of Green-land and Wineland (America). Kamban's last two plays are witty com-edies, *Komplekser* (Complexes, 1938), which attacks Freudian psy-chology, and *Grandezza* (1941), a satire on sensational journalism.

Kamban's works were especially well received in Germany, where he also worked as a stage director for a number of years. His connec-tions with Germany were interpreted, wrongly, as Nazi sympathies, and at the end of World War II he was executed by mistake by the Danish resistance movement.

Part III Between the World Wars

Chapter 6

Swedish Literature between the Wars

PROLETARIAN LITERATURE AND DEMOCRATIZATION

Even though great numbers of Swedish workers were in a revolutionary mood in 1917–18, there was no significant unrest. Rather, constitutional reform enacted universal suffrage and laid the foundation for the political influence of the Social-Democratic Party, an influence which steadily increased during the 1920s and 1930s. In 1919–20 Sweden experienced a general economic boom, after which a recession began. The country was plunged into an economic and social crisis, the general condition then improved again, until a new international economic crisis occurred late in the 1920s.

The democratization of Swedish society is clearly reflected in the literature. Around 1910 several writers emerged from the working class who were to lay the groundwork for portrayals of the lowest social strata, a dominant charactertistic of Swedish literature in the twentieth century. The realistic material used by these writers and their conception of humankind and society posed new problems for the creation of literature. In their choice of themes and literary techniques, the proletarian writers were closely allied with naturalism. For many Zola was the master; above all, they had been strongly influenced in their youth by younger naturalists, such as Maxim Gorki and Upton Sinclair, and a few also by the Scandinavian pioneer of proletarian writing, Martin Andersen Nexø.

The first representative of proletarian literature is Dan Andersson (1888–1920). The wide popularity of his poetry after his death is attributable chiefly to two collections, *Kolvaktarens visor* (1915; partly tr. as *Charcoal-Burner's Ballad*, 1943), and *Svarta ballader* (Black Ballads, 1917)—a mixture of realistic scenes and religious speculation. In prose, Martin Koch (1882–1940) was dominant; his epic work in the spirit of Gorki, such as the extensive family chronicle *Guds vackra värld* (God's Beautiful World, 1916), prefigured the proletarian literature of the 1930s. In this decade there emerged a whole group of authors with a proletarian background, who relate in autobiographical books their experiences in Swedish society *before* the time of the encompassing social reforms. Among them are Eyvind Johnson, Harry Martinson, and Vilhelm Moberg, as well as the two portraitists of the rural proletariat, Ivar Lo-Johansson and Jan Fridegård. Fridegård (1897–1968) was a strongly individualistic writer of ironic and satiric novels dealing with the conflicts of the poor with society—as in his major work, the autobiographical cycle about *Lars Hård* (1935–51). Lo-Johansson, on the other hand, pursues a more committed, documentary naturalism. His earliest works were travel books describing miners and gypsies, later published in one volume under the title *Vagabondliv* (Vagabond Life, 1949). In his novel *Godnatt, jord* (Good Night, Earth, 1933) Lo-Johansson (1901–   ) emerges as the first of the proletarian writers of the 1930s to depict poor farmhands as a *collective* social group. Of higher quality are the three volumes of *Statarnoveller* (Stories about Farmhands, 1936–41) describing the physical and psychological needs of this class. In a number of social novels Lo-Johansson continued his treatment of working-class problems. *Analfabeten* (The Illiterate, 1951) is the first in an eight-volume autobiographical series, which concludes with *Proletärförfattaren* (The Proletarian Writer, 1960). Since 1968 Lo-Johansson has concentrated on the short story in an impressive number of volumes, each connected with one of the seven mortal sins—examples of human folly. An eighth collection, *Ordets makt* (The Power of the World, 1973), focuses on the origin and history of speech and the written word. Lo-Johansson's increasing interest in history is evidenced by the work *Furstarna* (The Princes, 1974), subtitled "A Chronicle from Gustavus Vasa to Charles XII," and the short-story collection *Lastbara berättelser* (Depraved Stories, 1974).

Vilhelm Moberg

Moberg (1898–1973) was the first realistic depicter of the Swedish proletariat who was born into that class. His first successful novel, *Raskens* (1921), introduced the exploited farmhand into Swedish literature; it is an unsentimental story of a peasant soldier, his large family, and their daily fight against poverty and misery. Whereas this book contains no direct social criticism, the two novels about the farmer Adolf and his family, *Långt från landsvägen* (Far from the Highway, 1929) and *De knutna händerna* (Clenched Fists, 1930) are far more somber. Adolf is a conservative individualist who cannot accept any technological progress, a domestic tyrant whose children rebel against him and leave the farm. The individual's revolt against society and its traditions is also the subject of the novel *Mans kvinna* (Man's Woman, 1933), Moberg's contribution to the cult of eroticism in the 1930s (see p. 168). Facing the choice between duty and love, the main character, Märit, follows her instincts and decides to leave husband and home.

Moberg's contribution to the autobiographical writings of the 1930s, the trilogy about *Knut Toring* (1935–39; Eng. tr. *The Earth Is Ours*, 1940), explores the same main theme as the books of Lo-Johansson and Fridegård, one of the most important social problems of the twentieth century: the flight from the country to the city, resulting in a shortage of workers on the farms and a feeling of uprootedness among the new factory workers. The lengthy novel *Soldat med brutet gevär* (1944, Soldier with Broken Gun; Eng. adaptation *When I Was a Child*, 1956) also documents the history of the labor movement, in which Moberg himself took an active part. The novel closes with sharp criticism of the Swedish policy of neutrality during the war. This theme links the novel to his earlier historical novel about freedom, *Rid i natt!* (1941; Eng. tr. *Ride This Night!*, 1943) a markedly successful book in which Moberg, clearly referring to contemporary events, portrays the revolt of the Swedish farmers against the tyrannical domination of a German nobleman. His last novel, *Förrädarland* (Land of Traitors, 1967), is set in the same milieu and treats the sufferings of a peace-loving peasantry caused by discord among members of the upper class. This motif is also basic to his polemical history of Sweden, *Min svenska historia* (1970–71; Eng. tr. *A History of the Swedish People*, 1972–73).

After World War II Moberg composed his major work, the partly documentary prose epic about the emigration of Swedish farmers to the United States in the nineteenth century, *Romanen om utvandrarna* (1949–59; Eng. tr. *The Emigrants*, 1951, *Unto a Good Land*, 1954, *The Last Letter Home*, 1961; filmed by Jan Troell 1971–72). It is both a social depiction of enormous scope and a myth about the human search for happiness. In addition, the work offers a satirical analysis of the general background to the emigration: the Swedish bureaucracy and social hierarchy. This cycle was very popular because of Moberg's excellent mastery of the theme, because of the general validity of his observations, and because of his convincing narrative power.

For the young intelligentsia among the workers, the victory of the reformist wing of the Social-Democratic Party (see p. 151) meant an abrupt awakening from the dream of the revolution; this would become decisive for their world view in the following years. They discovered it was impossible to operate exclusively with the impersonal concept of the "masses," that the social problem was, above all, a personal one—a disappointment that resulted in general ennui. In addition, there was the effect of World War I upon cultural life, and the postwar mentality, familiar from world literature. All illusions were shattered, any belief in a sense and purpose to life became ludicrous. This nihilistic condition of the "lost generation" eventually was characteristic of all countries, for instance in the works of Hemingway, Malraux, and Remarque—in Denmark in the work of Tom Kristensen, in Iceland in that of Halldór Laxness, and in Norway in that of Aksel Sandemose.

Eyvind Johnson

Next to Pär Lagerkvist, Johnson (1900–76) is probably the Swedish author who gave the most accurate and interesting expression of this postwar attitude. Whereas Lagerkvist's existential anxiety was primarily on a metaphysical plane, Johnson had a more practical, social focus. His great series of novels about Olof Persson (1934–37; Eng. tr. of first part, *1914*, 1970) tells of Johnson's education from primary school on, his active participation in socialist organizations, and his experience as a manual worker; the work is no broad epic portrayal, but a series of excerpts from Olof's experiences, using a photo-montage technique. Johnson spent the years 1919–21 in Stockholm politically active but unemployed. During various stays in Germany and France from 1921 to 1930 he had experienced the European postwar misery as a worker and a correspondent. After the break with the socialism of his youth, which occurred in the year 1924, he began his literary career.

Johnson's early books were written when he was experiencing existential anxiety and defeat. They are coined in the hectic rhythm of expressionism, deal with hunger and isolation—Hamsun's influence is evident—and pathetically and indignantly decry social injustice. In his later works, moral accusations retreat in favor of a lyrically psychological, novelistic treatment. Through its basically gloomy mood, the novel *Minnas* (To Remember, 1928) is linked to Johnson's first creative period. Its narrative technique, employing the inner monologue of James Joyce's *Ulysses*, was a novelty in Sweden. In its penetrating study of a case of schizophrenia, the book turns toward the future.

Entirely in the new style is *Kommentar till ett stjärnfall* (Commentary on a Falling Star, 1929), an epic reshaping of Strindberg's *The Father*. All the characters represent different kinds of human inadequacies, from cynical weariness through lack of self-confidence to evil calculation. Here, too, the narrative technique is colored by the inner monologue.

Like all other European prose writers of his generation, Johnson was influenced by modern psychology, above all by Freud. Basic to his portrayal of characters is a Proustian analysis of recollection and the psychological dimension of time; but he was also spurred on by André Gide's *Les Faux-monnayeurs* (*The Counterfeiters*) and by his own delight in experimentation.

In the 1930s Johnson lived primarily in Sweden. In *Regn i gryningen* (Rain at Daybreak, 1933) he continued his social and cultural analysis, which became pointed cultural criticism in the manner of Freud and D. H. Lawrence. Gradually his creative works became more humanistic and democratic, as in the two political novels *Nattövning* (Night Maneuvers, 1938) and *Soldatens återkomst* (The Return of the Soldier, 1940), and above all in the trilogy about *Krilon* (1941–43). The previously anarchistic cultural critic passionately takes the side of democracy against fascism and national socialism. Johnson also takes a stand against the half-hearted policy of neutrality that Sweden had adopted. The battle that the real-estate broker Krilon and his friends in Stockholm are waging against the major enemies Jekau and Staph (the Soviet Union and Hitler's Germany) symbolizes not only the years of World War II, but the eternal struggle between right and might. This conflict is played out on a realistic level and takes on metaphysical dimensions. The trilogy thus becomes a somewhat grotesquely exaggerated, yet true, picture of the power mentality, and Krilon himself becomes an allegorical figure with Christlike traits. The deepest impression on the reader is made by the extraordinary inventiveness, the overpowering fantasy, and the occasionally vivid, sometimes subtle symbolism. In the detailed description of the external world Thomas Mann's influence is clear, but it is the symbolism that lifts the work above the time in which it was written. The Krilon trilogy is the most important monument in Swedish literature to the war and various attitudes toward *any* war.

After the war Johnson lived in Switzerland (1947–49) and in England (1949–50). During these years he wrote two historical novels that treat the basic theme of his mature work: the hopeless battle of the good and the right for a better world. *Strändernas svall* (1946, The Swell on the Beaches; Eng. tr. *Return to Ithaca*, 1952) is a reworking of Homer's *Odyssey*. When Johnson treats classical motifs, he does not conform to the idealizing realism of classical art, but reworks the myths from a modern point of view. He maintains the classical frame, but softens the firm outlines of the figures and shapes them as fragmented and vacillating; for instance, Odysseus becomes a reflective, self-critical man who belongs to our time, a man filled with doubts and inner turmoil. Very few of Johnson's books lack allusion to relationships and legends of antiquity. Homer's work in particular was very important to him. In the 1920s James Joyce actualized these themes in *Ulysses*; Thomas Mann's tetralogy *Joseph und seine Brüder* (Joseph and His Brothers), a mix of accurate archaeology and romantic irony, and Robert Graves's *I, Claudius* were also important influences.

Drömmar om rosor och eld (Dreams of Roses and Fire, 1949) anticipates Huxley's novel on the same subject, *The Devils of Loudon*. Johnson's novel is an expression of his development toward a basically pessimistic view of life. The priest Grainier, a victim of the witchcraft trial in France in 1634, is a hero of greater dimensions than Ulysses and more tragic because he recognizes his unavoidable fate.

With *Molnen över Metapontion* (Clouds over Metapontion, 1957), Johnson returned to classical themes. The greatest portion of the plot plays in southern Italy, incessantly swinging back and forth between events that happened 2300 years earlier—such as the persecutions under one of Syracuse's tyrants—the concentration camps of World War II, and the more peaceful world of the 1950s. Johnson intends thereby to show that freedom, security, and love are always threatened, that the progress of history is unpredictable and senseless.

His greatest novel on this theme is *Hans nådes tid* (1960; Eng. tr. *The Days of His Grace*, 1968), perhaps Johnson's most mature and unified work. The setting is Charlemagne's France. In a depressing manner Johnson portrays how, after rebelling against the emperor, several young men are variously transformed into irresolute tools in the hands of power or become petrified in their outlook. The basic tone is deeply pessimistic, the attitude toward the mendacity of power partly biting irony, partly rebellious defiance. Yet woven through this tragic fantasy is sympathy with the victims and admiration of the human capacity to intellectually resist in a world where justice and love exist only in dreams.

The narrative experiments are continued in *Livsdagen lång* (Life's Long Day, 1964); the novel is constructed not of a single plot, but of a number of stories from different epochs, held together by one character, the narrator Donatus. The theme of the book—that the interpretation of reality is dependent on this narrator—makes it a parallel to Enquist's and Delblanc's meta-novels of the same decade (see p. 288). *Favel ensam* (Favel Alone, 1968) is a pessimistic novel set in modern England, with flashbacks to the Nazi persecution of the Jews. In *Några steg mot tystnaden* (A Few Steps Toward Silence, 1973), Johnson returns to a more experimental way of writing. The novel shifts between several different time levels to illuminate an everpresent problem: the effort of humans and of Western humanism to retain integrity and dignity in the face of injustice and abusive power.

In 1957 Johnson was elected to the Swedish academy—an official recognition of the modernistic novel, to whose breakthrough he himself had decisively contributed. In 1974 he, with Harry Martinson, received the Nobel Prize. His work, which mirrors the ideological and technical development of the novel from Hamsun to Faulkner, is pervaded by the political and cultural debates of his time. He regarded the dissolution of the form of the novel as a necessary step in its development, and saw each of his novels as an experiment in expressing the dark and the bright sides of life.

PSYCHOLOGICAL REALISM

Besides the proletarian writers, there were several authors of bourgeois background who, like the generation of the first decade, employed traditional epic technique (see p. 122). In contrast to the earlier writers, however, they were strongly interested in the psychoanalytic method and view of humankind. Attention was focused on the irrational and instinctive.

Agnes von Krusenstjerna

Von Krusenstjerna (1894–1940) wrote a series of novels about Tony (1922–26) which are exemplary of this focus. She returned to this autobiographical material in her last, unfinished cycle, *Fattigadel* (Poor Nobility, 1935–38). The seven-volume novel *Fröknarna von Pahlen* (The Misses von Pahlen, 1930–35) is not primarily a satire on the nobility to which von Krusenstjerna herself belonged, but a proclamation—in the vein of Hjalmar Söderberg—of the desires of the flesh and the irretrievable loneliness of the soul, in von Krusenstjerna's books the soul of a woman in love. Von Krusenstjerna caused a sensation and a scandal with her very committed and egocentric writing, a forerunner of the literature of the 1930s and its cult of sexuality (see p. 168).

Olle Hedberg

Hedberg (1899–1974) gained recognition as the rational satirist of the Swedish middle class. Influenced by psychologist Alfred Adler, French moralist La Rochefoucauld, and Danish novelist Jacob Paludan, Hedberg wrote two lengthy novels about Karsten Kirsewetter (1937–39) and Bo Stensson Svenningsson (1941–45), in which he unveiled, with irony and penetrating psychological insight, the pettiness, envy, and hypocrisy of the bourgeois world. Hedberg's easily accessible style made his writing extremely popular, but also rather superficial, especially his later novels from the 1950s on. His last work, *Tänk att ha hela livet främför sig* (Imagine Having Your Entire Life Ahead of You), was published in 1974.

Walter Ljungquist and Tage Aurell

Ljungquist and Aurell, because their approach was experimental, did not receive recognition as important novelists until later. Ljungquist (1900–74) debuted with the novel *Ombyte av tåg* (Change of Trains, 1933), written in a concise Hemingway-like style. The writing in his later novels is more colorful and descriptive: *Azalea* (1948) and the series of novels, influenced by Rudolf Steiner's anthroposophy, about the writer Jerk Dandelin (1951ff), which concluded with the posthumously published *Sörj dina träd* (Mourn Your Trees, 1975).

The style of Aurell (1895–   ) is very compact. In novels like *Skillingtryck* (Broadsides, 1943) and the autobiographical *Viktor* (1955), as well as in the short-story collections *Smärre berättelser* (Smaller Stories, 1946) and *Nya berättelser* (New Stories, 1949), Aurell directs his attention to the neglected and unsuccessful elements in society, describing them objectively, in a manner reminiscent of the Icelandic saga, with its lack of direct psychological analysis.

TWO BREAKTHROUGH FIGURES

Most of the authors who made their appearance after the turn of the century were prose writers whose works reached a wider public than had earlier Swedish literature. Prose predominated until the 1930s. However, during and immediately after World War I a younger generation stepped forward, consisting primarily of lyric poets, although the novel and the short story were not completely neglected.

Birger Sjöberg

Sjöberg (1885–1929) grew up in a bourgeois milieu in the west Swedish town of Vänersborg and began his career as an idyllic, very popular troubadour, only to end it in isolation, brooding, and despair, which could be expressed only by stretching language to the utmost. A long artistic development led Sjöberg to his first success, *Fridas bok* (Frida's Book, 1922). These graceful songs derive from Sjöberg's numerous imitations of Bellman and Fröding; many are reworkings of poems that Sjöberg had written as early as 1903. The elegant form of the 1922 poems sharply contrasts with the turgid and high-flown philosophical torrent of words that flow from the half-educated singer of these songs. His love for the office girl Frida is expressed in images and words that naively exaggerate his admiration and parody his jealousy. The unique mix of tender poetry and comedy in this volume is based on this fiction. In only one poem are these good middle-class citizens pushed aside, in a fantasy about a funeral procession, "Bleka Dödens minut" ("Pale Death's Moment"), an elegiac death poem which shatters the idyll.

In several poems from *Frida's Book* the World War is mirrored. Its effects on Sweden are described in the novel *Kvartetten som sprängdes* (The Quartet That Was Broken Up, 1924). The setting is still the small town, but the idyll has now been dashed by the postwar economic crisis. The plot is set in the hectic years 1920–22; the quartet has broken up because its members, instead of playing chamber music, play the stock market. The work teems with secondary plots and characters, on the pattern of Charles Dickens; and, as in Dickens, the moods constantly shift between burlesque and tragedy, satire and sentimentality. The idyll was merely an illusion, although the large reading audience did not recognize this. It accepted *Kvartetten som sprängdes* with enthusiasm, not disturbed, as the critics were, by its excessively loose structure.

In contrast, Sjöberg's next collection of poems, *Kriser och kransar* (Crises and Wreaths, 1926), surprised and shocked the public; he suddenly showed an entirely new face, one tormented by anxiety and suffering. Knowing all of Sjöberg's literary works—in particular the posthumous volumes *Fridas andra bok* (Frida's Second Book, 1929), *Minnen från jorden* (Memories from the Earth, 1940), *Syntaxupproret* (The Syntax Revolt, 1955), and *Fridas tredje bok* (Frida's Third Book, 1956)—we can clearly see the connection between his idyllic and his tragic poetry. The motifs are the same throughout; only the perspective has changed. With original images, and symbols that are not always easy to grasp, Sjöberg in *Kriser och kransar* portrays life, taking as his point of departure its two central problems: the senselessness of existence and the impenetrability of death. This death motif is closely related to Sjöberg's mood of anxiety and opens religious perspectives, for death is present not only as a threat, but also as a liberator from the misery of life. Sjöberg attempts to penetrate this mystery, his language taking on a seeking and paradoxical tone. The stylistic traits characteristic of Sjöberg's writing, traceable to his reading of Shakespeare in his youth, correspond with those of expressionism: bold juxtapositions, personifications of abstract concepts, and a mixture of pure naturalism with the most tender poetry. With his first book Birger Sjöberg renewed the Swedish song tradition; with his last he introduced modernism into Swedish literature.

Pär Lagerkvist

The central figure, and the most versatile artistic talent of the 1920s, is Lagerkvist (1891–1974). He was born in Växjö, the son of a railroad official. In his autobiography, *Gäst hos verkligheten* (1925; Eng. tr. *Guest of Reality*, 1936 and later), he portrayed his unpretentious family life and the ineradicable impression that his parent's religiosity made on him. He himself stood, like a stranger, outside their world of firm conviction, outside their unproblematic life. During his time in school Lagerkvist was introduced to new ideas that brought him into opposition with society and religion. As a university student he wrote for left-wing radical newspapers and published a few prose works in which he was still seeking a personal form of expression.

Lagerkvist broke through as a lyricist in 1916 with a volume that bears the title *Ångest* (Anguish). The fear of death which had filled him as a child, the shattering experience of the World War, and a deep personal crisis had released in him a boundless feeling of anxiety. Everything is loneliness, eternity is empty, and God is silent: "Love is nothing. Anguish is everything / the anguish of living." Lagerkvist's originality lies neither in the symbolic language nor in the vocabulary. The new and remarkable thing, which makes him the first Swedish expressionist, is above all his use of classically simple language to express spontaneous, desperate moods.

During the war years Lagerkvist also wrote his first dramas, in which the same deep pessimism dominates. The three one-act plays *Den svåra stunden* (Eng. tr. *The Difficult Hour*, 1966), published with a theoretical manifesto against the naturalistic theater, *Teater* (Theater, 1918), portray people in the hour of their death. They find themselves at the boundary between two worlds, the plot in many places becoming a projection of the thoughts and fantasies of these dying people. The model is Strindberg, the author of *To Damascus* and the chamber plays. Greater artistic control of the expressionistic dramatic style is evident in *Himlens hemlighet* (Eng. tr. *The Secret of Heaven*, 1966) in the collection *Kaos* (Chaos, 1919). The piece is a nightmare, and the

stage represents a portion of the globe, populated by allegorical figures: cripples, the insane, and fools. To them comes a young man, the
first in the series of Lagerkvist's tragic heroes, who inquires about "the
meaning." The answer is that everything just revolves quickly; at the
end, in despair, he throws himself into the darkness that surrounds the
earth. The volume also contains lyrics under the collective title "I
stället för tro" ("In Place of Faith"), which include several of Lagerkvist's most exquisite personal poems, in which he expresses, in religious language, his longing for the experience of eternity as a part of
existence.

The longing to reconcile himself with life is even clearer in the prose
work *Det eviga leendet* (1920; Eng. tr. *The Eternal Smile*, 1934 and
later), which is constructed like a Renaissance narrative cycle. The
setting is the realm of the dead, where the dead tell of their life and
death, and philosophize about the meaning of life. They decide to
seek out God, to demand an explanation. God proves to be an old
forester who does not know why he created the earth and humankind. But then he devises a philosophy of life: devotion to duty and
moderation, which opens the way to fellowship with other people.
Through their encounter with him, the dead experience consolation
and precisely this fellowship: They experience goodness itself—the
eternal smile.

Lagerkvist's attempt to reconcile himself with life succeeds. The
new faith attains its consummate expression in two volumes of poems,
with the significant titles *Den lyckliges väg* (The Path of the Happy
One, 1921) and *Hjärtats sånger* (Songs of the Heart, 1926). These
poems, in which Lagerkvist often reaches back to traditional rhymed
verse forms, express how his experience of love changes his life and
conquers the anxious darkness of his youthful works. In other poems,
however, particularly in *Hjärtats*, reconciliation is absent. They bear
witness to the fact that Lagerkvist was unable to push aside the problem of suffering and evil. But the pain is not revealed, as it had been
earlier, in unarticulated lamentation; rather, it is lyrically expressed,
as in the introductory poem "Torso":

Only you, my bosom, is left,
you who can suffer,
you who can feel the depth of pain
but not complain.
My mouth is dust,
crumbled in a strange soil,

my throat is dust,
cannot call out its anguish.
Broken into fragments
my limbs lie
in the gravel of the road
to be trodden upon by all.

Tr. Marianne Forssblad

In the collection of stories *Onda sagor* (Evil Tales, 1924), light and darkness again combat each other; in *Det besegrade livet* (The Conquered Life, 1927), a collection of aphorisms inspired by Ekelund, and structured as a long monologue, the gap between humans and life becomes unbridgeable. But in this work, in the drama *Han som fick leva om sitt liv* (The Man Who Was Permitted to Relive His Life, 1928), one of Lagerkvist's greatest stage successes, and in the volume of realistic short stories *Kämpande ande* (Fighting Spirit, 1930), his faith in humans, who are placed in the cruel, irrational game of life, shines through.

The political crises of the 1930s are mirrored in Lagerkvist's writing. The aggression of the totalitarian states deepened the pessimism of this writer who was so sensitive to his times. But it also sharpened his will to fight for the humanistic cultural heritage. In 1933 he stepped forth as a committed contemporary writer with the novella *Bödeln* (Eng. tr. *The Hangman*, 1936 and later). The first part is set in a medieval village inn, the hangman a red-hooded mute figure who listens to the drunken artisans and peasants as they tell tales about the destructive power of evil. In the second part the scene is a dance hall in a fascist world of the present, where the hangman is again the silent observer. Here Lagerkvist has resurrected the primitive quality of the medieval period in an even more sinister way and has clothed his characters in modern attire. In the Middle Ages the hangman was watched with anxious interest; now he is celebrated. He reveals himself at the end as the timeless, but suffering, embodiment of evil; he is condemned for eternity to take the guilt of all human beings upon himself, without finding salvation, not even through God.

Lagerkvist always occupied himself with the existence of evil. In 1944, in the novel *Dvärgen* (Eng. tr. *The Dwarf*, 1945 and later), he made the psychology of the evil will the object of an ingenious investigation. In the diary of a dwarf at the court of an Italian Renaissance prince the times and people are mirrored. The dwarf is able to comprehend only inhumanity, gruesomeness, and power; he is the incarnation of evil, which survives humankind, an Anti-Christ figure. Since he is the tool, or even the cause, of all evil, he ends up in prison, where he waits cheerfully for his release, since he knows that the world will soon need him again. The dwarf becomes a counterpart to the hangman—simultaneously a human being and a characteristic of the human race. In this work, perhaps his best, Lagerkvist is more successful than he has ever been, effectively combining symbolism with realism and employing the highest forms of verbal expression. The dwarf, possessing the features and the three-dimensional figure of a human being, is clearly distinguished from the magnificent and extraordinarily vividly portrayed life of a historical epoch.

This great symbolic work was the first to bring Lagerkvist close to the reading public. International fame—and the Nobel Prize in 1951— came to him with the novel *Barabbas* (1950; Eng. tr. 1951 and later). Lagerkvist's struggle with suffering and the search for God is continued in the figure of the liberated robber who, incapable of loving or sacrificing, but filled with a vague longing for something beyond himself, becomes a symbol for the loneliness and the unquenchable drive for destruction in humankind. He is a chosen one, selected for a life of isolation. Barabbas would like to believe, but has no God to whom he can pray. He sees the empty grave, but not the resurrected Christ; he does not understand Christ's message of charity, but is still linked to him and has the words "Christos Jesus" scratched into the pendant that is the emblem of his slavery. And when Barabbas believes he is helping the Christians in Rome, when he helps to spread the fire that was started by the emperor, this deed becomes a kind of confession of faith. He would like to serve not the emperor, but the crucified God. Barabbas is not a Christian, but he dies with them. When he is hanging on the cross, he speaks into the silence: "To you I yield up my soul." To whom is he speaking? To God? The question remains unanswered.

With *Barabbas* Lagerkvist began a new phase in his writing. In six later volumes the seeking and meditative aspect became even more prominent. In the collection of poems entitled *Aftonland* (1953; Eng. tr. *Evening-Land*, 1975), which is simultaneously wistful, resigned, and vehemently questioning, the author confesses that he himself is a lonely stranger, expressing his longing for a distant God:

> That the restlessness of my heart may never cease,
> That I may never have peace.
> That I may never become reconciled with life, nor with death.
> That my path may last eternally with an unknown end.
>
> Tr. Marianne Forssblad

In *Sibyllan* (1956; Eng. tr. *The Sibyl*, 1958 and later) the theme is the encounter of human with God. Lagerkvist brings together an old seeress from Delphi and the wandering Jew Ahasuerus. When Ahasuerus, who was cursed by Christ, asks about the meaning of his fate, the seeress tells him the story of her life: As a young girl she was selected to be the Pythia of the oracle, and in this office she has found happiness, but also horror. For God is not merely exalted and noble, but also jealous and gruesome. She has experienced nothing of that God of love whom Ahasuerus has encountered in the shape of the Son of Man and has rejected.

Only at the end of *Ahasverus död* (1960; Eng. tr. *The Death of Ahasuerus*, 1962) does the restless wanderer find peace in a quiet monastery, where he experiences Christ not as the Son of God, but as an unhappy fellow human being. This novel and the two following, *Pilgrim på havet* (1962; Eng. tr. *Pilgrim at Sea*, 1964) and *Det heliga landet* (1964; Eng. tr. *The Holy Land*, 1966), treat of restless souls, of pilgrims. The setting is the vaguely described European Middle Ages. Ahasuerus has a comrade, Tobias, who is also an unwilling wanderer, an unharmonious and guiltladen man who is possessed by an irresistible urge to go to the Holy Land. After the death of Ahasuerus, Tobias goes to the Holy Land on a pirate's ship. When he arrives there, he encounters a desolate world, where the shepherds know nothing of gods and temple ruins bear witness to a forgotten faith. At the end Tobias does achieve the reconciliation for which he has been longing. A dream figure of the Holy Virgin, resembling a girl whom he had disgraced in his youth, appears to Tobias. He confesses his guilt to her, is forgiven, and dies in peace when he experiences her love.

Lagerkvist's last book, *Mariamne* (1967; Eng. tr. *Herod and Mariamne*, 1968), carries a similar message of love. It is a historic and symbolic narration of the universal tragedy: the masculine, egoistic man of power who is unable to find happiness through the help of female empathy. The title figure is the unhappy wife of Herod the Great. She is filled with goodness and manages for a time to soften his hardness, but her love cannot, in fact, alter him. Finally Herod has her killed, his regime becomes more brutal than ever, and he dies alone and hated.

In his late work Lagerkvist strove for the greatest possible simplicity. The novels are composed as a series of highly detailed pictures, the words forming clear, harmonious sentences. Lagerkvist, who was a pathfinder for Swedish literature in his youthful works, now achieved the classical ideal of art as the unartificial. He joined the classical tradition of the nineteenth century and the writing of Rydberg and Heidenstam. His work asks humankind a question of conscience by portraying the fundamental struggle between Good and Evil—or are these two powers unequally matched? Does it not end far too often with Herod having Mariamne killed? It is Pär Lagerkvist's simple wisdom that the actions of humans are motivated in their innermost beings: The author equates narcissism and evil, on the one hand, and selflessness and kindness on the other—a thought not far removed from the Sermon on the Mount.

LYRICISTS OF THE 1930s

World War I and the following world crisis proved that the old values were bankrupt. Predominant were the banishment of all illusions, the experience of the transitoriness of existence, and the presence of a strong apocalyptic atmosphere inspired by Oswald Spengler's cultural pessimism in *Der Untergang des Abendlandes* (The Decline of the West, 1918-22). In many works of the period, a bitter feeling of homelessness is manifest; writers brood over the meaning of existence or seek among new value systems—psychoanalysis, Marxism, or nonsectarian mysticism—a replacement for what they have lost.

Lyrics characteristic of the decade were written by Nils Ferlin, Karin Boye, and a group of academic poets, Hjalmar Gullberg, Johannes Edfelt, and Bertil Malmberg. Formally this "academic" poetry follows a traditional pattern and can be regarded as a reaction against the deliberate naivete of Lagerkvist's style and the free verse of the Fenno-Swedish modernists.

Hjalmar Gullberg

Formal virtuosity, not least in rhyme technique, is characteristic of the work of Gullberg (1898-1961). A master of form, his work ranges from elegant, sharp epigrammatic verse through melodious songs to classical cantatas. Gullberg sardonically mixed solemn language and everyday turns of phrase in his philosophical and confessional lyrics. This was, perhaps, fashionable—one model being Birger Sjöberg—but it was also the expression of inner conflicts, of passion with irony, feeling with intellectual skepticism. In spite of his lack of illusions and prevalent melancholy, Gullberg believed in the existence of spiritual values. In his early work, written in 1927, 1929, and 1932, a religious admixture is present, and in the collection *Att övervinna världen* (To Overcome the World, 1937) he shapes his tendency toward mysticism into purely Christian symbols, his religiosity never taking on the character of an established faith.

In the 1940s Gullberg found himself in the midst of a creative crisis, which he did not overcome until 1952 when he published *Dödsmask och lustgård* (Death Mask and Garden of Pleasure). Gullberg's view of life had changed. He abandoned his view of the poet as a prophet called upon by God, for he felt that God was infinitely far away. In one series of poems, Christian motifs are combined with classical myths. Even his imagery has changed, influenced by foreign and Swedish modernistic lyric poetry. For Gullberg it was a question of "finding a poetic language," which could describe "the naked human being, the demythologized and unstylized human being." *Terziner i okonstens tid* (Terza Rima in Inartistic Times, 1958), and the last collection, *Ögon, läppar* (Eyes, Lips, 1959), synthesize Gullberg's later, form-bound style and freer associative verse. The poems contain variations on and summaries of previous themes: the vocation of the poet, and doubts about that vocation, Gullberg's personal struggle with antiquity, on one hand, and Christianity, on the other, suffering and death. Against Gullberg's characteristic loneliness is set the feeling of a new-found human community, expressed in a series of love poems that are simple in form, introspective in mood, and musical in tone.

Johannes Edfelt

The early poetry by Edfelt (1904–   ) was strongly influenced by Gullberg. Not until the volume *Högmässa* (High Mass, 1934) did his personal, strongly pessimistic originality break through. It placed him in opposition to the primitivistic trend of the period, but it gave him relevance during the next decade. Edfelt's somber view of life dominates his collections *Hemliga slagfält* (Secret Battlefields, 1952), *Under Saturnus* (Beneath Saturn, 1956), and *Insyn* (Insight, 1962). In these a unique anti-metaphysical and satirical tone is heard, whereas *Ådernät* (Web of Veins, 1968) summarizes his entire work. In a number of prose poems and aphorisms, Edfelt's consciousness of death, which is present both as an external, unavoidable fact and as an inner, life-petrifying force, is expressed with convincing honesty.

Bertil Malmberg

The atmosphere of fear and rootlessness during the interwar period is also articulated in the poetry of Malmberg (1889–1958), which has its origin in Oscar Levertin and the German symbolists, notably Stefan George. Malmberg's poetry is not fully mature until after World War II in the volumes *Med cyklopöga* (With Cyclops' Eye, 1950) and *Lek med belysningar* (Play with Lights, 1953). The motifs have remained the same, but a development is noticeable from a late symbolic to a pure modernistic style—sketchlike, Ekelöf-influenced, observations about a shattered, eternally changing world.

Nils Ferlin

Closer to the period's pessimism stands Ferlin (1898–1961), whose poetry has a distinguished place in the Swedish ballad tradition of Fröding, Karlfeldt, and Dan Andersson. Ferlin's life and writing is an incarnation of the myth of the bohemian artist and is related to the writing of Villon and Bellman. Another point of departure is his occupation as a revue and cabaret writer, which inspired his use of the refrain and the surprising ends of poems which dominate his first collection, *En döddansares visor* (The Ballads of a Death-Dancer, 1930). Whereas here Ferlin's pessimism is still rather egocentric, a satirical note is added in his two best collections *Barfotabarn* (Barefoot Children, 1933) and *Goggles* (1938). A characteristic trait is his deep sympathy with forgotten misfits of society, often expressed through biblical imagery. Ferlin is a religious poet, even though rather critical of the established church. He never achieved a firm faith, but always brooded on the disquieting questions that deal with the meaning of a seemingly absurd world.

Karin Boye

A similar restlessness was present in the writing and life of Boye (1900–41), a life that ended in suicide. With religious earnestness and passionate tenacity, constantly driven to new solutions and horizons, she tested all the various messages of salvation of her time. She rebelled against the ecstatic Christianity of her youth; with the help of the heroic philosophy of Nietzsche and Ekelund, she sought to perfect her personality and to affirm even the darker side of life. This ideal characterizes her poetry collections entitled *Moln* (Clouds, 1922), *Gömda land* (Hidden Lands, 1924), and *Härdarna* (The Hearths, 1927), which are strongly influenced by Ekelund in their prophetic attitude, free rhythm, and choice of words.

Later Boye joined left-wing radical circles, became a persuaded disciple of psychoanalysis, and was unsuccessfully treated for depression several times. She later reported this development in her novel *Kris* (Crisis, 1934), one of the most disquieting religious books of the interwar period. In the following year *För trädets skull* (For the Sake of the Tree) was published, a volume of poems in which Boye attempted to create a unity of her divided nature, in verses alternating between moods of ecstatic affirmation of life and despair. A posthumous collection was selected and introduced by Hjalmar Gullberg, and published in 1941 under the title *De sju dödssynderna* (The Seven Deadly Sins), her most convincing work because of the depth and beauty of the lyric poems about love and death.

Among Karin Boye's prose works the most important is the utopian novel *Kallocain* (1940; Eng. tr. 1966), based on her impressions while traveling in Germany and the Soviet Union. *Kallocain* is related stylistically to Aldous Huxley's nightmare *Brave New World* (1932) and to Franz Kafka's novels; it depicts a totalitarian state in which total control of the masses has triumphed. All activities are societal, all private life is excluded. The inexorable system of controls achieves its highest point with the drug Kallocain, whose inventor, Leo Kall, narrates the story. The drug forces patients to betray their innermost thoughts, and gradually it becomes obvious that these are not always in line with state interests. When this truth drug has its effect on Linda, Leo's wife, and reveals tendencies counter to official policy, the dramatic conflict begins: the battle between loyalty to self and loyalty to the collective state. The novel ends tragically, but it is, like Karin Boye's lyric poetry, the expression of a defiant hope in the future of humanity.

PRIMITIVISM AND HUMANISM

Opposition in the 1920s to traditional moral concepts was an international phenomenon. One of the first representatives of this view was D. H. Lawrence, whose "sexual mysticism" strongly influenced Swedish literature for a number of years. A group of youth authors, called "The Primitivists," dreamed of a happier era resulting from the liberation of the life of instinct from conventional inhibitions. In 1929 five of them, all of a working-class background, published an anthology of modernistic poetry entitled *Fem unga* (Five Young Ones). The five were Artur Lundkvist, Harry Martinson, Gustav Sandgren (1904–   ), Erik Asklund (1908–   ), and Josef Kjellgren (1907–48), who wrote the first Swedish collective novel of importance, *"Smaragden"* ("The Emerald," 1939), depicting life onboard a freighter. The five were looking for contact with the older Swedish modernism, particularly with Fenno-Swedish modernism. They worked with Elmer Diktonius, and through his translations in *Ungt hav* (Young Sea, 1923) they encountered the modern American poets Edgar Lee Masters and Carl Sandburg. They differentiated themselves from earlier Swedish modernists by consistently worshiping instinctual drives, in the spirit of Freud and Lawrence, by their obvious interest in exotic themes and primitive peoples, and also by a stronger programmatic cult of the machine: "We will play life's new melody for humankind / the arousing, intensified rhythm of life, / quick, / bold, / steel-gleaming!" (Artur Lundkvist).

Artur Lundkvist

Lundkvist (1906–   ), the son of a small-scale farmer from the south Swedish region of Scania, grew up "in a no-man's land in the midst of farmers and workers." Soon, in opposition to his father as well as to the town, he assumed an attitude of protest, which he later directed against society and tradition. In his early work he was strongly influenced by the attitudes of Lawrence and in formal aspects by American poets like Whitman and Sandburg. Motifs from the big cities and life in the countryside characterize the collections *Glöd* (Glow, 1928), *Naket liv* (Naked Life, 1929), and *Vit man* (White Man, 1932), which demonstrate an ecstatic intoxication with life, as well as confidence in the instincts and desires of human beings. Religion and morality are foreign to him, and social reality is dissolved in a utopian dream world in which life blossoms in uninhibited freedom.

In Lundkvist's later collections of prose poems, such as *Nattens broar* (Bridges of the Night, 1936) and *Sirensång* (Song of the Sirens, 1937), romantic sensuousness yields to gloom. He is seeking the world of myths, and in dark and suggestive visions, along the lines of the program of the French symbolists, is trying to give expression to the unconscious life of the soul in a poetry that is scholarly and anything but spontaneous. However, in *Liv som gräs* (To Live Like Grass, 1954) and *Vindrosor, moteld* (Wind-Roses, Counterfire, 1955), he again turns toward an almost propagandistic reverence for sensuousness and the joy of life. The poems are filled with Lundkvist's faith in the power of the primitive and of poetry to change and renew life. They express a revolutionary criticism of sterile civilization, but also a search for community—now a central theme of his poetry. In Swedish literature Lundkvist's poems and imagery are epoch-making. He always writes in free rhythms that are close to lyrical prose; but, unfortunately, he is not a master of conciseness and restraint. Image is set next to image, sensuous impression next to sensuous impression, often in grandiose panoramas which can be tiring.

Lundkvist's fictional prose takes a variety of forms: naturalistic short stories such as *Berättelser för vilsekomna* (Stories for the Lost, 1961); novels like the historical *Snapphanens liv och död* (The Life and Death of a Guerrilla Fighter, 1968); semi-documentary narratives dealing with historical characters, used as a disguise for current issues, such as *Krigarens dikt* (The Poem of the Warrior, 1976), about Alexander the Great; and a genre combining prose and poetry, essays and aphorisms, as in *Det talande trädet* (The Talking Tree, 1960) and *Flykten och överlevandet* (The Escape and the Survival, 1977). The latter consists of a symbol-laden series of images, products of an exuberant fantasy, but full of precise observations. His search for reality led him on travels around the world, the result a great number of travel books. In several of these, *Vallmor från Taschkent* (Poppies from

Taschkent, 1952), and *Så lever kuba* (This Is the Way Cuba Lives, 1965), he declares his solidarity with the socialist world.

As the leading representative of primitivist literature, Artur Lundkvist occupies a significant position in Swedish literature, not least as a critic, essayist, and translator of foreign poetry. He prepared the way for the more recent American and Spanish literature. As early as 1932 he dealt with Whitman, Sandburg, Sherwood Anderson, O'Neill, Dos Passos, and Thomas Wolfe in his essay collection *Atlantvind* (Atlantic Wind); and as editor of the magazine *Karavan* (Caravan, 1934–35), he introduced Eliot, Lawrence, and Faulkner in Sweden. Lundkvist always wanted to introduce the newest trends in literature; he lacked both feeling for and interest in the past.

Harry Martinson

A more genuine and original poetic talent is Martinson (1904–78). When he was six his parents died, and thus began a constant migration from one farm to another. At sixteen he went to sea, where, before his literary debut, he lived as a stoker, day worker, and vagabond, making his way as far as South America and India. Martinson's early poetry shows great verbal imagination, but also indebtedness to Fröding and Kipling. He did not achieve his own style until the collection *Nomad* (1931); these poems treat of childhood, the sea and sailors, and, especially, nature. Like Lundkvist's poetry, they have a free rhythmical and rhymeless structure, bold imagery, and uninhibited associations. In detailed impressions of nature and apparently capricious observations, Martinson captures, with artful brevity and sharpness of delineation, the unity of the universe, the mirroring of the cosmos in the infinitesimal.

In the two travel books *Resor utan mål* (Aimless Travels, 1932) and *Kap Farväl* (1933; Eng. tr. *Cape Farewell*, 1934) Martinson achieves the same virtuosity as he had in his prose. The structure of the books is determined by the type and perspective of the experiences, not by his compulsion to describe particular routes. The sporadic commentary on social and cultural problems is held together by Martinson's utopia of the "world nomad," a symbol for the changeability of life.

The persuasive verbal fantasy that distinguishes all of Martinson's work reaches its full development in his autobiographical childhood recollections, *Nässlorna blomma* (1935; Eng. tr. *Flowering Nettle*, 1936) and *Vägen ut* (The Way Out, 1936), with which he reached a large reading public. Only then did he manage to liberate himself from his past, only then did his commitment to the problems of the political times of crisis result in an artistic turnaround. Vitalism and primitivism were no longer capable of inspiring Martinson; they had proved far too useful in the service of ideologies. A series of volumes of essays, whose observations of nature expand into large cultural perspectives and a positive philosophy of life, proved how Martinson had opened himself to the humanistic cultural tradition. In the name of nature and of humanity he battled against the glorification of effectiveness, of the mentality of competition, and of violence. The outbreak of World War II became for him first and foremost the result of the "civilization of violence," which was manifesting itself in the totalitarian states. Like several of the younger Swedish authors, he had a certain sympathy for the young Soviet nation, but faced the consequences of his new attitude in 1939, by voluntarily taking part in the Finnish Winter War against the Soviet Union.

In all of Martinson's works the human being stands at the center. This humanism is particularly noticeable in the poem cycle *Passad* (Trade Winds, 1945), in which he creates a grandiose picture of the fundamental division of western culture. Here Odysseus is contrasted with Robinson, that is, the humanist and poet is compared with the empiricist and scientist; Martinson considers it a catastrophe that these contrasts were never unified, that they were never synthesized in modern humankind. The trade wind becomes a symbol of the good will that is supposed to find the way to this unity, a way that leads to humankind itself:

> But new and wise explorers I have met
> have pointed inward
> toward the coasts of new Gondwana.
> And they have told me
> that hidden waves always wander there
> that oceans of riddles always flow there
> round never described islands of inner journeys
> and I have listened to them
> and sensed
> a new trade wind—a new land of Gondwana.
>
> Tr. Marianne Forssblad

In *Vägen till Klockrike* (1948, The Road to Klockrike; Eng. tr. *The Road*, 1955), Martinson takes up the theme again and shapes it with rogueish freedom and lyrical inventiveness. The structure of the work, a free succession of episodes, parallels the contents; the novel portrays the vagabond Bolle and other lost characters, their experiences and fates. Although the descriptions of setting and characters are excellent, it is the symbolic content that is essential. It is a novel about a man who places himself outside society and his times, but who finds inner equilibrium and reconciliation in the realm of meditation, nature, and the dream. In this book Martinson set down all that he had learned by living: the value of humanitarianism and the ability of humans to survive.

In the volumes of poems entitled *Cikada* (1953), *Gräsen i Thule* (The Grasses in Thule, 1958), and *Vagnen* (The Car, 1960) Martinson continued his protest against violence. In a series of artless nature poems and resigned meditations, he demonstrated his disgust for the life-style of people in an era of stepped-up pace and the atom bomb. In *Dikter om ljus och mörker* (Poems about Light and Darkness, 1971) and *Tuvor* (Tussocks, 1973) Martinson protested the exploitation and destruction of nature, and it became increasingly obvious in these collections that his artistic strength now lay in concrete observation. It is his poems dealing with the little things in nature—flowers, grass, insects—that most impress readers.

Cikada also contains twenty-nine songs that later became part of the verse epic *Aniara* (1956; Eng. tr. 1963), a vision of humankind on its way out of the world and beyond itself into eternity—the first work in Swedish that attempts to embrace astronomical reality in poetic form. Aniara is a spaceship that leaves an earth polluted with radioactivity. On the way to Mars the ship gets off course, owing to the asteroid Hondo—the name of the island upon which Hiroshima is located—and is thrown with its 8,000 emigrant passengers into an infinite trip through space. Aniara is the symbol of civilization, which transforms the powers of life that lie sleeping in the atoms into blind destructiveness. During the trip the course of cultures and religions is experienced, cults arise and are used as consolation, the songs of the earth become holy myths, until finally all is silent.

Aniara must not be understood only as prophesy. First, it is a new kind of lyric poetry, a cosmically and scientifically inspired space-travel poetry unique in world literature. But it also expresses purely artistic joy in description, in great and giddy cosmic perspectives, and contains ironic banality and various verbal effects. *Aniara* is one of the central accomplishments in the poetry of this century, a pioneering work that gained international attention, not least as an opera set to music by Karl-Birger Blomdahl with libretto by Erik Lindegren (see p. 258). Through his renewal of literary expression in this work Harry Martinson can take his place in Swedish literature beside the two other masters, Strindberg and Sjöberg. In 1974 he, with Eyvind Johnson, received the Nobel Prize.

Gunnar Ekelöf

As an experimenting modernist, Ekelöf (1907–68), born in Stockholm, exhibited in his early volumes of poems a certain intellectual kinship with the "Five Young Ones" (see p. 168), in particular with Lundkvist. On the other hand, he never embraced the gospel of primitivism, and he broke much more radically with the poetic formal tradition than did those poets who employed concrete and easily comprehensible images, and adhered closely to traditional syntax. Ekelöf's poetry presents a never-ending battle with three central human problems—the self, reality, and death—and attempts to reconcile these with one another. His experience of the surrounding world, and of life in general, is tragic. One way out of his conflict is the dream, the total dissolution of the self in mystical experience; another is merging with the universe, with life and death. Ekelöf's mysticism, colored by studies of oriental languages in London and Uppsala, is complicated, often paradoxical, filled with taut contrasts, and incomplete—which can also be said of the formal aspects of his poetry. His poems are never structurally complete, are never definitive expressions of thoughts and feelings.

In the late 1920s Ekelöf lived in Paris and there came into contact with the newest directions in the artistic life of the times, cubism and surrealism. Whereas his youthful poems were romantic and moody, modeled on Indian and Persian verse, his taste changed around 1929 in the direction of the radically modernistic, as demonstrated by his first book, *sent på jorden* (Late Arrival on Earth, 1932). These poems are a nihilistic revolt, not only against traditional poetry, but also against life; they flow into suicidal moods, thoughts of death, and visions of destruction. The collection was announced as being the first Swedish surrealistic poetry, a designation which Ekelöf accepted reluctantly since he, in contrast to the surrealists, controlled his free-flowing associations. His dreamlike imagistic language achieves a certain firmness through a kind of musical thematic technique, which emerges even more clearly in *Dedikation*.

In *Dedikation* (Dedication, 1934) the revolt against the traditional conception of reality has changed to belief in the task of the poet as a seer and redeemer in the spirit of Arthur Rimbaud. The collection is dominated by sumptuous imagery and a suggestive, lyrical rhythm, linking it to Swedish romanticism. In *Sorgen och stjärnan* (Sorrow and the Star, 1936), one finds a similar bright, but more accessible poetry, which is reminiscent of the Nordic ballad and contains larger compositions in which universality and isolation stand in antithetical contrast to each other.

Färjesång (Ferry Song, 1941) marks a new phase. One can point to the connection with earlier oriental poetry and philosophy, with Indian music, but T. S. Eliot also had a very significant influence on Ekelöf's style from this time on. The collection breaks with the surrealism of *Dedication* as well as with the easily accessible lyric poetry of *Sorrow and the Star*. Ekelöf had tried in his early work to turn from reality and in his later work to approach it again. Now he found a "third viewpoint, the objective one," dominant in *Non serviam* (1945) and *Om hösten* (In Autumn, 1951). He negates his self as a mere accidental and passive battlefield for the war of life. He seeks the unity behind everything, behind the self and the superficial variousness of reality, and elevates the border between life and death into a mystical experience of the dissolution of the self in the universe. He combines with this mysticism a sharp analysis of the contradictions of life.

Strountes (1955; a Frenchification of the Swedish expression "strunt," i.e., nonsense) consists of a series of fragmentary, apparently bagatelle-like poems and inspirations, in which Ekelöf, using satire and parody, humor and puns, explores both the possibilities of the linguistic material and the emptiness and senselessness of existence. In *Opus incertum* (1959) and *En natt i Otočac* (A Night in Otočac, 1961) he continues this antiaesthetic, even antipoetic direction; in despair over the poverty of life and of words, he sacrifices his rich and varied artistic resources in favor of an ascetic sketchiness. However, *A Night in Otočac* already signifies an advance toward a dearly acquired harmony. In the collection a great number of mutually irreconcilable concepts are considered, which the poet attempts to collect in a synthesis. The book ends in a tension-laden idyll:

> On the blue of the sky
> the clouds are colors
> for the wind's light brush.
> On earth they become shadows
> out of which dusk builds
> that realm of Hades
> where the dark violets grow.
>
> Tr. Marianne Forssblad

En Mölna-elegi (1960; Eng. tr. *A Mölna Elegy*, 1979) is the most unified of Ekelöf's works. Here he analyzes the self and its fantasies at that moment when the present is combined with the past and when the different layers of the self are revealed. The theme is introduced, varied, and interwoven throughout, as in a piece of music. The elegy also illustrates Ekelöf's relationship with the past. The poet in the first and last parts of the elegy experiences the situations that memory calls forth; the middle part is different. Greek and Latin quotations are printed on the left page, the Swedish text on the right. This resembles a free-flowing chain of associations in which the flood of words, reminiscences—of among others, the eighteenth-century Swedish mystic Emanuel Swedenborg and the Fenno-Swedish modernist Edith Södergran—recollections, thoughts, inspirations, and visions leads to purification in a consuming song of fire.

In the 1950s Ekelöf took several trips to the Mediterranean countries, resulting in frequent references to Mediterranean culture in his books. One volume resulted directly from his encounter with oriental culture: *Dīwān över Fursten av Emgión* (Divan over the Prince of Emgión, 1965), the first part of his major creative work, which also includes the collections *Sagan om Fatumeh* (The Tale of Fatumeh, 1966) and *Vägvisare till underjorden* (Guide to the Underworld, 1967). The poet transfers his conception of the present into a past world. Ekelöf portrays Byzantium in transition from antiquity to the Middle Ages, the blossoming of the culture in corrupt, mystical, and erotic decadence. The nucleus is a series of hymns and fantasies of the East Roman prince of Emgión about a madonna figure. She is Christian and heathen, the potentiality of all wishes, but also the disappointment of all longings. This figure is a kind of mythic conception, existing yet not actual, a camouflage of Ekelöf's own inspirations and his attitude as an artist. Ekelöf seeks to assert the identity of humankind through all times and cultures; in its universality his major work follows the same line as Martinson's *Aniara*. The main motif in the trilogy, however, is love; the theme is varied through symbolic pictures of woman as shadow, fate, virgin, and mother. Love eventually leads to abolishing the contradiction between life and death, death being recognized as part of a larger cycle.

Ekelöf is a learned poet. Like Eliot and Pound, he uses cultural history as material, as a constantly active reality. The two primary sources of his style are music and mysticism. He is the first Swedish poet to attempt to carry the vocabulary of music directly over to the language of literature. He frequently alludes to other poets, creating the effect of accord: Behind the written words one senses a more profound and more complicated connection. Ekelöf's conviction that human existence is senseless did not lead him to abandon the mystical attempt to break through, once and for all, the established limits of the self. A central thought in many of Ekelöf's poems is that the infinitely large, the cosmos, is constructed in the same way as the infinitely small, human cells. If one enters into the spirit of his world, one is often horrified by its hardness and despair. These are not confessions, but statements about what the world offers to humans in the chaotic present. But there are also wonderful sounds, fantasy-filled expressions, apparently without sense, or with that sense which the persons experiencing the poem can bring to it. Gunnar Ekelöf is the most difficult and the greatest modern poet in the Nordic countries.

Chapter 7

Norwegian Literature between the Wars

SOCIAL CRITICISM AND EXISTENTIAL UNCERTAINTY

Although Norway was able to maintain its external neutrality during World War I, many of the younger authors who appeared around 1920 were strongly influenced by the unsettling events of the period. They felt the ground shake beneath them, and they looked for a new stability. Since it was impossible to return to the time before 1914, they focused their hopes on the Communist Revolution of 1917.

Even before the war, the Norwegian labor movement had been revolutionary. Waste and excess, and inflation and lack of goods during the war years, were much more apparent here than in neighboring countries. Economic differences between the social groups after the financial crisis of 1920 and the general strike of 1921 were greater than ever.

Several writers embraced socialism, on the one hand, and Freud's theories, on the other (see p. 184). Among them were Arnulf Øverland, Sigurd Hoel, and Helge Krog (1889–1962), the last a Marxist drama critic and author of naturalistic and social dramas in the tradition of Ibsen and Heiberg. His works include *Underveis* (1931; Eng. tr. *On the Way*, 1939), and *Opbrudd* (1936; Eng. tr. *Break-Up*, 1939); he also wrote elegant and ironic comedies which have enjoyed great popularity in Scandinavia. These three writers joined the circle of young intellectuals writing for the journal *Mot Dag* (Toward Daybreak, 1921–36). However, most of them reacted with horror to the Moscow show

178 NORWEGIAN LITERATURE BETWEEN THE WARS

trials of the years 1936–38. Øverland particularly, in whom the proletariat had a sure advocate, clearly took another direction when the
trials and the following outbreak of war altered the ideological situation. Hoel, on the other hand, was much too ambivalent about the impending world revolution to gain poetic inspiration from that source.

Among the writers of the same age, Ronald Fangen (1895–1946)
was the only active opponent of the socialist trend. He too published
a journal, *Vor Verden* (Our World, 1923–32), in deliberate opposition
to *Toward Daybreak*. There was not really a group around Fangen, although many important authors were more in sympathy with him
than with Erling Falk (1887–1940), the editor of *Toward Daybreak*.
Among these authors were Sigrid Undset, Tarjei Vesaas, and the very
popular Sigurd Christiansen (1891–1947). Christiansen wrote two
novels, *To levende og en død* (1931; Eng. tr. *Two Living and One
Dead*, 1932) and *Agner i stormen* (1933; Eng. tr. *Chaff before the
Wind*, 1934), that made him his generation's most thorough portrayer
of ethical and religious conflicts. All these writers attempted to build
on the ethical values of prewar times, the most characteristic example
being Fangen himself. He wrote collections of critical essays and psychological novels, such as *Duel* (1932)—translated into ten languages
(Eng. tr. 1934)—and *Mannen som elsket rettferdigheten* (The Man Who
Loved Justice, 1934); in these works he attempted to combine the
liberal and conservative interpretations of society with a professing
Christian view of life. This attitude was manifest in his characters,
making them an interesting complement to those in Hoel's works.
Whereas Hoel had appropriated some of Freud's theories, Fangen was
influenced by Alfred Adler's psychology of the individual; if Hoel
found literary inspiration in, among other places, Hjalmar Söderberg's
fine-honed prose, Fangen—and Sigurd Christiansen—were particularly
stirred by Dostoevsky's thorough knowledge of human nature.

Cora Sandel

Outside all political groups stands Sandel (pseud. for Sara Fabricius,
1880–1974), who, like no other Norwegian writer, has been able to
interpret the inhibitions and feelings of inferiority of women placed
in a callous world. Her trilogy *Alberte og Jacob* (1926; Eng. tr. *Alberta and Jacob*, 1962), *Alberte og friheten* (1931; Eng. tr. *Alberta
and Freedom*, 1963), and *Bare Alberte* (1939; Eng. tr. *Alberta Alone*,
1965) is a compassionate depiction of the painful development of a
woman toward independence in a narrow petty-bourgeois milieu, a
development that finally leads to her liberation as an artist. In her
short stories Cora Sandel constantly returns to female characters who,

like Alberta, long for freedom and suffer in an unfeeling, hostile environment. The remarkable story, later dramatized, of the encounter of the dressmaker Katinka with a Swedish sailor in *Kranes konditori* (1945; Eng. tr. *Krane's Café*, 1968)—two lonesome and unconventional people who feel sympathy for and understanding of each other—is a variation of the Alberta motif, as is Cora Sandel's last novel, *Kjøp ikke Dondi* (1958, Don't Buy Dondi; Eng. tr. *The Leech*, 1960).

Arnulf Øverland

The only great lyricist in Norway during the 1930s, Øverland (1889–1968) certainly belongs to the generation of Wildenwey and Bull. However, the decisive influences on his work are from a different era. For no other Norwegian author did World War I, and even more the postwar period, signify such a sharp separation of past from present. His youthful poetry from 1911 to 1915 did not arouse particular attention from critics or the reading public. Death and isolation were very significant themes, and it was clear that Øverland was picking up where the lyric poetry of the 1890s left off. With *Brød og vin* (Bread and Wine, 1919) he dedicated himself to poetry about his own epoch. He fought against the Germany of his time and attacked with biting scorn the hunger blockade of the allies. The poetry of the self had given way to bloody portrayals from the battlefield hospitals; the aesthetic egocentric had become a moralist, prophet, and indignant satirist.

In the fall of 1922 Øverland began to write in *Toward Daybreak* (see p. 177) and adopted a socialist view of society. From his sense of fellowship with oppressed people during the war, it was only a short step to sympathy with the oppressed of all nations; in *Berget det blå* (Blue Mountain, 1927) this sympathy grows to full strength. The book is a collection dominated by profound intellectual poetry. It is introduced with the cycle "Riket er ditt!" ("Thine Is the Kingdom"), which portrays in biblical terms the slavery of humankind and the migration to the promised land of solidarity. Øverland was not particularly inclined toward Christianity and its teaching of reconciliation, but one thing notable is that he—the belligerent atheist—was bound more than most poets to religious symbols and wrote verses linked to a purely Christian world.

Øverland's next collection, *Hustavler* (Laws of Living, 1929), is the most varied of all his work. It consists of simple ethical poems about love of one's fellow humans, the blending of social and national elements in antichauvinistic patriotic hymns, and several self-critical revolutionary songs in which the longing of the poet is directed either toward a new era of brotherhood and justice or toward the unknown.

After Hitler's accession to power, Øverland was one of the first in Norway to recognize the threat. Precisely because he so loved German culture and felt ties to personalities like Heine, Schopenhauer, Nietzsche, his reaction was very strong. When the war broke out in 1939, he changed his attitude once again. He who had created a scandal with his Communist and anti-Christian agitation now gathered the Norwegian people together. His poems of resistance, not war poetry but lyrics of peace, circulated secretly and were not printed until 1945 in the collection *Vi overlever alt* (We Shall Live Through All), one of the most widely distributed volumes of poems in Scandinavia. The most famous was probably the visionary poem of the concentration camps, "Du må ikke sove" ("You Must Not Sleep"), and even today this poetry about war and brutality has value beyond that of the documentary. Øverland was already under arrest by the summer of 1941, and from the spring of 1942 until the end of the war he was in "protective custody"—still writing illegally—in the concentration camp at Sachsenhausen.

In *Tilbake til livet* (Back to Life, 1946) Øverland published lyric poems that did not fit into the framework of his previous collection. This volume contains his last revolutionary poem, "Masken" ("The Mask"), an existential speculation on the power of the unconscious and the problem of estrangement. Do earthly life and the human soul merely represent a reflection of a deeper, unknown world, an eternity toward which our minds should strive? This breath of platonic mysticism is never taken further. Øverland does not strive for any solution but concentrates on this world.

This link with reality is to be found above all in the volumes of poems entitled *Fiskeren og hans sjel* (The Fisherman and His Soul, 1950) and *Sverdet bak døren* (The Sword behind the Door, 1956), in which themes such as home and children—reflections of Øverland's own private relationships—are taken up for the first time in simple, somewhat monotonous language.

On the other hand, Øverland's last three collections contain a more complicated, symbolic, intellectual poetry. *Den rykende tande* (The Smoldering Wick, 1960) is in part a stocktaking of reality, seen with the clear vision of age. Old truths are shown in a new light, with altered contours, and Øverland describes them powerfully—when he is not resigned. Through the straightforward approach to death in *På Nebo bjerg* (On Nebo Mountain, 1962) and *Livets minutter* (The Minutes of Life, 1965), Øverland's late work takes on a unique tone. He writes about death, which he approaches through his aging, looks back self-appraisingly, and formulates his images of recollection with characteristic verbal precision and careful rhythm. It is the stern teaching of the old poet that the last and innermost things are not accessible. We surround the mystery and are ourselves surrounded by it.

Even in the postwar years Øverland took part in contemporary disputes with undiminished strength. He turned sharply against Soviet foreign policy and the powerlessness of the United Nations, intervened in the Norwegian language dispute in favor of the conservative *riksmål* (see p. 18), and described lyrical modernism as "speaking in tongues from Parnassus," a description that was regarded by many young writers as a betrayal of art. Øverland's lyric accomplishment has often been compared with that of Heine, he himself never concealing that the German poet was his immediate model. Like Heine, he was no formal experimenter, no artistic renovator. The most essential paradox of Arnulf Øverland's poetry is that, both in content and form, it is an antipoetic poetry. Nevertheless, it presents a wealth of nuances and simple greatness.

Sigurd Hoel

Hoel (1890–1960) was a narrator, a cool analyst and ironic commentator—one of the best literary critics and essayists in Norway. He, the son of a teacher, was born on a farm in the east Norwegian village of Nord-Odal. Without ever denying his home region and nationality, he became a confirmed modern, cosmopolitan intellectual figure. His background includes his home valley and Europe between the wars, the old peasant culture and that of the modern city.

Hoel's literary breakthrough, *Syndere i sommersol* (1927; Eng. tr. *Sinners in Summertime*, 1930), is a humorous satire about young postwar intellectuals, eager Freudians, who spend a summer together on an island. In contrast to the older, prejudiced generations, they believe themselves to be entirely free of all inhibitions and illusions; nevertheless, they bring with them ample amounts of jealousy, old-fashioned concepts of love, and confused feelings. Hoel is making particular fun of psychoanalysis, although he was most responsible for introducing the modern psychoanalytical form of the novel in Norway (see p. 184).

More significant is *En dag i oktober* (1931; Eng. tr. *One Day in October*, 1932), modeled on Elmer Rice's play *Street Scene* (1929) and the first Norwegian attempt to write a "collective novel." The plot is set in an apartment house in Oslo, the inhabitants being the "major character." On an October day they experience a shock: A young divorced woman in the house commits suicide, and readers witness the revelation of the miseries of her life. Her disappointing marriage had been dominated by anger and hate, pettiness and shabbiness. In a penetrating psychological study, which interrupts the collective form of the book and the classical unities of time, space, and action, the diary entries of her scientist husband Dr. Ravn, are presented, demonstrating how unsuited he, a man of the intellect, is for marriage. And still the author allows us to suspect, behind the careful report, another explanation for the unsuccessful marriage. For Ravn himself experiences moments of merciless self-examination in which he recognizes that he perhaps merely used science as a pretext to escape from his marriage.

In Hoel's most penetrating psychological work of the interwar period, *Fjorten dager før frostnettene* (Fourteen Days before the Frosty Nights, 1935), a central place is occupied by the motif of the man who deserts his beloved because he is incapable of love. On his fortieth birthday Dr. Holmen takes stock by asking himself the unpleasant question: "What have I had from my life?" He is a typical figure in Hoel's work: a man in his best years, who examines his life critically and discovers that the cause of his present emptiness and loneliness must be sought in the fateful failure of the love of his youth.

In *Arvestålet* (Ancestral Steel, 1941) Hoel shows a surprising knowledge of Norwegian folklore and tradition, indicating how deeply he was rooted in the old peasant culture. The novel is a preliminary study to the work that is possibly Hoel's greatest artistic achievement, *The Magic Ring*. Between these two books lie several novels dealing with events from World War II and the German occupation, as well as from the postwar era.

During the German occupation Hoel was forced to flee to Sweden in 1943. There he began *Møte ved milepelen* (1947; Eng. tr. *Meeting at the Milestone*, 1951), the book that asks an important question about the war years more emphatically than did any other Norwegian book: Why did so many Norwegians become traitors to their country? To what degree are we all responsible for this? In tragic portrayals of human beings who have bungled their lives, we experience how "someone can be condemned to ruin on account of an idée fixe, another because of a lifetime lie, a third because of the instincts that led him astray, a fourth because of unparalleled stupidity." Even the first-person narrator is not nearly as flawless as he believes himself to be. True, he has not betrayed his country, but he has done something equally fateful; he has betrayed his love. Like Holmen, he once experienced a great and liberating love; like him, he was too cowardly and inhibited to accept it, thus betraying the holiest thing in life. Later, punishment overtakes him: His son, born in secret, has become a collaborator. Thereby this child, who has been denied, becomes a symbol of the Naziism within ourselves: All of us bear the responsibility, or even the guilt, and are affected by fate. *Meeting at the Milestone* contains gripping descriptions of the occupation years, but is most absorbing because of its sophisticated structure and the constant shifts between different time planes, a technique that one finds even in Hoel's prewar novels. The past constantly breaks into the present of the novel in the form of reflections, recollections, and associations.

Two other works with retrospective structures are *Jeg er blitt glad i en annen* (I Have Fallen in Love with Someone Else, 1951), an uneven novel about the generation from *Sinners in Summertime* seen twenty-five years later, and *Stevnemøte med glemte år* (Assignation with Forgotten Years, 1954), which, like *Meeting at the Milestone*, analyzes the relationship between the dramatic events of 1940 and the following period. The main character is one of the deceased heroes of the battle against the German occupation forces. At the beginning of the story he has been dead for fourteen years. However, a group of people still live in his shadow, plagued by constantly growing doubts whether it is right that this man is able to exert such power over them. Gradually the comparisons between that time and the present organize themselves into a pattern different from the official one, forcing the friends of the dead man to come to terms with the self-betrayal in their own lives.

In Hoel's last novel, the powerful saga *Trollringen* (The Magic Ring, 1958), fantasy can again unfold freely, unburdened by the satiric comments on the period that pervade most novels contemporary with *The Magic Ring*. A gloomy and impoverished village milieu surrounds young Håvard, a stranger who marries the widow Rønnau. The marriage has begun with guilt and betrayal on both sides, and "the magic ring," the past which is taking revenge, captures him. Håvard had been engaged to a girl from his own community before Rønnau lured him into marriage by pretending to be pregnant with his child. After ten years of marriage Rønnau dies an accidental death and Håvard is accused of her murder. He finds the indictment a higher justice, for he incurred guilt by abandoning his fiancée. Thus begins a suspenseful plot, which ends as bitter tragedy.

The belief that acknowledging one's errors has a liberating effect underlies Hoel's fictional works and his essays. Like everything he created, his essays testify to a strong and sensitive intellectual gift, a barometer of the time which constantly and instantaneously registered everything new. As a journalist Hoel also intervened decisively in the political and literary life of the times.

IN THE SHADOW OF WORLD WAR II

Around 1930 a succession of new authors made their appearance: Tarjei Vesaas, Aksel Sandemose, Nordahl Grieg, and Johan Borgen. Their work was influenced by the period's economic crises and the growing political tension, and it was constantly attentive to the themes of the day. The ideological battle became more intense, the contrasts more sharply focused; the excesses of the dictatorships challenged these writers to a psychological investigation of human nature. Psychoanalysis, which had been introduced by Hoel in 1924, found a much wider and less critical audience in public discussion in Norway than in the other Nordic countries; it called forth a literature that turned against authoritarian upbringing and bourgeois morality, for instance in the works of Hoel and Sandemose. In other instances psychoanalysis had a superficial and vulgar effect. A reaction to this writing occurred as early as the beginning of the 1930s. Grieg mocked psychoanalysis and its disciples: Social criticism and political struggles were, in his opinion, far more important than psychological rarities.

Writers were much influenced by the many translations of modern foreign, above all American, literature. Particularly valuable was "Den gule serie" ("The Yellow Series"), edited by Hoel, in which more than fifty volumes were published between 1930 and 1940. Among the authors were Kafka, Faulkner, and Hemingway; on the other hand, a representative of primitivist neo-romanticism. D. H. Lawrence, was not translated until six years after his death. In general, one does not find in Norway or in the other Nordic countries, the "primitivism" that characterizes Swedish literature. On the other hand, in Norway apart from Vesaas's work, there is no romantic break with the realistic style, as there was in Denmark with Nis Petersen, Kaj Munk, and Karen Blixen, in Sweden with Harry Martinson, and in Finland with F. E. Sillanpää. Further, one does not find in Norwegian literature the sociological grasp of Danish authors like Hans Kirk and Knuth Becker, nor anything akin to the great autobiographical novels of such Swedish writers as Johnson, Fridegård, and Lo-Johansson, or Finnish writers such as Toivo Pekkanen.

Tarjei Vesaas

Vesaas (1897–1970), a farmer's son from Eastern Telemark, was the Norwegian author who broke most consistently with the realistic novel. The essential thing in Vesaas's books is not so much what the people say as what they leave unsaid, not so much what they think as what they feel and sense.

The lyrical, occasionally sentimental tone of the early works, the somewhat uncontoured portrayal of people, in part influenced by Selma Lagerlöf, gave way to strict realism and a tension-filled plot in *Dei svarte hestana* (The Black Horses, 1928). It is a novel in the popular tradition: Each of the characters is based on a single characteristic or passion, and the plot is constructed on a very concrete theme. The theme is the struggle between a passion for gambling and a passion for love, a struggle that takes place in the family of a prosperous farmer and that ends with the death of the main character and his wife's subsequent renunciation of the lover of her youth.

At the beginning of the 1930s Vesaas again drew near to a lyrical romantic style and wrote novels in which the borders between symbolism and realism, portrayal of people and milieu, were somewhat blurred. One such work is the rather long-winded tetralogy about *Klas Dyregodt* (1930–38). Common to these books is an impending mood of catastrophe, which becomes intensified in *Sandeltreet* (The Sandalwood Tree, 1933), a novel about the mystery of birth and death. In a style influenced by German expressionism, Vesaas expresses his fear of the approaching war in the pacifist drama *Ultimatum* (1934); however, this anxiety is rendered with greater artistic maturity only after 1940, influenced by international politics, in both the novels and the short stories. These works have earned for Vesaas a place among the most significant Scandinavian authors of the twentieth century.

In *Kimen* (1940; Eng. tr. *The Seed*, 1964) catastrophe spreads over a peaceful island community like a mass suggestion. The catastrophe is kindled in the portrayal of a merciless hunt for a mentally disturbed man who has killed a girl. Behind this external plot a universal drama is playing itself out: Hatred and the primitive desire for revenge achieve power over the people and seduce them into lynching the hunted man. Humanity arises, however, when the murderers recognize their guilt and accept it.

Vesaas's next novel, *Huset i mørkret* (1945; Eng. tr. *The House in the Dark*, 1976) is his postwar work that comes closest to the portrayal of the present. It is clearly a book about the occupation of Norway, yet the plot is elevated to an allegorical plane and simultaneously describes the essence of evil. Occupied Norway is symbolized by a large, inaccessible house with innumerable rooms and corridors, in whose center the "Arrow People" rule, and from which point they terrorize the other inhabitants. The author has eliminated all description, all external settings which could distract the reader, in order to concentrate on a portrayal of the human soul in its struggle with internal and external powers. He succeeds in creating stylized, general human types and scenes of simple and deep humanity.

In *Bleikeplassen* (The Bleaching Place, 1946) the realistic and symbolic are totally blended. The result is a suggestive world—penetrated by the longing for purity and truth—the setting for the battle between light and darkness, which ends in spiritual purification and salvation through death. Johan Tander is possessed by a passion for one of the young girls in his laundry; when another man becomes her lover, Tander perceives it as a crime against himself and believes he is justified in doing away with his rival. The people around him see the impending catastrophe, but only his wife Elise reacts to it and manages through her love to neutralize the demonic magic and burst the circle of hatred around her husband.

The combination of symbolism and realism is less convincingly executed in *Tårnet* (The Tower, 1948), a novel about adolescent love, and in *Signalet* (The Signal, 1950) the symbolic language seems too abstract and contrived. However, *Vårnatt* (1954; Eng. tr. *Spring Night*, 1964 and later) is a concrete, action-filled novel about the human process of maturing. Vesaas achieves mastery in *Brannen* (The Fire, 1961), a thoroughly poetic protest against evil—not in a single human being, but in the world. Only one character appears who has a name; Jon feels one day that someone is calling him. Like a refugee he is pursued from one experience of evil to another. The book is a shattering Kafkaesque nightmare about destructive power. But Jon's initiation into the depths of the human soul, and into a life in which terror reigns, transforms him when he experiences goodness and positive values. He comes to recognize that nothing can exist without this struggle between light and darkness, life and death. Humans have an absolute responsibility toward life and their fellow humans.

Fuglane (1957; Eng. tr. *The Birds*, 1968) is based on the same premise: When Mattis discovers the love between his sister Hege and the woodcutter Jørgen, he knows he is standing in their way. Because he is retarded he is entirely dependent on his sister. The situation becomes graver when the stranger appears one day and stays to live in the hut. As a result, Mattis places his life in the hands of fate: His death upon the water is a sacrifice for Hege and her love. *The Birds* is a study of a human being with a weak intellect and a pure heart. With extraordinary poetic power and psychological fantasy, Versaas has entered into the thoughts and feelings of such a person, into a world where everything is symbol and mystery.

Isolation and the mystery of salvation are again present in the novels *Is-slottet* (1963; Eng. tr. *The Ice Palace*, 1966 and later) and *Bruene*

(1966; Eng. tr. *The Bridges*, 1969 and later), the first, and more significant, being an ecstatic and suggestive vision. Two girls, Siss and Unn, are mutually attracted. A bond is created between them, through which they feel like one person. But behind their happiness lurks a religious anxiety that they have done something sinful. This awareness drives Unn out into the ice formations, into the "ice palace," never to return. The plot is basically only an introduction to what Vesaas actually wants to portray: the bond of the deserted Siss with her absent friend beyond death and the faith in their common secret. This bond prevents the previously extroverted Siss from re-establishing contact with her surroundings. Finally, when winter is past, Siss experiences liberation. She is liberated from the ice palace, in whose center sits the frozen girl, a symbol of the ice within humans, of the winter of the soul which can destroy us all.

The genre of the novel dominates Vesaas's work. But he emerges as one of the best short-story writers of Norway with his collections *Vindane* (The Winds, 1952) and *Ein vakker dag* (A Beautiful Day, 1959). The setting is mostly rural, and the characters are in constant contact with nature. The intermingling of the spiritual condition of the individual and the color and tone of the environment inspired Vesaas to create exceptional novellas, whether he is portraying the reaction of the primitive or the problem world of the modern intellectual. Particularly touching are his portrayals of children and their small but important world, their ability to grasp what grownups do not understand. Vesaas's novellas, in contrast to his novels, are more accessible, without ever being banal. Here, too, he is the great master of symbolism.

The same is true of Vesaas's last novel, suggestively titled *Båten om kvelden* (1968; Eng. tr. *The Boat in the Evening*, 1971). The sixteen sections are semi-autobiographical sketches, less experiences than recollections and images. The single parts blend into a musical and thematic pattern, into an image of the enigmatically miraculous and the mysteriously threatening elements in nature and in human existence.

It came as no surprise when, in 1946, Vesaas made his appearance as a lyricist with the collection *Kjeldene* (The Fountains) composed of poems that were conventional in form and content. As early as 1947 a new volume appeared, *Leiken og lynet* (The Game and the Lightning), in which his unique gift for creating symbols was evident. His style developed under the influence of Edith Södergran's poems in the three collections published in the period 1949 to 1956, followed in 1970 by his last collection *Liv ved straumen* (Life by the River). In these poems Vesaas achieved such conciseness and expressionistic power that he became one of the first and most original representatives of lyric modernism in Norway (see p. 297). By eliminating everything superfluous, and leaving only words and images that were bearers of associations, he created in his best poems a uniquely suggestive tension; in others, however, the extreme conciseness smothered the poetry.

The central motifs are the same as those in Vesaas's other work; the metaphysical evil of the time, the powers within and outside the uprooted person of the twentieth century, and the fear of catastrophe. Like Pär Lagerkvist in Sweden and Martin A. Hansen in Denmark, he created his own rich language of symbols, through which he expressed in a very intimate artistic way the tension of the times and the tension within himself. His creative work is an inspired attempt to approach as closely as possible the basic experiences that have exercised their power over his entire life, an attempt to capture the incomprehensible, the inexpressible.

Nordahl Grieg

A greater difference than that between Vesaas and Grieg (1902–43) is difficult to imagine. Vesaas's work is reflective and his favorite genre is the novel; Grieg is primarily a lyricist and dramatist who eagerly attempted to unite life and poetry. He went out into the world, as a sailor, vagabond, and journalist to find the material for his writing rather than plumbing the human intellect and psyche. His strong sense of his times sometimes swelled to a lyrically patriotic feeling, which he then translated into action. As a soldier, he was among the Norwegian troops who retreated northward in 1940; he fled with the government to England and was piloting a plane when he was shot down over Berlin. The manner of his death probably enhanced his reputation beyond what his talent really merits.

In 1927 Grieg had traveled as a war correspondent to China. From his impressions of the revolution there, he shaped the play *Barrabas* (1927). Here the question of the justification of power is illuminated through the contrasts of revolution/passive resistance and violence/pacifism. It is illustrated by a young man who has to choose between Barrabas and Jesus, and allows himself to be overpowered by the attraction of brutality into choosing Barrabas. The play has technical flaws, but as an expressionistic avant-garde piece, as a transplanting of Russian and German theatrical experiments in the 1920s, albeit a naive one, it is significant.

The socialistic radicalism of *Barrabas* is also present in the poetry collection *Norge i våre hjerter* (Norway in Our Hearts, 1929), but was entirely overlooked by the public. They noticed only the declamatory, patriotic effects, which made Grieg more popular than any other Norwegian poet since Wildenwey. But after a two-year stay in Moscow from 1932 to 1934, Grieg returned a persuaded communist, and his criticism of capitalist society became increasingly sharper. In the drama *Vår ære og vår makt* (Our Glory and Our Power, 1935) his criticism is implacable. In a series of scenes from the worlds of shipowners and sailors, Grieg employs a distinctly filmic technique to portray how profiteering Norwegian seafaring interests ruthlessly exploited sailors in World War I, sending them heedlessly to their death.

In 1937 Grieg traveled to Spain as a war correspondent. He incorporated his observations and experiences there in his major stage work, the drama of ideas entitled *Nederlaget* (1937; Eng. tr. *The Defeat*, 1944). It was trenchantly contemporary, although the background is the Franco-German war of 1870–71 and the unsuccessful uprising of the Communards in Paris. The play focuses on this defeat, caused by a lack of brutality on the part of the revolutionaries. Their leader, the idealistic humanist Varlin, wanted to achieve victory "not through killing or dying, but through the creation of justice." The cynical Rigault, on the other hand, proclaimed the necessity of terror and denunciation in the service of the revolution. The drama ends with the recognition that "good can conquer only through violence."

Grieg himself saw armed battle as necessary in the contemporary situation. He expressed this view in the journalistic novel *Ung må verden ennu være* (The World Must Still Be Young, 1938), set partly in Moscow, partly in war-desolated Spain. The English philologist Ashley, who is studying Russian manuscripts in Moscow, comes under the influence of the fanatic girl Kira, who obeys all party orders, and he becomes sympathetic toward communism. Because of the Moscow Trials, however, Ashley draws back and becomes for Grieg a representative of passive western European humanism, which merely discusses and does not act. By contrast, Grieg, in his need to subordinate himself to the collective and to party discipline, has drawn a wholly positive and forceful portrait of communist-party members. Aesthetically and substantively the part of the book set in Spain is weaker; it is merely a series of hastily written, very loosely connected sketches about the brutal reality of the civil war; it does not compare with Malraux's novel of Spain, *L'Espoir* (Man's Hope), and Hemingway's *For Whom the Bell Tolls.*

Grieg's activity in the later war years was varied. Through his radio appeals from England he became a focal figure and a stimulus in the Norwegian fight for freedom. His greatest accomplishment, however, is his war poems, collected after the liberation in a volume entitled *Friheten* (Freedom, 1943; Eng. tr. *All that is Mine Demand*, 1944). Grieg was the most popular poet of the time, after Øverland. He took the basic theme of *Norway in Our Hearts* and carried it further in a series of poems that are among the most significant that have been written about war and the fatherland: "17. Mai 1940" ("May 17, 1940"), "Godt år for Norge" ("Good Year for Norway"), and "På Tingvellir" ("On Tingvellir"). They are free of any burden of tradition and bombastic patriotism. Pervasive are a burning faith in the goodness of human beings, thoughts of peace, and love for the stubborn will to live among the ruins.

Aksel Sandemose

A position between the spiritual analysis of Hoel and the social criticism of Grieg is occupied by Sandemose (1899–1965). In his work he is fascinated by the struggle between the individual and the masses. Although he believes that environment is the explanation for everything, and believes it impossible for human beings to break out of this environmental causality through acts of will, he is an individualist and opposes the dogmatic views of materialism and psychoanalysis.

Sandemose was born in the north Danish town of Nykøbing into a poor family. After his confirmation, he ran away to sea. In 1923 he published his first work, *Fortællinger fra Labrador* (Stories from Labrador). This volume and his other books from the 1920s were written and published in Danish. They are based on the author's experiences as a sailor and on observations made by the new settlers in Canada and Labrador. They are strongly influenced by Johannes V. Jensen, Joseph Conrad, and Jack London, but already show the traits characteristic of Sandemose's mature work: original portrayals of the sea and an interest in the instinct-dominated life of the soul. In 1929 Sandemose moved to Norway, where his mother had been born, and from then on he wrote exclusively in Norwegian.

The novel *En sjømann går i land* (A Sailor Goes to Shore, 1931) is the first book about Espen Arnakke from the Danish city of Jante, the Nykøbing of Sandemose's childhood. Off Newfoundland Espen escapes from the ship on which he has led a tormented life, constantly fighting for recognition from his comrades. In Misery Harbor he becomes friends with "Big John," whom he admires and envies, but whom he murders in a crime of passion when "Big John" seduces his girlfriend. After the murder Espen flees to Canada, where he lives as a farmhand. Sandemose tells how he struggles with his nightmarish act and overcomes his uncertainty. To do this, he has to examine his earlier life and confess to all the concealed but recognizable causes of his murder of "Big John."

In *En flyktning krysser sitt spor* (1933; Eng. tr. *A Fugitive Crosses His Tracks*, 1936), Espen attempts seventeen years later to understand why he became a murderer; it emerges that the cause is rooted in his childhood. The novel is divided into many, mostly disconnected, sections, which are not arranged chronologically. Dark memories of Espen's infancy alternate with experiences of his childhood and youth, portrayals of the milieu in Jante with reflections of the mature man. The novel is a strong attack on provincialism, envy, the competitive mentality in society, and the system of reciprocal repression, which Sandemose calls the "Law of Jante."

In these years, when Sandemose was working on the story of Espen Arnakke, he also published *Klabautermannen* (The Banshee, 1932), the expanded and revised version of a work he had written as a youth in Denmark. The banshee, who appears to superstitious sailors and prophesies shipwreck, here becomes a symbol of existential anxiety, the major theme of this dark romantic tale being the inner shipwreck of human beings. The atmosphere of death and destruction becomes intensified in the next psychological novel of the sea, *Vi pynter oss med horn* (1936; Eng. tr. *Horns for Our Adornment*, 1938). With unvarnished naturalism, Sandemose depicts the relationships between the crew members of a schooner on its way to Newfoundland, while acutely analyzing their subconsciouses using Freudian methods.

In 1943, during the German occupation, Sandemose had to flee to Sweden. The political situation in Norway lent color to *Det svundne er en drøm* (The Vanished Is a Dream, 1944), a novel in the form of diary entries and reflections of the Norwegian-American John Torson. The entries treat of a 1938–40 visit to his homeland, which Torson had left after an unhappy love affair. The memory of the girl Agnes remains in his subconscious and forces him to return after many years to re-experience the past. The basic theme, characteristic of Sandemose's other books as well, is the youthful experience that haunts, hardens, and finally destroys a man. The point of departure of the plot is a crime, the tale a mystery story. While Torson is in Norway his younger brother is accused of and condemned to die for a mysterious murder which, it seems, Torson himself committed. Did he act in a half-conscious state? He himself does not know. Gradually, as he writes, recollections emerge and details come together in a frightening pattern that shows him to be the murderer.

In *Tjærehandleren* (The Tar Dealer, 1945) it is again the past that has determined the protagonist's rebellion against and spite toward society. Audun Hamre selected his profession only as a cover; in reality he is a thief and a marriage swindler. The reports of how he steals money from widows and elderly unmarried women are exciting, the novel reading like a thriller; but, above all, these deeds represent his revenge against society for his misfortune, and his intense hatred. This is rooted partly in his relationship with his father, partly in that with his former wife. Far from everyone he builds a house from his ill-gotten gains, in which he lives with his mother, the only person he really loves. When she dies, he is left in complete loneliness. What remains to him is his contempt for human beings and his nihilism.

Other novels dealing with people's secret instinctual drives that are rooted in the past include the war novel *Alice Atkinson og hennes elskere* (Alice Atkinson and Her Lovers, 1949), and Sandemose's last significant novel, *Varulven* (1958; Eng. tr. *The Werewolf*, 1966), a sequel to which, *Felicias bryllup* (Felicia's Wedding), appeared in 1961. The werewolf symbolizes the repressions that prevent people from living happy lives. Humankind is victimized by the werewolf, but is its creator as well. The werewolf is hidden in everybody, but perhaps least in the three main characters of the novel, the poet Erling Vik, the wealthy farmer Jan, and his wife, Felicia. However, even they are harmed by experiences of their youth. Erling cannot forget the school-girl Gulnare, the great, chaste love experience of his youth. Felicia cannot forget that at the age of seventeen she was abandoned by Er-ling. This becomes important for both of them, and for their relation-ship, when Erling later, after she is married to Jan, becomes her lover. But *The Werewolf* would not be a Sandemose novel if love were not wedded to murder, lust to death—the two poles around which his fantasy always circles. This tension is generated by Felicia's murder, the numerous and complicated motives for which go back to the pe-riod of the German occupation. All the characters in the book are po-tential murderers. They are under suspicion, but have alibis. They have not murdered Felicia in the legal sense, but possibly in the depths of their werewolf souls.

Aksel Sandemose is one of the few writers who seriously delved into the teachings of psychoanalysis and thereby became a writer. Like Strindberg and Dostoevsky, he discovered that the irrational is real; his writing is a constant attempt to track down this incompre-hensible element. The chaotic nature of his books is traceable solely to this monomaniacal obsession, which for him represented the fight for his own soul.

Johan Borgen

The writing of Borgen (1902-79) is also permeated by restlessness and emotion, a constantly shifting play of complicated moods; at the same time he is the most inventive stylist among the artists who made their appearance in the 1930s. The central problem of his characters is the question of identity, the question of whether personality is more than a social product, created by the expectations of society and our own need for concealment. His characters are outsiders who are unable to find their way in sober everyday reality and are always on a quest or in flight from the world that society has created for them, looking for another, deeper reality which they sense must exist. Such a person is described in Borgen's first novel, *Når alt kommer til alt* (All in All, 1934), which is at the same time a strong attack on the sophisticated facade of politeness and attentiveness that prevents people from saying what they mean and relieving their unhappy spirits, injured by deception and concealment.

All of Borgen's succeeding dramas and radio plays, some very unevenly written, attack hypocrisy and social and psychological conventions. The most important work is *Mens vi venter* (While We Are Waiting, 1938),—inspired by Pirandello—which with its theme of fear of isolation and emptiness is linked to the mood of his first novel. The central figure in this experimental masterpiece, "The Tired One," is unable to make decisions. He is always fleeing from choice; to choose himself would mean to determine his identity. Although the first-person narrator in *All in All* hoped that something meaningful would occur if only he could escape from everyday life, it is unnecessary for "The Tired One" to break with any kind of milieu. He has long since left it behind and knows of no formal existence to which he can return.

Borgen's last drama, *Frigjøringsdag* (Day of Liberation, 1963), is a play of the absurd, with a series of plots involving anonymous, everyday characters, which reveal human stupidity and evil.

Borgen's short stories, from his first Hamsun-influenced collection, *Mot mørket* (Toward Darkness, 1925), to *Trær alene i skogen* (Trees Alone in the Forest, 1969), demonstrate his mastery of this genre and are unsurpassed in more recent Norwegian literature. In almost all of these works, the basic theme is the significance of childhood and love. Borgen seems to be omniscient in his understanding of the psyche of a child, as for instance in the story "Fuglen og Fristeren" ("The Bird and the Temptor"), which consists of the retrospective stream-of-consciousness accounts of five people. He works convincingly with a complex motif: our secret kinship with those juvenile delinquents who commit some terrible act in a moment of ecstasy and later are very successful in life if their deeds are not discovered.

It is characteristic of Borgen's love stories, as in the volume *Noveller om kjærlighet* (Stories about Love, 1952), that they treat of a love in which psychic harmony is more important than physical, a love that can liberate humans in moments of ecstasy from influences and memories, not primarily through passion, but through tenderness and warmth.

Borgen is a master of representing sudden outbreaks of forgotten or suppressed spiritual powers. The primary goal for him is not to *tell* a story or to reproduce a picture of external reality; rather, his short stories are studies, sudden dives into the dark ravings of the spirit or of a dark past, spotlights on the ironic paradoxes of human existence.

The first volume of Borgen's major work, the trilogy about *Lillelord* (Little Lord, 1955), is the story of a boy, Wilfred Sagen, from the protected middle-class world of Oslo just before World War I. His mother is a widow who clings to the child in him, not realizing that this unnatural upbringing is having precisely the opposite effect: The forced innocence causes the boy to develop a sovereign ability to dissemble. Among the best parts of the novel are the portrayal of the relationship of mother and son, based on tyranny and confidence, self-deceit and tenderness. But the stronger those bonds become, the stronger becomes his need for freedom. Wilfred slides into an absorbing double life and is forced more and more to encapsulate his mysterious world in a shell of hard, cold egoism. The spoiled youth has developed into a lonely man, who conceals behind the mask of his manifest good upbringing an amoral and destructive character.

The first volume makes a strong impression on the reader because it moves from painstaking psychological analysis to a broad poetic drama of fate. However, this total impression seems to crumble into broad analyses of details in the sequel, *De mørke kilder* (The Dark Sources, 1956). This volume does not have nearly the strength and consistent quality of the first. Here Borgen follows Wilfred into the interwar period, a time spent in rather dubious circles in Oslo and Copenhagen. In *Vi har ham nå* (We Have Him Now, 1957), we encounter Wilfred at the beginning of World War II. The Germans are occupying Norway, and it is not surprising that Wilfred perceives in this situation a unique opportunity to set into motion a novel double game. The reader learns indirectly that he has betrayed his half-brother, but also that he has helped a group of Jewish refugees over the border to Sweden. It would be incorrect to call him a Nazi. He is first and foremost a man who lives outside easy commitment, who seeks the truth in every individual situation, a man without values, without faith. The voluminous trilogy ends on the morning when Norway is again free. The final punctuation is the revolver shot of Wilfred's suicide.

Borgen's next novel *"Jeg"* ("I," 1959), demonstrates that human

beings are made up of a jumble of possibilities, which they often vainly attempt to unite for a short time to create usable images of their
volatile personalities. Matias Roos is divided to the core of his being.
To confirm his existence he seeks a specific guilt. On the drive into
the city it happens: He runs over a child with his motorcycle. Or does
he? It becomes evident that no accident has occurred; the scene with
the maimed girl must have played itself out in his imagination. Or did
he really kill a child? The child within himself? He senses that his inner
division must have occurred sometime in his childhood, and he attempts to regain his innocence.

The novel *Blåtind* (Blue Peak, 1964) yields a new and fascinating
variation on the identity problem. One of the major characters is a
Jewish woman, Nathalie, who has lost her connection with her earlier
self through her experiences in the concentration camp. Now she
longs for security and stability, and marries a Swedish commissioner
of refugees, Peter Holmgren, in whom she finds the certainty she is
seeking. It is revealed, however, that Holmgren, in another and deeper
sense, is on a restless flight from himself, from the fear of his cowardly
self, to which he has never been able to reconcile himself. He is filled
with an urge to change, a longing for the inaccessible. Thus it is logical
that Holmgren finally must force himself to conquer Blue Peak, the
symbol of the inaccessible goal; during this attempt he perishes.

Borgen's next novel, *Den røde tåken* (1967; Eng. tr. *The Red Mist*,
1973), gathers many of his most characteristic themes in a form—an
inner monologue—dictated by strict artistic logic. Through the entire
book the reader follows one consciousness, behind whose restless
search for stability is concealed a lost self, which committed a double
crime. The nameless protagonist is a murderer fleeing back into the
past, to the place and moment of the crime. While he climbs up onto
the city's freedom monument, the line between past and present blurs;
when he reaches the top, only one thing remains—the leap into emptiness. During the fall, a miracle occurs: He who has been paralyzed
throughout his life by the infinite possibilities of freedom, now sees
the mist lifting; he is no longer several characters, but one.

Min arm, min tarm (My Arm, My Intestine, 1972) is another variation on Borgen's major theme: the human search for coherence and
wholeness in life. The main character is hospitalized and brings with
him a bottle of wine which causes the death of a fellow patient. The
feeling of guilt releases a process of self-examination which brings
about a complete change in his personality. However, in *Eksempler*
(Examples, 1974), a novel about the dissolution of a marriage, Borgen
reveals a skeptical attitude toward the possibilities of gaining any in-

tegrity of character. He gives special attention to the role that language plays in the couple's mutual distrust, to the linguistic evasion that furthers the process of petrification into "examples."

In all his novels Borgen thus continuously explores existential aspects of the human condition. He has no moral message to deliver; he is a writer who always feels the need to expand his art and abandon his positions, unlike many authors who entrench themselves behind the art form they have developed and the positions they have attained.

Chapter 8

Danish Literature between the Wars

EXPRESSIONISM AND DISILLUSIONMENT

The outbreak of World War I marked a more significant turning-point in Danish literature than in the literature of the other Nordic countries. The tension in Europe was evident in press releases about increasing military budgets and nationalistic proclamations. Still the public was surprised by the outbreak of war. Denmark's neutrality became the basis of a powerful economic upswing; it was a time of stock-market speculation and new wealth, but also a time of inflation and bankruptcy. The threat of war intensified the appreciation of life. A new generation of lyricists emerged spontaneously, ecstatically affirming the glory of existence. The two most prominent personalities of this group, Emil Bønnelycke and Tom Kristensen, published a series of attention-arousing collections of poems marked by materialistic individualism and colorful expressionism. They were still far removed from the German expressionists, who had formed their particular style amid war and revolution.

Emil Bønnelycke

"To bring the images to bursting, to make the lines explode against one another, to have the colors shreek through sheer power and splendor" is a program that Bønnelycke (1893–1953) realized in his most famous collection, *Asfaltens Sange* (Songs of the Asphalt, 1918). Untraditional prose poems, influenced by Johannes V. Jensen's youthful poetry and Walt Whitman's universal affirmation of life, testify to a glowing enthusiasm for the technology of the modern metropolis and for his own time. But this euphoria lasted only five years. The powerful reaction, a feeling of being condemned to silence or bitter disillusionment, set in around 1921 and can be noted in virtually all expressionistic writing. To be sure, this period had begun promisingly with regard to internal politics: The eight-hour work day was introduced in 1919, and Denmark was reunified with North Schleswig in 1920, which, however, was followed by demonstrations and strikes in Denmark. At the end of the war there was much criticism and skepticism, and no one had confidence in the uneasy peace.

The position of the artist was very uncertain, both socially and morally. The ideals of western culture, as well as the peace movement and humanism, had gone bankrupt; the best that one could hope for was that these ideals could be newly recognized and defined, if one did not prefer nihilism. This ideological chaos culminated around 1925 in fierce debate.

Otto Gelsted

Gelsted (1888–1968) confronted this confusion with a rational, critical intellect, schooled in Greek poetry and Kant's philosophy, and characterized by a scientific recognition of the logical connection of all things. He was the first to react artistically against the materialism of the war years in the poem "Reklameskibet" ("The Show Boat") and the subsequent collapse of the modern world view in "Bøn til den moderne Mentalitet" ("Prayer to the Modern Mentality"). Gelsted left art criticism and socialist journalism behind him when, in 1920, he introduced psychoanalysis in Denmark with a translation of Freud's *Das Unbewusste* (The Subconscious) at the same time he published his first volume of poems, *De evige Ting* (The Eternal Things), influenced by Johannes V. Jensen. The love poetry of this collection evinces a split between instinct and rational thought, a dualism that also dominates the volume *Jomfru Gloriant* (Virgin Gloriant, 1923). Henceforth Gelsted strove for clarity and harmony, a development that found its most flawless expression in the serene collection *Rejsen til Astrid* (The Journey to Astrid, 1927), and in the volumes from 1929 to 1961—a poetry strict in form, rich in motifs, balanced and concise. The youthful feeling of isolation and homelessness yielded to an experience of fellowship and an acceptance of fate.

Tom Kristensen

As the creator of a new poetic mentality, the central figure of the

1920s was unquestionably Bønnelycke; however, as a poet and an intellectual personality, Kristensen (1893–1974) was far more significant. He learned from Johannes V. Jensen's zest for life, Whitman's language, Sophus Claussen's verbal magic, and much from Bønnelycke, who was a model for the Copenhagen scenery and language in the early collections, *Fribytterdrømme* (Pirate Dreams, 1920) and *Mirakler* (Miracles, 1922). With a purely artistic attitude toward existence as the point of departure, Kristensen seeks here to give life to the events in a metropolis in a new poetic form. He transforms external reality into a festive orgy of screaming colors. This occurs not only when he loses himself in exotic fantasies, but also when he describes the brutal beauty of a fight in a billiard hall in a proletarian quarter of Copenhagen. Just as the colors are appreciated for their own sake, so is the sound of the words exploited in a purely aesthetic manner, intensified in the poem "Itokih" almost to Dadaism.

In the collection *Paafuglefjeren* (The Peacock Feather, 1922) Kristensen reworks new materials from a trip to China and Japan. He has broken here with the expressionistic style and has found a controlled form of expression, saturated with color, which approaches impressionism. But the external harmony only increased the tension in the homeless, individualistic soul of the poet. In long intellectual poems he struggled with serious questions concerning art and reality, life and death; in the monumental poem about human existence, "Henrettelsen" ("The Execution"), which consists of waiting passively for the blows of fate, the anxiety of the poet finds a colossal intensive form.

A year after his lyrical debut, Kristensen published a lengthy novel, *Livets Arabesk* (Arabesque of Life, 1921). Although he chose various settings in Copenhagen, the book is a long way from being realistic. It is, rather, a romantic expressionistic orgy of styles, a desperate expression of life as a repulsive absurdity, and thereby an indirect admission that the affirmation of life in *Pirate Dreams* was false.

The novel presents upper and lower classes as equally corrupt: After a communistic revolution, the proletarians merely imitate the degenerate bourgeois culture. To be sure *Arabesque of Life* is intended as a political novel, but the author quickly deserts the problems associated with that and engrosses himself in religious questions. These are linked to the main character, Dr. Baumann, and his longing for a "divine peace" in a feeling of collective community, a feeling which he seeks in vain in the sensations of the moment.

In the next novel, *En Anden* (Another, 1923), Kristensen portrays the growing up of a proletarian child. Valdemar Rasmussen, now a customs official in China, recalls his youth and everyday life in Copenhagen around 1910, in supple language which records coolly and precisely, with an artistry unsurpassed in the Danish literature of these years. Yet the harmony is only external, the feigning of an inner peace in the midst of restlessness. The problem is the same as in *Arabesque of Life*: to find himself, to shape one's own life. Although the view of humanity continues to be divided, Valdemar Rasmussen's retrospective glance at his fragmentary existence changes into the recognition that he is still the same person, alternately chasing his shadow and fleeing from it, trapped in the hopeless dream of being able to form into a personality his incomprehensible inner self.

In Kristensen's last novel, *Hærværk* (1930; Eng. tr. *Havoc*, 1968), the restlessness and despair are clearly exposed. The book can be read as an autobiography, as an artistic novel or *roman à clef*, or as a psychological study of the progressive decline of a human being. The motto reads: "Fear the soul, and do not worship it, for it is like a vice." The main motif of the book is the fear on the part of the main character, the literary critic Ole Jastrau, of becoming lost in the world and extinguished, the fear that he cannot find himself. This fear is portrayed in a poem as being "Asiatic in size"—a concentration of the mood of the "lost generation" (see p. 154). The method of self-liberation is neither communist nor Catholic, both of which scare off Jastrau with their logic; neither is it the sensations that Baumann sought (see p. 199); the solution is simply to destroy oneself. First his petty-bourgeois marriage comes apart, then he gives up his position at the newspaper. As the work progresses, the process of dissolution accelerates, with the help of alcohol. Jastrau in his decline experiences not only joy in his self-destruction, but also a kind of infinity. It is precisely this for which his soul thirsts—but against which the motto warns. Huxley and Joyce have been pointed to as models for *Havoc*. Certainly there are formal and stylistic resemblances to *Ulysses*: Like Joyce, Kristensen employs the inner monologue, and like the characters in Huxley's *Point Counter Point* (1928) Jastrau is constantly in search of his identity; but as far as sincerity and unsentimental examination of the postwar character is concerned, almost no other work in world literature can measure up to *Havoc*.

Kristensen published very few long works after the 1930s. But he was one of the most influential literary critics in Denmark. The point of departure of his reviews was always the immediate impression, his subjective view of the work. His reviews and essays are descriptive reports and, perhaps, portraits of the works and simultaneously of himself. *Den evige Uro* (The Eternal Restlessness, 1958) is the title of one of the numerous volumes of Kristensen's essays. It can be read as a longing for harmony, a longing that pervades all of his creative writing, as an expression of the tragedy of modern humankind. More acutely than his contemporaries, Tom Kristensen knows the rupture between tradition and war experience, a duality that underlies his despairing art.

Jacob Paludan

Next to Kristensen, Paludan (1896-1975) is the most typical writer of his generation; at the same time, both are its extremes. The two occupy themselves with the crisis of the postwar period. But while Kristensen feels the chaos within himself, Paludan is an observer who criticizes and condemns it from a conservative standpoint. From the beginning he was skeptical of the times, expecting only the worst; before anyone else, he saw that the 1930s were not really years of peace, but, rather, a period between wars.

During a trip to Ecuador and the United States (1920/21) Paludan was confronted with an aspect of Americanism, with the superficiality and commercialism that is linked to an obsessive concern with money. He protests this attitude in his debut work, the novel *De vestlige Veje* (The Western Roads, 1922), a pessimistic, somewhat abstract, condemnation of the present.

In *Søgelys* (Searchlight, 1923) the satire is directed with far greater effect against Danish conditions, though the work too clearly bears the stamp of its time. The time that the searchlight illuminates is "the century of mediocrity," or, more precisely, 1922, and the setting is a boarding house in Copenhagen. With omniscient asides the author mercilessly censures the guests and their soulless superficiality.

In *Fugle omkring Fyret* (1925; Eng. tr. *Birds around the Light*, 1928), Paludan demonstrates for the first time his ability to reshape current topics. The result is a social novel whose dramatic plot symbolizes the postwar period and its attempt to destroy nature and humanity. But the victims know how to revenge and assert themselves. Revenge comes when the sea destroys the new harbor, which was built as a financial speculation; assertiveness is present in the instinctively assured girl Bodil, who is inextricably bound to nature. In her Paludan created one of his positive female figures who embody elementary virtues like fidelity and selflessness, and are capable of liberating the often reflective and uncertain masculine figures.

In Paludan's next book, *Markerne modnes* (The Fields Ripen, 1927), a tragic novel dealing with art, his pessimism is more oppressive than it has been before. As usual, he works with distinct contrast and sharply defined types: the man of feeling and the man of pleasure. Ivar is drawn to music, Ralf to poetry. But their talents are never developed: Ivar does, to be sure, become a violinist and is on his way to becoming a virtuoso; but an inflamed finger interrupts his career. He loses his grip on reality and becomes an easy prey for the egoistic and frigid Ellinor, who is Paludan's most negative embodiment of female emancipation. Parallel to Ivar's story is Ralf's; he is the aristocrat who is assured and dominant in every situation. Whereas Ivar embodies the youth of 1914 who were negatively affected by the war, Ralf belongs to the pampered youth who were stimulated by it. Nevertheless, he too is about to experience his downfall.

In his major work *Jørgen Stein* (1932-33; Eng. tr. 1966), Paludan wrote the most significant novel of development in modern Danish literature. He shows how the war altered all of Danish life—in the countryside, the provinces, and in Copenhagen—and especially how difficult it was for the young to find a firm footing. Jørgen Stein's father is a representative of the old class of civil servants that belongs to the time before 1914; he is unable to comprehend what is happening when his world of nationalistic, conservative ideals collapses, and he himself is economically ruined. His oldest son, the lawyer Otto, exploits the situation as a speculator, but runs aground on the shoals of materialism and ends by committing suicide—a vivid and tragic illustration of life in the postwar period. The antithesis of this amoral man of the moment is the title character. His happy childhood is separated from the rest of his experiences by the outbreak of the war. In the spring of 1918 he recognizes that the hope which had been awakened by religion, reason, and democracy is doomed to disappointment. In Copenhagen, Jørgen studies first philosophy, then art history. He gives up his studies and tries journalism, but manages to achieve only inner resignation; he cannot find his way in the world at large or within himself. He is already in the shadow of the new world crisis when he meets the uncomplicated peasant girl Marie, who becomes his wife. He finds peace in the country, and at the end of the novel, when Marie is about to bear his child, he is rescued through a feeling of duty and responsibility toward his family.

Jørgen Stein, like Pontoppidan's *The Realm of the Dead*, ends with the consolation that life is invincible, even in the midst of destruction. Nevertheless, pessimism predominates. The great themes of the work are the decline of a culture and the futile goal of bringing oneself into harmony with the changing world. Jørgen represents the youth of the interwar period, its indifference, its terrifying insight into the relativity of all things—he, too, belongs to the "lost generation."

Jørgen Stein is Paludan's last novel. Like Kristensen, he was a productive critic and a thoroughly topical and versatile humanistic essayist.

In addition, he published several collections of satiric aphorisms in which he analyzed the thoughts basic to his fiction. Paludan's scorn of his present did not bring him to the point of uncritically singing the praises of the past. The leit-motif of his work is always the struggle for personal freedom, against any sort of spiritual tyranny, a motif which still attracts readers.

A LYRICAL INTERMEZZO

Around the middle of the 1920s the hectic debate about world views reached its zenith. One result of the great success of the expressionistic poets was the emergence of a new generation of lyricists, who attempted in various ways to find their footing in a changed world. The most distinguished artistic talents among them were Per Lange, Paul la Cour, and Jens August Schade.

Per Lange

The poetry of Lange (1901–   ) in the collections *Kaos og Stjærnen* (Chaos and the Star, 1926), *Forvandlinger* (Metamorphoses, 1929), and *Orfeus* (Orpheus, 1932) has erotic, mystical, and natural motifs permeated with a tragic idealism. Lange attempts to overcome the artistic and human dissolution of the period through clarity of thought and a clear, classical style.

Paul la Cour

La Cour (1902–56), on the other hand, in his poetry collections from the 1920s, *Den galliske Sommer* (Gallic Summer, 1927), *Den tredie Dag* (The Third Day, 1928), and the novel *Aske* (Ashes, 1929), tries to penetrate the inner being of nature and matter and his self in order to perceive the secret of existence.

La Cour's two main collections from the 1930s, *Dette er vort Liv* (This Is Our Life, 1939) and *Alt kræver jeg* (I Demand All, 1938), are dominated by feelings of guilt about the fate of Europe as the poet discerns the power of his own ruthless instinct. Simultaneously, there is a growing belief in the necessity of change. The result of la Cour's search beyond the intellect is presented in his major work, *Fragmenter af en Dagbog* (Fragments of a Diary, 1948), a mix of philosophical teaching, poetics, and poetry, which influenced many of the Danish poets of the 1940s and '50s. The collections from this period, *Levende Vande* (Living Waters, 1946) and *Mellem Bark og Ved* (Between Bark and Wood, 1950), correspond to the world of ideas expressed in the

Fragments: the unity of existence emerging from the meeting of the rational and irrational forces in art.

Jens August Schade

Schade (1903–78), in his turn, captures the tension between the infinite and finite in numerous volumes of surrealistic poetry, already fully developed in his first book, *den levende violin* (The Living Violin, 1926). Here a tragic feeling dominates, a sense of the insignificance of the self in the infinite universe. *Sjov i Danmark* (Fun in Denmark, 1928; "Sjov" is also the name of the hero) is partly an ironic autobiography, partly a satiric depiction of Denmark. All of the later collections, from *Hjertebogen* (The Heart Book, 1930) to *Overjordisk* (Supernatural, 1973), are characterized by daring and disrespectful love poems, erotic nature poems, and cosmic fantasies. They are permeated by Schade's all-embracing sexual message—the closest Danish literature has ever come to the primitivism of D. H. Lawrence—which is very strikingly expressed by the titles of Schade's two lyrical novels, *Den himmelske Elskov paa Jorden* (Heavenly Love on Earth, 1931) and *Mennesker mødes og sød Musik opstaar i Hjertet* (People Meet and Sweet Music Fills the Heart, 1944).

Gustaf Munch-Petersen

Somewhat younger, and more internationally oriented, was Munch-Petersen (1912–38), who was killed during the Spanish Civil War while serving as a volunteer on the Republican side. His first collection, *det nøgne menneske* (Naked Man, 1932), containing unrhymed poems, shows Munch-Petersen to be a modern writer, clearly influenced by French surrealism and the Fenno-Swedish modernists Diktonius and Södergran, whereas his ideas about human solidarity are founded on socialism. The volumes *det underste land* (The Land Below, 1933) and *nitten digte* (Nineteen Poems, 1937) sum up his social dream of community and happiness by laying bare the origin of the subconscious. Munch-Petersen created a concise, lyrical, image-filled poetry reminiscent of Ezra Pound's imagism, thereby becoming a forerunner of Danish modernistic poetry.

Most of these poets made their debuts in a period that was an interlude before world catastrophes. Their joy in life and their optimism soon retreated under the impact of the stock-market crash on Wall Street in 1929; the consequences reached Denmark a few years later, causing an unprecedented rate of unemployment. The national socialist takeover in Germany in 1933 also affected Danish literature. It was a period during which the primary problem of domestic politics was the struggle for subsistence, the problem of external politics, the fear of war and the longing for peace. This situation provoked a great number of socially realistic and critical novels; it also caused the writers to take a position against the threat from the south, a position that was national-Christian (Kaj Munk) or socialist (Hans Kirk), or pessimistic, the result of recognizing the almost nonexistent culture of the postwar years, the moral inadequacy of humankind, and the new danger (Nis Petersen).

The youth of the upper bourgeois class were particularly hit by this new pessimism. The mood found its clearest expression in Denmark in a novel by Knud Sønderby (1909–66), *Midt i en Jazztid* (In the Middle of a Jazz Age, 1931), written in a hard-boiled style influenced by Hemingway. Related is the novel *To Mennesker mødes* (Two People Meet, 1932), whose theme is the fearful power of human emotions. He skillfully deals with another problem in *En Kvinde er overflødig* (A Woman Is Superfluous, 1936, dramatized in 1942; Eng. tr. *A Woman Too Many*, 1955)—the generation gap, neither generation wanting to accept the life-style of the other.

IDEOLOGICAL CONFRONTATIONS

The most artistically convincing expression of the restlessness and the nihilism of the period is found in the work of Nis Petersen.

Nis Petersen

Petersen (1897–1943) was unable to find either ideological or material security, and drifted about as a vagabond and bohemian, succumbing to doubt and despair. He made his debut as a lyricist with the collection *Nattens Pibere* (The Pipers of the Night, 1926), in which these moods are already apparent. The title poem is the gloomiest, a fantasy in a cemetery, where the bats are the only living creatures: "Dead is the dead man, but doubly so, when bats / quivering above the gardens of the lifeless / cast a shadow full of scorn upon his hopelessness." The later collections, *En Drift Vers* (A Drove of Verse, 1933) and *Stykgods* (Mixed Cargo, 1940), are in the same mood, but changed from the rhetorical style influenced by Kipling and Wilde to plain verse of exquisite beauty.

In 1931 Petersen's major work appeared, *Sandalmagernes Gade* (Eng. tr. *The Street of the Sandalmakers*, 1933). The novel, translated into more than ten languages, is a broad portrayal of Rome during the time of the Emperor Marcus Aurelius. The feeling that dominates the characters is one of uprootedness and uncertainty. They live in a society that is in the process of dissolution. Values are constantly changing, and the ground is prepared for new religious and philosophical systems; prophecies of impending calamity and world destruction occupy the time, and the progress of life is given its hectic character by the plague that infests Rome. *The Street of the Sandalmakers* is superficially a historical novel; however, if one removes the Roman coloration, it is a contemporary novel. Ancient Rome resembles modern Copenhagen, and the author shows how both epochs stand in a negative relationship to the message of love contained in the gospels. The main character, Marcellus, a child of his times—related to Paludan's Jørgen Stein (see p. 202)—encounters the early persecutions of the Christians. He is not at all a martyr, but is killed accidentally. The author shows the fate of many other characters. All gradations of Roman society are represented, and the settings are vividly detailed, the result of exhaustive historical study and of brimming fantasy. The details are actualized through the use of ironic anachronisms and a modern, subjective form of speech.

Petersen's second novel, *Spildt Mælk* (1934; Eng. tr. *Spilt Milk*, 1935), is a disillusioned story of the Irish Civil War of 1922. From his later years stem four collections of short stories (1937–43), like his novels rather weak structurally, but all expressing his fascinating personality. Nis Petersen never attempts to identify with his characters. On the contrary, they are always seen from the outside, illuminated from all viewpoints; this technique does not allow for deep psychological analysis, but it does make possible a remarkable portrayal of people who long for love and who attempt to relate to an existence they cannot master.

Hans Kirk

The second significant prose work around 1930 was written by Kirk (1898–1962); this collective novel, *Fiskerne* (The Fishermen, 1928), is in the naturalistic tradition of Pontoppidan and Andersen Nexø. It tells of a group of families who have left the rough west coast of Jutland seeking a milder environment. They are clearly set off from the inhabitants of the new region. They have left a bleak area and highly dangerous work; but they bring with them a strongly puritanical Christianity, and they immediately begin to prosyletize. Although they enounter strong resistance, they succeed, owing to their cohesiveness and their strong faith, in conquering the community from within. They expel the Lutheran pastor in order to introduce their own pattern of life. The basic viewpoint of the novel is purely sociological and Marxist: The development of a society is portrayed, but the work rises above the level of agitation through its credible and realistic portrayal of human beings. However, this is not true of Kirk's next two novels, *Daglejerne* (Day Laborers, 1936) and *De ny Tider* (New Times, 1939), which describe the industrialization of an old village community and the resulting severe human and economic problems. In his last novels, *Slaven* (The Slave, 1948) and *Vredens Søn* (The Son of Wrath, 1950), Kirk departs from contemporary motifs, although drawing parallels to our times, especially the German occupation of Denmark in 1940-45.

Jørgen Nielsen

Despite the fact that a large segment of Kirk's work is critical and polemical, his human outlook is quite positive. This is not true of Nielsen (1902-45), another significant novelist of the 1930s. His view of life—found in his major works, the short-story collections *Lavt Land* (Low Country, 1929), *Vi umyndige* (We, the Dependents, 1934), and *Figurer i et Landskab* (Figures in a Landscape, 1944)—is marked by pessimism and resignation.

Aage Dons

Psychological analysis is the specialty of Dons (1903–   ). In his novels, such as *Soldaterbrønden* (1936; Eng. tr. *The Soldier's Well*, 1940), he describes the attempts of rootless, lonely human beings to overcome their isolation.

Hans Scherfig, Harald Herdal, and Knuth Becker

A blatant political tendency is obvious in the novels of Scherfig (1905-79), next to Kirk the most markedly Marxist writer of the period. For him the apparent absurdity of life is a sign of the corruption of capitalism; he portrays this corruption in a series of satirical and humorous novels, such as *Den forsvundne Fuldmægtig* (Head Clerk Disappeared, 1938), *Det forsømte Foraar* (Neglected Spring, 1940) and *Idealister* (1945; Eng. tr. *The Idealists*, 1949). Some social critics, such as Harald Herdal (1900-78) describe the misery of the big-city proletariat. Others, such as Knuth Becker (1891-1974), in his extensive autobiographical cycle of novels about the boy Kai Gøttsche (1932-56), direct their criticism at public institutions and the entire educational system. However, this primarily socialistic or communistic literature did not dominate the period, partly because the Moscow Trials (1936–38) had too terrifying an effect, even upon the most idealistic sympathizers. On the other hand, Danish theater experienced a hectic flowering.

DRAMA

Carl Erik Soya

The dramas by journalist Soya (1896–　) are characterized by brutal realism, as in *Parasitterne* (The Parasites, 1929), psychoanalytical experience, as in *Hvem er jeg?* (Who Am I?, 1932), and ruthless satire, as in *Umbabumba* (1935), directed at Nazi Germany. *Who Am I?* is the first comedy in a series of experimental dramas (1940–48) influenced by Pirandello and Abell, in which the author plays tricks with scenic illusions and the time dimension.

Kjeld Abell

More strongly related to the old naturalism was the early work of Abell (1901–61). In his successful dramas he attacked petty bourgeois existence in *Melodien, der blev væk* (1935; Eng. tr. *The Melody That Got Lost*, 1939) and child-rearing in *Eva aftjener sin Barnepligt* (Eva Does Her Duty, 1936), but also proclaimed a fighting humanism against the impending war in *Anna Sophie Hedvig* (1939; Eng. tr. 1944). The struggle against evil is a theme which is variably treated in two plays published during World War II, as well as in *Silkeborg* (1946), a tribute to the Danish resistance during the German occupation in 1940–45. The humanist's dilemma in a postwar world threatened by violence and destruction is analyzed in Abell's last plays, *Vetsera blomstrer ikke for enhver* (Vetsera Doesn't Bloom for Everybody, 1950), *Den blå Pekingeser* (The Blue Pekinese, 1954), and *Skriget* (The Cry, 1961). These are symbolic and philosophical dramas experimentally mingling dream and reality, past and present, in their protest against the negative forces.

Kaj Munk

The most interesting figure of the interwar period was the writer and pastor Munk (1889–1944). Within a few years he became the greatest preacher, the most discussed cultural personality, and undoubtedly the most significant modern dramatist of Danish literature, which outside of his work has only a few valuable plays. Because of Munk's contempt for the enfeebled democracies of the time, and his admiration for the ruthless, but self-sacrificing despots, he was very receptive to the new dictatorial ideologies. It was his hope that Denmark too would find its strong leader and that he could awaken the nation through his writing. He clung fast to fanatical hero worship, although he revised his opinion of Hitler and Mussolini even before the war. On April 9, 1940, he began the last phase of his work: the condemnation of the German occupation of Denmark. He was by nature defiant, and his path led inexorably toward catastrophe: On January 4, 1944, he was murdered by the Gestapo.

Munk's first major play, *En Idealist* (1928; An Idealist; Eng. tr. *Herod the King*, 1953), revealed a superior dramatic ability, seen here in his sharply delineated characters and powerful scenes, surprises, and effects. It contains three climaxes. First, the scene in Egypt, where King Herod is admitted to the presence of Cleopatra and Antony, and his tactical game leads to a triumphant conclusion. Second, the duel between Herod and Octavian, a masterpiece of dialectical fantasy and contrasting effects; finally, the concluding scene: the encounter of Herod with Mary and the Christ child, ending in Herod's death struggle. He is the idealist of the play, who sacrifices others and himself for an idea: his own power. But the piece is also characteristic of Munk's dualistic attitude toward life: the worldly hero-worshiper who, however, believes in God. In the drama about Herod he permits the battle of the king to become a struggle against God, which ends in Herod's defeat when he is unable to kill the Son of God.

The conflict of power with the Christian message of love recurs in *Han sidder ved Smeltediglen* (1938; Eng. tr. *He Sits at the Melting-Pot*, 1953). Here Munk portrays how God allows his power to work through a fragile human being, who thereby gains the strength to assert himself against the powerful in this world—in the actual situation, the Nazis—not in the service of truth, but in the service of love. And in Munk's last stage work on the theme of power, the masterful drama *Før Cannae* (1943; Eng. tr. *Before Cannae*, 1953), Hannibal, a boasting Hitler figure, stands facing the victorious ideals of humanity, as represented in Fabius.

After power, the second great motif in Munk's work is love. Usually the motifs are interwoven, often in sinister forms, as in *Herod the King*, when Herod sacrifices his beloved, and thus his happiness, to an idea. In *Cant* (1931; Eng. tr. 1953), the greed for power and craving for love balance each other. It is the most cheerful of Munk's dramas. At the same time, it is the play in which poetry finds its freest expression, a technically perfect virtuoso piece set at the court of Henry VIII, with colorful scenes modeled on Shakespeare and striking figures reminiscent of Schiller, although it lacks the personal involvement so characteristic of Munk's other plays.

The modern miracle play *Ordet* (1932; Eng. tr. *The Word*, 1953; filmed in 1955 by Carl Th. Dreyer) was Munk's greatest stage success and stands completely apart from Munk's other dramatic works. It contains a prophecy that was intended to shock the Sunday Christians and challenge the unbelievers. The problem: Is it possible in our modern era for God to give human beings such a strong faith that they can perform miracles? In contrast to Bjørnson's rationalizing miracle play *Beyond Our Power I* (see p. 29), the answer is affirmative. The mentally ill Johannes believes that he is Christ. In the final scene, surrounded by believers and unbelievers, and liberated from his madness, he resurrects his dead sister-in-law Inger through prayer and boundless faith.

Throughout his life Kaj Munk was an antagonist, challenging and confusing the public, provoking misunderstanding, a mix of prophet and fantast. In reality he was a man who consistently attempted to take up Ibsen's "ideal challenge," the strict challenge to himself to make actions match words, to risk his life for an idea.

A HIGH POINT IN PROSE WRITING

Karen Blixen

A writer who belongs to no definite epoch in literary history is Blixen, born Dinesen (1885–1962; pseudonyms Tania Blixen, Isak Dinesen, Pierre Andrézel). From 1914 to 1932 she lived in Kenya, where she headed her own coffee plantation, thus having no link with Denmark in the period between the wars. This probably explains why her breakthrough work, *Seven Gothic Tales*—published in 1934 in the United States and in 1935 in her own Danish translation as *Syv fantastiske Fortællinger*—was received in Denmark as something strange and new. Karen Blixen regularly wrote her works in English as well as in Danish.

Seven Gothic Tales made Blixen famous overnight. The collection was a reminder for Danish literature that not only social criticism, but also knowledge and fantasy belong to the poetic sphere. The volume is full of literary references to Danish romantic poets, to world classics, and not least to the Bible. Most of the stories have a cosmopolitan background and an aristocratic, historical setting—the eighteenth and nineteenth centuries. It is characteristic of Blixen's writing that the historical setting allows her to maintain a certain distance from her material and to clearly emphasize the fairytale-like quality of her stories. The fantastic element is linked with two main themes, love and dreams. The Eros theme appears in a prominent, but distorted fashion in "Aben" ("The Monkey"), where an abbess transforms herself into an ape, the symbol of unchecked passion, to bring two very different young people together. Erotic love also dominates in "Et Familieselskab i Helsingør" ("The Supper at Elsinore"), a thoroughgoing ghost story, in which longing and suppressed eroticism are analyzed. "Drømmerne" ("The Dreamers") attempts to show various stages and nuances of the dream as a kind of illusionary existence, to portray unhappy people who are either incapable or prevented from fulfilling the role assigned them by God. Here, as in other works, Karen Blixen elucidates the idea that God is an artist. To be sure, he can appear cruel, but human suffering is only a detail of a greater whole.

A contrast to the ironic, cynical, and artistic short stories is the autobiography *Den afrikanske Farm* (1937; Eng. tr. *Out of Africa*, 1937), which, as a result of its enthusiastic and accessible portrayals of Africa, was read by an even larger audience. There was a sequel much later, entitled *Skygger paa Græsset* (1960; Eng. tr. *Shadows on the Grass*, 1960 and later). In *Out of Africa*, Blixen tells of the idyllic life on her farm and marvelously describes nature, animals, and human life. The book ends, however, with a personal catastrophe, when she is forced to give up the farm because of poor economic conditions. The acceptance of this tragedy is at the same time the key to her view of life. She regards with contempt the person who complains about fate, or rebels against it. One should accept it, thereby asserting personal pride, rather than striving for happiness or good fortune that is not in accord with God's plan. The book is not merely an autobiographical report; it is a deliberately composed work of art, which is closely related to the short stories. It portrays the myth-creating fantasy of the natives, their piety and magic. The section entitled "Af en Emigrants Dagbog" ("From the Diary of an Emigrant") contains fantastic episodes that are fiction, and in her next volume of stories, Karen Blixen again makes contact with the world of tales and legends.

Borrowing from Shakespeare, she chose for her next volume the title *Vinter-Eventyr* (1942; Eng. tr. *Winter's Tales*, 1942 and later). In contrast to the earlier seven, these stories are more concise in form, softer in tone, and more varied in mood. They focus primarily on a single course of action or a single event, hence the author's perspective comes across more clearly. The setting is predominantly Nordic, and the time is closer to the present, but the view of life is the same. The highest point of the volume is "Sorg-Agre" ("Sorrow-Acre"), in which humans are portrayed as marionettes in the hands of God, and the lord of the estate, who causes an old mother to be worked to death as punishment for the misdeeds of her son, is seen as a divine stage manager. The human being must accept all of his or her fate, even the negative aspects. The comic game that God plays with the human being appears to him or her to be a tragedy. But this is not the decisive point; what is important is that one adhere to the rules of the game.

After publishing a thriller, *Gengældelsens Veje* (1944; Eng. tr. *The Angelic Avengers*, 1946 and later; *Roads of Retribution*, 1947), Blixen reappeared in 1957 with a new impressive work, *Sidste Fortællinger* (Eng. tr. *Last Tales*, 1957 and later). The setting is the Mediterranean countries. The outstanding "En Herregaardshistorie" ("A Country Tale") is a companion piece to "Sorrow-Acre" and deals with the recognition of the laws of human tragedy, which Kardinal Salviati, in "Kardinalens første Historie" ("The Cardinal's First Tale"), attempts to overcome through art. The invented story, he asserts, has its rules and conditions, like the story of life. In the fictional story one can obtain an answer to the cry, "Who am I?" It is the true essence of art that it exists autonomously and that its power is the elevating, the life-affirming and life-preserving.

The next year *Skæbne-Anekdoter* (1958; Eng. tr. *Anecdotes of Destiny*, 1958 and later) appeared. Here the fantastic element is set apart. The stories are not as demanding as the preceding ones, but beneath the exciting and entertaining surface are serious perspectives. The common themes of *Anecdotes of Destiny*—as well as of the post-humous story *Ehrengard* (1963; Eng. tr. 1963 and later)—are the relationship between art and life, and interference with fate. The most famous is "Babettes Gæstebud" ("Babette's Feast"), about the old cook who, for fourteen years, has had no opportunity to display her true essence in her art; at the memorial celebration for the deceased dean she executes her masterpiece in culinary art before guests who do not comprehend it. The two daughters of the dean see the banquet as grandiose proof of human devotion, whereas for Babette it is an expression of sovereign self-assertion and expanding of her identity, a matter between herself and God.

The story can also be understood as a paraphrase of Karen Blixen's relationship to her audience. Literary taste had taken another direction, but she gathered about herself a small circle of young artists, who were inspired and enchanted by her great personality. Thereby Karen Blixen and Martin A. Hansen became the most important Danish inspirers of the so-called *Heretica* movement (see p. 315); but even abroad her influence was significant, and many southern American writers, above all Carson McCullers and Truman Capote, have admitted that they are strongly indebted to her.

Karen Blixen's stories are characterized by detailed allegory. Technically they are partially imitative of earlier authors, but their fantasy is modern: Dreams transform themselves into reality and vice versa. Thoughts are transposed into paradoxes and romanticism is destroyed by irony. Behind the superb dialogue an inner coherence is suggested, in which existential problems are set up for debate—problems that are not illustrated by Blixen's characters but, rather, grow with them out of her narrative art. While she capriciously juggles the plot in the humorous sphere, she is compelled at the same time to have the strict laws of life govern her characters. In Karen Blixen's work, there is a constant alternation of and a constant interplay between the indulgent smile of humor and the sternness of tragedy; hence the both exciting and perplexing element in the stories, hence also the richness of her writing.

Hans Christian Branner

Like Karen Blixen, Branner (1903–66) adopted a free and skeptical attitude toward the ideological, moral, and social systems of his time. At the beginning of his career he did, to be sure, regard Freud's psychoanalytic theories among the great liberating events of his generation, but he was always an opponent of "psychoanalysis as a view of life," as he was always skeptical of Freudian attempts at therapy. Whereas the influence of psychoanalysis on Branner diminishes, that of existential philosophy increases; its central concepts of anxiety, responsibility, and loneliness come more and more into the foreground of his work.

Branner's first work, *Legetøj* (Toys, 1936) is a collective novel, dealing with deception and betrayal as they gain ground in a trading firm. The author is the omniscient narrator, who causes his characters, through their behavior, to reveal their innermost thoughts and follies. The sales manager Feddersen is the evil spirit and strong man of the firm, who seizes power through a system of terror and denunciation. Slowly the portrayal expands, the trading firm becoming a state and clear allusions being made to the rapid advance of Naziism in Germany. But one of the young employees, the medical student Martin Lind, who was previously a follower of Feddersen, slowly begins to doubt this system. And in Lind's crisis of conscience Branner depicts the humanistic process that represents a positive alternative to Feddersen's power ideology.

Drømmen om en Kvinde (Dream about a Woman, 1941) deals with human isolation, in particular with the two situations in life in which isolation is greatest, birth and death; it simultaneously demonstrates the necessity of human contact. Branner uses the stream-of-consciousness technique, which he often employed in his writing. He did not carry it through in as much detail as did James Joyce, for example; he combined it with inner monologue and flashbacks to explain the psychological makeup of his characters.

Dream about a Woman is Branner's most difficult book. There are very few events, but they are fundamental—a man dies, a woman bears a child. It is set at the outbreak of the war in 1939. There is no real plot and no environment through which the characters can reveal themselves. It is a collective novel without a main character, but with two contrasting figures—Merete, far advanced in pregnancy, and the lawyer Mortimer, who is suffering from cancer. Each of them, the woman of life and the man of death, has a long flashback of his or her life, which leads up to the present situation, in which Mortimer has driven to his hotel to die and Merete to the clinic to have her baby. Only now do they succeed in conquering the isolation which rests like an evil fate on all people, in their own ruined marriages.

Branner's short stories became the most popular of his works. The two collections *Om lidt er vi borte* (Soon We Are Gone, 1939) and *To Minutters Stilhed* (1944; Eng. tr. *Two Minutes of Silence*, 1966) deal with people's encounters with concepts in the face of which they are estranged and helpless: hatred, war, death, and, finally, the encounter of a man with a woman, of a child with the world of grownups. The same themes are found in Branner's novels, but it seems that in the shorter form, his talent found a particularly free play. Branner's ability to engross himself in the world of the child and to uncover an essential drama behind an apparently banal plot—abilities he had demonstrated earlier in the novel *Barnet leger ved Stranden* (The Child Plays on the Beach, 1937)—elevates the short stories of the first collection to the level of world literature. "Et Barn og en Mus" ("A Child and a Mouse") is the tragic story of a boy who has found a mouse in the attic and feeds it until the grownups set a trap and kill it. When he finds the mouse in the trap and is told that it is only sick, two new, horrible things have entered his world: deception and death. "Hannibals Træsko" ("Hannibal's Wooden Shoes") and "Iris" deal with sensitive children from poor families, whose encounters with arrogant upper-class children familiarize them with another of the evil inequities of life: class differences.

In *Two Minutes of Silence* three of the short stories deal with different stages of puberty; in most of the others, love is the main motif. The underlying idea is that a happy relationship between a man and a woman is the only salvation from isolation; the theme is demonstrated through the thoughts of the remaining partner, when death has just ended a marriage.

The theme of the short story *Angst* (Anguish, 1947) is the anxiety psychosis of the occupation period from 1940 to 1945. It treats of the frenzy that war forces upon human beings, of the attempts of a writer to comprehend this better than the people who are actively fighting, and of humanism before it unfolds. This humanism can be observed in all its phases in the novel *Rytteren* (1949; Eng. tr. *The Riding Master*, 1951; *The Mistress*, 1953). Four persons continue to be dominated by a deceased, power-seeking figure, the riding master Hubert. Branner analyzes the process that liberates Susanne, Hubert's former mistress, from a life of strict dependency. Whereas Hubert had turned into an animalistic tyrant to repress his feelings of fear and guilt, the inferior doctor, Clemens, succeeds in leading Susanne to a life of responsibility by neutralizing the guilt feelings of both of them through his own goodness and humanism.

The complex inner monologue that characterized Branner's art has given way in *The Riding Master* to short, striking dialogues and straight narrative. The book was significant not only as a psychological experiment; as an ethical message, it represented a shift of emphasis for Branner. Critics hailed it as a masterpiece.

World War II is the dark background for almost everything Branner wrote after 1939, but not until ten years after the war did he use the material that the war itself provided. In the novel *Ingen kender Natten* (1955; Eng. tr. *No Man Knows the Night*, 1958) he portrays two milieus: that of the resistance and that of the collaborators. The historical framework is, however, of minor significance; the novel is deeply concerned with the circumstances of an uprooted man who is dominated by nihilistic philosophy and Freudian psychology. The tragedy of the main character, the collaborator Tomas, is that he believes in nothing, but would like to believe. He traverses psychological and political spheres, but can settle nowhere. He attempts to find a kind of brotherhood with the young Communist Simon, who is fleeing the Gestapo. Whereas Simon, the representative of the secure and the robust, dies a meaningful death, it is Tomas's tragedy that he sacrifices his not very heroic life for a heroic task in which he is unable to believe.

Branner triumphed as a dramatist with *Søskende* (1952; Siblings; Eng. tr. *The Judge*, 1955). The three grown children of an old judge meet in his home because he has suffered a mortal heart attack. He had always been the silent, strict authority figure. His oldest son, Arthur, feels boundless admiration for him and has adapted perfectly to society, as an ambitious lawyer. The youngest son, Michael, has rebelled against his father and has plunged into the free life of a vagabond. Between these two brothers stands the sister, Irene—Branner's most beautiful portrait of a woman—who is in a loveless marriage to a wealthy, jealous man. She understands how to liberate her brothers from their inhibitions, to conjure up happy moments from their youth, and to awaken in them the dream of giving up everything to live together in a small house in the country. But when their father dies, it becomes clear that all three siblings are incapable of freeing themselves from the past.

Very different from this play is *Thermopylæ* (1958; Eng. tr. 1973), a drama of ideas in which Branner seriously analyzes the concept of humanism. The dominant character is the cultural historian Stefan Fischer. During the German occupation he gives provocative lectures on the history of democracy, although he knows he will be punished by the Germans. Fischer's great courage in the face of the senseless and inexorable drives him to an absurd martyr's death. He represents tolerance to such a great degree that he yields to the dominance of power when one of his sons becomes a Communist and the other a Nazi. His attitude thus demonstrates the dangerous consequences of tolerance, illustrating Branner's call for some limitation of freedom.

Branner is a pessimistic moralist whose creative work is based on the belief that modern humankind lives in a dangerous world and is entirely on its own. Still it was his conviction that responsibility and goodness could break the bonds of human isolation: "It is our task as human beings to take responsibility for one another, to stave off the worst, to love without being loved, without expecting forgiveness for anything."

Martin A. Hansen

Hansen (1909-55) a farmer's son from Sealand also began his career as a realistic social critic, but by the late 1940s had become a major advocate of religious and anti-naturalistic trends. With his two first related novels, *Nu opgiver han* (Now He Gives Up, 1935) and *Kolonien* (The Colony, 1937), written after his training as a teacher, Hansen ties into the social and provincial literature, treating the conflicts between old and new social structures in a peasant society.

A significant artistic step forward is the burlesque novel *Jonatans Rejse* (Jonatan's Journey, 1941), which contains elements of the world view that Hansen deepened in his remaining work. Hansen builds on the old fable of the blacksmith who sticks the devil into a bottle and thus is able to acquire all the splendors of the world. But the smith proves to be unselfish and wants to give the bottle to his king, so that the goodness flowing from it can be of use to everyone. So he goes on a trip to the capital, enters society, his experiences there being described in the novel. During his wanderings he is accompanied by the youth Askelad. In these two figures, the modern and the medieval world views conflict with each other. Jonatan embodies the harmonious medieval world resting on its traditions; Askelad, with his critical and analytical attitudes, symbolizes modern rationalism, whose victory is shown at the end of the book in a vision of destruction—in contrast to the smith who understands how to rein in evil, symbolized by the imprisoned devil.

In his next book, *Lykkelige Kristoffer* (1945; Eng. tr. *Lucky Kristoffer*, 1974), Hansen combines the picaresque-novel form with historical material. As with *Jonatan's Journey*, Cervantes's Don Quixote is the model here. The impoverished knight Kristoffer travels from southern Sweden to Copenhagen to perform mighty deeds, and dies a hero's death during a siege of the city in 1536. He is accompanied by his Uncle Paal, a thick-skinned, superstitious old warrior, by the monk Martin, the narrator of the story, and by Father Mattias, the representative of medieval cultural harmony. Yet the work is also a philosophical novel. It is not the decline of the medieval popular culture that is being described, but, rather, the collapse of the Middle Ages itself and its universal figures, the knight and the priest, who are being mocked and called into question.

Although Hansen had recognized God and Satan as realities as early as in *Jonatan's Journey*, here, in Dostoevskian fashion, he moves the struggle between them into the human heart. After World War II he transferred this conflict into the present, in the volume of short stories entitled *Tornebusken* (The Thornbush, 1946). The common theme is the spiritual transformation of human beings, influenced by shocking events, and the major occurrence is war, the sin symbolized by the title. The philosophical vision "Midsommerfesten" ("The Midsummer Festival") shows the path modern humans must take, willingly or unwillingly. They cannot recognize God, but through crime Satan can become a reality. The thought of evil and good as reciprocally essential emerges in the conversation between the demonic, mysterious Georg and Alma. When they encounter each other, Alma is nihilistically divided, on the verge of suicide. But because Georg awakens her love, he compels her back into life. As a sufferer, she serves Christ; as a tormenter, he serves Satan; when he departs, in an exorcism, he reveals Satan's innermost being. But Alma pleads with Christ—God is recognized through Satan—and she becomes his salvation, as Beatrice does for Dante, Gretchen for Faust.

Agerhønen (The Partridge, 1947) is also a carefully composed collection of short stories, with twelve stories in three sections. The middle section contains the most valuable tales. They tell of the evil, meaninglessness, and sterility of the adult world. "Offer" ("Sacrifice") deals with the topic of senseless death. It is a bleak story of two children who are buried alive to save a community from the plague. "Høstgildet" ("The Harvest Feast") describes how a youth dies when he is forced to drink too much brandy. A flickering hope is expressed by a half-believing pastor, who has the task of opening the soul of the dead child's father, a soul that is hardened by defiance. Meaninglessness also predominates in "Ventesalen" ("The Waiting Room"), a sharp attack on nihilism. An older woman is able to overcome the emptiness and malice of other persons because she is entirely at peace in her faith in God.

The Partridge is Hansen's most characteristic book. There is an intense interplay between thoughtfulness and simplicity, between confident stylistic composition and an intellectual compository talent, which also characterizes his most famous book and last fictional work, the radio novel *Løgneren* (1950; Eng. tr. *The Liar*, 1954 and later). *The Liar* represents perhaps the greatest success of a Danish book in the exacting belles-lettres. It is written in the form of a dairy. On a small island the sexton and teacher Johannes Vig sketches his life for a fictional confidant, Nathanael, that is, the reader, who, according to the Bible, was a man without deceit, unlike Johannes himself. He regards past events through recollection; that memory falsifies is one of the basic ideas in the book. Johannes loves his former student Annemari, but resists temptation, since she is engaged to Oluf, who is away on a trip to the mainland. He reacts too slowly when she breaks with Oluf, and she enters into a relationship with an engineer, Harry. As revenge, Johannes seduces the wife of a friend. Finally he, who has chosen loneliness, is suddenly faced with the task of giving back to this woman her faith in the meaning and beauty of life.

Hansen selects a doubter in order to proclaim optimism and faith in life, for *The Liar* also deals with a dilettante of faith, who struggles and conquers evil, to reach from the ethical to the religious stage. This struggle is also symbolized by the island, on which the story is set during a few days in spring when the ice is breaking up and contact with the mainland is reestablished—a symbol of resurrection. The book is characterized largely by subtle symbols, often taken from classical works. Everything evolves significantly, nothing happens too precipitously. *The Liar* is a work of genius, mingling poetic but precise descriptions of nature with religious philosophical meditations.

In Hansen's books an unusual strength and balance predominates, rooted in his constant will toward a harmonious view of life. Hansen demands a feeling of responsibility, which is shown in his only humorous book, *Jonatan's Journey*. Kristoffer's willingness to sacrifice himself elevates him to greatness. Neither the sacrifice nor the suffering is meaningless. This was the last problem Martin Hansen dealt with in his writing. He came to believe that suffering strikes all because it releases powers in us that lead beyond suffering. As a writer Hansen was actually a realist who was able to reproduce reality as only Johannes V. Jensen before him had done. He was not a sharp dialectician, but was bound to a tradition, to which his view of life bore testimony. It is in this context that one should also consider Hansen's poetic and historical ideas about the extinct, but still remembered, peasant culture, expressed in the essay collection *Tanker i en Skorsten* (Thoughts in a Chimney, 1948) and in *Orm og Tyr* (Serpent and Bull, 1952), which reconstructs, on the basis of architectural and literary monuments, ancestral belief from the period of Nordic antiquity up through the Middle Ages. Martin A. Hansen had the same philosophical bent as Kierkegaard, Dostoevsky, and Bergson, who sought to replace the utopian faith in progress and rational perception with a basic metaphysical viewpoint.

Chapter 9

Faroese Literature — A Survey

On the Faroese Islands, situated in the North Atlantic, Danish was the official language until 1948 when the islands became a self-governing region of Denmark. A major barrier to the development of the Faroese language was the absence of spelling rules, which were first developed in 1854 by V. U. Hammershaimb (1819-1909). Until then, literary tradition was primarily oral, consisting of riddles, tales, and ballads which were transmitted from one generation to another.

Modern Faroese literature began with patriotic and religious songs composed in the 1870s by Faroese students in Copenhagen and on the islands. The three major writers of this period were Fríðrikur Petersen, Jóannes Paturson, and Rasmus Effersøe. Fríðrikur Petersen (1853-1917), a politician and theologian, was unsurpassed as a writer of patriotic songs. His poem "Eg oyggjar veit" ("I Know Islands"), printed in the volume *Minnisútgáva* (Commemorative Edition, 1953), was for a long time used as the Faroese national anthem. Jóannes Paturson (1866-1946) became a leading figure in the Faroese liberation movement and founded in 1906 the first autonomist party, whose leader he remained until 1935. Patursson was a versatile and talented politician and author who wrote numerous articles on cultural and political topics. In addition, he created patriotic poetry, some of which was published in *Yrkingar* (Poems, 1932). He was much involved in preserving Faroese traditions and published several collections of songs and ballads. The same interest characterized Rasmus Effersøe (1857-1916), who in 1889 founded *Føringafelag* to protect Faroese language and culture; he also edited the first newspaper in Faroese (from 1890). Effersøe's writings were published in *Minnisútgáva* (Commemorative Edition, 1917–18), including his very popular patriotic songs and a number of dramas with motifs from history and daily life.

Only in the period after 1900 did a richer and more intimate form of poetry emerge. Its foremost representative was Jens H. O. Djurhuus (1881–1948), the major poet in Faroese literature, whose ornate and exclusive imagery has been compared with that of Aukrust in Norway, Einar Benediktsson in Iceland, and Leino in Finland. The keynote of *Yrkingar* (Poems, 1914; second enlarged edition, 1928), the first individual volume of poetry in Faroese, and *Nýggjar yrkingar* (New Poems, 1938) is doubt and pessimism, a result of the clash between the author's powerful, pathetic dream of beauty and petty, miserable reality. Completely different was his younger, more productive brother, Hans Andreas Djurhuus (1883–1951), a writer of popular and idyllic lyrical poetry, of which two selections, *Undir víðum lofti* (Under) Wide Skies) and *Yvir teigar og tún* (Over Field and Farmyard), were published in 1934 and 1936, respectively. Djurhuus was also the author of a volume of children's songs, *Barnarímur* (Children's Songs, 1915). In addition, he wrote fairy tales, epic poetry, and several dramas, such as the plays *Marita* (1908) and *Annika* (1917) with motifs from Faroese history and legends.

Faroese prose had its beginnings in Hammershaimb's edition of ballads and folk tales, *Færøsk Anthologi* (Faroese Anthology, 1886–91). Regin í Líð (pseudonym of Rasmus Rasmussen [1871–1962]), author of short stories and nature descriptions from about 1900 on, published the first Faroese novel in 1909; *Bábelstornið* (The Tower of Babel), a novel portraying three generations of a family, deals with the conflicts between Danish and Faroese, and especially between the peasants' traditional distrustful conservatism and reforming efforts within the political and economic sector.

The next generation of writers also experienced the clash between the vanishing peasant culture and the new social structure. This conflict forms the basis of a novel by Heðin Brú (pseudonym of Hans Jakob Jacobsen [1901–   ]), *Feðgar á ferð* (1940; Eng. tr. *The Old Man and His Sons*, 1970), a humorous portrayal of the reactions of an old Faroese to modern times. His two-volume novel *Longbrá* (Mirage, 1930) and *Fastatøkur* (Firm Grip, 1935) was the first Faroese work to depict the lives of sailors and fishermen. It tells the story of the boy Høgni, of his adolescence and break with his parents and his escape to the sea. Brú's talents as a portrayer of humans and nature were also developed in poems, published in the magazine *Varðin* (The

Cairn, 1921–) and in the short-story collections *Fjallaskuggin* (The Shadow of the Mountain, 1936), *Purkhús* (1966), and *Búravnurin* (Pantry-Pal, 1971). The novel *Leikum fagurt* (Let Us Play Prettily, 1963) deals with the political fanaticism on the islands before World War II, and *Men lívið lær* (But Life Laughs, 1970) is a historical novel set among peasants around 1800.

Brú's writing includes both detailed realistic descriptions of Faroese everyday life and symbolic narrative. He is undoubtedly the most stylistically talented of contemporary writers on the Faroe Islands. Brú not only preserves the ancient Faroese dialects, he also makes the language more viable through translations of foreign literature such as Shakespeare's plays.

Two of the most outstanding Scandinavian authors of the twentieth century are Faroese but write in Danish.

Jørgen-Frantz Jacobsen

The sole work of Jacobsen (1900–38) was published posthumously: The historical novel *Barbara* (1939; Eng. tr. 1948) builds on a local tradition from the eighteenth century. The book paints a fascinating portrait of a woman who completely follows her natural instincts–a Faroese Madame Bovary. She is the widow of two ministers and married to a third whom she abandons. Even though Barbara represents the tragic aspects of human relationships, she is the tubercular author's glorification of the precious qualities of life.

William Heinesen

The writing of Heinesen (1900–), who was born in Tórshavn where he has lived since 1932, has more facets than Jacobsen's, being both lyrical and epic. His poetic debut, *Arktiske Elegier* (Arctic Elegies, 1921), was heavily influenced by the symbolism of the 1890s. Like Heinesen's volumes of poetry written from 1924 to 1927, the collection expresses extreme individualism: The self–confronted with Faroese nature–faces loneliness and death in isolation. *Stjernerne vaagner* (The Stars Awaken, 1930) denotes a turning from mysticism toward social awareness; Heinesen finally broke with nature mysticism and individualism in favor of critical rationalism, influenced by Otto Gelsted and Hans Kirk, with *Den dunkle Sol* (The Dark Sun, 1936). This tendency increases in *Hymne og Harmsang* (Hymn and Song of Wrath, 1961), a book of radical cultural criticism. It is combined with Heinesen's predilection for cosmic nature in *Panorama med regnbue* (Panorama with Rainbow, 1972), a volume which effectively deals with a basic motif in his writing: how to overcome the antitheses of life/death and time/eternity.

In his prose Heinesen's social commitment is first noticeable in a number of realistic collective novels influenced by Kirk. The first, *Blæsende Gry* (Stormy Daybreak, 1934), gives a broad cross-section of a small island's community, the fight between old and new and the exploitation of the poor by wealthy merchants and shipowners. *Noatun* (1938; Eng. tr. *Niels Peter*, 1940) describes the individual's fight against such exploitation and—like Heinesen's poetry—his battle with harsh Faroese nature. The author's pessimism turns into deadly satire as he settles accounts with the profit-seekers and phrasemongers of World War II. In this novel, as well as in his masterpiece *De fortabte Spillemænd* (1950; Eng. tr. *The Lost Musicians*, 1971), Heinesen's profound imaginative power is fully released, combined in the latter with a grotesque sense of humor. Heinesen has now returned to the Tórshavn of his childhood and portrays a large gallery of eccentric musicians and poets far above the material world which, however, constantly poses a threat to them. The novel *Moder Syvstjerne* (The Pleiades, 1952) is a lyrical and philosophical hymn to women as the source of life and of all meaningful existence. Comic and tragic elements in human life are again ingeniously mingled in Heinesen's other major work, *Det gode Håb* (The Good Hope, 1964), an epistolary novel set in the seventeenth century, the darkest period in the islands' history, when they were heavily exploited by the Danes. Heinesen's own childhood provides the material for his latest work, *Tårnet ved verdens ende* (The Tower at the End of the World, 1976). In about seventy brief chapters the novel portrays Amaldus the Young and his dreams and fantasies. In reality, the work is the aging author's magnificent farewell to life, expressed in a lyrical, occasionally humorous, language, which hides deep sadness and resignation.

Heinesen is one of those remarkable authors, indeed one of the foremost within the Nordic countries, who succeeds, both as a poet with a cosmic vision and as a narrator of fabulous tales, in creating his own universe. Behind the external social and historical reality of the period pieces such as those in *Fortællinger fra Thorshavn* (Stories from Tórshavn, 1973), a selection of Heinesen's best short stories—he seeks the poetic experience that is the only thing of everlasting value in a changing world.

Among the writers of the next generation, Regin Dahl (1918–   ) has lived in Denmark since 1937 and writes in both Danish and Faroese. Since 1937 he has published seven volumes of poetry, of which the selection, *Ærinde uden betydning/Sneisaboð* (Errand without Meaning,

1970) is the most representative in its mix of current themes and old Faroese tradition; another selection, *Tríkirni* (Neglected Field) was published in 1978. Formally Dahl's books demonstrate a development from romantic symbolism toward classical modernism. The same can be said of the more subdued collection of poetry by Karsten Hoydal (1912–), *Myrkrið Reyða* (Red Darkness, 1946), *Syngjandi Grot* (Singing Stones, 1951), and *Vatnið og Ljosið* (The Waters and the Light, 1960). The volume *Teinur og Tal* (Talk on the Way, 1972) contains numerous translations from Edgar Lee Masters. The most versatile among the younger Faroese authors is Jens Pauli Heinesen (1932–) whose work includes, in addition to poetry, short stories, novels, and one drama. His major work is the cycle of novels *Tú upphavsins heimur* (Your Primordial World, 1962–66), which most convincingly elaborates the main motif of Heinesen's writings: the human attempt to gain power over others.

The most recent Faroese authors are primarily lyrical poets, the most experimental of these the very talented Steinbjørn B. Jacobsen (1937–), who has also published numerous children's books. He follows the strong Faroese tradition of nature poetry, and his condensed style is reminiscent of Ezra Pound's imagism and Japanese *haiku* poetry. Guðrið Helmsdal Nielsen (1941–), on the other hand, chooses a more sensitive, modernistic style in the manner of Edith Södergran for her nature poetry and a rather traditional approach reminiscent of Tove Ditlevsen for her love poems.

A neo-romantic atmosphere–also to be found in contemporary Danish literature–dominates the poems of Arnbjørn Danielsen (1947–) and Heðin M. Klein (1950–), whereas the political world figures importantly in the work of Jóannes Dalsgaard (1940–) as do everyday events and impressions in the work of Rói Patursson (1947–). Recent forms of "concrete" and "systematic" poetry (see p. 256) have found few representatives.

Chapter 10

Fenno-Swedish Modernism

After World War I a modernist breakthrough occurred in Fenno-Swedish literature which turned against the *flaneur* mentality and the older writers' aristocratic exclusiveness. Without forming any cohesive group, the young poets contributed to the periodical *Ultra* (1922), which in 1928 was succeeded by *Quosego* (1928–29). This modernism remained something of an underground movement during the 1920s, not manifest in the other Nordic countries. One must turn to the Anglo-American poets T. S. Eliot and Ezra Pound to find corresponding trends—*The Waste Land* was published in the same year as *Ultra*. Nevertheless, in the long run Fenno-Swedish modernism was to influence poetic developments in all the Nordic literatures.

Hagar Olsson, the new school's leading theoretician, polemicized against Arvid Mörne's "village romanticism," maintaining that the new movement was international in outlook. In 1923 Elmer Diktonius published a volume of translations of Sandburg, Masters, Pound, and Alfred Mombert, *Ungt hav* (Young Sea), and in 1925 Hagar Olsson a collection of essays, *Ny generation* (The New Generation) with portrayals of Joyce, Whitman, and Pirandello. Fenno-Swedish literature now became susceptible both to European, especially German, expressionism—with its emphasis on life's complexity and polarity—and to the current of anti-intellectualism and irrationalism that had found its philosopher in Henri Bergson. It is no coincidence that the work of the poets who prepared the way for modernism has strong elements of mysticism and romanticism.

Edith Södergran

The first and possibly greatest of the Fenno-Swedish modernists, Södergran (1892-1923) made her debut in 1916 with *Dikter* (Poems). Characteristic of this collection is a series of brief pictures of nature, in which her Karelian home village of Raivola is recognizable. Her landscape, however, is a dream landscape; as in the work of Vilhelm Ekelund, the natural and the spiritual are blended completely. Important in this first work are love poems based on a disappointing love experience of the poet:

> You searched for a flower
> and found a fruit.
> You searched for a spring
> and found an ocean.
> You searched for a woman
> and found a soul—
> you are disappointed.

Tr. Marianne Forssblad

Between Edith Södergran's first and second collections lie two years in which her life and her poetry changed decisively: The fact that her poetry did not gain recognition injured her deeply; the bloody events of 1917/18, the Russian revolution, and the Finnish Civil War inundated even Raivola; her tuberculosis worsened, but she defended herself against approaching death. Nietzsche's philosophy of the superman who conquers suffering mobilized her entire vitality and strength of will. Hymns to the beauty and richness of life alternate in the collections *Septemberlyran* (The September Lyre, 1918), *Rosenaltaret* (The Altar of Roses, 1919), and *Framtidens skugga* (Shadow of Future, 1920).

This exertion of strength led by 1920 to a crisis in which Södergran's Nietzschean affirmation of life and materialistic world view collapsed. She sought religious stability and finally found her way through Rudolf Steiner's anthroposophy to the Christ of the Gospels, where she experienced peace. Against this background, her last, profound, and transfigured poems of the posthumous collection *Landet som icke är* (The Land, Which is Not, 1925) assume greatness as a personal preparation for death.

Edith Södergran learned from the German prewar expressionism of Alfred Mombert and the Russian futurism of Vladimir Majakovski. Her poetic work points to the possibility of relaxing the sometimes

too tightly structured poetry of the 1890s, through greatly intensi-
fying poetic imagery.

Hagar Olsson

Personal experiences forced Edith Södergran's poetry into new and
original directions. This was also true of Olsson (1893–1978); a strong
preoccupation with contemporary problems was also an important
factor. Her early works contain attacks on literary fashion in Finland
at that time and a vague mysticism pervaded by an awareness of death.
This theme is present in Olsson's first book, the novel *Lars Thorman
och döden* (Lars Thorman and Death, 1916) and is fully developed in
the novel influenced by Lagerkvist, *Kvinnan och nåden* (A Woman
and Grace, 1919), which affirms the Christian belief that death is the
ultimate step to grace. Between 1926 and 1930 Olsson published
three novels and two plays in rapid succession. All are heavily experimental: Pirandello and the German expressionist Georg Kaiser are the
models for the plays; the prose of the novels is both surrealistic and
concisely journalistic. The themes are typical of the 1920s: pacificism,
Pan-Europeanism, functionalism, and, above all, collectivism. With
Chitambo (1933) she created her first major work, a partly autobiographical novel of development which demonstrates the futility of all
human action. In the poetic Karelian idyll *Träsnidaren och döden*
(1940; Eng. tr. *The Woodcarver and Death*, 1965) Olsson's mysticism
is fully expressed; her next work, an imitation of a Chinese legend,
Kinesisk utflykt (A Chinese Excursion, 1949), is set in a landscape of
dreams and memories, based on events from her own life that she
later describes in her autobiography published in 1963, *Möte med
kära gestalter* (Meeting Those Whom I Have Loved).

Elmer Diktonius

The third poet of the *Ultra* group is Diktonius (1896–1961), whose
artistic career began at the Academy of Music in Helsingfors, but who,
after a number of sharply criticized performances of expressionistic
compositions, chose the life of a writer. Diktonius made his literary
debut with a volume characteristic of his later work. The poems in
Min dikt (My Poetry, 1921), inspired by Vilhelm Ekelund, are concise and aphoristic, and are exclusively concerned with art and artistic
creation. Diktonius did not believe in art for art's sake and rejected
any purely aesthetic view of art. He thought art and everyday life
simply expressed two aspects of existence in continual interplay. The

opening poem, "Jaguaren" ("The Jaguar"), expresses the poet's Nietz-
sche-inspired program, brutality for the sake of life:

> We want to kill the screams of those without feeling
> the pity of those without heart
> the religiousness of those without faith
> the powerlessness of the strong
> the evil weakness of the good
> we want to give life through killing.

Tr. Marianne Forssblad

The same uncompromising stand, the same aesthetic radicalism, which
in the young Diktonius was accompanied by political radicalism, is
continued in *Hårda sånger* (Hard Songs, 1922), *Brödet och elden* (The
Bread and the Fire, 1923), *Taggiga lågor* (Barbed Flames, 1924), and
the breakthrough volume, *Stenkol* (Coke, 1927). The poet wants to
find a new, more naked reality and to see life free of its dead shell.

In the collection from 1930, *Stark men mörk* (Strong but Dark)
Diktonius experimented with a number of dadaist effects and simultaneously mobilized a humanistic attitude in the face of the political
catastrophies that were threatening. In addition, a social criticism is
present in a number of proletarian poems, together with a new positive attitude toward nature, undoubtedly influenced by Whitman,
evidenced by the titles of the volumes *Mull och moln* (Clods and
Clouds, 1934) and *Jordisk ömhet* (Earthly Gentleness, 1938). Here
the previously very aggressive poet unreservedly accepts the brighter
aspects of life, utilizing biblical motifs and shaping his poems with
broad, vigorous strokes, fascinated by the tiny miracles of nature,
which symbolize the eternal cycle of life and death. This turning to
nature and the idyllic is also present in the sketches from the countryside, *Onnela* (1925). These mark the beginning of Diktonius's prose
writing, which culminates in the pacifist novel *Janne Kubik* (1932),
the story of a communist during the civil war, which is related with a
wealth of naturalistic detail.

The idea of perishability underlies the childhood memories in the
collections *Varsel* (Forebodings, 1942) and *Annorlunda* (Otherwise,
1948). The poems are characterized by intimacy and warmth, and
also by a feeling of solidarity with all that is alive and growing. Diktonius's exuberant joy in life is sustained throughout his work, as the
title of his last book, *Novembervår* (November Spring, 1951) indicates.
The poems are enlivened by the spontaneous acceptance of the instinctive and vital forces of life, which is Diktonius's revolutionary
contribution to Fenno-Swedish poetry.

Gunnar Björling

The most singular and radical of the modernists was Björling (1887–1960). He was born in Helsingfors and was a well-known figure in the city's literary life when he made his debut in 1922 with *Vilande dag* (The Resting Day), a collection of prose poems echoing Vilhelm Ekelund and the Indian poet Rabintranath Tagore, who was very popular around 1920. It contains the basic elements of Björling's succeeding works: a relativist moral philosophy and a vision of life as something open and unfinished. As he attempted to capture life's boundlessness, Björling began to realize the limited expressive possibilities of language. He, therefore, constructed his own syntax, in which parts of sentences and suffixes were dropped. The method is fully developed in *Korset och löftet* (The Cross and the Promise, 1925), expressing—in Björling's own words—"a universal dada-individualism," which culminates in *Kiri-ra!* (1930). This volume reveals Björling to be the earliest and most consciously dadaist of the Nordic poets. After the publication of *Solgrönt* (Sungreen, 1933) nature became an increasingly important source of inspiration as Björling reacted against intellectualism and attempted to reestablish direct contact with the simplest forms of life. Here one finds ecstatic exclamations and sensitive poetry, impressionistic pictures of nature and monumental statements, quiet repose in the universe and ruthless self-examination, which, especially in *Fågel badar snart i vattnen* (The Bird Bathes Soon in the Waters, 1934) and *Men blåser violer på havet* (But Blowing Violets on the Sea, 1936) are played off against each other. From then on Björling published a book almost every year—poetry, aphorisms, and miniature essays—always in very concise form. Early nihilistic tendencies are replaced by mystical calmness, which, however, is interrupted by shrill dissonances. In the 1940s Björling published seven collections and in the early 1950s a volume each year, of which a representative selection, *Du jord du dag* (You Earth You Day), was published in 1957. The poems are increasingly laconic, and the psychological point of departure is still that words will never be able to render a complete picture of experience, a realization that is raised to a metaphysical level: Life is a fragment; when humans want to express something meaningful about life and death, they are mute or stammer helplessly.

Rabbe Enckell

In an article in *Quosego* (see p. 227) Enckell (1903–74), one of the main theoreticians of Fenno-Swedish modernism, formulated an artistic program which, although not revolutionary, was a clear rejection of traditional forms of art. His poetry differs from that of Södergran, Diktonius, and Björling in that it is neither visionary nor prophetic, neither violent nor ecstatic, but, rather, consists of delicate analyses of his feelings. In the first collections, *Dikter* (Poems, 1923) and *Flöjtblåsarlycka* (Flutist's Happiness, 1925), Enckell appears as a soft-spoken poet of love and nature, his descriptions of the latter being acute visual pictures. He looked for the aesthetic experience that was an expression of his cult of beauty, related to that of Vilhelm Ekelund; Obstfelder was the model for Enckell's free verses. Consistently Enckell related his observations to his own personality, letting himself color each detail, a technique that also characterizes his three self-searching prose volumes from the 1930s.

Enckell mastered the art of the miniature in *Vårens cistern* (Spring's Cistern, 1931) and *Tonbrädet* (The Soundboard, 1935). Several of the poems speak of "the lost anxiety of the heart, the winter-locked thought" and a tone of resignation prevails: "On earth happiness is prohibited." In the 1935 collection a fascination with classical motifs is manifest, this tendency becoming even more distinct in *Valvet* (The Vault, 1937) and *Lutad över brunnen* (Bent over the Well, 1942), in which Enckell uses Greek and Roman myths in poems with a certain rhetorical pomp, occasionally in classical meters. Simultaneously he began to write a series of Greek-inspired verse dramas, from *Orfeus och Eurydike* (Orpheus and Eurydice, 1938) to *Alkman* (1959), works that illuminate the often tragic relationship of humans and fate.

Andedräkt av koppar (A Breath of Copper, 1946) finally brought the author a larger audience, marking his breakthrough in Sweden. Included is the central philosophical poem "O spång av mellanord" ("O Steps of Words Between"), a long piece about language, life itself being represented by the "Words Between": "One finds nothing in life, / if one cannot find those words, / made transparent by that / which the spirit has in common with all and everything." Throughout the 1950s and up to his last collection, *Flyende spegel* (Fleeing Mirrors, 1974), Enckell published a number of volumes in which he employed additional classical motifs in small lyrical portraits or in dialogues—meditative, refined poetry which complements the visionary, romantic, provocative, and philosophical elements of Fenno-Swedish modernism with moderation, balance, and strong self-criticism. These elements also characterize the essay collections from *Relation i det personliga* (Personal Report, 1950) to *Tapetdörren* (The Wallpaper Door, 1968) in which he deals with aesthetic problems from the point of view of his exclusive and individualistic conception of art.

Chapter *11*

Social Realism and Innovation in Finland

TRADITIONAL AND EXPERIMENTAL PROSE

Prose literature in Finland between the two world wars was dominated by a number of authors writing in Finnish, who during the troubled years of the civil war rejected all neo-romantic slogans and addressed themselves to the needs and interests of the common people—in contrast to the work of the Fenno-Swedish poets. The result was a flourishing realistic prose literature, sharply contrasting with the earlier idealized descriptions of Finnish folk life.

Ilmari Kianto

The writing of Kianto (1874–1970) includes poems, novels, tales, plays, memoirs, and travel books, but he achieved his greatest artistic victory with his objective depictions of his northern Finnish native village and its population, which are outstanding period pieces. In *Punainen viiva* (The Red Line, 1909) the poor rural population is promised electoral reforms which, however, turn out to be an empty gesture; behind all the phrases, reality is as bleak as ever. Kianto's criticism is aimed at the upper class, but the communist agitator also gets his share. Although his tone is serious, Kianto always lets a humorous vein flow; in the novel *Ryysyrannan Jooseppi* (Jooseppi from Ryysyranta, 1924), a master of comic description is at work. Kianto does not refer to social issues in the book except for the problem of prohibition. The plots of both works are secondary; what Kianto focuses on is extreme poverty and its impact on everyday life in the backwoods.

Joel Lehtonen

Neither Kianto nor Joel Lehtonen (1881–1934) expects to see any substantial political change result from their social criticism. They blame a society that does not guide uneducated people and their main characters who entrench themselves behind their biases and resentments.

With the volume of short stories *Kuolleet omenapuut* (The Dead Apple Trees, 1918) Lehtonen became a mature artist. Many of the characters are taken from his earlier, uneven, works, written during the civil war. The idealistic bookstore-owner Aapeli Muttinen, a character from Lehtonen's first novel, *Kerran kesällä* (Once during the Summer, 1917), and the author's alter ego, buys the estate Putkinotko, on which he invites Juutas Käkriäinen, another important character in Lehtonen's literary gallery, to live. His major work, *Putkinotko* (1919–20), describes with festive, occasionally Rabelaisian humor the events of a single summer day among the twelve members of the lazy, dirty, and disorderly Käkriäinen family; their social and economic background is revealed, as is the failure of everything they try to do. The character portrayal and especially the dialogue are strongly naturalistic, but they are framed with impressionistic, colorful, mature descriptions which provide a contrast to the poverty and misery.

Characters from this novel also appear in Lehtonen's later works such as the novel *Rakastunut rampa* (A Cripple in Love, 1922), in which the individualism and hero worship of his early, neo-romantic works—influenced by Hamsun, Lagerlöf, and Nietzsche—are sharply rejected. From now on Lehtonen's writing is increasingly marked by his revolt against his own time. However, after *Putkinotko* he was incapable of creating the same balance in the struggle between the positive and negative sides of life. Most pessimistic is his last novel, *Henkien taistelu* (The Struggle of the Spirits, 1933), a series of loosely connected scenes from everyday life; the framework is a discussion between God and Satan about whether or not a completely good human can be forced to lose faith. This travesty on Le Sage's story of the devil on two sticks from 1707 becomes a caricature of time and life. All illusions are exposed, all masks torn off, pettiness and narrowness of mind have taken over. Undoubtedly Joel Lehtonen, an extremely incongruous and many-sided personality, is one of Finland's most exciting authors, who should occupy a central place in Nordic literature.

Maria Jotuni

A third author, Jotuni (1880–1943), also managed to give her harsh criticism of life a reconciling, humorous touch. Her posthumously published novel about the 1930s, *Huojuva talo* (A Tottering House, 1963), is now considered her major work. It is a story of an unhappy marriage, but, like Lehtonen's last book, it is a general protest against violence and injustice. Her most significant works are her short stories, which reach their culmination in the volumes *Rakkautta* (Love, 1907) and *Kun on tunteet* (The Feelings One Has, 1913), dealing with erotic motifs. The titles are ironic, for love is seen as selfish and marriage as a purely pecuniary arrangement. In an objective fashion, Maria Jotuni causes her female characters to become social accusations, thereby completing the task Minna Canth began in the 1880s. Jotuni's originality lies in her sensuous emancipation and subtle erotic psychology, which suggest that Herman Bang and Maupassant were her teachers.

Frans Eemil Sillanpää

The author of the interwar period who was most closely connected to his native soil—the area around Tampere (Tammerfors)—was undoubtedly Sillanpää (1888-1964). His four-year study of biology at the University of Helsinki influenced his view of life radically. He perceives humanity only in terms of nature, and nature is not only a biological fact but also a condition that stimulates our psychic sensations. The product of this condition, in which the self and nature merge—as in his first novel, *Elämä ja aurinko* (Life and the Sun, 1916)—is a refined, sensuous piece of art, for which Sillanpää had found inspiration in Hamsun and Maeterlinck.

In *Hurskas kurjuus* (1919; Eng. tr. *Meek Heritage*, 1938) the lyrical mood is replaced by disciplined objectivity. The novel depicts the miserable life of Juha Toivola, innocently executed during the civil war, a solitary, passive character, who simply drifted with events into the socialist movement and succumbed. Sillanpää's sympathetic attitude toward the communist Juha created a sensation, but the compassion and humanity of the book made it a classic description in Finnish literature of the bloody events. Sillanpää's next novel, *Nuorena nukkunut* (1931; Eng. tr. *The Maid Silja*, 1933; *Fallen Asleep while Young*, 1939) spread his fame abroad. The book deals with the destruction of an old peasant family, framed by sensitive, chiaroscuro descriptions of nature in summer. Contrasted with the poverty and illness of the main characters is their inner strength as they face death—the author's demonstration of the spirit's victory over matter.

The tone of Sillanpää's first novel is resumed in his novels of the 1930s, *Miehen tie* (The Way of Man, 1932) and *Ihmiset suviyössä* (1934; Eng. tr. *People in the Summer Night*, 1966). The first is a love story, set in a village against the backdrop of the vividly depicted seasonal changes; the second takes place during a few days and nights of summer, and offers a cross-section of human destiny. The narrative shifts from one character to another, stressing their relative importance and parallel destinies, and the events include all the processes of life: birth and death, young and mature love. The importance that Sillanpää places on love and sex as the ruling forces of all human life, together with his insistence that these forces have moral values which are unconnected to social rules, has suggested a comparison with D. H. Lawrence.

In the 1930s Sillanpää published two collections of short stories, *Virran pohjalta* (The Bottom of the River, 1933) and *Viidestoista* (The Fifteenth, 1936) and in 1941 a novel *Elokuu* (August). By that time he was regarded by the public as the greatest of the Finnish writers, and in 1939 he was awarded the only Nobel Prize for literature that Finland has received.

Volter Kilpi

Kilpi (1874–1939) made his debut around 1900 with three neoromantic novels, lyrical prose the philosophical content of which is traceable to Nietzsche and Schopenhauer. He then stopped writing and began working as a librarian at the University of Turku (Åbo), which opened in 1922. Kilpi returned to the literary scene in 1933 with the novel *Alastalon salissa* (In the Living Room of Alastalo), the most daring Finnish prose experiment of the interwar period. The external action of this two-volume work takes place in only six hours. Farmers of a Westfinnish coastal parish in the 1860s meet to discuss the purchase of a new ship. On the surface the novel is a didactic story about honesty and hard work like Kivi's *Seven Brothers*; and like it, there is an inner, mythical, dimension; the characters function not only in the present but also in the past, in the future, and on purely fictitious levels. Kilpi uses minute details of the setting, stream-of-consciousness, and inner monologue—reminiscent of Proust and Joyce —as he discloses the hopes and dreams as well as the negative qualities and conflicts of these people. Although there appears to be a firm class structure, an almost imperceptible but total power struggle takes place which Kilpi registers down to the smallest nuances to demonstrate the basic idea of the novel: the transitoriness of everything. Language becomes an important means in the process of cognition, and to find *le mot propre*, Kilpi uses not only dialect and proverbs, but also completely new constructions, which make the book almost impossible to translate.

The next two works are set in the same milieu as is *In the Living*

Room of Alastalo. The first story in the collection *Pitäjän pienempiä* (Small People in the Country, 1934), "Ylistalon tuvassa" ("In the Living Room of Ylistalo"), tells humorously what some sailors were doing in a neighboring house while the farmers of the previous novel were discussing important matters at Alastalo. The other stories, however, are less humorous and often deal with people who, through bad luck and their own fault, have ruined their lives. The action of the novel *Kirkolle* (On the Road to the Church, 1937)—the gathering of some churchgoers, their journey in a boat, and arrival at the church—takes place in three hours. Again the description of the individuals, their thoughts and feelings, is the main factor. The narrative moves between present and past, reminiscent of Proust, and branches off in discursive secondary episodes, ignoring syntactical rules.

Mika Waltari

Kilpi is undoubtedly the most exciting and original talent in Finnish prose ,and as such will always have a limited audience. More traditional and world famous is Waltari (1908–79). His best work—the trilogy *Mies ja haave* (A Man and a Dream, 1933), *Sielu ja liekki* (The Soul and the Flame, 1934), and *Palava nuoruus* (Burning Youth, 1935), published in one volume as *Isästä poikaan* (From Father to Son, 1942), about a family that settles in Helsinki, and *Vieras mies tuli taloon* (1937; Eng. tr. *A Stranger Came to the Farm*, 1952), a novel with a rural setting—were written in the 1930s. While employed by the Government Information Service during the war, Waltari wrote some wartime novels and in the postwar years up to 1964 six colorful and romantic historical novels which have made him the best-known Finnish author of all time. The novels were translated into most major languages, and the first, *Sinuhe, egyptiläinen* (1945; Eng. tr. *The Egyptian*, 1949) was filmed in Hollywood. Disguised by a historical facade, *The Egyptian* is an analysis of the disappointment and disillusionment after Finland's defeat by Russia in 1944.

More valuable than these purely entertaining novels are Waltari's short stories, in which sentimentality is modified by self-irony and a more skeptical view of life. The stories in *Kuun maisema* (1953; Eng. tr. *Moonscape and Other Stories*, 1954) and *Koiranheisipuu* (The Woodbine, 1961) are marked by a clearly pessimistic and resigned tone, a result of Waltari's disillusioning realization that humans are unable to measure up to his ideals: freedom of the individual, humanity, and tolerance.

Waltari was one of the few prose writers connected with the pamphlet *Tulenkantajat* (The Torchbearers, 1924)—a parallel to the Fenno-

Swedish *Ultra*—which eventually gave its name to an entire group of writers proclaiming as their program the love of life, an international outlook, and tolerance. Their proclamations, however, quickly faded in the face of the political events of the interwar period, when the "Lappo-Movement," originally the farmers' reaction against the leftist tendencies prevalent about 1930, signaled a new surge of nationalistic sentiment. Unlike the Fenno-Swedish modernists, the *Tulenkantajat* group left no lasting impression on literature.

The two self-taught authors Pentti Haanpää and Toivo Pekkanen belonged to the same generation as the *Tulenkantajat* writers but were not closely associated with this group.

Pentti Haanpää

Haanpää (1905–55) was notably a master of the short story; an excellent selection was published as *Jutut* (Stories) in 1946, in which Haanpää used a traditional realistic technique. His choice of motifs is limited: He depicts primarily lumberjacks of northern Finland, poor people who, like Haanpää himself, are strongly critical of society. The tone becomes more aggressive in the novel *Yhdeksän miehen saappaat* (The Boots of Nine Men, 1945), a disrespectful account of the Finnish army, which contains a series of episodes connected by a pair of boots passing from man to man. After World War II Haanpää wrote three collections of short stories, of which *Heta Rahko korkeassa iässä* (Heta Rahko at an Old Age, 1947) and *Atomintutkija* (The Nuclear Physicist, 1950) are among Haanpää's best works; the subjects range from the serious and tragic to humorous portraits of modest and energetic characters.

Toivo Pekkanen

Pekkanen (1902–57) is also a representative of the proletarian writers. He broke through with the partly autobiographical novel about a young worker entitled *Tehtaan varjossa* (In the Shadow of the Factory, 1932), a novel that has parallels in the proletarian literature of the other Nordic countries. In all of Pekkanen's works the importance of human spiritual progress is stressed. In the novel *Isänmaan ranta* (The Shore of My Country, 1937), which describes a strike among longshoremen at the end of the 1920s, he lets the human leader of the strike, Helminen, believe in peaceful social evolution and the spiritual maturing of the individual. A fascination with the fantastic and symbolic is obvious in the drama *Demoni* (The Demon, 1939), which deals with the problems of a genius, in the D. H. Lawrence-like novel about human subconscious powers, *Musta hurmio* (Black Ecstasy, 1939), and in the best of Pekkanen's short-story collections, *Mies ja punapartaiset herrat* (The Man and the Gentlemen with the Red Beards, 1950). Shortly before his death Pekkanen began his major work, a broadly planned cycle of novels of which three were published, *Aamuhämärä* (Dawn, 1948), *Toverukset* (Friends, 1948), and *Voittajat ja voitetut* (Victors and the Vanquished, 1952). The novels depict the industrial growth of the author's childhood town of Kotka. The narrative, however, is largely fictional, describing the personal relations, love affairs, and religious problems of Pekka, a young worker. Strictly autobiographical is *Lapsuuteni* (1953; Eng. tr. *My Childhood*, 1966).

Both Pekkanen and Haanpää are fine examples of the fact that the Finnish proletarian writers were far more individualistic than were their Nordic colleagues. They did not belong to any group or organization, but tried individually to find their own point of view, realizing that a feeling of solidarity is necessary but that it is even more crucial to strengthen one's own individuality.

THE CREATION OF MODERNISTIC POETRY

Uuno Kailas

The most remarkable poet of the *Tulenkantajat* group was Kailas (1901–33). Owing to poor mental and physical health he never finished his humanistic studies at the University of Helsinki, but lived a nomadic life until he died of tuberculosis. Kailas's early collections, *Tuuli ja tähkä* (The Wind and the Ear of Grain, 1922) and *Purjehtijat* (The Seafarers, 1925), bear witness to his knowledge of Baudelaire and expressionistic German poetry in their use of free verse and exotic imagery. In both volumes Kailas employs Christian symbols, though he seldom speaks of the relationship of humankind to divinity; for him the world was governed by blind fate. Obsessed as he was with the thought of death, Kailas was unable to find any comfort in philosophy or aesthetics, but attempted to overcome his obsession by equating it with sleep and dreams or simply accepting it as a word without meaning.

Silmästä silmään (Eye to Eye, 1926) brought Kailas before a large audience. It marks a transition in his art from free verse to more traditional forms, characterized by regular rhythm and rhyme, and shows his progressive introversion. The most important poems in this volume describe human destiny as a continuous and lonesome journey through the desert leaving behind a trail of blood. Although it seems a futile task, it remains for humans to struggle forward with beauty as the one and only guiding star. *Paljain jaloin* (Barefoot, 1928) evinces Kailas's increasingly strong feeling of pain and resignation—may fate treat him as it did the martyrs: "They are the torch that illuminates the chasm of the times, / they are the brazen serpent / and the blood on the doorpost / and the rainbow over the flood." In *Uni ja kuolema* (Sleep and Death, 1931) some of the motifs of the previous collections reappear in a more subdued manner. The volume is a poignant testimony to Kailas's feeling of alienation: "There is no door / for friends or visitors to come. / But two doors have I, / two: to dream and to death."

The tension Kailas felt was primarily ethical: a Christian dualism between spirit and matter, ideal and reality, guilt and atonement. His major poems are placed in the twilight zone between vigil and dream and become magnificent projections of the poet's feeling of guilt and fear of death. They belong to the most fascinating artistic achievements of modern European poetry.

Aaro Hellaakoski

An ethical element also dominates the writing of Hellaakoski (1893–1952) but in a much less speculative way. The son of a geography teacher in Oulu (Luleåborg), he published some works on geology and taught this subject for many years as a lecturer at the University of Helsinki and at a secondary school. In 1916 he published his first volume of poetry and continued to write poetry, while also writing essays and scientific works, until 1928. He did not resume the publication of poetry until 1943—when he was forced to by the shocking events of the war with Russia (see p. 255).

In his debut work, *Runoja* (Poems, 1916), Hellaakoski portrays the poet's struggle to acquire an artistic means of expression. The important part played by the creative will is expressed in *Me kaksi* (We Two, 1920) as a dialogue between reason and heart, a discussion between these two fundamentally different elements within the poet himself. The book also contains a number of tightly structured nature poems in which nature stands for liberation, offering Hellaakoski oblivion without demanding anything in return:

> Quietly like a dream
> July sails forth and away.
> Yesterday is long ago.
> Tomorrow is forgotten.
> From whence come, whereto gone?
>
> Tr. Marianne Forssblad

Jääpeili (The Ice Mirror, 1928), the only poetic work of the 1920s that can be considered parallel to those by the Fenno-Swedish modernists, is epoch-making not so much because of its typographical experiments but because of its innovative meters and varied content. Hellaakoski's modernism is based on his interest in pictorical art, especially cubism, and the influence of the French surrealist poet Apollinaire. The collection *Uusi runo* (New Poetry, 1943) initiates a period of brilliant creativity, culminating in *Sarjoja* (Suites, 1952), which places Hellaakoski among Finland's greatest lyrical poets of the postwar era. Poetry is now characterized by self-examination, the self becoming increasingly subordinate to a larger totality. In long meditative verses, reminiscent of Rilke's elegies and Eliot's quartets, Hellaakoski expresses a pantheistic experience of nature. A number of religiously colored poems and thoughts of death, inspired by illness, are also included. Hellaakoski concludes that humans can find ultimate truth only through contemplation, expression of undogmatic religiosity, and a fearless and straightforward waiting for death.

At the time of his death, Hellaakoski was one of the most significant writers in Finland, especially appreciated by the younger generation of authors.

P. Mustapää

In the work of Mustapää (pseudonym of Martti Henrikki Haavio [1899-1973]) Hellakoski's influence is evident: the rejection of traditional formal patterns and the refusal to adopt the fashions of the 1920s. Among the *Tulenkantajat* writers Mustapää represents a national tradition. In his early collections, *Laulu ihanista silmistä* (The Song about the Wonderful Eyes, 1925) and *Laulu vaakalinnusta* (The Song about the Griffin, 1927), he remained within the western Finnish cultural arena. As an internationally renowned folklorist, Mustapää was well acquainted not only with the *Kalevala* tradition but also with newer ballads and broadsides, whose style he slightly parodied to create a naive mode of expression. To this must be added the strong influence of Kipling and the two Swedish poets Karlfeldt and Sjöberg. Unlike Kailas and Hellaakoski, Mustapää did not find problems of guilt and conscience appealing. His view of life was rather relativistic, determined by his rejection of the demand for the impossible.

> A wise man understands without fail
> that a rose disappears from a branch
> and footsteps from a trail.
> —A wise man accepts.
>
> Tr. Marianne Forssblad

Not until *Jäähyväiset Arkadialle* (Farewell to Arcadia, 1945), *Linnustaja* (The Fowler, 1952), and *Tuuli Airistolta* (The Wind Blows from Airisto, 1969) did Mustapää create the rhythmic and metaphoric effects that so clearly point to new literary developments. The poems are light rhythmically and rather singable, but are filled with highly sensuous imagery reminiscent of Ezra Pound. Narrative elements are gradually pushed aside, the landscape is sketched with a few lines, and the text becomes suggestive of hidden undercurrents that bring together images that were separate. It is precisely by freeing the poem's inner structure from metrical rules and any epic moralizing and narcissistic elements that Mustapää was more innovative than any earlier Finnish poet.

Chapter 12

Renewal and Traditionalism in Iceland

THE CREATION OF MODERN POETRY

The economic upswing during World War I created a boom within manufacturing, trade, and the fishing industry. In Reykjavík a wealthy, conservative middle class of merchants and shipowners emerged; simultaneously the migration from countryside to city increased, resulting in a large proletariat, most of whom were employed in the fishing industry. Whereas 9,000 people lived in the cities in 1900, more than 20,000 did in 1915. As a counterbalance to the politically influential bourgeoisie, the farmers organized themselves in cooperative associations, and the workers founded their trade union in 1916, which passed its first test during the sailors' strike of the same year.

Icelandic poetry, which around 1900 had been largely traditional and romantic, after 1920 moved toward greater realism, stylistic flexibility, and receptiveness to foreign influences. An intense cult of the self, the present, and sexuality emerged, together with a greater political consciousness.

Stefán Sigurðsson frá Hvitadal

The first poems by Sigurðsson (1887–1933), *Söngvar förumannsins* (The Wanderer's Song, 1918) became a literary event. During a stay in Norway from 1912 to 1916 Sigurðsson had learned much of Vinje, Ibsen, and Wergeland, and had adapted their metric forms. His poetry was more personal than any enountered before in Iceland, revelations of all aspects of his emotional life. In a number of poems the joy of life dominates in tributes to youth and love:

> Oh, my dear, you remember what happened
> in the bright river of light.
> We were so young and intoxicated
> with the fragrance from the heart of the day.
>
> And ours were the moment and youth
> and the fire in manner and speech.
> We met again and again
> with the everthirsting lips of youth.
>
> Tr. Marianne Forssblad

But as a whole the collection moves between two basic tones: darkness (impotence) and light (love and happiness). Nowhere is this more masterfully done than in "Hjartarím" ("Heart Rhyme"), a poem profound in feeling and brilliant in form.

Sigurðsson's next book, *Oður einyrkjans* (The Song of the Lonesome Crofter, 1921), is colored by his life as a farmer. The poems are more earthy and objective, and the range of themes greater as the poet turned to folklore and fairy tales for inspiration. The deep strain of spirituality, notable in the first collection, along with worldliness and flaming passion was heightened by severe illness and became concretized in the strong religious feeling expressed in the closing poem, "Líf" ("Life"). This is one of his very best, containing a deeply felt and sincere declaration of faith; in 1923 he converted to Catholicism. A eulogy of the Catholic Church is found in his next work, *Heilög kirkja* (Holy Church, 1924), reminiscent of the sacred poetry of medieval Icelandic writers, masterful in its metrical excellence and lyrical sensitivity, which also characterizes Sigurðsson's collections of religious poetry of 1927, *Helsingjar* (Geese), and 1933, posthumously, *Anno Domini 1930*. In these collections, he increasingly utilized old Icelandic meters, a revealing testimony to the poet's deep roots in the native soil and tradition.

Davíð Stefánsson

Like Sigurðsson, Stefánsson (1895–1964) established his leading position among the young poets with his first collection, *Svartar fjaðrir* (Black Feathers, 1919). But Stefánsson was more characteristic of the changing times—an exaggerated worship of life contrasted with a destructive war and expressed in a dissolute fashion: "And so we dance and dance / and drink poisonous wine. / . . . I'll be the king of the devils, / and she'll be a queen of mine.'' Stefánsson has a broader range than Sigurðsson, freeing Icelandic poetry from its intricate and stereo-typed verse forms—an inheritance from the Skaldic poetry—replacing them with lighter, more flexible meters and simple language inspired by Icelandic folk ballads.

Stefánsson's second collection, *Kvæði* (Poems, 1922), contains subjective poetry written in the first person and a number of extensive and forceful narrative poems. A trip to Italy provided new motifs for this collection and the third, *Kveðjur* (Greetings, 1924); colorful and realistic descriptions of the social misery he had observed abroad dramatically contrast with the splendor of historic monuments. In the 1930s Stefánsson published two more volumes in which a note of social satire was increasingly audible; in 1947 *Ný kvæðabók* (A New Book of Poems) appeared containing his reactions to the war and disillusionment at the rearmament of the superpowers, in 1966 the posthumous collection *Síðustu ljó* (Last Poems).

As early as 1926 Stefánsson had written an unsuccessful play; in 1941 the humorous *Gullna hliðið* (Eng. tr. *The Golden Gate*, 1967), based on an Icelandic folk legend, became a great success, even abroad. He also wrote a novel *Sólon Íslandus* (1940), a story of a nineteenth-century vagabond, an ambitious artistic dreamer who, because of external circumstances is prevented from developing his talents.

The variety of motifs and forms, the straightforward language, his receptiveness, and the fact that his emotional life was the subject of many of his poems make Stefánsson one of the great renewers of Icelandic poetry.

Tómas Guðmundsson

This renewal was continued by Guðmundsson (1901–) who consistently combined neo-romantic poetic language with everyday language. Following a less than spectacular debut, Guðmundsson appeared in 1933 as a fully developed artist with *Fagra veröld* (Fair World) in which Reykjavík and its busy life became an important theme, the poet discovering there a new dimension of beauty. It is this worship of beauty that is characteristic of Guðmundsson's writing; both here and in the next collection, *Stjörnur vorsins* (Stars of Spring, 1940), it assumes a mystical dimension. The starting point is usually memories and dreams from the poet's youth mingled with the bitter realization that the adventures of the past can never be repeated.

Fljótið helga (The Holy River, 1950) was written during and after World War II and contains a number of polemic poems against Nazism. But the most effective poems express resignation at the transitoriness of life. In his best poetry—of which numerous collected editions, *Ljó asafn* (*Collected Poems*), were published between 1953 and 1974—Guðmundsson avoided social motifs that he found unpoetic. Instead, he constantly searched for beauty, the elusive idea of which he clothed in unique linguistic and rhythmic splendor.

Jóhannes úr Kötlum

The lyric and nature poetry written by Kötlum (pseud. of Jóhannes Bjarni Jónasson [1899–1972]) is in the national, romantic tradition of Einar Benediktsson. Less poetic, but far more convincing, are his satires on corrupt capitalistic society and his preaching of a new social system in *Ég læt sem ég sofi* (I Pretended I Was Asleep, 1932) and *Samt mun ég vaka* (Yet, I Will Stay Awake, 1935), marking his conversion to Communism. Although some of these poems are forceful and contain splendid passages, the message often overshadows the artistic quality. In *Hrímhvíta móðir* (Snowcapped Motherland, 1937) Kötlum surveys the history of Iceland in a series of poems about the men, women, and events that contributed most to the political and cultural progress of his country.

Hart er í heimi (World Is in Chaos, 1939) is largely concerned with the disturbing antidemocratic signs of war, and *Eilífðar smáblóm* (Eternity's Little Flower, 1940) and *Sól tér sortna* (Sun Turns Black, 1945) reflect this attitude, in particular expressing sympathy with occupied Norway and Denmark. In these volumes, as in all of Kötlum's writing, the poet is at his best when he turns his attention to themes of his own country, especially when he writes about rural life and old traditions. In the 1950s he published *Sóleyjarkvæði* (Sun Island Poems, 1952) and *Hlið hins himneska friðar* (The Portals of Heavenly Peace, 1953) both collections written in his old patriotic and pacifist manner. But with *Sjödægra* (Seven Day's Journey, 1955) Kötlum succeeded in blending the various elements of his work into splendid poetry, characterized by rich lyricism and mastery of form. *Óljóð* (Anti-Poems, 1962), on the other hand, express in a fragmented rhetorical style the revolutionary author's bitterness over social and political developments. The same tone characterizes *Ný og nið* (Crescent and Waning Moon, 1970), telling of Kötlum's expectations of the rebellious young. He also produced fine translations of Edith Sitwell, T. S. Eliot, Carl Sandburg, e. e. cummings, and Walt Whitman, collected in *Annarlegar tungur* (Strange Tongues, 1948).

HIGH POINTS IN PROSE WRITING

Four authors—Gunnar Gunnarsson, Kristmann Guðmundsson, Þorbergur Þórðarson, and Halldór Laxness—brought modern Icelandic prose to a high degree of sophistication during the late 1920s. With Guðmundur Kamban, these writers were mainly responsible for bringing the Icelandic novel up to the standards of world literature.

Gunnar Gunnarsson

Gunnarsson (1889–1975) lived in Denmark from 1897 to 1939. Even though he wrote in Danish during this period, all his works, consisting of more than forty volumes, deal exclusively with Icelandic topics. His first success was *Af Borgslægtens Historie* (1912-14, From the History of the Borg Family; Eng. tr. *Guest the One-Eyed*, 1920 and later), a recreation of the author's native Iceland seen at a romantic distance, a family saga whose central figure—the diabolical and power-seeking, but finally penitent priest Guest—turns into a legendary saint. The work became a bestseller and was the first Icelandic book to be made into a movie.

The idealistic optimism that had thus far marked Gunnarsson's work was badly shaken during World War I. The author began to search for the meaning of life, speculating on the responsibility of God and humankind. He wrote a number of philosophical problem novels and plays (1915-20), which take place among the then contemporary middle class in Iceland. The most important was the brilliantly structured novel *Salige er de enfoldige* (1920, Blessed Are the Poor in Spirit; Eng. tr. *Seven Days' Darkness*, 1930). The scene is Reykjavík in the fall of 1918, struck by an epidemic of Spanish influenza and a volcanic eruption; the plot is the struggle between a humanitarian doctor and his cynical opponent. The doctor is defeated and is taken to an insane asylum.

Gunnarsson eventually comes to a new faith in humankind by turning to the past—both his own and his country's. The speculative, heavy elements in style and content are now replaced by the spontaneous and simple in the series of novels *Kirken paa Bjærget* (1923-28, The Church on the Mountain; Eng. tr. of Parts 1-3, *Ships in the Sky*, and *The Night and the Dream*, 1938), memories of the author's life from his earliest childhood to his acceptance as a writer in Copenhagen. With *Jon Arason* (1930), the story of the last Catholic bishop, Gunnarsson resumed work on a monumental cycle of twelve novels relating the history of Iceland. The work was begun in 1918 with a description of the landnám period in *Edbrødre* (Eng. tr. *The Sworn Brothers*, 1919 and later) and concluded with *Graamand* (Gray Man, 1936). The masterpiece of the series is undoubtedly *Svartfugl* (1929, Black Gull; Eng. tr. *The Black Cliffs*, 1967), a story of crime and punishment set in the eighteenth century. Taken as a whole, the series tells of the founding of a nation, its development toward internal unity under responsible leadership, and the disintegration of this unity as a consequence of egotism and aggression.

After returning to Iceland Gunnarsson wrote *Heiðaharmur* (The Heath's Sorrow, 1940) and *Sálumessa* (Requiem, 1952), which portray the troubles of the poor farmers during the social transition into a modern urban society. The novella *Brimhenda* (approx. tr. *Sonata by the Sea*, 1954) also deals with human closeness to the soil and nature in general. Besides poems and essays, Gunnarsson wrote nine volumes of short stories, the most important of which, the novella *Advent* (1937; Eng. tr. 1939), became a bestseller in the United States as *The Good Shepherd* (1940), depicting the successful human struggle against the forces of nature.

Gunnar Gunnarsson's works evince an inept use of language, and his psychology is generally simplistic. But his books reached a large audience because of his humanistic attitude toward the fundamental problems of life. He dwelt on the questions of death, evil and good, guilt and atonement—religious motifs that never became sermons but were expressions of an observant and analytical mind.

Kristmann Guðmundsson

At a time when several Icelandic authors made a name for themselves in Denmark, Kristmann Guðmundsson (1902-   ) wrote his first important book in Norwegian, the short-story collection *Islandsk kjærlighet* (Icelandic Love, 1926), which was an immediate success; Guðmundsson soon became the most frequently translated Icelandic writer—into thirty-six languages in all. He is at his best when, as in the novel *Den første vår* (The First Spring, 1933), he writes about youthful, obsessive love, sometimes resulting in disillusion, sometimes on an optimistic note, as in the autobiographical novel *Hvite netter* (White Nights, 1934). *Brudekjolen* (1927; Eng. tr. *The Bridal Gown*, 1931) followed by *Livets morgen* (1929; Eng. tr. *Morning of Life*, 1936) and *Nátttröllið glottir* (The Night Troll Grins, 1943), are a series of family sagas with a well-constructed plot based on age-long rivalries between the members of influential families. Among these novels, *Morning of Life* is particularly outstanding, relating—as does Sigrid Undset's *Kristin Lavransdatter*—the story of a strong and nobel character pitted against fate, written with an intensity and conciseness reminiscent of the sagas.

Guðmundsson also wrote three historical novels. *Det hellige fjell* (The Holy Mountain, 1932) describes the old Norse and Irish settlement of his birthplace. *Gyðjan og uxinn* (1937; Eng. tr. *Winged Citadel*, 1940) is a romance set in Crete during the Mycenaean age—

though it is full of allusions to World War II politics—based on the idea of the psychological balance of instinctive passion and ennobling love. Here and in *Þokan rauða* (The Red Fog, 1950–52), which deals with the creator of the ancient *Völuspa* poem, the author approaches mystical idealism, which also marks his only volume of poetry, *Krist-mannskver* (Kristmann Poems, 1955). His works from the 1960s and 1970s are superficial and must be considered light entertainment.

Þorbergur Þórðarson

Guðmundsson's direct opposite was the older Þórðarson (1889–1974) who had tried life as a farmer, a fisherman, and a bohemian before publishing his first piece of writing, *Bréf til Láru* (Letters to Laura, 1924), essays on social, philosophical, and personal topics. Influenced by Upton Sinclair, these works ruthlessly attack capitalism, the church, and the Icelandic peasant culture, but they also reveal the author's own theories and fantasies in a number of autobiographical sketches.

Þórðarson's major achievements were the autobiographical novels *Íslenzkur aðall* (1938, Icelandic Nobility; Eng. tr. [partial] *In Search of My Beloved*, 1961 and later) and *Ofvitinn* (The Eccentric, 1940–41). Although realistically written and claiming to tell only the truth, they are highly imaginative works, containing outstanding period pieces full of eccentric characters and strange happenings. With the poetic and graceful *Sálmurinn um blómið* (The Hymn about the Flower, 1954–55), in which existence is described through the language and the eyes of a little girl, Þórðarson reveals himself once again as a poet with a fertile imagination but with no talent for innovation. His influence is due largely to his personal and varied style, paradoxical and shocking to traditional taste—he used foreign words and terms that before him were regarded as inappropriate. Typical of Þórðarson are self-irony and naivete, the contrasting attitudes that made his writing a milestone in Icelandic prose, forming a transition to the writing of Laxness.

Halldór Kiljan Laxness

After writing his first work, a romantic story influenced by Hamsun and Bjørnson, *Barn náttúrunnar* (Child of Nature, 1919), Laxness (1902–   ) visited Denmark and Sweden and stayed in Germany and Austria between 1921 and 1922. The confrontation with ancient European culture, in addition to the chaotic situation in the wake of the world war, intensified his search for a philosophy of life. Through his acquaintance with the Danish poet Johannes Jørgensen, Laxness came into contact with monastery life in Luxembourg, which led in 1923 to his conversion to Catholicism. In 1925 to 1926 he traveled through Italy, and here he composed his breakthrough work, *Vefarinn mikli frá Kasmír* (The Great Weaver from Kashmir, 1927). It is an expressionistic and autobiographical coming to terms with the times from a Catholic viewpoint, permeated with the restlessness and conflicting ideas of the postwar era, making Laxness the Icelandic representative of the so-called lost generation. The novel follows the hectic actions of an Icelandic poet and candidate for the priesthood through oriental mysticism and German philosophy, in particular Marx and Nietzsche, until he finally chooses God and the Church. However, the book also marks the beginning of the author's dissociation from Christianity.

Laxness visited the United States between 1927 and 1929, and tried his fortune as a movie-script writer in California. At this time he became personally acquainted with Upton Sinclair and read Sinclair Lewis. He thereby became aware of a complex of social problems that was to occupy him most of the following decade and that was already expressed in the first of the numerous and weighty volumes of critical essays, *Alþýðubókin* (The Book of the People, 1929). Here Laxness turned from psychology to purely socialist views; the central problem became the individual and that individual's relationship to the environment. In addition, he flayed the capitalistic society of the United States and the provinciality of his own countrymen. The first result of his new socialistic faith was a novel in two volumes, *Þú vínviður hreini* (O Thou Pure Wine, 1931) and *Fuglinn í fjörunni* (The Bird on the Beach, 1932; both volumes published together as *Salka Valka*, 1951; Eng. tr. 1936 and later) in which Laxness turned to the common people for inspiration. In a small fishing village the first trade union is established, a strike breaks out, and the domination of the local merchant is threatened. The political and social currents of the outside world change a number of destinies, among them that of the primitive child of nature Salka Valka, who is capable of dealing with all the difficulties and harshness of existence. *Sjálfstætt fólk* (1934–35; Eng. tr. *Independent People*, 1945 and later) is the story of the impoverished farmer Bjartur at the threshold of modernity, a giant of physical strength, betrayed by his own traditions and his stubborn individualism. Defiantly he moves farther out into the wilderness with his sick daughter, while his son joins the trade union in the city. In Salka Valka and Bjartur, Laxness created heroes; but the protagonist of *Heimsljós* (1937–40; Eng. tr. *World Light*, 1969) is a rather delicate, romantic poet, a genius, who was never able to develop fully because of his negative surroundings—the artist's eternal problem, placed in the framework of social criticism.

Íslandsklukkan (Iceland's Bell, 1943–46), a historical novel of the eighteenth century, has a related motif. It tells how the Old Icelandic heroic spirit of freedom was preserved throughout an oppressive age by the combined efforts of a stubborn and undefeatable small farmer and an enlightened collector of old Icelandic manuscripts, Árni Magnússon. The spiritual strength of the weak in society who are opposed to the constraint and display of force imposed by the ruling systems is seen in the perspective of world politics in *Gerpla* (1952; Eng. tr. *The Happy Warriors*, 1958), a grotesque travesty on the heroes of the *Fóstbrœðra saga*, aimed directly at contemporary history—a biting attack on the false and romantic heroic ideals of the time, on the worship of violence and power. Political callousness is also illuminated in *Atómstöðin* (1948; Eng. tr. *The Atom Station*, 1961), dealing with the discords that arose when in 1946 Iceland allowed the United States to maintain air bases in peacetime.

In 1932 Laxness made his first journey to Russia, which he wrote about very favorably in a travelogue. This positive attitude became even more pronounced during his second stay in 1937–38, during which he witnessed the Moscow trials, described in *Gerska æfintýrið* (The Russian Adventure, 1938). In the years after World War II Laxness's distinct individualism led him far away from the Russian adventure, with its spiritual and physical constraints. The break can be followed in his autobiography, *Skáldatími* (A Writer's Schooling, 1963). In his novels Laxness increasingly turned from social questions. In *Brekkukotsannáll* (1957, Annals of Brekkukot; Eng. tr. *The Fish Can Sing*, 1966) the first-person narrator describes in flashbacks the life of his grandparents in Reykjavík around 1900, a period when simple, traditional values were honored. However, these people, though deeply rooted in tradition, were allowing themselves to be deceived by myths. The point is illustrated by the farmer in Laxness's next novel, *Paradísarheimt* (1960; Eng. tr. *Paradise Reclaimed*, 1962). He leaves his homestead and family to travel to Utah, the promised land of the Mormons, but realizes his mistake and returns only to find the ruins of his old farm. The novel is a tribute to individual endeavor and individual freedom. This revolt against ideology is continued in Laxness's later novels, the humorous fable *Kristnihald undir jökli* (1968; Eng. tr. *Christianity at Glacier*, 1972) and the documentary novel *Innansveitarkrónika* (A Parish Chronicle, 1970), in which Laxness presents a number of vivid portraits and scenes of life from his home parish, based on the idea that one cannot remain faithful to anybody but oneself. In the humorous and satirical novel *Guðsgjafaþula* (A Rhyme of God's Gift, 1972), Laxness turns his criticism against his own time and castigates dilettantism in business and politics.

Laxness is also an excellent lyric poet whose only collection, *Kvæðakver* (Poems, 1930), is a surrealistic burlesque of traditionally romantic Icelandic poetry. He also wrote impressionistic, introspective short stories, influenced by Sigbjørn Obstfelder, and was a productive dramatist. He experimented with a symbolist mode of expression—which serves as a cover for sharp satire, as in *Silfurtúnglið* (The Silver Moon, 1954), directed at the commercial entertainment industry—and with an introverted, mystical approach, as in the comedies *Stompleikurinn* (The Chimney Play, 1961) and *Þrjónastofan Sólin* (The Knitting Workshop Called, "The Sun," 1962). His increasingly adamant rejection of the class struggle and materialism, a result of studying the Eastern philosophy of Taoism, dominates the comedy *Dúfnaveislan* (1966; Eng. tr. *The Pigeon Banquet*, 1973).

Halldór Laxness has never stagnated; he has always had the courage to give up accepted viewpoints, just as he has continuously chosen new artistic directions. Laxness has created his own style—characterized by humor, irony, and symbolism—by bringing together the literature of other countries and the native tradition of the saga. The highly poetic quality of his work is evident even in the most intensely realistic scenes, and his prose is highly imaginative, which is manifest in the large gallery of characters immortalized by strong stylization. His early works were dreamy and impressionistic; later he became more objective and put a greater emphasis on ethical questions. In the 1940s his language became terser, eventually approaching the dialogue style, which led to the dramatic experiments of the 1950s. In 1955 Halldór Laxness, the great innovator and the greatest Icelandic writer of the twentieth century, received the Nobel Prize for Literature.

Part IV Postwar Developments

Introduction

The turbulent years after the outbreak of World War II began with Finland's Winter War against Russia (1939–40) and continued with German aid to Finland (1941–44), the occupation of Denmark and Norway by German troops (1940–45), of the Faroese Islands and Iceland by the British (1940–45), and Sweden's armed neutrality. These events intensified the militant stance of Nordic writers. Literature, philosophical and polemical, did not reach its zenith until after the war.

Following the brutality and destructiveness of the war, the quest for a meaningful metaphysical and existential basis of life became a driving force in Nordic literature. It was a time of continuous political tension and nuclear threat, marked by international crisis and war: the Korean War from 1950 to 1953, the revolt in Hungary and the Suez crisis in 1956, the Vietnam War from 1958 to 1973, the Cuban crisis in 1962, the permanent state of war in the Middle East, the revolt in Prague in 1968, acts of terrorism, and the social and political problems of the third world—tragic events and conflicts that were increasingly reflected in Nordic literature.

World problems influenced the political situation in the Nordic countries. Denmark, Norway, and Iceland joined NATO in 1949, but Sweden remained committed to neutrality, an attitude manifest in the so-called third position espoused by numerous politically conscious writers—a neutral position between the two superpowers and their ideologies. Finland was forced to continue honoring its treaty of friendship with Russia, entered into in 1948, which restricted its foreign policy.

255

However, in numerous other ways the Nordic countries strove for closer cooperation with each other. In 1952 the Nordic Council was founded in an attempt to coordinate the legal, social, and cultural endeavors of the five countries. But an effort to establish close economic cooperation within NORDEK (The Nordic Economic Union) failed completely owing to the different political situations in the countries. Then, in 1959, Denmark, Norway, and Sweden became members of EFTA (European Free Trade Association); Denmark remained a member only until 1972, when a referendum called for the country to join the EEC (European Economic Community). In Norway, following a fierce debate in which numerous writers were involved, a similar referendum resulted in a rejection of the proposal that Norway join the Community.

Nordic literature became increasingly marked by a demand for political commitment, which reached its climax in the 1960s. Furthermore, the modern welfare state and growing materialism became the targets of sharp attacks, which were also aimed at the ivory-tower attitude, defended by some writers as the means of artistic survival. In addition, the 1960s brought a critical analysis of women's roles in a male-dominated society. As a consequence, a fierce debate arose about the artist's position and responsibility, a debate which led to a critical appraisal of the artist's relationship to the surrounding world and to his or her material, as well as to speculations on the communication process and the relationship of language and reality.

One group of writers emerged, whose work was experimental and not easily accessible, who dealt with language from a philosophical point of view. Their work eventually developed into the so-called concrete and systematic literature, which looked on language not only as a linguistic tool but also as a social and political system. Another group chose stylistic simplicity, a neo-realistic approach called the new simplicity, which had first appeared in Sweden around 1960 and later also had its representatives among writers of documentaries. These trends were more or less oriented to the political left, probably to a greater degree in Finland, Norway, and Sweden than in Denmark and Iceland, creating a strong reaction against any type of directive.

A recent development in Denmark has been a neo-romantic, imaginative trend focusing on an existential complex of problems and not associated with any ideological faction—an attitude also characteristic of a number of significant authors in the other Nordic countries.

Chapter *13*

Swedish Postwar Literature

During World War II the Swedish government adopted a neutral posture, which many regarded as opportunistic and cowardly. Although
the Swedish population experienced the war at a distance, its brutality
influenced an entire generation of writers and became their central
problem: One could no longer rely on national, religious, or even humanistic values. Anxiety and a feeling of powerlessness became the central experience of reality. Neutrality offered no possibility for political
action, but writing did: It became the arena for protesting violence.

Experiencing a chaotic existence, people turned from national and
social problems to existential questions; in the process a strong tendency toward mysticism is unmistakable. In the journal *40-tal* (The
40s, 1944–47) writers attempted to establish a link with foreign colleagues of the same generation. As literary models they took Kafka,
Rilke, and Eliot, and after the war Sartre and Camus as well. They
also found models in Swedish literature. The pessimism of the 1940s
found its indigenous basis in Hjalmar Gullberg's and Nils Ferlin's
anxiety-filled poetry of the 1930s; for their views of the task of literature and its use of musical structures, the authors could refer to
Ekelöf. Typical of the literature of the 1940s was the transition from
realism to symbolism, which had already begun in the interwar period.
The entertaining, social function of literature was negated, as was
everything particular or coincidental. Private and transient moods, a
narrow experience of the world, appeared valueless. Every line of a
poem was supposed to express a universal experience. To capture the

all-encompassing nature of consciousness, the poets of the 1940s employed rich metaphoric language; thus the poetic image, inspired by Eliot and Mallarmé, assumed a dominant position. This literature is not easily accessible, since it reflects a splintered and complex reality which can be rendered only in a fragmented or contrastive syntax—anticipated by the earlier Fenno-Swedish lyric poetry.

LYRIC POETRY OF THE 1940s

The artistic range of the period is best demonstrated in the works of two lyricists, Erik Lindegren and Karl Vennberg.

Erik Lindegren

The work of Lindegren (1910–68) is in many ways typical. In addition to the disillusioning experience of the time, there is a romantic attitude, an imaginative component reminiscent of French surrealism and Welsh poet Dylan Thomas.

Lindegren's poetry is set in an abstract universe. He sought above all to express an *inner* psychological reality in ecstatic rhetoric. His first collection was the conventional *Posthum ungdom* (Posthumous Youth, 1935). Later he became acquainted with Artur Lundkvist and the Fenno-Swedish modernists, and began work on the volume that was to become the path-breaking and unsurpassed lyric masterpiece of the 1940s, *mannen utan väg* (1942; Eng. tr. *The Man Without a Way*, 1969). It consists of forty unrhymed, symmetrical poems, almost every line of which is saturated with dissonant imagery. All the poems are equivalent; none contains the "meaning" of the entire volume any more fully than any other. The importance lies not in the literal meaning of the words, but in their overtones and their emotional content. Within the poems a difficult battle is being fought, a battle against absolute hopelessness and senselessness:

> The hand shivers from vertigo on the ladder of the stranglers
> greedy tears rustle in the nightingale's empty cage
> already mourning itself demands more victims of death
> even a train accident stammers forgive me
> a naked eye burns: short circuit
> and fate photographs yet another astonished corpse.
>
> Tr. Marianne Forssblad

Gradually the profile of one figure emerges, "the wanderer, who wanders always deeper into the world / and seeks his talisman from light and darkness," his road leads not into chaos or catastrophe, but into the courageous affirmation of life.

Man without a Road had a great influence on the younger writers but none of them went as far as Lindegren; in his two later collections, he turned again to more traditional forms. Even his pessimism abated gradually, particularly in *Sviter* (Suites, 1947). After an intense love experience, Lindegren wrote highly musical verses, rich in nuances; he experienced a renewed feeling for life and eventually turned to mysticism. In the poem "Hamlets himmelsfärd" ("Hamlet's Ascension") ecstatic religious experiences are united with apocalyptic fantasies, which had also been characteristic of *Man without a Road*. The tone in *Vinteroffer* (Winter Rites, 1954) is cooler by comparison and hints at a feeling of distance from the external world. When Erik Lindegren wrote his first great collection, he was an interpreter of the problems of the times. *Winter Rites* is introduced by a poem about Icarus, which shows human beings on the path away from reality; the first part of the volume is filled with such moods, of the flight into nothingness, of loneliness and death.

Karl Vennberg

Lindegren was the era's great, inspiring stylistic innovator, Vennberg (1910–   ) its critic and theoretician. His poetry is deliberately antiromantic and is linked to the concrete world picture of the natural sciences. He is a didactic poet who constantly occupies himself with the problems of intellectual life. His pessimism, like that of Lindegren, is created by the times. War propaganda had sharpened his distrust of catchwords and generalizations, a distrust that engendered a desire for clarity and skepticism toward various ideologies.

Vennberg had an unremarkable first work behind him when he published the collection *Halmfackla* (Straw Torch) in 1944; with *Tideräkning* (Chronology, 1945), it became the canon for an entire generation. Here one finds bitter skepticism toward all forms of faith and solutions to existential problems. In a series of ironic and scornful verses, Vennberg emphasizes that all teachings of salvation are merely the expression of selfish interests. He articulates his skeptical position in quick-witted, somewhat dry diction: "You have to evade / the outermost point / only there you can see / that the sea / drowns in the horizon / and that all sails are bewildered."

Vennberg could not maintain his distrust of all forms of realism. In the next collection, *Fiskefärd* (Fishing Trip, 1949), an almost idyllic mood of intimacy and warmth predominates, which yields in the religious poems to a hope for salvation. But this cheerful tone was only an intermezzo. In the 1950s, Vennberg became involved in daily politics as the advocate of the "third position" between the two superpowers—a view entirely in accord with his own poetics. In spite of this, he was no longer a "poet of the times." Personal feelings were given more space, and a tone of resignation predominated. In *Tillskrift* (Dedication, 1960) the author was closer than ever to overcoming his skepticism. This collection flows into a shattering appeal to the absent God, a confessional poem to religion, which, as in Lagerkvist's work, is a yearning for God. During the 1960s Vennberg displayed an increasing interest in current politics from a socialist viewpoint. In *Sju ord på tunnelbanan* (Seven Words in the Subway, 1971) he enjoined his fellow writers not to give up the critical attitude that dominated the 1960s, but to overcome the disappointment they experienced when their political analyses failed when confronted with reality—a viewpoint Vennberg vigorously defended in essays and public debate. *Vägen till Spånga Folkan* (The Road to Spånga Community Center, 1976) marked a return to the poet's private sphere. Retaining the artistic quality of his early collections, Vennberg attempts to conquer destructive thoughts of approaching death by mingling anguish and comedy. His latest poems, entitled *Visa solen ditt ansikte* (Show Your Face to the Sun, 1978), however, do not get beyond sentimental rhetoric.

Werner Aspenström

A tone of sarcasm and intellectual desperation similar to that in Vennberg's earlier volumes characterizes the collection *Skriket och tystnaden* (The Scream and the Silence, 1946) by Aspenström (1918-). However, Vennberg's somewhat dry, conversational style is replaced here by tighter form and more precise poetic expression. Aspenström's poetry contains nothing of Lindegren's often cryptical imagery; also, he does not attempt to shock, but instead to express purely and clearly. This tendency, developed into a more intimate tone and simple style influenced by legend and fairy tale, can be found in *Snölegend* (Snow Legend, 1949), *Litania* (1952), and *Hundarna* (The Dogs, 1954). *Litania* is a collection of miniature poems in a naive style, snapshots that contain not only minute details but also perspectives on infinity. In succeeding volumes, Aspenström takes his recurring symbols from nature—the brook, the tree, and the light, for instance in *Dikter under träden* (Poems under the Trees, 1956):

> Light's white waterfall
> through the cloud, through the branches
> and on the child's incessant questioning:
> why and why?

The little things of the world cannot
be explained. Not the grass
not the light's waterfall, the white,
inaudible.

Tr. Marianne Forssblad

But it is seldom a question of a relaxed idyll, and Aspenström's succeeding collections, *Om dagen om natten* (By Day by Night, 1961) and *Trappan* (The Staircase, 1964) are marked by an oscillation between unconcerned joy over familiar things and a bitter awareness of death. In Aspenström's succeeding collections, *Sommar* (Summer, 1968), *Inre* (Inner, 1969), *Under tiden* (Meanwhile, 1972), and *Jordvagga-himmelstak* (Earthcradle-Skyroof, 1973), the idyllic tone is increasingly disturbed by destructive irony. However, the poet's extraordinary linguistic precision remains intact and indeed reaches a new height of virtuosity in his latest collection, *Ordbok* (Dictionary, 1976).

In addition to lyric poetry, Werner Aspenström wrote a number of important lyrical, symbolic dramas, remarkable attempts at a Swedish Theater of the Absurd, which have been collected in *Teater* (1959–66). The lovely prose volume *Bäcken* (The Brook, 1958) contains an autobiographical description of childhood in the form of a series of short stories replete with poetry and humor.

Sven Alfons and Ragnar Thoursie

On the borderline between the 1940s and the less philosophical and pessimistic 1950s, are Sven Alfons (1918–) and Ragnar Thoursie (1919–), both reminiscent of Birger Sjöberg in their ironical attitude. Alfon's sparse work is characterized—as the title of his collection *Backspegel mot gryningen* (Rear-View Mirror toward Dawn, 1949) indicates—by a retrospective tendency, a romantic attempt to bridge the gap between past and future in order to reach a complete experience of the present. In *Ängelens bild* (The Angel's Picture, 1961) the ironic and everyday tone become an expression of the poet's simple, anti-intellectual view of life, in which the belief in art becomes the central point: "I have just about everything I need / life, death / but, my dear, please send me / send me / ultramarine."

In the first volume of poetry written by Ragnar Thoursie (1919–), *Emaljögat* (The Enamel Eye, 1945), the central position is occupied by poems that clearly have their points of departure in everyday situations. The social interest becomes stronger in Thoursie's second and latest collection, *Nya sidor och dagsljus* (New Pages and Daylight, 1952), in which he abandons his earlier symbolic and visionary style in favor of radical simplification of language. This trend corresponds to the poet's growing criticism of the Swedish welfare state, a criticism based on Thoursie's stand between individualism and socialism, similar to the "third position."

PROSE OF THE 1940s

Eyvind Johnson's novels burst the unities of time and space, thereby breaking with the realism of the 1930s—indeed they often reach a metaphysical level. However, the decisive break with naturalism came with the philosophical prose writers of the 1940s. Their models were the same as those of the lyricists: Kafka, Camus, and Sartre.

Lars Ahlin

The first of the new prose writers of the 1940s, Ahlin (1915–) belonged to the generation of young people who were at the point of entering the work force when the economic crisis of the early 1930s occurred, causing widespread unemployment. The resulting feeling of absolute disenfranchisement and social emptiness never left Ahlin.

His first book, *Tåbb med manifestet* (Tåbb with the Manifesto, 1943), deals with his unemployment; it also lays down the major points of his program. The young proletarian Tåbb is a "zero being," so he seeks a world view that will correspond to his life. He finds the theses of communism existentially inadequate; but in Lutheran theology he finds a teaching about point zero that speaks to him: The human being is intrinsically nothing, only a sinner to be judged according to his or her deeds.

In the clear, vivid descriptions of the workers' environment, Ahlin's mastery of realistic narrative technique finds it full expression. The same is true of Ahlin's short stories in *Inga ögon väntar mig* (No Eyes Await Me, 1944), which deal with the same motifs that are in his first book. But he does not content himself with being a good storyteller; on the contrary, in his later novels he turns away from any attempt to form an illusion of life and reality. The novel is intended as the meeting point for author and reader, where the reader takes an active part in a conversation and brings the events and problems of the narrated material into contact with his or her own experiences. Ahlin himself never takes a position in relation to his characters, but permits each to play out his or her role without formulating a value judgment.

This ideal is realized in *Min död är min* (My Death Is My Own, 1945). All the characters have somehow failed in their lives, a fact they attempt to conceal. The main character, Sylvan, is a "zero being." His wife has left him, and at the beginning he sees no alternative but to take his own life. But he recognizes his failure and from this recognition he attempts to establish a new contact with life and his fellow humans. He proclaims the gospel of love, to which Ahlin subscribes, a gospel of life-dispensing death, with "point zero" as the starting place. The book is an episodic novel: The same problems are illustrated by different individuals, fates, and events that are, in part, symbolic.

Ahlin attempts to put his theories into practice in the most extreme manner in his novel *Om* (If, About, Around, 1946). The situation of the sinful human is demonstrated here in the relationship of a degenerate and immoral father to his son, who attempts to reform him. The setting is the same as in *My Death Is My Own*, the northern Swedish city of Sundsvall where Ahlin spent his childhood, and the main character, now called Peter, closely resembles Sylvan.

After these two rather inaccessible novels, Ahlin dedicated himself for a time to uncomplicated work. In 1952; however, he returned to his earlier themes with a masterpiece entitled *Fromma mord* (Pious Murders). This new novel is an indictment of everything that makes it difficult to fulfill the commandments of conscience and love out of real emotion, and not merely on the basis of principle. Here Ahlin attempts to represent his Christian view of life. Structurally, the novel is reminiscent of *My Death Is My Own*; a series of brutal or melodramatic episodes, which are only scantily framed by an almost diffuse reality. In Ahlin's conception of the laws of the human world, of longing and of suffering, Luther and particularly Karl Barth play a decisive role—for instance, Barth's perception of the sanctity of humankind as an impossibility.

More accessible are the following three works, different in theme and mood but with basic similarities in style, setting, and structure. In *Kanelbiten* (Cinnamon Girl, 1953) Ahlin shows his mastery in his subtle analysis of the development of a child, Britt-Marie, into a woman, through stages of humiliation and wretchedness to absolute loneliness. The theme is that of undeserved suffering, expressed in a series of lyrically symbolic, stylized conversations which lack any illusion of reality. Like Britt-Marie, the main character in *Stora glömskan* (The Great Amnesia, 1954), the youth Zackarias feels a need to meet other people and to take an interest in them. This need is symbolized in his search for his bohemian father. The book, like *If, About, Around*, is constructed episodically of a series of subplots that illustrate one another and are held together by Zackarias. He also appears in *Natt i marknadstältet* (Night in the Market Tent, 1957), Ahlin's most harmoniously composed novel of ideas, which deals with the problems of human beings living together, problems that frustrate the attempt to obey the gospel of love. Love as an immortal part of our lives had already been the theme of the novel *Kvinna, kvinna* (Woman, Woman, 1955), and the two novels *Gilla gång* (Normal Course, 1958) and *Bark och löv* (Bark and Leaves, 1961), also analyze the intimations of eternity to be found in a love relationship.

Ahlin's personally formulated theology is eschatological. Therefore, most of his characters are amoral, and a major theme, as in Dostoevsky, is humiliation and suffering. It is the kind of spiritual and physical misery that is the precondition for the advent of an era of justice, in which God will rule. Only in love is the value of the human being experienced, a value that is above all degrees and hierarchies. Thus it is the task of the writer to formulate in words the common cause for those who cannot articulate it for themselves. In this striving to give new possibilities to the language and in his antipathy for naturalistic presentation, Lars Ahlin exerted a strong influence on the Swedish literature of the 1950s and '60s.

Stig Dagerman

Next to Ahlin, Dagerman (1923–54) is the most significant prose writer of the years immediately following the war. He was a contributor to the periodical *40-tal* and was regarded as the personification of the spirit of the 1940s. For him, too, point zero was a new start; but, although Ahlin's characters succeeded in overcoming fatal pessimism, Dagerman was never able to find a solution to human anxiety, which finally drove him to suicide.

In his first novel, *Ormen* (The Serpent, 1945), Dagerman writes of the terrors that spread among the soldiers in a barracks, symbolized by a snake that has escaped and is loose among them. The horror intensifies to terror, which drives the men to a feeling of community; but this is based on false suppositions. For the characters attempt to negate their fears instead of conquering them through a recognition of their power. The novel is far from realistic. Its characters are elements of a theme rather than three-dimensional figures; they are defined solely in terms of how they relate to the anxiety-ridden times.

The novel *De dömdas ö* (Island of the Condemned, 1946) also deals with people confronting the stress of the time. It is the account of seven shipwrecked people who are stranded on an uninhabited island where they face an agonizing death. The collective on the island is a microcosm of human life, of a distorted society. All are deranged by terror, and in their attempt to escape this they cling to one another;

however, no real sense of community can arise, for most of them are oppressed by secret guilt, character flaws, or egotism. Nevertheless, this nightmare—written in intense language influenced by Faulkner, with Kafkaesque symbolism—ends in a ray of hope: When the characters recognize the essence of their anxiety, they are able to overcome it, and through action and shared responsibility to transform it.

The short stories in the collection *Nattens lekar* (1947; Eng. tr. *The Games of Night*, 1959) are also permeated with fear and an atmosphere of death; they too were influenced by Kafka. In the novel *Bränt barn* (1948; Eng. tr. *A Burnt Child*, 1950) Dagerman abandons the symbolic world of his early works and describes realistically a motherless youth and his relationship to his father and his father's mistress—a psychological portrait of deception and betrayal, in an urban work setting.

Bröllopsbesvär (Wedding Troubles, 1949) was Dagerman's last book. The novel is set in a modern rural environment and is based on Dagerman's childhood recollections from the region of Uppland. It is rich in motifs and in rundown, unsympathetic and sometimes comical characters. The comedy is grotesque, for the world order of fear and meaninglessness has captured the people; there is no faith in positive fellowship.

In a short five years Stig Dagerman wrote all of his major works: In addition to novels and short stories, there were also a poetry collection, *Dagsedlar* (Duty Roster, 1954) and a series of dramas influenced by Lagerkvist, Camus, and Sartre, such as *Den dödsdömde* (1948; Eng. tr. *The Condemned*, 1951), which picked up motifs from the prose works. Dagerman was fascinated by current matters, and his prose provided an unshakable moral voice in his time, as he seriously attempted to make contact with present-day people.

Sivar Arnér

World War II caused a blossoming not only of metaphysical literature but also of works that raised ethical questions. The question of what is the people's attitude toward might and right was posed more and more frequently. Exemplary is the work of Arnér (1909–   ). His first collection of short stories, *Skon som krigaren bar* (The Shoe That the Warrior Wore, 1943), and his early novels, *Plånbok borttappad* (Wallet Lost, 1943) and *Knekt och klerk* (Soldier and Priest, 1945), portray the subordination of justice and spirit in the struggle with ruthless brutality, arriving at the painful recognition that total justice does not exist on earth, an insight that points to a higher reality.

Gradually the relationship between man and woman becomes one of the main themes in Arnér's work. The novel *Egil* (1948), written in the form of a concise Joycean monologue, follows the protagonist through an entire day in which nothing really happens. Flashbacks and reflections permit the reader to form an idea of Egil's character and his life in a Strindbergian matrimonial hell, a theme that is further elaborated in the novel *Han-Hon-Ingen* (He-She-Nobody, 1951).

Arnér's novels of the 1950s are characterized by the use of fairy tale and allegory. The novel *Fyra som var bröder* (Four Who Were Brothers, 1955) is a fairy tale in which modern society is symbolically represented. The four brothers personify different human types, of which only the mystic is portrayed sympathetically; he has achieved a total vision which reconciles the antitheses of life.

Current questions also occupy Arnér, and like many Swedish authors he favors the "third position." These questions are discussed in many of his novels, not least in *Four Who Were Brothers*, and also in a series of political allegories in the form of radio plays, *Fem hörspel* (Five Radio Plays, 1959). While writing these radio dramas Arnér did not produce short stories and novels. When his next short-story collection, *Finnas till* (To Exist, 1961), did appear, it was apparent that he had fought his way through to a new and more positive view of humanity, and to a warmer tone. Irony was now often balanced by rough humor, as seen in the novel *Nätet* (The Net, 1962). The main character is a homeless neurotic who feels himself persecuted by childhood memories. They surround him like a choking net, until he is cured by love.

In the 1960s Arnér wrote about the negative aspects of the welfare state. *Tvärbalk* (Cross-Beam, 1963) is a love story, but at the same time Arnér critically examines modern society as he compares the Swedish standard of living and life-style with conditions in the developing nations. A similar subject is dealt with in the novel *(Ett ett ett* (One one one, 1964), written in diary form.

The same distrust of fixed solutions, together with a relativistic world view—also to be found in the works of the younger Lars Gyllensten—is characteristic of Arnér's latest works, the novel *Byta människa* (Exchange a Person, 1972) and the short stories *Vattenvägar* (Waterways, 1973), here combined with political discussion. But behind the current perspective, a deeply irrational element is always discernible. In this respect Arnér is in harmony with the two other great prose writers of the 1940s, Ahlin and Dagerman. To a great degree he was influenced by the same contemporary events. However, Arnér cannot be counted in the inner circle of this generation of writers. In spite of his isolated attempts at symbolism, he was not an experimental author. He developed a from of realistic description, terse and somewhat dry, which made it possible for him to present psychological and moral subjects with convincing clarity and intensity—features that also distinguished Arnér's autobiographical series *Där är han* (There He Is, 1975), *Vilken kämpe* (What a Giant, 1976), and *Öppna dörrar* (Open Doors, 1978).

Thorsten Jonsson

Another trend in literature of the 1940s, anticipated by Walter Ljungquist, was strongly influenced by Hemingway. Instead of preoccupation with psychoanalysis and mysticism, the concern was to record the factual, the visible, and the verifiable. Emotions were not analyzed, they were demonstrated. Artur Lundkvist had published essays on modern American prose writers, but it was Thorsten Jonsson (1910-50)—his most important work is the volume of short stories *Fly till vatten och morgon* (Escape to Water and Tomorrow, 1941)—who effected the breakthrough of the laconic and objective American narrative to Swedish literature. Less successful because of its sentimentality and lack of convincing characters was the wartime novel *Konvoj* (Convoy, 1947). Even here, however, Jonsson did give his narrative art a filmlike quality—each detail sharply focused, the dialogue concise, and the action dramatic.

PROSE OF THE 1950s

The writing of the 1940s had proved to be a manifestation of a common style of attitude toward life; this was not true in the next decade. However, in the works of most of these writers, certain common traits can be noted: greater concern for aesthetics and more optimism. The most conspicuous feature of the literature of the 1950s was its lack of interest in social problems and criticism. Political questions were turned into moral and religious questions, the writers focused on aesthetic problems and, as indicated, a more optimistic view of life became predominant.

Lars Gyllensten

Gyllensten (1921–) is an exception. He took up in a highly original manner, the thoughts and attitudes of the 1940s and developed them further. His first two prose works, *Moderna myter* (Modern Myths, 1949) and *Det blå skeppet* (The Blue Ship, 1950) stand in a dialectical relationship to each other. *Modern Myths* consists of philosophical aphorisms and reflections delivered in an intellectual, ironic tone. Acting as a symbolic figure is the painter Hieronymus Bosch, who is regarded as the creator of myths that express a bitter and biting relativism. *The Blue Ship* is a highly structured story of a youth growing up on a boat, but it also contains rituals and myths, which recur in a series of romantic and sentimental variations.

Both approaches—the intellectual and analytical as well as the romantic and naive—represent two different world views. They are combined in the masterpiece *Barnabok* (Children's Book, 1952). The work is a psychologically intense and verbally exact portrayal of the progressive destruction of a marriage and the ruin of a human being; one perceives clearly that Gyllensten, a doctor by profession, derives his literary approach from his scientific method. The two views of life turn out to be antithetical, and the book demonstrates the impossibility of living in an inflexible either-or situation.

However, the novel *Senilia* (1956) points toward possibilities of accepting the world. Here, with clinical exactitude, Gyllensten registers the symptoms of aging in forty-year-old Torsten Lerr. The inner monologue of the main character predominates, although the author, on the model of Thomas Mann, is constantly present in a series of reflections. The transition of the protagonist from youth to middle age, the mutability, is perceived as a reconciling trait in an otherwise negative existence.

In *Senatorn* (The Senator, 1958) Gyllensten used a contemporary political subject as his point of departure. Here he presents, in a more clear and accessible manner than before, the ambivalence of the main character, Antonin Bhör, a high political official of a socialist satellite country whose ideology he has begun to question. It is Gyllensten's intention not only to demonstrate the injustice and repression of a totalitarian state, or how such a system can become the enemy of the human being, but to urge the necessity of destroying one's *own* system, to seek reality outside the self.

In Gyllensten's next two novels, well-known myths are reinterpreted. *Sokrates död* (The Death of Socrates, 1960) questions the value of the philosopher's heroic death; *Kains memoarer* (1963; Eng. tr. *The Testament of Cain*, 1967) defends Cain in a number of aphoristic texts dealing with a world in which truth is relative. Both works focus on a human being with an overpowering conviction, who will not hesitate to harm others in order to realize it. The humanist aspect of the *The Testament of Cain*—the fratricide itself is not accepted—is continued in *Lotus i Hades* (Lotus in Hades, 1966), a legendlike book about suffering and destruction, presenting situations which can be coped with only if human responsibility is not shirked. *Juvenilia* (1965) is set in contemporary Stockholm. The book demonstrates in ironic, tragic, and burlesque tones roles and attitudes that are to be interpreted morally and aesthetically. Thus neither the words nor the formulations are allowed to form too firm a pattern. The increased political activity and the spread of Marxist ideas in Swedish society forced Gyllensten to define further his viewpoints in his writings after the 1960s. The exceptions are two interrelated novels, *Palatset i parken* (The Palace in the Park, 1970) and *Grottan i öknen* (The Cave in the Desert, 1973), both based on the Orpheus and Eurydice theme, and the picaresque novel *I skuggan av Don Juan* (In the Shadow of Don Juan, 1976), which has the same approach as *The Death of Socrates* and *The Testament of Cain*. *Diarium spirituale* (1968)—"a fictitious, false-correct diary"—expresses the author's skepticism toward all rules and systems, whereas *Baklängesminnen* (Memories Backward, 1978) is a novel about humankind seen as a paradoxical combination of irreconcilable elements, hence unable to become whole beings. The two essay collections of 1971, *Ur min offentliga sektor* (From My Public Sector) and *Mänskan djuren all naturen* (Man, Animals, All of Nature) defend the freedom of the arts and the artist against the growing demand for political commitment. *Lapptäcken, livstecken* (Quilts, Signs of Life, 1976), containing excerpts from Gyllensten's books, sketches, and fragments, is an attempt to discipline the author's inspiration and imagination.

Lars Gyllensten's verbal fantasy is strikingly rich and moves effortlessly on all levels. He attempts to show human beings who are captured in an ideology. When the foundations begin to rock, they become uncertain and grope vainly for a foothold. Gyllensten's own alternative is philosphical relativism, a method of constant inquiry which he learned from the American philosopher Charles S. Pierce, a hesitant attitude that constitutes a polemic against any ideological system. Artistically this position results in a dialectical manner of writing—inspired by Kierkegaard—where the works contrast with each other and demonstrate various possibilities for action. Gyllensten's intellectual openness and artistic gifts have made him one of the most influential modern Swedish authors.

Like Gyllensten, Stig Claesson, and Pär Rådström basically distrust dogmatic ideologies.

Stig Claesson

The works of Claesson (1928–   ) cover an astonishingly wide range of motifs and settings. *Från nya världen* (From the New World, 1961) and *Min vän Charlie* (My Friend Charlie, 1973) are set in Canada. *Berättelse från Europa* (A Story from Europe, 1956) and *Att resa sig*

270 SWEDISH POSTWAR LITERATURE

upp och gå (To Rise and Walk, 1971) deal with postwar reconstruction in Italy and Yugoslavia. Claesson is also deeply concened with the problems of depopulation of the Swedish countryside in *Bönder* (Farmers, 1963) and *Vem älskar Yngve Frej?* (Who Loves Yngve Frej?, 1968). Claesson's most significant works are his portrayals of life in Stockholm, exemplified in the novel *Döden heter Konrad* (Death Is Named Konrad, 1967), a first-person account of approaching death, permeated by a disillusoned, fin-de-siècle attitude. This mood also characterizes the two novels *På palmblad och rosor* (On Palm Leaves and Roses, 1975) and *Henrietta ska du också glömma* (You Shall Also Forget Henrietta, 1977) which, like *Who Loves Yngve Frej?*, are set in the depopulated rural areas of Sweden and focus on apparently absurd but in fact highly symbolic events.

Pär Rådström

For Rådström (1925–63) the identity motif, the search for human relationships based not on illusions but on reality, serves as an important point of departure. In his first two novels, *Men inga blommor vissnade* (But No Flowers Withered, 1946) and *Stjärnan under kavajslaget* (The Star Beneath the Lapel, 1949), this quest takes place in a shadowy postwar Europe. These novels are written in the reflective, pessimistic tradition of the 1940s; the motif receives more original treatment in the novel cycle about the journalist Greg Bengtsson, the author's alter ego (1952–54).

Elements of self-examination also characterize the novel *Sommargästerna* (The Summer Guests, 1960), Rådström's most interesting book from the point of view of narrative technique. He tells of his meeting with his alter ego Paul Renberg, their summer vacation, and Renberg's disappearance and the search for him. In addition to roles and identities, *The Summer Guests* deals with the writing process, the writing of this specific novel. This process reflects how humans mature toward reality, which development, however, is threatened by misleading ideologies. The theme of roles and identities recurs in the novel *Översten* (The Colonel, 1961), where the hero is a PR (!) man named Peter Renner. In Rådström's last novel, *Mordet* (The Murder, 1962), he returns to the theme of human maturing. The crime is the murder of the part within ourselves that ties us to the past, which we must get rid of if we are to become whole individuals.

Birgitta Trotzig

The work of Trotzig (1929–) is of a completely different type.

Her books contain no ambiguities, they do not make reinterpretations possible. The short stories in her first volume, *Ur de älskandes liv* (From the Life of People Who Love, 1951), are composed in accordance with the aesthetic taste of the 1950s. Together with the prose poems *Bilder* (Pictures, 1954), they express a questioning emptiness, the answer to which is given in the historical novel *De utsatta* (The Outcasts, 1957). In very powerful but disciplined prose, Trotzig presents us with naturalistic scenes of human suffering and ravages from the seventeenth-century warstricken region of Scania, telling us that there is a demanding but just God who has promised not happiness, but consolation, and thereby a meaning to life.

Both *En berättelse från kusten* (A Story from the Coast, 1961) and *Sveket* (The Betrayal, 1966) are novels about misguided and repressed love, leaving humankind in petrified darkness; they are also pictures of human bestiality and, paradoxically, proclamations of God's grace. The title of the prose poems *Ordgränser* (Limits of Words, 1968) implies that the world is more evil than words can express. Through contrapuntally arranged scenes and fragments from Prague, Paris, and Toscana, Trotzig presents her vision of a chaotic and absurd civilization. The theme of the absence of language as a symbol of our almost hopeless existential situation also dominates the novel *Sjukdomen* (The Illness, 1972), a study of a single character, the farmhand Elje Ström. Elje is retarded and cannot express himself and comprehend his situation. His father sees that Elje is being driven deeper and deeper into insanity, but the father has no language with which to communicate his awareness, hence is unable to help. The illness becomes life itself.

Time and space are completely abandoned in the collection of tales *I kejsarens tid* (In the Time of the Emperor, 1975), myths, allegories, and metamorphoses woven around the theme of the fall of humankind and its possible salvation. *Berättelser* (Stories, 1977) deals with the almost constant absence of this salvation. Here Trotzig returns to the exposed human beings of her earlier works: the forgotten, the downtrodden, the silent, to whom the richness of life is revealed only rarely.

The world that Birgitta Trotzig depicts is dominated by cruelty. The only reconciling element is irrational love, which, however, is almost impossible to communicate. The absence of love is the basic idea permeating all of her work, leaving divine grace as the only alternative, as in the modern French novels of Mauriac and Bernanos. She herself belongs to this Catholic literary tradition and sees it as the writer's task—similar to that of the mystic—to give oneself up and place oneself in the service of the divine. Her invocative depictions of past and present physical hardship and suffering thus become a reflection of an inner spiritual world. Trotzig's mystical conception of art, based on her Catholic faith, combined with her exceptional linguistic sensitivity and intense creativity, make her one of the most original and exciting writers, not only in Scandinavia, but internationally.

Sven Fagerberg

Like Gyllensten and Rådström, Fagerberg (1918–   ) uses a rather complicated narrative technique. In his first book, *Höknatt* (Night of the Hawk, 1957), a book about the uncertain circumstances of a father's death and his son's search for the truth—the epic narrative is interrupted by dreams and poetic myths. Like Joyce, he combines an ancient erotic myth with a modern one, here reminiscent of Hamlet's family tragedy, using a bold alternation of cheerful irony and metaphysical seriousness.

Sven Fagerberg's writing is a continuous critical argument, permeated by Zen-Buddhist ideas, with the technological and bureaucratic Swedish society providing objects of meditation for readers. The novel *Svärdfäktarna* (The Sword Fencers, 1963) is set in present-day Sweden —a newspaper artist is its main character—and in legendary Japan. In *Det vitmålade hjärtat* (The White Painted Heart, 1966) Fagerberg alludes to Indian fairy tales and the Greek myth of Persephone's stay in the underworld. But even here the past is tied to the modern world, particularly through embittered criticism of the indifference of high finance toward human factors. Social criticism also permeates Fagerberg's novel *Tal till Hermes* (Speech to Hermes, 1977), which is modeled on Plato's dialogues and has a rather weak plot. A new trend becomes noticeable in the love story *Kassandra* (1976; written with Madeleine von Heland), in which Fagerberg, in a 3,000-year-old setting, analyzes modern humankind, which is not content with carnal love and material pleasures. The work is an attempt to demonstrate the power of the relationship between man and woman, which can overcome any external obstacle and which leads to liberation from traditional patterns of thought. This theme is also treated in Fagerberg's latest novel, *Maud Gonne och myterna om kvinnan* (Maud Gonne and the Myths about Women, 1978), based on the autobiography of W. B. Yeat's friend. It is an exuberant hymn in praise of woman.

Willy Kyrklund

Both Fagerberg's and Gyllensten's writings contain mythical elements. Kyrklund (1921–   ), originally a Fenno-Swedish writer, creates his own myths in the prose works *Tvåsam* (Twosome, 1949) and *Solange* (1951), dealing with human impotence in our highly rational era. Kyrklund brings his portrayal of the interplay of precisely observed everyday existence and ironic fantasies to its artistic climax in *Mästaren Ma* (The Master Ma, 1953), a collection of the thoughts of a fictitious Chinese philosopher about the haphazardness and transitoriness of life. Kyrklund continues with this theme in the volume of stories *Hermelinens död* (The Death of the Ermine, 1954). Kyrklund's most significant work is undoubtedly *Polyfem förvandlad* (The Changed Polyphemus, 1964), a collage of anecdotes, tales, and sketches, illuminating the process of change. In a world of *tristesse*, only love and the longing for truth remain, even though they, perhaps, are unattainable. Kyrklund demonstrates this further in *Den rätta känslan* (The Right Feeling, 1974), a volume of short stories more tightly structured than his previous books, and turns to bitterness and tragedy in the two closet dramas in the volume *Zebun-nisâ* (1977).

In the work of two authors of the 1950s, Sara Lidman and Pär Wästberg, an expanded international interest emerges; a link is established to the problems of the developing countries, a topic with which several other authors were to deal during the next decade.

Sara Lidman

The early works of Lidman (1923–   ), the collective novels *Tjärdalen* (The Tar Valley, 1953) and *Hjortronlandet* (The Land of Cloudberries, 1955), are set in the author's native Västerbotten and introduce literary neo-provincialism. Here one finds the human type, the outcast, that is present in her later books and the topics of guilt and responsibility, compulsion and encountering obstacles when one tries to help someone. The moralist viewpoint becomes more conspicuous in the two-volume novel *Regnspiran* (1958; Eng. tr. *The Rain Bird*, 1962) and *Bära mistel* (To Carry Mistletoe, 1960)—a high point in the modern psychological novel in Sweden. The agonizing love of Linda Stahl, the main female character, for a homosexual musician and the musician's position as an outsider are regarded as a semi-unconscious atonement for an earlier betrayal she committed in the sphere of love.

In the 1960s Sara Lidman turned her back on Swedish settings. Experiences from a stay in Africa in 1960–61 are reworked in the novels *Jag och min son* (I and My Son, 1961) and *Med fem diamanter* (With Five Diamonds, 1964). In these two books a Swedish technician is the fictional narrator, and there is a sharp attack on the politics of apartheid and bankrupt neutrality. Thus the topic is again betrayal and responsibility, here the moral betrayal of blacks by whites.

In the Vietnam conflict, Lidman took an early and firm stand against the United States. The results were the diary *Samtal i Hanoi* (Talks in Hanoi, 1966) and the collection of articles *Fåglarna i Nam Dinh* (The Birds in Nam Dinh, 1972), which, owing to their indignant and agitational tone, make any literary evaluation difficult.

In 1968 Lidman returned to a Swedish setting with *Gruva* (Mine), a piece of social reporting which takes a position on the strike of the miners in northern Sweden that year. *Mine* is conceived as a series of interviews with about forty workers, but the questions are omitted; we see only the responses, as the workers tell about themselves, their work, and their critical attitude toward society. It is a social system that Lidman wants to change, both here and in the drama *Marta, Marta* (1970). The neo-provincialism of Lidman's early work reemerges in her late novels, *Din tjänara hör* (Your Servant Listens, 1977) and *Vredens barn* (The Children of Wrath, 1979), two parts of a trilogy set in her childhood milieu, which focus primarily on human suffering and social questions rendered in a captivating epic narrative.

Pär Wästberg

A corresponding development is noticeable in the work of Wästberg (1933–). His early writings are artistically perfect, but somewhat disinterested portrayals of a dreamy childhood world. In the lyrical novel *Halva kungariket* (Half the Kingdom, 1955), about a young married couple and their contented but not at all naive way of experiencing the world, all poetic illusions are abandoned. In *Arvtagaren* (The Heir, 1958) Wästberg has the main character take an educational trip away from the Swedish idyll, so that he can portray the European postwar period and its characters. Wästberg himself went on educational trips —to America, Asia, and Africa. He became strongly involved in the cause of the Africans and wrote numerous newspaper articles, as well as two ironic and indignant eye-witness accounts, *Förbjudet område* (Forbidden Territory, 1960) and *På svarta listan* (Blacklisted, 1960).

In the trilogy *Vattenslottet* (The Water Castle, 1968), *Luftburen* (1969; Eng. tr. *The Air Cage*, 1972), and *Jordmånen* (1972, The Soil; Eng. tr. *Love's Gravity*, 1977) he attempts to create a synthesis of the discussions of freedom in his earlier work and returns the setting to Stockholm. It can be read as regional literature, in which the capital and its environment is described with an inexhaustible wealth of detail. But the trilogy has a wider perspective: The books are allegories of a country whose position in the world is beginning to change from that of an isolated province to that of a real power. They are also novels about a double love affair: One side is tradition, stasis, the other change, which can bring with it great erotic passion. Considered as a whole, this trilogy is Pär Wästberg's greatest work, displaying the entire range of his artistic ability.

Kurt Salomonson

The traditional, critical social novel is rarely present during the 1950s. An exception is the work of Salomonson (1929–   ), which forms an important link between the proletarian writers of the 1930s and the documentary reporters of the 1960s. Salomonson wrote a series of novels based on the underlying thesis that the solidarity of the working class, when confronted with the dictatorship of the big companies, becomes a mere illusion. Among these novels are *Grottorna* (The Caves, 1956)—based on an actual event, the compulsory transfer of some workers afflicted with silicosis—and the trilogy *Mannen utanför* (The Man Outside, 1958), *Sveket* (The Betrayal, 1959), and *Skiljevägen* (The Partition Wall, 1962).

Per Anders Fogelström

Rather than using political analysis and attack, novelist Fogelström (1917–   ) appeals to the sympathy and understanding of the reader. Fogelström, like Wästberg, quickly established himself as an outstanding portrayer of Stockholm, in the tradition of Strindberg, Söderberg, and especially Erik Asklund (see p. 168). Asklund's autobiographical series about Manne (1949–57) is the most important forerunner of Fogelström's five-volume novel cycle, a depiction of the development of Stockholm from 1860 to our time. The series opens with *Mina drömmars stad* (The City of My Dreams, 1960) and finishes in 1968 with *Stad i världen* (City in the World). Both *Ligister* (Street Gangs, 1949), which offers a fine analysis of the mentality of urban youth, and *Sommaren med Monika* (The Summer with Monika, 1951), dealing with the necessity of adjusting to the demands of everyday life, can be regarded as important preliminary studies to Fogelström's cycle. In the cycle, character delineation is more concise and thorough, and the social pathos rings truer. It is the first major depiction in Swedish literature of the poor farmworkers who were transformed into city people by the process of industrialization. With the publication in 1972 of *Upptäckarna* (The Explorers), Fogelström began one of the most widely read novel series of the 1970s, which concluded with *Besittarna* (The Proprietors) in 1977. Besides following the lives and careers of three boys from Stockholm, from the 1920s to the present, the books offer a brilliant social and political period piece, permeated by sympathetic insight.

Björn-Erik Höijer

Höijer (1907–), in his early writing, continues the realistic tendencies of the 1930s: two volumes of short stories, *Grått berg* (Gray Mountain, 1940) and *Stjärnklart* (Starry Night, 1943), and the novels *Bergfinken* (The Mountain Finch, 1944) and *Parentation* (Eulogy, 1945), deal with the northern Swedish mining communities. This milieu of Höijer's childhood is encountered again in some of his later novels, *Djävulens kalsonger* (The Underpants of the Devil, 1974) and *Gruvans ängel* (The Angel of the Mine, 1976); it serves solely as the background for subtle psychological portraits, influenced by Dostoevsky, in the otherwise autobiographical series of novels about the boy Martin (1950–63). Höijer moved away from social problems and increasingly occupied himself with moral issues, focusing on the conflict between good and evil. He found the solution in a mystical synthesis of the worldly and the supernatural, which he expressed in the novels *Rosenkransen* (The Wreath of Roses, 1953) and *Befriaren* (The Liberator, 1956). In these works, as well as in two other major novels, *Mannen på myren* (The Man on the Moors, 1957) and *Lavinen* (The Avalanche, 1961), the romantic worship of the heroic individual is manifest, which receives a more balanced treatment in his latest book, *Fjällvandring* (Mountain Hike, 1978).

Among Höijer's many—and uneven—works, the radio plays and dramas are of high quality; a selection was published in 1956. Usually they are variations on Höijer's favorite theme: the individual's relationship to his or her surroundings. One example is his major play *Isak Juntti hade många söner* (1954; Eng. tr. *Isak Juntti Had Many Sons*, 1973).

POETRY OF THE 1950s

The lyric poetry of the '50s was based on the poetics of the 1940s. The influence of Erik Lindegren in particular was noteworthy. Symbols—either sophisticated or naive—continued to play an important role, but the tone was less gloomy. Typical subjects were nature and love, described in poetic and playful language. Accordingly, Ezra Pound succeeded Eliot as an important source of inspiration. Characteristic of the decade is Bo Setterlind's attack on the 1940s as a period that he felt endangered the existence of poetry with its analytic approach to a humankind threatened with extinction. His book *Poeten och samhället* (The Poet and Society, 1954) is directed against any kind of social poetry.

Göran Printz-Påhlson

Critic Printz-Påhlson (1931–) demanded a new attitude toward language, an increased awareness of the problems of linguistic communication. Poetry should be regarded as a means of cognition, thus becoming "meta-poetry," which formulates its own conditions. These theories are reflected in *Solen i spegeln* (The Sun in the Mirror, 1958), a critical survey of the central problems of modern poetry. Printz-Påhlson's own poetry originates in the experience of a separation of language and reality, and bears strong traces of the interest in semantics and the philosophy of language that caught on around 1950. Technically his poems are quite brilliant, having many aspects in common with modern British poetry, notably that of William Empson, and they are often composed in complicated classical meters. Thus the sonnet forms the basic structure of the first collection, *Resan mellan poesi och poesi* (The Journey between Poetry and Poetry, 1955), which displays the poet's strong fascination with the scholarly and allusive. The problematic relationship of language and the outer world dominates the volume *Dikter för ett barn i vår tid* (Poems to a Child of Our Time, 1956); intellectual and surrealistic imagery is characteristic of these poems and of those in *Gradiva och andra dikter* (Gradiva and Other Poems, 1966), which are in the tradition of Gunnar Ekelöf's esoteric modernism, but include references to things current. The main theme, so characteristic of all of Printz-Påhlson's writing, deals with the poet's mission and responsibility in establishing a synthesis of words and life.

Majken Johansson

Johansson (1930–) also attempted to link reality and language. In her first collection, *Buskteater* (Popular Theater, 1952), the search for meaning and purpose in life underlies a number of humorous and burlesque, often anti-poetic and vulgar elements. There are obvious indications of her religious conversion, an account of which is given in the poetic autobiography *Från Magdala* (From Magdala, 1972), and which in 1959 caused her to join the Salvation Army. Johansson's collections from the 1960s, *Liksom överlämnad* (As If Abandoned, 1965) and *Omtal* (Spoken About, 1969) testify both to this religious breakthrough and to a greater involvement in the problem of everyday life. By establishing a tension between highly sophisticated awareness and naive childhood faith, Johansson made an important contribution to the renewal of Swedish religious poetry in the 1950s.

Bo Setterlind

Setterlind (1923–   ) cultivated a similar interest in poetry as a means of salvation. He was brought up in the spirit of the Free Church Movement, which strongly marked all of his extensive writing from the beginning. A central motif is the poet's personal experience of God, combined with a strong fascination with death, which he first expressed convincingly in the collection *Dikter från San Michele* (Poems from San Michele, 1954) and the novel *Alexandrine* (1952), set in a Swedenborgian land of death. Beginning with *Flickan och hinden* (The Girl and the Hind, 1955), a new trend is noticeable in Setterlind's poetry, away from the overexcited tone and toward more simple diction. Setterlind prefers to use the ballad meter and style, which gives his poetry a melodious intimacy reminiscent of Bo Bergman and Lagerkvist. Humankind's relationship to God has remained the major topic of Setterlind's poetry and his liturgical church plays (1966–69). Since the collection *Svävande över paniken* (Hovering above Panic, 1956), classic Christian mysticism has played an increasingly important role; it completely dominates Setterlind's latest volume, *Också fåglarna är fångar i sorgespelet* (The Birds Too Are Prisoners in the Tragedy, 1975), *Det ringer på dörren* (There Is a Ring on the Door, 1976), and *Mörkret och lovsången* (Darkness and the Hymn of Thanksgiving, 1978).

Östen Sjöstrand

Sjöstrand (1925–   ), on the other hand, was a religious mystic from the outset. He belongs to the metaphysical school of modernism, which he analyzes in his first essay collection, *Ande och verklighet* (Spirit and Reality, 1954). There are close affinities to the French poets Pierre Jouve, Pierre Emmanuel, and Paul Valery, and to Dylan Thomas, T. S. Eliot, and the Catholic American poet Robert Lowell. Sjöstrand shares the sense that music is a manifestation of the Absolute with such writers as Erik Lindegren and Gunnar Ekelöf, the last being the poet who exerted the strongest influence on him. Sjöstrand attempts to bring his poetry as close as possible to the substance of music in his striving toward the mystical experience of unity; that striving is expressed in the title of his first collection of poems, *unio* (1949):

> Freed of the community of the living
> I approached my life
> until the unity of the indivisible
> and the demand of death slipped away

and the days shrunk into today
and the universe became I.

Tr. Marianne Forssblad

To this main theme is added an element of social criticism in *In-vigelse* (Consecration, 1950), directed against the one-sided worship of materialism in the welfare society. Sjöstrand writes here in a generally more extroverted tone, which is also characteristic of the intense travel poems in *Främmande mörker, främmande ljus* (Strange Darkness, Strange Light, 1955). The imagery of the volume *Hemlöshet och hem* (Homelessness and Home, 1958) bears witness to Sjöstrand's unique interest in the natural sciences, which is also evident in the collections *En vinter i Norden* (A Winter in the North, 1963) and *I vattumannens tecken* (In the Sign of Aquarius, 1967); the latter is also influenced by astrology and Jung's discussion of fish symbolism. From now on Sjöstrand assigns to the poet and his work the elevated task of acting as a transmitter of knowledge and insight. This preoccupation with the problems of communication became particularly strong in the volume *Drömmen är ingen fasad* (The Dream Is No Facade, 1971), and is indicated in the title of Sjöstrand's latest collection, *Strömöverföring* (Transmission of Power, 1977). Here he continues the attempt to refine his linguistic tools, "to express the silent movements of the spirit and thereby also preserve the ability of human reaction"—an attempt which, in its religious, Catholic, context, distinguishes Sjöstrand as one of the great Christian poets of this century.

Lars Forssell

The catastrophic atmosphere of the 1940s is present in the first collection by Forssell (1928–   ), *Ryttaren* (The Rider, 1949); the volume contains compact and hermetic poems about transitoriness and death. Here, and even more in *Narren* (The Jester, 1952), which pursues the tragic themes of the first volume, Forssell's preference for employing masks and roles, and letting various figures act as his spokesperson is clear. This technique forms the transition to his career as a successful dramatist.

In his first play, *Kröningen* (1956; Eng. tr. *The Coronation*, 1964), he uses the ancient saga of Alcestis for his poetic portrayal of a hero who dares to be afraid. Such anti-heroes play an important role in Forssell's dramas. One example is King Gustav IV in the Brecht-inspired *Galenpannan* (1964; Eng. tr. *The Madcap*, 1973). The king is one of Forssell's fools, who serves as a mirror to humankind, demonstrating inflated emptiness and pitiful pettiness. Another valuable play is *Christina Alexandra* (1968), a psychological analysis of the seventeenth-century Swedish queen. The comedy *Borgaren och Marx* (The Citizen and Marx, 1970) and *Show* (1971), a play about American entertainer Lenny Bruce, are less significant.

Forssell published two translations of Ezra Pound's poems (1953, 1959), and his own poetry is indeed related to Pound's cryptic work. In the 1960s, however, Forssell turned from the complicated to the cabaretlike song. In *Röster* (Voices, 1964) this trend, and simultaneously Forssell's poetry, reached its zenith. The centerpiece of the collection is a series of poems that are spoken by the Russian dancer Nijinsky. He is also a spokesman for the basic mood in Forssell's poetry: the experience of emptiness and estrangement. Not until the volume *Ändå* (Yet, 1968) is this tone replaced by a more optimistic note, combined with a political attitude. "There is no reason for optimism. / There is no reason for pessimism. / There is reason for revolution," states Forssell in the volume *Oktoberdikter* (October Poems, 1971). His radical views are further elaborated in *Försök* (Attempts, 1972) and *Det möjliga* (The Possible, 1974), collections in which feelings of solidarity and confidence predominate, and they are given subtle treatment in his first novel, *De rika* (The Rich, 1976), a satirical portrayal of corruption and degeneration in an upper-class family.

Tomas Tranströmer

Among the most successful poetry collections of the 1950s are the slim volumes by Tranströmer (1931–). In *17 dikter* (17 Poems, 1954) he works primarily with impressions of nature from the archipelago around Stockholm, using many concrete details; the basic experience, however, is a power or movement in the cosmos, a universal coherence which occasionally takes on a religious dimension. His symbolic language is rich and concise, although the poems themselves are formally extremely simple. In Tranströmer's second collection, *Hemligheter på vägen* (Secrets on the Path, 1958), the poems are even more ascetic and at the same time more sophisticated, external themes being barely hinted at. *Den halvfärdiga himlen* (Half-Finished Heaven, 1962) and *Klanger och spår* (Sounds and Traces, 1966) are in the pessimistic mood of the earlier poems and are highly structured, unified pieces. The style is more simple than before, the world of images even less accessible.

Tranströmer had become more concrete in his poems of 1966, dealing with current political topics such as the war in Algeria. However, he is primarily interested not in ideological analyses but in moral questions concerning the individual in *Mörkerseende* (1970; Eng. tr. *Night Vision*, 1971) and *Stigar* (Paths, 1973). Tranströmer's vague political commitment is transformed into a discussion of the clash between the individual and society. The same theme informs the structure of *Östersjöar* (1974; Eng. tr. *Baltics*, 1975), a volume that embraces both spiritual reflections and political and historical perspectives on the Baltic Sea. In *Sanningsbarriären* (The Barrier to Truth, 1978) Tranströmer attempted to overcome his prevailing pessimistic world view by pointing to the possibilites of an existing supernatural world. Notes of consolation and confidence give the works both substance and resilience, marking a new development in his poetry.

Sandro Key-Åberg

Tranströmer belongs to the traditional symbolist school and has been criticized for having an uncommitted attitude. Key-Åberg (1922–   ), on the other hand, works with language effortlessly, with the intention of provoking the reader into opposing brutal reality. The ominous transitoriness and fragility of the body are dominant themes in his work from the outset. In the midst of life, we are embraced by death. This romantically shaded pessimism culminates in *Bittergök* (Bitter Fool, 1954). In his later poetry, Key-Åberg, without abandoning this dark vision, made a passionate appeal to people's sense of responsibility. Gradually he approached a sense of consolation, as seen, for instance, in the dialogue between God and humankind in the volume *Livets glädje* (The Joys of Life, 1960): "Love, my dear / is the rainbow which I see / shining between yours and / another human heart." The resignation that one senses in these lines is related to Birger Sjöberg's attitude; in fact, Sjöberg did exert some influence on Key-Åberg's style. In *Bildade människor* (Educated People, 1964), a collection of prose poems or choruses, Key-Åberg points out the negative aspects of existence, the baseness, the egoism, and the prejudices, expressed in superficial phrases in our everyday speech. These pieces were very popular—in stage presentation as well. The author developed them into short satirical sketches, such as *O* (1965; Eng. tr. *O*, 1970), which were presented in several European theaters. Key-Åberg's later plays include *Härliga tid som randas* (Wonderful Time That Is Approaching, 1968) and *Två slår den tredje* (Two Beat the Third, 1968), which deal with the daily threat of destruction, presented in a half-ironic play of words, whereas in *På sin höjd* (At the Most, 1972), Key-Åberg resumes the more melodramatic and intense approach of his earlier collections.

In 1976 Key-Åberg published his first novel, *De goda människorna*

(The Good People). Superficially it can be read as a realistic story about exploitation, politically as an allegory of the industrialized nation's taking advantage of the developing countries. In fact, the author sets out to give a highly ironic depiction of the Swedish welfare state, characterized by materialism and the attempt to manipulate its citizens.

POETRY OF THE 1960s

Since the definitive breakthrough of modern Swedish lyric poetry, the most important element has been a complex metaphoric and symbolic language. However, during the 1960s several poets, advocates of the "new simplicity," rebelled against the wealth of imagery. They demonstrated a renewed interest in simple lyrical language and an everyday style through which a complicated view of reality could be conveyed to the reader in a more accessible manner.

Göran Palm

It is poetry's role in the communication process that has constantly been stressed by the most significant spokesperson of the "new simplicity," Palm (1931–   ), both in his polemical literary criticism and in his poems. Thus his first collection, *Hundens besök* (The Visit of the Dog, 1961), contains deliberately simple, often aphoristic, poetry, which primarily conveys basic elements of reality; but, in fact, it treats of human isolation in a world determined by social gulfs. In *Världen ser dig* (The World Sees You, 1964) Palm demands that the poet abandon the traditional, aesthetic role and concentrate on creating contact and communication. Around 1965 Palm turned to the critical essay and published a number of "debate books." In *En orättvis betraktelse* (1966, An Unfair Observation; Eng. tr. *As Others See Us*, 1968) he depicts the highly developed industrial western world from the viewpoint of the underdeveloped countries. In *Indoktrineringen i Sverige* (Indoctrination in Sweden, 1968) he maintains that mass media and instructional materials favor a western antisocialist point of view; *Ett år på LM* (One Year at LM, 1972) and *Bokslut från LM* (Balance Sheet from LM, 1974) give a semi-documentary account of his experiences as a worker in a large industrial firm, L. M. Ericsson. In 1971 Palm returned to poetry with the volume *Varför har nätterna inga namn?* (Why Do the Nights Have No Name?), which is a thematic continuation of *The World Sees You*, but which transfers the responsibility from the poet to the politically awakened human being. With these books Palm followed a general development perceptible in all of Swedish literature, a turning to puritanical socialism.

Björn Håkanson

Håkanson (1937–   ) is also paradigmatic of the 1960s in his artistic development. Although his first collection of poems, *Rymd för ingenting* (Room for Nothing, 1962) was strongly influenced by Tranströmer and his next volume, *Mot centrum* (Toward Center, 1963), was an exercise in the methods of the "new simplicity," Håkanson took his language directly from everyday life, from ads and newspaper columns. His work lives in the moment and from the moment, having no aesthetic metaphysical intention. In his very distrust of language, he resolves that distrust and discovers new functional possibilities. Håkanson met the challenge of a politically involved literature with several collections: *Kärlek i Vita Huset* (Love in the White House, 1967), *Mellan två val* (Poems between Two Elections, 1969), and *Fronter i tredje världskriget* (Fronts in World War III, 1975), undogmatic formulations of his political creed. His politics also form the conclusion of his only novel, *Generalsekreteraren* (The Secretary-General, 1965), which describes the career of a secretary-general of the United Nations. At the same time, this very abstract and hermetic book is an extensive discussion of the possibilities of creating a world without problems, governed by responsibility and love, thereby making the author's function superfluous. Håkanson's viewpoints are most successfully formulated in the essay collection *Författarmakt* (The Writer's Power, 1970), which affirms his position as a leading theoretician in Swedish literature. In Håkanson's latest poetry collections, *Stängt för sammanträde* (Closed owing to a Meeting, 1976) and *Tjänstemannens son* (The Son of a Civil Servant, 1978), he violently protests against a welfare-state bureaucracy that denies the individual's moral responsibility and threatens the individual's life.

Göran Sonnevi

Much more direct in his political message is Sonnevi (1939–   ). He began his literary career with a volume of introverted, elegiac poetry entitled *Outförd* (Unfinished, 1961), which revolved around love and death, silence and extinction. The same motifs are present in *Abstrakta dikter* (Abstract Poems, 1963). A basic element in Sonnevi's poetry is his concept of the "structures," representing the principles that deprive life of its spontaneity and freshness. Language is one of these structures, and its power over our thoughts and notions is analyzed in *Ingrepp—modeller* (Intervention—Models, 1965). In addition, the collection contains Sonnevi's earliest political writing; his breakthrough as a political writer was accomplished with the separately published controversial poem "Om kriget i Vietnam" ("About the War in Vietnam," 1965). The author's revolutionary activism is apparent in the following titles: *Och nu!* (And Now!, 1967) and *Det måste gå* (It Has to Work, 1970); these works place Sonnevi beside Danish author Ivan Malinovski as one of the more convincing political writers of postwar Nordic literature. He utilizes shock effects with striking artistic results:

> Mummy, come
> and help me! My back
> is cold too, mummy,
> it's burning!
> Pour water on it
> and it will flare up!
> Then you won't be cold.

Tr. Marianne Forssblad

In *Det uavslutade språket* (The Unfinished Language, 1972) Sonnevi returns to his point of departure. To prevent a revolution, the ruling class manipulates language; it is the people's task, then, to break up this indoctrinating power structure through political action. *Det omöjliga* (The Impossible, 1975) and its sequel, *Språk; verktyg; eld* (Language; Tools; Fire, 1979) are Sonnevi's most significant poetry collections so far, daring and grandiose attempts to establish a synthesis of past and present human experiences in a captivating language, alternating between concrete, unpretentious expression and the highly abstract and speculative.

Preoccupation with the function of language leads not only to a literature critical of society, but also to a so-called concrete poetry: Words are employed as concrete, malleable material, freed of "sense" and "intention." The letters are arranged in patterns, and the words are exploited as sounds.

Pioneers of this direction were Öyvind Fahlström (1928-), who published the first manifesto of concrete poetry in the periodical *Odyssé* as early as 1953, and the poet and painter Carl Fredrik Reuterswärd (1934-). In his collection *På samma gång* (At the Same Time, 1961) he gave up syntax completely and arranged single words in a lyrical verbal tapestry that extended through the entire book. Not so much with satirical intent, but hoping to point out a new function of language, Reuterswärd composed a collage of newspaper excerpts entitled *VIP* (1963). He pushed his method to the extreme in *Prix Nobel* (1966), which consists entirely of punctuation marks.

Where Reuterswärd writes with the intention of provoking the reader, Bengt Emil Johnson (1936–) attempts above all to communicate his artistic experiences. For that reason he followed his volume *Gubbdrunkning* (The Drowning of an Old Man, 1965) with a phonograph record, in order to more vitally convey the printed word. *Tal till folket* (Speech to the People, 1975) is also an attempt to overcome all obstacles between poet and readers; readers are provoked by a confrontation with what is apparently a verbal hodgepodge, which is the starting point for a possible interpretation. In the collection *Rötmånad* (The Dog-Days, 1976), on the other hand, Johnson steps forth as the omniscient author who builds a linguistic structure on the associative power of language.

Åke Hodell (1919–) exemplifies in his work the growing political influence on the originally uncommitted genre of concretism. In *Igevär* (To Arms, 1963) and *General Bussig* (General Neat, 1964) he expresses his antimilitarism. *Orderbuch* (Order Book, 1965) and *CA 36715* (1965) are pseudo-documentaries, the first a portrayal of the fate of prisoners in a concentration camp, the second a diary of a prisoner in which the unreadable text is intended to convey his fear of extinction. Less subtle are *USS Pacific Ocean* (1968), accompanied by a phonograph record with a Black Power speech by Stokely Carmichael, and *Mr. Nixon's Dreams* (1970).

Erik Beckman

The political message is equally clear in the poetry collection by Beckman (1935–) entitled *Kyss Er!* (Kiss Yourself! 1969), containing satirical attacks on bourgeois indoctrination, a process in which language is considered the primary tool. The fight against language as a means of exploitation, and the insistence on an equality that is not primarily political or social but linguistic, are expressed in the novels *Någon, något* (Somebody, Something, 1964) and *Hertigens kartonger* (The Duke's Cardboard Boxes, 1965). The latter consists of 596 numbered prose texts, constituting both a walk through London and a movement through various linguistic possibilities. These are further explored in the novel *Inlandsbanan* (The Interior Railway, 1967), based on the theory that all linguistic elements are interchangeable. The long poem *Varifrån dom observeras* (From Where They Are Observed, 1966) is a demonstration of the arbitrary meaning of words.

The political aspect again becomes predominant in the novels *Kameler dricker vatten* (Camels Drink Water, 1971), which attacks the large multinational companies, and *Sakernas tillstånd* (The State of Affairs, 1973), concerning the individual's relationship to politics and the human possibility of finding freedom and happiness. Beckman is inclined to find the answer in communism, as he strongly emphasizes in the poems of *Tumme* (Thumb, 1974). In spite of his strong political preoccupation, Beckman still employs the technique and motifs of his early works. Words are freed from their traditional meanings, and they function in a code, having ambiguous, often inscrutable connotations. The same ambiguity characterizes Beckman's latest novel, *Jag känner igen mej* (I Recognize Myself, 1977), a harshly ironical portrayal of the world of politics rendered in the style of a fairy tale, and the poetry collection *Den kommunala kroppen* (The Municipal Body, 1979).

THE PROSE OF THE 1960s

The most important prose innovation is the French *nouveau roman*, represented by the works of Alain Robbe-Grillet, Michel Butor, and Nathalie Sarraute.

Torsten Ekbom

Robbe-Grillet in particular aroused great interest in Sweden and found a disciple in Ekbom (1938–   ), whose theoretical point of departure, like that of his Danish contemporary Svend Åge Madsen, was the idea that a book should not "contain" anything at all; an author is not supposed to be interested in *what* his characters perceive of their surroundings, but *how* they do so. *Spelöppning* (Opening of the Game, 1964) is a collage that the reader has to arrange; *Signalspelet* (The Signal Game, 1965) is a "prose machine" without any author, the basis of which is a Biggles-novel (popular boys' books by British author W. E. Johns) cut into pieces and put together again—picturing human existence as totally haphazard, subject to all kinds of manipulation. Ekbom's attempt to find an impersonal language that eliminates the author also characterizes *Spelmatriser för Operation Albatross* (Game Matrixes for Operation Albatross, 1966), dealing with the political aspects of computer science, and *En galakväll på Operan* (A Gala Performance at the Opera, 1969), a catalog of the world exhibition in London's Crystal Palace in 1897, but simultaneously a catalog of modernity and its myths. The political and ideological currents of the nineteenth century are the subject of Ekbom's latest work, the essay collection *Europeiska konserten* (European Concert, 1975), a stimulating, versatile, and spiritual exposé of ideas and human beings seen in an elegantly constructed cultural perspective.

Obviously Ekbom regards literature as a structure composed of linguistic signs. One implication of this view is particularly interesting, the relationship of the system of symbols to reality, which is described in an objective manner. This attitude led to the objectification of prose in all of Europe, culminating in the extensive use of a documentary and journalistic style. A Nordic pioneer in this area was the Dane Thorkild Hansen (see p. 343), but its most prominent representatives were in Sweden.

Per Olof Sundman

The early books of Sundman (1922–   ) were set in the northern part of Jämtländ. Among writers who lend a certain provincial style to their works (see p. 273), he soon established himself as one of the more important; however, he never limited himself to the provincial. His novels have social interest and are supported by existential questions. *Undersökningen* (The Investigation, 1958) illustrates his objective character portrayal. He has them appear, act, and speak in situations that are often very dramatic. Seldom, however, does he penetrate their innermost beings to render thoughts or feelings. The reader must attempt to make inferences about this. Thus the narrative proves how difficult if not impossible it is to reach an unambiguous truth about another person, since there is no objectively recordable reality.

The inaccessibility of truth is also the theme of *Skytten* (The Marksman, 1960), which is linked in theme and style to the preceding book. Sundman's treatment here also applies to the individual in his or her interpersonal relationships with other people.

The same sociological interest marks *Expeditionen* (1962; Eng. tr. *The Expedition*, 1962), in which Sundman abandons the scenery of Jämtland and works with historical material—Stanley's jungle expedition—investigating reciprocal relationships in a group of people isolated by their surroundings.

Ingenjör Andrées luftfärd (1967, Engineer Andrée's Balloon Flight; Eng. tr. *The Flight of the Eagle*, 1970) is a documentary report of a balloon trip from Spitzbergen to the North Pole in 1897, a flight that failed because it had been carelessly planned. Andrée was a firm believer in rising industrialism and attempted to combine his pioneering spirit with the new technology. Sundman tells his story with impressive discipline, in a taut, factual style, using notebooks of this tragic expedition. The work is not a psychological novel—we learn nothing about the physical and psychological burdens of the characters—and he does not yield to the temptation of treating his tragic material melodramatically or sentimentally. On the contrary, Sundman set out

to creat a double documentary by publishing the material for his preliminary research as *Ingen fruktan, intet hopp* (No Fear, No Hope,
1968). The simple, terse style of Sundman's documentary novels
reached its culmination in *Berättelsen om Såm* (The Story of Såm,
1977), based on the Icelandic *Hrafnkel's saga*, depicting a dramatic
family feud which Sundman shifts to a contemporary setting.

Per Olov Enquist

The difficulty of getting at the truth is also the topic of a novel by
Enquist (1934–   ), *Färdvägen* (The Direction of Travel, 1963), in
which the first-person narrator is the commentator. It is modeled on
the picaresque novel, a series of adventures, but it portrays a journey
through life; the different events of the trip stand for different alterna-
tives in life. Far more simple in form is Enquist's first great success,
which takes up a more complicated problem. *Magnetisörens femte
vinter* (The Fifth Winter of the Mesmerist, 1964) tells of a miracle
worker wandering in eighteenth-century Germany and his relationship to a skeptical doctor, who at first falls under the spell of the mes-
merizer, but soon discovers indications of fraud. He finds himself in
a moral conflict, since the mesmerist is able to save face even when his
fraudulence is exposed. The book thus becomes a report of the interplay of faith and mistrust, the irrational and reason.

The excellently structured novel *Hess* (1966) deals with the relationship of freedom and captivity. The book portrays a researcher
who is writing a treatise about Rudolf Hess and other people who
have the same name. Gradually he becomes fascinated by Hess and
identifies with him, although he simultaneously reports, with a certain
irony, his research methods, which are supposed to ensure that there
will be a distance between him and the object of his research.

As in *The Direction of Travel*, the author constantly questions his
own work, so that *Hess* also becomes a novel about writing a novel,
a so-called metanovel. With its linguistic and formal experiments, it
was, when published, one of the boldest, most challenging works of
modern Nordic prose.

But Enquist's international success did not occur until the publication of *Legionärerna* (1968; Eng. tr. *The Legionnaires*, 1973). The
background of this documentary novel is the surrender by the Swedish
government of the Baltic soldiers in German service to the Russians
in 1946, which aroused a storm of public protest. Enquist investigates
in detail what occurred in the months when these Baltic soldiers were
interned in Sweden. But *The Legionnaires* is more than a documentary,
for Enquist weaves his own personality into the presentation, which

becomes the object of constant revision and discussion. The delivery of the Baltic soldiers thus becomes an example of how the character of a political situation can be altered when one works one's way into it more deeply. Through the description of the political situation immediately after the war, the book becomes a description of the author's own situation; against the background of a multitude of historical facts, it turns into a book about the ignorance that is common to political amateur and professional, a book about the impossibility of truth and the attitude of intellectuals toward a world that concerns them, but in the face of which they feel like strangers.

Sekonden (The Second, 1971) also deals with the quest for identity. It contains numerous references to the novels of 1966 and 1968; like these, it is based on documentary material. On one level the novel is about sports, which Enquist sees as mirroring society and ideology. The narrator analyzes the question of why his father once cheated in order to win a contest, as he attempted to explain his own loneliness and lack of commitment in his relationship with an East German female athlete. The novel is both a philosophical discussion and a love story. *The Second* ranks high in recent Scandinavian prose. Enquist's ideological criticism of sports journalism, *Katedralen i München* (The Cathedral in Munich, 1972), concerning the Olympic Games in Munich, is only an interlude before his next great achievement, *Berättelser från de inställda upprorens tid* (Stories from the Time of the Canceled Revolts, 1974). This is a collection of short stories portraying various prison revolts in a capitalist society; some are subdued, others are carried out in desperate or absurd ways. The characters grope in the void, trying to reach reality. The dominant atmosphere of hopelessness is only a transitory stage—a possibility of reaching reality does exist, which points to a new trend in Enquist's writing. This is also indicated by his successful dramatic debut with *Tribadernas natt* (1975; Eng. tr. *The Night of the Tribades*, 1977), delineating the struggle between Strindberg and his wife, Siri von Essen, during the rehearsal of a play that is based on their lives. Their clash deals with the question of illusion versus reality, a question that, according to Enquist, should be the most pressing human concern.

In 1978 Enquist published a semi-documentary novel, *Musikanternas uttåg* (The Departure of the Musicians), in which he finally freed himself from the affected language characteristic of most of his previous works. The novel deals with the confrontation between the Social-Democratic Party and the Christian fundamentalists in the northern Sweden of Enquist's own childhood shortly after 1900. It analyzes prejudices, brutality, ignorance, and cruelty from a consistently objective point of view. By virtue of its complete mastery of topic, style, and epic narrative technique, the novel stands as one of Enquist's foremost works.

An alternative to the objectivity inspired by the *nouveau roman* is offered by the popular novelists Sven Delblanc and P. C. Jersild, who tell stories full of fantasy, partly burlesque, partly serious.

Sven Delblanc

The first novel by Delblanc (1931–), *Eremitkräftan* (The Hermit Crab, 1962), is a somewhat abstract allegory about the conditions of freedom in a totalitarian state and in a society in which indolence and irresponsibility prevail. In the broadly drawn story *Prästkappan* (The Cassock, 1963), Delblanc is able for the first time to bring his imaginative talents fully to the fore. The main character of the work, set in eighteenth-century Germany, is the discharged Pastor Hermann, who sets out into the world to find people who exemplify his high ideals. The most unbelievable events befall him, events which reveal that human honor and greatness are purely illusory. Hermann is forced to recognize that his venture is hopeless, to accept the fact that life will not offer him self-fulfillment. He becomes a hardened cynic, a living dead man.

The main character in *Homunculus* (1965; Eng. tr. 1969) is also a seeker with a mystical leaning toward the absolute, who comes into conflict with his surroundings and is forced to give up his plans. The Swede Sebastian has succeeded in chemically creating a human being, a homunculus. But when he learns that the two modern superpowers, the United States and Russia, as well as the Swedish government, are feverishly pursuing his secret in order to mass produce soldiers, he is forced to destroy his creation. The book is an unrestrained parody, but at the same time a pessimistic tale about the relationship between artist and society, and also about the plight of the individual defenseless in the face of power. *Nattresa* (Night Journey, 1967) offers a more positive solution to this complex of problems. The main character, Axel Weber, resists all the temptations of nihilism: the corruption of the arts, the human urge for submission, and the impossibility of gaining power, since this process is inevitably based on violence; thereby Weber reaches maturity and is able to act.

In *Åsnebrygga* (The Donkey's Bridge, 1969) Delblanc, like Enquist in *The Legionnaires*, voices his own doubts. It is an extreme example of the Swedish documentary novel. Whereas Sundman sets forth historical material about Andrée's balloon trip, and Enquist (*The Legionnaires*) and Sara Lidman (*Mine*) attempt to present actual circumstances objectively, it is Delblanc's intention to show through this fascinating book, which is, in fact, his own diary, how subjectively he relates to traditional objectivity. Here he deals with the observations of a Swedish guest professor during his stay at an American university (Berkeley). Delblanc does not assume the traditional stance of the narrator: He does not stand outside the story, but implicates himself to such a degree that he crosses the line between fiction and autobiography, thus demonstrating his independence of the reader. Delblanc does everything that a "real" author is not permitted to do. He abandons his role as a guest professor, confesses to being a man of the multitudes, but knows that he, the academician, is setting himself off as a lone wolf.

Delblanc's alter ego, Axel Weber, is the narrator of *Åminne* (Memorial, 1970), which is simultaneously a colorful, humorous picture of peasant life during the 1930s, a philosophical discussion, and a debate about narrative techniques. It was followed by *Stenfågel* (Stone Bird, 1973), *Vinteride* (Winter Lair, 1974), and *Stadsporten* (The Town Gate, 1976), novels that became more and more like chronicles, with fewer narrative experiments. The political and social analyses also gradually changed into a more psychological approach. In 1973 Delblanc pursued motifs and characters from *Night Journey* in the grotesque myth *Primavera*, written within a romantic and historical framework; he used a similar technique in the novel *Kastrater* (1975; Eng. tr. *The Castrati*, 1979), which discusses the everpresent question of the role of the artist, and his drama *Morgonstjärnan* (The Morning Star, 1977), which concerns an eighteenth-century peasant revolt. In *Grottmannen* (The Cave Man, 1977) Delblanc takes up the problem of a man caught between two cultures and his attempts to find himself. Delblanc's satire, aimed at Swedish cultural life, is both humorous and pointed, but it fails because of its grotesque exaggeration.

Per Christian Jersild

In the work of Jersild (1935–) the imaginative and the grotesque are combined with an interest in society, an interest shared by Delblanc, Sundman, and many other writers; but Jersild is a sharper satirist than they. *Räknelära* (Arithmetic Lesson, 1960) primarily contains lively and entertaining but in no way superficial tales about the computerized details and idiocies of the welfare state. Jersild's fine ear for jargon and trivia permits him to register all the nuances of everyday Swedish life; he is also capable of suddenly unleashing fantastic elements and confronting his superficial characters with experiences that throw a completely unexpected light on their situation.

This method is characteristic of many of Jersild's books; one example is *Ledig lördag* (Free Saturday, 1963), which concerns a trip on the subway. After a company party, two people are locked into a train car that rides around for several days on mysterious tracks. After the party they could have become a couple; now they have a Robinson Crusoe experience in the midst of modern communications technology, an evil dream in the technological world.

With the successful novel *Calvinols resa genom världen* (Calvinol's Trip through the World, 1965), Jersild turns his back on the Swedish milieu. Following the pattern of the classic satiric novel, he tells of the burlesque adventure of his hero, a charlatan, in various times and places. He takes part in the great Children's Crusade of 1212, represents King Gustav Adolf during the Thirty Years War, and undertakes a relief expedition in the bodily remains of a gigantic Russian dictator. Behind the apparently harmless episodes lies amusing but sharp ridicule of political and moral foolishness.

In 1970 Jersild continued this genre with *Drömpojken* (The Dream Boy), which analyzes, with farcical effects, a capitalist technological society. The hero is an engineer who wants to change his identity; however, this costs him an ear. The entire novel is a breathless description of the hero's furious chase through the world in search of a new one and a convincing demonstration of Jersild's ability to manipulate language as well as the reader.

Jersild reaches a high point in his writing with the novel *Grisjakten* (The Pig Hunt, 1968). It deals with the perfect civil servant who loyally carries out the orders of the system, without question or doubt. The government official Siljeberg is supposed to lead a project, the "De-pigification" of Gotland, with the same precision with which Hitler's bureaucrats administered the concentration camps. During the extermination maneuvers he finds a piglet that is dying of starvation. He decides to save the animal, since he feels they have a common fate. Exhausted, they seek refuge in a church, where the pig dies, and Siljeberg, who has gone insane, buries it.

Jersild focuses primarily on the individual's responsibility for his or her actions. In *Vi ses i Song My* (See You in Song My, 1970), the psychologist Nylander is employed by the General Staff and wonders whether he is thus contributing to the support of a suspect system. However, he is able to rationalize away his doubts in any situation, and thereby he indirectly becomes a victim of society's manipulation. Jersild again warns against such manipulation in *Djurdoktorn* (1973; Eng. tr. *The Animal Doctor*, 1975), a satirical novel set in the 1980s. It is a vision of a repressive system which absorbs the few revolts that occur by appealing to solidarity and understanding. In Jersild's latest novel, *Babels hus* (The House of Babel, 1978) we are only one year into the future, inside a gigantic, supermodern hospital. This gigantic monument to a misguided health policy is penetratingly analyzed by Jersild, who is himself a doctor. *The House of Babel* was among the most controversial books of that year, full of criticism, but with the underlying warmth that characterized *See You in Song My* and *The Animal Doctor*.

Lars Gustafsson

Gustafsson (1936–) stands outside the literary movements in fashion in Sweden. His work takes up the question of the identity of the human being, the relationship between the self and objects, and other philosophical problems, and investigates them with acuity and imagination. Gustafsson goes beyond the borders of human knowledge, approaching mysticism. He has found inspiration in the romantic works of Edgar Allan Poe and E. T. A. Hoffman, and tends to give his carefully composed novels a romantic form.

Thus his novel *Poeten Brumbergs sista dagar och död* (The Last Days and Death of the Poet Brumberg, 1959) is characterized as "a romantic tale"; it is composed as a mosaic from the literary legacy of the poet and philosopher Brumberg, made up of quotations from his renaissance novel and recollections and commentaries from his friends. The book concerns the contrast between the conventions that give stability to existence and the knowledge of boundlessness and multiplicity. Brumberg, that is to say Gustafsson, energetically defends the ambiguities in life and literature, as well as the relativity of truth.

In the allegorical novel *Bröderna* (The Brothers, 1960) Gustafsson takes up the question of how our environment markedly affects our personality and how it influences our conception of reality. The main character turns from the world and from objects, experiences a kind of religious mysticism, but discovers that he thereby loses his identity.

The relationship of the individual to his or her surroundings also occupies Gustafsson in his next two, more pessimistic, novels. The main character in *Följeslagarna* (The Companions, 1962) is a philosopher who writes about freedom of the will; he goes on an adventure-filled trip through Europe, which has some elements of the popular spy novel, without managing to comprehend the world from a non-materialistic position. Arenander, in *Den egentliga berättelsen om herr Arenander* (The Actual Story of Mr. Arenander, 1966), with his far-ranging scientific interests, is an ingeniously created representative of the person who believes that he can solve his problems with the help of natural science, but whose life ends in isolation and resignation.

In 1962 Gustafsson published the poem *Ballongfararna* (The Balloon Travelers), succeeded by the collections *Bröderna Wright uppsöker Kitty Hawk* (The Wright Brothers Visit Kitty Hawk, 1968) and *Kärleksförklaring till en sefardisk dam* (Declaration of Love to a Sephardic Lady, 1970)—self-examinations reminiscent both of Ekelöf's *A Mölna Elegy* and of Bjørnvig's *The Raven*. These volumes, and *Varma rum och kalla* (1972; Eng. tr. *Warm Rooms and Cold*, 1975), contain primarily variations on the themes of his novels: the relationships between fiction and reality, art and life, past and future.

Whereas Gustafsson's earlier works were marked by defeatism and bewilderment, a more pragmatic attitude is increasingly noticeable in his planned cycle of five novels. The cycle is entitled *Sprickorna i muren* (The Cracks in the Wall) and begins with *Herr Gustafsson själv* (Mr. Gustafsson Himself, 1971), a presentation of the narrator and his gradual confrontation with political reality, and continues with *Yllet* (The Wool, 1973) and *Familjefesten* (The Family Party, 1975), an analysis of the power structure in Sweden and its influence on the individual. In 1976 and 1978 Gustafsson published the last two volumes, the burlesque *Sigismund* and *En biodlares död* (The Death of a Bee-Keeper), the tragic but warm-hearted story of a man dying of cancer. In 1977 he also published the formally brilliant poetry collection *Sonetter* (Sonnets) and the light-hearted burlesque *Tennisspelarna* (The Tennis Players), set in Texas. All these works confirm Lars Gustafsson's central position in contemporary Swedish cultural life.

Chapter *14*

Norwegian Postwar Literature

World War II and the German occupation from 1940 to 1945 marked
a break in Norwegian literature. There was, in addition to love and
death, one theme that suddenly preoccupied everyone: Fatherland,
community, even the king became realities that were on all lips. Because Norwegian authors were writing about matters that affected the
public, they became critically important. By 1940 several books had
appeared whose plots were set entirely or in part during the war; a
novel by Nils Johan Rud (1908–), *Godt mot, menneske* (Take Courage, Man), was inspired by the war, and Tarjei Vesaas's *The Seed* (see
p. 185) was indirectly inspired by it. A hunger for reading was widespread. However, owing to censorship, this was satisfied only after the
liberation. Postwar literary life was marked by a flood of publications
and a great number of amateur publishers; even the established publishing houses seemed to have forgotten their experience and their
standards. A cultural debate flared, which was argued with fanatical
partisanship. Newspapers and journals split into two sharply divided
camps: naturalists, Voltaireans, and rationalists on one side, neo-
romantics and Christians on the other. In this rather provincial debate—one topic was Darwinism—two journals did manage to maintain
their standards: *Vinduet* (The Window, 1947–), neutral to a certain
extent, but unmistakably in sympathy with the radical side, and
Spektrum (Spectrum, 1946–54), around which there arose a conservative, Christian-anthroposophic circle. It was from this circle that
one of the more promising new writers, Jens Bjørneboe, emerged.

LYRIC POETRY, POSTWAR TO 1960

The most noteworthy aspect of Norwegian literature after the first coming to terms with war and occupation was the sudden shift to lyric poetry after 1948; there were very few new dramatic works, and prose, with the exception of Paal Brekke's novels, did not break with psychological realism until the 1960s, when it established contact with European modernism.

The climate in which the poets of the new generation began their work, still much overshadowed by the two older productive poets Wildenwey and Øverland, was the most adverse imaginable. During the occupation, literary life received no stimulation from the outside, and in the last years of the war virtually no books were published. Modernism had gained a foothold in Denmark in the work of Gustaf Munch-Petersen (1912–38) and in Ole Sarvig's *Green Poems* (1943), and Sweden had established contact with modern world literature through the metaphorical poetry of the 1940s—*Angst*, disintegration, and alienation were central themes. However, similar trends were barely present in Norway, and there was little demand for experimentation.

Rolf Jacobsen

There had been impulses toward renewal as early as the 1930s. In the collections *Jord og jern* (Earth and Iron, 1933) and *Vrimmel* (Multitude, 1935), Jacobsen (1907–   ), like Bønnelycke and earlier Johannes V. Jensen in Denmark, had attempted to incorporate all of modern civilization, technology, and urban life into a cluster of poetic themes; he perceived them not as antithetical to nature, but as natural parts of reality. After the war, Jacobsen wrote *Fjerntog* (Long-Distance Trains, 1951); his feelings for nature were now characterized by distance and disillusionment. In *Stillheten efterpå* (The Silence Afterward, 1965), *Headlines* (1969), and *Pass for dørene—dørene lukkes* (Beware of the Closing Doors, 1972) he expresses in somber language a strongly religious disgust with the results of the machine age. Although Jacobsen's initial contribution was related to the renewal of language—he was the first Norwegian poet to practice the principles of modern free verse—his later works placed more emphasis on imagery. *Pusteøvelse* (Breathing Exercise, 1975) opens with a vision of earth as seen from outer space and concludes with the refrain "everything passes": "My position, therefore, is easy: the observer's. Everything passes. Sit and watch." This attitude of passivity and reflection is stressed even more in *Tenk på noe annet* (Think of Something Else, 1979). Jacobsen's field of associations becomes increasingly more complicated; he creates bold images which he permits to work without interpretation, through their own power. He has become a significant Norwegian representative of imagistic poetry.

On the threshold of modernism stand Emil Boyson and Claes Gill.

Emil Boyson

Boyson (1897–1979) published *Sommertørst* (Summer Thirst), a highly experimental non-naturalistic novel, in 1927 and produced two more lyrical prose works during the 1930s. His major achievements, however, are the two volumes of poetry, *Gjemt i mørket* (Hidden in the Darkness, 1939) and *Gjenkjennelse* (Recognition, 1957), which blend philosophical reflections with sensuous images of love and beauty. Boyson was influenced by French symbolism and by Yeats and Eliot.

Claes Gill

The same two poets were the major models for the epoch-making collections by Gill (1910–73), *Fragment av et magisk liv* (Fragment of a Magic Life, 1939) and *Ord i jærn* (Works in Iron, 1942). He not only broke with traditional metrics, but, influenced by Eliot and Yeats, freed himself from traditional imagery and syntax. The metaphors pass in free succession, guided only by his often paradoxical experiences and associations.

For a long time Gill was an isolated phenomenon. Not until 1947 did Vesaas publish his volume of poems *The Game and the Lightning*, and in 1949 Reiss-Andersen his *Prinsen av Isola* (The Prince of Isola). Both clearly mark the beginning of a tendency toward modernism.

Gunnar Reiss-Andersen

The link with the Swedish modernists of the 1940s had a decisive effect on the development of Reiss-Andersen (1896–1964). His important writing was preceded by early work employing Wildenwey's and Bull's melodious rhythms and rhymes. His collections *Usynlige seil* (Invisible Sails, 1956) and *År på en strand* (Years upon a Beach, 1962), revealed him to be a poet with an exceptional talent for symbolic imagery. His last volume contains free, resounding, and consciousness-expanding poetry about the human being on the beach, at the border of infinity, of the unknown.

Paal Brekke

In 1949 Brekke (1923–   ) published a translation of Eliot's *The*

Waste Land and his own collection *Skyggefektning* (Shadowfencing), in which he attempted to explain the contemporary world picture. Brekke's intellectualism was schooled by Eliot and Pound, and influenced by Fenno-Swedish and modern Swedish literature, and it encountered rejection from critics and readers. His work is characterized not only by free rhythms, but also by bold syntactical tension and, above all, a modernistic vocabulary. Brekke's poetry is aptly described by the title of the first section, "Fragments of Chaos." The picture of reality that he holds up before us seems to be reflected in a shattered mirror. It confronts us with a world filled with emptiness and pain, which the poet conceals behind a mask of cynicism and scorn:

> Against the black and white of the wall mosaic
> are seen her toes with polished nails of red.
> My own foot next to them is thin,
> hairy. But made of the same precious stuff
> as hers. The same precious
> refuge for the worms.
>
> Our nakedness is a masquerade costume
> dressing a cry of loneliness.
> (. . .)
>
> Tr. Marianne Forssblad

After the negative reception of this collection, Brekke turned to prose (see p. 310). In 1957, however, he published another volume of lyric poetry which is thematically linked to the first collection, but marked by an even stronger inner tension. The volume *Løft min krone, vind fra intet* (Lift My Crown, Wind Out of Nothingness) shows that chaos and fragmentation increasingly dominate, but the creative will to overcome also emerges more clearly than before. Brekke frequently employs a "two-step technique": the contrastive interweaving of two entirely different themes. In *Roerne fra Itaka* (The Oarsmen of Ithaca, 1960) modern everyday life is described against the background of a classical motif; the effect is sometimes ironically satiric, above all in the poet's highlighting of the indifference and surrogate values of modern consumer society, and sometimes melodramatic, in poems about love, longing, and salvation.

In *Det skjeve smil i rosa* (The Wry Smile in Pink, 1965) anxiety again dominates. It is not a poetry collection in the usual sense, but a coherent nightmare with elements of so-called concrete poetry, dealing with the modern way of life and the indifference of human beings who wallow in commercialism and sexuality in the face of the possibility of their extinction. Moralistic sentiments also dominate the prose poems in *Granatmannen kommer* (The Grenade Man Is Coming, 1968). Inspired by the newspaper headlines about murder, war, and sexuality as a substitute for that love in which only poets believe, Brekke employs a collage-like form to demonstrate the power of evil, which lames us through the mass media. The mood of *The Wry Smile in Pink* is resumed in *Aftenen er stille* (The Evening is Quiet, 1972), in which Brekke, with sarcasm and irony, comments on the treatment of old people in the modern Norwegian welfare society.

Gunvor Hofmo

Like Brekke, Hofmo (1921–   ) experiences anxiety and isolation in the face of the cultural crisis. *Jeg vil hjem til menneskene* (I Want to Go Home to the People, 1946) shows both burning detestation of the madness of war and longing for a different reality. This craving for the transcendental leads her to Christianity, and much of her later poetry, such as *Blinde nattergaler* (Blind Nightingales, 1951), is strongly metaphysical. Hofmo's break with external social reality does not merely lead her from human fellowship; in her subjectivity she penetrates regions where the soul is delivered up to the powers of life and death. After finishing her fifth collection, *Testamente til en evighet* (A Will for Eternity, 1955), there was a pause of sixteen years before Hofmo returned to poetry with the volume *Gjest på jorden* (Guest on Earth, 1971). In that volume, in *Mellomspill* (Interlude, 1974), and in her collections *Hva fanger natten* (What Catches the Night, 1976) and *Det er sent* (It Is Late, 1978), the anguish of human existence is still the main theme, but a new, more reconciled view of life is present.

Tor Jonsson

In the works of Jonsson (1916–51) cultural pessimism and disillusionment are combined with a search for a new, positive attitude. His prose work *Nesler* (Nettles), published in two volumes in 1950 and 1952, is mainly journalistic essays attacking the social structure and the materialism of the old rural culture. Underlying the social criticism of Jonsson's three poetry collections, written in *nynorsk* (see p. 18), *Mogning i mørkret* (Maturing in the Darkness, 1943), *Berg ved blått vatn* (Rock by Blue Water, 1946), and *Jarnnetter* (Iron Nights, 1948), are currents of despair and loneliness. The poet's experience of a world filled with fear and hatred brings him, like Vesaas, to a realization of the evil and destructive forces in humans. Jonsson's final, posthumous, collection, *Ei dagbok for mitt hjarte* (A Diary for My Heart, 1951), contains some of the most forceful poems in Norwegian literature about death, the solution to Jonsson's problems, which he found, and chose himself.

Jan-Magnus Bruheim

Social responsibility as well as metaphysical problems are dealt with in the simple and lucid poetry of Bruheim (1914–   ). However, not until his third collection, *Yta og djupe* (The Surface and the Depth, 1945), did he break with the traditional poetic topics of loneliness and longing. In *På skålvekti* (On the Scales, 1947) he demonstrates the necessity of social responsibility and ethical commitment, whereas *Bilete med bakgrunn* (Picture with Background, 1957) analyzes the poet's relationship with traditional values, which he sees threatened by the atom bomb. Although fear about the future of humankind becomes increasingly important in Bruheim's later collections, *Stråler over stup* (Rays across the Abyss, 1963) and *Menneskehagen* (The Garden of Man, 1965), his volume *Ved kjelda* (At the Spring, 1972) treats a theme that is very common in present-day Nordic literature: the inability of language to capture reality. However, all of Bruheim's poems contain a certain indestructible faith in the human ability to survive, primarily through artistic creativity and moral responsibility. In *Du i meg* (You in Me, 1979) a mystical element is added which in some poems leads to a direct Christian message.

André Bjerke

Bjerke (1918–   ) is far removed from this religious and ethical vehemence. His early collections written during the war years were perceived as liberating, because of their positive attitude toward life. From the beginning, Bjerke was an elegant stylist and linguistic virtuoso. His verses remain supple even in the most difficult classical meters. They come into play particularly in the little epigrams on themes from everyday life, with inspired, pointed arguments that provoke the reader to smile rather than to cogitate.

In time, however, a polemical tone entered Bjerke's poetry, as for instance in the collection *Eskapader* (Escapades, 1948), whose title has a double meaning. It hints that one should not take light verses too earnestly, but is also a challenging play on the fashionable word "escapism." *En kylling under stjernerne* (A Chicken under the Stars, 1960) contains, in addition to polemical attacks on persons and institutions, the stirring farewell poem to his admired forerunner Herman

Wildenwey; there are also several virtuoso pieces in which Bjerke describes simple, but human, situations with consummate skill. He stayed with these themes in his poetry throughout the 1960s and in his latest collection, *Et strå i vind* (A Straw in the Wind, 1974). Among the favored targets of his irony are the rationalism and materialism of the period. He himself is one of the uncompromising spiritual figures in Norwegian literature, sympathizing with Øverland's posture in the argument about modern poetry (see p. 181).

Bjerke has thrown off the yoke of rationalism without seeking refuge in neo-romanticism. In his writing there arose again a Norwegian poetry that glorified sharp realism and that contained elements of the best linguistic tradition.

Jens Bjørneboe

The poetry of Bjørneboe (1920–76), with its historical themes and settings, belongs to this same classical tradition. In *Dikt* (Poems, 1951) and *Ariadne* (1953) the central goal is to demonstrate the sanctity of life, the concealed divine spark in creation. In religious language, Bjørneboe seeks to interpret the coherence in human development. Unfortunately, his poetry is often static, the images not conveying to the reader any liberating experience.

As Bjørneboe gradually turned his attention to writing novels (see p. 308) and plays, he chose current subjects. In the provoking and satiric attacks on the Norwegian prison system, *Til lykke med dagen* (Congratulations on the Day, 1965), Brecht's dramaturgy is introduced to Norway. *Fugleelskerne* (The Birdlovers, 1966) is directed against the sadism of war; the same pacifist tendency marks Bjørneboe's drama *Amputasjon* (Amputation, 1970), a parody of an authoritarian society's attempts to make deviant individuals adjust to the system. Bjørneboe returns to satire in his final work, the dramatic collage *Dongery* (1976), a burlesque and didactic piece about the mechanisms of consumption and profit in a capitalistic society.

Finn Bjørnseth

Bjørnseth (1924–73) also tried his hand at various genres. From the 1950s and 1960s stem a number of realistic novels and short-story collections, the focal point of which is an experience of either physical or metaphysical love. As a lyric poet, Bjørnseth wrote of different subjects. With his first volume, *Syv septimer* (Seven Seventh, 1954), he placed himself among the modernists by writing in an abstract, image-filled style, reflecting the threats of the cold war and the fear of a new Hiroshima. The dread of nuclear war also dominates the collections *Vuggevise for aftenlandet* (Lullaby for the Occident, 1962) and *Fordi* (Because, 1963); the lyricist and the narrator, the idealist and the social critic are brought together in the lyrical epic *Franceska* (1968), an exceptional piece that questions the grace of love. In his later years, Bjørnseth turned entirely to poetry. Skepticism and disillusionment mark *1970* (1970), whereas in *Logos* (1972) the Christian God is accepted as humankind's only means of salvation.

LYRICAL MODERNISM AFTER 1960

Olav H. Hauge

Around 1960 two of the most gifted young modernists, Stein Mehren and Georg Johannessen, appeared on the scene. Hauge (1908–), the third outstanding modernist poet, had written his first work in 1946—a collection of introspective, visionary poetry in the tradition of Aukrust, entitled *Glør i oska* (Embers in the Ashes). However, he was not recognized until the 1960s. By the time his second volume, *Under bergfallet* (Below the Avalanche, 1951) appeared, Hauge had broken with the abstract and romantic, and turned toward a physical experience of nature. Nature dominates the collections *Seint rodnar skog i djuvet* (Slowly Turn the Leaves in the Canyon, 1956) and *På ørnetuva* (On the Eagle's Hill, 1961), which are marked by a laconic, concise style undoubtedly influenced by Ezra Pound and Japanese *haiku* poetry. Hauge's symbolic use of nature almost disappears in *Dropar i austavind* (Drops in the Eastern Wind, 1966). Here the objects stand alone and speak for themselves. The sensitive feeling for nature in his early poems, which describe the harsh environment of fjords and mountains, is now replaced by a realism which finds almost aphoristic expression in the collection *Spør vinden* (Ask the Wind, 1971). Today Hauge represents both tradition and renewal in Norwegian poetry. He is self-taught—he learned English, German, and French on his own—and has done highly acclaimed translations of the French symbolists and the English and American modernists; he is decidedly more Europe-oriented than are most of his Norwegian fellow writers. He favors complicated meters and stanza patterns, but writes a conservative, strongly dialectical *nynorsk* (see p. 18).

Stein Mehren

A clearer line of development characterizes Mehren (1935–). In his first collection, *Gjennom stillheten en natt* (Through the Stillness of a Night, 1960), one finds the main themes of his poetry: the relationship of words to experience, the recognition of the environment and the self:

> Then we begin to talk
> I form words from words about words
> And you my love
> You begin already to fall in love with
> our love.
>
> Every word comes from childhood
> and infinitely far away from it
> we know already everything with words
> as if we were banished.
>
> For we can never forget that we are
> and only be ourselves
> May we always find ourselves.

Tr. Marianne Forssblad

Compared with Mehren's earlier collections, of which he regularly published one each year, *Vind Runer* (Wind Runes, 1967) contains nothing new. In addition to critical sections, conventional in viewpoint and expression, dealing with devalued language and pop culture, this volume contains valuable poems; in these, Mehren again occupies himself with overcoming the gap between object and symbol—the dilemma of the poet when he feels that words are only words.

Whereas *Tids alder* (Time's Age, 1966) was imitative, wordy modernism, *Aurora Det Niende Mørke* (Aurora, The Ninth Darkness, 1969) is an imposing formulation of the central problems in Mehren's work. The internal structure of the collection is a journey through transformations, a journey through language, various styles and forms of expressions that mirror one another. They are, however, held together by the same poetic personality, which corresponds to Mehren's idea of identity. The collection flows into an experience that is captured precisely in the language. Mehren's position as his generation's most significant lyric poet is confirmed by *Menneske bære ditt bilde frem* (Man Bring Your Picture Forth, 1975), *Trettende stjernebilde* (Thirteenth Constellation, 1977), and *Vintersolhverv* (Winter Solstice, 1979); these three volumes express the author's opinion that poetry is the only medium through which to take hold of reality. This opinion is particularly evident in Mehren's novels from the 1970s (see p. 310). Poetry should not be beauty and experience, but should serve to establish identity. Stein Mehren's lyric poetry is somewhat inaccessible, not least because of his bold symbolic language. Yet, like the two other Scandinavian lyric poets, Erik Lindegren and Thorkild Bjørnvig, he meets the reader half way through the magic musicality of his verses.

Peter R. Holm

Related to Mehren's hermetic modernism, but less preoccupied with the aesthetic aspects, are the poetry collections of Holm (1931–), whose first poems, explorations of the human mind, seem abstract and insubstantial. The volume *Stentid* (Stone Age, 1962) marks a stylistic renewal, with concrete and concise expressions of a love experience. More extroverted is *Diabos* (1968), which ironically lays bare the glossy and superficial world of advertising. *Sanndrømt* (Dreams Come True, 1971) and *Isglimt, glødepunkt* (Glance of Ice, Glow Point, 1972) contain a series of sophisticated lyrically exquisite nature poems— reflections of internal moods and thus a continuation of the classical symbolist tradition.

Georg Johannessen

The work of Johannessen (1931–) reveals a more outward-directed tendency, behind which one senses a moral, ideological world view. He too possesses a rich, image-filled creative talent and has written poetry of great metaphorical complexity; but he senses that traditional modernistic language does not capture reality. The simple title of his first collection, *Dikt 1959* (Poems 1959, 1959) reflects his demand for a poetry without superfluous decoration.

Johannessen expresses his protest against the wars and crimes of our times by occasionally using crass, even brutal effects: "I would like to have dead children on the paper, / between the lines I am writing." This is true of his two poetry collections *Ars moriendi* (1965)—a paraphrase of the seven deadly sins—and *Nye dikt* (New Poems, 1966). The same concept underlies his only play, *Kassandra* (1967), a moral drama of ideas. *Kassandra* is a passionate attempt to awaken an indifferent world heading for catastrophe, but it was staged in the style of a musical, with stark echoes of Aristophanes. Here Johannessen—and thus Norwegian dramaturgy—attains international visibility.

Simultaneous with Johannessen's neo-realistic poetry, the "new simplicity" and concrete poetry were gaining a foothold in Norway, as in the other Scandinavian countries, in the mid-1960s. These new poetic elements led to an emphasis on linguistics, on words and sounds, which eventually made letters and punctuation marks objects of poetic treatment.

Jan Erik Vold

One of the more talented representatives of this new poetry is Vold (1939–), a leading figure in the *Profil* rebellion (see p. 387). He is aware of his time and often excessively sensitive to the mood of the moment and the various forms of artistic expression. He made his artistic debut in 1965 with *Mellom speil og speil* (Between Mirror and Mirror), a collection of poems, including a number of figurative pieces about the search for a reality that is nonexistent—since the world consists of mirrors, of emptiness and deception. *Blikket* (The Glance, 1966) is a "concrete" collection, which too clearly recalls the poetry volume entitled *Statements* by the Danish poet Hans-Jørgen Nielsen. *Hekt* (Grab, 1966) is an experiment with the spoken language: In these harsh poems of the time, poems framed by the letter of an American soldier to his sister, Vold takes up a genre used particularly by younger Swedish authors who were critical of society.

Mor Godhjertas glade versjon. Ja (Mother Goodheart's Happy Version. Yes, 1968), like Mehren's *Aurora*, is a labyrinthian trip through language and fantasy, an unfolding of the self; whereas *Aurora* is a continuation of classical modernism, Vold's collection reads like a trip from a convoluted, concretistic linguistic system to a recognizable reality of the self. On the other hand, the volume *kykelipi* (1969) is characterized by a deep mistrust of words. This trend increases in the volume *Spor, snø* (Traces, Snow, 1970), in which Vold attempts to recreate an atmosphere of emptiness and inconstancy in short, three-line poems, inspired by Japanese *haiku* poetry. This "new simplicity" is continued in *Bok 8: Liv* (Book 8: Life, 1973) and *Buster brenner* (Buster Burns, 1976) and *S.* (1978); here it serves as an expression of the poet's apparently idyllic view of life. Some critics have mistakenly attacked this as escapism, tending to overlook Vold's serious commitment behind the linguistic virtuosity and burlesque fantasies, a commitment which becomes more obvious in *Sirkel, sirkel* (Circle, Circle, 1979), a volume of terse *haiku*-like poems based on experiences and impressions from a trip around the world.

PROSE, POSTWAR TO 1960

Although after the war most lyric poets had joined the modernistic school, which around 1950 manifested itself in the work of Paal Brekke and Tarjei Vesaas, traditional forms continued to dominate in prose. The courage and willingness to experiment with new forms of expression more appropriate to the portrayal of everyday life situations was, surprisingly, manifest more often in the older generation than in the younger. Without the innovative works of Borgen, Sandemose, and Vesaas, the postwar years would have been a period of crisis for Norwegian prose literature.

Egil Rasmussen and Gunnar Bull Gundersen

Borgen, with his novel *I* in 1959, wrote the prose that was then regarded as the most modern. His contemporary Egil Rasmussen (1903–64), who had written novels since 1934, also broke with realism at this time. In 1961 he published the prose work *Legenden om Lovella* (The Legend of Lovella)—an attempt to establish contact with the modern European surrealist and absurdist movements. A similar bold structure characterizes *Fabelnetter* (Fable Nights, 1961) by Gunnar Bull Gundersen (1929-   ). In contrast to Gundersen's earlier, realistic novels—*Om natten* (In the Night, 1956) and *Martin* (1959)—this book moves on various interrelated planes, with dreams and visions playing a significant role. The narrator is a writer who attempts to force his diary entries into an artistic form, thereby seeking a firm foothold in an existence that remains as fragmentary as his diary. Gundersen also uses the diary technique in *Judith* (1963), his finest novel, which is an analysis of the many and complex expressions of longing. The problem of the artist is the basic motif of the two introverted novels *Kjære Emanuel* (Dear Emanuel, 1965) and *Han som ville male havet* (He Who Wanted to Paint the Sea, 1968). Gundersen, however, abandoned the exclusive modernism of the 1960s with *Min reise til Egypt* (My Journey to Egypt, 1970), which deals with our consumer-oriented society, as well as with current foreign policy. This realistic trend is continued in Gundersen's only collection of poetry, *Skål blues* (Cheers Blues, 1972), and in his most recent novel, *De hjemløse* (The Homeless, 1977).

Sigurd Evensmo

Thematically, an ethical tradition dominated Norwegian postwar prose. Marked by the events of the war, the writers rebelled against the schematic division of human beings into courageous and cowardly, active and passive—out of the hard-won conviction that we are all equally responsible. Sigurd Hoel attempts in his novel *Meeting at the Milestone* to explain the causes of the Nazi mentality of those who betrayed their country. Younger authors also attacked this problem. One of them was Sigurd Evensmo (1912–78) in his *Oppbrudd etter midnatt* (Departure after Midnight, 1946), a somewhat glossy and superficial journalistic story about a wealthy fascist farmer whose feelings for his homeland bring him into conflict with the Germans. This novel is overshadowed by Evensmo's best book, *Englandsfarere* (1945; Eng. tr. *Boat for England*, 1947), one of the best-known Norwegian war novels, dealing with several resistance fighters who are captured on their flight, tortured, and executed. However, it is not tragic external fate that interests the author, but, rather, the varying motives that led them to these illegal deeds.

Evensmo's major work is his trilogy about Martin (1947–51), which is both a piece of social history and a psychological novel about a man who seeks solidarity and warmth, but who succumbs because of his ambivalence, which makes him appear indifferent and ruthless. After completing the trilogy, Evensmo turned to completely different types of books. *Gåten fra år null* (The Riddle from Year Zero, 1957) is one of the first Norwegian attempts at science fiction; *Femten døgn med Gordona* (Fifteen Days with Gordona, 1963) is a first-rate political thriller; and *Miraklet på Blindern* (The Miracle at Blindern, 1966) is a combination of both genres, set in 1984, clearly referring to George Orwell's horrific vision; however, Evensmo's novel ends optimistically at an international peace conference in Oslo. In 1976 Evensmo published the first volume of his memoirs, *Inn i din tid* (Into Your Time), followed by *Ut i kulda* (Out in the Cold) in 1978.

Torborg Nedreaas

Like Evensmo's first work, Nedreaas' (1906–) first book, the short-story collection *Bak skapet står øksen* (The Ax Is behind the Closet, 1945), deals with the German occupation. It relates the story of young girls who went astray during the war, Nedreaas taking up their defense. A similar sympathetic attitude characterizes her breakthrough novel, *Av måneskinn gror det ingenting* (Nothing Grows from Moonshine, 1947). The young girl who narrates her life is a victim of exploitation in a male-dominated society. The books about Herdis (1950–71) are based on the same theme and comprise a major work of modern Norwegian feminist literature, written without self-pity and sentimentality, but with sober and aggressive realism.

Finn Havrevold

Havrevold (1905–) deals with the relationship of isolation and violence in *Til de dristige* (To the Audacious, 1946) and *Walter den fredsommelige* (Walter the Peaceful, 1947). He sees the war as an expression, albeit a compromised one, of the desperate longing of the lonely, unloved human being, as a chance to flee oneself and to forget oneself in primitive brutality. In the 1950s Havrevold wrote a number of dramas, radio plays, and juvenile books of high quality. *Den ytterste dag* (Doomsday, 1963) and *Blå rytter* (Blue Knight, 1968) are pessimistic novels about human evil, raw lust, and stupidity, with symbolic implications. Lighter in tone, are *Pilen i lyset* (The Arrow in the Light, 1971) and *Under samme tak* (Under the Same Roof, 1972), in which the humanist position is given a chance; this approach is further developed in the novels *De nådeløse* (The Merciless, 1975) and *Vennskap* (Friendship, 1976). In 1977 Havrevold began his strongly autobiographical series of novels with *I fjor sommer* (Last Summer), continued with *Vinter i Vallegaten* (Winter in Vallegaten, 1978) and *Fars hus* (Fathers House, 1979).

Kåre Holt

In *Det store veiskillet* (The Great Crossroads, 1949), Holt (1917–) uses a single story to portray one person in three different situations: as a black marketeer, a Nazi informer, and a resistance fighter. His character traits remain the same; it is his choice that decides what his fate will be—an idea basic to several of Holt's books.

In the two-volume novel *Det stolte nederlag* (The Proud Defeat, 1956) and *Storm under morgenstjerne* (Storm beneath the Morning Star, 1958), this popular and productive author turned to a portrayal of the first socialist movement in Norway during the nineteenth century. With *Kongen* (The King) Holt began a trilogy about the medieval King Sverre (1965–69), influenced in its style and motifs by the sagas, but at the same time a modern work about the problem of identity and the relationship of power and responsibility. The philosophical novel *Oppstandelsen* (The Resurrection, 1971) deals with the same themes in a story about the resurrection of Christ. With *Farvel til en kvinne* (Good-bye to a Woman, 1972) Holt again returned to the period of the sagas, in a pessimistic portrayal of suppression, violence, and sexuality. In recent novels Holt has worked with documentary material. *Folket ved Svansjøen* (The People on Swan Lake, 1973) deals with a nearly extinct Lapp tribe, *Kappløbet* (The Race, 1974) with the polar explorer Roald Amundsen, *Sjøhelten* (The Naval Hero, 1975) with the eighteenth-century admiral Tordenskjold, and *Sønn av jord og himmel* (Son of Earth and Heaven, 1978) with the Norwegian missionary Hans Egede also called the Apostile of Greenland.

Jens Bjørneboe

An ethical commitment similar to Holt's characterizes the prose work of Bjørneboe (see p. 301). The subject of his first novel, *Før hanen galer* (Before the Cock Crows, 1952), is the terrifying reality of the medical experiments performed by doctors in the German concentration camps. Bjørneboe does not seek the causes of Nazism, but investigates the existence of the evil itself, which was created by the division between feeling and intellect. The novel is a vehement attack on modern natural science, which, in Bjørneboe's view, permits the human spirit to become alienated and stunted.

In *Jonas* (1955; Eng. tr. *The Last of These*, 1959) he directs his criticism at the failings of the Norwegian school system. He kindled a debate which became more intense with the publication of his next book, *Under en hårdere himmel* (Beneath a Harsher Sky, 1957), in which Bjørneboe characterizes as haphazard the prosecution of the Norwegian Nazis after the war. The human capacity for cruelty has continued to fascinate Bjørneboe, and he has treated the theme in his trilogy on "the history of bestiality," one of the most significant prose works of postwar Norwegian literature, *Frihetens øyeblikk* (1966; Eng. tr. *Moments of Freedom*, 1975), *Kruttårnet* (The Gunpowder Tower, 1969), and *Stillheten* (The Silence, 1973). This is a running chronicle of violence and torture. Horror is documented in the record kept by a court clerk; chapters of documentation alternate with chapters in which the author carries on discussions with God and various historical figures. The work contains elements of mythology, anthroposophy, and Jungian psychology, together with political polemics, baroque stories, and ironic fables. In *Haiene* (The Sharks, 1974), a novel about a ship's final voyage, Bjørneboe once again depicts human brutality, but one finds the implicit faint hope that the destructiveness of Western individualism will be replaced by a new sense of responsibility.

Bjørneboe has a journalist's ability to find "good material," that is, controversial material. In his polemical writings, with his quick-witted formulations, he occasionally reminds one of Øverland, yet he does not possess Øverland's conciseness and consistency. Bjørneboe intermittently propounded theories of anthroposophy, socialism, and anarchism, giving his books a disorganized character.

Agnar Mykle

Mykle (1915–) is another acknowledged *enfant terrible* of Norwegian literature. He possesses originality and verbal imagination, which he displays in the romantic novel *Tyven, tyven skal du hete* (1951, Thief, Thief, Is Your Name; Eng. tr. *The Hotel Room*, 1963 and later), in which Mykle emphatically proclaims the right to the free expression of sexuality. Similar tones are audible in the formless novels *Lasso rundt fru Luna* (1954; Eng. tr. *Lasso round the Moon*, 1960) and *Sangen om den røde rubin* (1956; Eng. tr. *The Song of the*

Red Ruby, 1961 and later); the latter was censored as being porno-graphic. The short humorous novel *Rubicon* (1965; Eng. tr. 1966 and later) demonstrates a greater narrative art and a keener awareness of details, characteristics that recall Mykle's model, Thomas Wolfe. The same elements are found in the two short stories on death and puberty published under the title *Largo* (1967).

Paal Brekke

The prose of Paal Brekke (see p. 298) is far more intellectual. His novels are no less experimental in form than his poetry. After the un-appreciative reception of the volume of poetry *Shadowfencing*, Brekke turned to prose. In 1951 he published the wordy and obscure novel *Aldrende Orfeus* (Aging Orpheus); in the style of James Joyce, he un-dertook an analysis of the generation gap before and after the war, making bitter attacks on conventional thought processes and ways of life.

Og hekken vokste kjempehøy (And the Hedge Grew Enormous, 1953) makes a clearer impression; here the psychological conflicts surrounding the theme of isolation are interwoven with an exciting murder plot. During the hunt for the murderer, it becomes increasingly clear that *all* of the characters in the book could be guilty, for *all* carry a murderer within themselves. This means that the main character is pulled into human fellowship and into an awareness of the shared re-sponsibility of all—a humanist message which can also be found in the novels of Kåre Holt.

PROSE MODERNISM

Stein Mehren

More esoteric, almost impenetrable, are Mehren's novels (see p. 302), *De utydelige* (The Obscure Ones, 1972) and *Titanene* (The Titans, 1974), two expansive, universal, and allegorical works that attempt to embrace all philosophical, social, and political aspects of the con-temporary period in Norway and Europe. "The obscure ones" are the humanist intellectuals who become lost in well-intentioned tolerance toward more extreme positions. Here, as in the public debate on the topic, Mehren rejects all political dogmatism and all demands upon the artist to change the world.

Terje Stigen

A similar imaginative approach, expressed in a more traditional form, is found in the work of Stigen (1922–　), whose voluminous lyrical, melancholy works are strongly influenced by Knut Hamsun. Like Hamsun's *Hunger*, Stigen's *Nøkkel til ukjent rom* (Key to the Unknown Room, 1953) tells of a supersensitive man who fluctuates between gallows humor and destruction, and only barely manages to escape misfortune. Like Hamsun, Stigen understands how to capture his characters half way between drama and reality, comedy and tragedy.

In the novel *Skygger på mitt hjerte* (Shadows on My Heart, 1952) Stigen had found the setting to which he constantly returned: northern Norway. Often it is a solitary island beneath the midnight sun, far removed from the restlessness of modern society, a haven for dreamers and refugees from life. The hero of the story is such a person. In his isolation he carries on conversations with himself, with the girl he loves, and with God, in the vain attempt to find a pattern in his life, and, like Karen Blixen's characters, to accept with resignation God's unfathomable game with humankind.

In *Vindstille underveis* (Calm Underway, 1956; Eng. tr. *An Interrupted Passage*, 1973) Stigen broke with the subjective form in favor of an epic narrative style. Four people in a fishing boat tell one another stories that appear to be unrelated. But gradually the reader discovers that they find their place in a larger pattern, in a mysterious game about love, longing, and fate.

In his succeeding novels, Stigen cultivated a more simple epic technique; for his main characters he selected uncomplicated men of action, who can live happily without any kind of crippling reflection. With *Det flyktige hjerte* (The Fickle Heart, 1967), perhaps Stigen's best work, he turned to historical material. The novel is set around 1800. The main character is a student of theology who is named as pastor north of the Arctic Circle. All his travel experiences are linked to the central theme of the book, love; love, however, is consistently portrayed as erotic perversion, for the feelings of the young pastor are distorted from the beginning. He uses them as a point of departure for his artistic development. Thus the novel treats a theme similar to Ibsen's dramatic epilogue *When We Dead Awaken*—the flight from human obligations into art, which is falsifying the life of the emotions.

Stigen goes even further back in history with *De tente lys* (The Lighted Candles, 1968), a novel set in the eleventh century, dealing with the desire for peace and necessary self-defense against a bloodthirsty enemy. *Min Marion* (My Marion, 1972) is a contemporary work about a current topic, the right of the handicapped to experience a love relationship, while the novel *Peter Johannes Lookhas* (1974) treats of the human inalienable right to follow individual conscience in a totalitarian society. In 1974 six of Stigen's radio plays were also published, under the title *Den røde sommerfugl* (The Red Butterfly) and three years later there followed another significant novel, *Avik-*

fjord (The Fjord of Avik, 1977), a *Bildungsroman* from northern Norway, followed by *Huset og byen* (The House and the City, 1978) and *Rekviem over en sommer* (Requiem over a Summer, 1979). A volume of Stigen's short stories, *Glasskulen* (1963), appeared in English as *The Crystal Ball* (1971).

Finn Carling

Stigen's realistic narrative contrasts sharply with the ingeniously constructed and symbol-filled prose of Carling (1925–   ). This is particularly true of the early novels, such as *Arenaen* (The Arena, 1951), *Piken og fuglen* (The Girl and the Bird, 1952), and *Fangen i det blå tårn* (Imprisoned in the Blue Tower, 1955). They all treat the same theme with artistic refinement, but with increasing despair: The artist betrays life by encapsulating himself from life or fleeing into dreams. In *Desertøren* (The Deserter, 1956) this theme, which Carling had introduced in his first book, *Broen* (The Bridge, 1949), precipitated an artistic crisis. *The Deserter*, together with *Sensommerdøgn* (Late Summer's Day, 1960), marked a turning point that led Carling to a more simple form. At the same time he concentrated in his novels on human beings who sought to break through the wall of isolation in their longing for a sense of community. He portrayed this endeavor in documentary studies of groups of social outsiders and in *Kometene* (The Comets, 1964), a novel, and *Gitrene* (The Bars, 1966), an abstract drama of ideas that employed complicated psychology to pursue the development of a feeling of love, as a being was transformed from animal to human.

In subsequent novels Carling resumed the technique of his books of the 1950s. In *Gjesten* (The Guest, 1970), a study of puberty, dream and reality merge. *Skip av sten* (Ship of Stone, 1971) is an allegorical settling of accounts with today's political theoreticians, who have forgotten the living human being. The documentary technique is again used in *Resten er taushet* (The Rest Is Silence, 1973), a book about death and our relationship to death, which brought Carling well-deserved success. *Fiendene* (The Enemies, 1974) contains brutal prose sketches and poems about violence, fear, and isolation, posted against a glimmer of solidarity in a vision of that future which may already be ours. In 1976 there followed the travelogue *Hvite skygger på svart bunn* (White Shadows on a Black Ground), poetic impressions of a journey to Africa. In 1977 Carling published a highly praised collection of short stories entitled *Marginalene* (The Marginals), in 1978 the travelogue from western Africa, *Mørke paralleller* (Dark Parallels).

Axel Jensen

A protest against our times, similar to that which forms the basis of

Carling's writing, but of lesser quality, is *Joacim* (1961), a novel by Jensen (1932–) in which the attack on commercialism and on the demands for efficiency is combined with Hamsun-like yearning for nature. Jensen's first book, *Ikaros* (1957; Eng. tr. *Icarus, a Young Man in the Sahara*, 1959) is a book with more facets, both a novel and a travelogue; it is the story of one of the angry young men who appeared in European literature in the 1950s. Driven by the need for a cognitive experience, and by anger against all ideologies, he flees into the Sahara to find a fixed point in another, spiritual reality.

After disappointments with his two novels *Line* (1959; Eng. tr. *A Girl I Knew*, 1962 and later) and *Joacim*, both of which can be classified as pure entertainment, there followed an artistic renewal with *Epp* (1965; Eng. tr. 1965 and later) a nightmarish story of a society of the future in which Epp, an anonymous man of the masses, portrays coolly and precisely an existence full of egoism, intolerance, and routine—an existence that remains unaltered in an altered world and thus is identical with our own. Jensen did not produce another book until 1974 when he published two books on India, the travelogue *Mor India* (Mother India) and the poetry collection *Onalila*. *Junior* (1978) and its sequel, *Senior* (1979), are somewhat insignificant collections of partly autobiographical prose sketches.

Finn Alnæs

In the foremost rank of contemporary Norwegian prose authors stands the philosophical writer Alnæs (1932–). Through his attempt to include the entire cosmos in his thinking, he seeks to show the insignificance of human beings in a demoralized and nihilistic period. His first novel, *Koloss* (Colossus, 1963), has as its theme the contrasts between three men. Brage is the natural man contrasted with the culturally spoiled Benthein and Stefan, who have been ennobled by culture. Brage's colossal strength changes suddenly into a power mentality or into great fantasies, outbreaks of feeling, and religious hallucinations. The plot is improbable and indescribable, and the style so verbally overpowering that it almost threatens to shatter the reader.

Alnæs's second novel *Gemini* (1968), shows that there were in Norway—as in most of the other Nordic countries—conflicts between exclusive modernism and a new documentary realism; the work is a polemical arugment against the times, and its material is derived from astronomy, treated in a factual, almost dry manner. The book is conceived as a dialogue between twin brothers, but is actually a monologue, since one brother lies unconscious in an iron lung; he is to be seen as the adjusted, conformist, and trite half of the writer. The "dialogue" treats the ethical and aesthetic position of the artist in a modern welfare society in sharply logical fashion, expressing concisely his deliberately conservative, defiant world view. This individualistic attitude is also defended in the didactic, almost allegorical novel *Festningen Faller* (The Fortress of Faller, 1971), which takes place in a futuristic no-man's-land. The fortress is occupied by a foreign power; the second in command, an ironical skeptic, is exposed to various ethical problems dealing with human responsibility and the duty, under specific circumstances, to disobey authority. Thus the novel becomes one more contribution to the general mistrust of officialdom and politics so common in the Nordic countries during the 1970s. In 1978 Alnæs published *Musica*, the first part of a novel cycle in eight volumes entitled *Ildfesten* (The Fire Feast), a family chronicle about trends of disintegration and adherence to tradition.

Chapter *15*

Danish Postwar Literature

The outbreak of World War II did not surprise the Danish public as much as the events of 1914 had. People had expected and feared the war; writers, in particular, had expressed the general anxiety and warned of the impending danger. Most Danish writers, whether socialists, conservatives, or nihilists, were decided opponents of national socialism and banded together to defend the culture of their country.

The occupation of Denmark in 1940 marked the beginning of a critical period for literature. The last remnants of the belief in cultural progress had vanished and human ideals seemed suspect. But the war years and the postwar period enriched the literature with inexhaustible themes which, however, did not find artistic expression until years later.

The Resistance between 1940 and 1945 occupied a less important place in Danish literature than in the literatures of the other occupied countries. Soya's (see p. 208) thinly disguised insect fable *En Gæst* (A Guest, 1941), Munk's (see p. 208) national drama *Niels Ebbesen* (1942), and books by Communist authors such as Andersen Nexø (see p. 140) were banned. After the general strike of 1943, many writers had to flee to Sweden; it was there that one of the most valuable works of this period was created: Otto Gelsted's (see p. 198) volume of *Emigrantdigte* (Emigrant Poems, 1945).

POETRY OF THE 1940s AND '50s

Although much of the prose was a direct continuation of the traditions of the 1930s, the poets made a decisive mark on the 1940s. Most of them contributed to the journal *Heretica* (1948-53), which occupied a "heretical" standpoint in relation to the dominant rationalism and materialism. *Heretica* thus became a reaction to the 1930s; an unmistakable parallel exists to the symbolists of the 1890s and their reaction to Brandes and his movement—with Helge Rode and later Karen Blixen as the connecting links and Martin A. Hansen as the leading personality. The common ground was the recognition of the "cultural crisis." A unified culture, like that of the Middle Ages, no longer existed, and the spiritual norms of earlier times had been succeeded by a less than all-embracing economical and political community. The poets painfully yearned for a change in the human spirit and waited for the culture to be rescued. Actually, they occupied themselves less with this hope than with anxiety and despair.

The structural crisis in poetry was linked to the absence of a common cultural base; obscurity was viewed as an integrating aspect of poetry, the poem as the bearer of a wisdom more highly valued than that which can be grasped by the intellect. Although this is the distinctive aesthetic of the period, many lyric poets followed tradition, writing rhymed, simple, and melancholy verse. One of these was Tove Ditlevsen (1918-76), whose major theme was human isolation in the big city. Other poets strove for clarity and austerity, for an analysis of the exact meaning behind the words. An example is the physicist Piet Hein (1905-   ), who made a late appearance as a poet; in his twenty volumes of *Gruk* (1940-63; Eng. tr. *Grooks*, vol. 1-6, 1966-78) he is exceptionally skillful with the epigrammatic play of words and ideas.

The writers most typical of the war period were Morten Nielsen and Halfdan Rasmussen.

Morten Nielsen

Nielsen (1922-24) wrote two poetry collections, *Krigere uden Vaaben* (Warriors without Weapons, 1943) and *Efterladte Digte* (Posthumous Poems, 1945) that show him to be a representative of a young generation devoid of illusions but willing to risk their lives for freedom. The everpresent fear in Nielsen's poetry is not of death, but of the inability to find meaning in life.

Halfdan Rasmussen

For Nielsen the Resistance movement served simply as the backdrop against which he matured as poet and human being. But it directly affected the writing of Rasmussen (1915-   ). The traditional, romantic poetry of his early collections changed under the impact of the war into contemporary, polemical poetry in *Digte under Besættelsen* (Poems during the Occupation, 1945); the most exquisite poems are based on the feeling of fellowship during the struggle. The postwar volumes from 1946 to 1949 are dominated by retrospective poems in which the dominant factors are the memories of the dead and the sense of guilt at still being alive. The gloomy brooding and the dread of a new war in *Aftenland* (Evening Country, 1950) are transformed in *Skoven* (The Forest, 1954) into a passion for nature, which is seen as the sole escape from fear and loneliness. This leads to more extroverted and realistic poetry in the travel book *Stilheden* (Tranquillity, 1962). Rasmussen gained his greatest popularity in later years through his numerous volumes of *Tosserier* (Tomfooleries, a selection from which was published in 1969), nonsense verse of great humor and stylistic significance.

Ole Sarvig

Among the *Heretica* poets, Sarvig (1921–) became particularly important with his broadly conceived poem cycle in six volumes; of these, *Grønne Digte* (Green Poems, 1943), *Jeghuset* (The House of Self, 1944), and *Menneske* (Man, 1948) represent the most important poetic accomplishments in Denmark during the 1940s. In this youthful poetry, whose modernistic and not very accessible imagistic language is related to abstract painting, Sarvig rendered a grandiose and coherent portrayal of modern humans in crisis at a cultural and historical turning point. The driving force of his poems is the search for resolution to this crisis. Beginning with his first nature poems, Sarvig's world of thoughts and ideas is constantly developing. Ancient religious symbols are reanimated and drawn into the poems, and in the end a sense of fellowship is regained.

The central texts of the *Green Poems* form a coherent metaphysics of history. The tone is often surprisingly harmonious, standing in absolute contrast to the mood of crisis in the collection *The House of Self*. Here the setting is new. The metropolis is discovered to be the place where modern humans meet their fate. It is a strange, desolate metropolis, with open areas and factories where human beings appear only as tiny, insignificant points.

This discordant crisis is overcome in *Man*, where the decisive themes are the experience of God and of love between man and woman. In the poem "I efteraaret og vinteren" ("In Autumn and in Winter"), one of the most disquieting poems of the 1940s, Sarvig expresses his religious feelings:

Maybe you live behind the city's
towers and shadowramps?
Do you light a fire behind the night's
foggy multitudes of light?
(. . .)
Are you behind the walls of fear?
Behind the boards of the floor?
Are you behind the dazzling stars?
Are you behind our thoughts?

Tr. Marianne Forssblad

Until writing his first novel, *Stenrosen* (The Rose of Stone, 1955), Sarvig had held firmly to the same theme: human beings and their time. *The Rose of Stone* is set in Berlin, a city that was destroyed because it was a manifestation of demonic modernism and is rebuilt in the old spirit. The main character, Endre Weber, personifies what Sarvig views as the basic problem: human alienation. Weber is aware of this, which makes it possible for him to begin a new life. But the process is fraught with uncertainty and dangers, symbolized by the severe injury that Weber sustains during a parachute jump, an injury that might be fatal.

De Sovende (The Sleepers, 1958) and *Havet under mit Vindue* (The Sea below My Window, 1960) have the framework of the detective novel. The traditional mystery is combined with the identity motif; solution of the crime is equivalent to acknowledging the power of evil and destruction, and finding the way to a new life. In *Limbo* (1963) the lyrical element predominates, at the expense of a more traditional novel structure. The book is a description of the waiting human being, of a woman and her dead husband's continued life in her soul. Normal time sequence is broken, and all narrative elements flow through the memories of this woman, transforming the novel into a vision of eternal love. The elements of suspense, although now completely devoid of metaphysical aspects, are found in the novel *Glem ikke* (Do Not Forget, 1972), a burlesque satire on Denmark. This work is completely overshadowed by *De rejsende* (The Travelers, 1978), Sarvig's most significant prose work, as exciting as a thriller, as lyrical as his best poetry, and powerful in its concise philosophical ideas. On one level the book relates a middle-aged Danish-American's attempts to settle accounts with his childhood myths; on a more profound level, it deals with the problem of finding oneself, one's identity in today's world. This basic motif in Sarvig's writing is also treated in *Forstadsdigte* (Suburban Poems, 1974), a retrospective cycle marking a return to his artistic point of departure: the cultural crisis, described in images of city life, which is overcome through a mystical experience of Christ and love.

Thorkild Bjørnvig

Sarvig perceived the mystery of love and grace as a liberation from chaos and uncertainty. For another lyricist from the *Heretica* group, Bjørnvig (1918–   ), it is faith in poetry that is of decisive significance. In his first collection, *Stjærnen bag Gavlen* (The Star behind the Gable, 1947), Eros is the dominant theme, the metamorphosis of a young love. Everything is governed by the law of transformation: departure, separation, death. The same themes recur in *Anubis* (1955) and *Figur og Ild* (Figure and Fire, 1959), in which Bjørnvig's diction has matured and has taken on greater musicality and substance. Both collections show that Bjørnvig is the best-schooled and most disciplined poet of his generation; he is a classicist who continues the poetic tradition of Per Lange, with reminiscences of Helge Rode and Rilke, whose poems Bjørnvig has masterfully translated into Danish.

The human being must live with the awareness that death is the unavoidable end. But in art the valuable moments of life can be captured; art can bring order and harmony to the chaos of existence. Gradually a concentrated philosophical poetry reflecting on the situation of the artist occupies an increasingly important place in Bjørnvig's writing, often in the form of literary portraits of, for example, Keats, Poe and Nietzsche. The question of the priority of life versus art is raised. However, Bjørnvig succeeds in combining Eros and creativity, intuition and cognition in the identity of the self.

Figure and Fire marks a transition for Bjørnvig to an artistic renewal, liberating his work from strict verse forms. This new freedom is unevenly expressed in *Vibrationer* (Vibrations, 1966) and is perfected in *Ravnen* (The Raven, 1968), an overpowering myth of the land of the soul. A fragmentary self passes through a crisis of love, identity, and guilt, reaching reconciliation and a sense of identity. The work, in which many of Bjørnvig's themes are expanded, is rewarding, but also difficult because of the powerfully concise expression and elaborate symbolism—on a par with Gunnar Ekelöf's mind-expanding poetry.

In the 1970s Bjørnvig created works that were more related to contemporary issues. The essay collection *Oprør mod neonguden* (Revolt against the Neon God, 1970) is a critical analysis of trends within the rebelliousness of the young. A great interest in ecological problems is expressed in the poetry volume *Delfinen* (The Dolphin, 1975). In his latest collection, *Morgenmørke* (Morning Darkness, 1977), Bjørnvig again turns inward to the sphere of his own personality, to the theme of identity inherent in love and other human relationships. The poems delineate a development from emptiness and longing to openness, balance, and maturity. Bjørnvig does not present primarily analyses of his private sphere; his inner experiences are seen against the background of nature and the cosmos, whereby he creates an exceptionally subtle correspondence between feelings and external reality.

Erik Knudsen

Like Bjørnvig, Knudsen (1922–   ) was a member of the *Heretica* group. However, after a short time, he broke with the journal and became associated with the Marxist journal *Dialog* (1950–62). He too expressed in his poems feelings of ambivalence, anxiety, and powerlessness in a "world full of sick gods." Knudsen achieved the full artistic expression of the battle between fear and hope in *Blomsten og Sværdet* (The Flower and the Sword, 1949), in which one finds verses on destruction and the powerlessness of the poet in a lifeless world: "Oh deaf sailors! Blind helmsmen! / Living brothers at the mast and rudder, / I call to you with water in my mouth." This cry for fellowship is an expression of Knudsen's conception of love as a world-altering power, which he places in opposition to the recognition that present-day humans cannot escape from "the black majesty of defeat." However, Knudsen is a fighter by nature. His naturalistic view of life is too strong to allow him to be brought to the point of mysticism or aestheticism—a view that finds its most convincing expression in the collection *Minotauros* (1955).

Erik Knudsen is the poet of his generation who most clearly altered his formal language to correspond to the aesthetic of literary modernism. Typical in this regard is *The Flower and the Sword*, employing Eliot's technique of allusions, which lends a many-faceted quality to the poetic experience. In his later collections of poems, *Sensation og stilhed* (Sensation and Silence, 1958) and *Journal* (1963), as well as in the satiric revue *Frihed—det bedste guld* (Freedom—the Best Gold, 1961), Knudsen proved himself as a socialistic and involved critic of society and culture. He maintained this role in a number of television plays which brought him considerable popularity. Knudsen always uses language as a tool for agitation—for instance, in the "Socialist Debate Book," *Babylon marcherer* (Babylon on March, 1970), in *Vietnam. Digte, taler og artikler* (Vietnam. Poems, Speeches, and Articles, 1973), directed against the American involvement in Vietnam and against capitalism in general, and in his latest poetry collection, *Forsøg på at gå* (Attempts to Walk, 1978).

Ole Wivel

The publisher of *Heretica*, Wivel (1921–   ), gradually moved toward a similar political engagement. He too acknowledged in his poems of the 1940s the rootlessness and anxiety of modern humankind, but he went a step further than Knudsen, to the point of acknowledging the Gospel. This curve of development, from a sense of catastrophe to the expectation of the Messiah, which is also found in Sarvig's work, can be followed from *Digte* (Poems, 1943), whose assured sense of form is influenced by Rilke and Per Lange, to *I Fiskens Tegn* (In the Sign of the Fish, 1948). Here Wivel achieves his artistic independence in poems that express his elegiac longing for a new God and a new Man. But contact with one's fellow humans can be established only when the individual dares to accept the conditions of his or her own life. The penetration of this isolation represents a kind of grace for Wivel, as it does for Sarvig: "Not to love one another / but loving to walk / beneath the same light of resurrection, / cheek to cheek."

Wivel's newer, confessional collections, *Jævndøgnselegier* (Equinoctial Elegies, 1949) and *Maanen* (The Moon, 1952), influenced by Eliot's writing, reveal that Wivel's world view, nourished by the dream of medieval cultural unity, also contains a longing for the cosmic, for the mysterious universe. In 1958 he published *Nike*; its atmosphere of change, its commitment to the present and to action, is indicated by a number of descriptive poems dealing with the contemporary nuclear threat and political crisis; in contrast to this, we find Wivel's proclamation of divine and human love. A similar tension can be observed in *Templet for Kybele* (The Temple for Cybele, 1961), where an unearthed marble torso of the goddess of fertility, a forgotten fragment, symbolizes the threat that hangs over human and external nature.

In Wivel's somewhat unclear collection *Gravskrifter* (Epigraphs, 1970), the common experience of all the poems is death, as in the series of Vietnam poems that introduce the volume and testify to the poet's movement toward topical political events. They are conceived as eyewitness accounts and monologues, which gives them a documentary character objectifying the horror and making the poems a confirmation of Wivel's now pessimistic belief in fate. Wivel returns to the more classic form of his earlier writing in his latest collection, *Danmark ligger her endnu* (Denmark Still Lies Here, 1979), and at the same time provides a striking illustration of a turning from the political writing of the 1960s to the recent neo-provincialism and romanticism in Danish literature.

Frank Jæger

The youngest of the *Heretica* poets, Jæger (1926–77), in his first volume of poems, was far removed from the sense of anxiety and isolation that characterized his older colleagues. *Dydige Digte* (Virtuous Poems, 1948) and *Morgenens Trompet* (Morning's Trumpet, 1949) show him to be a naive optimist who turns his back on bourgeois existence and ideological quarrels, and, joying in this life, dedicates himself to a simple life in nature. His fluent, improvisatory style with its surprising associations, his playfulness and humor, are similar to the literary reaction in Sweden to the 1940s; still, one finds in almost every collection some poems that betray feelings of powerlessness and isolation. His faith in life has turned into dread and negation, the warmth of heart has turned to coldness and hopelessness.

For his collections from the 1950s, *Havkarlens Sange* (Songs of the Merman, 1956) and *Cinna* (1959) Jæger selected a metrical, classical form. The tone has matured; peace, authority, and a new objectivity are perceptible, without diminishing the sensuous energy or the creative power. The nature poems possess the same charm, the same absorption in the setting, and the same rejection of abstraction as did the earlier poems. Love poems make up a greater portion of the new volumes, widening the artistic scope through their desperate expression of the powerlessness of the human being in the erotic realm. This increasing seriousness reaches its peak in *Idylia* (1967), Jæger's darkest and most austere book; its title should be understood to be ironic, with an undertone of ominous threat: "Above our millstone table the dark blue sky of Idylia. / The rat sits in the grass. Now it is sniffing at his foot."

The tension in Jæger's poetry between the idyllic and the demonic in nature can also be found in his prose. His first book is about the lackadaisical *Iners* (1950), which is conceived as a picaresque novel in the style of Eichendorff's *Aus dem Leben eines Taugenichts* (Memoirs of a Good-for-Nothing). In the first part of the book, the idyllic tone of the model predominates; but gradually Iners reveals himself as a brutal, not entirely true-hearted descendant of the romantic wanderer. The fantastic becomes unrestrained in the eighteen short tales of *Hverdagshistorier* (Everyday Stories, 1951). On the other hand, most of the short stories in *Kapellanen og andre Fortællinger* (The Chaplain and Other Stories, 1957) are modern realistic, psychological narratives with precise descriptions of settings, with humor and satire; the high point is the festive title story, influenced by Pontoppidan, about a mediocre Copenhagen theologian who, to his despair, is exiled into darkest Jutland and against all expectations finds contentment there (see p. 41).

The crisis in *Idylia* becomes more acute in the seven stories of *Provinser* (Provinces, 1972); the title indicates not only a geographical location, but also loneliness and isolation. In addition, the collection is a defense of the independent, spontaneous artist, rebelling against the political demands experienced by contemporary writers—a problem Jæger also takes up in his final work, the volume of essays and short stories entitled *Udsigt til Kronborg* (View toward Kronborg, 1976).

PROSE OF THE 1950s

The atmosphere of myth and fairy tale characteristic of many of Jæger's short stories is typical of several prose writers of the 1950s. Also characteristic is a renewed interest in Karen Blixen's writing, particularly noticeable in the works of Leif E. Christensen and W.-A. Linnemann. Both share the spiritual conviction that humans exist to realize God's plans.

Leif E. Christensen

In his first collection of short stories, *Tyven i Tjørnsted* (The Thief in Tjørnsted, 1951), Christensen (1924–) uses a Blixen-like, archaic language. In the philosophical war novel *Træslottet* (The Wooden Castle, 1964) he abandons this in favor of a style and structure inspired by the French *nouveau roman*. The novel *Drejebogen* (The Script, 1970) marks a turn toward more traditional, realistic and psychological depiction.

Willy-August Linnemann

The background for the work of Linnemann (1914–) is the conflict-filled South Schleswig region between Denmark and Germany, where he was born. One of Linnemann's early works was *Natten før Freden* (The Night before the Peace, 1945), a novel depicting the experiences of a young Schleswig man in the Resistance against the German occupation of 1940–45. His early works were succeeded by a five-volume cycle, *Europafortællinger* (European Stories, 1958–66), in which Linnemann mingled suspenseful narrative art with philosophical reflection. The framework is formed by the life stories of people hiding in a shelter during an air raid, attempting to find a pattern in their fate, the hidden face of God. Linnemann's seven-volume prose work (1968–74) is less philosophical, having more social criticism. In it he portrays seven members of an old Schleswig family, up to the present, which is depicted in the last volume, *Protestanten* (The Protestant, 1974). Despite a sharp protest against the custodianship and technocracy of the welfare state, and the longing for a new, more artistic era, which is again expressed in his later novels, *Bølgerne på fjorden* (The Waves on the Sound, 1977) and *Blæsten gennem gaderne* (The Wind through the Streets, 1978), one notes Linnemann's conviction that all is governed and overseen, an attitude that bestows a visionary character to this monumental work.

Albert Dam

Karen Blixen's demand that humankind must realize itself in its relation to fate is a recurring theme in the works of Dam (1880–1972), who did not receive recognition until he had fifty years of literary production behind him. Dam made his debut in 1906 with a story of a psychological triangle, *Mellem de to Søer* (Between the Two Lakes), which ends with a dramatically described murder. Criminality is also a theme in *Saa kom det ny Brødkorn* (Then the New Grain Came, 1934), on the surface a naturalistic regional novel, but in reality a symbolic treatment of the dualism of spirit and matter. *Morfars By* (Grandfather's Town, 1956) is a series of mythical stories about a parish and its inhabitants. Myths in which the action is concentrated in situations from the past, present, and visionary future of humankind are found in the short-story volumes *Syv Skilderier* (Seven Pictures, 1962) and *Menneskelinien* (The Line of Man, 1965). The same cultural-historical and anthropological point of view characterizes Dam's last stories, *Menneskekår* (Human Conditions, 1967), *Elleve Rids* (Eleven Sketches, 1968), and *Min Moder og hendes Sønner* (My Mother and Her Sons, 1969).

Two prose writers who were close to the *Heretica* movement are Erik Aalbæk Jensen and Tage Skou-Hansen.

Erik Aalbæk Jensen

The early novels by Jensen (1923–)–*Dommen* (The Sentence, 1949), *Dæmningen* (The Dam, 1952), and *Gertrud* (1956)—are based on the motif of human guilt feelings caused by evading the demands imposed by family and society. In his works from the 1970s, *Sagen* (The Case, 1971) and *Kridtstregen* (The Chalk Line, 1976), like the later writing of Leif E. Christensen and W.-A. Linnemann, he displays a tendency toward greater social commitment and uses documentary and eyewitness techniques.

Tage Skou-Hansen and Other Realists

The novels by Skou-Hansen (1925–) demonstrate the same development. His first work, *De nøgne Træer* (The Naked Trees, 1957), concerned the German occupation and debated the existential question of guilt and responsibility. In later novels, *På den anden side* (On the Other Side, 1965) and *Hjemkomst* (Homecoming, 1969), the same question is related to more ordinary events. The novels *Tredje halvleg* (Third Half, 1971) and *Medløberen* (The Follower, 1973) are partially set in the world of sports—a topic that had been dealt with from a more political viewpoint in a novel by P. O. Enquist in 1971.

In *Idrættens forræderi* (The Treason of Sports, 1973) Hans Lyngby Jepsen (1920–) also discusses the relationship between sports and society, continuing in his writing the traditional realism that has its base in the literature of the 1930s. The realistic and psychological portrayals of this decade are convincingly continued by the popular novelists Poul Ørum (1919–) and Henning Ipsen (1930–), both depicting neglected and powerless human beings unable to hold their own in an impersonal, bureaucratic society.

In addition to the fantastic and realistic strains in the prose of the 1950s, an experimental trend was also notable. If one speaks of the symbolist tradition in the work of the *Heretica* poets, one must also speak of the consistent modernism in prose that continued the existential line of the *Heretica* circle. These writers were more interested in abolishing the border between reality and the experience of that reality, and they made a deliberate effort to bring Danish literature into harmony with European modernism. The organ of this international orientation was the journal *Vindrosen* (The Compass, 1954–74).

Villy Sørensen

This modernism emerged in prose with the early works of Sørensen (1929–) and Peter Seeberg in 1953–54. The first two books written by Sørensen, *Sære historier* (1953, Strange Stories; Eng. tr. *Tiger in the Kitchen and Other Strange Stories*, 1969) and *Ufarlige historier* (Safe Stories, 1955) have a common theme: the unliberated, unrealized aspects of our selves and our attitude toward them. Clearly, the most important influence was German modernism, above all Hermann Broch, whose works Sørensen introduced in Denmark. The German teachers of the *poet* Villy Sørensen were Kafka and Thomas Mann. Mann's ironic retelling of myth is the model for the legends that form a special genre within Sørensen's short stories. However, Kafka's influence—in particular his short stories—seems to be of even greater significance. Sørensen's works are primarily existential interpretations; but in contrast to Kafka's exclusiveness, Sørensen is open and outward-directed.

His short stories, or rather tales, are certainly original, but in structure are linked to the tradition of this genre. They unite the apparently naive tone of Hans Christian Andersen with allegory and irony reminiscent of Karen Blixen. They are set in a world that is thoroughly absurd or ironic, usually in Danish affluent society. The main intention in Sørensen's work is to resist any tendency to absolutely demarcate the life of the intellect from the life of the instincts; he also refuses to accept only half the truth. A fantastic story about such acceptance is "Duo," which deals with Siamese twins who are both named Otto because the name is a palindrome. Other prose pieces have more of a science-fiction character, such as "Tigrene" ("The Tigers"); the plot is very similar to Ionesco's *Rhinocéros*, but actually deals with people's unconscious powers. Some of the stories can be superficially read as realistic descriptions, for instance "Hjemvejen" ("The Way Home"), but are, in fact, frightening Kafkaesque nightmares.

Not until 1964 did Sørensen's third volume of short stories appear, under the title *Formynderfortællinger* (Tales of Guardianship). All the stories—which are as strange and ominous as the earlier ones and are written in the same ironic style, full of puns and allusions—deal with the problem of guardianship. "Et formynderskabs historie" ("The Story of Guardianship") relates a segment of the history of the Habsburg family, and in the portrayal of the complicated struggle for power, the question is asked: What is guardianship? Tyranny or absolutism in the face of anarchy? These political perspectives are expanded in the legends of Judas and Paul to a treatment of the problem of free will versus necessity.

Villy Sørensen is a central figure in the Danish intellectual life of the postwar period. He decisively influenced the writers of his generation, less through short stories than through his aesthetic and philosophical essays. In these he analyzed the problems of the time and of individual human beings, and demanded critical examination of all previous assumptions. A series of outstanding essays shows how Sørensen combines German philosophical ideas (Heidegger) and psychoanalysis with the indigenous Kierkegaard tradition. *Oprør fra midten* (Revolt from the Center, 1978), a political vision of the future, of which Sørensen is the co-author, has placed him at the center of controversy and given rise to fierce accusations of totalitarianism.

Peter Seeberg

Whereas Sørensen's tales are a philosopher's thoughts clothed in

fantasy, the stories of Seeberg (1925–   ) arise from a profound observation of humankind. His idiomatic language and precise portrayal of
reality are characteristic of his first short story, "Spionen" ("The Spy,"
1954). It portrays a young man who is seeking community, but is too
reflective and analyzes other people so much that he cannot relate to
them. He is an outsider, isolated not only from his fellow humans but
from reality itself. This theme is present in everything Seeberg has
written.

His first novel, *Bipersonerne* (The Secondary Characters, 1956),
breaks with both traditional and symbolic realism. It portrays the life
of a group of foreign forced laborers in a German film studio during
the late years of World War II. There they live a strangely shadowy
everyday life, in the heart of the war drama and yet outside it—they
are secondary characters, anonymous people of the twentieth century.

In his major novel, *Fugls føde* (Bird Pickings, 1957), Seeberg deals
with conscious escapism. The main character, Tom, a writer, is a weak
dreamer, most of whose plans miscarry; at the same time, he possesses
a sharp awareness of human weaknesses and ruthlessly exploits these
weaknesses. A possible escape is offered by his old acquaintance Hiffs,
when Hiffs offers Tom a large sum of money if he can write something
real, thus challenging Tom to find a way out of nihilism. The following
lines come from Tom's attempt: "My eyes are blind, / my hands are
withered, / my mind is dominated by destruction." But Hiffs rejects
this apparently accurate self-analysis because Tom's honesty is merely
honest *indifference*.

Seeberg's short stories in *Eftersøgningen* (The Search, 1962) are reports of the search for something: for identity, truth, or reality—basic
themes that show the degree to which the short stories were written
in the tradition of absurdists like Beckett and Ionesco. It is noteworthy
that the stories in this collection possess their own world, their own
reality—that of human nature. The fictional tension is never triggered
by the plot or the situation, but by the language, in which Seeberg
demonstrates great stylistic virtuosity.

The novel *Hyrder* (Shepherds, 1970) is an apparently realistic story
about ordinary people in a provincial city. The basic idea of the book
is that we are one another's shepherds; inattention can cost the life
that is to be guarded. Seeberg illuminates the motives of people who
have chosen the profession of shepherds and opens perspectives on the
subject of responsibility and identity: How do we fulfill our responsibility toward others? Where does your self end and mine begin?

The relationship of humans to society is the theme of *Dinosaurusens
sene eftermiddag* (The Later Afternoon of the Dinosaur, 1974); revo-

328 DANISH POSTWAR LITERATURE

lutionary attempts to break the imposed social framework are rejected in favor of evolutionary development. Again Seeberg focuses on human existential alienation, symbolized by the split manner in which the characters perceive reality. However, this situation is not necessarily permanent, as demonstrated in *Argumenter for benådning* (Arguments for Mercy, 1976). In spite of our insignificance and impotence, it is possible through compassion and tolerance to overcome life's absurdity. This confidence in our ability to survive, less apparent in Seeberg's latest novel, *Ved havet* (At the Sea, 1978), places him among the great humanists of contemporary Nordic literature.

Leif Panduro

Less exclusive and much more productive is Panduro (1923–77), whose work almost always revolves around a certain type of human being—a person who is divided because he or she is tied to the past. In this, Panduro, like many other Danish writers, was influenced by Villy Sørensen, who points precisely to the psychological and social inadequacies of people. These form the theme of Panduro's modernistic monologue novel *Øgledage* (Saurian Days, 1961), in which the saurians represent the repressed elements in society and in the individual, the taboos and repressed aggressions. *Rend mig i traditionerne* (1958; Eng. tr. *Kick Me in the Traditions*, 1961) reveals Panduro's basic subject: the difficulties of puberty, that stage of life at which the human being capitulates to the ordered world of adults. Inspired by J. D. Salinger's *The Catcher in the Rye*, Panduro humorously describes a young boy's escape from school, his escapades in the city, and his imprisonment in a mental institution where he refuses to let himself become "normalized." Characters from this novel are found in *Fern fra Danmark* (Fern from Denmark, 1963), which poses the question of identity. The main character, a forty-year-old man, suffers from amnesia and searches for his identity, refusing to accept the role in society that everyone wants to impose upon him—a theme close to that in Max Frisch's novel *Stiller*.

The two succeeding books, in which Panduro moves from the subject of puberty to that of the schizophrenia of being grown up, are first-person novels, written, like all of Panduro's later works, in traditional prose; their narrators report how estranged they have become from their own selves. *Fejltagelsen* (The Error, 1964) deals with a hypochondriac who has fled from his present into illness, which is equivalent to a flight into irresponsibility. With all of his wretchedness, this neurotic, Marius, makes a sympathetic impression, whereas his healthy friend Hilmer is a frightening picture of normalcy. The bank manager

Morner, in *Den gale mand* (The Crazy Man, 1965) is a "normal" person who loses his grip and becomes a victim of the psychological process of disintegration, because he is too dependent on external conventional security. The insanity of normalcy is also the theme of the exciting, action-filled novel *Daniels anden verden* (The Other World of Daniel, 1970), which, like *Amatørerne* (The Amateurs, 1972), deals with the contrast between established society, i.e., the middle-aged generation, and revolutionary youth, which espouses necessary changes leading to a new way of life. *Vinduerne* (The Windows, 1971) is a case history of the eternal observer of existence, for whom life is a theatrical performance. *Den ubetænksomme elsker* (The Thoughtless Lover, 1973) is both a variation on the normal/abnormal theme and a captivating psychological thriller about love and responsibility, like Panduro's last novel, *Høfeber* (Hay Fever, 1975). In addition, he has written scripts for revues and films, a collection of short stories, *Den bedste af alle verdener* (The Best of All Worlds, 1974), and many television plays which reiterate the themes of the novels. *Farvel, Thomas* (Good-bye, Thomas, 1968), *I Adams verden* (In Adam's World, 1973) and *Louises hus* (Louise's House, 1977) are, in their skillful analyses of conflicts set in recognizable, everyday situations, culminations of Nordic television drama.

DRAMA AND POETRY OF THE 1960s

The political climate of the years immediately after the war had favored a poetry of impotence and fear, in which protest was expressed by a search for a sense of the cosmic or metaphysical. In the mid-1950s, however, a gradual focusing on social reality was perceptible. In the 1960s this trend was manifest both in an increased interest in the realistic drama of which Panduro's plays are typical and successful examples, and in an extroverted, experimental poetry.

Ernst Bruun Olsen

The greatest stage success was enjoyed by Olsen (1923–   ). His plays combine realism with fantasy and deal with current trends: *Teenagerlove* (1962), satirizing the cult of pop music, *Bal i den Borgerlige* (Middle-Class Ball, 1966), a political criticism of half-hearted socialism, and *Hvor gik Nora hen, da hun gik ud?* (Where Did Nora Go, When She Left? 1968), which combines a discussion of sex roles with socialism. The television plays *Til lykke, Hansen* (Congratulations Hansen, perf. 1971) and *Lille Mand farvel* (Good-bye Little Man, perf. 1975) are direct attacks on the capitalistic system.

Leif Petersen

Of greater artistic importance are the dramas for stage, radio, and television that Petersen (1934–) began in the 1960s, rooted in Pinter and Saroyan. Although his works are characterized by concrete, contemporary realism, he demonstrates a very special absurd humor, related to that of Villy Sørensen and Peter Seeberg, which exposes the human isolation behind the facade of the welfare state. This theme is also present in Petersen's plays of the 1970s, *Fremad* (Forward, perf. 1974) and *Nix pille* (Don't Touch, perf. 1976).

The real artistic innovation on the threshold of the 1960s was lyrical modernism, which to a great degree accepted the welfare society, commercialism, and the atom bomb. Whereas the 1950s were distinctly literary and nostalgic, the new poetry leaned challengingly toward the external appearances and jargons of society, confronting the irreconcilable elements of reality and sense impressions.

Klaus Rifbjerg

The lyrical blossoming of Danish poetry during the 1960s was largely attributable to Rifbjerg (1931–). His first book, *Under vejr med mig selv* (Getting Wind of Myself, 1956), is a humorous and verbally imaginative idyll in free verse; but in *Efterkrig* (Postwar, 1957) one senses a threatening emptiness in existence. This new direction found its most successful expression in the breakthrough collection *Konfrontation* (Confrontation, 1960), which conveys exclusively concrete experiences: "Empty, empty, empty—blessedly empty / is the world of everything but objects / living plunge, you and I / plunge in the continued moment of bursting / the only living thing: to stand opposite each other." An ecstatic element appears in the poem *Camouflage* (1961), a grandiose attempt to conquer reality through a voyage into the unconscious, back to the personal past, to myths and memories. Rifbjerg's technique is strictly associative. He plays with words, putting them into surprising combinations in a fragmented syntax.

The technique of confrontation is modified in his later poetry, but appears again in *Mytologi* (Mythology, 1970); these poems are based on a direct encounter of classical myth with modern conditions, or of the poet with the mythic hero. To illustrate the relationship between the public and modern art, *Portræt* (1963) presents a series of texts in which the words appear in different patterns, in an open style that appeals to readers for assistance. Another reaction against the lyrical style that Rifbjerg had introduced in *Confrontation*, is *Amagerdigte* (Amager Poems, 1965). Here his style is sober, reportorial, and matter-of-fact, inspired by the Swedish "new simplicity." He returns to the island of his birth, a suburb of Copenhagen, to reconstruct and reconquer the banal monotony of this lost time. The same private motif is also basic to *25 desperate digte* (25 Desperate Poems, 1974), a candid portrayal of the author himself. The objectivity of the Amager collection is continued in *Scener fra det daglige liv* (Scenes from Daily Life, 1973), a collection of colorful, realistic poems. The volume *Ved stranden* (At the Beach, 1976) resumes the uninhibited and expansive flights of fancy characteristic of the earlier works but in a new, original attitude of confrontation with nature.

Rifbjerg's almost sixty titles include not only poetry and prose, but also a number of scripts for revues and films, and less successful dramas, revealing the extent to which Rifbjerg's talent is tied to language rather than to the scenic and dramatic. Most of Rifbjerg's prose is traditional. Like Panduro's *Kick Me in the Traditions*, Rifbjerg's novel *Den kroniske uskyld* (Chronic Innocence, 1958) portrays the painful mystery of puberty. Innocence must be overcome, for the innocent person is unprotected and vulnerable. If this proves impossible, innocence is transferred into illness and the crisis of puberty becomes chronic. The novel ends in a catastrophe in which, basically, innocence itself is the guilty party. The same motif is present in many of the short stories of *Og andre historier* (And Other Stories, 1964), *Den syende jomfru* (The Sewing Virgin, 1972), *Sommer* (Summer, 1974), and *Det korte af det lange* (In Short, 1976), all less experimental than the collection of 1964.

The problems of insecure youth are also the subject of the novels *Arkivet* (The Archives, 1967) and *Lonni og Karl* (Lonni and Karl, 1968). The latter is a comic and satirical revolutionary fantasy, dedicated to Fidel Castro, the former a painstakingly factual account of two young men's everyday life. However, Rifbjerg is able to create an atmosphere of tension through his sophisticated use of language and symbols, a technique influenced by the French *nouveau roman* and resumed in the novel *En hugorm i solen* (A Viper in the Sun, 1974).

In a series of novels Rifbjerg psychologically explores the established adult world. *Operaelskeren* (1966; Eng. tr. *The Opera Lover*, 1970) portrays the love of the mathematics professor Franck for an opera singer, which eventually turns into a love of infidelity and ends in catastrophe. The story belongs to the Don Juan tradition: Franck is fascinated by the figure of the seducer and completely identifies with it. There is a series of warnings that dark powers are present in this fateful occurrence, such as snake symbols reminiscent of Frisch's novel *Homo Faber* (1957): A cool rationalist discovers that his previously well-ordered world is being manipulated by powers beyond his control. The full consequences of such a situation are experienced by the principal character of *Anna (jeg) Anna* (Anna (I) Anna, 1969), one of the major works in recent Danish literature. A diplomat's neurotic wife escapes from her luxurious life to travel with a young criminal hippie across Europe. This event is expressed both in sequences of poetic symbolism and in situations, recalling the popular novel, in which the couple is forced to flee the police.

The escape motif is also present in *Brevet til Gerda* (The Letter to Gerda, 1972), an anguished outcry against the static and passive, masking a fear of life that is, in reality, a fear of death. This theme, related to the theme of a journey back to one's human and social origins made possible when one is liberated from all suppressions, is repeated in the novel *Vejen ad hvilken* (The Road Along Which, 1975). In the complex *R. R.* (1972) Rifbjerg criticizes the crippling and leveling effects of rationalism to which the main character—a Faust-like figure—has sold his soul. A similar complexity characterizes *Kiks* (Miss, 1976), a satirical political novel in which Rifbjerg uses his earlier confrontation technique; on the other hand, *Dilettanterne* (The Dilettantes, 1973) and the "family chronicle" *De beskedne* (The Modest One, 1976), which tells of Danish everyday life during the 1950s and 1960s, are more accessible. Nevertheless, they all—including Rifbjerg's most recent and perhaps most significant novels, *Et bortvendt ansigt* (A Face Turned Away, 1977), *Tango* (1978), and *Joker* (1979)— confirm his position in Nordic literature as an exceptionally sensitive and prolific writer.

Jess Ørnsbo

In 1960, the same year that Rifbjerg's volume of poetry *Confrontation* came out, Ørnsbo (1932–) made his debut with *Digte* (Poems). The sense of social involvement found here is new to modernism; the point of departure is a worker's district in Copenhagen, but the locality is subordinated in a series of confrontations with the hopelessness and malice of modern urban existence; Ørnsbo aggressively attempts to contradict the heroic and melodramatic in life. As was true of Rifbjerg, vast amounts of realistic material were available to Ørnsbo. But he surpassed Rifbjerg in creating bold sensuous impressions and grotesque associations.

Ørnsbo's almost baroque metaphors were developed further in *Myter* (Myths, 1964), an attempt to expand the choice of motifs to include the subconscious. The decisive themes are: alienation, aggression, instincts, and death; they are described with piercing verbal effects, designed to add an existential and universal perspective to the factual description. An example is to be found in "De syges fordrivelse" ("The Banishment of the Ill"). Here scenes of destruction flow together in a symbolic picture of the removal of the undesired person, the situation of the victim: "Hour of blood serum / Relatives led away by corpses / squint-eyed ones led to the side."

Glaring stylistic effects also characterize Ørnsbo's two absurd plays, *Dværgen der blev væk* (The Dwarf Who Disappeared, 1968) and *Hypdangbok* (1969), in which Ørnsbo uses a compact verbal construction and grotesque caricatures, making staging a difficult task. More easily accessible are *Tusdigte* (Twilight Poems, 1966) and *Kongen er mulat, men hans søn er neger* (The King Is a Mulatto but His Son Is a Negro, 1971), twenty-four poems, desperate protests against inhumanity and violence. A similar attitude is expressed in the absurd story *Dullerdage* (Days of Duller, 1976), a combination of prose, dramatic monologue, and poetry. In *Digte uden arbejde* (Poems without Work, 1977) Ørnsbo returns to the motifs of his first work. In *Mobiliseringer* (Mobilizations, 1978) this social criticism is given political overtones in almost anarchic protest against a society in the process of dissolution.

Ivan Malinovski

For Malinovski (1926–   ) also the aesthetics of confrontation are a basic principle, a formal expression of his experience of the senselessness of existence. Like his teacher Erik Knudsen, he sees the world as divided into a series of antitheses. This pessimistic attitude and tragic conception of humanity, which is related to that of Ekelöf and the Swedish poetry of the 1940s, is hinted at in *Galgenfrist* (Short Respite, 1958), the first consistently modernist collection of poetry of the period.

Even less communicative is the catalog-like prose poetry in *Romerske bassiner* (Roman Basins, 1963), and the pithy, concentrated, *haiku*-like aphorisms in *Poetomatic* (1965). In the first collection, objects are seemingly juxtaposed in an attempt to paint a pathological picture of modern civilization. Underlying this picture is a meaningful linguistic structure based on poetic associations and word play. The left-wing poet reflects on the chaotic circumstances of humankind, which for him are a manifestation of Marx's theory of alienation. The second collection is also far removed from symbolic poetry. The mood alternates between nihilism and hope: "Should a person surrender if / and only because / death is reaching up to his knees."

Malinovski's revolutionary position emerges more clearly in *Leve som var der en fremtid og et håb* (Living as If There Were a Future and a Hope, 1968), in which his artistic method and attitude are unchanged. The authorial voice is unmistakable. In the atmosphere of constant tension—where the only certainty is irrepressible life in opposition to death—there rises, above the zero point of senselessness, an imperishable will to live, which leads the poet to political and social involvement. This theme is developed further in the volume *Kritik af tavsheden* (Critique of Silence, 1974), which, in addition, deals with the indoctrinating function of language—a theme found more frequently among contemporary Swedish writers than among their other Nordic colleagues.

With his keen verbal sense, Ivan Malinovski is an ideal translator. He translated from various languages a number of modern poets, such as Brecht, Mayakovsky, Neruda, Pound, and Trakl.

Jørgen Sonne

Sonne (1925–   ) has also done outstanding work as a translator, of, among others, Mallarmé, Rimbaud, and Villon. In other respects, however, he contrasts with Malinovski. Sonne's poetry is related to St.-John Perse, Eliot, Pound, and Ekelöf; like them, he moves within a broad tradition and alludes in his art to distant times and foreign cultures. Sonne's work is constantly developing in tone and intensity rather than thematically. His early poetry, strict in its form, is succeeded by experiments in a free style. The first three collections (1950–52) are still marked clearly by the postwar period's spiritual crisis and search for meaning. Religious themes emerge, a faith in vitality and love; however, in the fourth volume, *Italiensk suite* (Italian Suite, 1954), themes of destruction and decay predominate.

These works can be seen as talented introductions to *Krese* (Cycles, 1963), one of the most mature works of the 1960s. The book is divided into four sections, whose headings denote both duality and development: "Earlier and Now," "Muses and Museum," "Double Themes," and "Earlier and Since." It is an attempt to regain the primitive quality and wealth of feelings of childhood, through intellectual retrospection. The poems relate a maturing process that is at the same time the intellectual and poetic structure of the collection: The self dissolves and ceases to be a problem when the coherence of all things is recognized: "Thunder reigns in the cosmos / says the heart of the embryo." Duality is also present in the language, characterized by an ambiguity reminiscent of Ekelöf's *Strountes* and Pound's *Cantos*.

This same language is characteristic of Sonne's latest poems in *Huset* (The House, 1976), which are more emotionally forceful and complex than any of his other poems. He combines observations, reflections, and visions, in a long associative journey into fantasy, memory, and history, using a purely imagistic technique. Conversely, *Blå turist* (Blue Tourist, 1971), an ironic travel book about a naive photographer's confrontation with the realities of a developing country, is characterized by minute, precise descriptions of reality—such descriptions also characterize the poetry collection *Thai-noter* (Thai Notes, 1974).

Jørgen Gustava Brandt

Brandt (1929–) began his career as a member of the *Heretica* group, though he never accepted its demand for moral commitment. Since he also avoided taking a firm political stance in the decades following the founding of the movement, he was accused of pure aestheticism; the explanation for his attitude lies in his increasingly evident turn to religious mysticism. Brandt made his debut in 1949 with *Korn i Pelegs mark* (Grain on Peleg's Field), in which he struck some surrealistic notes that were not again sounded in Danish poetry until ten years later. Brandt worked with loosely linked associations to the Old Testament, to oriental mysticism, and to the apocalyptic poetry of Dylan Thomas. The material consists mainly of moods and feelings of a young urban person in the postwar years—as in Sarvig's writing. Although Sarvig sees the city as demonic and alienating, Brandt populates it with fantastic scenery, visions of Christ, experiences of nature and love, which combine spiritual and material realities.

The formally skillful, but somewhat impersonal collections of the 1950s were succeèded in 1960 by *Fragment af imorgen* (Fragment of Tomorrow). Narcissism is replaced by a perception that harmonizes the inner and outer world: "The night has directed her glance at me and recognizes herself." The inner balance of self-forgetfulness and a profound sense of identity is mirrored in the musical but somewhat melodramatic tone and in the broad reflective style reminiscent of T. S. Eliot. On the other hand, *Janushoved* (Head of Janus, 1962), which examines this balance in reference to everyday reality, signifies a turning away from declamation to free association, highly compatible with Brandt's extraordinary ability to create images. His poems are often formed of tireless descriptions of an object, through the details of which the poetic image is created. The poems in *Ateliers* (1967) are characterized by myths and religious symbols. In the collections *Vendinger* (Turns, 1971) and *Her omkring* (Around Here, 1974) Brandt uses such symbols to express his longing for a mystical rest in existence, a search which is reflected in the alternation of large and small texts, poetry and prose. This leads to the lyrical novels *Kvinden på Lüneburg hede* (The Woman on the Lüneburg Moors, 1969) and *Pink Champagne*, (1973) and culminates in the lyrical trilogy *Mit hjerte i København* (My Heart in Copenhagen, 1975), *Jatháram* (1976), and *Regnansigt* (Rain Face, 1976), an intense affirmation of life, intermingling past and present in remembrances and portraits. Brandt's writing is subtle and intellectual, with no direct involvement in current ideological problems. This is not a mark of aestheticism, but a philosophical point of view.

As in Sweden—although in Denmark it is more firmly grounded theoretically and linguistically—there arises around 1965, in addition to the "new simplicity," a tendency toward the concrete, in which words, functioning as signs, have intrinsic value. In prose one finds this tendency in Svend Åge Madsen's concise novel form; in poetry it is present in Malinovski's *Roman Basins*, in Benny Andersen's easily accessible writing, and, to an even greater degree, in the esoteric writing of Poul Borum and Per Højholt.

Benny Andersen

In *Den musikalske ål* (The Musical Eel, 1960), *Kamera med køkkenadgang* (Camera with Kitchen Access, 1962), and *Den indre bowlerhat* (The Inner Bowler Hat, 1964) Andersen (1929–) employs a witty, elegant form, in which the ambiguities of language create surprising and unexpected relationships, seen in the light of social attitudes. Andersen has a sympathetic understanding of the neglected and forlorn. He cultivates the portrait poem, in which the alienated human is presented, generally in a monologue. Indeed, his poetry collection of 1966 is entitled *Portrætgalleri* (Portrait Gallery), and similar portraits occur in his short-story collections *Puderne* (The Cushions, 1965) and *Tykke-Olsen m. fl.* (Fat Olsen and Others, 1968). During the debates concerning Denmark's entry into the European Economic Community, Andersen published the volume *Her i reservatet* (Here in the Reservation, 1971), an ironic and deliberately naive exposure of idyllic democracy. He again takes up the portrait in *Svantes viser* (Svante's Songs, 1972), for which Andersen wrote music as well as text—a very popular work. He cultivates the self-portrait in *Personlige papirer* (Personal Papers, 1974), an analysis of the poet's role. This personal element is also predominant in *Normader med noder* (Nomad with Notes, 1976), poetic and documentary texts from Andersen's life as a traveling musician during the 1950s. *Under begge øjne* (Under Both Eyes, 1978) marks a turn to purely existential questions, concluding with the acknowledgment that close human contact is the only way to lasting happiness.

Poul Borum

The perception of language, not only as a means of creating poetic symbols, but also as a means of cognition, has become an increasingly dominant idea in the work of Poul Borum (1934–   ). Since *Livslinier* (Life Lines, 1962) he has published one poetry volume yearly. His earlier collections, with deep roots in Fenno-Swedish and American modernism, attempt to embrace the quintessence of life, to describe or create in a fashion which ensures that something untried and unexpected will open up for the reader. A change toward a poetry analyzing the function of language marks *Kendsgerninger* (Facts, 1968). This change is completely accomplished in *Andethed* (Otherness, 1977); like *Facts*, this collection consists of brief poems, often inspired by music and art, in which the most delicate mood alternates with invocative exclamation, romantic atmosphere with concise statement.

Per Højholt

In his work, Højholt (1928–   ) experiments with all kinds of language: quotations, technical or self-coined words, and clichés. Paper and type are used as artistic materials, a cultivation of formal elements which in *Punkter* (Points, 1971) transforms the language into mere signs and closed symbols. *Volumen* (1974) is more open, a picture book with clusters of words, masterfully arranged as a collage designed to stimulate the reader's imagination.

Vagn Steen

The language of Steen and the younger major theoretician Hans-Jørgen Nielsen is more disciplined than Højholt's. Steen (1928–   ) focuses on problems of communication and the democratization of art. His first collection, *Digte?* (Poems? 1964), is a demonstration of various treatments of language in the form of jingles and linguistic tricks to stimulate the reader. This attempt reaches its extreme in *Skriv selv* (Write Yourself, 1965), a pad of blank pages. In the 1970s Steen expressed more personal experiences in his poetry, as in the love poems of *k. 24 digte til en* (k. 24 Poems for Somebody, 1973). However, he did not abandon his pedagogical and extroverted tendency, demonstrated in *Når lærerens kone er i brugsen* (When the Teacher's Wife Is in the Co-op, 1977).

Hans-Jørgen Nielsen

The early poetry volumes by Nielsen (1941) *at det at* (That It

That, 1965) and *konstateringer* (Statements, 1966), are academic exercises, which do not exploit any complicated syntactic possibilities or evince any trace of the humor characteristic of two of his models, Helmut Heissenbüttel and Bengt Emil Johnson. In Nielsen's later collections the mechanical and pedagogical aspects of his poetry are replaced by greater sensuousness and evocative power. In *Output* (1967) a philosophical, linguistic investigation of the relationship between word and reality, language is treated in a wholly unsophisticated manner. In *Fra luften i munden* (From the Air into the Mouth, 1968) the verses gain in substance and musicality, and now function in a romantic manner to expand the fantasy and spirit. Nielsen's major effort is the novel *Den mand der kalder sig Alvard* (1970), a work about language as the material behind which lies hidden a metaphysical attitude, clearly inspired by Zen Buddhism.

Inger Christensen

The high point of this tendency was achieved by Christensen (1935-   ). Although her novels *Evighedsmaskinen* (The Eternity Machine, 1964) and *Adorno* (1967) might be characterized as derivative and impersonal modernism, Christensen is an original lyric poet. The volumes *Lys* (Light, 1962) and *Græs* (Grass, 1963) focus on the disquieting world of writing, the fear of the loss of self during the creative act, and the function of the word. They pave the way for *Det* (It, 1969). The work is composed strictly symmetrically—3 x 8 x 8 poems—and exhibits a flowing verbal creativity in rhymed strophes, prose, and song lyrics. This creative process offers the possibility of *dis*covering the universe, although language itself is able to *cover* the world. Between language and experiences an infinite chasm exists; only the self combines words with objects and makes possible a movement from chaos to increasingly more refined differentiation within human life, a movement that is mirrored in the text. In *It* Christensen created a lasting monument to the 1960s, containing most of the important political, aesthetic, and existential questions of the decade. Christensen set out to create a synthesis of our interpretation of the surrounding world, and of the world itself—of art and reality—in the story *Det malede værelse* (The Painted Room, 1976), about the Italian Renaissance painter Mantegna. It is related by three different narrators, all of whom reach the conclusion that our world is in a constant process of creation, of which art is a highly integrated part.

PROSE MODERNISM

Around 1960 a milestone was reached in the history of Danish prose modernism. Modernism became a central focus of topical debate. Although many of the previous generation's novels were based on experiences of the war and occupation, the authors now turned to a topical, existential subject. This led to a transformation of the novel form, which was influenced by the *nouveau roman* of Robbe-Grillet and by Samuel Beckett; the influence can be found in both the absence of the traditional plot and the sharply defined distinction of the narrator from the characters in the novel.

Svend Åge Madsen

Clearly influenced by the *nouveau roman* is the novel by Madsen (1939–) entitled *Besøget* (The Visit, 1963), which contrasts two different narrative perspectives. The first part portrays the imprisonment of the narrator in a strange world in which the events are also symptoms of an inner condition. In the second part several scenes occur with the same characters; their actions and words are commented on in a pedantic, detached fashion, including observations about their motivations.

In the "non-novel" *Lystbilleder* (Pictures of Lust, 1964) the basic situation is again described from various viewpoints. In the first section of the book, which Madsen calls Chapter 0, a rape scene is reported indignantly. A repetition of the episode introduces Chapter 1, but this time it is reported with some experience of sexual pleasure. The remainder of the book is a series of short sections in which Madsen systematically attempts to define lust through various linguistic means.

In *Otte gange orphan* (Eight Times Orphan, 1965) the connection between the sections is indefinable. In seven independent stories told in the first person, seven mentally abnormal conditions are portrayed, in deliberately monotonous and image-free, but tension-filled language. The poetic, organizing mechanisms that function in these seven sections according to extreme, but still logical principles, no longer work in the eighth section; it is a completely disorganized expression of the chaotic personal state of the author when he starts to write.

Madsen's work has thus far followed the same line as that of the tragic modernist Beckett. Human identity, and with it the form of the novel, is reduced, little by little. With the novel in five independent volumes, *Tilføjelser* (Additions, 1967), this reduction is no longer depicted as human tragedy but as a totally given verbal abstraction.

The restrained humor in Madsen's puritanical writing breaks out in two novels: *Liget og lysten* (The Corpse and the Desire, 1968) was patterned on the popular novel, and *Tredje gang så tar vi ham* (We'll Get Him the Third Time, 1969) imitates the detective novel. Both, however, express the concept that literature is a system for creating a reality according to the ideas of the author, which are not given a priori. This problem is again discussed in *Sæt verden er til* (If the World Exists, 1971). In *Dage med Diam* (Days with Diam, 1972) readers have to combine the characters and the events to create the story they want to read, i.e., the reality they wish to experience. The same relative view of the world of fiction is present in *Jakkels vandring* (The Wandering of Jakkel, 1974), which brought about a renewal in Madsen's work, a result of which is the pseudo-documentary novel *Tugt og utugt i mellemtiden* (Decency and Indecency in the Meanwhile, 1976), a political, social, and psychological analysis of everyday life in Denmark in the 1970s.

Sven Holm

It is characteristic of Madsen and Holm (1940–   ) that political and social ideas emerge only gradually in their books. The title story in Holm's well-structured first book, *Den store fjende* (The Great Enemy, 1961), is a modern tale: Strategic military maneuvers and a destructive field battle stand in the foreground, but the entire book is actually a psychological study of persecution and duality of the self. Holm thereby made for himself a place in modern Danish literature among the "fantastic" tale-tellers—more a disciple of Villy Sørensen's than of Karen Blixen's. Influenced by the politicization of intellectual life in the following years, Holm widened his perspective to include the struggle for power among people in whom political and social relationships are mirrored.

This development can be observed clearly in his first novel, *Fra den nederste himmel* (From the Lowest Heaven, 1965), a broadly conceived attempt to write a political novel; the same development is also directly expressed in the three political allegories of his short-story collection *Rex* (1969), the other stories portraying the origin of power and aggression.

Between these two books, which represent an attempt to amalgamate existentialism with a kind of socialism, there lies the shattering science-fiction novel *Termush* (1967; Eng. tr. 1969); the book is composed of diary entries that register events in an isolated hotel. Here a group of people has sought refuge after World War III; they live in a universe of sterility and powerlessness, where human beings can survive with a minimum of feeling.

An entirely different character marks the apparently coincidental collage *Min elskede* (My Beloved, 1968). The conventional plot consists of several colorful, satiric chapters about mystical foreign agents; the actual concern, however, is the poet's fascinating dream of integrating language and reality. In the psychological and satiric novels *Syg og munter* (Sick and Merry, 1972), *Det private liv* (Private Life, 1974), and *Langt borte taler byen med min stemme* (Far Away the City Speaks with My Voice, 1976), the main theme is the relationship of social and personal traits in humans; the novels conclude with the melancholy realization that impotence and isolation prevail, even in sexual relationships, as Holm satirically demonstrates in his novel *Ægteskabsleg* (Marriage Game, 1977).

Preben Major Sørensen and Dorrit Willumsen

Other typical representatives of the fantastic narrative are Sørensen (1937–) and Dorrit Willumsen (1940–). With his first novel, *Ildmesteren* (The Fire Master, 1965), Sørensen placed himself in the tradition of Karen Blixen and Villy Sørensen, a position he has maintained with his masterpiece, the metaphysical novel *Af en ærkeengels erindringer* (From the Memoirs of an Archangel, 1976), a monologue by the fallen angel Lucifer. Willumsen deals with the confrontation between the two sexes, often from a grotesque and fantastic perspective; this is reflected in the title of her surrealistic novel *the krydderi acryl salær græshopper* (Tea, Spices, Acrylic, Fee, Grasshoppers, 1970), fantasy's protest against the lack of coherence in our world. The combination of confinement and unlimited freedom becomes a main motif in Willumsen's major work, the short-story collection *Modellen Coppelia* (The Model Coppelia, 1973), in which the characters mirror various stages of life. A similar structure is the basis of the satirical *En værtindes smil* (The Smile of a Hostess, 1974), in which the reader follows a number of passive human beings through nineteen chapters; they are victims of a society dominated by anonymous power structures and biological manipulations.

Willumsen's books delineate an existence characterized by alienation and depersonalization, resulting in an abstract atmosphere; the same prevails in the early writings of Cecil Bødker and Ulla Ryum.

Cecil Bødker

The poetry and prose of Bødker (1927) are marked from the early volumes by a tendency toward the mythical; *Luseblomster* (Dandelions, 1955) and *Fygende heste* (Flying Horses, 1956) are constructed as small fables, and the major poetry collection *Anadyomene* (1959) is a vision of the human fall and rebirth. In *I vædderens tegn* (Under the Sign of the Ram, 1968), however, the myths are more concretely mingled with details of nature. The development toward realism in Danish literature during the 1960s marks Bødker's prose. Her early short stories, published in *Øjet* (The Eye, 1961), also deal with the fall. A similar mythical complex of problems is found in *Tilstanden Harley* (The Condition of Harley, 1965), a novel about responsibility and irresponsibility, related to Seeberg's *Shepherds*, in which chronology, causality, and identity are absent. The stories of *Fortællinger omkring Tavs* (Stories around Tavs, 1971) have a semi-mythical setting. However, *En vrangmaske i vorherres strikketøj* (A Purl in Our Lord's Knitting, 1974), a description of a young boy's upbringing in a working-class milieu, evinces a growing and easily accessible realism. Bødker has published a number of outstanding and very popular children's books since 1967.

Ulla Ryum

The mythical element is also very strong in the writings of Ulla Ryum (1937–). However, she does not emulate Bødker and Svend Åge Madsen in their attempts to achieve the most precise language possible. Rather, she seeks to create a language of dreams, full of associations and ambiguity, reminiscent of the mood and method found in the works of the American writer Djuna Barnes. Ryum's main interest evolves around those tragic characters who have searched for meaning throughout a lifetime, but can find it only in death. Such a person is *Natsangersken* (The Night Singer, 1963), a fascinating psychological and symbolic portrait of a woman abandoned by life and love. One of the dominant themes in Ryum's writing is the unbridgeable gap between human beings. This tragic situation is thoroughly illustrated in *Latterfuglen* (The Laughing Jackass, 1965), a variation on the classical Orpheus myth, and in the two collections of short stories, *Tusindskove* (Thousand-Forests, 1969) and *Noter om idag og igår* (Notes about Today and Yesterday, 1971), both having a strange mingling of miracle and social realism. In *Jakelnatten* (The Night of the Puppet, 1967) the main theme is the person disappearing without a trace, a puppeteer whose deathbed monologue constitutes the largest part of the novel. In contrast to Ryum's fantastic and fabulous art are her dramas, which attack our dehumanized world. *Myterne* (The Myths, 1973) prepares the way for the author's demand for political and social solidarity, exemplified by *Natten, krigen* (The Night, the War, perf. 1975) and the radio play *Denne ene dag* (This One Day, perf. 1976).

NEO-REALISM

Thorkild Hansen

The neo-realistic trend that emerged around 1965 had a forerunner in Thorkild Hansen (1927-   ), whose first published documentaries were based on historical material. This in no way prevented him from participating in contemporary debate. He achieved his breakthrough in 1959 with *Pausesignaler* (Interval Signals), short prose pieces saturated with atmosphere and influenced by the author's Italian travels. Hansen achieved great success with *Det lykkelige Arabien* (1962; Eng. tr. *Arabia Felix*, 1964), based on impressions of two archaeological expeditions to Kuwait and the Nubian desert. The book is the exciting report of an eighteenth-century Danish expedition which was sent into the southwestern portion of the Arabian peninsula; it ended tragically, with only one of its six participants returning, the young scientist Carsten Niebuhr.

Arabia Felix had as its theme scientists who were torn from their cultural milieu. *Jens Munk* (1965; Eng. tr. *The Way to Hudson Bay*, 1970) deals with a primitive, but conscientious seaman and his bold, but unsuccessful attempt to find the Northwest Passage to India and China. Munk returned to Copenhagen in 1620, with only two of his crewmen; this tragic account, which forms the high point of the book, is the result of Hansen's research and creative fantasy, and is linked with the historical decline of Denmark in the seventeenth century. One senses an inner existential connection in the three parallel biographies of King Christian IV, Admiral Ove Giedde, and Jens Munk: None of the three is able to master the tasks that are set for him.

The theme of the trilogy *Slavernes kyst* (The Coast of the Slaves, 1967), *Slavernes skibe* (The Ships of the Slaves, 1968), and *Slavernes øer* (The Islands of the Slaves, 1970) is the slave trade, which was carried out both officially and privately by the Danes between the Gold Coast of Africa and the West Indies. Before he began writing the trilogy, Hansen traveled the slave traders' route, seeking out the places mentioned in the archival materials—the same methods he had employed in his two previous works. Most of his major characters are Danish officials, and in their varying temperaments and predispositions Hansen confronts the differing attitudes toward the slave trade. The trilogy became a polemic against the concept of the "convenient necessity" of slavery, and an attack on the fiction that Denmark, through its abolition of slavery in 1792, had proved itself a humanitarian state. That Hansen overstepped the bounds of objective reporting is obvious in the subjective style, the use of inner monologue and literary leit motifs. It is these features that raise the trilogy to the level of a masterpiece. Hansen combines a high degree of artistic creativity with skillful historical method. His significant position in recent Nordic literature is underlined by the publication of a three-volume work, *Processen mod Knut Hamsun* (The Trial against Knut Hamsun, 1978), a deeply committed and critical account of the treason trial of the famous Norwegian author after World War II.

The neo-realism of the 1960s, with its more traditional narrative technique, based on Thorkild Hansen and Swedish models, and on Mary McCarthy's novel *The Group*, not only created a new literary school, but also influenced a number of modernistic, experimental writers. Among them were Cecil Bødker, Leif E. Christensen, and Klaus Rifbjerg. This trend had already been anticipated by the novel *De nøjsomme* (The Modest, 1960) by Poul Vad (1927–   ), describing the "silent generation" of the 1950s, which had been too young to experience the exciting atmosphere of the German occupation and, therefore, felt that life had passed them by. The semi-documentary novel *Rubruk* (1972), about a thirteenth-century Franciscan monk, indicates Vad's increasing preoccupation with the imaginative; the trend reaches its climax in 1978 with *Kattens anatomi* (The Anatomy of a Cat), where the narrative structure is dissolved into numerous fantastic episodes and ambiguous dreams, in which Vad brilliantly manipulates time, place, and characters.

Anders Bodelsen

The most popular and productive of the neo-realists is Bodelsen (1937–   ), whose books are characterized by a detached narrative tone and great formal skill. These features emerge clearly for the first time in *Drivhuset* (The Greenhouse, 1965). Its fourteen mystery stories and detailed portrayal of the welfare state announce the two essential elements of the works that follow. The next collection of short stories, *Rama Sama* (1967; Eng. tr. 1973) also portrays the welfare society, but the author now penetrates with psychological analysis the journalistic and sociological details to the mystical connections underlying the material surface. The situations are no longer merely coincidental events, but disquieting conflicts that grow organically from the environment.

Bodelsen's novels of 1968—*Hændeligt uheld* (Unforeseen Contingency; Eng. tr. *Hit and Run, Run, Run*, 1970 and later; also as *One Down*, 1970) and *Tænk på et tal* (Eng. tr. *Think of a Number*, 1969; also as *The Silent Partner*, 1978)—continued in 1976 by *Pengene og livet* (Money and Life), cleverly combine the realistic novel with the thriller. *Frysepunktet* (1969; Eng. tr. *Freezing Point*, 1971) approaches science fiction. This book is a moral vision of the future. The major characters have themselves frozen and thawed several times in the course of the years, first to orient themselves in the future, then to flee this disappointing world, and finally to find death. Death, however, becomes only a deep sleep and thus a symbol for—but also a revolt against—the homelessness of the individual in the "brave new world."

In Bodelsen's writing—as in the work of most of the realistic authors—a change of viewpoint occurs at the close of the 1960s, resulting in an increased interest in the social mechanisms of society. *Bevisets stilling* (1973; Eng. tr. *Consider the Verdict*, 1976), based on a much-debated, contemporary criminal case, is the story of a taxi driver who has been wrongly accused of murder and who gradually becomes entangled in self-contradictions as he attempts to hide details of his personal life. When finally declared innocent, he is exhausted and dies of a heart attack. The novel thereby concludes in a violent accusation of the inhumanity of the judicial system.

The earlier short-story collection *Hjælp* (Help, 1971) contains stories about the human condition in modern society; in *Straus* (1971; Eng. tr. 1974), modern society is described as competitive and demanding success, leading to the ruin of a writer. In *Alt hvad du ønsker dig* (All That You Desire, 1974), however, the main character tries to escape society by using magic; the concluding moral of this modern tale is that reality has to be accepted as it is. This is demonstrated in *De gode tider* (The Good Times, 1977) and its sequel *År for år* (Year by Year, 1979) set in the 1960s and dealing rather didactically with the economic boom and the young generation's increasingly radical discussions about politics and economic systems. Because he deals with current themes and writes in a fluent journalistic style, Bodelsen is one of the most widely read authors in the Nordic countries.

Christian Kampmann

The prose of Kampmann (1939–) is also composed of critical studies of the middle-class way of life, but his psychological analysis is more acute. The novel *Sammen* (Together, 1967) consists of variations on the search for security and happiness in a middle-class Copenhagen environment. The encounter of two young people—their awkward and joyless love affair, and their separation—is precisely described in language reminiscent of illustrated magazines and is seen exclusively from the perspective of the characters. A similar, objective, somewhat hackneyed tone marks Kampmann's description in *Uden navn* (Without Name, 1969) of anonymous common people in a banal, failed marriage, and the attacks on their little world.

In *Nærved og næsten* (Near and Nearly, 1969), a major work of the 1960s, the social motif retreats behind existential problems: The work focuses on the attitudes of six married couples toward love, solitude, happiness, and death, and in particular on their despairing attempt to get close to other people. They all live comfortable and cultivated lives—but they are uncertain and unable to break out of their predetermined existence. Almost everything in this book is told from the standpoint of these people. However, in the second part, in which we follow young Georg through his childhood and youth, it is revealed that he was the narrator of the first part. The layers of reality flow into one another in a sophisticated manner, and the novel is elevated to the artistic orientation of the author himself as he relates to the characters and to reality.

Kampmann's moral stance is again clearly expressed in the short-story collection *Vi elsker mere* (We Love More, 1970), about people who are not able to bring their private moral concepts into harmony with the more liberal official attitude. The bitter truth is that freedom —rather, the belief that they have achieved freedom—estranges them from one another. They assume roles that lead them back into dependency.

Kampmann's most significant achievement is the cycle of novels about the greatness and decline of the Copenhagen bourgeoisie after World War II. The novels are *Visse hensyn* (Certain Considerations, 1973), *Faste forhold* (Firm Relationships, 1974), *Rene linjer* (Clean Lines, 1975), and *Andre måder* (Other Ways, 1975); they reflect the cold war era of the 1950s, the prosperity of the '60s, and finally the economic crisis of today. *Fornemmelser* (Feelings, 1977), *Videre trods alt* (Continue After All, 1979), and *I glimt* (In Glimpses, 1980) are autobiographical novels, descriptions of the social mechanisms that place the homosexual in a suppressed position. The skillful structure and superior character delineation of this documentary, and indeed of the entire body of Kampmann's work, confirm his position as one of the leading realistic authors of the Nordic countries.

Henrik Stangerup

Journalist, film-maker, and critic, Stangerup (1937–) deals primarily with problems caused by the modern welfare state. He broke through with the novel *Slangen i brystet* (The Snake in the Breast, 1969), in which the main character, a Danish journalist in Paris—a counterpart to Tom Kristensen's Ole Jastrau (see p. 200)—slowly disintegrates, owing to his lack of self-confidence. Description of the setting and satirical tone become more dominant in *Løgn over løgn*

(Lie upon Lie, 1971), which tells how the mass media exploit people and gradually become their caretakers. The title refers to the main character's hypocrisy, which is the result of his involvement in the mendacious world of the media; the novel becomes a sophisticated reflection on the author's attitude toward the very novel he has written. More direct are Stangerup's fierce attacks on the social and political development of society in *Manden der ville være skyldig* (The Man Who Wanted to Be Guilty, 1973), which combines the political novel with science fiction. Autobiographical features characterize *Fjenden i forkøbet* (Anticipating the Enemy, 1978), a novel in which Stangerup also attempts to describe the situation of modern humans in general.

Chapter *16*

Finnish Postwar Literature

The interwar depression struck Finland as hard as it did the other Nordic countries. Its effects were barely overcome when the nation was plunged into the devastations of World War II, a pawn of the superpowers. The Winter War against Russia under the command of Field Marshal Gustaf Mannerheim lasted from 1939 to 1940 and was continued from 1941 to 1944 with the support of Germany, which did not prevent Finland's defeat. This resulted in the loss of the province of Karelia, and the entire population of this province, 12% of the total population of Finland, had to relocate. Finland did manage to preserve her national identity; however, owing to her precarious geographical position it has had to carry on an extremely cautious politics of balance. Yet the country did join the United Nations and the Nordic Council in 1955, and became an associate member of the European Free Trade Association in 1961.

During the war years almost all literary activity ceased. The nationalistic spirit gave way to skepticism and disillusionment; the suffering of the nation seemed futile and its defeats resulted in a complete disintegration of values—heroic ideals and sacrifices were scoffed at. The war years cast their shadow over cultural life long after the fighting ended. The war, in particular the returning soldier, became the topic of numerous novels, of which very few have survived, among them Pentti Haanpää's *The Boots of Nine Men* (1945) and Väinö Linna's *The Unknown Soldier* (1954). The 1950s saw the emergence of a literature characterized by self-criticism, but on the whole authors shunned any participation in the debates on current political and social issues.

POETRY

Modernistic poetry did not gain a hold in Finland until the 1950s. These poets concentrated on ridding language of clichés and rhetoric in order to set rhythm and image free, and to make the diction more colloquial. (These tendencies appeared much earlier in Fenno-Swedish literature.) The leading force of this new poetry was Aila Meriluoto (1924–   ), who in the collection *Lasimaalaus* (The Stained Glass Picture, 1946) expressed her generation's sense of disillusionment and shattered ideals:

> We rise without a tomorrow,
> we rise mute, with hard eyes,
> with stone faces, with hearts of stone,
> like Our Lord of stone!
>
> Tr. Marrianne Forssblad

The major foreign impulses for Finnish postwar modernism came from the Swedish poets of the 1940s, especially Lindegren and Vennberg, and from Ezra Pound and T. S. Eliot, a selection of whose poems was translated in 1949. The influence of these foreign poets was combined with that of the native authors Hellaakoski, Mustapää, and Kailas, who exerted a considerable influence on the three transitional figures Lauri Viita, Juha Mannerkorpi, and Helvi Juvonen.

Lauri Viita

Viita (1916–65) managed in his successful first collection, *Betonimylläri* (A Miller of Concrete, 1947), to cope with the insecurity of the postwar years and the existence of clashing elements in life: Obstacles exist only to be overcome, and life has to be accepted even in its most frightening aspects. Viita's most important prose work, *Moreeni* (Moraine, 1950), based on childhood memories of the working-class milieu of Tampere (Tammerfors), is not a traditional social novel but a homage to the solid, hard-working, and anonymous human being on whom society is based. The collections from *Kukunor* (1949) to his latest poems in *Suutarikin suuri viisas* (A Shoemaker Is a Wise Man Too, 1961) demonstrate Viita's development from the more traditional to a modernism which is receptive to everyday concerns. Viita employs both spoken language and the old *Kalevala* meter in miniature poems in which the imagery and rhythm is highly original.

Juha Mannerkorpi

The poetry of Mannerkorpi (1915–   ) often focuses on metaphysial loneliness and pain as the fate of humans. These themes can be found in his earliest collection, *Lyhtypolku* (The Path of the Lanterns, 1946). Mannerkorpi is among the few Finnish writers who have views in common with French existentialism. The analysis of the human condition in a cruel and erratic world dominates the poetry volumes from the 1950s, his most significant short-story volume, *Sirkkeli* (The Circular Saw, 1956), and the novel *Jyrsijät* (The Rodents, 1958). In the 1960s Mannerkorpi translated Samuel Beckett; Beckett's influences on the novel *Matkalippuja kaikkiin juniin* (Tickets to All Trains, 1967) is obvious, whereas the French *nouveau roman* is the model for *Jälkikuva* (The Lingering Image, 1965). Although Mannerkorpi's early work constitutes an almost expressionistic postwar reaction, he stands today an isolated but recognized absurdist, who has consistently turned his back on the traditional psychological novel. In 1970 his novel *Suden-korento* (The Dragon-Fly), a menacing Kafkaesque nightmare about the individual's place in society, was awarded the national Finnish Literature Prize.

Helvi Juvonen

The religious outlook of interwar poet Uuno Kailas is carried on by Juvonen (1919–59), whose mysticism, originating in an experience of God's presence in nature, rapidly led her beyond the anguished, depressive poems of her first collection, *Kääpiöpuu* (The Dwarf Tree, 1949). Nature's miniature world, filled with warmth and innocence, which brings Juvonen to an understanding of the harmony existent in the universe, also forms the setting of the succeeding volumes. *Kuningas Kultatakki* (King Goldcoat, 1950) is her most experimental work; its religious poems evince the influence of the Bible and Finnish hymns, an influence also present in *Kalliopohja* (Bedrock, 1955). The intense, tightly composed texts of *Pohjajäätä* (Deep Ice, 1952) are continuations of Kailas's and Manninen's laconic style; in *Päivästä päivään* (From Day to Day, 1954) Juvonen uses a simple folksong-like style. In all of her writings she pursues the same themes: the hatred and lack of trust between humans, the importance of religious experience.

Much of Juvonen's poetry is in a traditional style, but her symbolic language is clearly modern, her imagery autonomous, making her work the most important transitional link to the modernism of the 1950s.

Eeva-Liisa Manner

The breakthrough of modernism occurred with the collection *Tämä matka* (This Journey, 1956) by Manner (1921–   ), a severe critique of overintellectualized modern civilization. It opens with a description of a state of isolation and alienation from everything natural, after which the poet, going back to the Cambrian geological period, retells the history of life to establish coherence between the past and the present. Loneliness is also the backdrop for the actions of the characters in Manner's verse play *Eros ja psykhe* (Eros and Psyche, 1959) and drama *Uuden vuoden yö* (New Year's Night, 1965). The poet sees a way out of the desolation in the experience of the solidarity of all things—not in a Christian way, like Juvonen's, but in a pantheistic one. This gradually leads her to a meditative attitude colored by ancient Chinese philosophy. The sources for Manner's next poetry collection, *Orfiset laulut* (Orphic Songs, 1960), a journey into the land of myth and the subconscious, include the Book of Revelation, medieval troubadour poetry, and astrology. She returns to Chinese models in *Niin vaihtuivat vuoden ajat* (So the Seasons Changed, 1964), meditative nature poems in a simple, concise style, contrasting with the image-filled, associative, and spontaneously flowing stanzas of *This Journey*. Manner discovered Spain as a social reality in *Kirjoitettu kivi* (The Written Stone, 1966) and, as a result, her style became more proselike, more distinctly colloquial. *Fahrenheit 121* (1968) mentions Vietnam and the Arab-Israeli conflict, but is actually an attempt to create an all-embracing metaphysical synthesis in a language that follows musical structures. The novel *Varokaa, voittajat* (Watch Out, Conqueror, 1972), a report on poverty and the resulting revolutionary mentality related in a lyrical style, bears witness to Manner's continued interest in Spain. Her poetry up to the 1970s is introspective and characterized by a purely philosophical and imaginative dream atmosphere. A complete change in style and outlook is evident in the playful work *Kamala kissa* (The Terrible Cat, 1976), influenced by T. S. Eliot's *Old Possum's Book of Practical Cats*, in which the animal's behavior humorously reflects that of human beings: *Kuolleet vedet* (Dead Waters, 1977) marks a return to the mystical perspectives of Manner's earlier poetry collections, demonstrating contemporary human estrangement from the natural.

Paavo Haavikko

Haavikko (1931–   ), the second modernistic poet of stature in the 1950s, following his first collection, *Tiet etäisyyksiin* (The Roads

That Lead Far Away, 1951), gradually consolidated his position through linguistic virtuosity, surprising juxtapositions of images and intense rhythmic expressions. His second collection is *Tuuliöinä* (In Windy Nights, 1953), the wind being the central symbol of restlessness in his writing. No one has written of the insecurity and relativism of human life more convincingly than Haavikko: "Every house is built by many but never finished / and history and mythical events are told again and again." In his poems Haavikko tends to use mythical and historical material, which reaches beyond the present far into the future. In his early work, history was colored by an uncommitted aloof romanticism; a social and political approach became clearer in *Synnyinmaa* (The Fatherland, 1955) and *Lehdet lehtiä* (Leaves Are Leaves, 1958), which anticipated the critical attitudes of the 1960s, as well as of Haavikko's own later poetry. In addition to political and social concerns he deals with the creative process itself. The confession of 1955, "Poetry, oh poetry, is my only fatherland, I speak of her, / she is my beloved who burst into song," also characterizes *Talvipalatsi* (The Winter Palace, 1959), "a journey through language," a highly sophisticated metapoetic tour de force. Haavikko is also highly productive as a dramatist and published in 1978 *Näytelmät* (Plays), a collection of his twelve works for the stage. In the plays *Münchhausen* (1960) and *Nuket* (The Puppets, 1960), in which Gogol's characters come to life and discuss matters with their creator, Haavikko approaches the theater of the absurd. In his prose, on the other hand, he treats a number of social and political issues, conveying a pessimistic view of a world filled with insignificant individuals and meaningless actions. *Yksityisiä asioita* (Private Matters, 1960) tells of a man who experiences the political events of 1918 only as an occasion for profitable business deals. *Toinen taivas ja maa* (Another Heaven and Earth, 1961) is about the breakup of a marriage and a woman driven to suicide, and *Vuodet* (The Years, 1962) draws a sharp and concise portrait of an alcoholic vagabond.

Puut, kaikki heidän vihreytensä (The Trees, All Their Greenness, 1966), a poetry collection characterized by intellectually progressive and politically conservative viewpoints, elaborated in an analysis of human power in the abstract, appeared in 1966. Criticism of fascism is the unifying element in the collection *Neljätoista hallitsijaa* (Fourteen Rulers, 1970), an attitude that also informs *Puhua, vastata, opettaa* (Speak, Answer, Learn, 1972), which is concerned with the destruction of the self in a conformist world. On the other hand, in *Kaksikymmentä ja yksi* (Twenty and One, 1974) Haavikko's inspiration was the *Kalevala*, and he alternated between modernistic language and the techniques of folk poetry. *Viiniä kirjoitusta* (Wine, Writing, 1976) is a collection of elegant and easily accessible poems about the inextricably interwoven motifs of life and death—an example of this stylistically innovative author's constant experimentation.

Lasse Heikkilä

A similar restlessness is reflected in the fragmentary poems of Heikkilä (1925–61). He published six volumes between his first collection, *Miekkalintu* (The Sword Bird, 1949), influenced by the Swedish poets of the 1940s, and his last work *Terra Mariana* (1959). The latter swings from aggressive intellectualism to religious meditation, influenced by Catholicism, occasionally leaning toward mysticism—an expression of the poet's search for stability.

Lassi Nummi

Far more conscious of poetic structure is Nummi (1928–). His ironic and reflective poetry and his melodious, romantic nature poems in the major volumes *Taivaan ja maan merkit* (The Signs of Heaven and Earth, 1956) and *Keskipäivä, delta* (Noon, Delta, 1967) are protests against the occasionally hermetic, factual, and concise poetry of the 1950s. Also, Nummi's latest poetry collection *Lähdössä tänään* (Departing Today, 1977) is characterized by traditional diction and deals with the death of a loved one and elaborate travel impressions of southern Europe.

Tuomas Anhava

A prominent representative of the hermetic, factual, and concise poetry of the 1950s is Anhava (1927–), whose poetry bears the marked influence of Eliot and Pound, from the first volume, *Runoja* (Poems, 1953) to *36 runoja* (36 Poems, 1958). In *Runoja 1961* (Poems, 1961) and *Kuudes kirja* (The Sixth Book, 1966), characterized by resignation in the face of an evil world, simplicity and conciseness is carried even further, now influenced by Japanese *haiku* poetry which Anhava has translated. Like Haavikko, Anhava is a skeptic: "I praise the uncertainty / and the courage / to evade the past and the subconscious." With his stern demand for quality, his respect for "le mot propre," Anhava became an example for a whole generation of Finnish poets.

Pentti Saarikoski

The poetry of the 1960s developed toward a clear political com-

mitment which eventually found expression in realistic everyday poetry. Both trends were introduced by Saarikoski (1937–), whose
writing reflects the entire literature of this and the following decade.
His poetry collections, *Maailmasta* (About the World, 1961) and *Mitä
tapahtuu todella?* (What Is Really Happening? 1962) comment directly on contemporary political events. Saarikoski is always skeptical,
even in his poems that openly embrace communism. It is characteristic that disorder and the threat of chaos are dominant themes in the
volume *Kuljen missä kuljen* (I Walk Where I Walk, 1965). His aversion
to absolute viewpoints and ideological authoritarianism—a stand parallel to that of the "third position" among Swedish writers—leads to
resignation and, surprisingly enough, to a number of miniature poems
about happy and unhappy love in *Laululta pois* (Away by Song by
Song, 1966) and *En soisi sen päättyvän* (I Wish It Would Not End,
1968).

Saarikoski's prose of this period is not as artistically significant as
his poetry. His first novel, *Ovat muistojemme lehdet kuolleet* (Dead
Are the Leaves of Our Memories, 1964), is a series of impressions
of and conversations in contemporary Helsinki, whereas both *Aika
Prahassa* (The Time in Prague, 1967) and *Kirje vaimolleni* (A Letter
to My Wife, 1968) are interior monologues describing brief stays in
Prague and Dublin. In the 1970s it became clear that Saarikoski no
longer wanted to commit himself politically. Symptomatic are his
translation activities—from Homer to James Joyce—and the poetry
volume *Alue* (The Area, 1973) in which he writes about his family,
his farm and its surroundings, a thoroughly private sphere. Linguistically this development is reflected in a change from an aphoristic to
a more supple, lyrical diction. The tension between Saarikoski's skepticism, which in the poetry collection *Tanssilattia vuorella* (The
Dancing-Floor on the Mountain, 1977) leads him to depict the contemporary world as a fossilized labyrinth, and his need to experience
faith and life as meaningful makes him the most agile of the younger
Finnish writers and the one with the widest scope.

Väinö Kirstinä

The work of Kirstinä (1936–), the second major lyrical poet of
the 1960s, is linguistically far more advanced than Saarikoski's, and
it is now clear that he is the most daring experimenter of the decade.
He made his debut in 1961 with *Lakeus* (The Plain), which employs
the exclusive, academic imagery of the 1950s. In *Puhetta* (Talk, 1963)
Kirstinä does a complete reversal, using obscene phrases, correct and
incorrect quotations, far-fetched associations, and excerpts from the

Helsinki telephone directory, in dadaist word series and sound combinations, pop art, and concrete poetry—expressions of the poet's determination not to stagnate in rigid attitudes. Similar is Kirstinä's collection *Luonnollinen tanssi* (The Natural Dance, 1965), containing a series of prose poems about the nuclear threat—a criticism of the entire atomic age, of a self-destructive, violent, and commercial civilization depicted in surrealistic visions. Kirstinä continued his protest against consumer society in his next volume, *Pitkän tähtäyksen LSD-suunnitelma* (Long-Range LSD Planning, 1967), which is structured in accordance with the cataloging system of public libraries. He seems to have found an escape in the secluded, idyllic life in nature, depicted with desperate humor in *Talo maalla* (A House in the Country, 1969), humor which in *Säännöstelty eutanasia* (Prescribed Euthanasia, 1973) emerges with increasing clarity as the poet's only weapon against a world so absurd that everyone must laugh to remain sane. In *Elämä ilman sijaista* (Life without a Substitute, 1977) Kirstinä focuses directly on the negative effects of technological progress depicting everyday life against the background of the industrialized city of Tampere (Tammerfors).

PROSE

The innovativeness so characteristic of Finnish postwar poetry is also true of the postwar prose, although it manifests itself at a slower pace.

Jorma Korpela

One of the first writers to deviate from traditional patterns was Korpela (1910–64). His participation in the war led him to speculate about the problems of suffering, guilt, and atonement, themes that point to Dostoevsky as Korpela's model. The basic ideas of his first work, *Martinmaa, mieshenkilö* (A Man Called Martinmaa, 1948), are characteristic of his work: A well-intentioned idealist tries to help people but only makes things worse, since he knows neither himself nor his motives. In *Tohtori Finckelman* (Doctor Finckelman, 1952) Korpela's most decisive break with traditional prose, the idealist has developed into a dangerous superman who terrorizes his surroundings and has to pay dearly for his power by completely losing contact with reality. In succeeding books Korpela used a more simple technique, but continued his speculations on the human abuse of power, now set in a war milieu. *Tunnustus* (The Confession, 1960) deals with the self-reproach of an officer who deliberately caused the death of a subordinate. Here, and in *Känttervatio* (The Outpost, 1964), the author examines the moral problems created by war from the point of view of the individual who feels responsibility for his or her actions. A religious sentiment now breaks through, leading to the biblical commandment of love and brotherhood. Besides this message Korpela's books reflect the destruction of a harmonious view of humankind, as well as depersonalization and human complexity, unpredictability, and greed for power.

Väinö Linna

The remaining postwar prose is primarily distinguished by its factual, concise style. War is generally seen as a personal experience, leading to a perception of the relativity of all values. Even when the narrative technique is realistic, as in the war novel by Linna (1920–), *Tuntematon sotilas* (1954; Eng. tr. *The Unknown Soldier*, 1957 and later), this relativity is present. Linna follows the destiny of a single platoon whose actions at the front are rendered in a vivid, realistic style uninfluenced by nationalistic myths. The novel became an immediate sensation; it sold in unprecedented numbers, was translated into several languages, and caused violent polemics in the press. Indeed, Linna strips war of its pathos, but his work is neither pacifistic nor defeatist. On the contrary, it contains a good dose of hero-worship, which places it in the tradition of J. L. Runeberg's *The Tales of Ensign Stål* (1848–60). Realism and humor are also the main elements in Linna's next work, the trilogy *Täällä Pohjantähden alla* (Here under the Polar Star, 1959-62). The author deals with the Civil War of 1918, speaking on behalf of the vanquished. Dramatic events are related from the point of view of the poorest people in a small western Finnish village and are based on Tolstoy's philosophy of history that the common people, not those in power, decide its course. Linna's style is simple. As in *The Unknown Soldier*, the reader is captivated by the lively dialogue and the masterful depictions of the mass scenes, which confirm Linna's position as a great epic narrator in the tradition of Kivi, Kianto, and Sillanpää.

Veijo Meri

Whereas Linna represents a more traditional trend within modern Finnish prose, Meri (1928–), more experimental, follows in the steps of Korpela. For Meri also the war and the military are basic themes. Although he was too young to take part in the fighting, he grew up the son of a noncommissioned officer in garrison towns, a background indirectly reflected in the novel *Irralliset* (The Rootless,

1959) and more directly in *Kersantin poika* (The Soldier's Boy, 1971). Meri often contrasts war's irrationality with the disciplined regimentation of military life. Both the reactions of the soldier and the events themselves become absurd; there is no normal relationship between cause and effect. This is demonstrated again in Meri's best-known novel, *Manillaköysi* (1957; Eng. tr. *The Manilla Rope*, 1967). The hero, Joose, smuggles home a piece of rope on his leave, enduring nightmarish trials and risking his life without understanding the motivations for his actions. Meri's soldiers are just as unwilling to comply with military rules as Linna's. Thus it is a deserter who is the main character in *Sujut* (Quits, 1961), a novel about the Russian military breakthrough in 1944. But Meri's characters lack the inner stability, which, after all, makes Linna's soldiers act correctly in decisive situations. They are overwhelmed by life's absurdity: for example, the chauffeur in *Everstin autonkuljettaja* (The Colonel's Driver, 1966), who has to drive back through half of Finland to pick up the briefcase his colonel has forgotten. The short-story collection *Tilanteita* (Situation, 1962) and the novels *Peiliin piirretty nainen* (The Woman in the Mirror, 1963) and *Suku* (The Family, 1968) are among Meri's few works with civilian subjects, showing him to be an outstanding anecdotal observer of the urban milieu.

Meri's prose, including the two short-story collections from 1972, *Leiri* (The Camp) and *Morsiamen sisar* (The Sister of the Bride), is mainly dialogue. From this stems his interest in drama as a mode of expression. Besides working as a playwright for radio and television, he has published three volumes of dramas since the mid-1960s; *Sotamies Jokisen vihkiloma* (The Marriage Leave of Private Jokinen, 1965) and the biographical *Aleksis Kivi* (1974) are the best known. Today Meri's works are regarded as classics of Finnish literature. In 1975 a four-volume selection of his works was published, including a number of previously unpublished short stories, and in 1976 he surprised his readers with a poetry collection, *Mielen lähtölaskenta* (The Mind's Countdown), containing poems written over many years.

Meri's realization that the riddles of the human mind cannot be explained makes him an objective recorder of reality; rather than analyzing his characters psychologically, he confines himself to describing events in their lives and their reactions to these occurrences.

Antti Hyry

The most typical representative of this purely factual style is Hyry (1931–), whose writing has been compared to the objective recital of facts in the works of Robbe-Grillet and the French *nouveau roman*.

Thus *Maailman laita* (The Edge of the World, 1967) simply describes a fishing trip in which a boat drifts away but is recovered the next day. Characteristic of this novel and of the short-story collection *Junamatkan kuvaus* (A Description of a Journey by Train, 1962) is Hyry's commitment to observable and concrete reality, with an emphasis on basic facts, to which his catalog-like, terse style is well suited. Childhood occupies a central place in his books. Directly autobiographical are *Kotona* (At Home, 1960), *Alakoulu* (The Lower Grades, 1965), and *Isä ja poika* (Father and Son, 1971), the setting of which is an untouched northern Finnish village. Hyry's view of life, which is distinctly religious, is personified by Niilo in the novel *Kevättä ja syksyä* (Spring and Fall, 1958), who experiences childhood as a paradise, a stage of life marked by the spontaneous experiencing of God and the world, a capacity that is lost in the sterile materialistic world of adults.

Pentti Holappa

Holappa (1927–   ) has a consciously French orientation. He lived for a long time in Paris and published a volume of excellent essays on modern French literature. Holappa made his debut as a poet in the 1950s and published three collections during this decade. Their somber, heavy imagery reflects the ambiguity of life, its undercurrents of superficial spirit of his time, an attitude which is also expressed in the collection *Viisikymmentäkaksi: Runoja* (Fifty-Two: Poems, 1979). As a prose writer, Holappa—like his Danish colleague Svend Åge Madsen—also focuses on the deceitfulness of phenomena. In the novel *Tinaa* (Tin, 1961) the same story is told in different ways to mislead the reader. In *Yksinäiset* (Alone, 1954) and *Perillisen ominaisuudet* (The Qualities of an Heir, 1963) reality is dissolved in alternative possible interpretations.

Eeva Joenpelto

The same critique of soulless, modern life, an attitude common among Finnish writers of the 1950s, characterizes the novels of Joenpelto (1921–   ), written in a concise, matter-of-fact style that avoids emotional overtones and authorial intrusion. She became recognized with her third novel, *Johannes vain* (Only Johannes, 1952), the central problem of which is the relation between material and spiritual values. Similar conflicts and complex ethical problems dominate Joenpelto's later works. In her mature novels, *Neito kulkee vetten päällä* (The Maid Is Walking on the Water, 1955) and *Kipinöivät vuodet* (The Sparkling Years, 1961) the action takes place on a farm located between an expanding urban area and a disappearing rural village. To the conflict between old and new life-styles is added—as usual in Joenpelto's writing—the generation gap. In her most important work of the 1960s, *Ritari metsien pimennosta* (The Knight from the Dark Forests, 1966), she paints a detailed portrait of an authoritarian public official who dedicates his life to Finnish-Russian relations and through whom a number of historically decisive events are filtered. This novel points toward the renewal of Joenpelto's work manifest in *Vatää kaikista ovista* (There Is a Draft from Every Door, 1974) and *Kuin kekäle kedessä* (Like Holding a Red-Hot Coal, 1976), and *Vetää kaikista ovista* (Rainy Salty Water, 1978), marked by psychologically varied character portrayals and a dramatic plot that takes place at the beginning of Finland's struggle for independence, when the country was divided into two camps. Underlying the individuals and their conflicts are universal mechanisms which direct the historical process; thus the novels are endowed with a mixture of objectivity and empathy reminiscent of Linna's work.

Paavo Rintala

Standing outside all literary groups is Rintala (1930–), in whose prose all the various trends of the 1950s are present. One of the most productive authors of the postwar period and its strongest moralist, Rintala dealt with religious and moral issues. He shared with Hyry the northern Finnish milieu and the view that urban humans were alienated —a religiously based judgment on our civilization. In his second novel, *Rikas ja köyhä* (The Rich and the Poor, 1955), he demonstrates the moral necessity of making the choice between spiritual and material values—a theme indicated by the title. Rintala observes the development of his own generation in the novels *Pojat* (The Boys, 1958) and *Pikkuvirkamiehen kuolema* (The Death of a Small Official, 1959) concerned with humans stagnating in a contemporary world of darkness and lies.

Rintala's books also include national self-criticism. In his much disputed trilogy, *Mummoni ja Mannerheim* (Grandmother and Mannerheim, 1960-62), Rintala attempts to dismiss the tenacious myths about Finland's national heroes during the Civil War and World War II; however, the major theme is the maturing of humans. Two human destinies are contrasted, originating in completely different social classes, but attaining an identical insight into the true values of life. Even stronger debate was aroused by *Sissiluutnantti* (1963, The Lieutenant of the Commandos; Eng. tr. *The Long Distance Patrol*,

1967) in which the unvarnished picture of the horrors of war is supported by the author's moral indignation, although he, no more than Linna, was a pacifist. The war is also the theme of *Sotilaiden äänet* (Soldier Voices, 1966), *Sodan ja rauhan äänet* (The Voices of the War and the Peace, 1967), and *Napapiirin äänet* (Voices from the Polar Circle, 1969), novels based on fragmentary but authentic interview material. In addition, Rintala put together a documentary about the siege of Leningrad during World War II, *Leningradin kohtalosinfonia* (Leningrad's Symphony of Fate, 1968), and wrote other accounts of major crises of the twentieth century, among these the first Nordic novels dealing exclusively with the Vietnam War, *Vietnamin kurjet* (The Cranes from Vietnam, 1971) and *Romeo ja Julia häränvuonna* (Romeo and Juliet in the Year of the Bull, 1974). This documentary trend, of which Rintala is the most talented representative in Finland, is continued with the novels *Kesäkuu 44* (June 44, 1974), *Se toinen Lili Marleen* (The Other Lili Marleen, 1975), and *Nahkapeitturien linjalla* (The Tanners' Line, 1976), attempts to reevaluate the events at the Finnish-Russian front during World War II.

Chapter 17

Fenno-Swedish Postwar Literature

In Fenno-Swedish literature the 1930s and '40s were a period of stagnation. The main contributions were made by the pioneers of the so-called Fenno-Swedish modernism (see p. 227), who now began to play an important role in the literary renewal of the other Nordic countries, especially Sweden. Among the few important new writers were the poet Ralf Parland and the prose writer Tito Colliander.

Ralf Parland

The first collection by Parland (1914–), *Avstånd* (Distance, 1938), was clearly influenced by Björling and Diktonius. Parland shared with Diktonius an active interest in music, and the poetry of the succeeding volumes is increasingly marked by rhythmic and thematic structures. The collections *Relief* (1950), *Eolita* (1956), and *Zodiaken* (The Zodiac, 1961) demonstrate Parland's pessimistic view of the modern world threatened by the atom bomb, expressed in cosmic images inspired by both modern science and oriental mysticism and poetry. The feeling of doom increases in the short-story volumes *Eros och elektronerna* (Eros and the Electrons, 1953) and *En apa for till himmelen* (A Monkey Went to Heaven, 1961)—satirical visions of the future written in the spirit of George Orwell. A further collection of short stories, *Regnbågens död* (The Death of the Rainbow) was published in 1970.

Tito Colliander

Colliander (1904–) is the first major representative of modern Fenno-Swedish prose. The son of a Finnish officer serving in the Russian army in St. Petersburg, he retained both his knowledge of the Russian language and an interest in Czarist Russia, tending to deal primarily with Russian emigrants living in Finland. A decisive literary influence was Dostoevsky. Early on Colliander was drawn to the Greek-Orthodox Church, and after his conversion he published several theological and confessional works. In the novels *Korståget* (The Crusade, 1937), set in Estonia, and *Förbarma dig* (Have Mercy, 1939), he penetrated the psychology of suffering, guilt, and atonement. The conflict between a desire for degradation and a longing for salvation is a basic theme, recurring in *Bliv till* (Come into Being, 1945). After having realized his Christian vocation in the 1950s, through teaching and religious writing, Colliander returned to belles lettres at the close of the decade with a poetry collection, *Glädjes möte* (The Meeting with Joy, 1957) and *Vi som är kvar* (We Who Are Left, 1959), a novel that manifests his continual dialogue with the problems of guilt. Of greater artistic quality is Colliander's eight-volume series of memoirs of 1964–73.

Eva Wichman

Wichman (1908–75) wrote both poetry and prose. Her breakthrough work, *Molnet såg mig* (The Cloud Saw Me, 1942), contains original and perceptive observations of nature, as well as satirical stories, mainly about middle-class pettiness. A distinct change occurs in the two short stories *Där vi går* (Where We Go, 1949). In these stories Wichman's spiritual attitude is more clearly defined and is directed toward specific social issues. Similarly, her poetry collections from the 1950s signaled a shift from the self-centeredness of the first volume of lyrics, *Ormöga* (Snake-Eye, 1946), to a radical, political commitment, as reflected in *Dikt i dag* (Poetry Today, 1951), and *De levande* (Those Who Live, 1954), which presents a simplistic communist ideology. A more balanced approach is discernible in the 1960s: The collections *Dikter* (Poems, 1960) and *Det sker med ens* (It Happens Suddenly, 1964) to some degree mark a return to Wichman's previous, exuberant but still highly disciplined poetic ambiguity and intense symbolic art, an expression of the author's experience of the tension-filled mystery of existence.

Solveig von Schoultz

Von Schoultz (1907–) is in many respects Eva Wichman's complete opposite. In place of a mystical basic experience she is guided by the instinctive cultivation of immediate reality; in contrast with Wich-

man's continuous striving for clarity and a form purged of any artificial effects, she employs epic, highly imaginative diction. This is evident in the collections *Min timme* (My Hour, 1940) and *Eko av ett rop*
(The Echo of a Call, 1945), in which the metaphors are clearly influenced by Karin Boye's poetry. In the later volumes, *Nätet* (The Net,
1956) and *Sänk ditt ljus* (Dim Your Light, 1963), von Schoultz strove
for a tighter, more experimental form, sustained by the everpresent
bitter realization of life's impermanence. The tensions of everyday life
also occupy her as a prose writer. In *De sju dagarna* (The Seven Days,
1942) and *Ingenting ovanligt* (Nothing Unusual, 1947) von Schoultz
analyses sensitive children and young people who must adjust to the
adult world; the acuity of her portraits matches that of her Danish
contemporary, H. C. Branner. In *Närmare någon* (Closer to Somebody,
1951) and *Även dina kameler* (Your Camels Also, 1965) she portrays
the conscious and unconscious aspects of women's minds. With the
exception of the philosophical poetry volume *De fyra flöjtspelarna*
(The Four Flutists, 1975), von Schoultz has continued to devote herself to prose. Most of the short stories of *Rymdbruden* (The Space
Bride, 1970) deal with the generation gap, whereas in *Där står du*
(There You Stand, 1973) she returns to her childhood in a fascinating
description of a young girl's strict family background and her confrontation with the more liberal life-styles of her friends. The short stories
of 1976, *Somliga mornar* (Some Mornings), are von Schoultz's contribution to recent Nordic feminist literature, posing the question: How
can a woman free herself from her purely physical ties to her child and
thereby also to the man who is the father of the child?

Bo Carpelan

Not until Carpelan (1926–) did Fenno-Swedish poets succeed in
going beyond the prewar traditions. In his early poetry collections,
Som en dunkel värme (Like a Dark Warmth, 1946), *Du mörka över-
levande* (Your Dark Survivor, 1947), and *Variationer* (Variations, 1950),
Carpelan employed elements from the Swedish poetry of the 1940s:
the dense, heavy imagery and pessimism typical of this decade. But
the basis of his work was the same as that of his contemporary Finnish
colleagues: the realization that human existence offered no stability,
that it was chaotic. The keynote is melancholy. The landscape of the
soul that Carpelan depicts is silent and dark, overshadowed by sadness and a consciousness of death: "Silence becomes dimmed and
earth is as close as a fleeting mist." *Objekt för ord* (An Object for
Words, 1954) clearly marked a change in Carpelan's position. He be-

gan to express more openness and confidence—reality regained its concreteness, which is particularly evident in the love poems. In *Landskapets förvandlingar* (The Transformations of the Landscape, 1957) and *Den svala dagen* (The Cool Day, 1961) the earlier spiritual landscapes become real. Carpelan abandons the private sphere, and simultaneously a change from "mysticism of words to mysticism of reality" takes place (Rabbe Enckell). The collection *Gården* (The Yard, 1969) revolves around an apartment complex and its inhabitants, seen through the eyes of a child. Out of the sharply focused portraits grows a total vision of humankind in all its frailty and debasement as well as its dignity. At the same time, Carpelan's language becomes more concrete and concise, developing into a rare formal mastery in his recent collections, *Källan* (The Spring, 1973) and *I de mörka rummen, i de ljusa* (In the Dark Rooms, in the Bright Ones, 1976).

Göran Stenius and Oscar Parland

Similar spiritual experiences form the basis of the novel *Klockorna i Rom* (1955; Eng. tr. *The Bells of Rome*, 1961) by Stenius (1909–   ), relating the story of his conversion to Catholicism. It is regarded as the best religious novel written in Finland after World War II. His major work, however, is the historical novel *Hungergropen* (The Hunger Pit, 1944), which describes life in Karelia during the war of 1808–09 (see p. 65); the novel is filled with color and atmosphere, as well as with drama and picturesque characters. Karelia is also the setting of the autobiographical novels by Oscar Parland (1912–   ), *Den förtrollade vägen* (The Enchanted Road, 1953) and *Tjurens år* (The Years of the Bull, 1962), masterful descriptions of the magic way in which a child experiences reality.

Walentin Chorell

Psychological analysis predominates in the work of Chorell (1912–   ). His early novels, *Calibans dag* (Caliban's Day, 1948), *Blindtrappan* (The Secret Stairs, 1949), and *Intim journal* (A Personal Diary, 1951) depict life as anguished, reminiscent of much contemporary Swedish poetry. Lighter in tone is the trilogy about *Miriam* (1954–58), which tells of a young woman who never loses courage or strength despite severe personal crises. As a playwright for the stage and for radio and television Chorell is famous in the Nordic countries. A central theme is treated in the play *Fabian öppnar portarna* (Fabian Opens the Gates, 1949): the conflict between the wealthy and the poor, between a conventional collective society and the lonesome rebel. *Madame* (1956) reveals the reactions of a former prima donna to aging and death, while *Systrarna* (1956; Eng. tr. *The Sisters*, 1971) and *Kattorna* (The Cats, 1961) are studies in erotic psychology. Usually Chorell's plays do not have a social message; rather, they are studies of the anxiety and unavoidable catastrophe of the individual. The existential drama of exceptional human beings, their conflicts with themselves and their surroundings, is also dealt with in Chorell's later novels. *Grodan* (The Frog, 1966) tells of a slightly handicapped girl at a day-care center, who causes consternation and chaos in other people's lives. In *Äggskalet* (The Egg Shell, 1972), *Knappen* (The Button, 1974), and *Livstycket* (A Piece of Life, 1976) Chorell depicts two young men in Helsingfors who experience the pressures of unsympathetic surroundings.

Tove Jansson

Jansson (1914–), artist and author of children's books, gained international fame with her stories about the Mumin trolls, e.g., *Kometjakten* (1947; Eng. tr. *Comet in Moominland*, 1951), *Muminpappans bravader* (1950; Eng. tr. *The Exploits of Moominpappa*, 1952 and later), *Trollvinter* (1957; Eng. tr. *Moominland Midwinter*, 1967), and *Sent i november* (1970; Eng. tr. *Moominvalley in November*, 1971). The stories also ran as serials in the daily newspapers and were presented as a television series. The world of these books, which have many adult readers, is a fairy-tale world often paralleling the world of the Fenno-Swedish upper class, a main motif being how evil can be overcome. In addition to her memoirs, *Bildhuggarens dotter* (1968; Eng. tr. *Sculptor's Daughter*, 1969), and *Sommarboken* (1972; Eng. tr. *The Summer Book*, 1975 and later), the best introduction to the Mumin world, Jansson wrote an outstanding novel about Florida, *Solstaden* (1974; Eng. tr. *Sun City*, 1976) dealing both with the loneliness of retired people in the midst of a hectic social life and with the young whose exuberant joy in life is based on their Christian faith.

Anna Bondestam

Bondestam (1907–) treats of advancing industrialization and the class struggle in her novels *Vägen till staden* (The Road to the City, 1957) and *Stadens bröd* (The Bread of the City, 1960), which are devoid of propaganda.

Leo Ågren

By contrast, the political novels by Ågren (1928–) anticipate social criticism after 1960. Like Lo-Johansson, Fridegård, and the other Swedish proletarian authors, Ågren experienced poverty; his description of the realities of oppression and privation, though strongly indignant, often have great artistic value. Ågren first succeeded with the trilogy *Kungsådern* (The Mainstream, 1957), *När gudarna dör* (When the Gods Die, 1959), and *Fädrens blod* (Ancestral Blood, 1961). Ågren tells the story of the peasant family Gersson from 1700 to the Civil War, in a very dramatic and concise fashion. The same conciseness marks the prose sketches of *Ballad* (A Ballad, 1962), which focuses with eruptive poetic force on the brutal oppression of religious freedom.

Jörn Donner

Political commitment also characterizes the career of Donner (1933–), leftist writer, critic, and film director, after he broke with his upper-middle-class milieu in the 1950s. Donner's novels of that decade are unconvincing, almost hysterical attacks on the degenerate values of the Helsingfors bourgeoisie. Of much higher quality are his travel books, *Rapport från Berlin* (Report from Berlin, 1958) and *Rapport från Donau* (Report from the Danube, 1962). *På ett sjukhus* (At a Hospital, 1960) consists of diary entries from his life as a conscientious objector. All three of these works are early contributions to the Nordic documentary. However, the matter-of-factness of these books is not matched in *Den nya boken om vårt land* (The New Book about Our Country, 1967), a critical but highly imprecise prediction of the future of Finland. In 1974 Donner published the first of a twelve-volume series, a Finnish counterpart to Thomas Mann's *Buddenbrooks* novel, *Nu måste du* (Now You Have To), dominated by dreary, lengthy analyses and reflections lacking any convincing character delineation. The same faults mark the sequels of 1976 and 1978, *Angelas krig* (Angela's War) and *Jakob och friheten* (Jakob and Freedom).

Christer Kihlman

Like Donner, Kihlman (1930–) is a strong critic of the social conventions of Finnish society. He made his debut with a book of poems, *Rummen vid havet* (The Rooms by the Sea), in 1951. His breakthrough came in 1960 with the novel *Se upp salige!* (Pay Heed, O Blest!), a satirical description of a small town and its self-centered Fenno-Swedish bougeoisie, weighed down by complex and occasionally diffuse psychological commentary delivered in stream-of-consciousness fashion. These same elements mark Kihlman's second novel, *Den blå modern* (The Blue Mother, 1963), which follows two brothers through childhood, revealing what is hidden beneath their superficial respectability. The novel is filled with explosive human emotions and transgresses the bounds of all of the period's sexual taboos. Kihlman's third novel, *Madeleine* (1965), follows one of the brothers through marital and alcoholic crises. The author conveys the latter's neurotic attitudes and self-analyses in a masterfully written interior monologue and in the sophisticated dialogue between the brother and his wife, which makes this Kihlman's most mature and balanced work thus far. He does not reach the same level in *Människan som skalv* (Man Who Tottered, 1971), a novel about alcoholic and sexual problems. But *Dyre prins* (Dearly Beloved Prince, 1975), both a humorous satire on the Finnish nouveau riche after World War II and a penetrating Dostoevskian psychological portrait, is a masterpiece of Nordic literature. This novel is one of the numerous analyses of barbaric Western men of power—from Scott Fitzgerald's *The Great Gatsby*, through Max Frisch's *Homo Faber*, to Klaus Rifbjerg's *The Operalover.*

Anders Cleve

The same intensity and commitment to his subject characterizes Cleve (1937-   ). He has been influenced primarily by Colliander, specifically by Colliander's attraction to the Greek Orthodox Church and his glowing prose style. Cleve first published two volumes of poetry, *Dagen* (The Day, 1955) and *Det bara ansiktet* (The Bare Face, 1956), and a book of short stories, *Gatstenar* (The Pavement, 1959). Both in this work and in the novel *Vit eld* (White Fire, 1962), the first volume of a trilogy, Helsingfors plays a major role. Physical sensations are continuously registered with brutal closeness and stunning effect. The milieu is the dreary outskirts of the working-class districts, wretched housing and back-street taverns, where the language is slangy and vulgar. Here, as in the sequels, *Påskägget* (The Easter Egg, 1966) and *Labyrint* (Labyrinth, 1971), Cleve employs diffuse, occasionally fragmentary language, through which he attempts to express the chaos from which he is trying to escape; the battle ends in a vision of love as the force capable of saving humans from meaninglessness.

Chapter *18*

Icelandic Postwar Literature

After World War II Icelandic writers became less insular. They became acquainted with more recent world literature, and numerous translations were published, especially of British and American writers such as Aldous Huxley, D. H. Lawrence, Ernest Hemingway, John Steinbeck, Erskine Caldwell, William Saroyan, and Sinclair Lewis. This international orientation was grounded in events during the war that, unlike World War I, had a direct effect on the country. Iceland was occupied by the British in 1940, then by the Americans in 1941. The most important political event of the decade was the proclamation of the republic on June 17, 1944 and the dissolution of the union with Denmark. The American occupation brought full employment and a high standard of living but also severe inflation. Farming had to be subsidized, and enormous amounts were invested in agriculture and trawler fleets. In 1946 Iceland became a member of the United Nations, received aid under the Marshall Plan, and, after a fierce internal fight, joined NATO in 1949, admitting an American garrison to the airbase of Keflavík.

In literature Halldór Laxness's development was symptomatic of the postwar period. After writing a dramatic, pessimistic account of the decadence of Icelandic culture owing to the crass materialism of the times, he turned to historical novels and increasingly occupied himself with questions of literary form. Some writers produced conventional epics, others began experimenting with style and language. In spite of the political optimism of 1944, a pessimistic note was sounded among the younger writers—inspired by the Swedish poetry of the 1940s—approaching an almost nihilistic feeling of despair. The term atómskáld, atom poet, was used to designate these writers, who usually employed unconventional free verse and impenetrable imagery.

POETRY

Steinn Steinarr

In poetry Steinarr (1908–58) led the experimentation in abstract styles. He began as a political poet with a rather traditional collection, *Rauður loginn brann* (Red Burned the Flame, 1934). His next volume, *Ljóð* (Poems, 1937), indicated a clear break with tradition, both ideologically and stylistically, and should be considered the first work of Icelandic lyrical modernism. The short, simple, and unrhymed poems express a radical skepticism based on a feeling of isolation and loneliness, and the realization of the absurdity of human existence. This nihilistic philosophy is even more pronounced in Steinarr's succeeding collections, with the programmatic titles *Spor í sandi* (Tracks in the Sand, 1940) and *Ferð án fyrirheits* (Journey without Promise, 1942), influenced by Carl Sandburg, modern abstract painting, and the Swedish modernists of the 1940s. These models also led Steinar to a number of typographical experiments, resulting in his most avant-garde work, the highly complex cycle of poems, *Tíminn og vatnið* (1948, enlarged ed. 1956; Eng. tr. *Time and Water*, 1972).

Snorri Hjartarson

Hjartarson (1906–   ) was also influenced by visual art; his language is permeated with metaphors from the world of nature. He, too, experimented with new forms and styles, though his point of departure was the neo-romantic world of ideas, which manifests itself in the formal beauty of his first collection, *Kvæði* (Poems, 1944), an intensely personal hymn to his native country. On the other hand, *Á Gnitaheiði* (On Gnita Heath, 1952), in which fear and anxiety are contrasted with the poet's earlier optimism, reflects the insecure postwar era; Snorri's syntax had become very intricate. Stylistically *Lauf og stjörnur* (Leaves and Stars, 1966) influenced by W. H. Auden, is free of these linguistic effects; in it Hjartarson expresses a deeply pessimistic attitude toward a world that has completely failed to meet the expectations of the poet.

Jón úr Vör

This trend toward simplicity, common in all Nordic countries during the 1960s, particularly characterizes Jón úr Vör (pseud. of Jón Jónsson [1917-]). In his first major collection, Þorpið (The Village, 1946), he presents in free verse a realistic picture of a remote fishing village and its poor inhabitants, being influenced by Swedish writers such as Artur Lundkvist. In his later collections, Með hljóðstaf (With Alliteration, 1951) and Maurildaskógur (The Phosphorescent Forest, 1965), he retains the concrete and precise language in a number of impressions of Reykjavík and in a series of poems dealing with the inability of humans to assert themselves socially and existentially in a threatening world, a realization which assumes a deep and bitterly pessimistic tone in Mjallhvítarkistan (Snow White's Coffin, 1968) and Vinarhús (House of Friends, 1972).

Hannes Sigfússon

Similar disillusionment and skepticism characterize the work of Sigfússon (1922-). His obscure and complex poetry in Dymbilvaka (Vigil during the Holy Week, 1949) is clearly influenced by T. S. Eliot, Gunnar Ekelöf, and the Swedish poets of the 1940s. Sprek á eldinn (Firewood, 1961) shows a way out of the pessimism of Sigfússon's early poetry and concludes in a vision of new and positive ways of life. He now demands of his readers full engagement in contemporary problems and maintains a radical position in Jarteikn (Omens, 1966), while employing easily accessible and more traditional verse forms in his effort to communicate with his readers.

Hannes Pétursson

Iceland's most important postwar lyrical poet, Pétursson (1931-) also began writing traditional verse. However, he, like Snorri Hjartarson, moved from the traditional to a more innovative, experimental method. Kvæðabók (Poems, 1955) is a mature and balanced first collection of great formal beauty. Gradually a feeling of alienation from the surrounding world took over, a feeling of universal transitoriness. The cult of beauty is replaced in Í sumardölum (In the Summer Valleys, 1959) and Stund og staðir (Time and Places, 1962) by the sentiment of helplessness which can be overcome only when the poet recaptures what is closest and most precious to him—the beauty of Iceland and his childhood memories. Thus the feeling of continuity, which Pétursson misses in his own time, is attained and expressed with exquisite artistry in Innlönd (Inner Regions, 1968). His poetry volume Rímblöð (Pages of Rhyme, 1971), the prose collection Ljóðabréf (Lyrical Epistles, 1973), and the documentary about a crime committed in northern Ireland a hundred years ago, Rauðamyrkur (Pitch

Darkness, 1973), are not of the same quality as the 1968 collection. His latest book, a collection of occasional poetry and essays, *Úr hugskoti* (Recollections, 1976), shows that Pétursson's work moved from the traditional to the innovative and back to the traditional.

Jón Óskar (Ásmundsson)

Among the "atom poets" Óskar (1921–   ) has perhaps been the most successful in combining a concise, self-centered poetry with nationalistic elements—particularly in his most valuable collection, *Nóttin á herðum okkar* (The Night on Our Shoulders, 1958). The same stylistic simplicity and melodious language characterize the novel *Leikir i fjörunni* (Games on the Beach, 1968), a valuable period portrait of Iceland's cultural climate before and after World War II, permeated with bitterness and pessimism. Óskar's well-written series of memoirs dealing with the same period has been published under the titles *Fundnir snillingar* (Sound Geniuses, 1969), *Hernámsáraskáld* (Poet of the Wounds of the Occupation, 1970), and *Gangstéttir i rigningu* (Sidewalks in the Rain, 1971).

PROSE

The return to Icelandic culture and nature as a remedy for existential anguish is also noticeable within prose, which is dominated into the 1960s by an epic, realistic tradition, rooted in a peasant society predating the technological revolution.

Guðmundur Daníelsson

Thus the setting of a novel by Daníelsson (1910–   ), *Á bökkum Bolafljóts* (On the Banks of the Bola River, 1940), is the southern lowlands where he was born, but the time is the past. His major novel, *Blindingsleikur* (Blind Man's Bluff, 1955), tells of the painful transition from old to new reflected in his heroes, who are strong but divided characters, doomed to failure owing to their inner contradictions. In reality Daníelsson is a romantic writer who does not always succeed in merging mythical elements with a realistic style. In spite of his narrative skill, his later novels, *Sonur minn Sinfjötli* (My Son Sinfjotli, 1961), *Turninn og teningurinn* (The Tower and the Dice, 1966), and *Vestangúlpur garró* (Strong Westerly Gale, 1977), are increasingly fragmentary, which the author tries to conceal through very stylized language verging on affectation.

Ólafur Jóhann Sigurðsson

Sigurðsson (1918–) is a much surer stylist. After having written a novel in the hard-boiled style of Hemingway, *Liggur vegurinn þangað* (Does the Road Lead There, 1940), he became noteworthy for richly nuanced, lyrical language combined with convincing psychological and realistic narrative. His most ambitious book, *Fjallið og draumurinn* (The Mountain and the Dream, 1944), is set in the provinces and contains overtones of social criticism. The sequel, *Vorköld jörð* (Spring Cool Earth, 1951), was published after the war, together with two collections of short stories, testifying to his remarkable ability to identify with the thoughts and living conditions of the poor and oppressed. This perceptiveness is displayed in the lyrical novella *Litbrigði jarðarinnar* (Earth Changing Color, 1947), a story of youthful love. In 1955 two more books were published, the short stories *Á vegamótum* (At the Crossroads) and the novel *Gangvirkið* (The Mechanism), continuing the social criticisim of *The Mountain and the Dream*. This tendency had developed into a bitter, strongly pessimistic critique of modern welfare society when, after seventeen years of near silence, Sigurðsson published the novel *Hreiðrið* (The Bird's Nest) in 1972. In 1976 he received the Literature Prize of the Nordic Council for his two poetry collections *Að laufferjum* (To the Ferryboats of Leaves, 1972) and *Að brunnum* (To the Wells, 1974), culminations of his work, combining contemporary social criticism with formal mastery and rich, poetic language.

Indriði G. Þorsteinsson

The feeling of alienation so typical of Sigurðsson's writing, the distaste for and bitterness toward the contemporary scene, also encountered in the works of Jón Óskar and Hannes Pétursson, is characteristic of the work of Þorsteinsson (1926–). His books focus on the social and psychological problems of people who have moved to the city from the country—he sees the later as the only source of permanent values—and who no longer belong anywhere. This motif serves as the basis of the novels *Sjötíu og níu af stöðinni* (Cab 79 on its Way, 1955), *Land og synir* (Land and Sons, 1963), *Þjófur í paradís* (A Thief in Paradise, 1967), and Þorsteinsson's major work, *Norðan við stríð* (North of the War, 1971), dealing with the Allied occupation of Iceland during World War II and its dismal consequences for the old peasant society: social decline, moral corruption, and, ultimately, total disintegration.

Thor Vilhjálmsson

The most significant stylistic renewal of Icelandic prose occurred in the work of Vilhjálmsson (1925–   ), influenced by Kafka and—following a stay in postwar Paris—by French existentialism. His pessimistic outlook, expressed in the title of his first piece, the prose sketches *Maðurinn er alltaf einn* (Man Is Always Alone, 1950), and likewise present in the short-story collection *Andlit í spegli dropans* (1957; Eng. tr. *Faces Reflected in a Drop*, 1966) also characterizes a number of travel descriptions he wrote in a cinematic style, rendering without moral value judgments highly detailed observations. In his first novel *Fljótt, fljótt sagði i fuglinn* (Fast, Fast Said the Bird, 1968), which deals with death and erotic love, the dimensions of personality, of time and space are absent. The novel has a very large gallery of characters from which he creates a history of human cruelty— from Christian martyrdom in the reign of Caligula to the Vietnam War. *Óp bjöllunnar* (The Scream of the Bug, 1970) enlarges on the themes of the previous work, relating with even greater stylistic brilliance, pleasure and pain in recurring scenes from history. Both works are major accomplishments in modern Nordic literature. More traditional is *Folda* (1972), a collection of three satirical short stories about Icelandic nationalism, whereas *Fuglaskottís* (Bird Dance, 1975) marks a return to the international setting of the previous works. The action unfolds during a twenty-four-hour stay in Rome and depicts a search by two Icelanders for two girls who have disappeared. The simple plot serves solely as a frame for a wealth of visionary and absurd happenings as well as wordy discussions about the state of the arts in modern society, the book being an almost impenetrable surrealistic piece of prose poetry.

A similar multitude of images distinguishes *Mánasigð* (Crescent Moon, 1976), which, like the earlier novels, deals with the contemporary human search for identity in a world beset by turmoil and change. Although in the earlier books the common bond of love was regarded as an end in itself, here the search remains unfinished—as it does in the works of Danish author Peter Seeberg—and is portayed as a nearly permanent, desirable condition, depicted with such artistic mastery that Vilhjálmsson stands out as his generation's most convincing prose writer.

Part V Recent Trends

Chapter 19

Recent Trends in Nordic Literature

SWEDEN

The general trend in the literature of the 1970s is an increasing skepticism toward the value of writing fiction as well as an attempt to establish new connections with reality, to express and encourage human contact and solidarity. With a growing political and social awareness, this solidarity embraces oppressed groups in Sweden and outside it. There is little truly experimental literature, but reportorial works flourish, whose task it is to present straightforward accounts of social and political reality. Sara Lidman—and Fenno-Swedish writer Jörn Donner—were forerunners, followed by Sven Lindqvist and Jan Myrdal.

Jan Myrdal

A work by Myrdal (1927–), *Rapport från kinesisk by* (1963; Eng. tr. *Report from a Chinese Village*, 1965) is a penetrating, lively picture of everyday life in China after the revolution; the results of the so-called cultural revolution are described in *Kina: revolutionen går vidare* (1970; Eng. tr. *China: the Revolution Continued*, 1970). *Kulturers korsväg* (The Crossroad of Culture, 1960) is both a travel description of Afghanistan and an attack on the romantic Western falsification of history. Myrdal continued in this genre in 1966 with *Turkmenistan*, analyzing Russia's politics in its Asiatic domains and attacking the Communists for their suppression of national minorities and with *Gates to Asia* (1971). Myrdal's extensive journalistic pieces are collected in five volumes of *Skriftställning* (Writings, 1968–75), in the books *Tal om hjälp* (Speeches about Help, 1971), containing articles about aid to developing countries, and *Lag utan ordning* (Law without Order, 1975), attacking the Swedish government. Related to this work is the novel *Karriär* (Career, 1975) which portrays four top politicians who are concerned only with pursuing their own careers and for whom public benefit has been turned into personal benefit.

Sven Lindqvist

Kina inifrån (Inside China, 1963), by Lindqvist (1932–), was published in the same year as Myrdal's first book about China. It relates the author's experiences in a country characterized by economic crises and the beginning of political tension with Russia. The objective tone of *Inside China* is replaced by one of personal commitment in *Myten om Wu Tao-tzu* (The Myth of Wu Tao-tzu, 1967)—a counterpart to Myrdal's *Samtida bekännelser* (Contemporary Confessions, 1964) in its portrayal of the dilemma that results from the destruction of a worldview based on European liberalism and individualism. *Slagskuggan* (1969; Eng. tr. *The Shadow*, 1972) and *Jord och makt i Sydamerika* (Property and Power in South America, 1974) mark a return to the genre of the critical report analyzing the exploitiveness of the United States, and separately published volume 2 of *Jord och makt* (The Dawn of the Earth, 1974) describes the plight of Latin-American farmhands.

REPORTORIAL LITERATURE

Sundman and Enquist write novels which skillfully and with great artistic effect mingle documentary and fiction, and Palm in his reportorial books indirectly analyzes the role of the author; but Myrdal's strictly political, anti-fictional attitude is continued by Carin Mannheimer (1934–) in *Rapport om kvinnor* (Report on Women, 1969), containing interviews with Swedish women, as well as by Sture Källberg (1928–). Källberg's *Rapport från medelsvensk stad: Västerås* (Report from an Average Swedish City: Västerås, 1969), the topic of which is the migration from rural areas to town, was succeeded by *Ackord* (Piece-Work, 1972, influenced by the American journalist Studs Terkel's *Division Street*, 1967), who in his turn had been inspired by Jan Myrdal. *Piece-Work* tells of the author's experiences in various work places and exemplifies a trend toward a reportorial literature written by the workers themselves. Instead of launching direct attacks against the capitalist system, the workers expose the destructive and humiliating mechanisms inherent in their daily work:

Rapport från en skurhink (Report from a Bucket, 1970) by Maja Ekelöf (1918–) was very successful; *Du, människa?* (You, Human Being?, 1972), by Marit Paulsen (1939–), demonstrates more persuasively how her job as a factory worker wore her out before she was thirty-four-years-old.

Per Gunnar Evander

The pseudo-documentary trend—an earlier example is Jersild's *The Pig Hunt*—consisting of the diary of a fictitious hero is taken up with great talent by Evander (1933–). Many of his novels are reconstructions of actual events, inquiries, and journalistic reports. *Sista dagen i Valle Hedmans liv* (The Last Day in Valle Hedman's Life, 1971) deals with the accidental death of the title character; it is based on evidence and police reports that are actually fabricated by the author. More complicated, but with a similar structure, is the novel *Berättelsen om Josef* (The Story of Joseph, 1972), which gradually develops into an intricate meta-novel, returning to the ideas of the epistolary novels *Bäste herr Evander* (Dear Mr. Evander, 1967) and *Tegelmästare Lundin* (Bricklayer Lundin, 1970), in both of which Evander discusses the question of truth: Is it possible to describe reality? Gradually Evander abandoned the neutral, factual, and slightly bureaucratic language of his earlier novels for a broad, more traditional epic technique, describing psychological processes; in the novels *Det sista äventyret* (The Last Adventure, 1973) and *Måndagarna med Fanny* (Mondays with Fanny, 1974) Evander's main characters are inhibited people who have difficulty expressing themselves and whose defective language becomes a mirror of their own defective life experience. With *Fallet Lillemor Holm* (The Case of Lillemor Holm, 1977) Evander, who has also written dramas and radio plays, returned to the theme of his 1972 novel: the plight of a novelist, which is related in a complicated narrative structure. Evander's latest novel, *Judas Iskariots knutna händer* (The Fists of Judas Iscariot, 1978), a lucid, matter-of-fact description of the last days in the life of Jesus seen through the eyes of Judas, seems to indicate a new trend in Evander's works.

Kerstin Ekman

More traditional and realistic in style is the work of Ekman (1933–), who began as a writer of crime fiction. In her novel *Menedarna* (The Perjurers, 1970) she portrays the Swedish strike leader, agitator, and song writer Joe Hill, who was executed in Salt Lake City, in 1916. In *Mörker och blåbärsris* (Darkness and Blueberry Bushes, 1972), influenced by Sara Lidman, Ekman wrote a novel about the underprivileged in modern welfare society. In *Häxringarna* (The Witches' Circles, 1974) and its sequels *Springkällan* (The Spring, 1976) and *Änglahuset* (The House of Angels, 1979) Ekman expands the scope of her work with a chronicle-like narrative of the period of industrialization, dealing with a multitude of characters and episodes. But above all these works are about women of various social levels, struggling in a male-dominated society.

Britt Arenander and Other Feminist Writers

With Arenander (1941–   ) social and political criticism takes on a more direct focus. Her novels *Steget* (The Step, 1968), *Off* (1969), and *Alla broar brända* (All Bridges Are Burned, 1971) revolve around a limited number of attitudes and human types: those who are ill at ease, those who are filled with a spirit of rebellion but cannot find a solution to their problems. Arenander's poetry collection *Dröm om verkligheten utanför Stockholm* (Dream about the Reality Outside Stockholm, 1974) also deals with human beings who are unable to adapt to any social system.

With the novel *Allt som finns att få* (All There Is to Get, 1976), about a woman who submits and adjusts to a man to such a degree that she almost extinguishes herself, and *Egen karta* (Our Own Map, 1979), Arenander has made a significant contribution to today's feminist literature. The collection of short stories *Kvinnor* (Women, 1975) by Ulla Isaksson (1916–   ) is among the more controversial feminist works. Recent Swedish feminist literature encompasses strong satires such as those by Margareta Sarri (1945–   )—*Ta dej en slav* (Get Yourself a Slave, 1975) is an example—and more objective analyses such as the account of a woman's isolation in her female role by Jörgen Eriksson (1934–   ), *Omständigheternas makt* (The Power of Circumstances, 1975). On a par with the artistic quality of Ulla Isaksson's book—and equally controversial—are two works by Kerstin Thorvall (1925–   ), *Det mest förbjudna* (The Most Forbidden, 1976) and *Oskuldens död* (The Death of Innocence, 1977), coming to terms with the sexual taboos of both this and the previous generation.

Like Kerstin Ekman, Björn Runeborg (1937–   ) follows a rather traditional epic line with the novels *Stenhugg* (Missing the Mark, 1970), dealing with the conflict between an enterprising newcomer and the defeatist and skeptical inhabitants of a village, and *Riddaren från Mjölby* (The Knight from Mjölby, 1977), a burlesque novel about a small merchant who attempts to combine idealism with free economic enterprise. In the novel *Valkamp* (Electoral Campaign, 1973) Runeborg deals with the problems of establishing a career. Lars Ardelius

(1926–   ) also employs this topic in his novel *Kronprinsarna* (The Crown Princes, 1972), the story of twins who by chance are brought up in different circumstances, one in the working class, the other in the upper class; their destinies become a mirror of society. *Och kungen var kung* (And the King Was King, 1976) is the first volume of a historical trilogy by Ardelius, followed in 1978 by *Tid och otid* (New Time and Bad Time) depicting large regions of nineteenth-century Sweden. It is characteristic of the renewed interest in that period which emerged during the mid-1970s. Bunny Ragnerstam (1944–   ) in his novels based on documentary material, *Innan dagen gryr* (Before the Day Dawns, 1974), *Uppbrottets timme* (The Hour of Departure, 1975), and *Vredens dag* (The Day of Wrath, 1977) deals with the city of Kristianstad in the 1880s. He attempts to demonstrate that the history of Sweden is that of the people, not of the king. This viewpoint is shared by Moberg and also forms the basis of several works by Hans Granlid (1926–   ), *Rackarsång* (Rascal Song, 1974) and *Flickan Kraft* (The Girl Kraft, 1975). Closer to our time—and dealing with the transformation and depopulation of the Swedish countryside—is *Agnarna i vinden* (Chaff in the Wind, 1976), the first volume of a novel cycle by Sture Källberg which was continued in 1977 with *I flock och ensam* (In a Horde and Alone), and in 1979 with *Den röda älven* (The Red River). After writing a volume of poetry, *Minnet i exil* (The Memory in Exile, 1964), Greek-born Theodor Kallifatides (1938–   ) made his debut as a novelist with *Utlänningar* (Foreigners, 1970), which treats the same motifs as do the poems, the author's emigration from his native country and his confrontation with Sweden. With *Bönder och herrar* (1973; Eng. tr. *Masters and Peasants*, 1977) Kallifatides began an epic tale of Greece during World War II which in 1975 was continued with *Plogen och svärdet* (The Plow and the Sword) and in 1977 concluded with *Den grymma freden* (The Cruel Peace), written in a vigorous and distinctive style, filled with secondary episodes and flashbacks which, however, do not disturb the narrative flow.

Staffan Seeberg

The more linguistically experimental trend, following the example of Torsten Ekbom, is represented by Seeberg (1938–   ). In *Vägen genom Vasaparken* (The Road through the Vasa Park, 1970) he abandons simple, descriptive prose, the language mirroring the sequence of events. He uses this same method in the science-fiction novel *Lungfisken* (The Lung Fish, 1971), set in Denmark in the year 2020, which deliberately exaggerates negative tendencies and possibilities within present society. *Cancerkandidaterna* (The Cancer Candidates,

1975) continues this criticism, being a stern reckoning with the exploitation of capitalistic society. Of greater artistic value is Seeberg's latest very imaginative and colorful novel, *Holobukk* (1977), in which the relationship between freedom and subjection, oppressors and oppressed, is penetratingly analyzed with great linquistic elegance.

Berit Bergström

Psychological analysis is employed by Bergström (1942-   ), whose novels revolve around the death motif, usually dressed in an absurdist form and set in a hospital, a Kafkaesque milieu. The main character of *Exekutionen* (The Execution, 1968) is a nurse who accidentally discovers that one of the patients is to be hanged for a traffic violation. The novel describes her futile and nightmarish efforts to have the execution stopped. Bergström's next novel, *En svensk dröm* (A Swedish Dream, 1970), also deals with the sentencing to death of the main character, Ingrid, who suffers from an incurable blood disease. Here, too, dreams, in which her panic is concentrated, occupy the central place. On the other hand, the heroine of *Brödet och stenarna* (The Bread and the Stones, 1973) is sentenced to live after having chosen suicide as her only way out of loneliness and isolation. The dissection that lays open the empty shell of Louise's emotional life is done with extraordinary skill. A similar skill characterizes Bergström's latest novel, *Stackars karl* (Poor Chap, 1977), the story of a man caught in a net of psychological difficulties.

In poetry a similar scope is noticeable, and it is obvious that the poetry of the 1970s, like the prose, continues some trends present in the previous decade. In particular, leftist political poetry has many representatives. Among the most significant are Peter Curman (1941-   ), with the collections *Hemmaliv* (Home Life, 1970), *Fönstren* (The Windows, 1972), and *Fåglarna* (The Birds, 1977); and Siv Arb (1931-   ) with the volumes *Burspråk* (Bay Window, 1971), *Dikter i mörker och ljus* (Poems in Darkness and Light, 1975), and *Under bara himlen* (Under the Open Sky, 1978). Jan Mårtenson (1944-   ) is the most significant writer of this political group. Whereas Mårtenson's first collection, *Dikter nu* (Poems Now, 1968), with its breadth and wealth of imagery, was strongly influenced by Lundkvist, tautness and precision characterize *Mellan oss* (Between Us, 1969) to a far greater degree. Here the poet's childhood memories are presented in a major work, continued in *Närmare* (Closer, 1972). The two collections also contain a number of political portraits. That Mårtenson has disparate points of departure for his political views is demonstrated by the title of the poetry collection *Jag erövrar världen tillsammans med Karl och bröderna Marx* (I Conquer the World Together with Karl and the Marx Brothers, 1973). Mårtenson's method is indirect, even in his very committed collection *Genvägar till galenskapen* (Shortcuts to Madness, 1979), his criticism always marked by warmth and fervor. As a result, he never resorts to proselytizing for his clearly expressed socialist position.

The early 1970s showed a marked increase in religious poetry, obviously products of the various religious currents that have emerged as an alternative to today's materialism. An unusual combination of Christianity and Marxism is represented by Elisabet Hermodsson (1927–) in the volumes *Disa Nilsons visor* (The Songs of Disa Nilson, 1974), a polemical counterpart to Birger Sjöberg's songs about Frida (see p. 159), and *Genom markens röda väst* (Through the Red Vest of the Field, 1975). Ylva Eggehorn (1940–) attempts to apply the biblical message to everyday situations in her collections *Jesus älskar dig* (Jesus Loves You, 1972) and *Han kommer* (He Comes, 1975), written in a simple, easily accessible style reminiscent of Bo Setterlind.

Tobias Berggren

The linguistic, philosophical trend within poetry is continued by the very talented Berggren (1940–); in his abstract first collection, *Det nödvändiga är inte klart* (The Necessary Is Not Certain, 1969), one finds the same speculations about the relationship between language and society as in Sonnevi's writing. Berggren clearly attempts to release language from the mental associations that bind one to old patterns. In *Den främmande tryggheten* (The Strange Security, 1971) he, like Sonnevi, speculates about the possibility of creating a language capable of bringing about change—thereby combining a political and a romantic attitude. The abstract, theoretical, and occasionally dry statements in these two works have completely disappeared in *Namn och grus* (Name and Gravel, 1973), a major work in modern Swedish poetry in which one finds the intense presence of the author. The volume mirrors a private crisis, expressed in a series of love poems dealing with the relationship between love and social life as well as in a large fantastic vision, "Resa i den integritetslösa världen" ("Journey through the World without Integrity"). The self is abandoned, naked, and defenseless in a chaotic unstable world. In a physically very tangible, highly sexual act of creation, the self, however, is embraced by and embraces "something" whispering: "You are somebody else somebody else somebody else." The journey toward rebirth has begun. A similar journey through the inferno toward light occurs in the collection *Resor i din tystnad* (Journeys in Your Silence, 1976), containing poems of extraordinary precision and visionary beauty, traits even more characteristic of Berggren's latest volume, *Bergsmusik* (Mountain Music, 1978).

Gunnar Harding

Less exclusive is the work of Harding (1940–), who in the preface to his selection *Poesi 1967-73* (Poetry 1967-73) mentions jazz and painting as important influences. Other major sources of inspiration are American Beat poetry, French surrealism, and the Russian author Majakovski. In addition, Harding stresses that his poetry is clearly visual, a characteristic that in his earlier works is linked to language, but gradually becomes associated with typography. The emphasis on the visual element, together with the poet's method of interweaving various themes, is not far removed from the style of the French surrealist Apollinaire. These traits also dominate his first collection, *Lokomotivet som frös fast* (The Locomotive That Became Stuck in Ice, 1967); the series of lyrical prose pieces, *The Fabulous Life of Guillaume Apollinaire* (1970) is a direct homage to the French poet.

In *Den svenske cyklistens sång* (The Song of the Swedish Cyclist, 1968) and *Blommor till James Dean* (Flower for James Dean, 1969) the influence of Walt Whitman and particularly Allen Ginsberg is clear—a result of a visit to the United States in 1968 which led to a love-hate attitude toward this country. The result was that Harding wrote a number of analyses of the power structure, often clothed in a historical guise, by drawing parallels between past and present. He used a similar technique in *Örnen har landat* (The Eagle Has Landed, 1970) to demonstrate that reality consists of clashing external and internal experiences, and that a multitude of events occur simultaneously—constituting Harding's poetic creed. The search for an all-encompassing unity, which extinguishes any boundary between the private and public spheres, so characteristic of this poet, is carried to its utmost degree in *Skallgång* (The Search, 1972). Various time periods and milieus are woven imperceptibly into an unbreakable unity, elevated above our technological everyday life in a number of melodious verses—the poet's effort to create living poetry in which the entire human being can be involved, all senses, organs, dreams, ideas. Harding has realized this program in his most convincing poetry collection, *Ballader* (Ballads, 1975), and in his first prose work *Luffaren Svarta Hästen* (The Tramp Black Horse, 1977). *Starnberger See* (The Lake of Starnberg, 1977), a sequence of thirty-two poems, marks a return to the methods of the 1970 collections; it is an imaginary biography blending fact and fiction, the subject this time being the mad King Ludwig II of Bavaria.

Lars Norén

Norén (1944–   ), also found inspiration for his early work in French surrealism, but especially in its predecessor Raymond Rousel and Rousel's attempt to create reality through language. Norén's early writing culminates in the hectic, image-laden, and visionary volume *Stupor. Nobody Knows You When You're Down and Out* (1968), the last volume in a series of autobiographical poetry collections since 1965; the background of the series is the poet's hospitalization for schizophrenia. In these works Norén deliberately recreated the apparently passive registering of impulses, voices, and images that had penetrated the mental emptiness resulting from his psychic paralysis.

In 1970 Norén published the first part of a trilogy, *Biskötarna* (The Beekeepers). This was followed in 1972 by *I den underjordiska himlen* (In the Underworld Heaven), an autobiographical novel with documentary elements dealing with human cruelty and vulnerability, replete with esoteric, symbolic structures, which, however, are splintered by highly realistic dialogue. The book demonstrates Norén's basic premise that dream and reality cannot be distinguished from each other. In his later poetry he attempts to avoid the too private sphere, which restrains his earlier spontaneity and turns his poetry in a more conventional direction. This can be traced from *Revolver* (1969), dealing in part with the Vietnam War, through *Solitära dikter* (Solitary Poems, 1972), to *Viltspeglar* (Mirrors of the Game, 1972), in which the poet abandons egotism and chaos for discipline and structure. *Kung Mej och andra dikter* (King Me and Other Poems, 1973) affirms this renewal. It contains mainly diary-like, short, lucid poems, into which the poet channels his very expressive and imaginative art. It is even more obvious that chaos has been overcome in the volumes *Dagliga och nattliga dikter* (Daily and Nightly Poems, 1974), *Dagbok augusti-oktober 1975* (Diary August-October 1975, 1976), and *Nattarbete* (Night Work, 1976). The longing for innocence and purity that permeates Norén's works of the 1960s has now been realized, with strong religious overtones, and is expressed here in his latest volume, *Order* (1978), with a linguistic virtuosity unequaled in Norén's generation.

Like Tobias Berggren and Gunnar Harding, Lars Norén cannot be placed in a specific literary category, nor can he be accused of any sectarian tendencies. Through their great artistic talent and wide scope these writers confirm the diversity of recent Swedish literature and

point toward the future, inspiring literary development in the years
to come.

NORWAY

Many of the most talented writers of contemporary Norwegian literature belonged to the group of writers who contributed to *Profil*
(1943–), originally a journal for philology students at the University
of Oslo. In 1966 it directed a sharp attack at the predominantly realistic
and psychological Norwegian literature and the aesthetizing literary
criticism. Sweden, with its more socially involved and experimental
trends, was considered the ideal. But very soon the rebellion took a
different, political direction, and *Profil* developed in the early 1970s
into an organ of Marxist literary theory in the service of the working
class.

Tor Obrestad

Obrestad (1938–) is the oldest of the *Profil* rebels and was for a
long time regarded as the central force. Both the poetry collection
Kollisjon (Collision, 1966) and the short-story volume *Vind* (Wind,
1966) take their point of departure from a highly personal, individualistic complex of problems, depicted in symbolic language influenced
by Kafka and Vesaas. In *Den norske løve* (The Norwegian Lion, 1970)
and *Stå sammen* (Stand Together, 1974) he abandons this exclusivity
and all aesthetic effects in favor of a direct, revolutionary message in
poems directed against both the United States and NATO and at social questions in Norwegian everyday life. The Marxist ideology is
conspicuous in Obrestad's most important work, the novel *Sauda!
Streik!* (Sauda! Strike!, 1972), a mix of documentary and fictional
material based on an illegal strike at an iron works which forced the
satisfaction of the workers' demands. A labor dispute also forms the
basis for the novel *Stå på!* (Get It On!, 1976). Here, as well as in
Obrestad's latest poetry collection, *Vinterdikt* (Winter Poem, 1979),
political propaganda frequently overwhelms aesthetic form.

Espen Haavardsholm

Obrestad's work developed from the individualistic and exclusive
to the extroverted and simple. Haavardsholm (1945–) was not quite
as successful in expressing his social message in a generally accessible
way. The novel *Munnene* (The Mouths, 1968), clearly influenced by
the Swede Björn Håkanson and the Dane Sven Holm, is based on the
dialectical interaction between the individual and the group. Haavards-

holm tells the story of four young people attempting to maintain their disillusioned view of life, marked by lack of identity and frustration, in a conscious revolt against the older generation. Complicated narrative structure is rejected in the short-story collection *Den avskyelige snømannen* (The Abominable Snowman, 1970) for a concise style in these stories of the triteness of humankind's relationship with a manipulative world. A direct coming to terms with this world—including the power structures in society—is formulated in the seven semidocumentary pieces comprising *Zink* (Zinc, 1971). In the political diary *Grip dagen* (Seize the Day, 1973) Haavardsholm directs a series of satirical and demagogic attacks on Norway's negotiations with the European Economic Community. Ideological overtones also predominate in *Historiens kraftlinjer* (The Lines of Power in History, 1975); this is more a political treatise than a novel about a young industrial worker's experiences in Albania and at home, and it poses the question of which road one should choose to reach socialism. This nonfictional approach is confined by Haavardsholm's collection of polemical prose works, reviews, and interviews, *Poesi, maktspråk* (Poetry, Language of Power, 1976). *Drift* (Instinct, 1980) is not a dogmatic political novel. It warns of the danger of making ideologies into religion. Haavardsholm tells of a young teacher based in an intellectual Communist setting who becomes disillusioned and loses his political commitment.

Dag Solstad

The most controversial—and the most talented—revolutionary Norwegian author is Solstad (1941–   ). He made his debut in 1965 with a series of short stories, *Spiraler* (Spirals), dealing with loneliness and isolation, which clearly were influenced by Kafka and the French absurdists. In 1967 there followed the collection *Svingstol* (A Turning Chair), characterized by a concise, terse style reminiscent of Vesaas, consisting of fragments of reality often rendered with provocative banality. On the other hand, the novel *Irr! Grønt!* (Patina! Green!, 1969) tells of the attempts of a peasant student to overcome his inhibitions; it is an eloquent but lengthy psychological experiment, characterized by an amassing of words reminiscent of James Joyce's technique. The title character in *Arild Asnes, 1970* (1971) is obsessed by the desire to escape his limited milieu, which results in his acknowledging the saving graces of the Marxist-Leninist ideology. Simultaneously the novel is an analysis of the plight of a socialist intellectual in contemporary Norway. Solstad writes with an intense commitment to his material. He believes in his topic and feels a solidarity with his hero that is reflected in the lively, imaginative language of the book. The same artistic qualities are found in *25. september-plassen* (The 25th of September Square, 1974), which chronicles the development of the working class in postwar Norway, from a time when the leadership of the labor movement was committed to reconstructing Norway in keeping with the ideals of socialism to a time when the concern for material comfort led to complacency and a policy of compromise. Less convincing are the first two parts of a trilogy, *Svik: førkrigsår* (Betrayal: Prewar Years, 1977) and *Krig: 1940* (War: 1940, 1978), social, realistic works marked by hollow pathos and flat character delineation, which resulted in Solstad being accused of preaching a harsh Communist line.

A number of other writers in the *Profil* group turned from the individualistic to the social, but refused, as Jan Erik Vold did (see p. 305), to enter the political battle.

Einar Økland

The first poetry collection by Økland (1940–   ), *Ein gul dag* (A Yellow Day, 1963), although somewhat personal in theme, pointed toward the simplicity and the commonplace which dominated the second half of the 1960s. *Vandreduene* (The Migrating Pigeons, 1968) sneeringly attacks traditional literature's use of symbol and metaphor. Økland sets his own tone in his "lyrical nature novel," *Amatør-album* (Amateur Album, 1969), which depicts the author's childhood and family, mingling poetry and documentary material. Økland combines prose, poetry, and drama in the scrapbook *Gull-alder* (Golden Age, 1972), in which he makes drastic associative leaps to reflect on his childhood and his role as a writer. Fiction and documentary are merged in *Stille stunder* (Quiet Times, 1974). Økland's poetry collection *Bronsehesten* (The Bronze Horse, 1975) is completely devoid of ideological commitment; underlying the description of an apparently trite reality is an analysis of language, or rather poetry, as our sole, if problematic, means of communication. All three works are permeated with that sound skepticism and self-irony which is missing in the work of many contemporary political authors. *Romantikk* (Romanticism, 1979) continues this trend, being a poetry collection of humor, irony, and ambiguity indirectly attacking political corruption.

Paal-Helge Haugen

The first two poetry collections by Haugen (1945–   ), *På botnen av ein mørk sommar* (On the Bottom of a Dark Summer, 1967) and *Sang-*

bok (Songbook, 1969), were strongly influenced by Chinese and Japanese poetry—Haugen had translated several collections. This is particularly noticeable in the number of concise observations of nature. However, it is as a novelist that Haugen gained his greatest success. In *Anne* (1968) the documentary approach is carried through consistently for the first time in Norwegian literature. It is the story of a girl who dies of tuberculosis at an early age. This tragic event is commented on with excerpts from medical books, a reader, and the Bible, alternating with short, lyrical fragments. Haugen's poetry collection from 1979, *Steingjerde* (Stone Fence), contains poems about his adolescence and about children as the only human beings who are able to meet the world openly.

Kjell Askildsen and Arild Kolstad

The political and social criticism that emerged toward the end of the 1960s is continued in the prose tradition by Kjell Askildsen (1929–). He wrote a conflict-filled love story from a revolutionary standpoint, focusing on women's liberation, *Kjære, kjære Oluf* (Dear, Dear Oluf, 1974). Less dogmatic is Arild Kolstad (1943–) in his social, realistic novel *Ruth* (1972). A stronger political awareness marks the sequel, *Gert* (1973), which illustrates how human communication is made impossible owing to the postwar era's obsession with gaining material prosperity. This motif is combined with suspense elements from the detective story in *Gruer—saken* (The Gruer—Case, 1974), about the war generation who made a career for themselves denying their working-class origins.

Bjørg Vik

A decidedly feminist writer, Vik (1935–) has focused her entire work on women's place in male-controlled society. However, the short-story collection *Kvinneakvariet* (The Women's Aquarium, 1972) and the drama *To akter for fem kvinner* (Two Acts for Five Women, 1974) ask whether women are responsible to a great extent for their present situation because they are much too willing to play a subordinate role. Less subdued and with stronger dramatic effects are the short stories in *Fortellinger om frihet* (Stories of Freedom, 1975) and the drama *Sorgenfri* (1978), a stoic account of love relationships in three settings and generations. *En håndfull lengsel* (A Handful of Longing, 1979) are short stories about people who accept their inner emptiness, attempt to reevaluate their lives, or feel that the small things give meaning to life.

Kjartan Fløgstad

Bjørg Vik is not a hopelessly biased propagandist, which makes her arguments more convincing. She shares this attitude with the very talented Fløgstad (1944-). After writing two highly emotional, symbolic poetry collections, he turned to motifs from his own life as a sailor and industrial worker in the short stories *Fangliner* (Painters, 1972) and the novel *Rasmus* (1974), written in a hard-boiled, matter-of-fact style. In addition, Fløgstad leveled strong attacks at contemporary prophets and fashionable trends. He had denounced them earlier in his collection of essays and short stories *Den hemmelege jubel* (The Secret Enthusiasm, 1970), in which poetry is held up as the ideal attitude toward life and the major human means of cognition. Fløgstad's latest novel, *Dalen Portland* (The Valley Portland, 1977), is written in the picaresque tradition and serves as a mirror of contemporary Norwegian society, which is portrayed in comic and tragic, fantastic and realistic ways.

Knut Faldbakken

The foremost representative of the psychological genre is Faldbakken (1941-). He treated the incest motif from a Freudian point of view in *Sin mors hus* (His Mother's House, 1969) and portrayed a middle-aged woman, thirsting for love, in *Maude danser* (Maude Dances, 1971), giving her certain vampire-like traits. Faldbakken made his decisive breakthrough with *Insektsommer* (Insect Summer, 1972). On the surface this novel is ironical, light entertainment, depicting a sixteen-year-old boy and his sexual experiences during a summer in the country. But underlying this story is another, a tragedy demonstrating how love can turn humans into ruthless beings. Faldbakken analyzes the decline of Western civilization particularly in his novel *Uår. Aftenlandet* (Famine. The Occident, 1974) and the sequel *Uår. Sweetwater* (Famine. Sweetwater, 1976), moving consistently on two levels: Underlying the entertaining and action-filled narrative is a complex, mythical pattern. *Adams dagbok* (The Diary of Adam, 1978) analyzes today's male—who appears in three variations—and his relations with women.

Tor Edvin Dahl

Pure documentaries are two works by Dahl (1943-): *Samene i dag— og i morgen* (The Samians Today—Tomorrow, 1970) and *Syv noveller om nødvendige mord* (Seven Short Stories about Necessary Murders, 1971); the latter title refers to the fact that love, not human beings, is strangled because of the roles and masks that contemporary society imposes on humans. However, the central character is a murderer in *Den andre* (The Other, 1972); Dahl has published several detective stories under the pseudonym David Torjussen. Like Faldbakken's *Insect Summer*, the novels *Guds tjener* (God's Servant, 1973) and *Bare for en dag* (Just for One Day, 1974) are many-faceted studies of puberty and the painful process of adjusting to the adult world. This psychological trend becomes predominant in *Hege og Lind* (Hege and Lind, 1974) and *Romanen om Eva* (The Novel about Eva, 1975); the apparently uncomplicated narrative conceals a conception of a world consisting of essential myths, which humans create in order to escape annihilating anxiety.

Gunnar Lunde

Characteristic of the short-story collections by Gunnar Lunde (1944-), *Flukten fra en flukt* (The Escape from an Escape, 1967), *Svart latter* (Black Laughter, 1969), *Sprell* (Wriggle, 1970), and *Liisa fra Finland* (Liisa from Finland, 1975) are a mix of realism and absurdity. The tritest, most common events are pursued to the utmost, creating effects of macabre, black humor. This technique is developed to perfection in *Drømmekvinnen* (The Dream Woman, 1970), on the surface a novel about marriage, which concludes, however, with the realization that life is so meaningless that it cannot be taken seriously. The novel *Angst—rytme* (Anxiety—Rhythm, 1973) marks a turning point in Lunde's writing. It is a forceful portrayal of our cowardly refusal to cope with daily fear and accept the reality that underlies it. A similar motif is treated in *Kanskje fins det fine dager* (Perhaps There Are Fine Days, 1976) and *Klovnens vakre død* (The Beautiful Death of the Clown, 1979), novels about the unwillingness of humans to embrace their fellow beings in full confidence.

The move into science fiction, combined with social criticism—anticipated by Sigurd Evensmo and Axel Jensen—occurs in the short-story collection *Rundt solen i ring* (Around the Sun in a Circle, 1967) written by Jon Bing and Tor Åge Bringsværd. Jon Bing (1944-) is primarily preoccupied with the situation of humans in a future, technological society described in *Komplex* (Complex, 1969). In the novel *Det myke landskapet* (The Soft Landscape, 1970) and the short stories *Knuteskrift* (Knot Writing, 1974), he explores the elements of science fiction in contemporary life, the elements of imagination that dominate our daily existence. Bing's style is occasionally as hard-boiled as a James Bond story, occasionally as poetic as a lyrical ballad. More satirical is Tor Åge Bringsværd (1939-), whose writing also displays

linguistic virtuosity. The novel *Bazar* (Bazaar, 1970) tells of the rebellion by status symbols in contemporary society, and one of the
stories in *Bløtkakemannen & Apache-pikene* (The Cream Cake Man
& the Apache Girls, 1972) depicts with burlesque humor a United
States in which the big businesses fight one another with wild-west
methods. Bringsværd's humor almost runs riot in *Den som har begge
beina på jorda står stille* (He Who Has Both Feet on the Ground Stands
Still, 1974), *Syvsoverskens dystre frokost* (The Somber Breakfast of
the Sleepy-Head, 1976), both with international settings primarily
New York, and *Pinocchio-papirene* (The Pinocchio-Papers, 1978).

Peder W. Cappelen

Cappelen (1931–), an exceptional dramatist, has emerged in contemporary Norwegian literature. He made his debut in 1960 with nature descriptions in epistolary form concerned with the function of
ritual, dream, and imagination in self-discovery and culture. High
points in this genre are: *Vidda på ny* (Return to the Mountain, 1974)
and the latest, *Fugl i en vår* (Birds in a Spring, 1979), in collaboration
with the painter Jens Johannesen. Similar topical concerns surface in
Cappelen's plays, which include short comedies for children based on
Asbjørnsen and Moe, full-length allegories based on folktales and
legends (*Tornerose, den sovende skjønnhet* [Briar Rose, the Sleeping
Beauty, 1968], *Trollspill* [Troll Play, 1975], *Hvittenland* [Whitten-
land, 1979]), and dramas based on myth, saga, and history (*Kark*,
1974, *Sverre—Berget og ordet* [Sverre—the Mountain and the Word,
1977], *Lucie—jomfru till Austråt* [Lucie—the Maiden of Austråt,
1980]). In his fiction Cappelen is influenced by Karen Blixen; his
drama has its closest affinity to Shakespeare, Strindberg, as well as
to the poetic drama of Claudel, Giraudoux, and Anouilh.

In poetry Tove Lie (1942–) consistently follows a symbolist, anti-
modernist trend, expressed convincingly and with great artistic discipline in the volumes *Syrinx* (1970), *Lotus* (1972), and *Vi sprang ut
av ild* (We Jumped from the Fire, 1979), her most convincing work
so far. Kjell Heggelund (1932–), on the other hand, consistently at-
temps to free himself of traditionalism by employing the language of
weekly tabloids and the advertising world in his poetry collected in
Dikt (Poems, 1977). Arvid Torgeir Lie (1938–) moved from nature
poetry to political propaganda with his collection *Skrive og tenke*
(Write and Think, 1971). He used increasingly nuanced modes of expression in the volumes *Sol og sekund* (Sun and Second, 1973), and
Sju svingar opp (Seven Sharp Curves, 1976). More uncompromising
is the straightforward, forceful poetry of Stig Holmås (1946–) in
the collections *Vi er mange* (We Are Many, 1970) and *Tenke på i*

morgen (Think of Tomorrow, 1972), works that also display a redeeming sense of humor, being both sarcastic and compassionate.
    As a contrast one should mention Arild Nyquist (1937-) and Arild Stubhaug (1948-); their subtle—occasionally sarcastic—way of describing everyday happenings is notable. This method creates surprising effects leading to new poetic dimensions and greater artistic excellence, and is a welcome addition to the anti-dogmatic trend that distinguishes contemporary Norwegian literature.

DENMARK

The works of two of the most significant young writers of the 1960s, Inger Christensen and Hans-Jørgen Nielsen, voiced the demand that humans no longer be defined according to set values but according to their relationship to society, an emphasis that continued into the 1970s.
    However, the more dogmatic demand of the 1960s for direct social and political commitment is also carried on in the so-called reportorial genre, in particular in feminist writing. The genre had a forerunner in the writings of Elsa Gress (1919-). Around 1970 a number of more militant books of interviews were published, influenced by the Swedish *Report on Women*, in which women's problems were interpreted from a social point of view: *Kvinder i hjemmet* (Women at Home, 1972), *Kvindernes bog* (Women's Book, 1972), and *Kvinder på fabrik* (Women in the Factories, 1973). Also the personal document in the manner of Maja Ekelöf's *Report from a Wash Bucket* was to play an important role in feminist Danish literature. Thus Grete Stenbæk Jensen (1925-) managed to stir public opinion with *Konen og æggene* (The Woman and the Eggs, 1973), which demonstrates with strong social commitment how the so-called welfare system has been able to create tolerable conditions for the single, industrial female worker.
    Documentary literature is represented in a number of studies of work environments done by collectives, students, and the workers themselves; it also influenced fictional writing. A novel by Jette Drewsen (1943-), *Hvad tænkte egentlig Arendse?* (What Did Arendse Actually Think?, 1972) deals with the problems of the middle-aged housewife; Jytte Borberg (1917-) in *Orange* (1972) and *Nu og aldrig* (Now and Never, 1979) writes about the liberated woman who uses all means available to her in society.

Ole Hyltoft

    With Jette Drewsen and Jytte Borberg we are close to neo-realism and the strictly narrative novel, which is carried on with great talent by

Hyltoft (1940–); thus far his work has been political satire. The short stories in *Revolutionens fortrop* (The Vanguard of Revolution, 1975) are polemically aimed at both bourgeois career-seekers and the opportunistic, intellectual clique which exploits socialism and Marxism for their own economic advancement. *Hvem er angst for den stygge ulv?* (Who Is Afraid of the Bad Wolf?, 1976) is a masterful combination of satire and international thriller; the main theme is a successful salesman's attempts at liberation: liberation from his own milieu, from the conventions of society, from the multinational firms—all of these combining to create the "wolf" of the title. Satire plays a lesser role in the outstanding two-volume novel *De befriede* (The Liberated, 1979) and *De besejrede* (The Vanquished, 1979), telling of the lives, hopes, and visions of a group of people who were young during World War II. They want to set themselves free from their working-class or bourgeois past, but discover how difficult it is to liberate themselves and thereby also the society of which they are a part.

Ebbe Kløvedal Reich

Thorkild Hansen's historical documentary is combined with polit-ical but undogmatic awareness in the works of Reich (1940–). His cultural historical novel about N. F. S. Grundtvig (see p. 4), *Frederik* (1972), was succeeded by *Rejsen til Messias* (The Travel to Messiah, 1974), a novel about "the origin of capitalism, Denmark's path of suffering toward absolutism and the first doubts of the Danish state church," with a fictitious main character surrounded by a multitude of historical figures; the book constitutes a rejection of both Marxist and scientific explanations of humankind, which is viewed from the perspective of mysticism. In 1977 Reich published his version of the Cimbrian march against Rome around 100 B.C., *Fæ og frænde* (Cattle and Kindsman), a tale related earlier by Johannes V. Jensen in *The Long Journey*, whose characters reappear in Reich's work. Clearly referring to the European Economic Community, Reich has Rome stand as the prototype from which every evil emanates: economic, political, and cultural imperialism, pollution, and the destruction of nature. The democratic Cimbrians are the opposite of Rome; despite this somewhat naive contrast, Reich is able to create a dialectical fantasy sustained by his usual bold imagination and linguistic mastery. These features also characterize his historical novel set in the Middle Ages, *Festen for Cæcilie* (The Feast for Cecilie, 1979).

Leif Hjernøe

Hjernøe (1938–) combines documentary material with an interest in linguistics and philosophy. *Romanen om Vitus Bering* (The Novel about Vitus Bering, 1972) thus consists of parallel tracks, containing, respectively, a documentary of the life of a Danish explorer, a series of philosophical reflections on language, and various counterparts to contemporary events seen in the light of the book's historical episodes. According to Hjernøe, the writing process is an obstacle to expressing anything original. This artistic dilemma is exemplified in *Hverdag* (Everyday, 1976), impenetrable multitude of linguistic possibilities and structures. Hjernøe's model is Michel Butor, with his interpretattion of the relativity of time.

Henrik Bjelke

Bjelke (1937–   ) is clearly indebted to James Joyce in his major work, the myth of rebirth, *Saturn* (1974), about a divided self and its wanderings through the present and the world of myth. It is primarily literature as a writing process that fascinates Bjelke, with all its inherent possibilities for illusion and allusion, a point of view that increasingly dominates his works from the novel *Trap* (1970) to the short-story collection *Yoyo* (1976).

More accessible and less problematic are the inventive poems and lyrical prose works by Steen Kaalø (1945–   ), expressions of a neo-romantic current in contemporary Danish literature. To a certain degree this also distinguishes the poetry collections by Henrik Nord-brandt (1945–   ), whose favorite setting is the Near East. The longing for greater openness and an attempt to dispel human isolation is a general theme in Nordbrandt's writing, reaching a climax in the collection *Opbrud og ankomster* (Departures and Arrivals, 1974). Whereas nature and seasonal changes permeate the earlier volumes, love becomes increasingly predominant in the collections *Ode til blæksprutten* (Ode to the Octopus, 1975), *Glas* (Glass, 1976), and *Guds hus* (1977; Eng. tr. *God's House*, 1979). They contain elaborate, sensitive, and philosophical poetry which is difficult to label owing to its diversity.

The social realism of the 1930s is continued by Ulrik Gräs (1940–   ) in a number of novels about the working class. A similar proletarian milieu is depicted in the poetry collections by Lean Nielsen (1935–), *Slægtsdigte* (Family Poems, 1974), *ballader om vold og ømhed* (Ballads of Violence and Tenderness, 1976), and *barnedigte* (Children's Poems, 1979), forming the background for his direct exhortation to revolution. But often the demand for a new society is expressed as a romantic, revolutionary dream.

Vagn Lundbye

This dream is realized in *Smukke tabere* (1970), a lyrical novel by

Lundbye (1933–), the title of which is a direct translation of Leonard Cohen's *Beautiful Losers.* The first-person narrator, who keeps a diary, experiences something like religious fellowship with a partisan group on its way to blow up a reactor; the book constitutes the Beat Generation's dream of a collective, sustained by melodious, resplendent language. The ideal cultural situation is represented by the North American Indians, described in *Her ligger min Yucca frugt* (Here Lies My Yucca Fruit, 1972) and *Den indianske tanke* (The Indian Idea, 1974), the product of the author's imagination and history. In the first two parts of a planned trilogy, *Tilbage til Anholt* (Back to Anholt, 1978) and *Hvalfisken* (The Whale, 1980), Lundbye's perspective has become universal through his call for a return to "the original condition—a life-style between light and darkness, cold and warmth, closeness and cosmos. An existence of giving and taking which began far out in the world and ended far out in the world. An endless flow of life and nature and death."

Rolf Gjedsted

Another typical representative of this romantic, sensitive trend is Gjedsted (1947–). He made his debut in 1969 with *Englefronten* (The Angel Front), lyrical science-fiction stories that illustrate his idea of the poet as prophet or magician. Even more experimental in their absolute worship of beauty are *Krigen er smuk* (The War Is Beautiful, 1970) and *Skønhedsreservatet* (The Beauty Reservation, 1973), inspired by William S. Burroughs, Eastern mysticism, drugs, and popular literature. Gjedsted's most recent book, *Rejsen, rummet og ritualet* (The Journey, the Space and the Ritual, 1976), is an ambitious, romantic, surrealistic attempt to illuminate a number of existential situations with the help of the author's own writing process. Idyllic, pastoral moods alternate with images of violence and death, but destruction is poeticized and transformed into dreams and visions of strange exotic beauty and decadence.

Beauty as a psychedelic experience, combined with elements of science fiction, is depicted by Knud Holten (1945–) and Anders Westenholz (1936–). Greater interest in things social is expressed by the more traditional, realistic authors Ole Henrik Laub (1937–) and Paul Thomas Brandt (1943–), and the more linguistically oriented authors Dan Turèll (1946–), who in 1975 had a popular breakthrough with his memoirs *Vangedebilleder* (Pictures from Vangede), Jens Smærup Sørensen (1946–), and Kristen Bjørnkjær (1943–). In 1976 Bjørnkjær published one of the most significant poetry volumes of the 1970s, *Kærestesorg* (Lover's Grief), which recreates the joys and sorrows of love in simple, almost colloquial language. In several plays and short films Bjørnkjær deals with a series of social problems seen from a clearly socialist viewpoint.

Marianne Larsen

Social and political engagement is also obvious in the talented work of Larsen (1951–), although it is less so in her early surrealistic collections than in the volumes from 1974 and 1976, *Billedtekster* (Captions) and *Det må siges enkelt* (It Must Be Said Simply), which cover specific political concepts such as sexual politics, class struggle, and imperialism in a lucid, powerful style. A recurring theme is an inability to express oneself, which is typical of oppressed and socially powerless groups. The same motif is present in Larsen's first prose work, the short-story collection *Under jordskælvet i Argentina* (During the Earthquake in Argentina, 1978). Here, however, silence is functional: The woman who in the poems most frequently expressed her impotence through silent screams, now speaks by being silent, which has revolutionary implications.

Vita Andersen

This awareness of present issues is combined with a more intimate tone in the writing of Andersen (1944–) one of the more popular of the new authors of the 1970s. Her first poetry collection, *Tryghedsnarkomaner* (Security Addicts, 1977), revolves around experiences from childhood and places of work, experiences of love and loneliness. These motifs reappear in the short stories *Hold kæft og vær smuk* (Shut Up and Be Beautiful, 1978).

These young writers—more names could have been mentioned— together with the more established authors, promise that Danish literature will in the 1980s sustain the versatility and talent characteristic of the previous decade.

FINLAND

The general economic growth in all Nordic countries during the 1960s had far-reaching effects in Finland, since it caused heavy emigration of workers to the industrialized southern regions of Finland and to Sweden, contributing to a depopulization of the already sparsely populated northern provinces. In 1966 a Communist-supported government was established, resulting in severe internal political tension. The leftist movements became increasingly radicalized, directing their protests first against the Vietnam War, then against conditions in Greece and Chile, and later expanding their opposition to encompass the en-

tire capitalistic system. The oil crisis of 1973 produced numerous re-
strictions and price increases, and confidence in the blessings of technology and industrial progress was replaced by a growing awareness
of the importance of resources. Environmental issues became a major
topic—at the beginning less in literature than in the mass media, small
debate theaters, and the press.

Among the leading authors of the 1970s were Pentti Saarikoski
and Väinö Kirstinä, who also played a dominant role in the previous
decade. They abandoned their earlier political stands and exclusive,
linguistic experimentation for more private motifs and simpler language. However, a sophisticated preoccupation with language and a
stronger philosophical emphasis is found in the works of Jyrki Pellinen
(1940-   ). The prose poems *Kuuskajaskari* (1964) and *Niin päinvastoin
kuin kukaan* (So on the Contrary Than Nobody, 1965) are primarily
labyrinthine incursions into the world of words, whereas the more
concise poems *Tässä yhteiskunnassa on paha nukkua* (You Cannot
Sleep Well in This Society, 1966) are more traditional, with refined
natural description and romantic melancholy. This tendency away
from meta-poetry and toward more ordinary language is continued in
the volume *Toisin sanoen kuuntelet* (In Other Words, You Are Listen-
ing, 1969). In his collections of the 1970s Pellinen showed a development toward surreal romanticism and mysticism; this trend, which has
added to the interesting aspects of his writing, led to his latest work,
Kertosäkeiden laulu (The Song of Refrains, 1976). This cyclic poem
is a prolonged, melancholy search for the self, a pensive dialogue with
the poet's mirror image.

The protest literature of the 1960s is continued in the work of Kari
Aronpuro (1940-   ), which is openly satirical of a number of social
and political situations in and outside Finland. This literature reached
its culmination in the work of Matti Rossi (1934-   ), whose first collection, *Näytelmän henkilöt* (The Characters in the Play, 1965) contains the most artistically varied poems on the Vietnam War in Finnish
literature. The dogmatic attitude in Rossi's two collections *Agitprop*
(1972) and *Soi kivinen lanka* (Sword, Wire of Stone, 1974) marks the
peak of the radical politicizing of poetry in Finland.

The wave of report and debate literature that reached its crest around
1970 parallels the revolutionary attitude within poetry. Apart from
Matti Rossi's book about South America, *Väkivallan vuosi* (The Year
of Violence, 1970), and the accusatory report on textile workers by
Marja-Leena Mikkola (1939-   ), *Raskas puuvilla* (Heavy Cotton,
1971), it is primarily journalists who are authors of works in this
genre—in contrast to the situation in neighboring Sweden where major writers are involved. Mikkola is also one of the few Finnish con-

tributors to Nordic feminist literature, with her short-story collections *Lääkärin rouva* (The Wife of the Doctor, 1972) and *Suistomaalla* (By the Delta, 1977), and a number of social songs and cabaret pieces. At present she is also regarded as one of Finland's leading authors of children's books. Less radical, and with a slightly satirical tone, are the empathic depictions of social needs in the novels of Samuli Paronen (1917–74). The novels, *Huone puutalossa* (A Room in a Wooden Shed, 1971) and *Kapina* (The Revolt, 1973), are traditional, realistic prose.

Hannu Salama

The foremost representative of this style is Salama (1936–   ), whose early works attracted little attention. The novel *Juhannustanssit* (The Midsummernight Dance, 1964) aroused strong public debate because of its ostensibly blasphemous passages. The novel tells of a midsummer celebration in a small village when some of the big-city celebrants, while intoxicated, become involved in a fatal traffic accident. In spite of some poorly written passages, Salama has managed to convey the brutal behavior and vulgar language of his characters to great effect, contrasting it with the poetically portrayed summer night. In some of the stories in *Kenttäläinen käy talossa* (Kenttäläinen Comes to Visit, 1967) the author relates his experiences in this literary controversy. Salama's obstinate individualism, exemplary of the increased subjectivity of the 1960s, is present in the novel *Minä, Olli ja Orvokki* (I, Olli, and Orvokki, 1967), a Dostoevskian study of the growth of evil among a group of eccentrics alienated from society. The novel by far outdoes *The Midsummernight Dance* in naturalistic detail and coarseness. His next major work, *Siinä näkijä missä tekijä* (Appears after a Thaw, 1972), tells of the activities of a Communist resistance group during World War II. In spite of Salama's positive attitude toward the central characters—and toward the working class in general—he does not automatically turn into flawless heroes those who fight for socialism. As a critical realist Salama is distinctly aware of his characters' mistakes and weaknesses as well as the group's inner conflicts. His objective outlook is further refined in the first volume of a planned series about contemporary Finland, *Kosti Herhiläisen perunkirjoitus* (Kosti Herhiläisen's Inventory, 1976). With pessimism and occasionally cynicism it portrays a man who has lost his assuredness and searches for something in his past to enable him to face the present.

As a proletarian writer Salama has a kindred spirit in Alpo Ruuth (1943–   ). Ruuth's major work thus far, *Kotimaa* (The Native Country, 1974)—a narrative that alternates between realism and the grotesque—focuses on a problematic condition within Finnish society in the early 1960s: chronic unemployment which forces the main character of the novel to leave for Sweden. Like Ruuth, Lassi Sinkkonen (1937–76) wrote novels set in a working-class milieu. *Sumuruisku* (Fog Spray, 1968) describes a Communist-led business enterprise and its human and organizational problems. *Solveigin laulu* (Solveig's Song, 1970) and its sequel *Solveig ja Jussi* (Solveig and Jussi, 1973) offer a broader picture of the postwar Helsinki proletariat, drawn with affection and humor. But Sinkkonen is at his best when he portrays women with tender and sympathetic erotic realism both in these works and in the autobiographical *Mutta minulla ei olisi rakkautta* (But I Shouldn't Have Love, 1972). Sinkkonen's last novel, *Sirkkelisirkus* (The Circle Circus, 1975), on the other hand, is a dark pessimistic and occasionally desperate story of broken and bitter human beings hovering on the outskirts of welfare society. Woman here is degraded to a sex object, society pits violence against violence.

A new element in the prose of the 1970s, which has its counterpart in the "new simplicity" within poetry, is the return of the provincial narrative, a rediscovery of long-forgotten cultural traditions. Inspiration and motifs come from folk literature, the *Kalevala*, authors like Kivi, and the neo-romanticism of the turn of the century.

In the novels of Eeva Kilpi (1928–), such as *Häätanhu* (Wedding Dance, 1973), and short stories, such as *Kesä ja keski-ikäinen nainen* (Summer and the Middle-Aged Woman, 1970), the village, reflecting a Rousseau-inspired dream, is depicted as a place of security and the safeguard of a more profound, more genuine life-style. A work by Leo Kalervo (1924–), *Kiinitys menneeseen* (Mortgage in the Past, 1967), defends the traditional values of the village as opposed to the destructive forces of war. In the novels *Tuppisuu suomalainen* (A Reticent Finn, 1969) and *Pihlamäkeläiset* (The People from Pihlamäki, 1974) the author contrasts rural and urban life. The city, a place of increased centralization and impersonal efficiency, is strongly attacked in a novel cycle by Eino Säisä (1935–), *Kukkivat roudan maat* (The Lands of Flowering Frost, 1971), a cross-section of Finnish society seen from the perspective of the countryside. The social and emotional problems caused by the shift of population from the country to the city are a predominant theme in the popular novels by Heikki Turunen (1945–), *Simpauttaja* (The Dabster, 1973), *Joensuun Elli* (Elli of Joensuu, 1974), and *Kivenpyörittäjän kylä* (The Stoneroller's Village, 1976). All the novels are set in the author's home region of North Karelia, the part of Finland that has suffered most acutely from the mechanization of traditional occupations.

The young poets have turned to a simple style and intimate atmosphere, a care for detail and a predominant interest in nature, partly motivated by opposition to the materialistic values of the welfare society. Thus when Tommy Tabermann (1947–) in 1970 published his first volume of poetry, *Ruusuja Rosa Luxemburgille* (Roses for Rosa Luxemburg), critics looking for dogmatic political verse were highly disappointed. They found sensitive and romantic poetry about nature and young love, themes that Tabermann also treats with successful diversity in his most recent collections, *Kaipaus* (Yearning, 1976), *Anna minä kumoan vielä tämän maljan* (Let Me Drink Up This Cup Still, 1977), and *Kipeästi keinuu keinumme* (Painfully We Sway in our Swing, 1979). Tabermann, however, deals with many other aspects of human life, no doubt influenced by the life of the industrial town of Karjaa where he lives, an influence which can also be clearly seen in his first novel, *Suudelma* (The Kiss, 1977).

Jarkko Laine (1947–) uses the features of popular culture to attack the welfare-society culture. The tone of his collection *Viidenpennin Hamlet* (Five-Penny Hamlet, 1976) is critical and skeptical, but is balanced by a strong element of humor and puns. Laine is international in outlook: His poems—some of which are in English—refer to writers such as Baudelaire, Dante, Eliot, Hesse, Mayakovsky, and Orwell. Defiance of any dogmatism or systematization is also characteristic of his novel *Futari* (The Soccer Player, 1977).

A very talented nature poet is Risto Rasa (1954–). In his collections *Metsän seinä on vain vihreä ovi* (The Forest Wall Is Only a Green Door, 1971) and *Kulkurivarpunen* (The Vagabond Sparrow, 1973) he concentrates on the little things and the ways of nature which he considers essential components in human life. In the collection *Hiljaa, nyt se laulaa* (Quiet, It's Singing, 1974), a number of romantic love poems are included.

This neo-provincialism and a fascination with the cultural heritage—political writer Matti Rossi (see p. 400) uses the ancient *Kalevala* meter in his poetry collection *Laulu tummana tulevi* (The Song Comes Darkly, 1976), and the work of older authors like Haavikko, Meri, Saarikoski, and Kirstinä also bears this influence—should, perhaps, be interpreted as a reaction against the uncritical and sensational treatment by the mass media of both commercial and ideological trends. In any case, these impulses created an in-depth analysis of national identity which has resulted in the significant artistic renewal of postwar Finnish literature.

FENNO-SWEDISH LITERATURE

It is clear that contemporary Fenno-Swedish literature has abandoned the aestheticizing tendencies of earlier decades in favor of simple, more accessible and less self-absorbed subjects. Writers now desire to embrace all social and political realities, as demonstrated by Claes Andersson (1937–). In *Det är inte lätt att vara villaägare i dessa tider* (It Isn't Easy to Be a House Owner Today, 1969) and *Bli, tilsammans* (Become, Together, 1971) he interweaves debate poems and poems of love and personal happiness, alternating subjectiveness and external issues. The same dialectic freedom also distinguishes the collections *Rumskamrater* (Room Mates, 1974) and *Genom sprickorna i vårt ansikte* (Through the Cracks in Our Face, 1977). Andersson discusses the leftist movement from various perspectives in the novel *Den fagraste vår* (The Fairest Spring, 1976) and expands on the need for increased human responsibility. Such an attitude is far removed from the Marxist tendencies in the two uncompromising, aphoristic poetry collections *Massmöte på jorden* (Mass Meeting on Earth, 1972) and *Han kommer, han kommer* (He Comes, He Comes, 1973) by Gösta Ågren (1936–), one of the few Fenno-Swedish writers with direct political involvement.

Tom Sandell (1937–), who began by imitating French surrealism, has also developed into a sharp critic of his times, with the poetry collections *Dikter* (Poems, 1969) and *Just det, dvs. livet* (Exactly That, i.e., Life, 1970). However, the succeeding novels, *Obeväpnad till tänderna* (Unarmed to the Teeth, 1971) and *Du* (You, 1973), are expressions of a more meditative, philosophical approach. Lars Huldén (1926–) combines such an attitude with liberating and unique humor, employing witty and varied language in terse stanzas structured around coincidences. Selected poems by Huldén were published as *Långdansen* (The Long Dance) in 1976; they show, together with his first prose work *Hus* (House, 1979), the influence on his writing of his East Bothnian home region, its local dialect and folklore.

Neo-provincialism is represented to an even greater extent by a series of self-taught authors, who possess a significant epic talent. Olaf Granholm (1924–), a former traveling salesman, draws on his own experiences as a farmer. In his novels *Bässpojken* (The Goat Boy, 1971) and *Spånskottaren* (The Shingle Sweeper, 1973) he paints pictures of human fate around an East Bothnian lumbermill during World War II. In 1966 Anni Blomqvist (1909–), wife of an Åland fisherman, began a dramatic epic tale, set in the archipelago, about two people's obstinate battle with their harsh surroundings. Almost each year since her debut, Anni Blomqvist has published a sequel in this very popular series.

Märta and Henrik Tikkanen

The two most striking new writers of the 1970s were the married couple Märta and Henrik Tikkanen. Märta (1935–) made her debut in 1970 with *Nu imorron* (Now Tomorrow), a novel about Fredrika and Anders, two people who are united in a bond of passion but who each guards his or her right to independence and a separate life. Although the main emphasis here is on personal issues, the set of problems in the sequel, *Ingenmansland* (No Man's Land, 1972), is somewhat different. Fredrika is no longer able to ignore the injustices of a male-dominated society and the violence in the world, and she becomes increasingly radical and revolutionary. Märta Tikkanen again speaks for the oppressed, including the situation of the modern woman, in *Vem bryr sig om Doris Mihailov* (Who Cares For Doris Mihailov, 1974) and *Män kan inte våldtas* (Men Cannot be Raped, 1975)—the latter made into a film by Jörn Donner (see p. 368). The two novels are written in flexible, lively prose, with a place for both warmth and pithiness. The same elements characterize her poetry collection *Århundradets kärlekssaga* (The Love Story of the Century, 1978), which in precise direct language offers a penetrating portrayal of conflicts in love, married life and work.

When in 1975 Henrik Tikkanen (1924–) published the first part of his confessions, *Brändövägen 8 Brändö. Tel. 35* (Eng. tr. *A Winter's Day*, 1980), followed by *Bävervägen 11 Hertonäs* (1976) and *Mariegatan 26 Kronohagen* (1977)—the titles refer to three important addresses in his life—he upset a large part of the reading public and achieved his literary breakthrough in Sweden. But the three volumes are more than egocentric and scandalous works about the rottenness of the Fenno-Swedish upper class in general and Tikkanen's family in particular. They are primarily attacks on firmly entrenched taboos based on the theme of the family curse. Tikkanen reveals the human degradation and dissolution of his parents and exposes his own sexual exploits and inherited alcoholism with a mixture of ironic taunting and deep tragedy. The third part depicts the author's happy but stormy marriage to Märta, the bright star in his pessimistic world—a counterpart to Dante's Beatrice, Goethe's Gretchen, and Ibsen's Solvejg. More extroverted is Tikkanen's novel *30-åriga kriget* (The 30-Year War, 1977) about a Finnish soldier, forgotten at the border of the North Karelian wilderness after the war against Russia, who, as an obedient, patriotic defender, refuses to accept the fact that the war has ended—a fast-moving, strongly satirical and pacifistic declaration.

Through their intensity, determined involvement, and brilliant use of all the resources of language, the Tikkanens and the earlier writers Anders Cleve and Christer Kihlman stand as the most fascinating exponents of contemporary Fenno-Swedish literature.

ICELAND

In the late 1960s there was a considerable upsurge of leftist literature, turning in particular against foreign political and economic influences. In her social realistic novel *Snaran* (The Trap, 1968) Jacobína Sigurðardóttir (1918–) raises the problem of domination by multinational corporations. Foreign influence is also treated by Svava Jacobsdóttir (1930–) in her satirical novel *Leigjandinn* (The Tenant, 1969), but here it is clothed in symbolic and absurd language. Superficially the novel tells of a married couple and their unexpected tenant, but in reality the narrative deals with the relationship between Icelanders and the American military stationed in Keflavík.

Guðbergur Bergsson

A similar satirical and critical tone is increasingly predominant in the writing of another of today's most talented Icelandic authors, Bergsson (1932–). His novel *Tómas Jónsson, metsölubok* (Tómas Jónsson, Bestseller, 1966) is regarded as one of the most revolutionary works in Icelandic literature since Laxness's novel *The Great Weaver from Kashmir*. All limits between inner and outer reality are swept away, personality is dissolved or transformed into other characters in this book about physical decay, darkness, and death. *Ástir samlyndra hjóna* (The Love of a Harmoniously Married Couple, 1967) depicts, occasionally with morbid humor, contemporary Iceland with its threatening conformity. The novel also contains a strong attack on the United States and the American relationship with Icelanders in general. This political motif recurs in Bergsson's next book, *Anna* (1969), set, as are the others, in a small fishing village close to Keflavík. The language is more traditional than in Bergsson's earlier writing, in spite of the novel's very intricate structure. The events take place in a family consisting of three generations, in which each individual reflects upon the present from his or her personal point of view. The narrative is strongly satirical, and Bergsson uses every possibility to emphasize the trivial and disgusting in each of the people, deliberately presenting a distorted picture of a gray and boring reality. An almost absurd culmination of his contempt is reached when the family is visited by three ladies who were married in the United States and were sent home at the expense of the government, telling of their experiences abroad.

The combination of absurdity and reality similarly forms the basis of Bergsson's short-story collection *Hvað er eldi guðs* (What Does God Eat, 1970) and creates mythical traits in the two-volume novel *það sefur í djúpinu* (It Sleeps in the Depth, 1973) and its sequel *það rís úr djúpinu* (It Rises from the Depth, 1976), again revolving around the grotesque and repulsive elements of life. The period of these works is the postwar era, but—as in all of Bergsson's works—it is transformed by a strange timelessness. The main character, Anna, the title character of the novel of 1969, appears with her family in almost all of Bergsson's works—a typical feature in his work which should be considered a continuous series of attempts to give spiritual embodiment to concrete reality. His method consists of apparently surpassing reality to disclose the extreme, grotesque, and negative in everyday life, a technique that makes Bergsson the leading experimenter in Icelandic prose today.

Poetry in the 1970s slowly followed the same trends as did the prose. It continued to emphasize problems of a subjective nature and questions about moral values; only gradually did poetry become politically committed and manifest experimental forms. Nature is—as always—a major motif in modern Icelandic poetry. Yet one of the more promising younger poets, Þorsteinn frá Hamri (pseudonym of Þorsteinn Jónsson [1938–]), is able to join new and old, both linguistically and philosophically.

Þorsteinn frá Hamri

In his writing the classical past is assimilated with the present, in a flexible, modern, and rhythmic language. It is a period marked by the presence of the American base in Keflavík and by the Vietnam War, both of which the poet ironically repudiates through political radicalism linked with nationalistic pathos—a typical combination in Icelandic literature. Hamri's preoccupation with the national tradition— history, literature, and folklore—resulted in a number of optimistic and well-balanced poetry collections during the 1960s. His growing awareness that the hermetic style of lyrical modernism had established a decisive barrier in the communication process led in 1972 to the strongly pessimistic poems *Veðrahjálmur* (Sun Rings); they constitute a dream about the possibilities of human fellowship, a vision which is almost impossible to maintain when confronted with the present shattered world view: "Only startled out of sleep / we have a presentiment of two values / human and human." This search for truly lasting values forms the basic theme of Hamri's lyrical novel *Möttull konungur eða Caterpillar* (King Cloak or Caterpillar, 1974), in which he succeeds in combining motifs from myth, folk legend, and contemporary everyday life.

Pétur Gunnarsson

A more obvious social and political consciousness is found in the work of Gunnarsson (1947–), a typical representative of the postwar generation who stepped forward around 1975 and spoke for a political activism that appears most convincing when combined with a linguistic and stylistic renewal, an attempt to utilize spoken language and generally known references in plain, everyday works. Gunnarsson's collection *Splunkunýr dagur* (A Brand-New Day, 1973) is indeed based on the optimistic realization that the world is inconstant and life is a continuous happening. In the novel *Punktur, punktur, komma, strik* (Period, Period, Comma, Dash, 1976) this attitude is blended with a clear insight into social implications. With swift and humorous brush strokes he paints an overview of postwar developments in Iceland, and beyond this in the whole Western world from World War II to the Vietnam War. The young Andri and his friends are born into systems and roles that are beyond their control, but against which they rebel.

Sigurður Pálsson

The same generation speaks in the linguistically skillful poems by Pálsson (1948–), *Ljóð vega salt* (Poems on the See-Saw, 1975). He has verve and freshness in common with Pétur Gunnarsson, and both utilize obviously autobiographical material. In his poems Pálsson presents a number of half-nostalgic, half-mocking scences from his childhood in the country, his school years and various odd jobs. But he is never narcissistic. Rather, the description of his youth becomes the point of departure for his emotional and intellectual position toward a new, far more complicated reality.

As in the other Nordic countries, the feminist cause is a part of this reality. In *Feilnóta í fimmtu sinfóníunni* (The Wrong Chord in the Fifth Symphony, 1975), a novel by Jökull Jakobsson (1933–), the narrator is an upper-class woman who tells of her futile rebellion against her social and sexual roles, and her career-minded husband. Her attempts to recapture freedom and youth through love affairs and excursions into the drug-infested habitats of the young are primarily related ironically and humorously, genuinely balancing the novel's strong tone of lyricism and pathos. More brutal and harsh is the world portrayed in *Eftirþankar Jóhönnu* (Jóhanna's Afterthoughts, 1975), by Vésteinn Lúðvíksson (1944–), an attempt to analyze the established female role from a social point of view. Jóhanna, a forty-year-old divorced mother of five, tells of her latest love affair with Hörður, whom she has helped to commit suicide. Neither one can or will accept the traditional social and sexual roles. Jóhanna rebels, whereas Hörður gives up and succumbs; both are unable to overcome the roles imposed by society which have defined and destroyed their lives.

The universal perspective of the novel makes it less narrow than the feminist literature of other countries and is an excellent example of the nondogmatic attitude that characterizes the principal authors in the five Nordic nations, giving their literature its wide scope, high quality, and promising possibilities for the future.

Bibliography

Bibliography

This bibliography is selective and focuses mainly on works in English that provide further bibliographical references. Monographs and articles dealing with individual authors are listed alphabetically under the authors' names and include only material in English.

ABBREVIATIONS

ASR: *The American-Scandinavian Review*; since 1975 *Scandinavian Review*.
BA: *Books Abroad*; since 1977 *World Literature Today*.
BF: *Books from Finland*.
PPNCFL: *Proceedings: Pacific Northwest Council on Foreign Languages, Part 1: Foreign Literatures*; since 1980 *Selecta*.
Scan: *Scandinavica*.
ScanR: *Scandinavian Review*.
SS: *Scandinavian Studies*.
WLT: *World Literature Today*.

BIBLIOGRAPHIES

Scandinavian Literature

A list of five hundred books by Scandinavians and about Scandinavia, 2nd ed. New York: The American-Scandinavian Foundation, 1923.
MLA international bibliography of books and articles on the modern languages and literatures. New York: The Modern Language Association of America, 1921ff. [Includes sections on Scandinavia.]
Ng, Maria and Michael S. Batts. *Scandinavian literature in English translation 1928-1977*. Vancouver, B.C.: The Canadian Association of University Teachers of German, 1978.

Scandinavia: a bibliographic survey of literature. Washington D.C.: United States. Dept. of the Army. U.S. Government Printing Office, 1975.
Scandinavian Studies. Lawrence, Kansas, 1911ff. [Includes bibliographies.]
Scandinavica. London/New York, 1962ff. [Includes bibliographies.]
Skard, Sigmund. *Report on the Scandinavian collection.* Washington, D.C.: U.S. Library of Congress, 1944.
The year's work in modern language studies. London: The Modern Humanities Research Association, 1929/30ff. [Includes sections on Scandinavia.]
Tiblin, Mariann and Susan Larson-Fleming. *Scandinavia in English. An annual bibliography of humanities and social sciences 1978.* Minneapolis: Center for Northwest European Language and Area Studies, University of Minnesota, 1980.

Denmark

Bredsdorff, Elias. *Danish literature in English translation.* Westport, Conn.: Greenwood Press, 1973. [Reprint of 1950 ed.]
Dania polyglotta. Literature on Denmark in languages other than Danish and books of Danish interest published abroad. An annual bibliography. Copenhagen: The Royal Library, 1946ff.
Dansk bogfortegnelse 1841ff. Copenhagen: Gad, 1861ff.
Denmark. Literature, language, history, society, education, arts. A select bibliography. Copenhagen: The Royal Library, 1966.
Jørgensen, Aage. *Dansk litteraturhistorisk bibliografi 1967ff.* Copenhagen: Akademisk Forlag, 1968ff.
Jørgensen, Aage. *Contributions in foreign languages to Danish literary history 1961-1970. A bibliography.* Aarhus: Akademisk Boghandel, 1971.
Mitchell, P. M. *A bibliographical guide to Danish literature.* Copenhagen: Ejnar Munksgaard, 1951.
Munch-Petersen, Erland. *A guide to Danish bibliography.* Copenhagen: The Royal School of Librarianship, 1965.
Ober, Kenneth H. *Contributions in Dutch, English, Faroese, German, Icelandic, Italian, and Slavic languages to Danish literary history 1925-1970: A provisional bibliography.* Copenhagen: Det kongelige Bibliotek, 1976.

Faroe Islands

Færøsk bogfortegnelse 1841ff. Copenhagen: Gad 1861ff. [Published in *Dansk bogfortegnelse* or as a supplement to *Dansk bogfortegnelse.*]
Fors Bergström, Ejnar. *Den färöiska boken. En nordisk kulturinsats: språket och litteraturen, en översikt. Dokumentation och data 6.* Stockholm: Kungliga biblioteket, 1974.

Finland

Aaltonen, Hilkka. *Books in English on Finland.* Turku: Turku University Library, 1964.
Books from Finland. Helsinki: Helsinki University Library, 1967ff.
Suomen kirjallisuus. Finlands litteratur. The Finnish national bibliography, 1544ff. Helsinki: Helsingin Yliopiston Kirjasto, 1877ff.
Suomessa ilmestyneen kirjallisuuden aineenmukainen uutuusluettelo. Systematisk katalog över i Finland utkommen litteratur. Helsinki: Akateeminen kirjakauppa, 1945ff.
Rosvall, Toivo David, "A bibliography of Finnish literature in England." *BA* 9 (1935), 394-95.

Iceland

Bókmenntaskrá skírnis, 1968ff. Reykjavík: Hið Íslenzka Bókmenntafjelag, 1969ff.

Islands bogfortegnelse 1899-1934. Copenhagen: Gad, 1899-1934. [Published irregularly in *Dansk bogfortegnelse* or as a supplement to that publication.]

Jósepsson, Bragi. *Icelandic culture and education: An annotated bibliography.* Research bulletin 1. Bowling Green, Ky.: Western Kentucky University, 1968.

Landsbókasafn Islands. Islenzk bókaskrá. The Icelandic national bibliography, 1974ff. Reykjavík: Landsbókasafn Islands, 1976ff.

Mitchell, P. M. and Kenneth H. Ober. *Bibliography of modern Icelandic literature in translation. Including works written by Icelanders in other languages. Islandica* 40. Ithaca, N.Y. and London: Cornell University Press, 1975.

Reykjavík. Landsbókasafnið. Árbók, 1944-1973. Reykjavík: Landsbókasafnið, 1945-75. [A national bibliography is in a special section entitled *Íslenzk rit.*]

Norway

Grønland, Erling. *Norway in English: Books on Norway and by Norwegians in English 1936-1959. A bibliography, including a survey of Norwegian literature in English translation from 1742 to 1959.* Oslo: Norwegian Universities Press, 1961.

Naess, Harald S. *Norwegian literary bibliography 1956-70: Norsk litteraturhistorisk bibliografi 1956-70.* Oslo: Universitetsforlaget, 1975.

Norsk bogfortegnelse. The Norwegian national bibliography, 1814ff. Kristiania, Oslo: Den norske bokhandlerforening, 1848ff.

Norsk litterær årbok. Oslo: Det Norske Samlaget, 1966ff. [Includes bibliographies.]

Norwegian scholarly books 1825-1967. Oslo: Universitetsforlaget, 1968.

Øksnevad, Reidar. *Norsk litteraturhistorisk bibliografi 1900-1945.* Oslo: Gyldendal, 1951.

Øksnevad, Reidar. *Norsk litteraturhistorisk bibliografi 1946-1955.* Oslo: Gyldendal, 1958.

Pettersen, Hjalmar, ed. *Bibliotheca Norvegica, 1-4.* Christiania: Cammermeyer, 1899-1924.

Sweden

Holmbäck, Bure. *About Sweden, 1900-1963; a bibliographical outline.* Compiled with the assistance of Ulla-Märta Abrahamson and Mariann Tiblin. [Stockholm, 1968.] (In *Sweden illustrated.* Stockholm, v. 15 (1968), pp. 1-94.)

Josephson, Aksel G. S. *A List of Swedish books 1875-1925.* New York: Bonniers, 1927.

Suecana extranea. Böcker om Sverige och svensk skönlitteratur på främmande språk/Books on Sweden and Swedish literature in foreign languages, 1963-66. Stockholm: The Swedish Institute, 1968ff. Stockholm: Kungliga Biblioteket, 1968ff.

Svensk bokförtekning. Arskatalog. The Swedish national bibliography. Stockholm: Svensk bokhandel, 1913ff.

Svensk bokkatalog, 1866ff. Stockholm: Svenska bokförläggareföreningen, 1878ff.

Svensk litteraturhistorisk bibliografi. Uppsala: Svenska litteratursällskapet, 1880ff. [In *Samlaren; tidskrift för svensk litteraturhistorisk forskning,* 1880ff.]

LITERARY HISTORY

Scandinavian Literature

Biztray, George. "Documentarism and the modern Scandinavian novel." *SS* 48 (1976), 71-83.

Blankner, Frederika et al. *The history of the Scandinavian literatures*. New York: Dial Press, 1938.

Borelius, Hilma. *Die nordischen Literaturen*. Potsdam: Akademische Verlagsgesellschaft Athenaion, 1931.

Bredsdorff, Elias, Brita Mortensen, and Ronald Popperwell. *An introduction to Scandinavian literature from the earliest time to our day*. Westport, Conn.: Greenwood Press, 1970. [Reprint of 1951 ed.]

Brennecke, Detlef, ed. *Aspekte der skandinavischen Gegenwartsliteratur*. Heidelberg: C. Winter Universitätsverlag, 1978.

Brøndsted, Mogens, ed. *Nordens litteratur*, 1-2. Copenhagen: Gyldendal, 1972 / Oslo: Gyldendal, 1972 / Lund: Gleerup, 1972.

Fonsmark, Henning B., ed. *Nordisk litteratur før 1914*. 5th ed. Copenhagen: Politiken, 1975.

Friese, Wilhelm. *Nordische Literaturen im 20. Jahrhundert*. Stuttgart: Kröner, 1971.

Gabrieli, Mario. *Le letterature della Scandinavica: Danese, Norvegese, Svedese, Islandese*. 2nd aug. ed. Firenze: Sansoni / Milano: Accademia, 1969.

Kotas, Walter H. *Die skandinavische Literatur der Gegenwart seit 1870*. Wiesbaden: Dioskuren Verlag, 1925.

Larsen, Hanna A. *Scandinavian Literature*. Chicago: American Library Association, 1930.

Marker, Frederic J. and Lise-Lone. *The Scandinavian theatre: A short history*. Oxford: Blackwell / Totowa, N.J.: Rowman and Littlefield, 1975.

Mawby, Janet. *Writers and politics in modern Scandinavia*. London: Hodder and Stoughton, 1978.

Printz-Påhlson, Göran. "Concepts of criticism in Scandinavia 1960-67." *Scan.* 7 (1968), 1-30.

Runnquist, Åke. *Moderna nordiska författare*. Stockholm: Forum, 1966.

Sandvej, Knud, ed. *Vor tids Hvem-Skrev-Hvad. Efter 1914*, 1-2. 3rd ed. Copenhagen: Politiken, 1968.

Scandinavica 12 (1973), Supplement. [Special issue on contemporary Scandinavian poetry.]

Schoolfield, George C. "Tradition and innovation in the Occidental lyric of last decade. VI. Canals on Mars: the recent Scandinavian lyric." *BA* 36 (1962) 9-19, 117-24.

Topsøe-Jensen, H. G. *Scandinavian literature from Brandes to our day*. New York: The American-Scandinavian Foundation / W. W. Norton and Company, 1929.

Vowles, Richard B. "A half century of Scandinavian drama." *Drama Survey* (Minneapolis) 1 (1961), 178-94.

Denmark

Borum, Poul. *Danish literature*. Copenhagen: Det danske Selskab, 1979.

Brandt, Jørgen Gustava. *Præsentation. 40 danske digtere efter krigen*. Copenhagen: Gyldendal, 1964.

Brostrøm, Torben and Mette Winge, eds. *Danske digtere i det 20. århundrede*, 1-5. Copenhagen: Gad, 1980ff.

Brøndsted, Mogens and Sven Møller Kristensen. *Danmarks litteratur*. 3rd ed. Copenhagen: Gyldendal, 1975.

Claudi, Jørgen. *Contemporary Danish authors, with a brief outline of Danish literature*. Copenhagen: Det danske Selskab, 1952.

Durand, Frédéric. *Histoire de la littérature danoise*. Paris: Aubier-Montaigne / Copenhagen: Gyldendal, 1967.

Kjærgaard, Helge. *Die dänische Literatur der neuesten Zeit (1871-1933)*. Copenhagen: Levin and Munksgaard, 1934.

Marx, Leonie. "Literary experimentation in a time of transition: The Danish short story after 1945." *SS* 49 (1977), 131-54.

Mitchell, P. M. *A history of Danish literature*. 2nd aug. ed. New York: Kraus-Thomson, 1971.
Møller Kristensen, Sven. *Dansk litteratur 1918-52*. 7th ed. Med tillæg 1952-64. Copenhagen: Munksgaard, 1965.
Nielsen, Frederik and Ole Restrup, eds. *Danske digtere i det 20. århundrede*, 1-3. Copenhagen: Gad, 1965-66.
Petersen, Carl S. and Vilhelm Andersen. *Illustreret dansk litteraturhistorie*, 1-4. Copenhagen: Gyldendal, 1924-34.
Ravn, Ole. *Dansk litteratur 1920-75*, 1-2. Copenhagen: Gjellerup, 1976.
Roger-Henrichsen, Gudmund. *A Decade of Danish literature 1960-70*. Copenhagen: The Ministry of Foreign Affairs, 1972.
Svendsen, Hanne Marie and Werner. *Geschichte der dänischen Literatur*. Neumünster: Karl Wachholtz / Copenhagen: Gyldendal, 1964.
Thomsen, Ejnar. *Dansk litteratur efter 1870 med sideblik til det øvrige Norden*. Copenhagen: Rosenkilde and Bagger, 1965. [Reprint of 1935 ed.]
Traustedt, P. H., ed. *Dansk litteraturhistorie*, 1-6. 2nd aug. ed. Copenhagen: Politiken, 1976-77.
Vosmar, Jørn, ed. *Modernismen i dansk litteratur*. 2nd ed. Copenhagen: Fremad, 1969.
Woel, Cai M. *Dansk litteraturhistorie 1900-1950*, 1-2. Odense: Arnkrone, 1956.

Faroe Islands

Brønner, Hedin. *Three Faroese novelists*. New York: Twayne, 1973.
Brønner, Hedin. "The short story in the Faroe Isles." *SS* 49 (1977), 155-79.
Jacobsen, Ole. "Nyere digtning" in *Færøerne*, 2, 100-21. Copenhagen: Det danske Forlag, 1958.
Krenn, Ernst. *Die Entwicklung der foeroyischen Literatur*. Urbana, Ill.: University of Illinois Press, 1940.
Matras, Christian. *Føroysk bókmentasøga*. Copenhagen: Føroya málfélag, 1935.

Finland

Ahokas, Jaakko. "The short story in Finnish literature." *BF* 3:3 (1969), 2-6.
Ahokas, Jaakko. "Finnish drama and culture." *Michigan Academician* 3:3 (1971), 45-53.
Ahokas, Jaakko. *A history of Finnish literature*. Bloomington: Indiana University, Research Center for the Language Sciences for The American-Scandinavian Foundation, New York, 1973.
Dauenhauer, Richard. "The literature of Finland." *Literary Review* 14 (1970), 5-27.
Dauenhauer, Richard and Philip Binham. *Snow in May: An anthology of Finnish writing, 1945-72*. Rutherford, N.J.: Fairleigh Dickinson University Press, 1978. [Included are sections on Finnish literature.]
Finnish and Baltic history and literatures. Cambridge, Mass.: Harvard University Press, 1972.
Havu, I [lmari] and Th[omas] Warburton. *Finlands litteratur 1900-1950*, 1-2. Stockholm: Örnkrona [1958].
Holmqvist, Bengt. *Modern finlandssvensk litteratur*. Stockholm: Natur och Kultur, 1951.
Huldén, Lars et al. *Finlands svenska litteratur*, 1ff. Helsingfors: Söderström, 1968ff. [Forthcoming.]
Ivask, Ivar, ed. *The two literatures of Finland. World Literature Today*, 54:1. Norman, Oklahoma: University of Oklahoma Press, 1980.
Laitinen, Kai. *Finlands moderna litteratur; konturer, huvudlinjer, resultat, 1917-1967*. Stockholm: Forum, 1968.
Landquist, John. *Modern svensk litteratur i Finland*. Stockholm: Natur och Kultur, 1929.

Lindström, Hans. *Finlandssvensk nittonhundratalslitteratur*. Stockholm: Sveriges Finlands-föreningars riksförbund, 1965.

Nummi, Lassi. "Zur Situation des Schrifttums im heutigen Finland." *Ausblick* 24 (1973), 30–38.

Rubulis, Aleksis. *Baltic literature. A survey of Finnish, Estonian, Latvian, and Lithuanian literatures*. Notre Dame, Indiana: University of Notre Dame Press, 1970.

Saarinen, E. "Movements in modern Finnish literature." *The Norseman*, 14 (1956), 278–84.

Sandell, Tom. "Finland's Swedish-language literature in 1970–73." *BF* 9:1 (1975), 2–7.

Sarajas, Annamari. "Contemporary Finnish writing." *BA*, 29 (1955), 149–54.

Scandinavica 15 (1976), supplement. [A special issue on Fenno-Swedish literature.]

Schoolfield, George C. "The post-war novel of Swedish Finland." *SS* 34 (1962), 85–110.

Schoolfield, George C. "Some reflections on Finland's literature." *BF* 6:3 (1972), 2–7.

Svedberg, Ingmar. "Political poetry in modern Finnish literature." *BF* 3:2 (1969), 2–7.

Tarkiainen, Viljo. *Finsk litteraturhistoria*. Helsingfors: Söderström, 1950.

Waltari, Mika. "The Finnish literature of today." *BA*, 10 (1936), 268–69.

Iceland

Andrésson, Kristinn E. *Íslenzkar nútímabókmenntir 1918-1948*. Reykjavík: Mál og menning, 1949. Swedish ed. by Peter Hallberg. *Det moderna Islands litteratur 1918-1948*. Stockholm: Kooperative förbundets bokförlag, 1955.

Beck, Richard. *History of Icelandic poets 1800-1940. Islandica* 34. Ithaca, N.Y.: Cornell University Press, 1950.

Chapman, Kenneth G. "From Edda to Atom: A brief look at contemporary Icelandic poetry." *BA* 38 (1964), 5-10.

Einarsson, Stefán. *History of Icelandic prose writers 1800-1940. Islandica* 32-33. Ithaca, N.Y.: Cornell University Press, 1948.

Einarsson, Stefán. *A history of Icelandic literature*. New York: The Johns Hopkins Press for The American-Scandinavian Foundation, 1957.

Einarsson, Stefán. *Íslensk bókmenntasaga, 874-1960*. Reykjavík: Snæbjörn Jónsson, 1961.

Gislason, Bjarni M. *Islands litteratur efter sagatiden, ca. 1400-1948*. Copenhagen: Aschehoug, 1949.

Hallmundsson, Hallberg. "Years of growth: The Icelandic theater 1956-60." *ASR* 49 (1961) 145-51.

Magnússon, Sigurður A. "Icelandic literature: Preserver of national culture." *Mosaic* 1 (1968), 83-93.

Magnússon, Sigurður A. "Den politiske efterkrigsroman i Island." *Horisont* (Vasa) 17 (1970), 18-26.

Magnússon, Sigurður A. "The modern Icelandic novel: From isolation to political awareness." *Mosaic* 4 (1970), 133-43.

Nordal, Sigurður. *Utsikt over Islands litteratur i det 19. og 20. århundre*. Oslo: Aschehoug, 1927.

Norway

Beyer, Edvard, ed. *Norges litteraturhistorie*, 1-6. Oslo: J. W. Cappelen, 1974-75.

Beyer, Harald. *A history of Norwegian literature*. New York: New York University Press for The American-Scandinavian Foundation, New York, 1956.

Beyer, Harald and Edvard. *Norsk litteraturhistorie*. 4th rev. and aug. ed. Oslo: Aschehoug, 1978.

Bull, Francis et al. *Norsk litteraturhistorie*, 1-6. 2nd ed. Oslo: Aschehoug, 1957-63.

Christiansen, Hjalmar. *Norwegische Literaturgeschichte von der Edda bis zur Gegenwart: ein Überblick.* Berlin: Die Quintessenz, 1953.

Dahl, Willy. *Stil og struktur; utviklingslinjer i norsk prosa gjennom 150 år.* 2nd revised ed. Oslo: Universitetsforlaget, 1969.

Dahl, Willy. *Nytt norsk forfatterleksikon.* Oslo: Gyldendal, 1971.

Dahl, Willy. *Fra 40-tall til 70-tall. Norsk prosa gjennom et kvart århundres etterkrigstid.* 2nd revised ed. Oslo: Gyldendal, 1973.

Downs, Brian W. *Modern Norwegian literature 1860-1918.* Cambridge: Cambridge University Press, 1966.

Elster, Kristian. *Illustrert norsk litteraturhistorie,* 1-6. 2nd ed. Oslo: Gyldendal, 1934-35.

Groth, Helge. *Hovedlinjer i mellomkrigstidens litteratur.* Bergen: John Griegs bogtr., 1947.

Grøndahl, Ingebright C. *Chapters in Norwegian literature.* London: Gyldendal, 1923.

Houm, Philip. *Norges litteratur. Fra 1914 till 1950-årene.* 2nd ed. Oslo: Aschehoug, 1976.

Jorgenson, Theodore. *History of Norwegian literature.* New York: Haskell House, 1970. [Reprint of 1933 ed.]

Lescoffier, Jean. *Histoire de la Littérature Norvégienne.* Paris: Société d'édition "Les Belles Lettres," 1952.

Mawby, Janet. "The Norwegian novel today." *Scan.* 14 (1975), 101-13.

Naess, Harald. "From Hoel to Haavardsholm: Norwegian literature since World War II." *Literary Review* (Fairleigh Dickinson University) 12 (1969), 133-48.

Støverud, Torbjørn. *Milestones of Norwegian literature.* Oslo: Tanum, 1967.

Sweden

Björck, Staffan et al. *Litteraturhistoria i fickformat. Svensk diktning från 80-tal till 60-tal.* Stockholm: Liber, 1967.

Boor, Helmut de. *Schwedische Literatur.* Breslau: F. Hirt, 1924.

Brandell, Gunnar and Jan Stenkvist. *Svensk litteratur 1870-1970,* 1-3. Stockholm: Aldus, 1974-75.

Brostrøm, Torben. *Modern svensk litteratur 1940-72.* Stockholm: Aldus, 1974.

Engman, Bo et al. *Litteraturlexikon: svensk litteratur under 100 år.* Stockholm: Natur och Kultur, 1974.

Gustafson, Alrik. *A history of Swedish literature.* Minneapolis: University of Minnesota Press for The American-Scandinavian Foundation, New York, 1961.

Gustafsson, Lars. *Forays into Swedish poetry.* Austin and London: University of Texas Press, 1978.

Hedlund, Tom. *Mitt i 70-talet. 15 yngre svenska författare presenteras.* Stockholm: Forum, 1975.

Hilleström, Gustaf. *Swedish theater during five decades.* Stockholm: Svenska Institutet, 1962.

Lagerlöf, Karl-Erik. *Samtal med 60-talister.* Stockholm: Bonniers, 1965.

Lagerlöf, Karl-Erik, ed. *Femtitalet i backspegeln.* Stockholm: Aldus / Bonniers, 1968.

Lagerlöf, Karl-Erik. *Strömkantringens år och andra essäer om den nya litteraturen.* Stockholm: PAN/Norstedt, 1975.

Linder, Erik Hj. *Fem decennier av nittonhundratalet,* 1-2. 4th aug. ed. Stockholm: Natur och Kultur, 1965-66. Also included as volume 5 of *Ny illustrerad svensk litteraturhistoria;* see Tigerstedt entry.

Matsson, Ragnar. *Svensk 30-tal. Krisen och litteraturen.* Stockholm: Gidlund / Solna: Seelig, 1975.

Runnquist, Åke. *Moderna svenska författare.* 2nd ed. Stockholm: Forum, 1967.

Schück, Henrik and Karl Warburg. *Illustrerad svensk litteraturhistoria,* 1-8. Stockholm: Rabén och Sjögren, 1926-49.

Schück, Henrik. *Histoire de la littérature suédoise*. Paris: Éditions E. Leroux, 1923.
Scobbie, Irene, ed. *Essays on Swedish literature. From 1880 to the present day*. Aberdeen: University of Aberdeen, 1978.
Svenskt litteraturlexikon. 2nd ed. Lund: Gleerup, 1970.
Tigerstedt, E. N., ed. *Ny illustrerad svensk litteraturhistoria*, 1–4. 2nd aug. ed. Stockholm: Natur och Kultur, 1967.
Tigerstedt, E. N. *Svensk litteraturhistoria*. 3rd ed. Stockholm: Natur och Kultur, 1967.
Vowles, Richard B. "Post-war Swedish poetry: The other side of anguish." *Western Humanities Review* 15 (1961) 355–48.
Wizelius, Ingemar. *Swedish literature 1956–60*. Stockholm: The Swedish Institute, 1960.

ANTHOLOGIES IN ENGLISH
Scandinavian Literature

Allwood, Martin S. *Twentieth century Scandinavian poetry. The development of poetry in Iceland, Denmark, Norway, Sweden and Finland, 1900–1950*. Copenhagen: Gyldendal, 1950.
Allwood, Martin S. and Lindsay Lafford. *Scandinavian songs and ballads*. 4th ed. Mullsjö: Anglo-American Center, 1957.
Bannister, Estrid. *Scandinavian short stories: A selection of Swedish, Norwegian and Danish stories*. Harmondsworth/New York: Penguin Books, 1943.
Gosse, Edmund and W. A. Craigie. *The Oxford book of Scandinavian verse, 17th century-20th century*. Oxford: The Clarendon Press, 1925.
Hallmundsson, Hallberg. *An anthology of Scandinavian literature from the viking period to the twentieth century*. New York: Collier, 1965.
Krook, Anna Sofia. *Songs of the north. A collection of poems*. Helsingfors: Söderström and Co., 1926.
Modern Scandinavian plays. New York: Liveright Publishing Corporation for The American-Scandinavian Foundation, 1954.
Radio plays from Denmark, Finland, Norway, Sweden, awarded prizes in the Scandinavian radio play contest held in 1969. Stockholm: Sveriges Radio, 1971.
Scandinavian plays of the twentieth century, 1–3. Princeton: Princeton University Press for The American-Scandinavian Foundation, New York, 1944–51.
Sprinchorn, Evert. *The genius of the Scandinavian theatre*. New York: New American Library, 1964.
Stories by foreign authors. Scandinavia. New York: C. Scribner's Sons, 1898.
Wells, Henry W. *Five modern Scandinavian plays*. New York: Twayne/The American-Scandinavian Foundation, 1971.
Willoughby, Robert. *Masterpieces of the modern Scandinavian theatre*. New York: Collier, 1967.

Denmark

Bredsdorff, Elias. *Contemporary Danish plays*. Freeport, N.Y.: Books for Libraries Press, 1970. [Reprint of 1955 ed.]
Bredsdorff, Elias. *Contemporary Danish prose*. Westport, Conn.: Greenwood Press, 1974. [Reprint of 1958 ed.]
Five Danish poets. Loanhead, Scot.: M. MacDonald, 1973.
Friis, Oluf. *A book of Danish verse*. New York: The American-Scandinavian Foundation, 1922.

Heepe, Evelyn. *Swans of the North and short stories by modern Danish authors*. Copenhagen: Gad, 1953.
Heepe, Evelyn and Niels Heltberg. *Modern Danish authors*. Folcroft, Pa.: Folcroft Library Editions, 1974. [Reprint of 1946 ed.]
Holm, Sven. *The devil's instrument and other Danish stories*. London: Peter Owen, 1971.
Jansen, F. J. Billeskov and P. M. Mitchell. *Anthology of Danish literature*. Carbondale: Southern Illinois University Press, 1971.
Jensen, Line et al. *Contemporary Danish poetry*. Boston: Twayne / Copenhagen: Gyldendal, 1977.
Keigwin, Richard P. *The Jutland wind and other verse from the Danish peninsula*. Oxford: Basil Blackwell, 1944.
Keigwin, Richard P. *In Denmark I was born. A little book of Danish verse*. Copenhagen: Høst og Søn, 1948.
Koefoed, H. A. *Modern Danish prose*. Copenhagen: Høst og Søn, 1955.
Larsen, Hanna Astrup. *Denmark's best stories*. New York: The American-Scandinavian Foundation / W. W. Norton and Company, 1928.
Mitchell, P. M. and Kenneth H. Ober. *The Royal guest and other classical Danish narrative*. Chicago: University of Chicago Press, 1977.
Modern Danish writers. Adam International Review. London: June 1948 [special issue].
Modern Nordic plays. Denmark. New York: Twayne / Oslo: Universitetsforlaget, 1974.
Mogensen, Knud K. *Modern Danish poems*. New York: Bonniers / Copenhagen: Høst and Son, 1949.
Stork, Charles W. *A second book of Danish verse*. Freeport, N.Y.: Books for Libraries Press, 1968. [Reprint of 1947 ed.]

Faroe Islands

Brønner, Hedin. *Faroese short stories*. New York: Twayne / The American-Scandinavian Foundation, 1972.

Finland

Dauenhauer, Richard and Philip Binham. *Snow in May: An anthology of Finnish writing, 1945–72*. Rutherford, N.J.: Fairleigh Dickinson University Press, 1978.
Modern Nordic Plays. Finland. New York: Twayne / Oslo: Universitetsforlaget, 1973.
Schoolfield, George C. *Swedo-Finnish short stories*. New York: Twayne / The American-Scandinavian Foundation, 1974.
The Literary Review, 14:1. Rutherford, N.J.: Fairleigh Dickinson University, 1970.
Tompuri, Elli. *Voices from Finland. An anthology of Finland's verse and prose in English, Finnish and Swedish*. Helsinki: Sanoma Osakeyhtiö, 1947.

Iceland

Beck, Richard. *Icelandic lyrics*. Reykjavík: Litbrá, 1956. [Reprint of 1930 ed.]
Beck, Richard. *Icelandic poems and stories*. Freeport, N.Y.: Books for Libraries Press, 1968. [Reprint of 1943 ed.]
Benedikz, Eiríkur. *An anthology of Icelandic poetry*. Reykjavík: The Ministry of Education, 1969.
Bjarnason, Paul. *Odes and echoes*. Vancouver, B.C.: privately published, 1954.
Bjarnason, Paul. *More echoes: Being translations mainly from the Icelandic*. Vancouver, B.C.: privately published, 1962.

Boucher, Alan. *Poems of today. From twenty-five modern Icelandic poets.* 2nd ed. Reykja-
    vík: Iceland Review Library, 1974.

Boucher, Alan. *Short stories of today. By twelve modern Icelandic authors.* 2nd ed. Reykja-
    vík: Iceland Review Library, 1976.

Firchow, Evelyn S. *Icelandic short stories.* Boston: Twayne / New York: The American-
    Scandinavian Foundation, 1975.

Johnson, Jacobina. *Northern lights. Icelandic poems.* Reykjavík: Bókaútgáfa Menningarsjóðs,
    1959.

Kirkconnell, Watson. *The North American book of Icelandic verse.* New York and Montreal:
    Louis Carrier and Alan Isles, 1930.

Modern Nordic plays. Iceland. New York: Twayne / Oslo: Universitetsforlaget, 1973.

Pétursson, Ásgeir and Steingrímur Þorsteinsson. *Seven Icelandic short stories.* Reykjavík:
    The Ministry of Education, 1960.

Norway

Allwood, Inga Wilhelmsen. *Modern Norwegian poems.* New York: Bonniers, 1949.

Five Norwegian poets. Loanhead, Scot.: M. MacDonald, 1976.

Gathorne-Hardy, G. M. *The spirit of Norway: Norwegian war poems.* London: The Royal
    Norwegian Information Office, 1944.

Larsen, Hanna Astrup. *Told in Norway.* Freeport, N.Y.: Books for Libraries Press, 1971.
    [Reprint of 1927 ed. also published as *Norway's best stories.*]

Modern Nordic plays. Norway. New York: Twayne / Oslo: Universitetsforlaget, 1974.

Stork, Charles W. *Anthology of Norwegian lyrics.* Freeport, N.Y.: Books for Libraries Press,
    1968. [Reprint of 1942 ed.]

Sweden

Ahlberg, Fred. *Masterpieces of Swedish poetry.* Tujunga, Calif.: Cecil L. Anderson, 1952.

Allwood, Martin S. et al. *Modern Swedish poems.* Rock Island, Ill.: The Augustana Book
    Concern, 1948.

Allwood, Martin S. and Lindsay Lafford. *Swedish songs and ballads.* New York: Bonniers,
    1950.

Bäckström, Lars and Göran Palm. *Sweden writes; contemporary poetry and prose.* Stock-
    holm: Prisma / The Swedish Institute, 1965.

Bly, Robert. *Friends, you drank some darkness. Three Swedish poets.* Boston: Beacon Press,
    1975.

Brandberg, Paul. *A Swedish reader.* London: Athlone Press, 1953.

Five Swedish poets. New York: Spirit Press, 1972.

Fleischer, Frederic. *Seven Swedish poets.* Malmö: Bo Cavefors, 1963.

Fleischer, Frederic. *Eight Swedish poets.* Malmö: Bo Cavefors, 1969.

Hannay, Carolyn and J. M. Nosworthy. *Some Swedish poets.* Stockholm: The Swedish Insti-
    tute, 1958.

Harding, Gunnar and Anselm Hollo, eds. *Modern Swedish poetry in translation.* Minneapolis:
    University of Minnesota Press, 1979.

Lagerlöf, Karl-Erik, ed. *Modern Swedish prose in translation.* Minneapolis: University of Min-
    nesota Press, 1979.

Larsen, Hanna Astrup. *Sweden's best stories.* New York: The American-Scandinavian Foun-
    dation / W. W. Norton, 1928.

Locock, Charles D. *A selection from modern Swedish poetry.* London: Allen and Unwin,
    1929 / New York: Macmillan, 1930.

Locock, Charles D. *Modern Swedish poetry.* London: H. and W. Brown, 1936.

McLean, Reginald J. *A book of Swedish verse*. London: Athlone Press, 1968.
Modern Nordic Plays. Sweden. New York: Twayne / Oslo: Universitetsforlaget, 1973.
Modern Swedish short stories. Plainview, N.Y.: Books for Libraries Press, 1974. [Reprint of 1934 ed.]
Stork, Charles W. *Modern Swedish masterpieces*. New York: E. P. Dutton, 1923.
Stork, Charles W. *Anthology of Swedish lyrics from 1750–1925*. 2nd rev. and aug. ed. New York: The American-Scandinavian Foundation / London: H. Milford, Oxford University Press, 1930.
Wästberg, Per, ed. *An anthology of modern Swedish literature*. Cross-Cultural Communications. Merrick, New York, 1979.

HISTORY AND CIVILIZATION
Scandinavian Literature

Anderson, Stanley. *The Nordic Council: A study of Scandinavian regionalism*. Seattle: University of Washington Press, 1967.
Connery, Donald S. *The Scandinavians*. New York: Simon and Schuster, 1966.
Derry, T. K. *A history of Scandinavia: Norway, Sweden, Denmark, Finland, and Iceland*. Minneapolis: University of Minnesota Press for The American-Scandinavian Foundation, 1979.
Holst, Johann J. *Five roads to Nordic security*. Oslo: Universitetsforlaget, 1973.
Laurin, Carl et al. *Scandinavian art*. New York: The American-Scandinavian Foundation / London: H. Milford, Oxford University Press, 1922.
Scott, Franklin D. *The United States and Scandinavia*. 2nd rev. and aug. ed. Cambridge, Mass.: Harvard University Press, 1950.
Scott, Franklin D. *Scandinavia*. Cambridge, Mass.: Harvard University Press, 1975.
Skårdal, Dorothy Burton. *The divided heart: Scandinavian immigrant experience through literary sources*. Lincoln: University of Nebraska Press, 1974.

Denmark

Hvidt, Kristian. *Flight to America. The social background of 300,000 Danish Emigrants*. New York, San Francisco, London: Academic Press, 1975.
Jones, W. Glyn. *Denmark*. New York: Praeger / London: Benn, 1970.
Oakley, Stewart. *The story of Denmark*. London: Faber and Faber, 1972.

Faroe Islands

West, John W. *Faroe: the emergence of a nation*. London: C. Hurst / New York: P. S. Eriksson, 1972.

Finland

Kirby, D. G. *Finland in the twentieth century: A history and an interpretation*. Minneapolis: University of Minnesota Press, 1979.
Wuorinen, John H. *A history of Finland*. 2nd ed. New York and London: Columbia University Press for The American-Scandinavian Foundation, New York, 1965.

Iceland

Magnússon, Sigurður A. *Northern sphinx: Iceland and the Icelanders from the settlement to the present*. Montreal: McGill-Queen's University Press, 1977.

Nordal, J. and V. Kristinsson, eds. *Iceland 874-1974*. Reykjavík: Central Bank of Iceland, 1975.
Tomasson, Richard F. *Iceland. The first new society*. Minneapolis: University of Minnesota Press, 1980.

Norway

Derry, T. K. *A history of modern Norway, 1814-1972*. Oxford: Clarendon Press, 1973.
Popperwell, Ronald. *Norway*. London: Ernest Benn, 1972.
Semmingsen, Ingrid. *Norway to America. A history of the migration*. Minneapolis: University of Minnesota Press, 1978.

Sweden

Koblik, Steven, ed. *Sweden's development from poverty to affluence, 1750-1970*. Minneapolis: University of Minnesota Press, 1975.
Runblom, Harald and Hans Norman, eds. *From Sweden to America. A history of the migration*. Minneapolis: University of Minnesota Press / Uppsala: University of Uppsala, 1976.
Samuelsson, Kurt. *From great power to welfare state: 300 years of Swedish social development*. London: Allen and Unwin, 1968.
Scott, Franklin D. *Sweden: The nation's history*. Minneapolis: University of Minnesota Press, 1977.

MONOGRAPHS AND ARTICLES ON INDIVIDUAL AUTHORS

Aakjæt, Jeppe

Westergaard, W. "Jeppe Aakjæt." *ASR* 12 (1924), 665-69.

Abell, Kjeld

Madsen, Børge Gedsø. "Leading motifs in the dramas of Kjeld Abell." *SS* 33 (1961), 127-36.
Marker, Frederick J. *Kjeld Abell*. Boston: Twayne, 1976.

Ahlin, Lars

Lundell, Torborg. "Lars Ahlin's concept of the writer as identificator and förbedjare." *Scan* 14 (1975), 27-35.
Lundell, Torborg. *Lars Ahlin*. Boston: Twayne, 1977.

Andersen, Benny

Marx, Leonie. "Exercises in living: Benny Andersen's literary perspectives." *WLT* 52 (1978), 550-54.

Andersen, Tryggve

Schiff, Timothy. "Tryggve Andersen's novel Mot kvæld and its motto." *SS* 48 (1976), 146-55.
Schiff, Timothy. "Moral equivocality in the works of Tryggve Andersen." *SS* 50 (1978), 249-68.
Undset, Sigrid. "Tryggve Andersen." *ASR* 33 (1945), 19-31.

Andersson, Claes

Warburton, Thomas. "Claes Andersson: The poet as the progressive." *BF* 13:3 (1979), 94-96.

Andersson, Dan

Schleef, Caroline. "Dan Andersson: Charcoal-burner and poet (1888-1920)." *ASR* 42 (1954), 231-37.
Stensland, Per G. "Dan Andersson: Pilgrim and poet." *ASR* 31 (1943), 249-52.

Aspenström, Werner

Sjöberg, Leif. "Werner Aspenström: A writer for all seasons." *ASR* 57 (1969), 385-92.
Törnqvist, Egil. "Poet in the space age: A theme in Aspenström's plays." *SS* 39 (1967), 1-15.

Bang, Herman

Gustafson, Alrik. "Degenerate heredity and family tradition in Herman Bang's Haabløse Slægter." *Journal of English and Germanic Philology* 40 (1941), 364-90.
Hermannsen, Mogens. "Herman Bang." *ASR* 45 (1957), 170-72.
Simonsen, Sofus E. "Herman Bang: Life and theme." *Germanic Notes* 3:5 (1972), 34-37.

Benedictsson, Victoria

Borland, Harold. "Ernst Ahlgren: Novelist in theory and practice." *Scan* 13 (1974), 97-106.

Bendiktsson, Einar

Beck, Richard. "Iceland's 'Poet Laureate'." *BA* 10 (1936), 270-71.
Beck, Richard. "The dean of Icelandic poets." *ASR* 27 (1939), 341-42.

Bergman, Hjalmar

Gustafson, Alrik. "Hjalmar Bergman's 'accounting' with the Swedish middle-classes." *Samlaren* 36 (1955), 64-76.
Linder, Erik H. *Hjalmar Bergman.* Boston: Twayne, 1975.
Mischler, William. "A reading of Hjalmar Bergman's story 'Konstapel Wiliam'." *Scan* 10 (1971), 33-41.
Petheric, Karin. *Hjalmar Bergman: Markurells i Wadköping.* Studies in Swedish Literature 4. Hull, 1975.
Sprinchorn, Evert. "Hjalmar Bergman." *Tulane Drama Review* 6:2 (1961), 117-27.
Stevenson, Sarah A. "Comedy and tragedy in 'Markurells i Wadköping'." *Edda* (1974), 191-200.
Vowles, Richard B. "Bergman, Branner and off-stage dying." *SS* 33 (1961), 1-9.

Björling, Gunnar

Nilsson, Kim. "Semantic devices in Gunnar Björling's poetry." *Michigan Germanic Studies* 3:1 (1977), 54-73.

Bjørneboe, Jens

Hoberman, John M. "The political imagination of Jens Bjørneboe: A study of *Under en hårdere himmel.*" *SS* 48 (1976), 52-70.

Bjørnson, Bjørnstjerne

Downs, Brian W. "Bjørnson and tragedy." *Scan* 1 (1962), 17-28.
Foster, George F. "The message of Bjørnson." *Open Court* 38 (1924), 321-38.
Larson, Harold. *Bjørnstjerne Bjørnson: A study in Norwegian nationalism.* New York: King's Crown Press, 1944.

Larson, Harold and Einar Haugen. "Bjørnson and America—a critical review." *SS* 13 (1934), 1–12.

Malone, Kemp. "Bjørnson and his plays." *Forum* (Houston) 3:6 (1961), 13–16.

Noreng, Harald. "Bjørnson research: A survey." *Scan* 4 (1965), 1–15.

Palmer, Arthur H. "Bjørnson and the United States." *SS* 5 (1918–19), 102–9.

Payne, William H. *Bjørnstjerne Bjørnson, 1832–1910.* Chicago: A. C. McClury and Co., 1910.

Sehmsdorf, Henning. "Bjørnson's *Trond* and popular tradition." *SS* 41 (1969), 56–66.

Sehmsdorf, Henning. "The self in isolation: A new reading of Bjørnson's *Arne.*" *SS* 45 (1973), 310–23.

Sturtevant, Albert M. "Bjørnson's Maria Stuart i Skotland." *SS* 4 (1917), 203–19.

Sturtevant, Albert M. "Some critical notes on Bjørnson's Halte Hulda." *SS* 10 (1929), 79–86.

Blixen, Karen

Billy, Ted. "Werther avenged: Isak Dinesen's 'The Poet'." *West Virginia University Philological Papers* 24 (1978), 62–67.

Brink, J. R. "Hamlet or Timon: Isak Dinesen's 'Deluge at Norderney'." *International Fiction Review* 5 (1978), 148–50.

Burstein, Janet H. "Two locked caskets: Selfhood and 'otherness' in the work of Isak Dinesen." *Texas Studies in Literature and Language* 20 (1978), 615–32.

Daler, John Kent von. "Lessons in symbolism read from Isak Dinesen." *Language and Literature* 2:1 (1973), 71–85.

Dinesen, Thomas. *My sister: Isak Dinesen.* London: Michael Joseph, 1975.

Hannah, Donald. *'Isak Dinesen' and Karen Blixen: The mask and the reality.* London: Putnam and Co., 1971.

Johannesen, Eric O. "Isak Dinesen and Selma Lagerlöf." *SS* 32 (1960), 18–26.

Johannesen, Eric O. *The world of Isak Dinesen.* Seattle: University of Washington Press, 1961.

Landy, Marcia. "Anecdote and destiny: Isak Dinesen and the storyteller." *Massachusetts Review* 19 (1978), 389–406.

Langbaum, Robert. *The gaiety of vision: A study of Isak Dinesen's art.* London: Chatto and Windus, 1964.

Lydenberg, Robin. "Against the law of gravity: Female adolescence in Isak Dinesen's *Seven Gothic Tales.*" *Modern Fiction Studies* 24 (1978–79), 521–32.

Migel, Parmenia. *Titania: The biography of Isak Dinesen.* New York: Random House, 1967 / London: Michael Joseph, 1968.

Schouw, H. Wayne. "Karen Blixen and Martin A. Hansen: Art, ethics, and the human condition." *SS* 52 (1980), 16–31.

Svendsen, Clara, ed. *Isak Dinesen: A memorial.* New York: Random House, 1965.

Svendsen, Clara and Frans Lasson. *The life and destiny of Karen Blixen.* New York: Random House, 1970.

Weed, Merry. "*Märchen* and legend techniques of narration in two 'tales' of Isak Dinesen." *Journal of the Folklore Institute* (Bloomington, Ind.) 15 (1978), 23–44.

Whissen, Thomas R. *Isak Dinesen's aesthetics.* Port Washington, N.Y.: Kennikat Press, 1973.

Whissen, Thomas R. "The bow of the Lord: Isak Dinesen's portrait of the artist." *SS* 46 (1974), 47–58.

Whissen, Thomas R. "Without fear: Isak Dinesen's *Winter's Tales* and occupied Denmark." *International Fiction Review* 3 (1976), 57–61.

Bojer, Johan

Gad, Carl. *Johan Bojer: The man and his works.* Westport, Conn.: Greenwood Press, 1974. [Reprint of 1920 ed.]

Lödrup, H. P. "Johan Bojer." *ASR* 14 (1927), 207-11.
Porterfield, Allen W. "America reads Johan Bojer." *ASR* 9 (1921), 477-81.

Borgen, Johan

Birn, Randi M. "The quest for authenticity in three novels by Johan Borgen." *Mosaic* 4:2 (1970), 91-99.
Birn, Randi M. "Dream and reality in Johan Borgen's short stories." *SS* 46 (1974), 59-72.
Birn, Randi M. *Johan Borgen*. New York: Twayne, 1974.
Mischler, William. "Metaphor and metonymy in Johan Borgen's *Eksempler*." *Scan* 16 (1977), 11-21.

Boye, Karin

Tegen, Gunhild. "Karin Boye in memoriam." *ASR* 30 (1942), 240-43.
Vowles, Richard B. "Ripeness is all: A study in Karin Boye's poetry." *Bulletin of the American-Swedish Institute* (Minneapolis) (spring 1952), 3-7.

Brandes, Georg

Asmundsson, Doris R. "America meets Georg Brandes." *ScanR* 65 (1977), 4-10.
Larsen, Sven A. "Georg Brandes' views on American literature." *SS* 22 (1950), 161-65.
Moritzen, Julius. *Georg Brandes in life and letters*. Newark, N.J.: D. S. Colyer, 1922.
Møller Kristensen, Sven. "Georg Brandes research: A survey." *Scan* 2 (1963), 121-32.
Nolin, Bertil. *Georg Brandes*. Boston: Twayne, 1976.
Shelander, Asaph R. "Georg Brandes." *ASR* 2, November (1914), 30-32.
Shelander, Asaph R. "Brandes in America." *ASR* 2, November (1914), 33-36.

Branner, Hans Christian

Markey, Thomas L. "Hans Christian Branner: An encomium." *Scan* 7 (1968), 39-51.
Markey, Thomas L. *Hans Christian Branner*. New York: Twayne, 1973.
Vowles, Richard B. "Bergman, Branner, and off-stage dying." *SS* 33 (1961), 1-9.

Brú, Heðin

Brønner, Hedin. "Heðin Brú: Faroese novelist." *ASR* 59 (1971), 351-59.

Bull, Olaf

Elster, Kristian. "Three lyrical poets of Norway." *ASR* 13 (1925), 653-63.

Cappelen, Peder W.

Sehmsdorf, Henning K. "Folktale and allegory: Peder W. Cappelen's *Briar Rose. The Sleeping Beauty*." *PPNCFL* 30 (1979), 122-26.
Sehmsdorf, Henning K. "History and idea in Peder W. Cappelen's *Kark*." *Selecta* 1 (1980), 83-86.
Sehmsdorf, Henning K. "Strindberg's *Ett drömspel* and Cappelen's *Sverre-Berget og ordet*." *Festschrift to Walter Johnson*. Chapel Hill: University of North Carolina Press, 1980, forthcoming.
Sehmsdorf, Henning K. "The allegory of a new beginning: Peder W. Cappelen's *Hvittenland*." *Selecta* 32 (1981), forthcoming.

Carpelan, Bo

Ahokas, Jaakko. "Two poets of Finland: Paavo Haavikko and Bo Carpelan." *BA* 46 (1972), 37-43.

Chorell, Walentin

Salminen, Johannes. "Walentin Chorell: An appreciation." *ASR* 56 (1968), 136–39.
Warburton, Thomas. "Literary portraits: Walentin Chorell." *BF* 3:3 (1969), 11–12.

Colliander, Tito

Warburton, Thomas. "Literary portraits: Tito Colliander." *BF* 2:1 (1968), 6–7.

Dagerman, Stig

Bergmann, S. A. "Blinded by darkness: A study of the novels and plays of Stig Dagerman." *Delta* 11 (1957), 16–31.
Fleisher, Frederic. "Stig Dagerman: In memoriam." *BA* 39 (1955), 165.
Thompson, Laurie. "Stig Dagerman's 'Vår nattliga badort': An interpretation." *Scan* 13 (1974), 117–27.
Thompson, Laurie. "In fear and trembling: A study of Stig Dagerman's imagery." *Erfahrung und Überlieferung: Festschrift for C. P. Magill.* Cardiff: University of Wales Press, 1974, 206–22.
Thompson, Laurie. *Stig Dagerman: Nattens lekar.* Studies in Swedish Literature 5. 2nd ed. Hull, 1979.
Thompson, Laurie. "Stig Dagerman and politics." *Scan* 19 (1980), 39–56.

Delblanc, Sven

Sjöberg, Leif. "Delblanc's *Homunculus*: Some magic elements." *Germanic Review* 49 (1974), 105–24.
Vowles, Richard B. "Myth in Sweden: Sven Delblanc's *Homunculus*." *BA* 48 (1974), 20–25.

Diktonius, Elmer

Petheric, Karin. "Four Finland-Swedish prose modernists (. . .)." *Scan* 15 (1976), 45–62.
Schoolfield, George C. "Elmer Diktonius and Edgar Lee Masters." *Americana-Norvegica* 3. Oslo: Universitetsforlaget, 1971, 307–27.
Schoolfield, George C. "Elmer Diktonius as a music critic." *Scan* 15 (1976), 29–44.

Dinesen, Isak; see Blixen, Karen

Donner, Jörn

"Jörn Donner writes 'for adults'." *BF* 2:1 (1968), 9–10.

Duun, Olav

Birkeland, Bjarte. "Olav Duun." *Scan* 10 (1971), 112–21.
Carleton, Phillips D. "Olav Duun: Spokesman of peasants." *ASR* 16 (1928), 741–42.
Thompson, Lawrence. "Olav Duun: 1876–1939." *BA* 14 (1940), 128–31.

Ekelöf, Gunnar

Ekner, Reidar. "Gunnar Ekelöf: The poet as a trickster." *SS* 42 (1970), 410–18.
Hunter, Grace. "Two contemporary Swedish poets." *Prairie Schooner* 27 (1955), 57–67.
Shideler, Ross P. "An analysis of Gunnar Ekelöf's 'Röster under jorden'." *Scan* 9 (1970), 95–114.
Shideler, Ross P. "'The glassclear eye of dreams' in twentieth-century Swedish poetry." *WLT* 51 (1977), 530–34.
Sjöberg, Leif. "Gunnar Ekelöf's 'Tag och skriv': A reader's commentary." *SS* 35 (1963), 307–24.

Sjöberg, Leif. "Allusions in the first part of *En Mölna-Elegi.*" *SS* 37 (1965), 293–323.
Sjöberg, Leif. "Allusions in the last part of *En Mölna-Elegi.*" *Germanic Review* 40 (1965, 132–49.
Sjöberg, Leif. "Gunnar Ekelöf: Poet and Outsider." *ASR* 53 (1965), 140–46.
Sjöberg, Leif. "Gunnar Ekelöf: Swedish poet." *BA* 41 (1967), 291–93.
Sjöberg, Leif. "A note on poems by Ekelöf." *SS* 39 (1967), 147–52.
Sjöberg, Leif. "The later poems of Gunnar Ekelöf: *Dīwān* and *Fatumeh.*" *Mosaic* 4:2 (1971), 101–15.
Sjöberg, Leif. *A reader's guide to Ekelöf's A Mölna elegy.* New York: Twayne, 1973.
Vowles, Richard B. "Gunnar Ekelöf: Swedish eclectic." *Western Humanities Review* 6 (1952), 53–58.

Ekelund, Vilhelm

Gustafson, Alrik. "Two early Fröding imitations: Vilhelm Ekelund's 'Skördefest' and 'I pilhäcken'." *Journal of English and Germanic Philology* 35 (1936), 566–80.

Enckell, Rabbe

Petheric, Karin. "Four Finland-Swedish prose modernists (. . .)." *Scan* 15 (1976), 45–62.
Schoolfield, George C. "Rabbe Enckell's 'Mot Itaka'." *Germanic Notes* 7 (1976), 17–22, 36–39.

Enquist, Per Olov

Shideler, Ross P. "The Swedish short story: Per Olov Enquist." *SS* 49 (1977), 241–62.
Shideler, Ross P. "Putting together the puzzle in Per Olov Enquist's *Sekonden.*" *SS* 49 (1977), 311–29.

Falkberget, Johan

Beck, Richard. "Johan Falkberget." *SS* 16 (1941), 304–16.
Beck, Richard. "Johan Falkberget: A great social novelist." *ASR* 38 (1950), 248–51.
Beck, Richard. "Johan Falkberget at seventy." *BA* 25 (1951), 24–25.
Raastad, Ottar. "Johan Falkberget: An appreciation." *ASR* 58 (1970), 153–62.

Fangen, Ronald

Govig, Stewart D. "Ronald Fangen: A Christian humanist." *ASR* 49 (1961), 152–59.
Thompson, Lawrence. "Ronald Fangen: 1895-1946." *BA* 20 (1946), 367–70.

Ferlin, Nils

Vowles, Richard B. "Nils Ferlin: The poet as clown and scapegoat." *The Norseman* 12 (1954), 424–29.

Forssell, Lars

Carlson, Harry G. "Lars Forssell: Poet in the theater." *SS* 37 (1965), 31–57.

Fridegård, Jan

Graves, Peter. *Jan Fridegård: Lars Hård.* Studies in Swedish Literature 8. Hull, 1977.

Fröding, Gustaf

Fleisher, Frederic. "Gustaf Fröding: 1860-1911." *ASR* 42 (1954), 303–8.
Flygt, Sten G. "Gustaf Fröding's conception of eros." *Germanic Review* 25 (1950), 109–23.
Johnson, Walter. "Fröding and the dramatic monologue." *SS* 24 (1952), 141–48.

Vickner, Edwin J. "A study in Fröding." SS 21 (1949), 65–78.

Garborg, Arne

Larsen, Hanna A. "Arne Garborg." ASR 12 (1924), 275–83.
Lillehei, Ingebrigt L. "Some of the earlier writings of Garborg." SS 2 (1914–15), 181–95.
Lillehei, Ingebrigt. "The language and main idea of Arne Garborg's works." SS 3 (1916), 134–99. [Reprinted as A study in the language and the main ideas of Arne Garborg's works. Urbana, Ill., 1916.]
Sjåvik, Jan. "Form and theme in Arne Garborg's Mannfolk and Hjaa ho Mor." Selecta 1 (1980), 87–90.
Wiehr, Josef. "Arne Garborg." SS 5 (1917–18), 275–96.

Geijerstam, Gustaf af

Rapp, Esther H. "Gustaf af Geijerstam in the field of the psychological novel." SS 8 (1925), 239–48.

Gjellerup, Karl

Zberae, Nicolae. "Karl Gjellerup: A master of expression of Indian thought." Indo-Asian Culture 19:1 (1970), 30–33.

Grieg, Nordahl

Dahlie, Hallvard. "On Nordahl Grieg's The Ship Sails On." International Fiction Review 2 (1975), 49–53.
Koht, Halvdan. "Nordahl Grieg." ASR 30 (1942), 32–40.

Guðmundsson, Kristmann

Einarsson, Stefán. "Five Icelandic novelists." BA 16 (1942), 254–59.

Guðmundsson, Tómas

Ringler, Richard N. "The poems of Tómas Guðmundsson." ScanR 63 (1975), 27–39.

Gullberg, Hjalmar

Vowles, Richard B. "Hjalmar Gullberg: An ancient and a modern." SS 24 (1952), 111–18.

Gunnarsson, Gunnar

Beck, Richard. "Gunnar Gunnarsson: Some observations." Scandinavian Studies. Essays presented to Dr. Henry G. Leach. Seattle: University of Washington Press for The American-Scandinavian Foundation, New York, 1965, 293–301.
Einarsson, Stefán. "Gunnar Gunnarsson: An Icelandic author." Jón Bjarnason Academy Yearbook (1940), 9–24.
Einarsson, Stefán. "The return of an Icelander." ASR 29 (1941), 235–37.
Einarsson, Stefán. "Five Icelandic novelists." BA 16 (1942), 254–59.

Gustafsson, Lars

Sandstroem, Yvonne L. "The machine theme in some poems by Lars Gustafsson." SS 44 (1974), 210–23.

Gyllensten, Lars

Haack, Elsbeth G. "Semantic detour: A post-structuralist study of Lars Gyllensten's text Senilia." PPNCFL 30 (1979), 119–21.

Isaksson, Hans. *Lars Gyllensten*. Boston: Twayne, 1978.

Sjöberg, Leif. "Lars Gyllensten: Master of arts and sciences." *ASR* 55 (1967), 158–62.

Haanpää, Pentti

Laitinen, Kai. "Escape from the vicious circle: An introduction to Pentti Haanpää." *BF* 10:3–4 (1976), 55–58.

Haavikko, Paavo

Ahokas, Jaakko. "Two poets of Finland: Paavo Haavikko and Bo Carpelan." *BA* 46 (1972), 37–43.

Binham, Philip. "Dreams each within each: The Finnish poet Paavo Haavikko." *BA* 50 (1976), 337–41.

Binham, Philip. "A poet's playground: The collected plays of Paavo Haavikko." *WLT* 53 (1979), 244–45.

Dauenhauer, Richard. "The view from the aspen grove: Paavo Haavikko in national and international context." *Snow in May: An anthology of Finnish writing, 1945–72.* Rutherford, N.J.: Fairleigh Dickinson University Press, 1978, 67–97.

Kinnunen, Aarne. "The writer and his works: An interview with Paavo Haavikko." *BF* 11 (1977), 166–72.

Laitinen, Kai. "How things are: Paavo Haavikko and his poetry." *BA* 43 (1969), 41–46.

Hallström, Per

Dahlström, C. E. W. L. "Hallström's impressionism in *A secret Idyll*." *Publications of the Modern Language Association of America* 46 (1931), 930–39.

Hamsun, Knut

Andersen, Arlow W. "Knut Hamsun's America." *Norwegian-American Studies* (Northfield) 23 (1967), 175–203.

Beck, Richard. "Knut Hamsun at seventy-five." *BA* 8 (1934), 387–89.

Gustafson, Alrik. "Hamsun's 'Growth of the Soil'." *ASR* 27 (1939), 199–214.

Gustafson, Alrik. "Man and the soil: Knut Hamsun." *Six Scandinavian novelists.* New York: Biblo and Tannen, 1969, 226–85. [Reprint of 1940 ed.]

Haugen, Einar, "Knut Hamsun and the nazis." *BA* 15 (1941), 17–22.

Hyllested, C. C. "Knut Hamsun: An appreciation." *ASR* 2, March (1914), 13–17.

Klieneberger, H. R. "The Norwegian contribution to the modern novel: Knut Hamsun and Sigrid Undset." *Durham University Journal* 18 (1957), 70–78.

Knaplund, Paul. "Knut Hamsun: Triumph and tragedy." *Modern Age* (Chicago) 9 (1965), 165–74.

Larsen, Hanna A. "Knut Hamsun." *ASR* 9 (1921), 448–57.

Larsen, Hanna A. *Knut Hamsun.* New York: Knopf, 1922 / London: Gyldendal, 1923.

McFarlane, J. W. "The whisper of the blood: A study of Knut Hamsun's early novels." *Publications of the Modern Language Association of America* 71 (1956), 563–94.

Mischler, William. "Ignorance, knowledge and resistance to knowledge in Hamsun's *Sult*." *Edda* (1974), 161–77.

Naess, Harald. "The three Hamsuns: The changing attitude in recent criticism." *SS* 32 (1960), 129–39.

Naess, Harald. "A strange meeting and Hamsun's *Mysterier*." *SS* 36 (1964), 48–58.

Naess, Harald. "Knut Hamsun and America." *SS* 39 (1967), 305–28.

Naess, Harald. "American attitudes to Knut Hamsun." *Americana-Norvegica* 3 (1971), 338–60.

Naess, Harald. "Who was Hamsun's hero?" *The hero in Scandinavian literature*. Austin and London: University of Texas Press, 1975, 63-86.

Naess, Harald. "The image of the nineteenth century Midwest in Knut Hamsun's writings." *Norwegian influence on the Upper Midwest*. Duluth: University of Minnesota-Duluth, 1976, 50-53.

Nilson, Sten Sparre. "Knut Hamsun, England, and America." *Scan* 1 (1962), 124-36.

Popperwell, Ronald G. "Interrelatedness in Hamsun's *Mysterier*." *SS* 38 (1966) 295-301.

Ruud, M. B. "Knut Hamsun." *SS* 3 (1916), 241-52.

Sehmsdorf, Henning. "Knut Hamsun's *Pan*: Myth and symbol." *Edda* (1974), 345-403.

Simpson, Allen. "Knut Hamsun's anti-semitism." *Edda* (1977), 273-93.

Turco, Alfred. "Hamsun's *Pan* and the riddle of 'Glahn's death'." *Scan* 19 (1980), 13-30.

Unruh, Kathryn I. "The long dark summer in *Segelfoss Town*." *Edda* (1977), 263-72.

Waal, Carla. "Hamsun's *Ved Rigets Port* on the Norwegian stage." *SS* 41 (1969), 138-49.

Waal, Carla. "The plays of Knut Hamsun." *Quarterly Journal of Speech* 57 (1971), 75-82.

Wiehr, Josef. *Knut Hamsun: His personality and his outlook upon life*. Northampton, Mass.: *Smith College Studies in Modern Languages* 3:1-2, 1922.

Hansen, Martin Alfred

Ingwersen, Faith and Niels. *Martin A. Hansen*. Boston: Twayne, 1976.

Printz-Påhlson, Göran. "*The Liar*: The paradox of fictional communication in Martin A. Hansen." *SS* 36 (1964), 263-80.

Schouw, H. Wayne. "Kierkegaardian perspectives in Martin A. Hansen's *The Liar*." *Critique: Studies in Modern Fiction* 15:3 (1973), 53-65.

Schouw, H. Wayne. "Karen Blixen and Martin A. Hansen: Art, ethics, and the human condition." *SS* 52 (1980), 16-31.

Vowles, Richard B. "Martin A. Hansen: Danish craftsman and mystic." *Accent* 17 (1957), 43-44.

Hansson, Ola

Hume, David R. "The first five years of Ola Hansson's literary exile 1888-93." *Facts of Scandinavian Literature*. (*Germanische Forschungsketten* 2.) Lexington, Ky.: Apra Press, 1974, 32-39.

Hauge, Alfred

Flatin, Kjetil A. "The rising sun and the lark on the quilt: Quest and defiance in Alfred Hauge's *Cleng Peerson* trilogy." *PPNCFL* 27 (1976), 133-36.

Hauge, Olav H.

Hanson, Katherine. "Nature imagery in Olav H. Hauge's poetry." *PPNCFL* 29 (1978), 114-18.

Heidenstam, Verner von

Berg, Ruben G: son. "Verner von Heidenstam." *ASR* 5 (1917), 160-68.

Gustafson, Alrik. "Nationalism reinterpreted: Verner von Heidenstam." *Six Scandinavian Novelists*. New York: Biblo and Tannen, 1969, 123-76. [Reprint of 1940 ed.]

Stork, Charles W. "Verner von Heidenstam." *ASR* 49 (1961), 39-44.

Heinesen, William

Brønner, Hedin. "William Heinesen: Faroese voice–Danish pen." *ASR* 61 (1973), 142-54.

Jones, W. Glyn. "*Noatun* and the collective novel." *SS* 41 (1969), 217-30.

Jones, W. Glyn. "William Heinesen and the myth of conflict." *Scan* 9 (1970), 81-94.

Jones, W. Glyn. *William Heinesen.* New York: Twayne, 1974.
Jones, W. Glyn. "*Tårnet ved verdens ende*: A restatement and an extension." *SS* 50 (1978), 19–30.

Hoel, Sigurd

Grunt, Olav P. "Sigurd Hoel." *ASF* 41 (1953), 31–38.

Huldén, Lars

Jones, W. Glyn. "Introduction." *BF* 2:2 (1977), 140–42.

Ibsen, Henrik

Andersen, Annette. "Ibsen in America." *SS* 14 (1937), 65–109, 115–55.
Anderson, Andrew R. "Ibsen and the classical world." *Classical Journal* 11 (1916), 216–25.
Arestad, Sverre. "Ibsen in America: 1936–46." *SS* 14 (1952), 93–110.
Arestad, Sverre. "*Little Eyolf* and human responsibility." *SS* 32 (1960), 140–52.
Bentley, Eric. *In search of theater.* New York: Alfred A. Knopf, 1953, 365–77.
Bentley, Eric. *The playwright as thinker.* 7th ed. New York: Meridian Books, 1960, 75–106.
Bradbrook, Muriel C. *Ibsen the Norwegian: A revaluation.* London: Chatto and Windus, 1946.
Clurman, Harold. *Ibsen.* New York: Collier Books, 1977.
Contemporary approaches to Ibsen. Proceedings of the First International Ibsen Seminar, Oslo, August 1965. Ed. Daniel Haakonsen. Oslo: Universitetsforlaget, 1966.
Contemporary approaches to Ibsen 2. Proceedings of the Second International Ibsen Seminar, Cambridge, August 1970. Ed. Daniel Haakonsen. Oslo: Universitetsforlaget, 1971.
Contemporary approaches to Ibsen 3. Reports from the Third International Ibsen Seminar, Bergen, 1975. Ed. Daniel Haakonsen et al. Oslo: Universitetsforlaget, 1977.
Downs, Brian W. *Ibsen: The intellectual background.* Cambridge: University Press, 1948. [Reprint of 1946 ed.]
Downs, Brian W. *A study of six plays by Ibsen.* Cambridge: University Press, 1950.
Egan, Michael. *Ibsen: The critical heritage.* London: Routledge, 1972.
Eikeland, P. J., ed. *Ibsen studies.* Northfield, Mn.: St. Olaf College Press, 1934.
Fife, Robert H. and Ansten Anstensen. "Henrik Ibsen on the American stage." *ASR* 16 (1928), 218–28.
Firkins, Ina Ten Eyck. *Henrik Ibsen: A bibliography of criticism and biography.* New York: H. W. Wilson Co., 1921.
Fjelde, Rolf. *Ibsen: A collection of critical essays.* Englewood Cliffs, N.J.: Prentice-Hall, 1965.
Flaxman, Seymour L. "The debt of Williams and Miller to Ibsen and Strindberg." *Comparative Literature Studies* (Special Advance Issue, 1963), 51–60.
Flores, Angel, ed. *Henrik Ibsen: A Marxist analysis.* New York: The Critics Group, 1937.
Franc, Miriam A. *Ibsen in England.* Boston: Four Seas, 1919.
Goodman, Randolph. "Playwriting with a third eye: Fun and games with Albee, Ibsen and Strindberg." *Columbia University Forum* 10 (1967), 18–22.
Gray, Ronald. *Ibsen—a dissenting view: A study of the last twelve plays.* Cambridge: University Press, 1977.
Hansen, Karin S. *Henrik Ibsen, 1828-1978: A filmography.* Oslo: Norsk Filminstitutt, 1978.
Haugen, Einar. *Ibsen's drama: Author to audience.* Minneapolis: University of Minnesota Press, 1979.
Heiberg, Hans. *Ibsen: A portrait of the artist.* Coral Gables, Fla.: University of Miami Press, 1969.
Hurt, James. *Catiline's dream: An essay on Ibsen's plays.* Urbana: University of Illinois Press, 1972.

Ibsen, Bergliot. *The three Ibsens*. London and New York: Hutchinson, 1951 / New York: The American Scandinavian Foundation, 1952.

Johnston, Brian. *The Ibsen cycle: The design of the plays from Pillars of Society to When We Dead Awaken*. Boston: Twayne, 1975.

Johnston, Brian. "The poetry of *An Enemy of the People*." *Scan* 18 (1979), 109-22.

Johnston, Brian. *To the third empire: Ibsen's early drama*. Minneapolis: University of Minnesota Press, 1980.

Jorgensen, Theodore. *Henrik Ibsen: A study in art and personality*. Westport, Conn.: Greenwood Press, 1978. [Reprint of 1945 ed.]

Koht, Halvdan. *Life of Ibsen*. New York: Blom, 1971.

Lavrin, Janko. *Ibsen: An approach*. London: Methuen, 1950.

Lee, Jennette. *The Ibsen secret: A key to the prose dramas of Henrik Ibsen*. New York: Putnam's, 1907.

Lucas, F. L. *The drama of Ibsen and Strindberg*. New York: Macmillan, 1962.

MacFall, Haldane. *Ibsen: The man, his art and his significance*. Norwood, Pa.: Norwood Eds., 1978. [Reprint of 1907 ed.]

McFarlane, James. "Recent trends in Ibsen scholarship and criticism." *Scan* 2 (1963), 108-21.

McFarlane, James, ed. *Henrik Ibsen: A critical anthology*. London: Penguin, 1970.

Meyer, Hans G. *Henrik Ibsen* (with appendix on American productions by Leonard S. Klein, pp. 185-90). New York: Ungar, 1972.

Meyer, Michael. *Ibsen: A biography*. New York: Doubleday, 1971.

Modern Drama 21:4 (1978). [Special issue on Henrik Ibsen.]

Northam, John. *Ibsen's dramatic method*. London: Faber, 1952.

Northam, John. *Ibsen: A critical study*. Cambridge: University Press, 1973.

Popperwell, Ronald G. "Ibsen's female characters." *Scan* 19 (1980), 5-12.

Roberts, Richard E. *Henrik Ibsen: A critical study*. Philadelphia: R. West, 1978. [Reprint of 1912 ed.]

Scandinavian Review 66:4 (1978). [Special issue on Henrik Ibsen.]

Scandinavian Studies 51:4 (1979). [Special issue on Henrik Ibsen.]

Sehmsdorf, Henning K. "Two Legends about St. Olaf, the masterbuilder." *Edda* (1967), 263-71.

Shaw, George B. *The quintessence of Ibsenism: Now completed to the death of Ibsen*. London: Constable, 1913.

Tennant, P. F. D. *Ibsen's dramatic technique*. Cambridge: University Press, 1948.

Tysdahl, B. J. *Joyce and Ibsen: A study in literary influence*. Oslo and New York: Norwegian Universities Press, 1968.

Weigand, Hermann J. *The modern Ibsen: A reconsideration*. New York: Holt, 1925.

Jacobsen, Jens Peter

Arestad, Sverre. "J. P. Jacobsen's *Niels Lyhne*." *Scandinavian Studies. Essays presented to Dr. Henry G. Leach*. Seattle: University of Washington Press for The American-Scandinavian Foundation, New York, 1965, 202-12.

Gustafson, Alrik. "Toward decadence: Jens Peter Jacobsen." *Six Scandinavian Novelists*. New York: Biblo and Tannen, 1969, 73-122. [Reprint of 1940 ed.]

Ingwersen, Niels. "Problematic protagonists: *Marie Grubbe* and *Niels Lyhne*." *The hero in Scandinavian literature*. Austin and London: University of Texas Press, 1975, 39-61.

Jensen, Niels Lyhne. *Jens Peter Jacobsen*. Boston: Twayne, 1980.

Knudsen, Dagmar. "J. P. Jacobsen." *ASR* 5 (1917), 265-69.

Madsen, Børge Gedsø. "J. P. Jacobsen reconsidered." *ASR* 50 (1962), 272-79.

Jacobsen, Jørgen-Frantz

Brønner, Hedin. "Jørgen-Frantz Jacobsen and *Barbara*." *ASR* 61 (1973), 39-45.

Jacobsen, Rolf

Naess, Harald. "The poetry of Rolf Jacobsen." *ASR* 62 (1974), 265-69.

Jæger, Frank

Hugus, Frank. "The dilemma of the artists in selected prose works of Frank Jæger." *SS* 47 (1975), 52-65.

Jakobsdóttir, Svava

Magnússon, Sigurður A. and Dennis Auburn Hill. "The Icelandic short story: Svava Jacobsdóttir." *SS* 49 (1977), 208-16.

Jansson, Tove

Jones, W. Glyn. "Tove Jansson: My books and my characters." *BF* 12:3 (1978), 90-97.

Jensen, Aksel

Sehmsdorf, Henning. "Aksel Jensen's *Epp*: Science Fiction as social satire." *PPNCFL* 25 (1974), 118-21.

Jensen, Johannes Vilhelm

Friis, Oluf. "Johannes V. Jensen." *Scan* 1 (1962), 114-23.
Ingwersen, Niels. "America as setting and symbol in Johannes V. Jensen's early work." *American-Norvegica* 3 (1971), 272-93.
Marcus, Aage. "Johannes V. Jensen." *ASR* 20 (1932), 340-47.
Nielsen, Marion L. *Denmark's Johannes V. Jensen.* Utah State Agricultural College Monograph Series, 3, 1955.
Nyholm, Jens. "The Nobel Prize goes Nordic." *BA* 19 (1945), 131-35.
Toksvig, Signe. "Johannes V. Jensen." *ASR* 31 (1943), 343-46.

Johnson, Eyvind

Bäckström, Lars. "Eyvind Johnson, Per Olof Sundman, and Sara Lidman: An introduction." *Contemporary Literature* 12 (1971), 242-51.
Orton, Gavin. "Eyvind Johnson: An introduction." *Scan* 5 (1966), 111-23.
Orton, Gavin. *Eyvind Johnson.* New York: Twayne, 1972.
Orton, Gavin. *Eyvind Johnson: Nu var det 1914.* Studies in Swedish literature 1. Hull, 1974.
Sjöberg, Leif. "Eyvind Johnson." *ASR* 56 (1968), 369-78.
Sjöberg, Leif. "The 1974 Nobel Prize in literature: Eyvind Johnson and Harry Martinson." *BA* 49 (1975), 407-21.
Warme, Lars G. "Eyvind Johnson's *Några steg mot tystnaden:* An apologia." *SS* 49 (1977), 452-63.

Järnefelt, Arvid

Kolehmainen, John I. "When Finland's Tolstoy met his Russian master." *American Slavic and East European Review* 16 (1957), 534-41.

Jørgensen, Johannes

Jones, W. Glyn. "Johannes Jørgensen and his apologetics." *SS* 32 (1960), 27-36.

Jones, W. Glyn. "Some personal aspects of Johannes Jørgensen's prose." *Modern Language Review* 55 (1960), 399-410.

Jones, W. Glyn. "The early novels of Jørgensen." *SS* 36 (1964), 103-17.

Jones, W. Glyn. "Johannes Jørgensen in the centenary of his birth." *Scan* 5 (1966), 100-10.

Jones, W. Glyn. *Johannes Jørgensen.* New York: Twayne, 1969.

Nugent, Robert. "Jørgensen's devotional verse: A contemporary act of faith." *Renascence* 15 (1963), 79-81.

Kamban, Guðmundur

Einarsson, Stefán. "Five Icelandic novelists." *BA* 16 (1942), 254-59.

Karlfeldt, Erik Axel

Fleisher, Frederic. "The vagabond in the life and poetry of Erik Axel Karlfeldt." *SS* 26 (1954), 25-27.

Hildeman, Karl-Ivar. "The evolution of 'Längtan heter min arvedel'." *SS* 31 (1959), 47-64.

Hildeman, Karl-Ivar. "Erik Axel Karlfeldt: An evaluation." *SS* 40 (1968), 81-94.

Larson, Carl. "Erik Axel Karlfeldt: Poet of Dalecarlia." *ASR* 13 (1925), 15-20.

Stork, Charles W. "Erik Axel Karlfeldt." *ASR* 19 (1931), 581-94.

Uppvall, A. J. "The poetic art of Erik Axel Karlfeldt." *Germanic Review* 2 (1927), 244-61.

Kielland, Alexander

Sturtevant, Albert M. "Notes on Alexander Kielland." *SS* 11 (1931), 90-99.

Sturtevant, Albert M. "*Skipper Worse* and the Haugianere." *SS* 11 (1931), 229-39.

Sturtevant, Albert M. "Regarding the chronology of events in Kielland's novels." *SS* 12 (1933), 101-9.

Kihlman, Christer

Sarajas, Annamari. "A reading experience: 'Man who tottered'." *BF* 6:1 (1972), 13-14.

Svedberg, Ingmar. "Extending the bounds of reality: An approach to the work of Christer Kihlman." *BF* 10:1-2 (1976), 7-10.

Kilpi, Eeva

Kilpi, Eeva. "Summer and the authoress." *BF* 5:1 (1971), 2-3.

Savolainen, Erkki. "Eeva Kilpi and her erotical novel." *Look at Finland* 1 (1973), 58-61.

Kinck, Hans E.

Bukdahl, Jørgen. "Hans E. Kinck." *ASR* 15 (1927), 589-94.

Kristensen, Tom

Byram, M. S. "The reality of Tom Kristensen's Hærværk." *Scan* 15 (1976), 29-37.

Byram, M. S. "*Ulysses* in Copenhagen: James Joyce and Tom Kristensen." *James Joyce Quarterly* (University of Tulsa) 14 (1977), 186-90.

Byram, M. S. "Tom Kristensen's *Livets Arabesk* seen as a political gesture." *Scan* 16 (1977), 109-18.

Krog, Helge

Arestad, Sverre. "Helge Krog and the problem play." *SS* 37 (1965), 332-51.

Krusenstjerna, Agnes von

Jones, Llewellyn. "Agnes von Krusenstjerna: A Swedish Proust." *BA* 23 (1949), 10–14.

Kvaran, Einar H.

Beck, Richard. "Einar H. Kvaran: An Icelandic novelist and dramatist." *Poet Lore* 43 (1936), 56–63.

Lagerkvist, Pär

Ahlenius, Holger. "The dramatic work of Pär Lagerkvist." *ASR* 28 (1940), 301–8.
Åhnebrink, Lars. "Pär Lagerkvist: A seeker and a humanist." *Pacific Spectator* 6 (1952), 400–12.
Benson, Adolph A. "Pär Lagerkvist: Nobel Laureate." *College English* 13 (1953), 417–24.
Bloch, Adèle. "The mythical female in the fictional work of Pär Lagerkvist." *International Fiction Review* 1:1 (1974), 48–53.
Braybrooke, Neville. "Lagerkvist and his *Barrabas*." *Queen's Quarterly* 59 (1952), 367–72.
Buckman, Thomas R. "Pär Lagerkvist and the Swedish theater." *Tulane Drama Review* 6:2 (1961), 60–89.
Ellestad, Everett M. "Lagerkvist and cubism: A study of theory and practice." *SS* 45 (1973), 38–53.
Gustafson, Walter W. "Pär Lagerkvist and his symbols." *BA* 26 (1952), 20–23.
Gustafson, Walter W. "The patterns of the work of Pär Lagerkvist." *SS* 26 (1954), 12–16.
Gustafson, Walter W. "Pär Lagerkvist and archaic art." *SS* 27 (1955), 64–70.
Gustafson, Walter W. "*Sibyllan* and the patterns of Lagerkvist's works." *SS* 30 (1958), 131–36.
Jackson, Naomi. "The fragmented mirror: Lagerkvist's *The Dwarf*." *Discourse* 8 (1965), 185–93.
Johannesson, Eric O. "Pär Lagerkvist and the art of rebellion." *SS* 30 (1958), 19–29.
Kattsoff, Louis O. "Encounter with God in the novellas of Pär Lagerkvist." *Discourse* 9 (1966), 378–88.
Kehl, D. G. "The chiaroscuro world of Pär Lagerkvist." *Modern Fiction Studies* 15 (1969), 241–50.
Linnér, Sven. "Pär Lagerkvist's *The Eternal Smile* and *The Sibyl*." *SS* 37 (1965), 160–67.
Mjöberg, Jöran. "Pär Lagerkvist and the ancient Greek drama." *SS* 25 (1953), 46–51.
Ramsey, Roger. "Pär Lagerkvist: *The Dwarf* and dogma." *Mosaic* 5:3 (1972), 97–106.
Rovinsky, Robert T. "The path to self-realization: An analysis of Lagerkvist's *Livet* (1911)." *SS* 45 (1973), 107–27.
Ryberg, Anders. *Pär Lagerkvist in translation: A bibliography*. Stockholm: Bonniers, 1964.
Scandinavica 10 (1971), supplement. [Special issue on Pär Lagerkvist.]
Scobbie, Irene. "Contrasting characters in *Barrabas*." *SS* 32 (1960), 212–20.
Scobbie, Irene. *Pär Lagerkvist: An introduction*. Stockholm: The Swedish Institute, 1962.
Scobbie, Irene. "Strindberg and Lagerkvist." *Modern Drama* 7 (1964), 126–34.
Scobbie, Irene. "An interpretation of Lagerkvist's *Mariamne*." *SS* 45 (1973), 128–34.
Scobbie, Irene. *Pär Lagerkvist: Gäst hos verkligheten*. Studies in Swedish Literature 2. 2nd ed. Hull, 1976.
Sjöberg, Leif. *Pär Lagerkvist*. Columbia Essays on Modern Writers 74. New York: Columbia University Press, 1976.
Spector, Robert. "The Limbo world of Pär Lagerkvist." *ASR* 43 (1955), 271–74.
Spector, Robert. "Lagerkvist and existentialism." *SS* 32 (1960), 203–11.
Spector, Robert. "Lagerkvist's uses of deformity." *SS* 33 (1961), 209–17.

Spector, Robert. "Pär Lagerkvist's dialogue of the soul." *Scandinavian Studies. Essays presented to Dr. Henry G. Leach.* Seattle: University of Washington Press for The American-Scandinavian Foundation, New York, 1965, 302-10.

Spector, Robert. "Lagerkvist's short fiction." *ASR* 57 (1969), 260-65.

Spector, Robert. *Pär Lagerkvist.* New York: Twayne, 1973.

Swanson, Roy A. "Evil and love in Lagerkvist's crucifixion cycle." *SS* 38 (1966), 302-17.

Vowles, Richard B. "The fiction of Pär Lagerkvist." *Western Humanities Review* 8 (1954), 111-17.

Weathers, Winston. *Pär Lagerkvist: A critical essay.* Grand Rapids: Eerdmans, 1968.

Lagerlöf, Selma

Afzelius, Nils. "The scandalous Selma Lagerlöf." *Scan* 5 (1966), 91-99.

Berendsohn, Walter A. *Selma Lagerlöf: Her life and work.* Port Washington, N.Y.: Kennikat Press, 1968.

Danielson, Larry W. "The uses of demonic folk tradition in Selma Lagerlöf's *Gösta Berlings saga.*" *Western Folklore* 34 (1975), 187-99.

De Vrieze, F. S. *Fact and fiction in the autobiographical works of Selma Lagerlöf.* Assen: Royal Van Gorcum Ltd., 1958.

Green, Brita. *Selma Lagerlöf: Herr Arnes penningar.* Studies in Swedish Literature 9. Hull, 1977.

Gustafson, Alrik. "Saga and legend of a province: Selma Lagerlöf." *Six Scandinavian novelists.* Biblo and Tannen, 1969, 177-225. [Reprint of 1940 ed.]

Gustafson, Walter W. "Selma Lagerlöf: A confession of faith." *Bulletin from the American Swedish Institute* 6:2 (1951), 12-16.

Johannesson, Eric O. "Isak Dinesen and Selma Lagerlöf." *SS* 32 (1960), 18-26.

Lagerroth, Erland. "The narrative art of Selma Lagerlöf: Two problems." *SS* 33 (1961), 10-17.

Lagerroth, Erland. "Selma Lagerlöf research, 1900-1964: A survey and an orientation." *SS* 37 (1965), 1-30.

Lagerroth, Ulla-Britta. "The troll in man: A Lagerlöf motif." *SS* 40 (1968), 51-60.

Larsen, Hanna A. "Selma Lagerlöf." *ASR* 23 (1935), 7-19, 113-28, 207-22, 309-26.

Larsen, Hanna A. *Selma Lagerlöf.* Garden City, N.Y.: Doubleday, Doran and Co., 1936.

Maule, Harry E. *Selma Lagerlöf: The woman, her work, her message.* Garden City, N.Y.: Doubleday, Page and Co., 1917.

Monroe, Elisabeth. "Selma Lagerlöf's art." *ASR* 28 (1940), 143-47.

Monroe, Elisabeth. "Provincial art in Selma Lagerlöf." In *The novel and society: A critical study of the modern novel.* Chapel Hill, N.C.: University of North Carolina Press, 1941, 88-110.

Pehrson, Elsa. "Glimpses from the hidden workshop of Selma Lagerlöf." *ASR* 33 (1945), 41-44.

Laxness, Halldór K.

Einarsson, Stefán. "Five Icelandic novelists." *BA* 16 (1942), 254-59.

Hallberg, Peter. *Halldór Laxness.* New York: Twayne, 1971.

Jacobs, Fred R. "Halldór Laxness and America: A bibilography." *The Serif* (Kent, Ohio) 10:4 (1973), 24-34.

Magnússon, Sigurður A. "Halldór K. Laxness: Iceland's first Nobel Prize winner." *ASR* 44 (1956), 13-18.

Pálsson, Hermann. "Beyond *The Atom Station.*" *Ideas and ideologies.* Reykjavík: University of Iceland, 1975, 317-29.

Ringler, Richard N. "Christianity in the slopes of the glacier." *BA* 44 (1970), 54–55.
Thompson, Lawrence S. "Halldór K. Laxness." *BA* 28 (1954), 298–99.

Lehtonen, Joel

Tarkka, Pekka. "Joel Lehtonen and Putkinotko." *BF* 11:4 (1977), 239–45.

Leino, Eino

Sarajas, Annamari. "Eino Leino 1878–1926." *BF* 12:2 (1978), 40–46.

Levertin, Oscar

Murdock, Eleanor E. "Oscar Levertin: Swedish critic of French realism." *Contemporary Literature* 5 (1953), 137–50.

Lidman, Sara

Bäckström, Lars. "Eyvind Johnson, Per Olof Sundman, and Sara Lidman: An introduction." *Contemporary Literature* 12 (1971), 242–51.
Borland, Harold H. "Sara Lidman's progress: A critical survey of six novels." *SS* 39 (1967), 97–114.
Borland, Harold H. "Sara Lidman: Novelist and moralist." *Svensk Litteraturtidskrift* 36:1 (1973), 27–34.
[Dembo, L. S.] "An interview with Sara Lidman." *Contemporary Literature* 12 (1971), 252–57.

Lie, Jonas

Gustafson, Alrik. "Impressionistic realism: Jonas Lie." *Six Scandinavian novelists*. New York: Biblo and Tannen, 1969, 25–72. [Reprint of 1940 ed.]
Larsen, Hanna A. "Jonas Lie (1833–1909)." *ASR* 21 (1933), 461–71.
Lyngstad, Sverre. *Jonas Lie*. Boston: Twayne, 1977.
Lyngstad, Sverre. "The vortex and related imagery in Jonas Lie's fiction." *SS* 51 (1979), 211–48.
Wiehr, Josef. "The women characters of Jonas Lie." *Journal of English and Germanic Philology* 28 (1929), 41–71, 244–62.

Lindegren, Erik

Ekner, Reidar. "The artist as the eye of a needle." *SS* 42 (1970), 1–13.
Steene, Birgitta. "Erik Lindegren: An assessment." *BA* 49 (1975), 29–32.
Vowles, Richard B. "Sweden's modern muse: Exploded sonnets and panic poetry." *Kentucky Foreign Language Quarterly* 2 (1955), 132–40.

Linna, Väinö

Laitinen, Kai. "Väinö Linna and Veijo Meri: Two aspects of war." *BA* 36 (1962), 365–67.
Rintala, Marvin. "Väinö Linna and the Finnish condition." *Journal of Baltic Studies* 8 (1977), 223–31.
Saarikoski, Marjukka. "What Väinö Linna thinks on his 50th birthday, December 20, 1970" [interview]. *BF* 5:1 (1971), 9–10.
Varpio, Yrjö. "Väinö Linna: A classic in his own time." *BF* 11:3 (1977), 192–97.

Lo-Johansson, Ivar

Paulsson, Jan-Anders. "Ivar Lo-Johansson: Crusader for social justice." *ASR* 59 (1971), 21–31.

Lundkvist, Artur

Sjöberg, Leif. "An interview with Artur Lundkvist." *BA* 50 (1976), 329-36.
Vowles, Richard B. "From Pan to panic: The poetry of Artur Lundkvist." *New Mexico Quarterly* 22 (1952), 288-96.
Vowles, Richard B. "Sweden's modern muse: Exploded sonnets and panic poetry." *Kentucky Foreign Language Quarterly* 2 (1955), 134-38.

Manner, Eeva-Liisa

Ahokas, Jaakko. "Eeva-Liisa Manner: Dropping from reality into life." *BA* 47 (1973), 60-65.
Sala, Kaarina. "Eeva-Liisa Manner: A literary portrait." *Snow in May: An anthology of Finnish writing, 1945-72.* Rutherford, N.J.: Fairleigh Dickinson University Press, 1978, 58-59.

Martinson, Harry

Bergmann, S. A. "Harry Martinson and science." *Proceedings of the Fifth International Study Conference on Scandinavian Literature.* London, 1966, 99-120.
Hunter, Grace. "Two contemporary Swedish poets." *Prairie Schooner* 27 (1955), 57-67.
Johannesson, Eric O. "Aniara: Poetry and the poet in the modern world." *SS* 32 (1960), 185-202.
Sjöberg, Leif. "Harry Martinson: Writer in quest of harmony." *ASR* 60 (1972), 360-71.
Sjöberg, Leif. "Harry Martinson: From vagabond to space explorer." *BA* 48 (1974), 476-85.
Sjöberg, Leif. "The 1974 Nobel Prize in literature: Eyvind Johnson and Harry Martinson." *BA* 49 (1975), 407-21.
Steene, Birgitta. "The role of the mima: A note on Martinson's *Aniara.*" *Scandinavian Studies. Essays presented to Dr. Henry G. Leach.* Seattle: University of Washington Press for The American-Scandinavian Foundation, New York, 1965, 311-19.
Tideström, Gunnar. "Harry Martinson's 'Aniara'." *Scan* 13 (1974), 1-17.
Vowles, Richard B. "Harry Martinson: Sweden's seaman poet." *BA* 25 (1951), 332-35.

Mehren, Stein

Naess, Harald. "Stein Mehren: Dialectic poet of light and dreams." *BA* 47 (1973), 66-70.

Meri, Veijo

Laitinen, Kai. "Väinö Linna and Veijo Meri: Two aspects of war." *BA* 36 (1962), 365-67.
Stormbom, Nils B. "Veijo Meri and the new Finnish novel." *ASR* 55 (1967), 264-69.

Mikkola, Marja-Leena

Hannula, Risto. "Literary portrait: Marja-Leena Mikkola." *BF* 4:2 (1970), 8-9.

Moberg, Vilhelm

Alexis, Gerhard T. "Moberg's immigrant trilogy: A dubious conclusion." *SS* 38 (1966), 20-25.
Alexis, Gerhard T. "Sweden to Minnesota: Vilhelm Moberg's fictional reconstruction." *American Quarterly* 18 (1966), 81-94.
Eidevall, Gunnar. "The Swedes in Moberg's trilogy." *Swedish Pioneer Historical Quarterly* 39 (1978), 69-78.
Elmen, Paul. "Religious motifs in 'The Emigrants'." *Swedish Pioneer Historical Quarterly* 24 (1973), 139-45.
Gustafson, Alrik. "'A Dream Worth Dying for—': The price of freedom in Vilhelm Moberg's recent novels." *ASR* 30 (1942), 296-307.
Holmes, Philip. *Vilhelm Moberg: Utvandrarna.* Studies in Swedish Literature 6. Hull, 1976.

Holmes, Philip. *Vilhelm Moberg*. Boston: Twayne, 1980.
Johnson, Walter. "Moberg's *Emigrants* and the naturalistic tradition." *SS* 25 (1953), 134–46.
Orton, Gavin and Philip Holmes. "Memoirs of an idealist: Vilhelm Moberg's *Soldat med brutet gevär*." *SS* 48 (1976), 29–51.
Winther, Sophus K. "Moberg and a new genre for the emigrant novel." *SS* 34 (1962), 170–82.

Munch-Petersen, Gustaf

Mitchell, P. M. "The English poetry of Gustaf Munch-Petersen." *Orbis Litterarum* 22 (1967), 352–62.

Munk, Kaj

Arestad, Sverre. "Kaj Munk as a dramatist (1898–1944)." *SS* 26 (1954), 151–76.
Bang, Carol K. "Kaj Munk's autobiography." *ASR* 33 (1945), 45–50.
Harcourt, Melville. "Kaj Munk." In *Portraits of destiny*. New York: Sheed and Ward, 1969, 1–47.
Schmidt, Robert. "Kaj Munk: A new Danish dramatist." *ASR* 21 (1933), 227–32.
Thompson, Lawrence. "The actuality of Kaj Munk's dramas." *BA* 15 (1941), 267–72.
Thompson, Lawrence. "A voice death has not silenced." *BA* 18 (1944), 126–27.

Mustapää, P.

Ahokas, Jaakko. "No serious songs: P. Mustapää, poet and professor." *WLT* 54 (1980), 38–40.

Nexø, Martin Andersen

Koefoed, H. A. "Martin Andersen Nexø: Some viewpoints." *Scan* 4 (1965), 27–37.
Madsen, Clara. "The social philosophy of Martin Andersen Nexø." *SS* 12 (1932), 1–9.
Thompson, Lawrence S. "Martin Andersen Nexø: 1869–1954." *BA* 28 (1954), 423–24.
Toksvig, Signe. "Martin Andersen Nexø." *ASR* 11 (1923), 345–50.

Nielsen, Jørgen

Madsen, Børge G. "*Lavt land* and its debt to *Himmerlandshistorier*." *SS* 31 (1959), 121–28.

Obstfelder, Sigbjørn

Norseng, Mary Kay. "Obstfelder's prose poem in general and in particular." *SS* 50 (1978), 177–85.
Schoolfield, George C. "Sigbjørn Obstfelder: A study in idealism." *Edda* (1957), 193–223.

Olsson, Hagar

"Hagar Olsson: 1893–1978." *BF* 12:1 (1978), 33.
Petheric, Karin. "Four Finland-Swedish prose modernists (. . .)." *Scan* 15 (1976), 63–72.
Schoolfield, George C. "Hagar Olsson's *Chitambo*: Anniversary thoughts on names and structure." *SS* 45 (1973), 223–62.
Stormborg, N.-B. "Inward journey: The works of Hagar Olsson." *ASR* 52 (1964), 261–65.
Törnqvist, Egil. "Hagar Olsson's first play." *Scan* 15 (1978), 63–72.

Øverland, Arnulf

Grunt, Olav P. "The poet and the world: The case of Arnulf Øverland." *ASR* 33 (1945), 233–43.
Houm, Philip. "Arnulf Øverland." *ASR* 61 (1973), 268–72.

Palm, Göran

Stendahl, Brita K. "In Sweden everybody reads the bulletin." *BA* 42 (1968), 209-11.

Paludan, Jacob

Heltberg, Niels. "Jacob Paludan." *ASR* 40 (1952), 142-45.

Panduro, Leif

Hugus, Frank. "The King's new clothes: The irreverent portrayal of royalty in the works of Leif Panduro and Finn Søeborg." *SS* 51 (1979), 162-76.

Pontoppidan, Henrik

Ekman, Ernst. "Henrik Pontoppidan as a critic of modern Danish society." *SS* 29 (1957), 170-83.

Geismar, Oscar. "Henrik Pontoppidan." *ASR* 21 (1933), 7-12.

Gray, Charlotte S. "From opposition to identification: Social and psychological structure behind Henrik Pontoppidan's literary development." *SS* 51 (1979), 273-84.

Jones, W. Glyn. "Henrik Pontoppidan: The church and Christianity after 1900." *SS* 30 (1958), 191-97.

Larsen, Hanna A. "Pontoppidan of Denmark." *ASR* 31 (1943), 231-39.

Mitchell, P. M. *Henrik Pontoppidan*. Boston: Twayne, 1979.

Ober, Kenneth H. "The incomplete self in Pontoppidan's *De Dødes Rige*." *SS* 50 (1978), 396-402.

Rifbjerg, Klaus

Gray, Charlotte S. "Klaus Rifbjerg: A contemporary Danish writer." *BA* 49 (1975), 25-28.

Rintala, Paavo

Tarkka, Pekka. "Paavo Rintala: A literary portrait." *BF* 3:1 (1969), 8-9.

Rølvaag, Ole Edvart

Eckstein, Neil T. "The social criticism of Ole Edvart Rølvaag." *Norwegian-American Studies* 24 (1970), 112-36.

Eckstein, Neil T. "*Giants in the Earth* as saga." *Where the West begins: Essays on Middle Border and Siouxland writing, in honor of Herbert Krause*. Sioux Falls, S.D.: Augustana College, 1978, 34-41.

Haugrud, Raychel A. "Rølvaag's search for Soria Moria." *Norwegian-American Studies* 26 (1974), 103-17.

Jordahl, O. "Folkloristic influence upon Rølvaag's youth." *Western Folklore* 34 (1975), 1-15.

Jorgenson, Theodore and Nora O. Solum. *Ole Edvart Rølvaag: A biography*. New York and London: Harper and Brothers, 1939.

Kaye, Frances W. "Literary pilgrimages on the Middle Border." *Prairie Schooner* 52 (1978), 281-89.

Laverty, Carroll D. "Rølvaag's creation of the sense of doom in *Giants in the Earth*." *South Central Bulletin* 27:4 (1967), 45-50.

Olson, Julius E. "Rølvaag's novels of Norwegian pioneer life in the Dakotas." *SS* 9 (1926-27), 45-55.

Paulson, Kristoffer F. "Berdahl family history and Rølvaag's immigrant trilogy." *Norwegian-American Studies* (Northfield) 27 (1977), 55-76.

Reaske, Herbert E. *Rølvaag's Giants in the Earth*. New York: Monarch Press, 1965.
Reigstad, Paul M. *Rølvaag: His life and art*. Lincoln: University of Nebraska Press, 1972.
Simonson, Harold P. "Rølvaag and Kierkegaard." *SS* 49 (1977), 67–80.
Thorson, Gerald, ed. *Ole Rølvaag: Artist and cultural leader*. Northfield, Mn.: St. Olaf College Press, 1976.

Saarikoski, Pentti

Simonsuuri, Kirsti. "Myth and material in the poetry of Pentti Saarikoski since 1958." *WLT* 54 (1980), 41–46.
Tarkka, Pekka. "Introduction." *BF* 11:4 (1977), 232-34.

Salama, Hannu

Tarkka, Pekka. "Hannu Salama: A writer between the social classes." *WLT* 54 (1980), 28–32.

Sandel, Cora

Polak, Ada. "Cora Sandel and *Alberte*." *The Norseman* 15 (1957), 352–57.

Sandemose, Aksel

Nielsen, Erling. "Aksel Sandemose: Investigator of the mystery of human nature." *Scan* 8 (1969), 1–18.

Sarvig, Ole

Rossel, Sven H. "Crisis and redemption: An introduction to the writings of Ole Sarvig." *WLT* 53 (1979), 606-9.

Scherfig, Hans

Kristensen, Sven Møller. "How to castigate your public—and write best sellers." *Danish Journal* 76 (1973), 26–29.

Schildt, Runar

Schoolfield, George C. "Runar Schildt and Swedish Finland." *SS* 32 (1960), 7–17.
Zuck, Virpi. "The use of models as tools in literary criticism." *PPNCFL* 27 (1976), 137–40.
Zuck, Virpi. "The Finno-Swedish short story: Runar Schildt." *SS* 49 (1977), 180–207.

Seeberg, Peter

Rossel, Sven H. "The search for reality: A study in Peter Seeberg's prose writings." *PPNCFL* 27 (1976), 126–29.

Sigurjónsson, Jóhann

Larsen, Hanna A. "Eyvind of the Hills." *ASR* 4 (1916), 346–49.
Magoun, F. P. "Jóhann Sigurjónsson's *Fjalla-Eyvindur*: Source, chronology, and geography." *Publications of The Modern Language Association of America* 61 (1946), 269–92.

Sinkkonen, Lassi

Sievänen-Allen, Ritva. "Everyday song." *BF* 5:3 (1971), 2-3.

Sjöberg, Birger

Engblom, Carl J. "Birger Sjöberg." *ASR* 47 (1959), 159–63.

Sjöstrand, Östen

Bergsten, Staffan. "Östen Sjöstrand's *Aquarius* poetry." *Mosaic* 4:2 (1970), 117–30.

Bergsten, Staffan. *Östen Sjöstrand.* New York: Twayne, 1974.

Sjöberg, Leif. "After these epiphanies" [interview]. *ScanR* 68 (1980), 30–36.

Söderberg, Hjalmar

Butt, Wolfgang. *Hjalmar Söderberg: Martin Bircks ungdom.* Studies in Swedish Literature 7. Hull, 1976.

Geddes, Tom. *Hjalmar Söderberg: Doktor Glas.* Studies in Swedish Literature 3. Hull, 1975.

Hedberg, Johannes. "A coincidence according to the Gospel of St. James." *Moderna språk* (Stockholm) 72 (1978), 1–11.

Lofmark, Carl. *Hjalmar Söderberg: Historietter.* Studies in Swedish Literature 10. Hull, 1977.

Lofmark, Carl. "Hjalmar Söderberg (1869–1941): A Swedish freethinker." *Question* 11 (1978), 3–14.

Söderberg, Eugénie. "Hjalmar Söderberg." *ASR* 29 (1941), 334–37.

Södergran, Edith

Hird, Gladys. "Edith Södergran: A pioneer of Finland-Swedish modernism." *BF* 12:1 (1978), 4–7.

Schoolfield, George C. "Edith Södergran's 'Wallensteinprofil'." *Scandinavian Studies. Essays presented to Dr. Henry G. Leach.* Seattle: University of Washington Press for The American-Scandinavian Foundation, New York, 1965, 278–92.

Solstad, Dag

Sehmsdorf, Henning. "From individualism to Communism: The political and esthetic transformation of Dag Solstad's authorship." *PPNCFL* 27 (1976), 130–32.

Stefánsson, Davið

Beck, Richard. "Davið Stefánsson: Icelandic national poet." *BA* 42 (1968), 222–25.

Einarsson, Stefán. "Davið Stefánsson." *ASR* 55 (1967), 34–40.

Stenius, Göran

Jones, W. Glyn. "Göran Stenius' philosophical novels." *Scan* 16 (1977), 93–108.

Stephansson, Stephan G.

Beck, Richard. "An Icelandic poet-pioneer." *ASR* 17 (1929), 424–25.

Beck, Richard. "Stephan G. Stephansson." *ASR* 44 (1956), 151–56.

Cawley, F. Stanton. "The greatest poet of the western world: Stephan G. Stephansson." *SS* 15 (1938), 99–109.

Strindberg, August

Allen, James L. "Symbol and meaning in Strindberg's *Crime and Crime.*" *Modern Drama* 9 (1966), 62–73.

Bandy, Stephen C. "Strindberg's biblical sources for *The Ghost Sonata.*" *SS* 40 (1968), 200–9.

Benston, Alice N. "From naturalism to the *Dream Play*: A study of the evolution of Strindberg's unique theatrical form." *Modern Drama* 7 (1965), 382–98.

Bentley, Eric. *In search of theater.* New York: Alfred A. Knopf, 1953, 134–43.

Bentley, Eric. *The playwright as thinker.* 7th ed. New York: Meridian Books, 1960, 158–80.

Bentley, Eric. "The ironic Strindberg." In Sprinchorn, Evert, ed. *The genius of the Scandinavian theater.* New York: New American Library, 1964, 599–603.

Bergeron, David M. "Strindberg's *Easter*: A musical play." *University Review* 33 (1967), 219–25.

Bergholz, Harry. "Strindberg's anthologies of American humorists, bibliographically identified." *SS* 47 (1971), 335–43.

Blackwell, Marilyn J., ed. *Festschrift to Walter Johnson.* Chapel Hill: University of North Carolina Press, forthcoming.

Block, Haskell. "Strindberg and the symbolist drama." *Modern Drama* 5 (1962), 314–22.

Borland, Harold H. "The dramatic quality of Strindberg's novels." *Modern Drama* 5 (1962), 299–305.

Brandell, Gunnar. *Strindberg in Inferno.* Cambridge, Mass.: Harvard University Press, 1974.

Bronsen, David. "*The Dance of Death* and the possibility of laughter." *Drama Survey* 6 (1967), 31–44.

Brustein, Robert. *The theatre of revolt.* Boston: Little, Brown and Co., 1964, 85–134.

Bryer, Jackson, R. "Strindberg 1951–1962: A bibliography." *Modern Drama* (1962), 269–75.

Bulman, Joan. *Strindberg and Shakespeare.* London: Jonathan Cape, 1933.

Carlson, Harry G. "Ambiguity and archetypes in Strindberg's *Romantic Organist.*" *SS* 48 (1976), 256–71.

Dahlström, Carl E. W. L. *Strindberg's dramatic expressionism.* 2nd ed. New York: B. Blom, 1965.

Deer, Irving. "Strindberg's dream vision: Prelude to film." *Criticism* 14 (1972), 253–65.

Dukore, Bernard F. "Strindberg: The real and the surreal." *Modern Drama* 5 (1962), 331–34.

Flaxman, Seymour L. "The debt of Williams and Miller to Ibsen and Strindberg." *Comparative Literature Studies* (Special Advance Issue, 1963), 51–60.

Freedman, Morris. "Strindberg's positive nihilism." *Drama Survey* 2 (1963), 288–96.

Goodman, Randolph. "Playwriting with a third eye: Fun and games with Albee, Ibsen and Strindberg." *Columbia University Forum* 10 (1967), 18–22.

Gustafson, Alrik. "Six recent doctoral dissertations on Strindberg." *Modern Philology* 52 (1954), 52–56.

Hamilton, Mary G. "Strindberg's alchemical way of the cross." *Mosaic* 7:4 (1974), 139–53.

Hartman, Murray. " Strindberg and O'Neill." *Educational Theatre Journal* 18 (1966), 216–23.

Hauptman, Ira. "Strindberg's realistic plays." *Yale Theatre* 5:3 (1974), 87–94.

Hayes, Stephen G. and Jules Zentner. "Strindberg's *Miss Julie*: Lilacs and beer." *SS* 45 (1973), 59–64.

Hildeman, Karl-Ivar. "Strindberg, *The Dance of Death* and revenge." *SS* 35 (1963), 267–94.

Jarvi, Raymond. "Strindberg's *The Ghost Sonata* and sonata form." *Mosaic* 5:4 (1972), 69–84.

Jarvi, Raymond. "*Ett drömspel*: A symphony for the stage." *SS* 44 (1972), 28–42.

Jarvi, Raymond. "'Svarta handsken': A lyrical fantasy for the stage." *Scan* 12 (1973), 17–25.

Johannesson, Eric O. "*Syndabocken*: Strindberg's last novel." *SS* 35 (1963), 1–28.

Johannesson, Eric O. "Strindberg's *Taklagsöl*: An early experiment in the psychological novel." *SS* 35 (1963), 223–38.

Johannesson, Eric O. *The novels of August Strindberg.* Berkeley: University of California Press, 1968.

Johnson, Walter. "Strindberg and the Dance Macabre." *Modern Drama* 3 (1960), 8–15.

Johnson, Walter, "*Creditors* reexamined." *Modern Drama* 5 (1962), 281–90.

Johnson, Walter, *Strindberg and the historical drama.* Seattle: University of Washington Press, 1963.

Johnson, Walter. "*Gustaf Adolf* revised." *Scandinavian Studies. Essays presented to Dr. Henry G. Leach.* Seattle: University of Washington Press for The American-Scandinavian Foundation, New York, 1965, 136–46.

Johnson, Walter. "*A Dream Play*: Plans and fulfilment." *Scan* 10 (1971), 103-11.

Johnson, Walter. *August Strindberg*. Boston: Twayne, 1976.

Kaufman, K. J. "Strindberg: The absence of irony." *Drama Survey* 3 (1964), 436-76.

Kaufman, Michael W. "Strindberg's historical imagination: *Erik XIV*." *Comparative Drama* 9 (1975), 318-31.

Lamm, Martin. "Strindberg and the theatre." *Tulane Drama Review* 6 (1961), 132-39.

Lamm, Martin. *August Strindberg*. New York: B. Blom, 1971.

Lapisardi, Frederick S. "The same enemies: Notes in certain similarities between Yeats and Strindberg." *Modern Drama* 12 (1969), 146-54.

Lawson, Stephen R. "Strindberg's *Dream Play* and *Ghost Sonata*." *Yale Theatre* 5:3 (1974), 95-102.

Lide, Barbara. "Strindberg and Molière: Parallels, influence, image." In *Molière and the Commonwealth of letters: Patrimony and posterity*. Jackson: Mississippi University Press, 1975.

Lide, Barbara. "The young idealist and the fat old clown: Development of the tragicomical in Strindberg's *Mäster Olof*." *SS* 51 (1979), 13-24.

Lindstöm, Göran. "Strindberg studies 1915-1962." *Scan* 2 (1963), 27-50.

Lucas, F. L. *The drama of Ibsen and Strindberg*. New York: Macmillan, 1962.

Lyons, Charles R. "The archetypal action of male submission in Strindberg's *The Father*." *SS* 36 (1964), 218-32.

McGill, V. L. *August Strindberg*. 2nd ed. New York: Russell, 1965.

Madsen, Børge G. "Naturalism in transition: Strindberg's "cynical" tragedy *The Bond*." *Modern Drama* 5 (1962), 291-98.

Madsen, Børge G. *Strindberg's naturalistic theatre: Its relation to French naturalism*. Seattle: University of Washington Press, 1962.

Mays, Milton A. "Strindberg's *Ghost Sonata*: Parodied fairy tale on Original Sin." *Modern Drama* 10 (1967), 189-94.

Milton, John. "A restless pilgrim: Strindberg in *The Inferno*." *Modern Drama* 5 (1962), 306-13.

Modern Drama 5:3 (1962). [Special issue on August Strindberg.]

Mortensen, Brita and Brian W. Downs. *Strindberg: An introduction to his life and work*. 2nd ed. Cambridge: University Press, 1965.

Oster, Rose-Marie. "Hamm and Hummel: Beckett and Strindberg on the human condition." *SS* 41 (1969), 330-43.

Parker, Gerald. "The spectator seized by the theatre: Strindberg's *The Ghost Sonata*." *Modern Drama* 14 (1972), 373-86.

Plasberg, Elaine. "Strindberg and the new poetics." *Modern Drama* 15 (1972), 1-14.

Raphael, Robert. "Strindberg and Wagner." *Scandinavian Studies. Essays presented to Dr. Henry G. Leach*. Seattle: University of Washington Press for The American-Scandinavian Foundation, New York, 1965, 260-68.

Rapp, Esther H. "Strindberg's reception in England and America." *SS* 23 (1951), 1-22, 49-59, 109-37.

Reinert, Otto, comp. *Strindberg: A collection of critical essays*. Englewood Cliffs, N.J.: Prentice-Hall, 1971.

Roth, Marc A. "Strindberg's historical role-players." *Scan* 18 (1979), 123-40.

Scandinavian Review 64:3 (1978). [Special issue on August Strindberg.]

Scanlan, David. "*The Road to Damascus, Part One: A skeptic's Everyman*." *Modern Drama* 5 (1962), 343-51.

Scobbie, Irene. "Strindberg and Lagerkvist." *Modern Drama* 7 (1964), 126-34.

Sehmsdorf, Henning. "August Strindberg's *Swanwhite* and Scandinavian folk poetry: Idea and form." *The Barat Review* 1 (1966), 98-104.

Sehmsdorf, Henning; see under Cappelen, Peder W.

Senelick, Laurence. "Strindberg, Antoine and Lugné-Poë: A study in cross purposes." *Modern Drama 15 (1973), 391–402.

Smedmark, C. R. ed. Essays on Strindberg. Stockholm: Strindberg Society, 1966.

Sprinchorn, Evert. "The logic of A Dreamplay." Modern Drama 5 (1962), 352–65.

Sprinchorn, Evert. "Strindberg and the greater naturalism." Tulane Drama Review 13 (1968), 119–29.

Sprinchorn, Evert. "The Zola of the occult: Strindberg's experimental method." Modern Drama 17 (1974), 250–66.

Sprinchorn, Evert. "Strindberg and the wit to go mad." SS 48 (1976), 247–55.

Sprinchorn, Evert. "Hell and Purgatory in Strindberg." SS 50 (1978), 371–80.

Steene, Birgitta. "Shakespearean elements in historical plays of Strindberg." Journal of Comparative Literature 11 (1959), 209–20.

Steene, Birgitta. The greatest fire: A study of August Strindberg. Carbondale: Southern Illinois University Press, 1973.

Steene, Birgitta. "The ambiguous feminist." ScanR 64 (1978), 27–31.

Steene, Birgitta. "August Strindberg in America 1963–1979: A bibliographical assessment." Festschrift to Walter Johnson. Chapel Hill: University of North Carolina Press, 1981. Forthcoming.

Stockenström, Göran. "The journey from the Isle of Life to the Isle of the Dead: The idea of reconciliation in The Ghost Sonata." SS 50 (1978), 133–49.

Syndergaard, Larry E. "The Skogsrå of folklore and Strindberg's The Crown Bride." Comparative Drama 6 (1972–73), 310–22.

Taylor, Marion A. "A note on Strindberg's The Dance of Death and Albee's Who's afraid of Virginia Woolf?" Papers on Language and Literature 2 (1966), 187–88.

Törnquist, Egil. "Strindberg's The Stronger." SS 42 (1970), 297–308.

Törnquist, Egil. "Miss Julie and O'Neill." Modern Drama 19 (1976), 351–64.

Uppvall, Axel Johan. August Strindberg: A psychoanalytic study with special reference to the Oedipus complex. Boston: R. G. Badger, 1920.

Vincentia, Sister M. O. P. "Wagnerism in Road to Damascus." Modern Drama 5 (1962), 335–43.

Vowles, Richard B. "Strindberg's Isle of the Dead." Modern Drama 5 (1962), 366–78.

White, Kenneth S. "Visions of a transfigured humanity: Strindberg and Lenormand." Modern Drama 5 (1962), 323–30.

Winther, Sophus K. "Strindberg and O'Neill: A study of influence." SS 31 (1959), 103–20.

World Theatre 11:1 (1962). [Special issue on August Strindberg.]

Sundman, Per Olof

Bäckström, Lars. "Eyvind Johnson, Per Olof Sundman, and Sara Lidman: An introduction." Contemporary Literature 12 (1971), 242–51.

[Dembo, L. S.] "An interview with Per Olof Sundman." Contemporary Literature 12 (1971), 267–75.

Sjöberg, Leif. "Per Olof Sundman and the uses of reality." ASR 59 (1971), 145–54.

Sjöberg, Leif. "Per Olof Sundman: The writer as a reasonably unbiased observer." BA 47 (1973), 253–60.

Warme, Lars G. "Per Olof Sundman and the French New Novel: Influence or coincidence." SS 50 (1978), 403–13.

Warme, Lars G. "The quests in the works of Per Olof Sundman." PPNCFL 28 (1978), 108–11.

Tranströmer, Tomas

Fulton, Robin. "The poetry of Tomas Tranströmer." Scan 12 (1973), supplement, 107–23.

Sellin, Eric. "The African relevance of Tomas Tranströmer's 'En simmande mörk gestalt'." Scan 7 (1968), 53–55.

Sellin, Eric. "Tomas Tranströmer and the cosmic image." *SS* 43 (1971), 241–50.
Sellin, Eric. "Tomas Tranströmer: Traffiker in miracles." *BA* 46 (1972), 44–48.
Sjöberg, Leif. "The poetry of Tomas Tranströmer." *ASR* 60 (1972), 37–42.
Steene, Birgitta. "Vision and reality in the poetry of Tomas Tranströmer." *SS* 37 (1965), 236–44.
Swahn, Sven Christer. "Tomas Tranströmer." *BA* 37 (1963), 402–3.

Undset, Sigrid

Bayerschmidt, Carl F. *Sigrid Undset*. New York: Twayne, 1970.
Beck, Richard. "Sigrid Undset and her novels on medieval life." *BA* 24 (1950), 5–10.
Dunn, Mary M. *"The Master of Hestviken*: A new reading." *SS* 38 (1966), 281–94.
Dunn, Mary M. *"The Master of Hestviken*: A new reading II." *SS* 40 (1968), 210–24.
Gustafson, Alrik. "Christian ethics in a pagan world: Sigrid Undset." *Six Scandinavian novelists*. New York: Biblo and Tannen, 1969, 286–361. [Reprint of 1940 ed.]
Klieneberger, H. R. "The Norwegian contribution to the modern novel: Knut Hamsun and Sigrid Undset." *Durham University Journal* 18 (1957), 70–78.
Larsen, Hanna A. "Sigrid Undset: I. Modern works; II. Medieval works." *ASR* 17 (1929), 344–52, 406–14.
McCarthy, Colman J. "Sigrid Undset." *Critic* 32 (1974), 58–64.
Monroe, N. Elisabeth. "Technique in Undset's medieval novels." *Renascence* 4 (1951), 53–57.
Vinde, Victor. *Sigrid Undset: A Nordic moralist*. Seattle: University of Washington Book Store, 1930.
Winsnes, A. H. *Sigrid Undset: A study in Christian realism*. New York: Sheed and Ward, 1953.

Vesaas, Tarjei

Beyer, Edvard. "Tarjei Vesaas." *Scan* 3 (1964), 97–109.
Chapman, Kenneth G. "Basic themes and motives in Vesaas' earliest writing." *SS* 41 (1969), 126–37.
Chapman, Kenneth G. *Tarjei Vesaas*. New York: Twayne, 1970.
Stendahl, Brita K. "Tarjei Vesaas: A friend." *BA* 42 (1968), 537–39.

Vik, Bjørg

Waal, Carla. "The Norwegian short story: Bjørg Vik." *SS* 49 (1977), 217–40.

Vilhjálmsson, Thor

Hallberg, Peter. "The one who sees: The Icelandic writer Thor Vilhjálmsson." *BA* 47 (1973), 54–59.

Vogt, Nils Collett

Elster, Kristian. "Three lyrical poets of Norway." *ASR* 13 (1925), 653–63.

Waltari, Mika

Laitinen, Kai. "The human voice." *BF* 13:3 (1979), 85–88.

Wied, Gustav

Watkins, John B. C. "The life and works of Gustav Wied." *Cornell University Abstracts of Theses*, 1944, 29–32.

Wildenwey, Herman

Elster, Kristian. "Three lyrical poets of Norway." *ASR* 13 (1925), 653–63.

Index

Index

INDEX   473